MEDIEVAL RUSSIA

A Source Book, 850–1700

THIRD EDITION

MEDIEVAL RUSSIA

A Source Book, 850–1700

THIRD EDITION

Edited by

BASIL DMYTRYSHYN

Professor Emeritus, Portland State University

Harcourt Brace Jovanovich College Publishers
Fort Worth   Philadelphia   San Diego
New York   Orlando   Austin   San Antonio
Toronto   Montreal   London   Sydney   Tokyo

MOSCOVIA VRB
tius Ruf

MOSCVÆ VRBIS
LOCA INSIGNIORA.

1. Magni Ducis arx, dicta Czargorod.
2. Magni Ducis conclauia noua.
3. Ecclesia S. Michaelis.
4. Aula, siue atrium vel Palatium Patriarchæ.
5. Conclaue, seu cænaculum è latere exstructum, è quo magnus Dux populo se conspiciendum præbet, aut inde Principis Edicta populo proclamantur.
6. Tabernæ siue pergula, in quibus diuersi generis animalium pelles, aliæque merces diuenduntur.
7. Curia ciuium, et Cancellaria prope quas Vnguentorum officinæ, seu Pharmacopolia.
8. Legatorum externorum Aula siue Hospitium.
9. Carceres seu Custodiæ reorum.
10. Tabernæ pictorum.
11. Externorum Mercatorum Aula siue Hospitium.
12. Forum in quo fœnum et diuersi generis tentoria seu domunculæ venduntur.
13. Aquæ calidæ seu Thermæ.
14. Magni Ducis hortus.
15. Peganiski ie soro seu lacus.
16. Equile M. Ducis.
17. Armamentarium.
18. Forum equarium.
19. Domus Fusoria.
20. Glinski aula.

urbis dicta Kitajgorod

suo circumdata muro, dicta Bielgorod

Tertia pars urbis versus Septentrionem vocata Skorodum.

To the Memory
of My Parents

Publisher	Ted Buchholz
Acquisitions Editor	David Tatom
Developmental Editor	Martin Lewis
Senior Project Editor	Dawn Youngblood
Production Manager	Kenneth Dunaway
Art & Design Supervisor	John Ritland
Text Design	Impressions Publishing Services, Inc.
Cover Design	John Ritland

Library of Congress Cataloging-in-Publication Data

Medieval Russia : a source book, 850–1700 / edited by Basil Dmytryshyn. — 3rd ed.
p.   cm.
Includes bibliographical references.
ISBN 0-03-033422-5
1. Soviet Union—History—Sources.   I. Dmytryshyn, Basil, 1925–.
DK3.D56 1990   90-4555
947-dc20   CIP

Requests for permission to make copies of any part of the work should be mailed to:
Copyrights and Permissions Department, Harcourt Brace Jovanovich, Inc.
6277 Sea Harbor Drive, Orlando, FL 32887.

Address for editorial correspondence: Harcourt Brace Jovanovich, Inc.
301 Commerce Street, Suite 3700,
Fort Worth, TX 76102

Address for orders: Harcourt Brace Jovanovich, Inc. , 6277 Sea Harbor Drive,
Orlando, FL 32887.
1-800-782-4479, or 1-800-433-0001 (in Florida)

PRINTED IN THE UNITED STATES OF AMERICA

1 2 3 4 090 9 8 7 6 5 4 3 2

Harcourt Brace Jovanovich, Inc.
The Dryden Press
Saunders College Publishing

Preface
to the
Third Edition

The main objective of this new edition is the same as that of its two predecessors, to make available to the student, the general reader, and the scholar
who is not a specialist extensive, illustrative source material on political, social,
economic, religious, cultural, legal, and other matters faced by peoples of
various principalities of Medieval Rus/Russia from approximately A.D. 850
to A.D. 1700.

The new edition has been completely reorganized and redesigned. It consists
of three Parts and includes 70 entries. The first Part, subtitled KIEVAN RUS,
has twenty-one entries (six of which are new) and treats various principalities
of Kievan Rus up to the fourteenth century. The second Part, subtitled
MONGOL YOKE, has ten entries (four of which are new) and deals with
various aspects of Mongol conquest and domination of Rus principalities from
1237 to 1480. The third Part, subtitled MUSCOVY, includes thirty-nine
entries that reflect the rise of the Principality of Muscovy-Rus into Russia
from 1325 to 1700.

To accommodate the new material it was necessary to delete a few entries
from the second edition. The challenge was enormous, and it is hoped that
the users of this edition will be pleased with the final product, which also
includes an updated bibliography and rich illustrative material.

I wish to express my gratitude to the editors of Holt, Rinehart and Winston,
Inc., for suggesting that I prepare the third edition. In particular, I wish to
thank David Tatom, Acquisitions Editor; Martin Lewis, Developmental Editor; and Dawn Youngblood, Senior Project Editor, for their encouragement,
patience, and understanding. Special thanks also goes to Leon Unruh, who
proofread *Medieval Russia* so knowledgably and meticulously. My thanks go
likewise to many of my colleagues who have, over the years, offered ideas
and, in some instances, specific suggestions for new entries. Unfortunately,
space limitations prevented me from incorporating many of their excellent
suggestions. However, I would like to thank the reviewers of the third edition:
Seymour Becker, Rutgers University; Chester Dunning, Texas A&M Uni-

versity; Orysia Karapinka, University of Pittsburgh; Thomas S. Noonan, University of Minnesota; and Richard Robbins, University of New Mexico.

Finally, my special thanks go to my wife Virginia who, as she has done on numerous occasions before, helped me to proofread the new material and put it through the word processor.

Basil Dmytryshyn

Green Valley, Arizona
May 1990

Preface
to the
Second Edition

The purpose of the new edition is to enrich this collection of sources through new documentary material. In pursuit of that goal several lengthy documents have been added, ranging from a tenth century Arab description of "Rus" to eyewitness accounts of bloody disturbances that engulfed Muscovy in the middle of the seventeenth century. It is hoped that the inclusion of this new material will fill some of the gaps of the first edition and thereby make this volume more meaningful and useful to all interested students of the history of Rus and of Russia before Peter the Great.

Basil Dmytryshyn

Portland, Oregon
September 1972

Preface
to the
First Edition

Medieval Russia: A Source Book is a collection of basic sources on political, social, economic, and cultural life in medieval Russia, and is designed for the student, the general reader, and the scholar who is not a specialist. It is neither a text nor a substitute for a text, but an attempt to furnish what a more formal volume cannot offer—extensive, illustrative source material to amplify and enrich the text.

The selections fall into two main categories: excerpts from chronicles, letters, and official instructions written or issued by medieval Russians; and observations of, or commentaries on, the customs, habits, and ideas of the Russian people as recorded by their European contemporaries. Each of the forty-one selections is preceded by a brief introduction aimed at making the article more meaningful by placing it in its proper historical perspective.

The task of selecting representative documents that would contribute to a greater understanding of Russian medieval history was not an easy one, especially when dealing with such a complex and unwieldy subject. Some readers may feel that their areas of interest have been under-represented, but this is unavoidable in any effort to survey some eight hundred years of history in one volume. Space, too, was a problem, for complete documents (or documents as nearly complete as practicable) were preferred to brief excerpts so that the reader might achieve greater insight into the important events of the country's past.

Wherever possible existing translations of documents were used; some of these appeared in rare or expensive editions and are now out of print or not readily available. Such translations are reproduced here in their original form. Because there is no uniform way to transliterate from Cyrillic to Roman characters, the selections translated by different scholars show a diversity in the spellings of certain Russian names.

Many documents of this collection, however, appear here in English for the first time. Because of considerable difference in syntax and style, translation of these documents presented several technical difficulties and many passages required some adaptation to modern English. The same solution, regarding spelling and transliteration, was applied to a number of documents written in sixteenth-century English. In all my own translations I have aimed for accuracy instead of poetic or elegant rendition, and I have adhered to the system of transliteration used by the Library of Congress, with only minor exceptions. Thus, all Russian proper names ending in и й have been rendered as -ii- (Shuiskii); the Russian ю has been rendered throughout as -iu- (Iurii); and the Russian я has been rendered as -ia- (Iaroslav). An exception to this rule is the word бояр , which, because of the widely used English spelling, has been rendered as *boyar*. Apostrophes have been excluded and plurals of all untranslatable Russian words (*voevodas, dengas*) have been anglicized. A glossary listing unfamiliar expressions and terms not readily translatable has been appended, as well as three genealogical tables of Russian princes and tsars from 862 to 1917 and a chronological table.

It is a pleasant custom among scholars to thank all those who have made possible the appearance of a work. I acknowledge my indebtedness to the following institutions and individuals: the Research Committee of Portland State College for financial assistance that helped defray travel expenses for the selection of material from the Russian collection at the University of California Library at Berkeley; the University of Illinois Research Board for providing a research assistant, Barry Hoffman, who assisted me in the preparation of the bibliography; the publishers who kindly permitted me to reprint selections from previously translated material (individually acknowledged under each item); my colleagues at Portland State College for their interest and encouragement; and Mrs. Elizabeth Phelps, Mrs. Deanna Bozeman, and Miss Doris Jamison, who volunteered their typing services.

Lastly, I owe more than I can express to my wife Virginia, who has read this manuscript with a keen eye and whose critical judgment has helped to improve it. It is for this and many other reasons that this volume is dedicated to her.

Basil Dmytryshyn

Portland, Oregon
June 1966

Contents

Maps

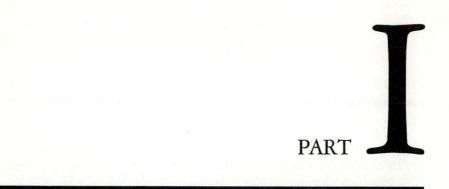

PART I

Kievan Rus

1

The Distribution
of Medieval Slavs

Our knowledge of the original home of the Slavs, like that of most people in their preliterary development, is nebulous. One of the most vital sources of the early history of eastern Slavs is *Povest Vremennykh Let* (The Tale of Bygone Years), also known as *Nachalnaia Letopis* or the *Primary Chronicle*. Modern scholarship has established that the *Primary Chronicle* was compiled between 1037 and 1118 by monks of the Kievan Crypt Monastery. Among its many contributors were Nikon, who recorded events from 1060 to 1073, some of which were eyewitness accounts; and Nestor, who in the year 1113 gave the *Primary Chronicle* its present form. Since Nestor's version was subsequently used by other chroniclers, until the nineteenth century the *Primary Chronicle* was known as the *Chronicle of Nestor*. Although Nestor's original edition has not been preserved we have two later editions of his work: the *Lavrentian Chronicle*, prepared in 1377 for a prince in Suzdal, and the *Hypatian Chronicle*, which dates from the middle of the fifteenth century and was discovered in the Hypatian Monastery at Kostroma.

The *Primary Chronicle*, as well as similar medieval records of Russian history, is a mixture of religious writings, legend, fact, and fiction. Except for the introduction, it is organized on a yearly basis beginning with the year 852 (or 6360 according to the old Byzantine calendar used in Russia until 1699). The *Chronicle* contains many brief entries as well as lengthy and colorful accounts of wars, feuds, agreements, and other developments.

These are the narratives of bygone years regarding the origin of the land of Rus, who first began to rule in Kiev, and from what source the land Rus had its beginning. . . .

For many years the Slavs lived beside the Danube, where the Hungarian and Bulgarian lands now lie. From among these Slavs, parties scattered throughout the country and were known by appropriate names, according to the places where they settled. Thus some came and settled by the river Morava,

---

Reprinted by permission of the publishers from Samuel H. Cross, "The Russian Primary Chronicle," *Harvard Studies and Notes in Philology and Literature* (Cambridge, Mass., Harvard University Press, 1930), vol. 12, pp. 136–142.

and were named Moravians, while others were called Czechs. Among these same Slavs are included the White Croats, the Serbs, and the Khorutanians. For when the Vlakhs attacked the Danubian Slavs, settled among them, and did them violence, the latter came and made their homes by the Vistula, and were then called Lyakhs. Of these same Lyakhs some were called Polyanians, some Lutichians, some Mazovians, and still others Pomorians. Certain Slavs settled also on the Dnieper, and were likewise called Polyanians. Still others were named Derevlians, because they lived in the forests. Some also lived between the Pripet and the Dvina, and were known as Dregovichians. Other tribes resided along the Dvina and were called Polotians on account of a small stream called the Polota, which flows into the Dvina. It was from this same stream that they were named Polotians. The Slavs also dwelt about Lake Ilmen, and were known there by their appropriate name. They built a city which they called Novgorod. Still others had their homes along the Desna, the Sem, and the Sula, and were called Severians. Thus the Slavic race was divided, and its language was known as Slavic.

When the Polyanians lived by themselves among the hills, a trade-route connected the Varangians with the Greeks. Starting from Greece, this route proceeds along the Dnieper, above which a portage leads to the Lovat. By following the Lovat, the great lake Ilmen is reached. The river Volkhov flows out of this lake and enters the great lake Nevo. The mouth of this lake opens into the Varangian Sea. Over this sea goes the route to Rome, and on from Rome overseas to Tsargrad. The Pontus, into which flows the river Dnieper, may be reached from that point. The Dnieper itself rises in the upland forest, and flows southward. The Dvina has its source in the same forest, but flows northward and empties into the Varangian Sea. The Volga rises in the same forest, but flows to the east, and discharges through seventeen mouths into the Caspian Sea. It is possible by this route to the eastward to reach the Bulgars and the Caspians, and thus attain the region of Shem. Along the Dvina runs the route to the Varangians, whence one may reach Rome, and go on from there to the race of Ham. But the Dnieper flows through various mouths into the Pontus. This sea, beside which taught St. Andrew, Peter's brother, is called the Russian Sea. . . .

The Polyanians lived apart and governed their families, for thus far they were brethren, and each one lived with his gens on his own lands, ruling over his kinsfolk. There were three brothers, Kii, Shchek, and Khoriv, and their sister was named Lybed. Kii lived upon the hill where the Borich trail now is, and Shchek dwelt upon the hill now named Shchekovitza, while on the third resided Khoriv, after whom this hill is named Khorevitza. They built a town and named it Kiev after their oldest brother. Around the town lay a wood and a great pine forest in which they used to catch wild beasts. These

men were wise and prudent; they were called Polyanians, and there are Polyanians descended from them living in Kiev to this day.

Some ignorant persons have claimed that Kii was a ferryman, for near Kiev
there was at that time a ferry from the other side of the river, in consequence
of which people used to say, "To Kii's ferry." Now if Kii had been a mere
ferryman, he would never have gone to Tsargrad. He was then the chief of
his kin, and it is related what great honor he received from the Emperor
when he went to visit him. On his homeward journey, he arrived at the
Danube. The place pleased him, and he built a small town, wishing to dwell
there with his kinsfolk. But those who lived near by would not grant him
this privilege. Yet even now the dwellers by the Danube call this town Kievetz.
When Kii returned to Kiev, his native city, he ended his life there; and his
brothers Shchek and Khoriv, as well as their sister Lybed, died there also.

After the death of these three brothers, their gens assumed the supremacy
among the Polyanians. The Derevlians possessed a principality of their own,

as did also the Dregovichians, while the Slavs had their own authority in Novgorod, and another principality existed on the Polota, where the Polotians dwell. Beyond them reside the Krivichians, who live at the head waters of the Volga, the Dvina, and the Dnieper, and whose city is Smolensk. It is there that the Krivichians dwell; and beyond them are the Severians. At Byelo-Ozero are situated the Ves, and on the lake of Rostov, the Merya, and on Lake Kleshchino the Merya also. Along the river Oka (which flows into the Volga), Muroma, the Cheremisians, and Mordva preserve their native languages. For the Slavic race in Rus includes only the Polyanians, the Derevlians, the people of Novgorod, the Polotians, the Dregovichians, the Severians, and the Buzhians, who live along the River Bug and were later called Volhynians. The following are other tribes which pay tribute to Rus: Chud, Merya, Ves, Muroma, Cheremis, Mordva, Perm, Pechera, Yam, Litva, Zimegola, Kors, Narva, and Liv. These tribes have their own languages and belong to the race of Japheth, which inhabits the lands of the north.

Now while the Slavs dwelt along the Danube, as we have said, there came from among the Scythians, that is, from the Khazars, a people called Bulgars, who settled on the Danube and oppressed the Slavs. Afterward came the White Huns, who inherited the Slavic country. For these Huns first appeared in the reign of the Emperor Heraclius, who campaigned against Chosroes, the Emperor of Persia. The Avars, who attacked Heraclius the Emperor and nearly captured him, also lived at this period. They made war upon the Slavs, and harassed the Dulebians, who were themselves Slavs. They even did violence to the Dulebian women. . . . The Avars were large in stature and proud of spirit, and God destroyed them. They all perished, and not one Avar survived. There is to this day a proverb in Rus which runs, "They perished like the Avars." Neither race nor heir of them remains. The Pechenegs came after them; and the Black Huns passed by Kiev later during the time of Olga.

Thus the Polyanians, who belong to the Slavic race, lived apart, as we have said, and called themselves Polyanians. The Derevlians, who are likewise Slavs, lived by themselves and adopted this tribal name. But the Radimichians and the Vyatichians sprang from the Lyakhs. There were in fact among the Lyakhs two brothers, one named Radim and the other Vyatko. Radim settled on the Sozh, where the people are known as Radimichians, and Vyatko with his family settled on the Oka. The people there were named Vyatichians after him. Thus the Polyanians, the Derevlians, the Severians, the Radimichians, the Vyatichians, and the Croats lived at peace. The Dulebians dwelt along the Bug, where the Volhynians now are found, but the Ulichians and the Tivercians lived by the Dniester, and extended as far as the Danube. There was a multitude of them, for they inhabited the banks of the Dniester almost down to the sea, and to this day there are cities in that locality which still belong to them. Hence they are called Great Scythia by the Greeks.

These Slavic tribes preserved their own customs, the law of their forefathers, and their traditions, each observing their individual usages. For the Polyanians retained the mild and peaceful customs of their ancestors, and showed respect for their daughters-in-law and their sisters, as well as for their mothers and fathers. For their mothers-in-law and their brothers-in-law they also entertained great reverence. They observed a fixed marriage custom, under which the groom's brother did not fetch the bride, but she was brought to the bridegroom in the evening, and on the next morning his gifts were presented.

The Derevlians, on the other hand, existed in bestial fashion, and lived like cattle. They killed one another, ate every impure thing, and there was no marriage among them, but instead they seized upon maidens by capture. The Radimichians, the Vyatichians, and the Severians had the same customs. They lived in the forest like any wild beast, and ate every unclean thing. They spoke obscenely before their fathers and their daughters-in-law. There were no marriages among them, but simply festivals among the villages. When the people gathered together for games, for dancing, and for all other devilish amusements, the men on these occasions carried off wives for themselves, and each took any woman with whom he had arrived at an understanding. Whenever a death occurred, a feast was held over the corpse, and then a great pyre was constructed, on which the deceased was laid and burned. After the bones were collected, they were placed in a small urn and set upon a post by the roadside, even as the Vyatichians do to this day. Such customs were observed by the Krivichians and the other pagans, since they did not know the law of God, but made a law unto themselves.

❧ *2* ❧

The Coming of the Varangians

The political history of the early Kievan state began with the Normans, or Vikings, whom the Greeks called Varangians. According to the *Primary Chronicle*, the Varangians established a firm foothold in northeastern

---

Reprinted by permission of the publishers from Samuel H. Cross, "The Russian Primary Chronicle," *Harvard Studies and Notes in Philology and Literature* (Cambridge, Mass., Harvard University Press, 1930), vol. 12, pp. 144–147.

Europe (Novgorod) about 862 A.D. From here, under the leadership of Riurik, they gradually brought other areas under their control, and by 880 the entire Dnieper Basin, including the city of Kiev, was Varangian-dominated. The dynasty that Riurik established controlled the destiny of Kiev, and subsequently of Moscow, until 1598 when Feodor, the son of Ivan the Terrible, died without leaving an heir.

In the eighteenth century the Norman origin of the Kievan state gave rise to the so-called Normanist theory, which argued that the Normans gave Kiev not only its government but its culture as well. This view was soon challenged by anti-Normanist scholars who emphasized the Slavic origins of the Kievan state. During the past two hundred years both camps have produced many scholarly works in support of their positions. As a result of this investigation, both views have undergone considerable modification, but the two theories still attract avid followers.

6367 (859). The Varangians from beyond the sea imposed tribute upon the Chuds, the Slavs, the Merians, the Ves, and the Krivichians. But the Khazars imposed it upon the Polyanians, the Severians, and the Vyatichians, and collected a squirrel skin and a beaver skin from each hearth.

6368–6370 (860–862). The tributaries of the Varangians drove them back beyond the sea and, refusing them further tribute, set out to govern themselves. There was no law among them, but tribe arose against tribe. Discord thus ensued among them, and they began to war one against another. They said to themselves, "Let us seek a prince who may rule over us, and judge us according to the law." They accordingly went overseas to the Varangian Russes. These particular Varangians were known as Russes, just as some are called Swedes, and others Normans, Angles, and Goths, for they were thus named. The Chuds, the Slavs, and the Krivichians then said to the people of Rus, "Our whole land is great and rich, but there is no order in it. Come to rule and reign over us." They thus selected three brothers, with their kinsfolk, who took with them all the Russes and migrated. The oldest, Rurik, located himself in Novgorod; the second, Sineus, in Byeloozero; and the third, Truvor, in Izborsk. On account of these Varangians, the district of Novgorod became known as the land of Rus. The present inhabitants of Novgorod are descended from the Varangian race, but aforetime they were Slavs.

After two years, Sineus and his brother Truvor died, and Rurik assumed the sole authority. He assigned cities to his followers. Polotzk to one, Rostov to another, and to another, Byeloozero. In these cities, there are thus Varangian colonists, but the first settlers were, in Novgorod, Slavs; in Polotzk, Krivichians; at Byeloozero, Ves; in Rostov, Merians; and in Murom, Muromians. Rurik had dominion over all these districts.

With Rurik there were two men who did not belong to his kin, but were *boyars*. They obtained permission to go to Tsargrad with their families. They thus sailed down the Dnieper, and in the course of their journey they saw a small city on a hill. Upon their inquiry as to whose town it was, they were informed that three brothers, Kii, Shchek, and Khoriv, had once built the city, but that since their deaths, their descendants were living there as tributaries of the Khazars. Oskold and Dir remained in this city, and after gathering together many Varangians, they established their domination over the country of the Polyanians at the same time that Rurik was ruling at Novgorod. . . .

6378–6387 (870–879). On his deathbed, Rurik bequeathed his realm to Oleg, who belonged to his kin, and entrusted to Oleg's hands his son Igor, for he was very young.

6388–6390 (880–882). Oleg set forth, taking with him many warriors from among the Varangians, the Chuds, the Slavs, the Merians, and the Krivichians. He thus arrived with his Krivichians before Smolensk, took the city, and set up a garrison there. Thence he went on and captured Lyubech, where he also established a garrison. He then came to the hills of Kiev, and saw how Oskold and Dir reigned there. He hid his warriors in the boats, left some others behind, and went forward himself bearing the child Igor. He thus came to the foot of the Hunnish hill, and after concealing his troops, he sent messengers to Oskold and Dir, representing himself as a stranger on his way to Greece on an errand for Oleg and for Igor, the Prince's son, and requesting that they should come forth to greet them as members of their race. Oskold and Dir straightway came forth. Then all the soldiery jumped out of the boats, and Oleg said to Oskold and Dir, "You are not princes nor even of princely stock, but I am of princely birth." Igor was then brought forward, and Oleg announced that he was the son of Rurik. They killed Oskold and Dir, and after carrying them to the hill, they buried them there, on the hill now known as Hunnish, where the castle of Olma stands. Over that tomb Olma built a church dedicated to St. Nicholas, but Dir's tomb is behind St. Irene's. Oleg set himself up as prince in Kiev, and declared that it should be the mother of Russian cities. Varangians and Slavs accompanied him and his retainers were called Russes. Oleg began to build stockaded towns, and imposed tribute on the Slavs, the Krivichians, and the Merians. He commanded that Novgorod should pay the Varangians tribute to the amount of 300 *grivni* a year for the preservation of peace. This tribute was paid to the Varangians until the death of Yaroslav.

6391 (883). Oleg began military operations against the Derevlians, and after conquering them, he imposed upon them the tribute of a black marten skin apiece.

6392 (884). Oleg attacked the Severians, and conquered them. He imposed a light tribute upon them and forbade their further payment of tribute to the Khazars, on the ground that there was no reason for them to pay it as long as the Khazars were his enemies.

6393 (885). Oleg sent messengers to the Radimichians to inquire to whom they paid tribute. Upon their reply that they paid tribute to the Khazars, he directed them to render it to himself instead, and they accordingly paid him a *shilling* apiece, the same amount that they had paid the Khazars. Thus Oleg established his authority over the Polyanians, the Derevlians, the Severians, and the Radimichians, but he waged war with the Uluchians and the Tivercians.

⚓ 3 ⚓

Byzantine-Kievan Relations

Following their conquest of the Dnieper Basin the Varangians established lively relations with Constantinople, which was the center of Byzantine civilization. They gained some concessions from the Greeks through trade and treaties, others through military conquests and destruction. The *Primary Chronicle* gives vivid and detailed accounts of both approaches. Regardless of the means employed, Kiev's relations with Constantinople before the middle of the tenth century grew and became one of the basic foundations of Kievan economic prosperity and cultural greatness. In addition to war booty, the Kievans returned from Constantinople with an alphabet, calendar, Christian concepts—in short, culture. Because of these strong ties the subsequent decline of Constantinople (in the twelfth and thirteenth centuries) exerted a powerful influence on the decline of Kiev.

6371–6374 (863–866). Oskold and Dir attacked the Greeks during the fourteenth year of the reign of the Emperor Michael. When the Emperor had set forth against the Saracens and had arrived at the Black River the eparch sent him word that the Russes were approaching Tsargrad, and the Emperor turned back. Upon arriving inside the strait, the Russes made a great massacre

---

Reprinted by permission of the publishers from Samuel H. Cross, "The Russian Primary Chronicle," *Harvard Studies and Notes in Philology and Literature* (Cambridge, Mass., Harvard University Press, 1930), vol. 12, pp. 145–146, 149–155, 157–159, 160–164.

of the Christians, and attacked Tsargrad in two hundred boats. The Emperor succeeded with difficulty in entering the city. The people prayed all night with the Patriarch Photius at the Church of the Holy Virgin in Blachernae. They also sang hymns and carried the sacred vestment of the Virgin to dip it in the sea. The weather was still, and the sea was calm, but a storm of wind came up, and when great waves straightway rose, confusing the boats of the godless Russes, it threw them upon the shore and broke them up, so that few escaped such destruction. The survivors then returned to their native land. . . .

6412–6415 (904-907). Leaving Igor in Kiev, Oleg attacked the Greeks. He took with him a multitude of Varangians, Slavs, Chuds, Krivichians, Merians, Polyanians, Severians, Derevlians, Radimichians, Croats, Dulebians, and Tivercians, who are Torks. All these tribes are known as Great Scythia by the Greeks. With this entire force, Oleg sallied forth by horse and by ship, and the number of his vessels was two thousand. He arrived before Tsargrad, but the Greeks fortified the strait and closed up the city. Oleg disembarked upon the shore, and ordered his soldiery to beach the ships. They waged war around the city, and accomplished much slaughter of the Greeks. They also destroyed many palaces and burned the churches. Of the prisoners they captured, some they beheaded, some they tortured, some they shot, and still others they cast into the sea. The Russes inflicted many other woes upon the Greeks after the usual manner of soldiers. Oleg commanded his warriors to make wheels which they attached to the ships, and when the wind was favorable, they spread the sails and bore down upon the city from the open country. When the Greeks beheld this, they were afraid, and sending messengers to Oleg, they implored him not to destroy the city and offered to submit to such tribute as he should desire. Thus Oleg halted his troops. The Greeks then brought out to him food and wine, but he would not accept it, for it was mixed with poison. Then the Greeks were terrified, and exclaimed, "This is not Oleg, but St. Demetrius whom God has sent upon us." So Oleg demanded that they pay tribute for his two thousand ships at the rate of twelve *grivni* per man, with forty men reckoned to a ship.

The Greeks assented to these terms and prayed for peace lest Oleg should conquer the land of Greece. Retiring thus a short distance from the city, Oleg concluded a peace with the Greek Emperors Leo and Alexander, and sent into the city to them Karl, Farulf, Vermund, Hrollaf, and Steinvith, with instructions to receive the tribute. The Greeks promised to satisfy their requirements. Oleg demanded that they should give to the troops on the two thousand ships twelve *grivni* per bench, and pay in addition the sums required for the various Russian cities: first Kiev, then Chernigov, Pereyaslavl, Polotzk, Rostov, Lyubech, and the other towns. In these cities lived princes subject to Oleg.

The Russes proposed the following terms: "The Russes who come hither shall receive as much grain as they require. Whosoever come as merchants shall receive supplies for six months, including bread, wine, meat, fish, and fruit. Baths shall be prepared for them in any volume they require. When the Russes return homeward, they shall receive from your Emperor food, anchors, cordage, and sails, and whatever else is needful for the journey." The Greeks accepted these stipulations, and the Emperors and all the courtiers declared: "If Russes come hither without merchandise, they shall receive no provisions. Your prince shall personally lay injunction upon such Russes as journey hither that they shall do no violence in the towns and throughout our territory. Such Russes as arrive here shall dwell in the St. Mamas quarter. Our government will send officers to record their names, and they shall then receive their monthly allowance, first the natives of Kiev, then those from Chernigov, Pereyaslavl, and the other cities. They shall not enter the city save through one gate, unarmed and fifty at a time, escorted by soldiers of the Emperor. They may purchase wares according to their requirements and tax-free."

Thus the Emperors Leo and Alexander made peace with Oleg, and after agreeing upon the tribute and mutually binding themselves by oath, they kissed the cross, and invited Oleg and his men to swear an oath likewise. According to the religion of the Russes, the latter swore by their weapons and by their god Perun, as well as by Volos, the god of cattle, and thus confirmed the treaty.

Oleg gave orders that silken sails should be made for the Russes and linen ones for the Slavs, and his demand was satisfied. The Russes hung their shields upon the gates as a sign of victory, and Oleg then departed from Tsargrad. The Russes unfurled their silken sails and the Slavs their sails of linen, but the wind tore them. Then the Slavs said, "Let us keep our canvas ones; linen sails are not made for the Slavs." So Oleg came to Kiev, bearing palls, gold, fruit, and wine, along with every sort of adornment. The people called Oleg "the Sage," for they were but pagans, and therefore ignorant. . . .

6420 (912). Oleg despatched his vassals to make peace and to draw up a treaty between the Greeks and the Russes. His envoys thus made declaration:

"We of the Rus nation: Karl, Ingjald, Farulf, Vermund, Hrollaf, Gunnar, Harold, Karni, Frithleif, Hroarr, Angantyr, Throand, Leithulf, Fast, and Steinvith, are sent by Oleg, Great Prince of Rus, and by all the glorious *boyars* under his sway unto you, Leo and Alexander and Constantine, great Autocrats in God, Emperors of the Greeks, for the maintenance and proclamation of the long-standing amity which joins Greeks and Russes, in accordance with the desire of our Great Princes and at their command, and in behalf of all those Russes who are subject to the hand of our Prince.

"Our serenity, above all desirous, through God's help, of maintaining and proclaiming such amicable relations as now exist between Christians and Russians, has often deemed it proper to publish and confirm this amity not merely in words but also in writing and under a firm oath sworn upon our weapons according to our religion and our law. As we previously agreed in the name of God's peace and amity, the articles of this convention are as follows:

"First, that we shall conclude a peace with you Greeks, and love each other with all our heart and will, and as far as lies in our power, prevent any subject of our serene Princes from committing any crime or misdemeanor. Rather shall we exert ourselves as far as possible to maintain as irrevocable and immutable henceforth and forever the amity thus proclaimed by our agreement with you Greeks and ratified by signature and oath. May you Greeks on your part maintain as irrevocable and immutable henceforth and forever the same amity toward our serene Princes of Rus and toward all the subjects of our serene Prince.

"In the matter of stipulations concerning damage, we subscribe to the following provisions:

"If clear proofs exist, there shall be a true declaration of such proofs. But if no credence attach to such declaration, the dissenting party shall take oath to this effect, and after he shall have taken oath according to his faith, a penalty shall be assessed in proportion to the trespass committed.

"Whatsoever Russ kills a Christian, or whatsoever Christian kills a Russ shall die, since he has committed murder. If any man flee after committing a murder, in the case that he is well-to-do, the nearest relative of the victim shall receive a legal portion of the culprit's property, while the wife of the victim shall receive a like amount, which is legally due her. But if the defendant is poor and has escaped, he shall be under distress until he returns or until he dies.

"If any man strike another with a sword or assault him with any other sort of weapon, he shall, according to Russian law, pay five pounds of silver for such blow or assault. If the defendant is poor he shall pay as much as he is able, and be deprived even of the very clothes he wears, and he shall also declare upon oath that he has no one to aid him. Thereafter the case against him shall be withdrawn.

"If any Russ commit a theft against a Christian, or vice versa, and should the transgressor be caught in the act by the victim of the loss, in case the culprit is killed in the process of committing the theft, no penalty shall be exacted for his death by either Greeks or Russes. The victim of the loss shall recover the stolen property. If the thief surrenders, he shall be taken and bound by the one upon whom the theft was committed, and the culprit shall return whatever he has dared to appropriate, making at the same time threefold restitution for it.

"If on the pretext of instituting a search, any person, whether Greek or Russ, employs abusive treatment or violence and appropriates some article by force, he shall repay three times its value.

"If a ship is detained by high winds upon a foreign shore, and one of us Russes is near by, the ship with its cargo shall be revictualed and sent on to Christian territory. We will pilot it through every dangerous passage until it arrives at a place of safety. But if any such ship thus detained by storm or by some terrestrial obstacle cannot possibly reach its destination, we Russes will extend aid to the crew of this ship, and conduct them with their merchandise in all security, in case such an event takes place near Greek territory. But if such an accident befalls near the Russian shore, the ship's cargo shall be disposed of, and we Russes will remove whatever can be disposed of for the account of the owners. Then, when we proceed to Greece with merchandise or upon an embassy to your Emperor, we shall render up honorably the price of the sold cargo of the ship. But if anyone on that ship is killed or maltreated by us Russes, or if any object is stolen, then those who have committed such acts shall be subject to the aforesaid penalty.

"From this time forth, if a prisoner of either nation is in durance either of the Russes or of the Greeks, and then sold into another country, any Russ or Greek who happens to be in that locality shall purchase the prisoner and return the person thus purchased to his own native country. The purchaser shall be indemnified for the amount thus expended, or else the value of the prisoner's daily labor shall be reckoned toward the purchase money. If any Russ be taken prisoner by the Greeks, he shall likewise be sent back to his native land, and his purchase price shall be repaid, as has been stipulated, according to his value.

"Whenever you find it necessary to declare war, or when you are conducting a campaign, providing any Russes desirous of honoring your Emperor come at any time and wish to remain in his service, they shall be permitted in this respect to act according to their desire.

"If a Russian prisoner from any region is sold among the Christians, or if any Christian prisoner is sold among the Russes, he shall be ransomed for twenty *bezants* and returned to his native land.

"In case a Russian slave is stolen or escapes or is sold under compulsion, and if a Russ institutes a claim to this effect which is substantiated, the slave shall be returned to Rus. If a merchant loses a slave and institutes a complaint, he shall search for this slave until he is found, but if any person refuses to allow him to make this search, the local officer shall forfeit his right of perquisition.

"With respect to the Russes professionally engaged in Greece under the orders of the Christian Emperor, if any one of them dies without setting his property in order and has no kinsfolk there, his estate shall be returned to his surviving relatives in Rus. But if he makes some disposition of his goods, the person whom he has designated in writing as his heir shall receive the property of which he thus disposed. This shall be the due process of inheritance in the cases of Russes engaging in trade, of casual travelers in Greece, and of those having debts outstanding there.

"If a criminal takes refuge in Greece, the Russes shall make complaint to the Christian Empire, and such criminal shall be arrested and returned to Rus regardless of his protests. The Russes shall perform the same service for the Greeks whenever the occasion arises.

"As a convention and an inviolable pledge binding equally upon you Greeks and upon us Russes, we have caused the present treaty to be transcribed in the handwriting of Ivan upon a double parchment, bearing your Emperor's and our own signatures, to be promulgated and handed to our envoys in the name of the Holy Cross and the Holy and Indivisible Trinity of your one true God. According to our own faith and the custom of our nation, we have sworn to your Emperor, who rules over you by the grace of God, that we will neither violate ourselves, nor allow any of our subjects to violate the peace and amity assured by the articles thus concluded between us. We have also given to your government an identic document for the mutual ratification of the same convention in order to confirm and promulgate the treaty thus concluded between us this second of September, in the year of Creation 6420 (912)."

The Emperor Leo honored the Russian envoys with gifts of gold, palls, and robes, and placed his vassals at their disposition to show them the beauties of the churches, the golden palace, and the riches contained therein. They thus showed the Russes much gold and many palls and jewels, together with the relics of our Lord's Passion: the crown, the nails, and the purple robe, as well as the bones of the Saints. They also instructed the Russes in their faith, and expounded to them the true belief. Thus the Emperor dismissed them to their native land with great honor. The envoys sent by Oleg returned to Kiev, and reported to him all the utterances of both Emperors. They recounted how they had made peace and established a covenant between Greece and Rus, confirmed by oaths inviolable for the subjects of both countries.

Thus Oleg ruled in Kiev, and dwelt at peace with all nations. . . .

6421 (913). Igor succeeded Oleg and began his reign. At the same time began the reign of Constantine, son of Leo and son-in-law of Romanus. . . .

6443–6449 (935–941). Igor attacked the Greeks, and the Bulgarians sent word to the Emperor that the Russes were advancing upon Tsargrad with ten thousand vessels. The Russes set out across the sea, and began to ravage Bithynia. They waged war along the Pontus as far as Heraclea and Paphlagonia, and laid waste the entire region of Nicomedia, burning everything along the gulf. Of the people they captured, some they butchered, others they set up as targets and shot at, some they seized upon, and after binding their hands behind their backs, they drove iron nails through their heads. Many sacred churches they gave to the flames, while they burned many monasteries and villages, and took no little booty on both sides of the sea. Then, when the army came out of the east, Pamphilus the Domestic with forty thousand men, Phocas the Patrician with the Macedonians, and Theodore the General with the Thracians, supported by other illustrious nobles, surrounded the Russes. After taking counsel, the latter threw themselves upon the Greeks, and as the conflict between them was desperate, the Greeks experienced difficulty in winning the upper hand. The Russes returned at evening to their companions, embarked at night upon their vessels, and fled away. Theophanes pursued them in boats with Greek fire, and dropped it through pipes upon the Russian ships, so that a strange miracle was offered to view.

The Russes upon seeing the flames, cast themselves into the seawater, being anxious to escape, but the survivors returned home. When they came once more to their native land, where each one recounted to his kinsfolk the course of events and described the fire launched from the ships, they related that the Greeks had in their possession the lightning from heaven, and had set them on fire by pouring it forth, so that the Russes could not conquer them. Upon his return, Igor began to collect a great army, and sent many messengers after the Varangians beyond the sea, inviting them to attack the Greeks, for he desired to make war upon them. . . .

6452 (944). After collecting many warriors among the Varangians, the Russes, the Polyanians, the Slavs, the Krivichians, the Tivercians, and the Pechenegs, and receiving hostages from them, Igor advanced upon the Greeks by ship and by horse, thirsting for revenge. The Khersonians, upon hearing of this expedition, reported to Romanus that the Russes were advancing with innumerable ships and covered the sea with their vessels. Likewise the Bulgarians sent tidings to the effect that the Russes were on the way, and that they had won the Pechenegs for their allies. When the Emperor heard this news, he sent to Igor his best *boyars* to entreat him to come no nearer, but rather to accept the tribute which Oleg had received, and to the amount of which something should even be added. He likewise sent palls and much gold to the Pechenegs.

Now Igor, when he came to the Danube, called together his retinue, and after some reflection communicated to them the Emperor's offer. Igor's retinue then replied, "If the Emperor speaks thus, what do we desire beyond receiving gold, silver, and palls without having to fight for them? Who knows who will be victorious, we or he? Who has the sea for his ally? For we are not marching by land, but through the depths of the sea. Death lies in wait for us all." Igor heeded them, and bade the Pechenegs ravage Bulgaria. He himself, after receiving from the Greeks gold and palls sufficient for his whole army, returned again and came to Kiev in his native land.

6453 (945). Romanus, Constantine, and Stephen sent envoys to Igor to renew the previous treaty, and Igor discussed the matter with them. Igor sent his own envoys to Romanus, and the Emperor called together his *boyars* and his nobles. The Russian envoys were introduced and bidden to speak, and it was commanded that the remarks of both parties should be inscribed upon parchment like the previous agreement existing under Romanus, Constantine, and Stephen, the most Christian princes. . . .

[*The Greeks stipulated:*] "The Great Prince of Rus and his *boyars* shall send to Greece to the great Greek Emperors as many ships as they desire with their agents and merchants, according to the prevailing usage. The agents have hitherto carried gold seals, and the merchants silver ones. But your Prince has now made known that he will forward a certificate to our government, and any agents or merchants thus sent by the Russians shall be provided with such a certificate to the effect that a given number of ships has been despatched. By this means we shall be assured that they come with peaceful intent.

"But if such persons come uncertificated and are surrendered to us, we shall detain and hold them until we notify your Prince. If they do not surrender, but offer resistance, they shall be killed, and indemnity for their death shall not be exacted by your Prince. If, however, they flee to Rus, we shall so inform your Prince, and he shall deal with them as he sees fit.

"If Russes come without merchandise, they shall not be entitled to receive monthly allowances. Your Prince shall moreover prohibit his agents and such other Russes as come hither from the commission of violence in our villages and territory. Such Russes as come hither shall dwell by St. Mamas's Church. Our authorities shall note their names, and they shall then receive their monthly allowance, the agents the amount proper to their position, and the merchants the usual amount: first, those from the city of Kiev, then those from Chernigov and Pereyaslavl. They shall enter the city through one gate in groups of fifty without weapons, and shall dispose of their merchandise as they require, after which they shall depart. An officer of our government shall guard them, in order that, if any Russ or Greek does wrong, he may redress it.

"When the Russes enter the city, they shall not have the right to buy silk above the value of fifty *bezants*. Whoever purchases such silks shall exhibit them to the imperial officer, who will stamp and return them. When the

Russes depart hence, they shall receive from us as many provisions as they require for the journey, and what they need for their ships (as has been previously determined), and they shall return home in safety. They shall not have the privilege of wintering in the St. Mamas quarter.

"If any slave runs away from Rus and flees into the territory of our Empire, or escapes from the St. Mamas quarter, he shall be apprehended if he be in Greek territory. If he is not found, the Christian Russes shall so swear according to their faith, and the non-Christians after their custom, and they shall then receive from us their due, two pieces of silk per slave, according to previous stipulations. If, among the people of our Empire, whether from our city or elsewhere, any slave of ours escapes among you and takes anything with him, the Russes shall send him back again. If what he has appropriated is intact, the finder shall receive two *bezants* from its value.

"If any Russ attempts to commit theft upon subjects of our Empire, he who so acts shall be severely punished, and he shall pay double the value of what he has stolen. If a Greek so transgress against a Russ, he shall receive the same punishment that the latter would suffer for a like offence. If a Russ commits a theft upon a Greek, or a Greek upon a Russ, he must return not only the stolen article, but also its value. If the stolen article is found to have been sold, he shall return double the price, and also shall be punished both by Greek law and custom and by the law of the Russes.

"If the Russes bring in young men or grown girls who have been taken as prisoners from our dominions, the Greeks shall pay a ransom of ten *bezants* each and recover the captives. If the latter are of middle age, the Greeks shall recover them on payment of eight *bezants* each. But in the case that the captives are old persons or young children, the ransom shall be five *bezants*. If any Russes are found laboring as slaves in Greece, providing they are prisoners of war, the Russes shall ransom them for ten *bezants* each. But if a Greek has actually purchased any such prisoner, and so declares under oath, he shall receive in return the full purchase price paid for the prisoner.

"In the matter of the country of Kherson and all the cities in that region, the Prince of Rus shall not have the right to harass these localities, nor shall that district be subject to you. If the Prince of Rus calls on us for soldiers wherewith to wage war, we agree to supply him with any number required.

"In case the Russes find a Greek ship cast ashore, they shall not harm it, and if any person remove any object therefrom, or enslave a member of the crew, or kill him, he shall be amenable to both Russian and Greek law. If Russian subjects meet with Khersonian fishermen at the mouth of the Dnieper, they shall not harm them in any wise. The Russes shall, moreover, not have the right to winter at the mouth of the Dnieper, either at Byelobereg or by St. Eleutherius, but when autumn comes, they shall return home to Rus.

Regarding the Black Bulgarians, who come and ravage the Kherson district, we enjoin the prince of Rus not to allow them to injure that region.

"If any crime is committed by a Greek subject to our Empire, the Russes shall not have the right to punish him, but according to the legislation of our Empire, he shall suffer in proportion to his misdeed.

"If a Christian kill a Russ, or a Russ a Christian, he who has committed the murder shall be held by the relatives of the deceased that they may kill him. If he who has committed murder runs away and escapes, the relatives of the murdered man shall receive the murderer's property in the case that he is wealthy. But if the escaped culprit is poor, he shall be pursued till found, and when he is found, he shall be executed.

"If a Russ assault a Greek, or a Greek a Russ, with sword, spear, or any other weapon, he who has committed this crime shall pay five pounds of silver according to the Russian law, but if he is poor, all his available property shall be sold, even to the garments he walks in, and these too shall be taken from him. Finally he shall swear upon his faith that he has no possessions, and then he shall be released.

"If our government shall desire of you military assistance for use against our adversaries, they shall communicate with your Great Prince, and he shall send us as many soldiers as we require. From this fact, other countries shall learn what amity the Greeks and the Russes entertain toward each other. . . ."

The agents sent by Igor returned to him with the Greek envoys, and reported all the words of the Emperor Romanus. Then Igor called the Greek envoys before him and bade them report what injunction the Emperor had laid upon them. The Emperor's envoys replied, "The Emperor has sent us. He loves peace, and desires to maintain concord and amity with the Prince of Rus. Your envoys have received the pledge of our Emperors, and they have sent us to receive your oath and that of your followers." Igor promised to comply with their request.

In the morning, Igor summoned the envoys, and went to a hill on which there was a statue of Perun. The Russes laid down their weapons, their shields, and their gold ornaments, and Igor and his people took oath (at least such as were pagans), while the Christian Russes took oath in the Church of St. Elias, which is by the stream, in the vicinity of the place Pasynetz and of the Khazars. This was, in fact, a cathedral church, since many of the Varangians were Christians.

Igor, after confirming the treaty with the Greeks, dismissed their envoys, bestowing upon them furs, slaves, and wax, and sent them away. The envoys then returned to the Emperor, and reported all the words of Igor and his affection for the Greeks. Thus Igor began to rule in Kiev, enjoying peaceful relations with all nations.

⚔ *4* ⚔

Porphyrogenitus' Description of the Voyage Down the Dnieper River

The commercial and military expeditions to the Black Sea and Constantinople via the Dnieper River represented a test of endurance for the Varangians, and later the Kievans. The most hazardous part of the journey was the passage through the treacherous cataracts on the lower Dnieper which were usually surrounded by hostile nomads such as the Pechenegs.

The following account by Byzantine Emperor Constantine Porphyrogenitus (911–959) also includes additional information about the Kievan state in the tenth century, the Pechenegs, the Bulgars, and other peoples.

The single-straked ships which come down from outer Russia to Constantinople are from Novgorod, where Sviatoslav, son of Igor, prince of Russia, had his seat, and others from the city of Smolensk and from Teliutza [Liubech] and Chernigov and from Busegrad [Vyshegrad]. All these come down the river Dnieper, and are collected together at the city of Kiev, also called Sambatas. Their Slav tributaries, the so-called Krivichians and the Lenzanines and the rest of the Slavonic regions, cut the single-strakers on their mountains in time of winter, and when they have fastened them together, as spring approaches, and the ice melts, they bring them on to the neighboring lakes. And since these lakes debouch into the river Dnieper, they enter thence on to this same river, and come down to Kiev, and draw the ships along to be fitted out, and sell them to the Russians. The Russians buy these bottoms only, furnishing them with oars and rowlocks and other tackle from their old single-strakers, which they dismantle; and so they fit them out. And in the month of June they move off down the river Dnieper and come to Vitichev, which is a tributary city of the Russians, and there they gather during two or three days; and when all the single-strakers are collected together, then they set out, and come down the said Dnieper river. And first they come to

---

From *Constantine Porphyrogenitus de Administrado Imperio* (Constantine Porphyrogenitus on Administration of the Empire). Greek text edited by Gy Moravcsik. Translated by R. J. H. Jenkins (Budapest, 1949), pp. 57–63, alternate. Items in brackets are mine.

the first barrage, called Essoupi, which means in Russian and Slavonic "Do not sleep!". The barrage itself is as narrow as the width of the Polo-ground; in the middle of it are rooted high rocks, which stand out like islands. Against these, then, comes the water and wells up and dashes down over the other side, with a mighty and terrific din. Therefore the Russians do not venture to pass between them, but put in to the bank hard by, disembarking the men on to dry land but leaving the rest of the goods on board the single-strakers. They then strip and, feeling with their feet to avoid striking on a rock, . . . This they do, some at the prow, some amidship, while others again, in the stern, punt with poles; and with all this careful procedure they pass this first barrage, edging round under the river-bank. When they have passed this barrage, they re-embark the others from the dry land and sail away, and come down to the second barrage, called in Russian Oulvorsi, and in Slavonic Ostrovouniprach, which means "the Island of the Barrage." This one is like the first, awkward and not to be passed through. Once again they disembark the men and convey the single-strakers past, as on the first occasion. Similarly they pass the third barrage also, called Gelandri, which means in Slavonic "Noise of the Barrage," and then the fourth barrage, the big one, called in Russian Aeifor, and in Slavonic Neasit, because the pelicans nest in the stones of the barrage. At this barrage all put into land prow foremost, and those who are deputed to keep the watch with them get out, and off they go, these men, and keep vigilant watch for the Pechenegs. The remainder, taking up the goods which they have on board the single-strakers, conduct the slaves in their chains past by land, six miles, until they are through the barrage. Then, partly dragging their single-strakers, partly porting them on their shoulders, they convey them to the far side of the barrage; and then, putting them on the river and loading up their baggage, they embark themselves, and again sail off in them. When they come to the fifth barrage, called in Russian Varouforos, and in Slavonic Voulniprach, because it forms a large lake, they again convey their single-strakers through at the edges of the river, as at the first and second barrages, and arrive at the sixth barrage, called in Russian Leanti, and in Slavonoc Veroutzi, that is "the Boiling of the Water," and this too they pass similarly. And thence they sail away to the seventh barrage, called in Russian Stroukoun, and in Slavonic Naprezi, which means "Little Barrage." This they pass at the so-called ford of Krarion, where the Chersonites cross over from Russia and the Pechenegs to Cherson; which ford is as wide as the Hippodrome, and is as high from below up to where the friends *of the Pechenegs* survey the scene as an arrow might reach of one shooting from bottom to top. It is at this point, therefore, that the Pechenegs come down and attack the Russians. After traversing this place, they reach the island called St. Gregory, on which island they perform their sacrifices because a gigantic oak tree stands there; and they sacrifice live cocks. Arrows, too, they peg in round about, and others bread and meat, or something of whatever each may have, as is their custom. They also throw lots regarding the cocks, whether to slaughter them, or to eat them as well, or to leave them alive. From this island onwards the Russians do not fear the Pechenegs until they reach the river Selinas. So then they start off thence and sail for four days, until they reach the lake which forms the mouth of the river, on which is the island of St. Aitherios. Arrived at this island, they rest themselves there for two or three days. And they re-equip their single-strakers with such tackle as is needed, sails and masts and rudders, which they bring with them. Since this lake is the mouth of this river, as has been said, and carries on down to the sea, and the island of St. Aitherios lies on the sea, they come thence to the Dniester river, and having got safely there they rest again. But when the weather is propitious, they put to sea and come to the river called Aspros, and after resting there too in like manner, they again set out and come to the Selinas, to the so-called branch of the Danube river. And until they are past the river Selinas, the Pechenegs keep pace with them. And if it happens that the sea cast a single-straker on shore, they all put in to land, in order to present a united opposition to the Pechenegs. But after the Selinas they fear nobody, but, entering the territory of Bulgaria, they come to the mouth of the Danube. From the Danube they proceed to the Konopas, and from the Konopas to Constantia, *and from Constantia* to the river Varna, and from Varna they come to the river Ditzina, all of which are Bulgarian territory. From the Ditzina they reach the district of Mesembria, and there at last their voyage, fraught with such travail and terror, such difficulty and danger, is at an end. The severe manner of life of these same Russians in winter-time is as follows. When the month of November begins, the chiefs together with all the Russians at once leave Kiev and go off on the "poliudie," which means "rounds," that is, to the Slavonic regions of the Vervians and Dregovichians and Krivichians and Severians and the rest of the Slavs who are tributaries of the Russians. There they are maintained throughout the winter, but then once more, starting from the month of April, when the ice of the Dnieper river melts, they come back to Kiev. They then pick up their single-strakers, as has been said above, and fit them out, and come down to Romania {i.e., the Byzantine Empire}.

⚔ 5 ⚔

Olga's Vengeance

Varangian conquest of the Dnieper Basin had positive as well as negative features. For instance, it brought political unity to the area, but it also imposed increased tribute. The *Primary Chronicle* records frequent complaints and even open rebellions against the excessive tribute demanded by the new masters, the most interesting of which occurred in 945 when the Derevlians killed Prince Igor (912–945). Igor's wife, Olga (945–957), avenged the death of her husband by killing the important men of the Derevlians and then destroying their cities. Because of her subsequent acceptance of Christianity, Olga was canonized by the Orthodox Church. It is to be noted that her punishment of the Derevlians reflected little saintliness.

6453 (945). In this year, Igor's retinue said to him, "The servants of Sveinald are adorned with weapons and fine raiment, but we are naked. Go forth with us, oh Prince, after tribute, that both you and we may profit thereby." Igor heeded their words, and he attacked Dereva in search of tribute. He demanded the previous tribute, and collected it by violence from the people with the assistance of his followers. After thus gathering the tribute, he returned to his city. On his homeward way, he said to his followers, after some reflection, "Go forward with the tribute. I shall turn back, and rejoin you later." He dismissed his retainers on their journey homeward, but being desirous of still greater booty, he returned on his tracks with a few of his vassals.

The Derevlians heard that he was again approaching, and consulted with Mal, their prince, saying, "If a wolf comes among the sheep, he will take away the whole flock one by one, unless he be killed. If we do not thus kill him now, he will destroy us all." They then sent forward to Igor inquiring why he had returned, since he had collected all the tribute. But Igor did not heed them, and the Derevlians came forth from the city of Izkorosten, and slew Igor and his company, for the number of the latter were few. So Igor was buried, and his tomb is near the city of Izkorosten in Dereva even to this day.

Reprinted by permission of the publishers from Samuel H. Cross, "The Russian Primary Chronicle," *Harvard Studies and Notes in Philology and Literature* (Cambridge, Mass., Harvard University Press, 1930), vol. 12, pp. 164–168.

But Olga [Igor's wife] was in Kiev with her son, the boy Svyatoslav. . . .
The Derevlians then said, "See, we have killed the Prince of Rus. Let us take
his wife Olga for our Prince Mal, and then we shall obtain possession of
Svyatoslav, and work our will upon him." So they sent their best men, twenty
in number, to Olga by boat, and they arrived below Borichev in their boat.
At that time, the water flowed below the heights of Kiev, and the inhabitants
did not live in the valley, but upon the heights. The city of Kiev was on the
present site of the palace of Gordiat and Nicephorus, and the prince's palace
was in the city where the palace of Vratislav and Chud now stands, while
the ferry was outside the city. Without the city there stood another palace,
where the palace of the Cantors is now situated, behind the Church of the
Holy Virgin upon the heights. This was a palace with a stone hall.

Olga was informed that the Derevlians had arrived, and summoned them
to her presence with a gracious welcome. When the Derevlians had thus
announced their arrival, Olga replied with an inquiry as to the reason of their
coming. The Derevlians then announced that their tribe had sent them to
report that they had slain her husband, because he was like a wolf, crafty and
ravening, but that their princes, who had thus preserved the land of Dereva,
were good and that Olga should come and marry their Prince Mal. For the
name of the Prince of Dereva was Mal.

Olga made this reply, "Your proposal is pleasing to me; indeed, my husband cannot rise again from the dead. But I desire to honor you tomorrow
in the presence of my people. Return now to your boat, and remain there
with an aspect of arrogance. I shall send for you on the morrow, and you
shall say, 'We will not ride on horses nor go on foot; carry us in our boat.'
And you shall be carried in your boat." Thus she dismissed them to their
vessel.

Now Olga gave command that a large deep ditch should be dug in the
castle with the hall, outside the city. Thus, on the morrow, Olga, as she sat
in the hall, sent for the strangers, and her messengers approached them and
said, "Olga summons you to great honor." But they replied, "We will not
ride on horseback nor in wagons, nor go on foot; carry us in our boat." The
people of Kiev then lamented, "Slavery is our lot. Our Prince is killed, and
our Princess intends to marry their prince." So they carried the Derevlians in
their boat. The latter sat on the cross-benches in great robes, puffed up with
pride. They thus were borne into the court before Olga, and when the men
had brought the Derevlians in, they dropped them into the trench along with
the boat. Olga bent over and inquired whether they found the honor to their
taste. They answered that it was worse than the death of Igor. She then
commanded that they should be buried alive, and they were thus buried.

Olga then sent messages to the Derevlians to the effect that, if they really required her presence, they should send after her their distinguished men, so that she might go to their Prince with due honor, for otherwise her people in Kiev would not let her go. When the Derevlians heard this message, they gathered together the best men who governed the land of Dereva, and sent them to her. When the Derevlians arrived, Olga commanded that a bath should be made ready, and invited them to appear before her after they had bathed. The bathhouse was then heated, and the Derevlians entered in to bathe. Olga's men closed up the bathhouse behind them, and she gave orders to set it on fire from the doors, so that the Derevlians were all burned to death.

Olga then sent to the Derevlians the following message: "I am now coming to you, so prepare great quantities of mead in the city where you killed my husband, that I may weep over his grave and hold a funeral feast for him." When they heard these words, they gathered great quantities of honey, and brewed mead. Taking a small escort, Olga made the journey with ease, and upon her arrival at Igor's tomb, she wept for her husband. She bade her followers pile up a great mound, and when they had piled it up, she also gave command that a funeral feast should be held. Thereupon the Derevlians sat down to drink, and Olga bade her followers wait upon them.

The Derevlians inquired of Olga where the retinue was which they had sent to meet her. She replied that they were following with her husband's bodyguard. When the Derevlians were drunk, she bade her followers fall upon them, and went about herself egging on her retinue to the massacre of the Derevlians. So they cut down five thousand of them; but Olga returned to Kiev and prepared an army to attack the survivors.

6454 (946). Olga, together with her son Svyatoslav, gathered a large and valiant army, and proceeded to attack the land of the Derevlians. The latter came out to meet her troops, and when both forces were ready for combat, Svyatoslav cast his spear against the Derevlians. But the spear pierced the ears of the horse, and struck the horse's foot, for the prince was but a child. Then Sveinald and Asmund said, "The prince has already begun battle; press on, vassals, after the prince." Thus they conquered the Derevlians, with the result that the latter fled, and shut themselves up in their cities.

Olga hastened with her son to the city of Izkorosten, for it was there that her husband had been slain, and they laid siege to the city. The Derevlians barricaded themselves within the city, and fought valiantly from it, for they realized that they had killed the prince, and to what fate they would in consequence surrender.

Olga remained there a year without being able to take the city, and then she thought out this plan. She sent into the town the following message:

"Why do you persist in holding out? All your cities have surrendered to me and submitted to tribute, so that the inhabitants now cultivate their fields and their lands in peace. But you had rather die of hunger, without submitting to tribute." The Derevlians replied that they would be glad to submit to tribute, but that she was still bent on avenging her husband. Olga then answered, "Since I have already avenged the misfortune of my husband twice on the occasions when your messengers came to Kiev, and a third time when I held a funeral feast for him, I do not desire further revenge, but am anxious to receive a small tribute. After I have made peace with you, I shall return home again."

The Derevlians then inquired what she desired of them, and expressed their readiness to pay honey and furs. Olga retorted that at the moment they had neither honey nor furs, but that she had one small request to make. "Give me three pigeons," she said, "and three sparrows from each house. I do not desire to impose a heavy tribute, like my husband, but I require only this small gift from you, for you are impoverished by the siege." The Derevlians rejoiced, and collected from each house three pigeons and three sparrows, which they sent to Olga with their greetings. Olga then instructed them, in view of their submission, to return to their city, promising that on the morrow she would depart and return to her own capital. The Derevlians reentered their city with gladness, and when they reported to the inhabitants, the people of the town rejoiced.

Now Olga gave to each soldier in her army a pigeon or sparrow, and ordered them to attach by a thread to each pigeon and sparrow a match bound with small pieces of cloth. When night fell, Olga bade her soldiers release the pigeons and the sparrows. So the birds flew to their nests, the pigeons to the cotes, and the sparrows under the eaves. Thus the dove-cotes, the coops, the porches, and the haymows were set on fire. There was not a house that was not consumed, and it was impossible to extinguish the flames, because all the houses caught fire at once. The people fled from the city, and Olga ordered her soldiers to catch them. Thus she took the city and burned it, and captured the elders of the city. Some of the other captives she killed, while she gave others as slaves to her followers. The remnant she left to pay tribute.

She imposed upon them a heavy tribute, two parts of which went to Kiev, and the third to Olga in Vyshegorod; for Vyshegorod was Olga's city. She then passed through the land of Dereva, accompanied by her son and her retinue, establishing laws and tribute. Her residences and hunting-preserves are there still. Then she returned with her son to Kiev, her city, where she remained one year.

⚔ 6 ⚔

Sviatoslav's Conquests

The early Varangian princes of Kiev were brave and colorful conquerors. None, however, matched the qualities of Prince Sviatoslav (957–972). In search of spoils and glory, he enlisted the aid of other bold adventurers and, moving with extraordinary speed, destroyed the Empire of the Khazars along the Volga before turning against the Bulgars and the Greeks to seek more fortunes in the Balkans. As a result of these military exploits, Sviatoslav elevated Kiev's power to unprecedented heights. The triumph was short-lived, for the downfall of the Khazar Empire in the East created a political vacuum and attracted the nomadic Pechenegs who overran the area north of the Black Sea, disrupted Kievan-Byzantine trade and, in 972, ambushed and killed Sviatoslav.

6464–6472 (956–964). When Prince Svyatoslav had grown up and matured, he began to collect a numerous and valiant army. Stepping light as a leopard, he undertook many campaigns. Upon his expeditions he carried with him neither wagons nor kettles, and boiled no meat, but cut off small strips of horseflesh, game, or beef and ate it after roasting it on the coals. Nor did he have a tent, but he spread out a garment under him, and set his saddle under his head; and all his retinue did likewise. He sent messengers to the other lands announcing his intention to attack them. He went to the Oka and the Volga, and on coming in contact with the Vyatichians, he inquired of them to whom they paid tribute. They made answer that they paid a silverpiece per ploughshare to the Khazars.

6473 (965). Svyatoslav sallied forth against the Khazars. When they heard of his approach, they went out to meet him with their Prince, the Kagan, and the armies came to blows. When the battle thus took place, Svyatoslav defeated the Khazars and took their city of Byelavyezha. He also conquered the Yasians and the Kassogians.

6474 (966). Svyatoslav conquered the Vyatichians and made them his tributaries.

6475 (967). Svyatoslav marched to the Danube to attack the Bulgarians.

Reprinted by permission of the publishers from Samuel H. Cross, "The Russian Primary Chronicle," *Harvard Studies and Notes in Philology and Literature* (Cambridge, Mass., Harvard University Press, 1930), vol. 12, pp. 170–177.

When they fought together, Svyatoslav overcame the Bulgarians, and captured eighty towns along the Danube. He took up his residence there, and ruled in Pereyaslavetz, receiving tribute from the Greeks.

6476 (968). While Svyatoslav was at Pereyaslavetz, the Pechenegs invaded Rus for the first time. So Olga shut herself up in the city of Kiev with her grandsons, Yaropolk, Oleg, and Vladimir. The nomads besieged the city with a great force. They surrounded it with an innumerable multitude, so that it was impossible to escape or send messages from the city, and the inhabitants were weak from hunger and thirst. Those who had gathered on the other side of the Dnieper in their boats remained on that side, and not one of them could enter Kiev, while no one could cross over to them from the city itself. . . .

But the people of Kiev sent to Svyatoslav, saying, "Oh Prince, you visit and observe foreign lands. But while you neglect your own country, the Pechenegs have all but taken us captive, along with your mother and your children as well. Unless you return to protect us, they will attack us again, if you have no pity on your native land, on your mother in her old age, and on your children." When Svyatoslav heard these words, he quickly bestrode his charger, and returned to Kiev with his retinue. He kissed his mother and his children, and regretted what they had suffered at the hands of the Pechenegs. He therefore collected an army, and drove the Pechenegs out into the steppes. Thus there was peace.

6477 (969). Svyatoslav announced to his mother and his *boyars*, "I do not care to remain in Kiev, but should prefer to live in Pereyaslavetz on the Danube, since that is the centre of my realm, where all riches are concentrated: gold, silks, wine, and various fruits from Greece, silver and horses from Hungary and Bohemia, and from Rus furs, wax, honey, and slaves. . . ."

6478 (970). Svyatoslav set up Yaropolk in Kiev and Oleg in Dereva. At this time came the people of Novgorod asking for themselves a prince. "If you will not come to us," said they, "then we will choose a prince of our own." So Svyatoslav promised them that a prince should be designated, but Yaropolk and Oleg both refused, so that Dobrynya suggested that the post should be offered to Vladimir . . . The citizens of Novgorod thus requested Svyatoslav to designate Vladimir, and he granted their request. The Novgorodians took Vladimir to be their prince, and he went forth to Novgorod with Dobrynya his uncle. But Svyatoslav departed thence to Pereyaslavetz.

6479 (971). Svyatoslav arrived before Pereyaslavetz, and the Bulgarians fortified themselves in the city. They made one sally against Svyatoslav; there was great carnage, and the Bulgarians came off victors. But Svyatoslav cried to his soldiery, "We seem to be conquered here already. Let us fight bravely, brothers and companions!" Toward evening, Svyatoslav finally gained the upper hand, and took the city by storm. He then sent messages to the Greeks, announcing his intention to march against them and capture their city, as he had taken Pereyaslavetz. The Greeks replied that they were in no position to offer resistance, and therefore begged him to accept tribute instead for himself and his soldiery, requesting him to notify them how many Russes there were, so that they might pay so much per head. The Greeks made this proposition to deceive the Russes, for the Greeks are crafty even to the present day. Svyatoslav replied that his force numbered twenty thousand, adding ten thousand to the actual number, for there were really but ten thousand Russes. So the Greeks armed one hundred thousand men to attack Svyatoslav, and paid no tribute.

Svyatoslav advanced against the Greeks, who came out to meet the Russes. When the Russes perceived their approach, they were terrified at the multitude of the Greek soldiery, and Svyatoslav remarked, "Now we have no place whither we may flee. Whether we will or no, we must give battle. Let us not disgrace Rus, but rather sacrifice our lives, lest we be dishonored. For if we flee, we shall be disgraced. We must not take to flight, but we will resist boldly, and I will march before you. If my head falls, then look to yourselves." Then his vassals replied, "Wherever your head falls, there we too will lay down our own." So the Russes went into battle, and the carnage was great. Svyatoslav came out victor, but the Greeks fled. Then Svyatoslav advanced toward the capital fighting as he went, and destroying towns that stand deserted even to the present time.

The Emperor summoned his *boyars* to the palace, and inquired what they should do, for they could not withstand Svyatoslav's onslaught. The *boyars* advised that he should be tempted with gifts, to discover whether Svyatoslav liked gold and silks. So they sent to Svyatoslav gold and silks, carried by a clever envoy. To the latter they gave command to look well upon his eyes, his face, and his spirit. The envoy took the gifts, and went out to Svyatoslav. It was reported to the Prince that Greeks had come bringing greetings, and he ordered that they should be introduced. They then came near and greeted him, laying before him the gold and silks. Svyatoslav, without noticing the presents, bade his servants keep them. So the envoys returned before the Emperor; and the Emperor summoned his *boyars*. Then the envoys reported that when they had come before Svyatoslav and offered their gifts, he had taken no notice of them, but had ordered them to be retained. Then another courtier said, "Try him a second time; send him arms."

This suggestion was adopted, and they sent to Svyatoslav a sword and other accoutrements which were duly brought before him. The Prince accepted these gifts, which he praised and admired, and returned his greetings to the Emperor. The envoys went back to the Emperor and reported what had occurred. Then the *boyars* remarked, "This man must be fierce, since he pays no heed to riches, but accepts arms. Submit to tribute." The Emperor accordingly requested Svyatoslav to approach no nearer, but to accept tribute instead. For Svyatoslav had indeed almost reached Tsargrad. So the Greeks paid him tribute, and he took also the share of those Russes who had been slain, promising that their families should receive it. He accepted many gifts besides, and returned to Pereyaslavetz with great acclaim.

Upon observing the small number of his troops, Svyatoslav reflected that if haply the Greeks attacked him by surprise, they would kill his retinue and himself. For many warriors had perished on the expedition. So he resolved to return to Rus for reinforcements. He then sent envoys to the Emperor in Silistria (for the Emperor was then at that place) indicating his intention to maintain peaceful and friendly relations. When the Emperor heard this message, he rejoiced, and sent to Svyatoslav gifts even more valuable than the former ones. Svyatoslav accepted these gifts, and on taking counsel with his retinue declared, "If we do not make peace with the Emperor, and he discovers how few of us there are, the Greeks will come and besiege us in our city. Rus is far away, and the Pechenegs are hostile to us. So who will give us aid? Let us rather make peace with the Emperor, for the Greeks have offered tribute; let that suffice. But if the Emperor stops paying tribute, we shall once more collect troops in Rus in still greater numbers, and march again on Tsargrad." His speech pleased his followers, and they sent their chief men to the Emperor. The envoys arrived in Silistria, and reported to the Emperor. He summoned them before him on the following day, and gave them permission to state their errand. They then replied, "Thus says our Prince: 'I desire to maintain true amity with the Greek Emperor henceforth and forever.'" The Emperor rejoiced, and commanded his scribe to set down on parchment the words of Svyatoslav. One envoy recited all his words, and the scribe wrote them down. . . .

After making peace with the Greeks, Svyatoslav journeyed by boat to the cataracts of the Dnieper, and the general, Sveinald, advised him to ride around the falls on horseback, for the Pechenegs were encamped in the vicinity. The Prince did not heed him, but went on by boat. The people of Pereyaslavetz informed the Pechenegs that Svyatoslav was returning to Rus after seizing from the Greeks great riches and immense booty, but that his troop was small. When the Pechenegs heard this news, they ambuscaded the cataracts, so that when Svyatoslav arrived it was impossible to pass them. So the Prince decided to winter in Byelobereg, but the Russes had no rations, so that there was a severe famine, and they paid as much as half a *grivna* for a horse's head. But Svyatoslav wintered there nevertheless.

When spring came, in 6480 (972), Svyatoslav approached the cataracts, where Kurya, Prince of the Pechenegs, attacked him; and Svyatoslav was

killed. The nomads took his head, and made a cup out of his skull, overlaying
it with gold, and they drank from it.

❧ 7 ❧

<h1 style="text-align:center">*The Acceptance
of Christianity*</h1>

Christianity was introduced into Kievan Rus long before Prince Vladimir
(980–1015) adopted it as the official religion of the state. There was,
for instance, a Christian church in Kiev during the reign of Igor. As
noted earlier, Igor's wife Olga, by embracing Christianity, became a saint
of the Orthodox Church and many merchants, as well as warriors of
Kievan princes, were either converts to or had an acquaintance with the
new faith.

The *Primary Chronicle* reports, in one narrative, many different legends
concerning the adoption of Christianity, as well as several traditional
accounts of the baptism of Prince Vladimir. It is ironic that no one knows
exactly where or even when Vladimir was baptized, whether in 988 or
989. Following his conversion, Vladimir imposed the new faith on his
subjects. In some places this imposition was peaceful; in others, force had
to be used. The adoption of Christianity from Constantinople opened
Kiev to widespread Byzantine cultural influence.

6494 (986). Vladimir was visited by Bulgarians of Mohammedan faith. . . .
Then came the Germans, asserting that they were come as emissaries of the
Pope. . . . The Jewish Khazars heard of these missions, and came them-
selves. . . . Then the Greeks sent to Vladimir a scholar. . . .

6495 (987). Vladimir summoned together his vassals and the city elders,
and said to them, "Behold, the Bulgarians came before me urging me to
accept their religion. Then came the Germans and praised their own faith;
and after them came the Jews. Finally the Greeks appeared, criticizing all
other faiths but commending their own, and they spoke at length, telling the

---

Reprinted by permission of the publishers from Samuel H. Cross, "The Russian Primary
Chronicle," *Harvard Studies and Notes in Philology and Literature* (Cambridge, Mass., Harvard
University Press, 1930), vol. 12, pp. 183–184, 197–201, 204–205, 210–211, 213.

history of the whole world from its beginning. Their words were artful, and it was wondrous to listen and pleasant to hear them. They preach the existence of another world. 'Whoever adopts our religion and then dies shall arise and live forever. But whosoever embraces another faith, shall be consumed with fire in the next world.' What is your opinion on this subject, and what do you answer?" The vassals and the elders replied, "You know, oh Prince, that no man condemns his own possessions, but praises them instead. If you desire to make certain, you have servants at your disposal. Send them to inquire about the ritual of each and how he worships God."

Their counsel pleased the Prince and all the people, so that they chose good and wise men to the number of ten, and directed them to go first among the Bulgarians and inspect their faith. The emissaries went their way, and when they arrived at their destination they beheld the disgraceful actions of the Bulgarians and their worship in the mosque; then they returned to their own country. Vladimir then instructed them to go likewise among the Germans, and examine their faith, and finally to visit the Greeks. They thus went into Germany, and after viewing the German ceremonial, they proceeded to Tsargrad, where they appeared before the Emperor. He inquired on what mission they had come, and they reported to him all that had occurred. When the Emperor heard their words, he rejoiced, and did them great honor on that very day.

On the morrow, the Emperor sent a message to the Patriarch to inform him that a Russian delegation had arrived to examine the Greek faith, and directed him to prepare the church and the clergy, and to array himself in his sacerdotal robes, so that the Russes might behold the glory of the God of the Greeks. When the Patriarch received these commands, he bade the clergy assemble, and they performed the customary rites. They burned incense, and the choirs sang hymns. The Emperor accompanied the Russes to the church, and placed them in a wide space, calling their attention to the beauty of the edifice, the chanting, and the offices of the archpriest and the ministry of the deacons, while he explained to them the worship of his God. The Russes were astonished and in their wonder praised the Greek ceremonial. Then the Emperors Basil and Constantine invited the envoys to their presence, and said, "Go hence to your native country," and thus dismissed them with valuable presents and great honor.

Thus they returned to their own country, and the Prince called together his vassals and the elders. Vladimir then announced the return of the envoys who had been sent out, and suggested that their report be heard. He thus commanded them to speak out before his vassals. The envoys reported, "When we journeyed among the Bulgarians, we beheld how they worship in their temple, called a mosque, while they stand ungirt. The Bulgarian bows, sits down, looks hither and thither like one possessed, and there is no happiness among them, but instead only sorrow and a dreadful stench. Their religion is not good. Then we went among the Germans, and saw them performing many ceremonies in their temples; but we beheld no glory there. Then we went on to Greece, and the Greeks led us to the edifices where they worship their God, and we knew not whether we were in heaven or on earth. For on earth there is no such splendor or such beauty, and we are at a loss how to describe it. We only know that God dwells there among men, and their service is fairer than the ceremonies of other nations. For we cannot forget that beauty. Every man, after tasting something sweet, is afterward unwilling to accept that which is bitter, and therefore we cannot dwell longer here." Then the vassals spoke and said, "If the Greek faith were evil, it would not have been adopted by your grandmother Olga, who was wiser than all other men." Vladimir then inquired where they should all accept baptism, and they replied that the decision rested with him.

After a year had passed, in 6496 (988), Vladimir marched with an armed force against Kherson, a Greek city. . . . Vladimir and his retinue entered the city, and he sent messages to the Emperors Basil and Constantine, saying, "Behold, I have captured your glorious city. I have also heard that you have an unwedded sister. Unless you give her to me to wife, I shall deal with your own city as I have Kherson." When the Emperors heard this message, they were troubled, and replied, "It is not meet for Christians to give in marriage to pagans. If you are baptized, you shall have her to wife, inherit the kingdom of God, and be our companion in the faith. Unless you do so, however, we cannot give you our sister in marriage." When Vladimir learned their response, he directed the envoys of the Emperors to report to the latter that he was willing to accept baptism, having already given some study to their religion, and that the Greek faith and ritual, as described by the emissaries sent to examine it, had pleased him well. When the Emperors heard this report, they rejoiced, and persuaded their sister Anna to consent to the match. They then requested Vladimir to submit to baptism before they should send their sister to him, but Vladimir desired that the princess should herself bring priests to baptize him. The Emperors complied with his request, and sent forth their sister, accompanied by some dignitaries and priests. Anna, however, departed with reluctance. "It is as if I were setting out into captivity," she lamented; "better were it for me to die here." But her brothers protested, "Through your agency God turns the land of Rus to repentance, and you will relieve Greece from the danger of grievous war. Do you not see how much evil the Russes have already brought upon the Greeks? If you do not set out, they may bring on us the same misfortunes." It was thus that they overcame her hesitation only with great difficulty. The Princess embarked upon a ship, and after tearfully embracing her kinsfolk, she set forth across the sea and arrived at Kherson. The natives came forth to greet her, and conducted her into the city, where they settled her in the palace.

By divine agency, Vladimir was suffering at that moment from a disease of the eyes, and could see nothing, being in great distress. The Princess declared to him that if he desired to be relieved of this disease, he should be baptized with all speed, otherwise it could not be cured. When Vladimir heard her message, he said, "If this proves true, then of a surety is the God of the Christians great," and gave orders that he should be baptized. The Bishop of Kherson, together with the Princess's priests, after announcing the tidings, baptized Vladimir, and as the Bishop laid his hand upon him, he straightway received his sight. Upon experiencing this miraculous cure, Vladimir glorified God, saying, "I have now perceived the one true God." When his followers beheld this miracle, many of them were also baptized.

Vladimir was baptized in the Church of St. Basil, which stands at Kherson upon a square in the center of the city, where the Khersonians trade. The palace of Vladimir stands beside this church to this day, and the palace of the Princess is behind the altar. After his baptism, Vladimir took the Princess in marriage. Those who do not know the truth say he was baptized in Kiev, while others assert this event took place in Vasiliev, while still others mention other places.

After Vladimir was baptized, the priests explained to him the tenets of the Christian faith, urging him to avoid the deceit of heretics. . . .

Hereupon Vladimir took the Princess and Anastasius and the priests of Kherson, together with the relics of St. Clement and of Phoebus his disciple, and selected also sacred vessels and images for the service. In Kherson he thus founded a church on the mound which had been heaped up in the midst of the city with the earth removed from his embankment; this church is standing at the present day. Vladimir also found and appropriated two bronze statues and four bronze horses, which now stand behind the Church of the Holy Virgin, and which the ignorant think are made of marble. As a wedding present for the Princess, he gave Kherson over to the Greeks again and then departed for Kiev.

When the Prince arrived at his capital, he directed that the idols should be overthrown, and that some should be cut to pieces and others burned with fire. He thus ordered that Perun should be bound to a horse's tail and dragged along Borichev to the river. He appointed twelve men to beat the idol with sticks, not because he thought the wood was sensitive, but to affront the demon who had deceived man in this guise, that he might receive chastisement at the hands of men. . . . While the idol was being dragged along the stream to the Dnieper, the unbelievers wept over it, for they had not yet received holy baptism. After they had thus dragged the idol along, they cast it into the Dnieper. But Vladimir had given this injunction, "If it halts anywhere, then push it out from the bank, until it goes over the falls. Then let it loose." His command was duly obeyed. . . .

Thereafter Vladimir sent heralds throughout the whole city to proclaim that if any inhabitant, rich or poor, did not betake himself to the river, he would risk the Prince's displeasure. When the people heard these words, they wept for joy, and exclaimed in their enthusiasm, "If this were not good, the Prince and his *boyars* would not have accepted it." On the morrow, the Prince went forth to the Dnieper with the priests of the Princess and those from Kherson, and a countless multitude assembled. They all went into the water; some stood up to their necks, others to their breasts, the younger near the bank, some of them holding children in their arms, while the adults waded farther out. The priests stood by and offered prayers. . . .

When the people were baptized, they returned each to his own abode. Vladimir, rejoicing that he and his subjects now knew God himself, . . . ordained that churches should be built and established where pagan idols had previously stood. He thus founded the Church of St. Basil on the hill where the idol of Perun and the other images had been set, and where the Prince and the people had offered their sacrifices. He began to found churches and to assign priests throughout the cities, and to invite the people to accept baptism in all the cities and towns.

He took the children of the best families, and sent them to schools for instruction in book-learning. The mothers of these children wept bitterly over them, for they were not yet strong in faith, but mourned as for the dead. . . . Vladimir was enlightened, and his sons and his country with him. . . .

6497 (989). After these events, Vladimir lived in the Christian faith. With the intention of building a church dedicated to the Holy Virgin, he sent and imported artisans from Greece. After he had begun to build, and the structure was completed, he adorned it with images, and entrusted it to Anastasius of Kherson. He appointed Khersonian priests to serve in it, and bestowed upon this church all the images, vessels, and crosses which he had taken in that city. . . .

[6502–6504 (994–996)] . . . [Vladimir] invited each beggar and poor man to come to the Prince's palace and receive whatever he needed, both food and drink, and marten skins from the treasury.

With the thought that the weak and the sick could not easily reach his palace, he arranged that wagons should be brought in, and after having them loaded with bread, meat, fish, various fruits, mead in casks, and *kvass*, he ordered them driven out through the city. The drivers were under instruction to call out, "Where is there a poor man or a beggar who cannot walk?" To such they distributed according to their necessities. Moreover, he caused a feast to be prepared each week in his palace for his subjects, and invited the *boyars*, the court officers, the centurians, the decurions, and the distinguished citizens, either in the presence of the Prince or in his absence. There was much meat, beef, and game, and an abundance of all victuals. On one occasion, however, after the guests were drunk, they began to grumble against the Prince, complaining that they were mistreated because he allowed them to eat with wooden spoons instead of silver ones. When Vladimir heard of their complaint, he ordered that silver spoons should be molded for his retinue to eat with, remarking that with silver and gold he could not secure a retinue, but that with a retinue he was in a position to win these treasures, even as his grandfather and his father had sought riches with their followers. For Vladimir was fond of his followers, and consulted them concerning matters of administration, wars, and government. He lived at peace with the neighboring Princes, Boleslav of Poland, Stephen of Hungary and Udalrich of Bohemia, and there was amity and friendship among them.

While Vladimir was thus dwelling in the fear of God, the number of bandits increased, and the bishops, calling to his attention the multiplication of robbers, inquired why he did not punish them. The Prince answered that he feared the sin entailed. They replied that he was appointed of God for the chastisement of malefactors and for the practice of mercy toward the righteous, so that it was entirely fitting for him to punish a robber condignly, but only after due process of law. Vladimir accordingly abolished *wergild* and set out to punish the brigands. The bishops and the elders then suggested that as wars were frequent, the *wergild* might be properly spent for the purchase of arms and horses, to which Vladimir assented. Thus Vladimir lived according to the prescriptions of his father and his grandfather. . . .

When the people heard of this [Vladimir's death on July 15, 1015], they assembled in multitudes and mourned him, the *boyars* as the defender of their country, the poor as their protector and benefactor. They laid him in a marble coffin and preserved the body of the blessed Prince amid their mourning.

He is the new Constantine of mighty Rome, who baptized himself and his subjects; for the Prince of Rus imitated the acts of Constantine himself. . . . Vladimir died in the orthodox faith. He effaced his sins by repentance and by almsgiving, which is better than all things else.

⚓ 8 ⚓

Ruskaia Pravda:
The Short Version

One of the most important legal sources on Kievan history is a document
called *Ruskaia Pravda*, or *Rus Justice*. There are two basic versions of
this document—short and expanded. The short version includes the old
Pravda of Iaroslav, which appeared in the 1030s, and the *Pravda* of
Iaroslav's sons, which appeared in the 1070s. The expanded version,
which includes many of the points of the short version plus additional
items, appeared at the end of the twelfth or early in the thirteenth century.
In reading the document, note that economic questions and problems of
property relationships occupy a prominent place.

Article 1

If a man kills a man, the brother is to avenge his brother; the son, his father;
or the father, his son; or nephews, their uncles; and if there is no avenger
[the murderer pays] forty *grivnas* fine; if [the killed man] is a [Kievan] Russian,
or a member of the *druzhina* [retinue], or a merchant, or a sheriff, or an agent
of the prince, or even an *izgoi* [serf], or a [Novgorodian] Slav, the fine is forty
grivnas.

Article 2

If a man is bleeding or is blue from bruises, he does not need any eyewitness;
if he has no sign [of injury] he is to produce an eyewitness; if he cannot, the
matter ends there; if he cannot avenge himself he is to receive three *grivnas*,
while the physician is to get an honorarium.

Article 3

If a person hits another with a stick, or a rod, or a fist, or a bowl, or a
[drinking] horn, or the dull side of a sword, he is to pay twelve *grivnas* fine;
if the offender is not hit back [by his victim], he must pay, and there the
matter ends.

From M. N. Tikhomirov, *Posobie dlia izucheniia Russkoi Pravdy* (An Aid for the Study of
Russian Justice) (Moscow, Izdatelstvo Moskovskogo Universiteta, 1953), pp. 75–86. Translation mine. Items in brackets are mine.

Article 4

If a person strikes another with an unsheathed sword, or with the hilt of a sword, he pays twelve *grivnas* for the offense.

Article 5

If a person hits [another's] arm and the arm is severed or shrinks, he pays forty *grivnas* fine. And if he hits the leg [but does not sever it], and then he [the victim] becomes lame, let both [parties] reach an agreement.

Article 6

And if a finger is cut off, three *grivnas* for the offense.

Article 7

For the mustache twelve *grivnas*; and for the beard twelve *grivnas*.

Article 8

If anyone unsheathes his sword, but does not hit, he pays one *grivna* fine.

Article 9

If a man pulls another man toward himself or pushes him away and [the offended] brings two witnesses, the fine is three *grivnas*; if he should be a Varangian or a Kolbiag, an oath is to be taken.

Article 10

If anyone conceals a runaway slave of a Varangian or a Kolbiag for three days, and if it is discovered on the third day, the original owner gets back his slave and three *grivnas* for the offense.

Article 11

If anyone rides another's horse without the owner's permission, he has to pay three *grivnas*.

Article 12

If anyone steals another's horse, or weapon, or clothes, and the owner recognizes it within his township, he gets back his property and three *grivnas* for the offense.

Article 13

If anyone should recognize his stolen property, he should neither take it nor say to a person, "This is mine"; he should say as follows: "Let us go to the place where you got it"; if he will not go immediately, he must post bond within five days.

Article 14

If a business partner should demand money from his associate and the latter should demur, he must be brought to a court of twelve men; and if it should be established that he [the associate] cheated, the partner shall receive his share and three *grivnas* for the offense.

Article 15

If the original owner should recognize his [runaway] slave and should want him back, the present owner shall lead him to the party from whom he purchased the slave, and he may go the second party; and should the matter go to the third party, the third party should be told: "Give me back my slave, and try to get your money back [from the fourth party] with the aid of an eyewitness."

Article 16

If a slave should hit a free man and then hide in the house of his master, and the master should be unwilling to give him up, the slave must be seized and his master must pay twelve *grivnas* fine; and the offended free man may beat that slave wherever he finds him.

Article 17

And if anyone should break [someone's] spear, or shield, or damage his clothes, and then should want to keep [these items], he must pay for them; and if he should insist on returning the damaged article he must pay for the value of that article.

The Law of the Rus Land enacted at a meeting of Princes Iziaslav, Vsevolod, and Sviatoslav, and the advisors Kosniachko, Pereneg, Nikifor of Kiev, Chudin, and Mikula.

Article 18

Should a bailiff be killed deliberately, the killer must pay eighty *grivnas* fine; the people are not to pay; and for [the murder of] a prince's adjutant, eighty *grivnas*.

Article 19

And if a bailiff is killed in a highway attack and the people do not search for the killer, the fine will be paid by that locality where the killed official is found.

Article 20

Should a bailiff be killed near a barn, or near a horse [stable], or a livestock [shed], or [trying to prevent] rustling of cattle, the murderer should be killed like a dog; the same law is applicable to the murderer of a steward.

Article 21

And for a prince's steward, eighty *grivnas*; and for a master of the stable [killed] near his livestock, also eighty *grivnas*, as decreed by Iziaslav when the Dorogobuzhians killed his master of the stable.

Article 22

For [the murder of] an elder of a prince's village, or for a field overseer, twelve *grivnas*; and for the helper of a steward, five *grivnas*.

Article 23

And for the killing of a peasant or a slave, five *grivnas*.

Article 24

And if a slave-nurse or her son is killed, twelve *grivnas*.

Article 25

And for [the killing of] a prince's horse, if the latter has a brand, three *grivnas*, and for a peasant's horse, two *grivnas*.

Article 26

And for a mare, sixty *rezanas*; for an ox, one *grivna*; for a cow, forty *rezanas*; for a three-year-old cow, fifteen *kunas*; for a yearling [heifer], one-half *grivna*; for a calf, five *rezanas*; for a yearling ewe, one *nogata*; and for a yearling ram, one *nogata*.

Article 27

If anyone should abduct someone's male or female slave, he has to pay twelve *grivnas* for the offense.

Article 28

If a man should come bleeding or bruised, he needs no witness.

Article 29

And whoever steals either a horse or an ox, or robs a barn, if he is alone he has to pay one *grivna* and thirty *rezanas*; if there were as many as eighteen thieves, each pays three *grivnas* and thirty *rezanas*.

Article 30

And if anyone damages or burns a prince's bee hive, three *grivnas*.

Article 31

And if anyone should torture a peasant, without the prince's order, three *grivnas* for the offense.

Article 32
And [for the torture of] a bailiff, a steward, or a sheriff, twelve *grivnas*.

Article 33
And whoever should plow over the property line or destroy a property mark, twelve *grivnas* for the offense.

Article 34
And whoever steals a boat, he has to pay [the owner] thirty *rezanas* for the boat, and sixty *rezanas* fine.

Article 35
And for [the theft of] a dove or a chicken, nine *kunas*.

Article 36
And for [the theft of] a duck, a goose, a crane, or a swan, thirty *rezanas* and a fine of sixty *rezanas*.

Article 37
And if anyone steals someone's hunting dog, or a hawk, or a falcon, three *grivnas* for the offense.

Article 38
If anyone should kill a thief in his own yard, or at the barn, or at the stable, he is [justly] killed; if, however, anyone detains the thief till daylight, he must bring him to the prince's court; and should he [the thief] be killed, and should people see that the thief was bound, the killer must pay for him.

Article 39
If anyone should steal hay, nine *kunas*; and for wood, nine *kunas*.

Article 40
If a gang of ten thieves should steal an ewe, or a goat, or a pig, each must pay a fine of sixty *rezanas*.

Article 41
And whoever should apprehend a thief receives ten *rezanas*; and a sheriff receives fifteen *kunas* from three *grivnas* [of fines collected]; fifteen *kunas* go [to the Church] as tithe; and the prince receives three *grivnas*. And from twelve *grivnas* of theft, the apprehender of the thief will receive seventy *kunas*; [the Church] two *grivnas* as tithe; and the prince ten *grivnas*.

Article 42

The following is the tax collecting custom: the collectors [during their journey] should receive seven buckets of malt, a ram or some other meat or two *nogatas*; and on Wednesday one *rezana* or cheese; the same on Friday; and as much bread and millet as they can eat; and two chickens per day; and shelter for four of their horses and feed for them, as much as they can eat; the collectors should [collect] sixty *grivnas*, ten *rezanas*, twelve *veveritsas*, and a *grivna* in advance; and during Lent collectors should receive fish and should get seven *rezanas* for fish; during a week they should receive fifteen *kunas* and food as much as they can eat; tax collectors should complete their task in one week; such is Iaroslav's decree.

Article 43

The following is the code of bridge builders: when they complete a bridge, they should receive for their work one *nogota*; also one *nogata* for every span; and if an old bridge needs repair of several planks, three, or four, or five, the same payment.

≉ 9 ≉

The Church Statute of Kiev

A few years after he became a convert to Christianity, Vladimir granted the Church many rights and privileges. His son and successor, Iaroslav the Wise, bestowed upon the Church additional favors. The original copies of these two vital documents have not been preserved. There do exist, however, two editions of Iaroslav's "Church Statute"—the West Rus, or what may be appropriately called the early edition, and the East Rus, or late edition. Both appeared many decades after the original document was issued and as a consequence include within their provisions a number of later practices and expressions.

I, Grand Prince Iaroslav, son of Vladimir, in accordance with the wish of my

---

From *Polnoe Sobranie Russkikh Letopisei* (Complete Collection of Russian Chronicles) 2d edition (Moscow-Leningrad: 1925), vol. V, pp. 120–122. Translation mine. Items in brackets are mine.

father, have conferred with Metropolitan Illarion and have prepared [this] Church Statute because [I believe that] there are matters that belong neither to [the exclusive] jurisdiction of the prince nor to that of the *boyars*. I have granted this jurisdiction, as embodied in the present rules of the Church Statute, to the metropolitan and the bishops. [These rules shall be valid] in all towns and in all territories wherever Christianity prevails.

1. Whoever shall carry away and then violate a maiden, if she is a daughter of an [influential] *boyar*, shall pay her five *grivnas* of gold for her indignity, and the bishop shall receive five *grivnas* of gold; if she is a daughter of a less [influential] *boyar* [she shall receive for her indignity] only one *grivna* of gold and the bishop [shall receive] one *grivna* of gold; and if she is a daughter [only] of a distinguished person she shall receive for her indignity five *grivnas* of silver and the bishop shall receive five *grivnas* of silver. The kidnappers shall [in addition] pay one *grivna* of silver to the bishop. The prince shall administer the justice [in these matters in accordance with ancient customs and traditions].

2. Whoever shall violate a daughter of an [influential] *boyar* or an [influential] *boyar's* wife shall pay her five *grivnas* of gold for her indignity, and five [*grivnas* of gold] to the bishop; [violated daughters and/or wives] of less influential *boyars* [shall receive] one *grivna* of gold [for their indignities] and the bishop shall receive one *grivna* of gold; [violated daughters and/or wives] of distinguished citizens shall receive three *rubles* [for their indignities] and the bishop shall receive three *rubles*; [violated daughters and/or wives] of commoners shall receive fifteen *grivnas* [for their indignities] and the bishop shall receive fifteen *grivnas*.* The prince shall administer justice [in these matters in accordance with ancient customs and traditions].

3. If, without any valid reason, a distinguished *boyar* puts his wife away, she shall receive three gold *grivnas* for her indignity and the bishop shall receive three gold *grivnas*; for the same action [the wife of] a distinguished citizen shall receive three *rubles* and the bishop shall receive three *rubles*; for the same action [the wife] of a commoner shall receive fifteen *grivnas* and the bishop shall receive fifteen *grivnas*. The prince shall administer justice [in these matters in accordance with ancient customs and traditions.].

4. If a daughter who has her father and mother [still living] should give birth to an illegitimate child, she should be reprimanded [by the bishop] and then placed in the bishop's court. The family may then ransom her out.

5. If someone should entice a maiden to his dwelling and then force her to have sexual intercourse with others, the bishop shall receive three *grivnas*

*Note those portions of the "Statute" which must belong to a later edition, since neither *rubles* nor *grivnas* without precious metals were in use in Kievan Rus (Ed.).

[for this crime] and the maiden [shall receive three *grivnas*] for her dishonor. All the participants who dishonored her shall be fined one *ruble*. The prince shall administer justice [in this matter in accordance with ancient customs and traditions].

6. If a husband should force his wife into prostitution, this is a religious crime. The prince [however] shall administer justice [in this case in accordance with ancient customs and traditions].

7. Should a husband marry another woman without divorcing his wife, the bishop shall have the jurisdiction in this matter. The new wife shall be placed in the bishop's court and the husband shall be made to live with his [first] wife.

8. Should a wife become very ill, or become blind, or be afflicted with a prolonged illness, [her husband] shall not be allowed to divorce her; the same rule shall apply to the husband [in case of his illness].

9. If the godfather should have sexual intercourse with the mother [of his godchild], the bishop shall receive one *grivna* of gold and at his discretion he shall also impose [an appropriate] penance.

10. The bishop shall receive 100 *grivnas* as the fine from whomever sets a dwelling, or a barn, or anything else afire. The prince shall have the jurisdiction [in this matter in accordance with ancient customs and traditions].

11. The bishop shall receive 100 *grivnas* as the fine from whomever shall have sexual intercourse with his sister. The bishop shall also impose [an appropriate] penance. The punishment for this crime shall be administered in accordance with [the existing] laws.

12. The bishop shall receive eighty *grivnas* from whomever marries a close blood relative. The bishop shall separate them and impose [an appropriate] penance.

13. The bishop shall receive forty *grivnas* from whomever shall live with two wives. The second wife shall be placed in the bishop's court and the husband shall be made to live with his lawful wife. Should he later abuse her in any way he shall be imprisoned.

14. If a husband and wife decide to separate voluntarily, the bishop shall receive twelve *grivnas*. If they were not married legally [in the Church] the bishop shall receive only six *grivnas*.

15. The bishop shall receive 100 *grivnas* from whomever shall have sexual intercourse with a nun.

16. The bishop shall receive twelve *grivnas* from whomever shall commit sodomy. He shall also impose [an appropriate] penance.

17. If a father-in-law should have sexual intercourse with his daughter-in-law, the bishop shall receive 100 *grivnas*; in accordance with the [existing] law he shall also impose [an appropriate] penance.

18. The bishop shall receive thirty *grivnas* from whomever shall marry two sisters.

19. If a brother-in-law should have sexual intercourse with his sister-in-law the bishop shall receive thirty *grivnas*.

20. The bishop shall receive forty *grivnas* from whomever shall have sexual intercourse with his stepmother.

21. Should two brothers be married to the same woman, the bishop shall receive 100 *grivnas* and the woman shall be sent to the bishop's court.

22. If a maiden does not want to marry and her father and mother force her into it, and if she then does some harm to herself, her father and mother are guilty and must pay the bishop a fine; the same applies to the young lad [she was forced to marry].

23. If someone should refer to the wife of an influential *boyar* as a prostitute, for her dishonor she shall receive five *grivnas* of gold and the bishop shall receive five *grivnas* of gold. The prince will have the jurisdiction in this case [in accordance with ancient customs and traditions]. [For the same dishonor the wife] of a less influential *boyar* shall receive three *grivnas* of gold and the bishop shall receive three *grivnas* of gold. [For the same dishonor the wife] of an [influential] city dweller shall receive three *grivnas* of silver. [For the same dishonor the wife] of a village [commoner] shall receive one *grivna* of silver and the bishop shall receive one *grivna* of silver.

24. If someone should cut another's hair or his beard, the bishop shall receive twelve *grivnas*. The prince shall have the jurisdiction in this case [in accordance with ancient customs and traditions].

25. If a man and/or his wife steal hemp or flax or any other crops, the bishop and the prince shall exercise joint jurisdiction in such cases.

26. If a man and/or his wife steal white garments, or cloth, or clothing, or linens, the bishop and the prince shall exercise joint jurisdiction in such cases.

27. The prince and the bishop shall equally divide fines from marriage or engagement fights or killings.

28. Should two men fight like women, [that is, should they] bite and scratch one another, the bishop shall receive three *grivnas*.

29. If a man should beat a strange woman [without any cause], she shall be compensated for her dishonor in accordance with the prevailing laws, and the bishop shall receive six *grivnas*.

30. If a son beats his father or his mother, the local representative of the prince shall punish him. The bishop, however, shall have the jurisdiction [over the son].

31. If a maiden wants to marry someone and her father and her mother refuse to give her their consent and if she [then] inflicts some harm to herself,

the bishop shall have the jurisdiction over her father and over her mother and also over the lad [she intended to marry].

32. If a monk, or a nun, or a priest and his wife, or a woman who bakes the sacramental bread commit any crime, the bishop shall have [exclusive] jurisdiction over them.

33. The bishop shall have [exclusive] jurisdiction over priests and monks who become intoxicated.

34. If a monk or a nun should abandon their vows the bishop shall have [exclusive] jurisdiction over their cases, and he shall also impose on them an [appropriate] penalty.

35. Local officials of the prince shall have no jurisdiction over crimes committed by a bishop's servants, the church people, and those living within monasteries. Crimes committed by these people shall be under the exclusive jurisdiction of the bishop's officials as is also their property.

36. Whoever shall violate this decree of mine, be they my sons, or my grandsons, or my great-grandsons, or any member of my family, or any *boyar,* whosoever shall infringe this order of things or shall interfere with the jurisdiction of the metropolitan, or that of the Church, or that of the bishops in their dioceses, he shall be subject to the rules of the Holy Fathers and shall be punished accordingly. Whoever shall interfere with the jurisdiction of the Church shall be excommunicated and condemned in accordance with the decrees of the Holy Fathers and of the Council of Nicea.

10

Metropolitan Hilarion's Eulogy of Prince Vladimir and Prince Iaroslav

Little is known of the background of Metropolitan Hilarion. Based on his literary heritage, he was a well-educated cleric, was familiar with Greek, Roman, Christian and Byzantine history, and was very conscious of the importance of the Kievan state.

Source: A. V. Gorskii, ed., *Pamiatniki dukhovnoi literatury vremen velikogo kniazia Iaroslava I* [Sources on Spiritual Literature in the Times of Grand Prince Iaroslav I], (Moscow, 1844), as reprinted in *Anthology of Old Russian Literature*, edited by Ad. Stender-Petersen in Collaboration with Stefan Congrat-Butlar (New York, Columbia University Press), pp. 111–112). Translation mine. Reprinted with permission of Columbia University Press.

It seems that Hilarion composed his eulogy sometime between 1037 and 1050; that is, when he still was a presbyter of Prince Iaroslav's private church in Berestovo. The eulogy is not only to Prince Vladimir, who accepted and imposed Christianity on Kiev in 988, but also to Prince Iaroslav, Vladimir's son, who continued the process. There is no doubt that because Hilarion insisted that the Kievan Church must enjoy the same dignity, rights and status as the Byzantine Church, at the height of his dispute with Constantinople, Prince Iaroslav appointed him the first Slavic prelate to be a Metropolitan of Kiev.

. . . With panegyric voices, Rome praises [Saints] Peter and Paul because they brought to them [the Romans] the belief in Jesus Christ, the Son of God. Asia, Ephesus [the ancient city in Asia Minor] and Patmos [an island in the Dedocanese archipelago] praise John the Theologian. India praises Thomas; Egypt praises Mark. All countries, cities and people honor and venerate their teachers who introduced them to the Orthodox Faith.

Let us, therefore, to the best of our abilities, praise humbly our great and wonder-creating teacher and mentor, the great *kagan* [leader] of our land [Prince] Vladimir, grandson of the sage Igor and son of the illustrious Sviatoslav, who, during his life, ruled with courage and bravery, became famous in many lands, and his victories and vigor are remembered and praised even today.

And they [that is, Igor, Sviatoslav, and Vladimir] did not rule a poor or unknown country. They ruled Rus, which is well-known and respected by everyone throughout the world. . . .

[Vladimir!] The blessed one! An excellent testimony of your true faith is the Holy Church of the Blessed Virgin Mary, Mother of God, which you built on Orthodox foundations and where your valiant body now rests awaiting the archangel's trumpets.

Another excellent testimony [to your efforts] is your son Iurii [that is, Iaroslav the Wise, 1015–54, whose Christian name was Iurii], whom God has designated heir to your throne. He [Iaroslav] does not violate your laws; he reconfirms them. He does not belittle your pious works; on the contrary, he expands them. He has not undone [any of your works]; he has reinforced them. He has built a great and holy church [St. Sophia] to honor God's omniscience in order to sanctify your city. He has decorated it with all kinds of beautiful things, including gold and silver, precious stones and sacred vessels. That church is marvelous and famous in all neighboring countries. There is no other like it in all countries to the north, east or west. He [Iaroslav] has bestowed the crown of glory on your illustrious city of Kiev. He also has turned your city and your people to the Holy Mother of God who is ever ready to assist Christians. . .

Venerable Prince! [Vladimir!]. Arise from your grave. Arise and shake off your sleep. You are not dead. You are only asleep till the resurrection day. Arise! You are not dead! You cannot die because you believe in Christ, the Giver of life to the entire world. Shake off your sleep! Open up your eyes so you may see honors the Lord has bestowed on you and what you have passed on to your sons. Arise and look at your son Iurii! Look at your beloved son whom God has brought forth from your loins. Look at him embellishing the throne of your land! Rejoice [at all of this] and be happy! Also look at Irina, the pious wife of your son. Look at your grandchildren and your great-grandchildren. See how they live and how God has taken care of them; how they preserve devotion in your tradition; how they partake of the Sacraments of the Holy Church; how they glorify Christ and how they respect His Holy name. [Arise] and see your city radiating with grandeur. See the blossoming of churches; see the flourishing of Christianity; see the city adorned with holy icons, gleaming, flagrant with thyme, praising God and filling the air with sacred songs! And after you have seen all of this, rejoice, be content and praise the good Lord, the Creator of all and of everything!

❧ *11* ❧

The Struggle for Succession

The Varangians introduced many innovations to Kievan Rus—constructive as well as destructive. Of the latter, the most famed was the struggle for succession. Following the death of each Grand Prince, beginning with Sviatoslav in 972, the country experienced prolonged and bitter quarreling and fighting among the princes until one victor emerged. These feuds exhausted the country's resources, disrupted trade, forced people to flee certain areas, invited foreign intrusions, and contributed in innumerable ways to the downfall of the Kievan state.

Reprinted by permission of the publishers from Samuel H. Cross, "The Russian Primary Chronicle," *Harvard Studies and Notes in Philology and Literature* (Cambridge, Mass., Harvard University Press, 1930), vol. 12, pp. 177–180, 214–225, 231–232, 235, 238–239, 245, 255.

6484–6485 (976–977). Yaropolk marched against his brother Oleg into the district of Dereva. Oleg sallied out to meet him, and they came to blows. When the companies fought, Yaropolk overcame Oleg. Where Oleg fled with his warriors into the town called Vruchi, there was a bridge across a moat to the city gates, and as the soldiery pressed hard on each other's heels, they fell into the moat. Oleg also was pushed from the bridge into the ditch; many men fell in, and the horses crushed the soldiers.

When Yaropolk entered his brother's city, he seized the latter's property, and sent in search of him. Upon looking for Oleg, Yaropolk's men were unable to find him, until one native of Dereva reported that he had seen Oleg pushed off the bridge the night before. So Yaropolk sent men to look for his brother. They dragged bodies from the moat from morning till noon, and found Oleg also under the other corpses. They carried him away and laid him upon a rug. Then Yaropolk came and wept over him. . . . So they buried Oleg in the city of Vruchi, and his tomb is there to this day. Yaropolk seized his property. . . . When Vladimir in Novgorod heard that Yaropolk had killed Oleg, he was afraid, and fled abroad. Then Yaropolk sent his viceroys to Novgorod, and was thus the sole ruler in Rus.

6486–6488 (978–980). Vladimir returned to Novgorod with Varangian allies, and instructed the viceroys of Yaropolk to return to the latter and inform him that Vladimir was advancing against him prepared to fight. . . .

Vladimir came to Kiev with a large force. Yaropolk could not resist him, but shut himself up in Kiev with his people and with Blud. Vladimir came to a halt at Dorogozhichi, and entrenched himself between there and Kapichi; his earthwork is there to this day. Vladimir then sent treacherous proposals to Blud, Yaropolk's general, saying, "Be my friend; if I kill my brother, I will regard you as my father, and you shall have much honor from me. It was not I who began to fight with my brother, but he, and I was for that reason overcome by fear, and therefore have come against him." Blud replied to the messengers of Vladimir that he would join with him in sincere friendship. . . .

Blud shut himself up with Yaropolk with the intention of betraying him, and he sent frequent messages to Vladimir, urging him to storm the city while he himself planned how he might kill Yaropolk. But on account of the citizens, it was not possible to kill him. So Blud, not being able to destroy him thus, contrived it by means of a ruse, while he urged the prince not to go forth from the city to fight. Thus he craftily suggested to Yaropolk that the people of Kiev were sending messages to invite Vladimir to approach the town so that they might betray Yaropolk into his hands, and advised him to flee from the city. Yaropolk heeded his suggestion, and he fled from Vladimir. He then shut himself up in the city of Rodnya at the mouth of the Ros, while Vladimir entered the city of Kiev, and then laid siege to Yaropolk at Rodnya. There was great famine there and we have to this day a proverb which speaks of famine as in Rodnya.

Blud then said to Yaropolk, "Do you see what a large force your brother has? We cannot overcome them. Make peace with your brother." He spoke thus plotting treachery against him. But Yaropolk assented. Blud then sent word to Vladimir that he would bring Yaropolk before him in accordance with his wishes. Vladimir, upon hearing these tidings, went to his father's castle with the hall . . . and settled there with his retinue. Blud next induced Yaropolk to appear before his brother and express his readiness to accept any terms he might offer. Yaropolk thus went in person to Vladimir, though he had been previously warned by Varyazhko not to go. "My prince," said he, "they will kill you. Flee rather to the Pechenegs and collect an army." But the Prince heeded him not. Yaropolk came accordingly before Vladimir, and when he entered the door, two Varangians stabbed him under the arms with their swords, while Blud shut the doors and would not allow his men to follow him. Thus Yaropolk was slain. . . . Vladimir then began to reign alone in Kiev. . . .

[Vladimir had twelve sons: Izyaslav, Mstislav, Yaroslav, Sudislav, Vsevolod, Svyatopolk, Vysheslav, Svyatoslav, Stanislav, Boris, Pozvizd, and Gleb. In 1015, following Vladimir's death] Svyatopolk settled in Kiev . . . and after calling together all the inhabitants of Kiev, he began to distribute largess among them. They accepted it, but their hearts were not with him, because their brethren were with Boris. When Boris returned with the army, after meeting the Pechenegs, he received the news that his father was dead. He mourned deeply for him, for he was beloved of his father before all the rest.

When he came to the Alta, he halted. His father's retainers then urged him to take his place in Kiev on his father's throne, since he had at his disposal the latter's retainers and troops. But Boris protested, "Be it not for me to raise my hand against my elder brother. Now that my father has passed away, let him take the place of my father in my heart." When the soldiery heard these words, they departed from him, and Boris remained with his servants.

But Svyatopolk was filled with lawlessness. Adopting the device of Cain, he sent messages to Boris that he desired to live at peace with him, and would increase the territory he had received from his father. But he plotted against him how he might kill him. So Svyatopolk came by night to Vyshegorod. After secretly summoning to his presence Putsha and the *boyars* of the town, he inquired of them whether they were wholeheartedly devoted to him. Putsha and the men of Vyshegorod replied, "We are ready to lay down our lives for you." He then commanded them to say nothing to any man, but to go and kill his brother Boris. They straightway promised to execute his order. . . .

These emissaries came to the Alta . . . fell upon him [Boris] like wild beasts about the tent, and overcame him by piercing him with lances. They also overpowered his servant, who cast himself upon his body. . . .

The desperados, after attacking Boris, wrapped him in a canvas, loaded him upon a wagon, and dragged him off, though he was still alive. When the impious Svyatopolk saw that he was still breathing, he sent two Varangians to finish him. When they came and saw that he was still alive, one of them drew his sword and plunged it into his heart. . . .

The desperate murderers, godless wretches that they were, returned to Svyatopolk in hope of commendation. The names of these contemners of the law are Putsha, Taletz, Elovit, and Lyashko. . . .

The impious Svyatopolk then reflected, "Behold, I have killed Boris; now how can I kill Gleb?" Adopting once more Cain's device, he craftily sent messages to Gleb to the effect that he should come quickly, because his father was very ill and desired his presence. Gleb quickly mounted his horse, and set out with a small company, for he was obedient to his father. When he came to the Volga, his horse stumbled in a ditch on the plain, and broke his leg. He arrived at Smolensk, and setting out thence at dawn, he embarked in a boat on the Smyadyn. At this time Yaroslav received from Predslava the tidings of their father's death, and he sent word to Gleb that he should not set out, because his father was dead and his brother had been murdered by Svyatopolk. Upon receiving these tidings, Gleb burst into tears, and mourned for his father, but still more deeply for his brother. . . .

While he was thus praying amid his tears, there suddenly arrived those sent by Svyatopolk for Gleb's destruction. These emissaries seized Gleb's boat, and drew their weapons. The servants of Gleb were terrified, and the impious messenger, Goryaser, gave orders that they should slay Gleb with despatch. Then Gleb's cook, Torchin by name, seized a knife, and stabbed Gleb. . . .

After Gleb had been slain, his body was thrown upon the shore between two tree-trunks, but afterward they took him and carried him away, to bury him beside his brother Boris in the Church of St. Basil. . . .

Now the impious and evil Svyatopolk killed Svyatoslav in the Hungarian mountains, after causing him to be pursued as he fled into Hungary. Then he began to reflect how he would kill all his brethren and rule alone in Rus. . . .

The impious Svyatopolk thus began his reign in Kiev. Assembling the people, he began to distribute skins to some and furs to others, and thus dissipated a large sum.

When Yaroslav heard of his father's death, he had many Varangians under his command, and they offered violence to the inhabitants of Novgorod and to their wives. The men of Novgorod then rose and killed the Varangians in their market place. Yaroslav was angry, and departing to Rakom, he took up his abode in the castle. Then he sent messengers to Novgorod with the comment that the death of his retainers was beyond remedy, but at the same time he summoned before him the chief men of the city who had massacred the Varangians, and craftily killed them. The same night news came from Kiev sent by his sister, Predslava, to the effect that his father was dead, that Svyatopolk had settled in Kiev after killing Boris, and was now endeavoring to compass the death of Gleb, and she warned Yaroslav to be exceedingly on his guard against Svyatopolk. When Yaroslav heard these tidings, he grieved for his father and his retainers.

On the morrow, he collected the remnant of the men of Novgorod and regretfully lamented, "Alas for my beloved retainers, whom I yesterday caused to be killed! You would indeed be useful in the present crisis." He wiped away his tears, and informed his subjects in the assembly that his father was dead, and that Svyatopolk had settled in Kiev after killing his brethren. Then the men of Novgorod said, "We can still fight for you, oh Prince, even though our brethren are slain." So Yaroslav collected one thousand Varangians and forty thousand other soldiers, and marched against Svyatopolk. . . . When Svyatopolk learned that Yaroslav was on his way, he prepared an innumerable army of Russes and Pechenegs, and marched out toward Lyubech on one side of the Dnieper, while Yaroslav was on the opposite bank.

6524 (1016). Yaroslav arrived before Kiev, and the brothers stood over against each other on both banks of the Dnieper, but neither party dared attack. They remained thus face to face for three months. Then Svyatopolk's general rode out along the shore and scoffed at the men of Novgorod, shouting, "Why did you come hither with this crooked-shanks, you carpenters? We shall put you to work on our houses." When the men of Novgorod heard this taunt, they declared to Yaroslav, "Tomorrow we will cross over to them, and whoever will not go with us we will kill." Now it was already beginning to freeze. Svyatopolk was stationed between two lakes, and caroused with his retinue the whole night through; Yaroslav on the morrow marshaled his troops, and crossed over toward dawn. His forces disembarked on the shore and pushed the boats out from the bank. The two armies advanced to the attack, and met upon the field. The carnage was terrible. Because of the lake, the Pechenegs could bring no aid, and Yaroslav's troops drove Svyatopolk with his followers toward it. When the latter went out upon the ice, it broke under them, and Yaroslav began to win the upper hand. Svyatopolk then fled among the Lyakhs, while Yaroslav established himself in Kiev upon the throne of his father and his grandfather. . . .

6526 (1018). Boleslav attacked Yaroslav with Svyatopolk and his Lyakhs.

After collecting Russes, Varangians, and Slavs, Yaroslav marched forth against Boleslav and Svyatopolk, and upon arriving at Volyn, they camped on both sides of the river Bug. . . .

Then Yaroslav fled with four men to Novgorod, and Boleslav entered Kiev in company with Svyatopolk. Boleslav ordered that his force should be dispersed to forage throughout the cities, and so it was done. When Yaroslav arrived at Novgorod in his flight, he planned to escape overseas, but the viceroy Constantine, son of Dobrynya, together with the men of Novgorod, destroyed his boats, protesting that they wished to fight once more against Boleslav and Svyatopolk. They set out to gather funds at the rate of four skins per man, ten *grivni* from each elder, and eighteen *grivni* from each *boyar*. With these funds they recruited Varangians whom they imported, and thus collected for Yaroslav a large army.

While Boleslav was settled in Kiev, the impious Svyatopolk ordered that any Lyakhs found in the city should be killed, and so the Lyakhs were slain. Then Boleslav fled from Kiev, taking with him the property and the *boyars* of Yaroslav, as well as the latter's two sisters, and made Anastasius steward of the property, for the latter had won his confidence by his flattery. He took with him a large company, and having appropriated to himself the cities of Cherven, he returned to his native land. Svyatopolk thus reigned alone in Kiev, but Yaroslav attacked him again, and Svyatopolk fled among the Pechenegs.

6527 (1019). Svyatopolk advanced with a large force of Pecheneg supporters, and Yaroslav collected a multitude of soldiery, and went forth against him to the Alta River. . . . The two armies attacked, and the plain of the Alta was covered with the multitudinous soldiery of both forces. It was then Friday. As the sun rose, they met in battle, and the carnage was terrible, such as had never before occurred in Rus. The soldiers fought hand to hand and slaughtered each other. Three times they clashed, so that blood flowed in the valley. Toward evening Yaroslav conquered, and Svyatopolk fled. . . . He could not endure to stay in one place, but fled through the land of the Lyakhs, pursued by the wrath of God. Upon reaching the wilderness between Poland and Bohemia, he ended his life in an evil fashion. . . .

6529 (1021). Bryachislav, son of Izyaslav, grandson of Vladimir, came and captured Novgorod, and having taken the people of Novgorod and their property, he returned to Polotzk. When he arrived at the Sudomir River, Yaroslav came thither from Kiev on the seventh day. He conquered Bryachislav, and returned the people of Novgorod to their city, while Bryachislav fled to Polotzk.

6530 (1022). Yaroslav came to Brest. At this time Mstislav, who was in Tmutorakan, attacked the Kassogians. . . .

6531 (1023). Mstislav marched against Yaroslav with a force of Khazars and Kassogians.

6532 (1024). While Yaroslav was at Novgorod, Mstislav arrived before Kiev from Tmutorakan, but the inhabitants of Kiev would not admit him. He thus departed thence and established himself upon the throne of Chernigov, while Yaroslav was at Novgorod. In this year, magicians appeared in Suzdal, and killed old people by satanic inspiration and devil worship, saying that they would spoil the harvest. There was great confusion and famine throughout all that country. The whole population went along the Volga to the Bulgarians, from whom they bought grain and thus sustained themselves. . . . Then Mstislav proposed to Yaroslav that the latter, as the eldest brother, should remain in Kiev, while the Chernigov district should belong to Mstislav. But Yaroslav did not dare to return to Kiev until they were properly reconciled. So Mstislav settled in Chernigov, and Yaroslav in Novgorod, though Kiev was occupied by subjects of Yaroslav.

6534 (1026). Yaroslav recruited many soldiers and arrived at Kiev, where he made peace with his brother Mstislav near Gorodetz. They divided Rus according to the course of the Dnieper. Yaroslav took the Kiev side, and Mstislav the other. They thus began to live in peace and fraternal amity. Strife and tumult ceased, and there was a great calm in the land. . . .

[In 1036 Mstislav died and] Yaroslav assumed the entire sovereignty, and was the sole ruler in the land of Rus. . . .

6562 (1054). Yaroslav, Great Prince of Rus, passed away. While he was yet alive, he admonished his sons [Izyaslav, Svyatoslav, Vsevolod, Vyacheslav, Vysheslav, and Igor] with these words: "My sons, I am about to quit this world. Love one another, since ye are brothers by one father and mother. If ye dwell in amity with one another, God will dwell among you, and will subject your enemies to you, and ye will live at peace. But if ye dwell in envy and dissension, quarreling with one another, then ye will perish yourselves and bring to ruin the land of your ancestors, which they won at the price of great effort. Wherefore remain rather at peace, brother heeding brother. The throne of Kiev I bequeath to my eldest son, your brother Izyaslav. Heed him as ye have heeded me, that he may take my place among you. To Svyatoslav I give Chernigov, to Vsevolod Pereyaslavl, *to Igor the city of Vladimir*, and to Vyacheslav Smolensk." Thus he divided the cities among them commanding them not to violate one another's boundaries, not to despoil one another. He laid upon Izyaslav the injunction to aid the party wronged, in case one brother should attack another. Thus he admonished his sons to dwell in amity. . . .

[Following Yaroslav's death in February, 1054] Izyaslav then took up his abode at Kiev, with Svyatoslav in Chernigov, Vsevolod at Pereyaslavl, Igor in Vladimir, and Vyacheslav at Smolensk. . . .

6564–6565 (1056–1057). Vyacheslav, son of Yaroslav, died at Smolensk, and Igor took up his abode in Smolensk, moving over from Vladimir. . . .

6567 (1059). Izyaslav, Svyatoslav, and Vsevolod liberated their uncle Sudislav from the prison where he had been confined for twenty-four years, and after they had obtained his oath of fealty, he took the monastic habit. . . .

6575 (1067). Vseslav, the son of Bryacheslav of Polotzk, undertook a campaign and captured Novgorod. Izyaslav, Svyatoslav, and Vsevolod, the three sons of Yaroslav, though it was the dead of winter, collected a force and set forth against him. They arrived before Minsk, but the citizens barricaded themselves in the city. Then the brethren captured it, put the men to the sword, sold the women and children into slavery, and proceeded to the Nemiga. Vseslav came forward to meet them. The two forces thus collided at the Nemiga, on March 3, with heavy snow on ground. They thus attacked and the carnage was severe. The casualties were numerous, but Izyaslav, Svyatoslav, and Vsevolod won the day, while Vseslav sought safety in flight. On July 10 following, Izyaslav, Svyatoslav, and Vsevolod took oath as to their peaceful intentions and offered Vseslav safe conduct if he would join them. He put his confidence in their sworn oath, and crossed the Dnieper by boat. Izyaslav preceded Vseslav into their tent, and contrary to their oath, the brethren thus took Vseslav captive at Rsha near Smolensk. Izyaslav then brought Vseslav to Kiev and there threw him and his two sons into prison. . . .

[In 1068 a general discontent occurred in Kiev]. The mob then gave a shout and went off to Vseslav's prison. When Izyaslav beheld their action, he fled with Vsevolod from the palace. But on September 15, the people thus haled Vseslav from his dungeon, and set him up in the midst of the Prince's palace. They then pillaged the palace, seizing a huge amount of gold and silver, furs, and marten skins. Izyaslav made his escape to Poland. . . .

6577 (1069). Reinforced by Boleslav [of Poland], Izyaslav marched to attack Vseslav, who went forth to meet them, and arrived at Byelgorod. But during the night he hid himself from the men of Kiev, and fled from Byelgorod to Polotzk. Then the men of Kiev saw on the morrow that their prince had fled, they returned to Kiev, and after calling an assembly, they sent messages to Svyatoslav and Vsevolod saying, "We did wrong in expelling our Prince, and now he leads the Poles against us. Return to your father's city.' If you refuse to return, then we have no alternative but to burn our city and depart to Greece." Svyatoslav replied, "We shall communicate with our brother. If he marches upon you with the Poles to destroy you, we shall fight against him, and not allow him to destroy our father's city. If his intentions are peaceful, then he shall approach with a small troop." Then the people of Kiev were pacified.

Svyatoslav and Vsevolod then sent messengers to Izyaslav, announcing that Vseslav had fled, and requesting him accordingly not to lead his Poles in attack upon Kiev, because no one was really opposing him. They also let it be understood that if he intended to nurse his wrath and destroy the city, they would be properly concerned for the ancestral capital. When Izyaslav received these tidings, he left the Poles and came forward, accompanied only by Boleslav himself and a small Polish escort. He sent his son Mstislav ahead of him into Kiev, and upon the latter's arrival, he slew those who had freed Vseslav, to the number of seventy, blinded others, and executed without any investigation others, who were entirely innocent. When Izyaslav arrived at the city, the inhabitants went forth to welcome him, and the men of Kiev received him as their Prince. He scattered the Poles to forage, and then had them secretly killed. Boleslav then returned to his native country. Izyaslav transferred the market place to the hill, and drove Vseslav out of Polotzk, where he set up his own son Mstislav. But the latter soon died, and Izyaslav enthroned in his stead his brother Svyatopolk, since Vseslav was fled. . . .

6581 (1073). The devil stirred up strife among these brothers, the sons of Yaroslav. When disagreement thus ensued among them, Svyatoslav and Vsevolod united against Izyaslav. The latter left Kiev, but Svyatoslav and Vsevolod arrived there upon March 22 and established themselves on the throne at Berestovoye, though they thus transgressed against their father's injunction. Svyatoslav was the instigator of his brother's expulsion, for he desired more power. He misled Vsevolod by asserting that Izyaslav was entering into an alliance with Vseslav for the purpose of attacking them, and by this means he irritated Vsevolod against Izyaslav. Now Izyaslav took considerable treasure with him on his flight into Poland with the intention of recruiting supporters there. But the Poles robbed him of all his property, and expelled him from their boundaries. Svyatoslav thus ruled in Kiev after the expulsion of his brother, and thus broke the injunction of his father and of God. . . .

6585 (1077). Izyaslav advanced with Polish support, and Vsevolod went forth against him. Boris settled at Chernigov on May 4; his reign lasted eighty days until he fled to join Roman in Tmutorakan. Vsevolod went to Volyn to attack his brother Izyaslav. Peace was concluded, so that Izyaslav came and settled in Kiev on July 15. Oleg, the son of Svyatoslav, was with Vsevolod at Chernigov.

6586 (1078). Oleg, son of Svyatoslav, fled from Vsevolod to Tmutorakan on April 10. In this year, Gleb, the son of Svyatoslav, was killed in Zavolochye. . . .

While Svyatopolk, the son of Izyaslav, was ruling at Novgorod in his stead, and while Yaropolk was reigning in Vyshegorod and Vladimir at Smolensk, Oleg and Boris led the pagans to attack Rus, and fell upon Vsevolod with their Polovcian reinforcements. Vsevolod advanced to meet them as far as the Sozh. The Polovcians then vanquished the Russes, and many lost their lives. Ivan, son of Zhiroslav, and Tuki, the brother of Chud, along with Porei and many others, met their death there on August 28. Oleg and Boris arrived before Chernigov, thinking they had won, and they visited much harm upon the land of Rus.

❦ *12* ❦

The Struggle with the Nomads

Next to the struggle for succession, the most important factor contributing to the downfall of Kiev was the struggle with intruding Asiatic nomads— the Pechenegs, the Torks, the Polovtsians, and others. The nomads were attracted to the area by its favorable climate and topography as well as its political disunity. Nomadic attacks disrupted trade with Constantinople, caused depopulation of the Kievan realm, exhausted resources of the country, and on many occasions played a significant role in internal feuds. In fact, between 1060 and 1210, the country was invaded by the Polovtsians over fifty times.

6476 (968). While Svyatoslav was at Pereyaslavetz, the Pechenegs invaded Rus for the first time. So Olga shut herself up in the city of Kiev with her grandsons, Yaropolk, Oleg, and Vladimir. The nomads besieged the city with a great force. They surrounded it with an innumerable multitude, so that it was impossible to escape or send messages from the city, and the inhabitants were weak from hunger and thirst. . . .

But the people of Kiev sent to Svyatoslav [nevertheless, a messenger], saying,

---

Reprinted by permission of the publishers from Samuel H. Cross, "The Russian Primary Chronicle," *Harvard Studies and Notes in Philology and Literature* (Cambridge, Mass., Harvard University Press, 1930), vol. 12, pp. 171–172, 177, 207–209, 211–212, 225–226, 233, 235, 239, 255, 258, 265–268, 270, 272–274, 292–296.

"Oh Prince, you visit and observe foreign lands. But while you neglect your own country, the Pechenegs have all but taken us captive, along with your mother and your children as well. Unless you return to protect us, they will attack us again, if you have no pity on your native land, on your mother in her old age, and on your children." When Svyatoslav heard these words, he quickly bestrode his charger, and returned to Kiev with his retinue. He kissed his mother and his children, and regretted what they had suffered at the hands of the Pechenegs. He therefore collected an army, and drove the Pechenegs out into the steppes. Thus there was peace. . . .

After making peace with the Greeks [in 971], Svyatoslav journeyed by boat to the cataracts of the Dnieper, and the general, Sveinald, advised him to ride around the falls on horseback, for the Pechenegs were encamped in the vicinity. The Prince did not heed him, but went on by boat. The people of Pereyaslavetz informed the Pechenegs that Svyatoslav was returning to Rus after seizing from the Greeks great riches and immense booty, but that his troop was small. When the Pechenegs heard this news, they ambuscaded the cataracts, so that when Svyatoslav arrived it was impossible to pass them. So the Prince decided to winter in Byelobereg, but the Russes had no rations, so that there was a severe famine, and they paid as much as half a *grivna* for a horse's head. But Svyatoslav wintered there nevertheless.

When spring came, in 6480 (972), Svyatoslav approached the cataracts, where Kurya, Prince of the Pechenegs, attacked him; and Svyatoslav was killed. The nomads took his head, and made a cup out of his skull, overlaying it with gold, and they drank from it. . . .

6500 (992). Vladimir attacked the Croats. When he had returned from the Croatian War, the Pechenegs arrived on the opposite side of the Dnieper from the direction of the Sula. Vladimir set forth against them, and encountered them on the banks of the Trubezh, where Pereyaslavl now stands. Vladimir took up his position on the near side, and the Pechenegs theirs on the other, and the Russes did not venture to the farther shore any more than their foes did to this side of the river. The prince of the Pechenegs came down to the river bank, and calling to Vladimir, proposed to him, "Send one of your warriors, and I will detail one of mine, that they may do battle together. If your vassal conquers mine, let us not fight together for three years to come. But if our champion wins, let us fight three years in succession." Then each prince returned to his own force.

Vladimir returned to his camp, and sent heralds through it to inquire whether there was no man who would fight with the champion of the Pechenegs. But none was found anywhere. On the morrow, the Pechenegs arrived, bringing their champion; but on our side there was none. Vladimir now began to be concerned as he sought a champion throughout his whole army. Then there came to the Prince an old man who said to him, "Oh Prince, I have a younger son at home. I came forth with four others, but he abides by the hearth. Since his childhood, there has been no man who could vanquish him. One day, when I reprimanded him while he was tanning a hide, he flew into a rage at me and tore the leather to bits in his hands." When the Prince heard these words, he rejoiced, and summoned the youth. So he was brought before the Prince, and the Prince informed him of all that had occurred. Then the youth said, "Oh Prince, I know not whether I be capable of this feat; wherefore let them test me. Is there no large and strong bull hereabouts?" Such a bull was soon found, and he directed them to anger the animal. The men put hot irons on him, and then let him go. The bull ran past the youth, and he seized the beast's flank with his hand. He thus pulled off the skin along with as much flesh as he could grasp. Then Vladimir remarked, "You are well qualified to do combat with the champion."

On the morrow the Pechenegs approached, and began to shout, "Is there no champion available? See, ours is ready!" Vladimir had given orders that night to rest upon their arms, and at dawn the two champions went forth. The Pechenegs had sent out their man, who was gigantic and fearsome. Vladimir sent forward his champion, and when the Pecheneg saw him, he laughed, for he was of but moderate size. A space was duly measured off between the two armies, and the warriors were allowed to attack each other. They came to grips, and seized upon each other with violence. But the Russ crushed the Pecheneg to death in his arms, and cast him upon the ground. The Russes raised a cheer, and the Pechenegs took to flight. The Russes pursued them, cut them down, and drove them away. In his joy, Vladimir founded a city on this river bank, and called it Pereyaslavl, because this youth had won glory there. Vladimir made him and his father great men, and then returned to Kiev with victory and great renown. . . .

Then [between 994–996] the Pechenegs came to Vasiliev, and Vladimir went forth against them with a small company. When the troops met, he could not withstand the enemy, so he fled, and took position under a bridge, where he concealed himself with difficulty from the foe. . . .

6505 (997). When Vladimir went to Novgorod after upland troops with which to fight the Pechenegs (for there was desperate and constant conflict with them), the latter, on perceiving that for the moment there was no prince at hand, came and beset Byelgorod. They allowed no sally from the city, and great famine prevailed. Vladimir could not bring succor, for he had no troops with him, and the number of the Pechenegs was great. The siege was thus prolonged, and the famine grew increasingly severe. . . .

6523 (1015). . . . When Vladimir fell ill, Boris [his son] was with him at the time. Since the Pechenegs were attacking the Russes, he sent Boris out against them, for he himself was very sick. . . .

[1034–1036]. While Yaroslav was still at Novgorod, news came to him that the Pechenegs were besieging Kiev. He then collected a large army of Varangians and Slavs, returned to Kiev, and entered his city. The Pechenegs were innumerable. Yaroslav made a sally from the city and marshaled his forces, placing the Varangians in the center, the men of Kiev on the right flank, and the men of Novgorod on the left. When they had taken position before the city, the Pechenegs advanced, and they met on the spot where the metropolitan Church of St. Sophia now stands. At that time, as a matter of fact, there were fields outside the city. The combat was fierce, but toward evening Yaroslav with difficulty won the upper hand. The Pechenegs fled in various directions, but as they did not know in what quarter to flee, they were drowned, some in the Syetoml, some in other streams, while the remnant of them is fleeing yet. . . .

6569 (1061). The Polovcians invaded Rus for the first time. On February 2, Vsevolod went forth against them. When they met in battle, the Polovcians defeated Vsevolod, but after the combat they retired. This was the first evil done by these pagan and godless foes. Their prince was Iskal. . . .

6576 (1068). A multitude of those nomads known as the Polovcians attacked the land of Rus, and Izyaslav, Svyatoslav, and Vsevolod went forth against them as far as the Alta. They joined battle in the dead of night, but since God had let loose the pagans upon us because of our transgressions, the Russian princes fled and the Polovcians were victorious. . . .

6579 (1071). The Polovcians raided about Rostovetz and Neyatin. . . .

[6586 (1078)]. While Svyatopolk, the son of Izyaslav, was ruling at Novgorod in his stead, and while Yaropolk was reigning in Vyshegorod and Vladimir at Smolensk, Oleg and Boris led the pagans to attack Rus, and fell upon Vsevolod with their Polovcian reinforcements. Vsevolod advanced to meet them as far as the Sozh. The Polovcians then vanquished the Russes, and many lost their lives. . . .

6587 (1079). Roman advanced with Polovcian forces as far as Voin, but Vsevolod remained near Pereyaslavl and made peace with the Polovcians. . . .

6588 (1080). The Torks of Pereyaslavl made an attack upon Rus. Vsevolod sent forth his son Vladimir, who went out and conquered them. . . .

[In the spring of 1093] the Polovcians attacked Rus, but when they learned that Vsevolod was dead, they sent propositions for peace to Svyatopolk. Without consulting with the numerous adherents of his father and his uncle, but taking counsel only with those who had accompanied him to the capital, Svyatopolk seized the Polovcian envoys and cast them into prison. When the Polovcians heard of this outrage, they immediately declared war. A large force

of them thus laid siege to the city of Torchesk. Being desirous of peace
Svyatopolk released the Polovcian envoys.

The Polovcians, however, were not anxious for peace, and continued their
attacks. Svyatopolk then set out to recruit a force with the intention of attacking them. The wise men advised him not to oppose the nomads, since
his force was small. He replied that he had eight hundred of his followers
who could easily withstand him. Other rash advisers urged him to pursue
his project, but the wiser heads informed him that even if he had a force of
eight thousand, it would be none too strong. They reminded him that the
country was already impoverished by war and taxes, and suggested that he
should ask his cousin Vladimir for aid. Svyatopolk followed their advice, and
sent to Vladimir a request for assistance. Vladimir assembled his troops, and
requested his brother Rostislav at Pereyaslavl to give Svyatopolk his support
as well. When Vladimir arrived at Kiev, the cousins met at St. Michael's,
and composed between them their quarrels and disagreements. They were
thus reconciled, and kissed the Cross to seal their compact. While the Polovcians were ravaging the countryside, the wise counsellors said to the princes,
"Why do you allow discord to part you? Behold, the pagans lay waste the
land of Rus. You may arrive at an understanding at some later time, but for
the present go out and meet the pagans either to conclude a peace or to wage
war." Vladimir favored a peace, but Svyatopolk was for war.

Svyatopolk, Vladimir, and Rostislav thus proceeded to Trepol. They arrived
at the Stugna, and before crossing the river, they called their followers into
consultation and began to deliberate. Vladimir suggested that in view of the
present danger they had better remain on the near side of the river and make
peace with the Polovcians. Yan and the other prudent men supported this
opinion, but the men of Kiev were not in accord with it, and urged the
crossing of the river because they were eager to fight. This counsel found
favor, and they crossed the river Stugna, which at the moment was considerably
swollen. After marshaling their troops, Svyatopolk, Vladimir, and Rostislav
then moved forward. Svyatopolk marched on the right wing, Vladimir on
the left, and Rostislav led the centre. When they had passed Trepol, they
passed the rampart. Then the Polovcians advanced to the attack with their
bowmen in the van. When our men took position between the ramparts, the
pagans set up their standards, and the bowmen advanced from their en-
campment. The Polovcians reached the rampart, raised their standards, and
first attacked Svyatopolk, whose troop they broke up. Svyatopolk made a firm
stand, but his soldiers fled without resisting the pagan onslaught, and he
himself was obliged to flee also. The Polovcians then attacked Vladimir. The
battle was fierce, and Vladimir took to flight with Rostislav. In their flight,
they arrived at the river Stugna, and dived in. Rostislav straightway began

to drown before Vladimir's very eyes. He was anxious to save his brother, and almost perished himself in the attempt. But Rostislav, the son of Vsevolod, thus met his death.

Vladimir swam the river with a small escort, for many of his troop and his *boyars* had fallen. When he arrived at the other bank of the Dnieper, he bewailed his brother and his vassals, and thus returned to Chernigov heavy with sorrow. Svyatopolk escaped to Trepol and there barricaded himself. He remained there till evening, and during the night departed for Kiev.

Upon perceiving their victory, the Polovcians scattered upon marauding expeditions throughout the countryside, while others returned to Torchesk. . . . While the Polovcians were besieging Torchesk, the inhabitants resisted and fought boldly from the town, so that they killed many of the enemy. The Polovcians then began to press them hard and cut off their water supply, so that the inhabitants weakened from hunger and thirst. They thus sent messages to Svyatopolk to inform him that unless he sent them food supplies they would be obliged to surrender. Svyatopolk despatched the supplies, but because of the multitude of the besiegers it was impossible to introduce them into the town. When the enemy had thus beleaguered the town for nine weeks, they divided into two parties, one of which remained near the city to prosecute the siege, while the rest marched toward Kiev and scattered on raiding parties between Kiev and Vyshegorod. Svyatopolk sallied forth as far as Zhelan, where the two forces advanced to the attack. When the battle-lines met, a fierce combat ensued, but our men fled before the pagans, and many perished, even a larger number than at Trepol. Svyatopolk arrived at Kiev with two companions, and the Polovcians returned to Torchesk. . . .

6602 (1094). Svyatopolk made peace with the Polovcians, and took to wife the daughter of their prince Tugortkan. In this same year, Oleg arrived from Tmutorakan before Chernigov with a force of Polovcians. Vladimir fortified himself in the city. Oleg then approached and burned the environs, including the monasteries. Vladimir made peace with Oleg, and departed from Chernigov to occupy his father's throne in Pereyaslavl, while Oleg took possession of the city that had been his own father's. The Polovcians committed many depredations in the vicinity of Chernigov, and Oleg made no attempt to restrain them for the reason that he himself had inspired their raids. This was, in fact, the third time that he had led a force of pagans to attack Rus. . . .

In this same year [1095], the Polovcians appeared before Yuryev. They besieged the city for a whole year, and had almost reduced it when Svyatopolk succeeded in pacifying them. The Polovcians returned beyond the Ros, and the citizens of Yuryev abandoned their town and fled to Kiev. Svyatopolk ordered that a town should be built on the hill of Vitichev, and he bade the Bishop Marinus settle there with the people from Yuryev, Sakov, and other refugees from various localities. The Polovcians then burned the deserted town of Yuryev. . . .

At this time [1096], Bonyak and his Polovcians appeared before Kiev on a Sunday evening, and while ravaging the environs, they burned the prince's palace at Berestovoye. Kurya and another band of Polovcians ravaged simultaneously the environs of Pereyaslavl, and burned Ustye on May 24. . . .

In this same month, Tugortkan, the father-in-law of Svyatopolk, came to Pereyaslavl and laid siege to the city. The inhabitants fortified themselves for resistance, while Svyatopolk and Vladimir advanced against him down the west bank of the Dnieper. They arrived at Zarub and crossed the river without being detected by the Polovcians, for God protected them. They then marshaled their forces and advanced toward the city. When the inhabitants observed their approach, they rejoiced, and came forth to meet them, while the Polovcians were standing on the other bank of the Trubezh in battle array. Svyatopolk and Vladimir immediately crossed the river to engage the Polovcians. Vladimir first intended to reform his troop, but they did not await his command, and instead spurred up their horses against their adversaries. When the Polovcians beheld their charge, they turned in flight, and our men pursued the foemen, cutting down their opponents. Upon this day the Lord performed a great deliverance. The aliens were thus conquered on July 19. Their prince Tugortkan was killed, and many others of our enemies fell. On the morrow, they found the dead body of Tugortkan, and Svyatopolk, respecting him as his father-in-law even though he was a foe, brought him to Kiev and buried him at Berestovoye, between the road to Berestovoye and the road to the monastery.

On Thursday, the twentieth of this same month, Bonyak, that godless, mangy thief and bandit, came suddenly to Kiev for the second time. The Polovcians almost entered the city, burned the suburbs about the town, and then attacked the monastery. After burning the monasteries of Stephen and Germanus together with the neighboring villages, they came to the Crypt Monastery while we were resting in our cells after matins, and they howled about the monastery. They planted two standards before the monastery gates, and we fled, some of us behind the building of the monastery, and others to its various rooms. The godless sons of Ishmael slew the brethren in the monastery and wandered about among the cells, breaking down the doors, and they carried off whatever they found in the various rooms. Then they set fire to the shrine of the Holy Virgin. Upon arriving before the church, they thus set fire to the south and the north doors, and upon making their way into the chapel near the grave of Theodosius, they seized the eikons, burned the doors, and blasphemed against God and our faith. . . .

[In 1102–1103 Svyatoslav and Vladimir] resolved to attack the Polovcians and invade their territory. . . . They then sent to Oleg and David and invited them to make a life-or-death stand against the Polovcians. David accepted, but Oleg opposed the campaign on the ground that he was unwell. Vladimir then embraced his cousin, and proceeded to Pereyaslavl, whither he was followed by Svyatopolk, David son of Svyatoslav, David son of Vseslav, Mstislav grandson of Igor, Vyacheslav son of Yaropolk, and Yaropolk son of Vladimir. They advanced on horseback and by boat, arrived below the cataracts, and halted by the rapids at the island of Khortich. They then mounted their horses, and when the foot soldiers had disembarked from the boats, they traveled across country for four days, and arrived at Suten.

When the Polovcians learned that the Russes were on their way, they collected innumerable forces and began to deliberate. Urusoba proposed that the Polovcians should make peace with the Russes, since the latter would offer the nomads a violent combat in view of the fact that the Polovcians had done much scathe to Rus. The younger chiefs replied to Urusoba that even if he was afraid of the Russes, they were not dismayed, for after conquering the Russes, they would invade their country and take their cities, and they wondered who would protect the Russes against them. . . .

The Polovcians advanced, and sent Altunapa in front as a vanguard, since he was celebrated among them for his courage. The Russian princes likewise sent forward their advance party. They thus surprised the vanguard of Altunapa, upon whom they fell, slaying him and his followers. Not one of them escaped, for the Russes slew them all. The nomad troops came on like the trees of the forest, and their mass was impenetrable. The Russes straightway advanced to meet them. Now God on high inspired an awful fear in the Polovcians, so that terror and trembling beset them at the sight of the Russian forces, and they wavered. Even their steeds possessed no more swiftness of foot. But our soldiery, both foot and horse, advanced joyously to the combat.

Upon beholding the effort of the Russes against them, the Polovcians fled before the Russian troops without even waiting to meet them, and our men gave chase and cut them down. On April 4, God thus performed a great salvation and bestowed upon us a mighty victory over our foes. Upon this expedition twenty Polovcian princes were slain: Urusoba, Kchi, Arslanapa, Kitanopa, Kuman, Asup, Kurtek, Chenegrepa, Surbar, and many other princes. Beldyuz was taken captive.

The kinsmen then rested since they had overcome their foes. They brought Beldyuz before Svyatopolk, and the Polovcian chief offered to pay gold and silver, horses and cattle as his ransom. Svyatoslav then sent him to Vladimir. When he stood before him, Vladimir inquired, "Have you noticed how your former oath has brought you to ruin? Though you often gave pledges, you continued to harass the land of Rus. Why did you not admonish your sons and your kinsfolk not to violate their oaths by the shedding of Christian blood? Your blood be upon your own head." He then directed that the Polovcian should be killed, and they cut him to pieces.

Thereafter all the kinsmen gathered together, and Vladimir exclaimed, "This is the day that the Lord hath made, let us rejoice and be glad in it. For the Lord hath freed us from our foes and put down our enemies, and crushed the serpents' heads. He hath given them as food to the men of Rus." They thus seized sheep and cattle, horses and camels, tents with booty and slaves, and with the tents they captured Pechenegs and Torks. They then returned to Rus carrying great spoil, with glory and a great victory won. . . .

6614 (1106). The Polovcians raided in the vicinity of Zarechesk, and Svyatopolk sent Yan, son of Vyshata, his brother Putyata, and Ivan the Khazar, son of Zakhari, to pursue them. They drove off the Polovcians and took some spoil. . . .

[In May, 1107], Bonyak raided and seized many horses in the vicinity of Pereyaslavl. In the same year, Bonyak and old Sharukan and many other chieftains came and laid siege to Lubny. Svyatopolk, Vladimir, Oleg, Svyatoslav, Mstislav, Vycheslav, and Yaropolk marched out to attack them at this town. At the sixth hour of the day, they crossed the Sula and shouted at the foe. The Polovcians were terrified, and because of their fear could not even raise a standard, but seized their horses and fled, while their foot-soldiers took to flight also. Our men then began to cut them down as they pursued them, and took others captive. They drove them thus nearly to the Khorol. They thus slew Taz, Bonyak's brother, while Sharukan barely escaped. On August 12, the Polovcians abandoned their camp after the capture of which the Russian soldiery returned home with a great victory. . . .

6618 (1110). In the spring, Svyatopolk, Vladimir, and David marched forth to attack the Polovcians, but returned after reaching the Voin.

⚔ *13* ⚔

The Testament of Vladimir Monomakh

Vladimir Monomakh (1113–1125) was one of the most energetic rulers of Kiev. He was greatly admired by the people, and feared by the feuding princes and nomadic raiders. His wise but firm policies curtailed lawlessness and civil strife, and his very strong impression on the Polovtsians during his adult life succeeded in reducing their attacks on Rus. Monomakh was also a true Christian prince. He advised his children to have faith in God and to show this faith in good deeds, to love peace, to be humble, to protect the weak, to be hospitable and generous, to shun idleness, and to depend upon themselves.

I, wretched man that I am, named Vasili at my baptism by my pious and glorious grandsire Yaroslav, but commonly known by my Russian name Vladimir, and surnamed Monomakh by my beloved father and mother . . . and for the sake of Christian people, for I was many times saved from all distress through his mercy and through the prayers of my father.

As I sat upon my sledge, I meditated in my heart and praised God, who has led me, a sinner, even to this day. Let not my sons or anyone else who happens to read this brief discourse laugh at its contents. But rather let any one of my sons who takes my words to heart and is not disposed to laziness conduct himself according to my counsel. First, for the sake of God and your own souls, retain the fear of God in your hearts, and give alms generously, for such liberality is the root of all good. If this document displeases anyone, let him not be angry, but rather let him believe that, in my old age, I talked nonsense as I sat upon my sledge. For emissaries from my kinsmen met me on the Volga with the message, "Join with us quickly, that we may expel the sons of Rostislav, and seize their possessions. If you do not join us, we shall act for our own advantage, and you may conduct yourself as you deem best." I replied, "At the risk of your wrath, I cannot go with you or break my oath."

Reprinted by permission of the publishers from Samuel H. Cross, "The Russian Primary Chronicle," *Harvard Studies and Notes in Philology and Literature* (Cambridge, Mass., Harvard University Press, 1930), vol. 12, pp. 301–309.

When I had dismissed the emissaries, in my sorrow I took up the Psalter, and when I opened it this passage struck my eye: "Why art thou cast down, my soul? Why dost thou disquiet me?" *etc.* (*Ps.* xliii, 5.) I collected these precious words and arranged them in order and copied them. If the last passage does not please you, then accept the first. "Why art thou sorrowful, my soul? Why dost thou disquiet me? Hope in God, for I will confess to him." . . .

It was thus that Basil, after gathering together young men who were pure in heart and untainted in body, inculcated in them a brief and a meek conversation and the word of God in right measure. He taught them to eat and to drink without unseemly noise; to be silent in the presence of the aged; to listen with profit to the wise; to humble themselves before their elders; to live in charity with their equals and their inferiors; to speak without guile, but to understand much; not to be immoderate in their language, nor to insult others in their conversation; not to laugh excessively; to respect the aged; to refrain from converse with shameless women; to cast their eyes downward and their souls upward; and to walk and not to leap. He taught them to respect all established authorities which are honored of all men. If any one of you can render a service to another, let him expect his recompense from God, and he shall thus enjoy eternal blessing.

Oh sovereign Mother of God! Take away pride and presumption from my poor heart, lest I be exalted in this empty life by the vanity of this world. Let the faithful learn to strive with pious effort. According to the word of the Gospel, learn to govern your eyes, to curb your tongue, to moderate your temper, to subdue your body, to restrain your wrath; and to cherish pure thoughts, exerting yourself in good works for the Lord's sake. When robbed, avenge not; when hated or persecuted, endure; when affronted, pray. Destroy sin, render justice to the orphan, protect the widow. "Come let us reason together, saith the Lord; if your sins be as scarlet, I will make them white as snow." (*Is.* i, 18.)

The dayspring of fasting shall shine forth, and likewise the light of repentance. Let us purify ourselves, my brethren, from every corporal and spiritual blemish, and, as we call upon our Creator, let us say, "Glory to thee, lover of mankind!" In truth, my children, understand how merciful, yea, how supremely merciful is God, the lover of mankind. Being of human stock, we are so sinful and mortal that, when anyone does us evil, we desire to destroy him and to shed his blood speedily. But our Lord, the ruler of life and death, suffers our sins to be higher than our heads, and yet he loves us all our lives as a father loves his son whom he chastens and then summons once more to his embrace.

Thus our Lord has promised us the victory over our enemies through three means of conquering and overcoming them: repentance, tears, and almsgiving. My children, the commandment of God to conquer your sins by these three means is not severe. But I implore you for God's sake, be not lazy, nor forget these three means. For they are not difficult of attainment. Not through solitude nor an ascetic life, nor by such fasting as other good men endure, but through easy efforts may you thus obtain the mercy of God. . . .

As you read these words, my sons, praise God who has shown us his mercy and admonished you through the medium of my poor wit. Give heed to me, and accept a half of my instruction if you are not disposed to adopt it all. When God softens your hearts, shed tears for your sins, and pray, "As thou hast taken pity upon the adulteress, the robber and the publican, have pity also upon us sinners," and utter these words both in the church and before you retire to rest. If it is in any way possible, fail not one single night to kneel to the ground three times, in the case that you cannot do so more often. Forget not nor be remiss in this observance, for by his nightly worship and hymn man conquers the devil, and by this means expiates what sins he has committed during the day. When you are riding forth upon your horse, if you have no special subject of conversation with a companion and cannot utter some other prayer, then exclaim without ceasing, "Kyrie eleison!" within yourselves. This is the best prayer of all, and infinitely better than thinking evil thoughts. Above all things, forget not the poor, but support them to the extent of your means. Give to the orphan, protect the widow, and permit the mighty to destroy no man. Take not the life of the just or the unjust, nor permit him to be killed. Destroy no Christian soul even though he be guilty of murder.

When you speak either good or evil, swear not by the name of God, nor cross yourselves, for that is unnecessary. Whenever you kiss the Cross to confirm an oath made to your brethren or to any other man, first test your heart as to whether you can abide by your word, then kiss the Cross, and after once having given your oath, abide by it, lest you destroy your souls by its violation.

Receive with affection the blessing of bishops, priests, and priors, and shun them not, but rather, according to your means, love and help them, that you may receive from them their intercession in the presence of God. Above all things, admit no pride in your hearts and minds, but say, "We are but mortal; today we live and tomorrow we shall be in the grave. All that thou hast given us is not ours, but thine, and thou hast but lent it to us for a few days." Hoard not the treasures of earth, for therein lies great sin. Honor the ancient as your father, and the youth as your brother.

Be not lax in the discipline of your homes, but rather attend to all matters yourselves. Rely not upon your steward or your servant, lest they who visit you ridicule your house or your table. When you set out to war, be not inactive, depend not upon your captains, nor waste your time in drinking, eating, or sleeping. Set the sentries yourselves, and take your rest only after you have posted them at night at every important point about your troops; then take your rest, but arise early. Do not put off your accoutrements without a quick glance about you, for a man may thus perish suddenly through his own carelessness. Guard against lying, drunkenness, and vice, for therein perish soul and body. When journeying anywhere by road through your domain, do not permit your followers or another's company to visit violence upon the villages or upon the dwellings, lest men revile you. Wherever you go, as often as you halt, give the beggar to eat and to drink. Furthermore, honor the stranger, if not with a gift, at least with food and drink, whencesoever he comes to you, be he simple, or noble, or an emissary. For travelers give a man a universal reputation as generous or niggardly.

Visit the sick, and accompany the dead, for we are all but mortal. Pass no man without a greeting; give him a kindly word. Love your wives, but grant them no power over you. This is the end of all things: to hold the fear of God above all else. If you forget all my admonition, read this counsel frequently. Then I shall be without disgrace, and you shall profit thereby.

Forget not what useful knowledge you possess, and acquire that with which you are not acquainted, even as my father, though he remained at home in his own country, still understood five languages. For by this means honor is acquired in other lands. Laziness is the mother of all evil; what a man knows, he forgets, and what he does not know he does not learn. In the practice of good works, you cannot neglect any item of good conduct.

First of all, go to church; let not the rising sun find you in your bed. For this was my father's habit, and it is likewise the custom of all good and perfect men. After rendering praise to God at matins, as you look upon the rising sun, refer praise to God with gladness once again, saying, "Thou hast lightened my eyes, oh Christ my God, thou hast given me thy bright light. Grant me increase, oh Lord, in the years to come, so that, as I repent my sins and order my life righteously, I may thus continue to praise God." Then sit and deliberate with your retainers, or render justice to the people, or ride out for hunting or for pleasure, or else lie down to sleep. Sleep is established by God for noonday repose, since birds and beasts and men then rest from their labors.

I now narrate to you, my sons, the fatigue I have endured on journeys and hunts for fifty-three years. First I rode to Rostov through the Vyatichians, whither my father had sent me while he himself went to Kursk. (1073) Second, to Smolensk with Stavko the son of Skordyata; he then went to Brest with Izyaslav, and sent me to Smolensk. From Smolensk, I rode on to Vladimir.

In that same winter, my brethren sent me to Brest to the place which they had burned, and there I watched their city. Then I went to my father in Pereyaslavl, and after Easter, from Pereyaslavl to Vladimir to make peace with the Poles at Suteiska. Thence back to Vladimir again in the summer.

Then Svyatoslav sent me to Poland; after going beyond Glogau to the Czechish forest, I traveled four months in that country. (1076) In this year, my oldest child was born in Novgorod. Thence I went to Turov, in the spring to Pereyaslavl again, and then back to Turov. Svyatoslav then died, and I again went to Smolensk, and thence during the same winter to Novgorod, and in the spring to help Gleb. In the summer, I went with my father to Polotzk, and during the second winter before Polotzk the city was burned. He then went to Novgorod, while I, supported by Polovcians, marched against Odresk, carrying on constant warfare, and thence traveled to Chernigov. (1077) Then, on my return from Smolensk, I rejoined my father in Chernigov a second time.

Then Oleg came from Vladimir, and I invited him to dinner with my father at the Red Palace in Chernigov, and I gave my father three hundred *grivni* of gold. Upon leaving Smolensk, I fought my way through the Polovcian forces, and arrived at Pereyaslavl, where I found my father newly arrived from a raid. Then I rode with my father and Izyaslav to Chernigov to fight with Boris, and we conquered Boris and Oleg. (1078) Then we went to Pereyaslavl, and remained in Obrov. Vseslav at that juncture fired Smolensk. I set forth with men from Chernigov and two horses, but we did not catch Vseslav at Smolensk. On this pursuit of Vseslav, I burned the countryside and ravaged as far as Lukaml and Logozhsk, then attacked Dryutesk, and returned to Chernigov.

In the winter of that year, the Polovcians devastated the whole of Starodub. I marched with men of Chernigov against the Polovcians. At the Desna, we seized the princes Asaduk and Sauk, and killed their followers. The next day, behind Novgorod, we scattered the powerful force of Belkatgin, and took their swords and all their booty. We then went for two winters among the Vyatichians to attack Khodota and his son. The first winter, I went to Korden, and then to Mikulen in pursuit of the sons of Izyaslav, whom we did not catch. In that spring we joined with Yaropolk at Brody.

The following summer, we chased the Polovcians beyond the Khorol, after they had captured Goroshin. During the autumn, in company with men of Chernigov, as well as Polovcians and Chityeyeviches, we captured the city and left in it neither slaves nor cattle. (1084) In that winter, we went to Brody to join Yaropolk, and concluded an important pact of friendship. In that winter, my father set me up to rule in Pereyaslavl, and we crossed the Supoi.

While we were on our way to the town of Priluk, we suddenly encountered the Polovcian chieftains with eight thousand men. We were ready and willing to fight with them, but we had sent our equipment ahead with the baggage train, and we therefore entered the town. They thus captured alive only Semtsya and a few peasants. Our men, on the other hand, killed or captured a large number of them. They did not even dare to lead away their mounts, and during the night fled to the Sula. On the following day, which was Sunday, we arrived at Byela Vyezha. With the aid of God and of the Holy Virgin, our troops killed nine hundred Polovcians, and captured the two princes Asin and Sakza, the brothers of Bagubars, and only two men of their force escaped. We then pursued the Polovcians to Svyatoslavl, thence to Torchesk, and still further to Yuryev. (1086) Then again, on the east bank of the Dnieper, we once more defeated the Polovcians at Krasnoye. In company with Rostislav, we subsequently captured their camp at Varin. I then went to Vladimir and set up Yaropolk as prince, but he soon died.

(1093) After the death of my father, Svyatopolk and I together fought until evening with the Polovcians at the Sula in the vicinity of Khalep, and then made peace with Tugortkan and other Polovcian chiefs. We took from Gleb's followers all their troops. (1094) Oleg subsequently attacked me in Chernigov with Polovcian support; my troops fought with him for eight days by the small entrenchment and would not let him inside the outworks. I took pity on the souls of our Christian subjects, and upon the burned villages and monasteries, and said, "It is not for the pagans to boast." I therefore gave my kinsman my father's place, and retired myself to my father's domain of Pereyaslavl. We left Chernigov on the day of St. Boris, and rode through the Polovcians in a company of not more than a hundred together with the women and children. The Polovcians showed their teeth at us, as they stood like wolves at the fords and in the hills. But God and St. Boris did not deliver us up to them as their prey, so that we arrived at Pereyaslavl unscathed.

I remained in Pereyaslavl three summers and winters with my retainers, and endured great distress through war and famine. We attacked the Polovcian forces behind Rimov, and God stood by us, so that we defeated them and took many captives. We overthrew the troops of Itlar, and after marching beyond Goltav, we captured their camp. We now attacked Oleg at Starodub, because he had made common cause with the Polovcians. In pursuit of Bonyak, we advanced to the Bug and later beyond the Ros in company with Svyatoslav. (1095) After reaching Smolensk, we became reconciled with David.

We set out a second time from Voronitza. At this juncture, the Torks and the Chityeyeviches came from among the Polovcians to attack us, so that we advanced against them to the Sula. We then returned again to Rostov for the winter, and three winters later I returned to Smolensk. Thence I went to Rostov.

A second time, Svyatopolk and I pursued Bonyak, but the nomads escaped and we did not catch them. Thereupon we again followed Bonyak beyond the Ros, yet did not overtake him. During the winter, I traveled to Smolensk, but left there on Easter Day. George's mother passed away. In the summer, I went to Pereyaslavl, and assembled my kinsmen together. Bonyak with his entire force of Polovcians approached Kosnyatin, and we sallied forth from Pereyaslavl to meet them as far as the Sula. By God's help, we were able to make peace with Ayepa, and after receiving his daughter as hostage, we proceeded to Smolensk. Thence we journeyed to Rostov. On departing thence, I again attacked the Polovcians under Urusoba in company with Svyatopolk, and God aided us. Then I again attacked Bonyak at Lubno, and God again vouchsafed us his aid. In company with Svyatopolk, I set out once more upon a campaign. With Svyatopolk and David, I later went as far as the Don, and God granted us his aid.

Ayepa and Bonyak had approached Vyrev with the intention of capturing it. I advanced to meet them as far as Romny with Oleg and my sons. When the nomads learned of our coming, they fled. Then we marched to attack Gleb at Smolensk, because he had captured our retainers. (1116) God aided us, and we accomplished our purpose. Thereupon we marched to attack Yaroslav son of Svyatopolk at Vladimir, since we were no longer disposed to endure his malice. (1117) On one occasion, I rode at full speed in one day from Chernigov to join my father in Kiev. Among all my campaigns, there are eighty-three long ones, and I do not count the minor adventures.

I concluded nineteen peace treaties with the Polovcians with or without my father's aid, and dispensed much of my cattle and my garments. I freed from their captivity the best Polovcian princes, including two brothers of Sharukan, three brothers of Bagubars, four brothers of Ovchin, and one hundred of their foremost leaders. Of other chieftains whom God delivered alive into my hands, I took captive, killed, and had cast into the river Slavlya Koxus and his son, Aklan, Burchevich, Azgului prince of Tarev, and fifteen other young chieftains, and at the same time not less then two hundred of the leading prisoners were likewise killed, and cast into the same river.

I devoted much energy to hunting as long as I reigned in Chernigov and made excursions from that city. Until the present year, in fact, I without difficulty used all my strength in hunting, not to mention other hunting expeditions around Turov, since I had been accustomed to chase every sort of game while in my father's company.

At Chernigov, I even bound wild horses with my bare hands or captured ten or twenty live horses with the lasso, and besides that, while riding along the Ros, I caught these same wild horses barehanded. Two bisons tossed me and my horse on their horns, a stag once gored me, one elk stamped upon me, while another gored me, a boar once tore my sword from my thigh, a bear on one occasion bit my kneecap, and another wild beast jumped on my flank and threw my horse with me. But God preserved me unharmed.

I often fell from my horse, fractured my skull twice, and in my youth injured my arms and legs when I did not reck of my life or spare my head. In war and at the hunt, by night and by day, in heat and in cold, I did whatever my servant had to do, and gave myself no rest. Without relying on lieutenants or messengers, I did whatever was necessary; I looked to every disposition in my household. At the hunt, I posted the hunters, and I looked after the stables, the falcons, and the hawks. I did not allow the mighty to distress the common peasant or the poverty-stricken widow, and interested myself in the church administration and service.

Let not my sons or whoever else reads this document criticize me. I do not commend my own boldness, but I praise God and glorify his memory because he guarded me, a sinful and a wretched man, for so many years in these dangerous vicissitudes, and did not make me inactive or useless for all the necessary works of man. As you read this screed, prepare yourselves for all good works, and glorify God among his saints. Without fear of death, of war, or of wild beasts, do a man's work, my sons, as God sets it before you. If I suffered no ill from war, from wild beasts, from flood, or from falling from my horse, then surely no one can harm you and destroy you, unless that too be destined of God. But if death comes from God, then neither father, nor mother, nor brethren can hinder it, and though it is prudent to be constantly upon one's guard, the protection of God is fairer than the protection of man.

⚒ *15* ⚒

The Assassination of Prince Bogoliubskii and a Popular Revolt in Vladimir

Practically all principalities of Kievan Rus experienced violence at one time or another. The turmoil stemmed from the endless princely feuds, from the nearly constant invasions by nomads from Asia, from the fre-

Source: V. I. Lebedev, et al., eds., *Khrestomatiia po istorii SSSR. S drevneishikh vremen do kontsa XVII veka* (A Source Book on the History of the USSR. From Ancient Times to the End of the XVIIth Century) 3rd. ed. (Moscow, Ministry of Education, 1949), vol. I, pp. 90–94 and 96. Translation mine.

quent attacks of Rus principalities by such western neighbors as Sweden, Livonian Knights, Lithuania, Poland, and Hungary, and from the internal clashes between "the haves" and "the have nots." So frequent and bloody indeed were these problems that contemporary observers attributed them to God's punishment for peoples' sins.

One such example of blood-letting occurred in the 1170s in the principality of Vladimir-Suzdal, considered by many Russian historians to be the cradle of firm princely rule that laid the foundation of subsequent princely autocracy in Muscovy. The principal target of this particular violence was Prince Andrei Bogoliubskii, who had sacked Kiev in 1169 and taken most of its movable treasures to Vladimir-Suzdal. In 1174 he was assassinated by a group of his own *boyars* who apparently resented his haughty and arrogant behavior. His sudden demise precipitated a massive popular uprising throughout the principality. The upheaval ended two years later with the emergence of Prince Vsevolod (1176–1212), known in history as "the Big Nest" on account of his large family.

The Assassination of Prince Andrei Bogoliubskii, 1174

[Prince Andrei] had a loyal servant named Iakim. From someone Iakim heard that the prince had ordered the execution of that person's brother. Thanks to the devil's advice, he [the would-be victim] managed to escape and told his brothers, the evil conspirators, as follows: "Today he had sentenced that person to death; tomorrow he will do the same to us. Let us join to do away with the prince." And so, like Judas did to Jesus, they decided to assassinate him that night.

When night fell they grabbed their weapons and, like ferocious animals, they moved to carry out their intent. But when they approached his sleeping quarters they were overwhelmed with fear and fright. They fled from the entrance hall to wine cellar where they drank spirits. There the devil entertained them, offered them his service, and encouraged them in their design. Emboldened by spirits, they returned to the entrance hall.

The leaders of the assassination plot were: Peter, son-in-law of [*boyar*] Kuchka, Ambal Iasin, the keeper of [prince's] keys, and Iakim Kuchkovich. The total number of conspirators, who on that day joined the plot that was conceived by the damned Peter, Kuchka's son-in-law, was twenty. On Saturday night, the Eve of Holy Apostles Peter and Paul, like wild animals, the conspirators approached the bedroom of Prince Andrei, of blessed memory. One of the conspirators stopped at the door and shouted: "Lord! Lord!" The prince replied: "Who is there?" And he answered: "Prokopii!" [Andrei's favored servant]. And the prince said, "Oh, young fellow! Not Prokopii."

When the conspirators heard the prince's words, they rushed to the door and began to pound on it and, using force, they tore it down. [Andrei] of blessed memory jumped out from his bed and tried to reach for his sword; but it was not there. That day, the key keeper Ambal took it away. That sword once belonged to St. Boris.

Two of the accursed men rushed inside the bedroom and began to wrestle with the prince. They thought that they had the prince on the floor and by mistake stabbed one of their own co-conspirators. When they saw the prince standing, they began to fight with him. Because he was a strong man, they used swords and sabers and wounded him with a spear. The prince told them: "Woe unto you, dishonest creatures! You are resembling Goriaser [the killer of Boris and Gleb in 1015]. What wrong have I done to you? If you will shed my blood here on earth, let God punish you for it and for my having provided for you."

The dishonest conspirators thought that they had killed the prince. They took their wounded co-conspirator and left with fear. The prince tried to pursue them but started to hiccup and moan on account of his wound in the heart and so he returned to the entrance hall. When they heard his voice, they returned. When they came to his bedroom, one of them said: "I think I saw the prince going from the entrance hall downstairs." And they said: "Let us find him." And so they went searching for him. But he was not where they thought he went. He was dead. They said: "We will perish! Let us search for him quickly!" They lit candles, and by following his blood drops, they found him. . . . He was murdered on Saturday night.

Before they departed early Sunday morning, which commemorated the twelve apostles, the accursed murdered Prokopii, the prince's loyal servitor. Then they went through the prince's rooms and took his gold, precious stones, pearls, ornaments, and all of his best possessions. They gave all of that loot to their mounted warriors who departed before sunrise. The conspirators dressed themselves in the prince's battle gear and began to assemble the prince's warriors telling them: "The military retinue from Vladimir will attack us soon." And while they were preparing themselves for a battle, they also sent a messenger to Vladimir with the following instruction: "Why are you preparing to attack us? We want to conclude peace with you. We did not plan his murder alone. You, too, were involved in the conspiracy." But the people in Vladimir replied: "If anyone [here] conspired with you, let him join you. We do not want to have any part of it." And so they went their separate ways. There followed such an awful pillaging that eyes could not stand to bear it.

Then on the spot of the murder scene there appeared a certain Kuzma from Kiev. The prince's body was no longer where he was murdered. And Kuzma began to ask: "Where is the body of the slain Lord?" And they replied: "He has been taken to the garden, but you will not be able to bury his body because we want to throw it to the dogs. We will consider anyone who will try to bury him as our enemy and we will kill him too." Kuzma began to cry over the prince's body saying: "My Lord! You either did not recognize your dirty and pernicious enemies or you failed to overpower them the same way you triumphed in the past over the heathen Bulgars." This way he remembered him.

Then there appeared Ambal, the key keeper. He was an Iasin [by background] and had keys to the entire princely household. The prince entrusted everything to him. After he glanced at him, Kuzma said: "Traitor Ambal! Put a rug or something else under as well as some cover over the body of our lord." But Ambal replied: "Go away. We want to throw him to the dogs." To this Kuzma replied: "Oh, you heretic! So you want to throw him to the dogs. Do you not remember what clothes you had when you came here? Now you are dressed in velvet clothes while the prince lies uncovered. I beg you, toss something [to cover his body]." Ambal then tossed a small rug and a mantle with which Kuzma covered the prince and took his body inside a church. And he said: "Open the church for me." And they replied: "Leave his body here in the entrance [of the church]. It must be a great grief for you." [The assassins] were drunk. . . . And so they placed his corpse in the entrance of the church and covered it with a mantle. There he lay for two days and three nights. On the third came Arsenii, abbot of the monastery of Saints Kuzma and Demian, and said: "How long should we allow the body of this prince to lie here? Open the church so I can perform a funeral service and we can bury him. And as soon as this riot is over, the people from Vladimir will come and take him there." And the clergy from the Bogoliubovo Cathedral appeared, took his body inside the church, and then placed it in a stone grave and, together with Abbott Arsenii, celebrated the funeral service.

An Uprising in Bogoliubovo and Vladimir in 1175

The inhabitants of Bogoliubovo pillaged the prince's manor and homes of craftsmen who worked with gold and silver. They took away clothes, silk material, and an enormous amount of other goods. They also perpetrated great damage to the prince's estates. They pillaged the homes of town officials and stewards and killed them, along with lesser officials of the prince whose homes they pillaged. They were unaware of the old saying: "A society that is governed by laws experiences many problems." Villagers joined in the pillage. The turmoil also affected Vladimir. But when a priest, dressed in his vestments and carrying an icon of the Holy Mother of God, went through city streets, the pillaging stopped. . . .

On Friday, the 6th [of July, 1175], the inhabitants of Vladimir told Abbott Feodul and Luka, priest [of the Church] of the Holy Mother of God: "Prepare a stretcher! We want to bring the body of Andrei, Grand Prince and our Lord." And they told the priest: "Gather all of your clergy, put on your vestments, assemble at the Silver Gate with the icon of the Holy Mother of God, and wait there for the arrival of the prince's remains." Abbott Feodul did what was requested of him. He and the clergy of the Vladimir church of the Holy Mother of God, together with many inhabitants of Vladimir, went to Bogoliubovo, exhumed the prince's body and brought it to Vladimir with dignity and a great amount of sorrow.

Shortly thereafter a [mysterious] sign began to appear in Bogoliubovo. People could not be restrained. They all cried and their tears prevented them from seeing clearly. In the distance it was possible to hear a moan. With tears in their eyes everyone lamented, saying: "Lord! When you went to Kiev, to the Cathedral [of St. Sophia] and to the city's Golden Gate, [whose treasures] you have brought [to Bogoliubovo], and then you ordered that a church be built in Iaroslav, you said: "I want to build a church as beautiful as [Kiev's] Golden Gate so it may stand as a memorial to my principality." He was mourned in this manner.

In the year 1176, when the Rostislavichi princes ruled Rostov lands, they distributed many townships to lesser Rus officials from Kiev. The latter, using judicial fees, caused many hardships to the inhabitants of Vladimir. Because the Rostislavich princes were young and inexperienced, they listened to the advice of their *boyars* who taught them how to acquire a property that belonged to others. . . . And the inhabitants of Vladimir said: "We have invited these princes and have sworn our allegiance to them. Unfortunately, their behavior indicates that they do intend to stay here for a long time. They not only plunder the entire territory, but churches as well. Brothers! Let us take care of ourselves!" Then they dispatched their emissaries to Rostov and Suzdal, explaining their grievances to them. The latter sympathized with them, but offered no concrete help. [Local] *boyars* offered their firm support for their princes. . . .

☙ *15* ☙

The Tale of the Host of Igor

It was during the Kievan period of Russian history that lay literature, in addition to chronicles and church literature, made a formal appearance. Of this lay literature, the most important representative, which subsequently became a national classic, is *Slovo o polku Igoreve,* or *The Tale of the Host of Igor.* This poetic description of an unsuccessful campaign against the Polovtsians in 1185 by Prince Igor of Novgorod-Seversk (1180–1202) was composed by an anonymous author at the end of the twelfth century. The original copy of this classic has not been preserved. In 1795 Count A. I. Musin-Pushkin discovered a sixteenth century manuscript of the *Slovo,* but that manuscript was destroyed in the great Moscow fire of 1812. Fortunately, a copy which had been prepared for Catherine II survived, and the present translation, aiming more for accuracy than for poetic rendition, was made from that copy.

Brothers, might it not be proper for us
To begin in ancient diction
A mournful tale of the campaign of Igor,
Igor, son of Sviatoslav?[1]
Let us begin this song, however,
As told in contemporary epics
And not as conceived by Boian.[2]
For the prophetic Boian,
Whenever he wished to compose a song for someone,
He wandered in his thoughts
[Like a nightingale] over the tree,
Like a gray wolf across the land
And like a blue eagle beneath the clouds.

You know how they [determined] to sing of wars of early times;
They released ten falcons upon a flock of swans;

From *Slovo o polku Igoreve, Igoria syna Sviatoslavlia vnuka Olgova (The Tale of the Host of Igor, Igor Son of Sviatoslav, Oleg's Grandson)* (Moscow, Gosudarstvennoe Izdatelstvo Khudozhestvennoi Literatury, 1954). Translation mine.

And whose falcon was first, his song was sung first!
Be it to Iaroslav the Elder[3] or Mstislav the Brave,[4]
Who slew Rededia[5] before the Kasog troops,
Or to Roman the Fair,[6] son of Sviatoslav.
Brothers, Boian really did not release ten falcons upon a flock of swans,
He only placed his prophetic fingers on the living strings
And they themselves murmured glory to the princes.

Brothers, let us begin this tale
From Vladimir the Elder[7] to our Igor,
Who tightened his mind with firmness,
Sharpened his heart with manliness,
And imbued with fighting spirit
Led his brave troops against the land of the Polovtsians
For the sake of the Russian land.
Then Igor looked up at the bright sun
And saw his warriors covered with darkness.
And Igor spoke to his troops:
"Brothers and soldiers!
It would be better for us to perish than to surrender.
Brothers, let us mount our swift horses
And gaze at the blue Don!"
The Prince was inclined to visit the Great Don
But an ominous sign blocked his desire.
"I wish," he said, "to break my spear
With you, Russian people, at the frontier of the Polovtsian land!
I want either to die or be able to drink a helmetful of the Don!"

O Boian, nightingale of old times
If you could sing of those wars
Hopping like a nightingale over the tree of thought,
Flying in thought beneath the clouds,
Weaving all glories of those times,
And racing along the Troian Trail[8] across the plains to the mountains!
You should sing the song of Igor, the grandson of Oleg!
The storm did not carry falcons across the wide fields!
Flocks of daws fly toward the Great Don!
You prophetic Boian, grandson of Veles,[9] should sing of this.

Horses neigh beyond the Sula [River]
Glory rings in Kiev,
Trumpets call in Novgorod [Seversk],

Banners stand in Putivl,[10]
Igor awaits his dear brother Vsevolod.[11]

And the Wild Bull Vsevolod told him:
"Igor, you are my only brother, my bright light!
We both are sons of Sviatoslav!
Brother, saddle your swift horses
For mine have already been saddled
And are waiting for you near Kursk!
My men of Kursk are famous fighters!
They were swaddled under the trumpets,
They were brought up under helmets,
They were nourished by the point of the spear,
They are familiar with all the roads,
They know all the ravines,
Their bows are strung tight,
Their quivers are open,
Their sabres are sharpened,
They lope like gray wolves in the field,
Seeking honor for themselves and glory for their prince!"
Then Prince Igor set his foot in the golden stirrup
And rode out into the open field.
The sun covered his way with darkness
The night, ominously moaning unto him, awakened the birds.
The herds of animals howl.
The Deva[12] calls from atop the trees
And commands the unknown land to listen:
The Volga, the [Azov] Seashore and the Sula land,
And Surozh and Korsun,[13]
And you, idol of Tmutorokan.
But meanwhile, the Polovtsians run over untrodden roads to the Great Don,
Their wagons squeak at midnight like dispersed swans.

Igor leads his warriors to the Don.
The birds in oak trees portend his misfortunes
The wolves howl of the menace in the ravines
The eagles with their clatter summon beasts to a bony feast,
The foxes yelp at the crimson shields.
O Russian land! You are so far behind the mountains.
Darkness of the night came!
The dawn began to break!
The mist has covered the fields,

The nightingales have stopped their chatter,
The daws have silenced their sounds.
With their shields the Russians have divided the great field
Seeking honor for themselves and glory for their prince.

At dawn Friday they trampled the pagan troops of the Polovtsians
And dispersing themselves like arrows over the field
They seized the fair Polovtsian maidens,
And with them also gold, and brocades, and precious samites.
Using Polovtsian caparisons, mantles, fur coats, and other items
They made bridges over bogs and marshes.
But the crimson flag with a white banner
And a crimson forelock with a silver hilt
Went to the Brave [Igor], son of Sviatoslav.
Oleg's brave family slumbers in the field
It has flown too far!
It was born to be insulted
Neither by a falcon nor by a hawk
Nor by you, black raven, pagan Polovtsian!
Gzak runs like a gray wolf
And Konchak[14] prepares a track for him to the Great Don.
Next day, early in the morning, red stars herald the dawn.
From the sea come black clouds
In an attempt to cover the four suns.
They flicker with blue lightning
And a great thunder can be heard.
The rain of arrows comes from the Great Don.
Here spears shall break
Here too sabres shall blunt
Against the Polovtsian helmets,
At the Kaiala River near the Great Don.
O Russian land, you are so far beyond the mountains!

Now the winds, Stribog's[15] grandsons,
Blow arrows from the sea
Against the brave troops of Igor!
The earth trembles
The rivers flow turbidly
Dust covers the fields
The banners proclaim:
Polovtsians are coming from the Don, from the Sea,
And from all sides!

Russian forces retreated!
The sons of demons divided the field with their [war] cries
While the brave Russians [divided it] with their crimson shields.
Fierce Bull Vsevolod!
Stand your ground
Dart your arrows at [enemy] soldiers
Crash through their helmets with the sword of steel!
You, Bull, wherever you charge, gleaming with your golden helmet
There lie pagan heads of the Polovtsians.
You, fierce Bull Vsevolod
Cut Avar helmets[16] with tempered sabres!
Brothers, will any injury matter to one
Who has forgotten about life and honors,
The city of Chernigov and the golden throne of his fathers
And the wants and habits of Gleb's daughter, his beautiful wife?

There have been Troian's ages
Gone are the years of Iaroslav
There have been wars of Oleg
Oleg,[17] son of Sviatoslav,
That Oleg forged sedition with a sword
And dispersed arrows over the land.
He set his foot in the golden stirrup in the city of Tmutorokan,
Old Great Iaroslav,[18] and the son of Vsevolod,[19] heard of his fame!
While prince Vladimir every morning stopped his ears in Chernigov.
Lust for glory brought to judgment Boris, son of Viacheslav.[20]
They buried him in a green horse blanket
For an offense against Oleg, the brave young prince.
From the Kaiala River after the beating
Supported by Hungarian cavalry
Sviatopolk[21] brought his father to the Church of St. Sophia in Kiev.
Then, during the reign of Boris, son of Gorislav
Feuds started and intensified
And grandsons of Dazhbog[22] lost their lives.
Princely feuds killed a whole generation!
Across the Russian land seldom were then heard songs of ploughmen
But often did the ravens croak
While dividing corpses among themselves,
And while jackdaws chattered in their tongue:
"Let us fly to a feast!"

Thus it was in those battles and in those wars.
But no one has heard of this kind of war.

From morning till evening
From evening till dawn
Fly tempered arrows
Clang sabres against the helmets
Crack steel spears
In an unknown field
Amidst the Polovtsian land!
Under {horses} hooves the black soil
Was covered with bones
And saturated with blood
And trouble came to the Russian land!
Do I seem to hear a noise and ringing
Early before the dawn?
Igor is turning his troops back!
He is sorry for his dear brother Vsevolod!
They fought one day,
They fought another,
And on the third day around noon
Igor's banners fell!
Here the brothers parted on the banks of the swift Kaiala
Here too the bloody wine ran out
And here the brave Russians finished the feast.
(They got their guests drunk)
And themselves fell in defense of the Russian land!
The grass wilts because of the sorrow
And the tree bends down because of grief!
Brothers, a sad time has descended!
A wilderness has covered our strength.
Forces of Dazhbog's grandsons have been wounded!
Misfortune has descended on the land of Troian like a maiden
Who flapped her swan wings
Over the blue sea and by the Don.
Gone are the days of abundance,
Over are princely wars against the infidel!
Now brother said to brother:
This is mine and that is mine also!
And the princes began to argue about trifles
As if they were great things.
And they began to create discord among themselves!
And from all sides the pagans invaded the Russian land victoriously.
Oh, falcon, you have gone too far to the sea in slaying birds!

Igor's brave troops cannot be resurrected!
The mourners began to weep
And sorrow spread throughout the Russian land
Spreading among the Russian people embers in a glowing horn!
Russian women wept, saying:
"We shall never be able to visualize our dear husbands
Nor to think of them nor even to see them!
Much gold and silver has been lost!"
Brothers, Kiev groaned from sorrow,
Chernigov from disaster,
Anguish engulfed the Russian land.
Deep sorrow spread over Russian lands.
Princes brought the discord upon themselves
While the pagans made victorious inroads into the Russian land
Collecting from each household a tribute of one squirrel's skin.

Thus those two brave sons of Sviatoslav
Igor and Vsevolod started the feud,
Which their mighty father,
Sviatoslav the Dread,[23] the Grand Prince of Kiev, stopped.
Sviatoslav was a terror!
He defeated enemies with his mighty forces
And with swords of steel!
He invaded the Polovtsian land
Trampled [their] hills and ravines
Muddled [their] rivers and lakes
And drained their creeks and marshes.
Like a hurricane he seized
The pagan Kobiak[24] on the shore of the sea
From amidst the mighty Polovtsian forces!
Kobiak found himself in the city of Kiev
[Prisoner] in the Court of Sviatoslav!

Germans and Wends,
Greeks and Moravians,
Sing glory to Sviatoslav,
But reproach Prince Igor,
Who lost an army at the bottom of the Kaiala, the Polovtsian River,
Now filled with the Russian gold.
There Prince Igor exchanged his golden saddle for a slave's saddle.
They removed the ramparts in the cities,
And all joy came to an end.

Sviatoslav had a sad dream:
"This night," he said, "in the Kievan hills early in the evening
You dressed me up in a black cloth on a bed of yew.
You gave me [to drink] blue wine mixed with bitters
And from hollow quivers you poured out
Into my lap a great treasure of the pagans
And then you flattered me.
My gold-plated throne was empty—without a prince!
And on the outskirts of Plesensk the ill-boding crows
Chattered from dusk through the night.
They flew into the Kisan Forest
And I could not drive them away to the blue sea."
And the *boyars* said to the prince:
"Prince, grief has captivated your mind
Because two falcons have flown off the golden
Ancestral throne in search of the city of Tmutorokan,
Or perhaps to drink a helmetful of the Don.
But the pagan sabres have clipped the falcons' wings
And the birds themselves are now entangled in an iron mesh.
Darkness came on the third day.
Two suns faded out.
Two crimson pillars were extinguished
And with them two young moons, Oleg and Sviatoslav,
Were covered with darkness.
On the Kaiala River darkness covered the world!
Polovtsians spread over the Russian land like a brood of panthers
And submerged it into the sea [of blood],
And a great uproar went up in the Khan's [camp]!
Disgrace transcended glory,
Slavery crashed down upon freedom,
Deva burst back to earth.
Beautiful Gothic maidens
Burst into a song on the shore of the blue sea,
Tinkling with the Russian gold
They sing of the time of Bus!
They glorify the vengeance of Shurokan![25]
While our troops are thirsty after joy."

Then, mingled with tears, the Great Sviatoslav spoke a golden word:
"Oh, my sons, Igor and Vsevolod," he said,
"Too early you started to harass the land of the Polovtsians

In seach of personal glory!
You have conquered ingloriously!
Ingloriously, too, you have shed pagan blood!
Your brave hearts were forged of hard steel
And tempered in violence!
But what have you done to my silver gray hair?
I see no more the might of my powerful,
Rich and war-experienced brother Iaroslav[26]
With his forces of Chernigov
And with his [mercenaries] Moguts, Tatrans, and Shilberans,
And Topchaks, Revugas, and Olbers![27]
[In the past] they conquered enemy forces without shields
Using only swords and war cries,
All for the glory of their ancestors!
But you have said: 'Let us be our own heroes!
Let us capture the glory of the future
And divide the glory of the past!'
Brothers, is there any wonder when an old man feels young again?
When a falcon molts
He chases the birds on high
And permits no harm to befall his nest.
But there is great trouble! [Other] princes will not aid me."
Gloomy times have arrived.
Inhabitants of Romen[28] cry under the Polovtsian swords
While Prince Vladimir is wounded.
Grief and misfortune has befallen Gleb's sons.
Where are you Great Prince Vsevolod?[29]
Do you intend to come from far away
To defend the golden throne of your ancestors?
You are strong enough to scatter the Volga with the oars [of your fleet]
And empty the Don with the helmets [of your soldiers].
If you were here with us then a female slave would go for one *nogata*
And a male slave for one *rezana*.[30]
With [the help of] the courageous sons of Gleb [Prince of Riazan]
You can shoot live arrows over dry land.
And you valiant Riurik and David![31]
Did not your golden helmets float in blood?
Do not your brave warriors roar like wild bulls
When wounded by steel swords in an unknown prairie?
Lords, set your feet in the golden stirrups
To avenge the outrage of our time, for the Russian land,

For the wounds of Igor, the brave son of Sviatoslav!
You Iaroslav Osmomysl [Eight-minded] of Galicia![32]
You sit high on your throne wrought of gold!
With your strong forces you defend the Hungarian mountains,
You block the path to the [Hungarian] king,
Close the gates on the Danube River,
And toss stones over the clouds.
Your rule extends all the way to the Danube.
All lands stand in fear of you.
You can open the gates of Kiev,
And from your ancestral golden throne
You can shoot at the sultans beyond the [Russian] land.
Lord, shoot at Konchak, the pagan slave,
For Russian land, for the wounds of Igor, the brave son of Sviatoslav!
And you brave Roman and Mstislav![33]
[In the past] your courage has led you to great deeds.
To accomplish a vital task you fly on high,
Literally like a falcon that rides the winds
As he tries to overcome the bird!
Under your Latin [*i.e.,* West European] helmets you have iron breast plates!
Your forces have shaken the earth,
Including many countries ruled by the Khan.
Lithuanians, Iatvigians, Deremelians[34]
And Polovtsians have dropped their spears
And bowed their heads under your swords of steel!

For Prince Igor, however, the sun has stopped shining.
And the tree has ominously shed its foliage.
[The enemy] has divided cities along the Ros and Sula Rivers
While Igor's brave forces cannot be resurrected.
Princes, the Don calls you!
The Don calls princes to victory!
Brave princes, descendants of Oleg, are ready for war!
You Ingvar and Vsevolod[35] and you three sons of Mstislav,
You are six-winged falcons of good family
Did you not gain your power through a [military] victory?
Where are your golden helmets
And Polish lances and shields?
Close the prairie gates with your sharp arrows
For Russian land, for the wounds of Igor, the brave son of Sviatoslav!

The silver stream of the Sula River
Flows no more [and does not protect] the city of Pereiaslavl.

And even the Dvina flows muddily
Towards the stern men of Polotsk
As a result of the pagans' war cries.
Only Iziaslav,[36] son of Vasilko
Clanged his sharp swords against Lithuanian helmets
Only to defame the glory of his grandfather Vseslav,[37]
And to fall on the bloody grass beneath the crimson shields
Cut down by Lithuanian swords.
And from his death bed he said:
"Prince, the wings of birds have covered your warriors
And the beasts have begun to lick their blood."
Neither brothers Briachislav[38] nor Vsevolod were there.
[Iziaslav] alone released his precious soul
From a brave body through a golden *gorget*!
All voices became silent!
All joy came to an end!
[Only] the trumpets of Gorodets resounded!
You Iaroslav,[39] and all your grandsons of Vseslav,[40]
The time has come to lower your banners
And to sheathe your dented swords.
You have deviated from the glory of your ancestors.
By your feuds you have enticed the pagans
Against the Russian land, against the possessions of Vseslav.
Your feuds, indeed, brought violence from the Polovtsian land.

During the seventh age of Troian
Vseslav casts lots for a maiden he loved.
With the aid of crutches he mounted a horse
And galloped to the city of Kiev,
Where with his lance he touched the golden throne of Kiev.
[Then] like a wild beast under cover of blue mist,
He galloped at midnight from Belgorod.
Clinging to a horse, by morning he opened the gates of Novgorod.[41]
He destroyed Iaroslav's glory!
And like a wolf he leaped from Dudutki to the Nemiga River.
On the Nemiga they spread sheafs of heads
And threshed them with flails of steel.[42]
They sacrificed lives on the threshing floor
And winnowed souls from their bodies.
The bloody banks of the Nemiga
Were not planted with grain

But with bones of Russia's sons!
Prince Vseslav judged the people
And sold cities of [other] princes.
But at night he prowled like a werewolf.
He reached Tmutorokan from Kiev
Before the cock could crow.
Like a werewolf he crossed the path of the Great Hors.[43]
The bells of St. Sophia of Polotsk tolled matins for him
And he could hear these bells ringing in Kiev!
Though a wise soul lived in his mighty body,
He often suffered misfortunes.
The prophetic Boian once wisely foretold of him:
"Neither a crafty, nor a clever man
Though he be swifter than a bird
Can escape divine judgment."
Oh, Russian land, you must mourn
And recall your early times and your early princes!
The Old Vladimir should not have been nailed to the Kievan hills.
Some of his banners now belong to Riurik,
And others to David!
They are worn now by oxen as they plow the soil
While the lances sing their song at the Danube River.

One can hear the voice of Iaroslavna.[44]
Like a cuckoo she sings early in the morning:
"Like a cuckoo," she says, "I will fly along the Danube
I will dip my beaver sleeve in the Kaiala River
And will cleanse the bleeding wounds of the prince
On his mighty body."
In the morning Iaroslavna cries again
Along the walls of Putivl, saying:
"Oh, wind, great wind!
Why, lord, do you blow so fiercely?
Why do you carry on your light wings
Khan's arrows against the forces of my beloved?
Are you not satisfied with blowing the clouds up high
Or with rocking ships upon the blue sea?
Why, lord, did you scatter my happiness
Over the feather grass [of the prairie]?"

In the morning Iaroslavna cries again
Along the walls of Putivl, saying:

"Oh, Dnieper, famed river!
You have pierced the stone mountains
Of the Polovtsian land!
You have carried Sviatoslav's boats against Kobiak's forces.
Bring, oh lord, my beloved to me
So that I might stop sending tears every morning to the sea."
In the morning Iaroslavna cries again
Along the city walls of Putivl, saying:
"You bright, you beautiful sun!
You warm everyone equally,
You are beautiful equally to all.
Why did you, oh lord, spread your burning rays
On the forces of my beloved?
Why did your rays increase their thirst in a waterless prairie
And thereby close their quivers with misfortune?"
The sea splashed [with fury] at midnight
Hurricanes advance through the mist.
Gods shows the road to Igor,
From the Polovtsian to the Russian land,
To the ancestral golden throne.
The evening glow now has faded.
Igor sleeps, Igor keeps vigil.
In his thought Igor surveys the land
From the Great Don to the Little Donets.
At midnight the horse was ready.
Across the river Ovlur[45] whistled
A warning for the prince to get ready.
Prince Igor will not remain a prisoner!
As he called, the earth trembled,
The grass rustled,
And the Polovtsian tents began to stir.
Like an ermine Prince Igor sped to the reeds
And like a white duck he swam across the water.
Then he leaped on a swift horse,
Jumped off it like a roaming wolf,
Sped towards the valley of the Donets,
Flew like a falcon under the clouds
Killing geese and swans for breakfast, lunch, and dinner.
When Igor flew like a falcon
Ovlur followed him like a wolf,
Shaking off the cold dew.

They both exhausted their horses.
The Donets said: "Prince Igor!
Great glory awaits you.
[Great] disappointment awaits Konchak,
While happiness is in store for the Russian land."
And Igor replied: "Oh, Donets!
Great glory awaits you, too,
For rocking a prince on your waves,
For spreading for him green grass
Along your silver banks,
For covering him with warm haze
Under the shadow of a green tree,
For disguising him on water as a white duck,
As a seagull on the stream,
And as a black duck in the air."
"Entirely different," he said, "is the Stugna River.[46]
Its stream is weak.
Because it has swallowed up other rivers
Its mouth is also wide.
The Dnieper imprisoned young prince Rostislav[47]
On the bottom of its banks.
And Rostislav's mother mourns the young prince.
Flowers have withered from sorrow,
While trees have bent to the ground in grief."

This is not the chattering of the magpies,
It is Gzak and Konchak following Igor's trail.
Crows did not caw at that time,
The daws became silent
And even magpies stopped chattering.
Everything crawled on all fours,
And with their noise the woodpeckers showed the way to the river,
And nightingales with their gay song announced the dawn.
Said Gzak to Konchak:
"If the falcon should reach the nest
We will shoot the falconet[48] with our gilded arrows."
And Konchak replied to Gzak:
"If the falcon should reach the nest
We will enmesh the falconet with [the charms of] a beautiful girl."
And said Gzak again to Konchak:
"If we enmesh him with [the charms of] a beautiful girl,

We will lose both the falconet and the beautiful girl,
And the birds will start fighting us in the Polovtsian land."
Boian, the song-maker of old times,
Said the following of the wars of Sviatoslav,
The grandson of Iaroslav, son of Oleg:
"It is difficult for a head to be without shoulders
It is equally difficult for a body to be without the head."
It is difficult for the Russian land to be without Igor.
The sun shines in the sky.
Prince Igor has returned to the Russian land.
Maidens sing on the Danube
Their voices reach Kiev across the sea.
Igor rides along the Borichev[49]
[To the church of] the Holy Virgin of Pirogoshch.[50]
The countryside is rejoicing,
Cities are jubilant,
Singing songs first to the old princes
And then to the young.
Let us sing glory to Igor, son of Sviatoslav,
To Wild Bull Vsevolod,
To Vladimir, son of Igor.
Hail to the princes and their troops
Who fight against pagan forces for Christendom.
Glory to the princes and to their troops—Amen.

Notes

1. Prince of Novgorod-Seversk, 1180–1198; later, Prince of Chernigov; died in 1202.
2. An ancient bard.
3. Also known as Iaroslav the Wise; Prince of Kiev, 1019–1054.
4. Brother of Iaroslav; Prince of Tmutorokan, a principality located between the Black and Azov Seas.
5. Prince of the Kasogs (Cherkess); slain by Mstislav in 1022.
6. Prince of Tmutorokan; killed in 1079.
7. Apparently Vladimir the Great; Prince of Kiev, 980–1015.
8. Apparently a reference to Roman Emperor Trajan (98–117), during whose reign present-day Rumania was brought under Roman influence.
9. A Kievan pagan deity; a protector of artists and singers.
10. A city on the Seim River.
11. Brother of Igor; Prince of Kursk.
12. A demon bird of Oriental mythology; a cross between an owl and a peacock.
13. Greek cities in Crimea.
14. Gzak and Konchak were Polovtsian *khans*.

15. The ancient Kievan god of the wind.

16. Made by the Avars in East Caucasus and had a sharp apical point.

17. Prince of Chernigov, 1075–1115; often responsible for the Polovtsian invasions of Kiev territories.

18. Prince of Kiev, 1019–1054.

19. Apparently Vladimir Monomakh; Prince of Kiev, 1113–1125.

20. Prince of Smolensk; killed in 1078 near Chernigov.

21. Prince of Kiev, 1093–1113.

22. A Kievan pagan deity; sun god.

23. Prince of Kiev, 1177–1194.

24. A Polovtsian *khan*; taken prisoner by Prince Sviatoslav of Kiev in 1184.

25. A Polovtsian *khan*; grandfather of Konchak; defeated by Kievan forces in 1107.

26. Prince of Chernigov; died in 1198.

27. Turkic tribes who settled in the principality of Chernigov.

28. A city in the principality of Pereiaslavl; besieged by Konchak.

29. Prince of Vladimir, 1176–1212; also known as "the Big Nest" because of his large family.

30. *Nogata* and *rezana* were monetary units in Medieval Russia.

31. Riurik, Prince of Belgorod, died in 1215; David, Prince of Smolensk, died in 1198.

32. Prince of Galicia, 1152–1187; apparently spoke eight languages.

33. Roman, Prince of Volyn, 1172–1205; Mstislav, brother of Roman, died in 1226.

34. Lithuanian tribes.

35. Sons of the Prince of Lutsk.

36. A Prince of Polotsk; killed by the Lithuanians in 1162.

37. Prince of Polotsk, 1044–1101.

38. Prince of Iziaslavl, near Polotsk.

39. Prince of Turov.

40. A Prince of Polotsk and Kiev; died in 1101; was considered a sorcerer.

41. Vseslav attacked Novgorod in 1069.

42. Vseslav was defeated in 1067 on the Nemiga River by Iziaslav, Sviatoslav, and Vsevolod.

43. Great Hors was a pagan deity, perhaps a sun god.

44. Wife of Prince Igor.

45. Ovlur, a Polovtsian guard who aided Igor in his escape.

46. A tributary of the Dnieper; located south of Kiev.

47. Brother of Vladimir Monomakh, drowned in 1093 in the Stugna River.

48. Refers to Igor's son Vladimir, who remained a prisoner of the Polovtsians.

49. The Dnieper River.

50. A church built in 1136 to house an icon brought to Kiev from Constantinople.

⚔ *16* ⚔

Daniel's Plea for Forgiveness

No one knows for certain who Daniel, author of this plea for forgiveness, was. Based on the content of the account, he must have been a young man of a well-to-do family in the city of Pereiaslav. It is clear that he was a well-educated and gifted man who, for some reason, had fallen into disgrace and wanted to regain his former social status. The plea, addressed to Prince Iaroslav Vsevolodovich (1213–36), abounds in references to the Bible, history, common sense, and folkish wisdom. It contains valuable information on social, economic, cultural, and moral matters of Kievan society. It is critical of the corruption, abuses, and many other ills of the day and singles out *boyars*, monks, and women for special criticism. The plea defends human dignity and argues that every individual should be judged primarily on his intellectual qualities. Daniel's plea, therefore, is an important document in the intellectual history of Kievan Rus on the eve of the Mongol invasion.

. . . Lord! My Prince! Please remember me during your reign. I am your servant and son of your servant. Lord! I see many individuals who are being taken care of by your generosity, in the same way the sun warms up everything. I am the only one who is growing in the shade like a single weed on whom the sun does not shine and the rain does not fall. I seem to walk in darkness, because every day and every night I am separated from your sight. Lord! Give me your ear! Listen to my words and forgive all of my transgressions!

Lord! My Prince! By the generosity of your home and the abundance of your table you take care of everybody. Like a deer searching for water I am only asking for your mercy. I feel like a dead tree standing along a road that every passerby wants to cut down. Everyone is also insulting me and I feel that your wrath is not only pursuing but closing in on me.

Lord! My Prince! A well-to-do person is known everywhere, including in a foreign city. No one identifies a poor man when he walks in his home town.

From N. N. Zarubin, ed., *Pamiatniki drevnerusskoi literatury* (Sources of Old Russian Literature) (Leningrad: 1932), vol. VIII, as reprinted in *Anthology of Old Russian Literature*, Edited by Ad. Stender-Petersen in collaboration with Stefan Congrat-Butlar. (New York: Columbia University Press, 1954), pp. 142–152. Translation mine. Words in brackets are mine. Reprinted with permission of Columbia University Press.

Whenever a rich person talks, everyone listens and his pronouncements are applauded sky-high. But when a poor man says something everyone jumps on him. In short, those who wear glittering clothes are perceived as honest speakers.

Lord! My Prince! Do not judge me by my external appearance. Look instead at my inner qualities. My clothes are poor, but my intellectual qualities are rich. I am a young person but have a mature intellect. In my thoughts I soar in the air like an eagle.

Lord! My Prince! Allow me to see your face, to hear your sweet voice, to see your mouth pronounce sweet phrases and to view your handsome appearance. Your messages resemble those coming from an early paradise. . . .

Lord! My Prince! Do not look at me the way a wolf looks at a lamb. Look at me instead the way a mother looks at her offspring. Look at birds! They do not plant; they do not harvest; and they do not store their food in a granary. They rely on God's mercy. Do not allow your hand to be diverted away from helping the poor. For it is written: "Give to those who ask you for help and be generous to those who beg," if you wish to enter the kingdom of heaven. It is also written: Tell your problems to your lord and he will take care of them. . . .

Lord! My Prince! I do not consider myself to be a brave warrior. But I am quite eloquent in my expressions. I collect daring as well as unifying ideas. [Based on Solomon's wisdom] it seems that it is better to have one good idea than to have ten useless thoughts. . . .

Lord! My Prince! I have not been brought up in Athens nor have I been tutored by philosophers. Like a honey bee I have been gathering all sorts of information and from it I have developed a thirst for knowledge in order to fathom the depth of the sea.

Lord! My Prince! Do not abandon me the same way my father and my mother abandoned me! My Lord! Please accept me [as your servant] and offer me your generosity!

Lord! My Prince! An oak tree grows strong because it has many roots. Our city [grows strong] on account of your rule.

Lord! My Prince! The captain is the head of a ship. You, Prince, are the leader of your people. Someone who has seen an army without a good prince has remarked: "I have seen a large animal without a head." Husbands are heads of their wives; a prince is the leader of husbands; and God is the supreme authority of princes. Like a richly-ornamented brocade that is speckled with many threads of silk in order to adorn a beautiful face, so, you, our Prince are held in high esteem by our wise *boyars* and by many people. You also are well-known in other countries.

Like a fishing net that does not hold water but can catch many fish, so you, too, our Prince, have no riches because you distribute them to men of influence and the brave to keep them around. You cannot gain good men with gold, but with good men you can acquire gold, silver, and cities. . . . Water is the mother of all fish. You, our Prince, are [the father] of your people. Spring adorns the landscape with its flowers. You, our Prince, embellish us with your generosity.

Lord! My Prince! I have been in a great need and grief and have suffered greatly under a working yoke. I have experienced every evil thing. I would rather wear bast shoes in your home than wear red-leather boots in a *boyar* home. I would prefer serving you in sack clothes than wear purple clothes in a *boyar* home. . . . I would rather drink water in your home than drink mead in a *boyar* home. I would rather eat a sparrow at your table than a lamb shoulder at the table of evil masters. . . .

Lord! My Prince! For some people Pereiaslav [is a great city]; for me it is a city of sorrow. For some Bogoliubovo [is a great place]; for me it is a bitter grief. For some Beloozero [is a clear water lake]; for me it is a lake of tar. For some Lake Lach [is a pleasant place]; for me it is a place where I cried a lot and where my growth stopped. My friends and my relatives have disassociated themselves from me because I have been unable to place rich food in front of them. Some continue to be my friends and even sit at my table and drink my mead. But at every opportune or adverse moment they turn into enemies and try to push me off balance.

Outwardly, they feel sorry for me; but in their hearts they enjoy my misfortune. Consequently, I do not trust any of my friends. I do not expect to receive any help from them or from my brother. Whatever I have they want to consume with me. But, when I do not have anything to share with them, they immediately distance themselves from me. Lord! My Prince! I beseech you! Please protect me from ruin. Prince Rostislav [brother of Vladimir Monomakh, 1113–1125] was right when he said: "I would rather die than inherit the principality of Kursk." The same expression applies to an ordinary individual. It is better to die than to live in misery. . . .

Lord! My Prince! I beseech you; please make it possible for me to see your face and experience your generosity in order to escape my present poverty, the source of all evil. . . . I am calling upon you with the voice of the prodigal son who said: "Please remember me and save me." I ask you for the same favor. Son of the Great Prince Vsevolod [Iaroslav's father, who died in 1212], do not let me cry and do not deprive me of your mercy the way Adam was deprived of heaven. Please pass some of your generosity to me in order to ease my poverty and allow me to be able to praise my ruler. . . .

Lord! My Prince! Rust devours iron. Grief does the same thing to the human mind. A phrase that is repeated too frequently loses its meaning.

Similarly, a human being becomes poor thanks to many misfortunes. . . . It seems that a person usually notices a small [particle of] dust in another person's eye, but that same person cannot see a big twig in his own eye. Everyone is scheming and cunning about the misery of others, but they are incapable of thinking and taking care of their own problems. . . .

Lord! My Prince! Do not disavow your suffering servant. Do not deprive me of my life! Similarly, as the fate of a female servant is in the hands of her master, so too is my fate in your hands, since I am your servant and son of your servant. Whenever you feast on different courses of a meal, please remember me eating dry bread. Whenever you are enjoying a sweet drink and are dressed in your splendid attire, please remember me dressed in a coarse garment made of sack cloth. When you relax on your soft bed, remember me laying under one rag. . . .

Lord! My Prince! The eagle is the lord over all birds; sturgeon over all fish; lion over all animals; and you, Prince, over all inhabitants of Pereiaslav. Who is not frightened whenever a lion roars? So too, Prince, who is not scared whenever you speak? Everybody is terrified whenever a snake hisses. So too, you, our Prince, instill fear in everybody because of your military might. Women prefer the glitter of gold. My Prince, your people prefer you. The human body is nourished through its veins. Prince! We are nourished by your [wise] rule. Prince! Young birds rejoice with the approach of the spring. Children find comfort with their mothers. We are very satisfied with you. . . .

Lord! My Prince! Every nobleman expects to receive honor and mercy from his prince in order to prevent them from roaming around in distress like a person circling an aurochs with an axe or someone trying to drive away a demon with a cowl. But who can determine what is good? No one can. Similarly as no one can shoot an arrow straight without feathering it, so too no one can gain honor through laziness. Vicious lies never bring any good. You will never triumph fighting with a dog over a bone. Those who have never experienced the suffocating power of the smoke cannot fully appreciate the warmth of the fire. The quality of gold is tested by fire; human endurance is tested by suffering. . . .

But, Prince, you may ask: "Do you agree with everything that you have said? Is that all?" [My answer is simple.] If I knew how to steal, I may not have offended you as much as it appears. A maiden loses its virginity through her licentiousness; a man loses his honor through theft.

But, Prince, you also may reply: "When you marry into a rich family, you must sing a given song and must partake of a certain food." But I will reply that I would rather have a high fever, because with time I can rid myself of it, than to live and suffer for the rest of my life with a vicious wife. Once I saw an evil-minded woman embellished with gold and have told her: "You do not need that gold.'' I would rather smelt iron ore than to live with an evil-minded wife. An evil-minded wife is like a scratch: it itches here and it hurts there. I also once saw an old woman who had an evil appearance, was cross-eyed, resembled a devil, was a loud-mouth, and evil-minded, and when she looked in a mirror, I told her: ''Don't look in that mirror, look instead at a scab. . . .''

Or, perhaps, you Prince will reply: ''Get tonsured!'' [To this advice I will respond as follows]: I have not seen a dead person riding on a pig, nor have I seen a devil making love to an old woman. I have not eaten figs grown on an oak nor grapes grown on a linden tree. I would rather die now than enter a monastery in order to please God. There is a saying: ''It may be possible to deceive worldly authorities, but it is impossible to deceive God.'' One must never lie to God nor play games with the Supreme Being. Unfortunately, there are many monks who have formally severed their connections with this world but who continue to enjoy all worldly pleasures, and like dogs they try to reconsume their waste. Like gluttonous dogs they invade villages and homes of influential people. Wherever there is a wedding or any celebration you will encounter monks, nuns, and other free loaders. For the sake of appearance, all of them put on an angelic appearance. Actually, they practice licentiousness and while in theory they exhibit a saintly dignity, in practice their behavior is reprehensible. . . .

ꙮ *17* ꙮ

A Discourse Concerning
The Ruin of Rus Land

One of the most intriguing pieces of medieval Rus literature is *A Discourse Concerning the Ruin of Rus Land*. It was discovered in 1892 in a Pskov monastery among manuscripts dating to the fifteenth century. Scholars

From X. M. Lopar'ov, ed., *Pamiatniki drevnei pismennosti i iskustva* [Sources on Ancient Literature and Art] (St. Petersburg: 1892), vol. LXXXVI, as reprinted in *Anthology of Old Russian Literature,* Edited by Ad. Stender-Petersen in collaboration with Stefan Congrat-Butlar. (New York: Columbia University Press, 1954), pp. 175–176. Translation mine. Words in brackets are mine. Reprinted with permission of Columbia University Press.

have been unable to identify the author of the *Discourse,* or to pinpoint
the date of its composition. Based on internal evidence, however, many
feel that it was written sometime between 1223, the year the Mongols
defeated Rus forces at Kalka, and 1246, the year Prince Iaroslav of
Vladimir-Suzdal, father of Alexander Nevskii, died. This approximate
date can be deduced from references to the glorious days of the past
when Rus principalities, whenever they used their resources and forces
wisely, were rich, powerful and influential in Eastern Europe. While the
Discourse makes no mention of Mongol invasion, the message is clear: A
cataclysmic change has occurred in the status of all Rus principalities.

Because in the original copy, the *Discourse* immediately preceded *The
Life of Alexander Nevskii,* some scholars consider *Discourse* to be a preface
to *The Life.* But differences between the two in style and language are
so pronounced that it is difficult to accept this interpretation. Indeed,
the literary style and language suggest that the unknown author of the
Discourse may have been influenced by *The Tale of the Host of Igor.*

Oh, shiny bright and beautifully adorned Rus Land!
You abound in lakes, rivers, and local springs;
In steep mountains and high hillocks;
In clear forests and wonderful meadows;
In diverse beasts and in countless birds;
In great cities and in amazing villages;
In many monasteries and churches;
In stern princes, honest *boyars* and noble people!
You, Rus land, abound in everything!
Oh, you Orthodox Christian faith!

[Rus! Your territories extend] from
Here to Hungary and to the Poles;
[And from them] to the Czechs;
And from the Czechs to the Iatvigians [a Lithuanian tribe];
And from the Iatvigians to Lithuania and to the Germans [that is,
the Livonian Crusading Order based in the city of Riga]
And from the Germans to Karelia [present-day southern part of Finland];
And from Karelia to Ustiug, inhabited by the heathen Toimitsi [a little known
Finno-Ugric tribe along the Toima River, tributary of Northern Dvina] all
the way to the White Sea; And from the White Sea to the Bulgars [present-
day region of the Chuvash and Bashkir Autonomous Republics of the RSFSR];
And from the Bulgars to the Bultars [a little known tribe that inhabited the
region east of the Volga and possibly the Oka Rivers; and from the Burtas
to the Cheremissians;
And from them to the Mordvinians

* * *

With God's help, all that territory was brought under Christian control by

Grand Prince Vsevolod [The Big Nest, 1176–1212], father of Iurii [Dolgorukii, 1219–1236], Prince of Kiev, and by his grandfather Volodimir Monomakh [1113–1125], who was so feared that Polovtsian mothers invoked his name to frighten their children in cradles.

* * *

[During that time] the Lithuanians did not dare to leave
Their marshes, and the Hungarians reinforced
Their cities with iron gates to prevent attack by
The Great Volodimir.
The Germans rejoyced because they were far-away, beyond the blue sea [the Baltic]; while the Burtasians, the Cheremissians, and the Vadians [perhaps the Votiaks, a Finno-Ugric tribe that inhabited the region along the Viatka River],
And the Mordvinians served as beekeepers for Prince Volodimir [Monomakh].
Greek [that is, Byzantine] Emperor Manuel [1143–1180]
Respected [the Grand Prince of Rus] and sent generous gifts
To him in order to prevent Grand Prince Volodimir
From attacking Constantinople.
Nevertheless, during that time [of conquest and influence]
Commoners [in Rus] suffered very much from the end of the reign of Iaroslav the Great [1019–1054] to Volodimir [Monomakh, 1113–1125] and on to the present Prince Iaroslav [1236–1246],
And his brother Iurii, Prince of Volodimir [1219–1236].

☙ 18 ❧

A Biography of
Prince Alexander Nevskii

One of the more colorful among Rus princes on the eve of and immediately following the Mongol invasion was Alexander Iaroslavich, known in history as Nevskii, who served first as Prince of Novgorod and, after

---

From V. Mansikka, *Pamiatniki drevnei pesmennosti i iskustva* (Sources on Ancient Literature and Art) (St. Petersburg), vol. CLXXX, as reprinted in *Anthology of Old Russian Literature* Edited by Ad. Stender-Petersen in collaboration with Stefan Congrat-Butlar. (New York: Columbia University Press, 1954), pp. 100–108. Translation mine. Words in brackets are mine.

his father's death, also as Grand Prince of Vladimir-Suzdal (1252–1263). The available evidence indicates that Alexander was a wise and courageous man and an inspiring leader. Thanks to his efforts, the Novgorodians successfully thwarted attempts by Swedish, German, and Lithuanian forces to impose their control over strategically vital Novgorod. Alexander also dealt realistically with the Mongol masters. Because of his achievements, he emerged as a great national hero not only of pre-revolutionary Russia but of the Soviet Union as well.

The following excerpts were translated from an account by an anonymous biographer who, through his close family ties, was familiar with the chronology of Alexander's life and who respected and admired Alexander very much. The biography is a secular rather than a religious account. It portrays Alexander as an ideal prince and warrior endowed with the best intellectual and physical qualities.

Let us tell a story about his bravery and life. Oh, Lord, our Jesus Christ, Son of God! I, humble, sinful and unworthy person, write about the life of a great prince, Alexander Iaroslavich [Prince of Novgorod and Grand Prince of Vladimir-Suzdal, 1252–1263], grandson of [Prince] Vsevolod [the Big Nest, 1176–1212]. Because I have heard [stories] from my parents and have personally seen him grow I would like to recount his saintly, honest and illustrious life. . . .

By God's will Prince Alexander Iaroslavich was born to his pious, humble and very gentle father, Grand Prince Iaroslav [Vsevolodovich, who ruled Kiev and Vladimir-Suzdal from 1236 to 1246] and his pious mother Feodosiia. . . . His [Alexander's] physical appearance was unlike that of any other man. His voice resounded like a trumpet. His face resembled that of Joseph [son of Jacob], whom the Egyptian pharaoh designated as Egypt's co-ruler. He [Alexander] was as strong as Sampson and as wise as Solomon. God granted him the bravery of Roman Emperor Vespasian [69–79], son of Emperor Nero, who subdued the land of Judea. . . . [Like Vespasian] Alexander Iaroslavich was unconquerable in combat.

* * *

Then a representative of a West [European] country, [actually the German Order of the Knights of the Holy Cross of Livonia] who call themselves God's servants, visited [Alexander] to see his unusual stature, similarly as the ancient Queen of Sheba came to King Solomon to hear his wisdom. So when this [West European] named Andrias [Welwen, the Grand Master of the Order] met Prince Alexander Iaroslavich, upon his return home he said the following: "I have visited many countries and have mastered many languages, but I have never seen anyone among kings and princes [like Prince Alexander Iaroslavich].

When a ruler of the northern part of the Roman Empire [actually it was Birger Jarl, Regent of Sweden during the reign of King Eric] heard about the gallantry of Prince Alexander Iaroslavich, he said: "I will go and conquer Alexander's country." And so he assembled a large force, put his men aboard many ships, and sailed this mighty military armada to the Neva River. He was overwhelmed by his madness. In his arrogance, he dispatched envoys to Prince Alexander Iaroslavich in Novgorod the Great with the following message: "Do you dare resist me? I came here to conquer your country!"

When Prince Alexander heard those words his heart became inflamed. He went to the Cathedral of Saint Sophia [in Novgorod], knelt before the altar, and with tears in his eyes began to pray to God. . . . After he finished his prayer, he rose and saluted Archbishop Spiridon who blessed him and wished him well. Then Alexander Iaroslavich left the Cathedral, wiped his tears, and began to strengthen his military force. Then he said: "God represents righteousness, not military might!". . . Then, without waiting, he joined his small military unit. He did not trust its capability. Instead, he entrusted his fate to the Holy Trinity.

It is difficult to visualize how his honest and great father [Grand Prince] Iaroslav would have responded to the challenge his son Prince Alexander Iaroslavich was now facing. There was no one available to send the [sad] news to his father in Kiev. Fortunately, many able warriors came forward as did many Novgorodians because the Grand Prince asked for their help. Six hundred men joined him on Sunday [July 15, 1240] to commemorate the day of the Holy Fathers and an additional thirty came to commemorate the [Fourth Ecumenical] Council of Chalcedon as well as to honor the names of Sts. Cyril and Julitta and St. Prince Vladimir, who brought Christianity to Rus. He [Alexander] also had great faith in the holy martyrs, Boris and Gleb.

There was a man named Peglusi, an elder from Izhersk [south of the Neva River on the Gulf of Finland]. He was entrusted with the surveillance of the sea shore. He was baptized [into Orthodox Christianity] but continued to live with his pagan fellow-tribesmen. At his baptism he received the name Philip. He lived piously and fasted every Wednesday and Friday. . . .

He then spotted a military force advancing against Prince Alexander Iaroslavich, whom he informed about the strength and the size of the enemy's force and he spent the entire night observing the enemy's approach. At sunrise he heard a violent noise at sea and spotted a single boat sailing, and aboard stood Boris and Gleb in their purple robes. . . . And Boris said to Gleb: "Brother Gleb, tell our oarsmen to row fast so we can help our relative, Grand Prince Alexander Iaroslavich."

When Peglusi saw this miracle and heard the voice of such a martyr [as Boris], he stood there petrified. . . . But soon Prince Alexander Iaroslavich appeared. When Peglusi saw him he told the Grand Prince about his unique experience. The Prince told him not to tell anyone about it. Encouraged by the news, he [Alexander] advanced against the enemy early in the morning. And there was a great slaughter of the Romans [that is, Swedes]. Many of them, including their leader, sent out an official peace appeal, signed by their code of arms.

There were six great brave, strong warriors in Alexander's camp who stood firmly with him. One was Gavrilo Aleksich. He sailed aboard a boat and when he spotted the [enemy] king, he grabbed his sword, [and] sailed his boat towards the king's vessel where he disembarked. Then he approached him and tossed him and his horse to sea. . . . Another man of Novgorod was Sbyslav Iakunovich, who, wielding his axe and exhibiting no fear, charged the enemy many times. He killed many enemy warriors with his axe. Prince Alexander Iaroslavich was very impressed by Sbyslav's strength and bravery. The third man was Jacob, native of Polotsk. He was the master of the Prince's hounds. With his sword he charged enemy units, distinguished himself, and the Prince congratulated him for it. The fourth was a man from Novgorod named Misha. He advanced on foot against the enemy and destroyed three boats. The fifth was a young man named Sava who attacked the tent of the enemy king and brought it down. When Prince Alexander's warriors saw the enemy's tent collapsing, they rejoiced. The sixth man was Ratmir, a servant [of the Prince]. He was not mounted but tried to take care of the wounded and he died because he himself was wounded several times.

I heard about these events from my Lord, Prince Alexander Iaroslavich, and from others who participated in the slaughter. . . . After he triumphed over the king at the mouth of the Izhera River [a tributary of the Neva], Prince Alexander Iaroslavich surveyed the casualties of his forces and decreed that all dead be put aboard vessels and buried at sea. . . .

A year following Prince Alexander's victory, another force came from the West and besieged his patrimonial city of Alexandrov. Prince Alexander at once went to meet the enemy. He drove the enemy away, killed many, and brought some as prisoners, but released them later as a sign of his peaceful intentions.

In the third year after he triumphed over the [enemy] king, Alexander advanced, in winter time, with large forces against German-held territories. . . . He captured Pskov and took many of their officials as prisoners of war. Prince Alexander Iaroslavich removed enemy officials from their posts and freed the city of Pskov from enslavement. He campaigned in the vicinity of Pskov, destroyed many towns, took many prisoners, and killed others. Some enemy leaders hid in the city in an effort to capture Prince Alexander Iaroslavich alive.

When enemy forces advanced, they encountered forward units of Prince Alexander. The Prince then resolved to meet the enemy. The encounter took place at the Chudskoe ozero [Lake Peipus]. Both forces had a multitude of warriors. To assist Alexander, his father, Grand Prince Iaroslav, dispatched a strong force led by his younger son Andrei. Like King David in antiquity, Prince Alexander had a multitude of brave men. . . .

It was Saturday. The battle started at sunrise and there was an enormous slaughter. The clash of lances and the sound of breaking swords resounded in the still of the icy lake. No one could see the ice because it was covered with blood. I heard this story from an eyewitness. . . .

Prince Alexander Iaroslavich returned from his triumph in great glory. His forces captured many prisoners and many horses, called *rydeli*. When Prince Alexander Iaroslavich went to the city of Pskov, he was met by *igumens* and priests dressed in festive robes and carrying crosses, and by a multitude of citizens. They thanked God and sang songs glorifying their Lord, Prince Alexander. . . . His name soon became famous from Lake Peipus to the Arabian mountains [Caucasus?] and from the Baltic to Rome.

Meanwhile, the Lithuanians increased their [hostile] activities and began to cause difficulties in the Alexandrov region which they terrorized. He [Alexander] advanced against them, defeated seven of their units, and killed many of their princes and *voevodas* [military commanders]. He captured some with his own hands. Others, who were using profane language, he tied to the tails of his horses. Subsequently they [Lithuanians] feared his name.

At about that time there appeared in the East a powerful ruler [Batu Khan, Master of the Golden Horde], who conquered many nations from East to West. When he heard of the brave and famous Prince Alexander Iaroslavich, he sent to him an envoy with the following message: "Alexander! Don't you know that God has allowed me to conquer many nations? You are the only one who has refused to submit to my command. If you wish to spare your land [from destruction], come to me at once and see first hand the glory of my empire."

After the death of his father [Iaroslav, in 1246], Prince Alexander Iaroslavich came with a great force to Vladimir [the capital of the Principality of Vladimir-Suzdal]. His arrival was momentous. The news of his coming spread along the Volga region and women of the Mohabit [a Finnish tribe] tried to scare their children by saying: "[Behave!] Prince Alexander Iaroslavich is coming!"

Grand Prince Alexander Iaroslavich reflected [about Batu Khan's statement] and after consulting and receiving blessing from Bishop Cyril of Rostov, he [Alexander] left to meet the Emperor [Batu Khan]. When Emperor Batu saw Alexander, he told his nobles: "Now that I have seen him, I know that there

is no person in his land equal to this prince." He [Batu Khan] then released
Alexander with great honors. Subsequently, Emperor Batu became angry at
Prince Andrei, younger brother [of Alexander], and sent against him his
military commander Nevrui who terrorized the Principality of Suzdal. After
he paid tribute in [the town of] Nerv, Grand Prince Alexander ordered that
a church be constructed on the site. There he also founded a city and invited
frightened people to settle in it. . . .

Once there even came Papal envoys from the great city of Rome with a
message for Prince Alexander Iaroslavich. The Papal message said: "Prince!
We have heard that you are honest and unusual and that your land is glorious
and great. For that reason we would like to dispatch to you two of our twelve
cardinals who are quite eloquent so you can hear their teachings." Grand
Prince Alexander Iaroslavich consulted with his knowledgeable advisors and
told the Papal envoys as follows: "I am very familiar with events from Adam
to the deluge and from there to the division of mankind; and from there to
the beginnings of Abraham and from Abraham to the crossing of the Red
Sea by the Israelites; and from the Exodus to the death of David; and from
the reign of Solomon to Augustus; and from the birth of Christ to His
crucifixion and resurrection; and from His resurrection and His ascension to
heaven to the reign of Constantine I; and from the First to the Seventh
[Councils of Nicea]." Then he added: "I do not need your teachings!" And
they returned home. . . .

Then, there developed a great misery. It was caused by the heathens. Many
people fought among themselves. Grand Prince Alexander Iaroslavich went
to Emperor [Batu Khan] to request his assistance for the needy people. He
also sent his younger brother Iaroslav and his son Dmitrii with the men of
Novgorod to guard against [a possible attack by] Western countries. He also
dispatched his own forces to join them. Iaroslav and his nephew advanced
with this mighty force and destroyed the German city of Iuriev [the present-
day Estonian city of Tartu] and returned home with many prisoners and with
great honor.

Meanwhile, Grand Prince Alexander Iaroslavich returned from his visit to
the heathens [the capital of Batu Khan]. After he reached Nizhnii Novgorod,
he became ill. . . . Grand Prince Alexander Iaroslavich was a devout believer
in God. Before he departed the earthly for the heavenly kingdom, he expressed
a desire to enter monastic life. God granted him his wish. . . . He died on
November 14 [1263], on St. Philip's day. . . . His noble body was then taken
to Vladimir. The Metropolitan, his assistants, princes, *boyars*, and all people,
humble and great, met the funeral procession at Bogoliubovo with candles
and censers. There was a tumultuous crowd pressure because everyone wanted

to see his body. Everyone wept and there was much shouting such as had never been heard before. It resembled an earthquake.

Then a miracle, which is worthy of attention, occurred. After the church service over his noble remains was completed, Metropolitan Cyril [of Kiev, who then spent most of his time in Vladimir] reached for his [Alexander's] hand in order to place therein a religious *gramota* [a document testifying that he was a good Christian]. The Prince extended his arm, as if he were alive, and took the *gramota* from the Metropolitan. There was great astonishment and excitement among those who were present there. His noble body was placed to rest in the Church of the Holy Virgin Mary on November 23, [1263]. . . .

⚔ *19* ⚔

Galicia-Volyn in the Thirteenth Century

In the second half of the twelfth century Kievan Rus experienced simultaneously two interrelated developments: the gradual withering away of the importance of the city of Kiev as the political, economic, and cultural center of the realm, and the territorial disintegration of the realm into a number of independent principalities. While each principality retained many of the Kievan practices, customs, and institutions, each principality also evolved a new way of life under the impact of local peculiarities. To the west and southwest of Kiev the most important principality was Galicia (called Halych in this reading)-Volyn, whose political fortune followed a somewhat erratic and at times a turbulent course. The brief history of Galicia-Volyn is marred by internal instability and foreign invasions. The principality seems to have suffered an overdose of both problems in the thirteenth century during the early reign of Prince Daniel and his brother, Vasilko.

This happened in the year 6735 [1227]. Let us tell of countless battles, of great hardships, of frequent wars, of great treasons, of frequent uprisings, and

From *Polnoe Sobranie Russkikh Letopisei* (Complete Collection of Russian Chronicles), 2d edition (St. Petersburg: 1908), vol. II, cols. 750 ff. Translation mine. Words in brackets are mine.

of many upheavals. From their youth on [Prince Daniel and his brother, Vasilko] had no peace.

When Iaroslav [Iziaslavich] ruled in Lutsk, Daniel went on a pilgrimage to Zhidichin to pray to St. Nicholas, and was invited by Iaroslav to come to Lutsk. Daniel's *boyars* then advised him: "Take Lutsk and imprison their prince." He replied, however: "I came here to pray to St. Nicholas and hence I cannot take such a step." Daniel went then to Vladimir where he assembled an army and dispatched it against Iaroslav [of Lutsk]. It was led by [the following warriors of Daniel:] J. Andrei, Viacheslav, Gavriil, and Ivan. When Iaroslav left the city he was seized, together with his wife. He was captured by Aleksei Oreshko, who had a swift horse and captured him before he was able to reach the city. The people of Lutsk organized their city defenses, but when Daniel and Vasilko came there next day, they surrendered. Daniel gave Lutsk and [the town of] Perepsonitsa to his brother, Vasilko; earlier he had given him [the town of] Brest.

Then the Iatvigians [a Lithuanian tribe] began to war around the town of Brest, but they were defeated by the warriors from Vladimir [Volynskii]. Two Iatvigian [warriors], Shutr Moindunich and Stegut Zebrovich, attacked Daniel's armies and Shutr was killed by Daniel and Viacheslav; while Stegut was killed by Shelv. When the Iatvigians started to retreat, Daniel pursued them and inflicted four wounds on Netr; he even knocked a spear from his hand. Vasilko pursued him and suddenly someone shouted very loudly: "Your brother is fighting in the rear!" Vasilko returned immediately and came to the rescue of his brother. This enabled Netr to escape and the other Iatvigians dispersed. But let us leave this story and return to an earlier account.

Daniel dispatched [his *tysiatskii*] Demian to his father-in-law with the following message: "The people of Pinsk should not rule [the town of] Czartorysk; I will not tolerate this." Demian brought Daniel [the following message from Daniel's father-in-law]: "My son, I made a mistake when I did not give you the city of Halych; I gave it to a member of a different dynasty thanks to the treacherous advice of Sudislav, who deceived me. But, God willing, we shall march against him. I will bring with me the Polovtsians and you come with your warriors. If God helps us, you will take Halych and I will seize the lower valley [of the Dniester River]. You are right concerning the problem of Czartorysk." Demian returned [with this message] on Saturday before Easter [1227]. On Easter Sunday Daniel and Vasilko came to Czartorysk and during the next night they laid siege to the town. An arrow released from the city wall killed Daniel's horse. On the following day after circling the town, Miroslav and Demian told the princes: "God has placed your enemies into your hands." Daniel then ordered [his forces] to approach the town and they took it. The ruling prince of the town was taken prisoner. . . .

This happened in the year 6737 [1229]. Leszek, the Grand Prince of Poland, was killed in the *sejm* [parliament] by Sviatopolk Ovdovich and Vladislav in accordance with a scheme that had been prepared by treacherous aristocrats. After [Leszek's] death, his brother Konrad invited Daniel and Vasilko to a conference and requested them to come to his aid. They agreed and advanced jointly against Vladislav the Elder. They went to war in person, and in Brest they appointed [Prince] Vladimir of Pinsk and the people from the towns of Ugrovsk and Brest to protect the country from the Iatvigians [during their absence].

At that time the Lithuanians attacked the Poles in peace time and they approached Brest. Vladimir of Pinsk told them: "You say that you are peaceful; but in my judgment you are not." He then advanced against them and with him also went the people of Brest and they defeated them.

Meanwhile Daniel and Vasilko joined Konrad, and after consultations they advanced to [the city of] Kalusz. They reached the Wieprz River in the evening and the morning they crossed the Prosna River and advanced to the city [of Kalusz]. It rained very heavily that night, and noting that no one opposed them they took many people prisoner and destroyed everything. Rus armies advanced to Milicz and Stary Gród, captured several villages belonging to Vladislav and took many people into captivity. Then they returned to their camp to decide how they should advance against the city [of Kalusz] and how they should fight. Their Polish friends did not want to fight [just then].

Next day Daniel and Vasilko advanced with their armies against the city. Konrad liked the style of combat used by Rus forces and encouraged his Poles to fight. However, they did not want to do it. Daniel and Vasilko approached the gates of Kalusz and sent Miroslav's and other units to approach it from the opposite direction.

The city was surrounded by a river. Along its banks grew willow and sallow trees. The latter were so thick that it was impossible to determine who was fighting whom and where. When one unit retreated from the battle line, others advanced toward them and when these retreated, new units advanced against them. Because of this situation, the city was not captured that day. Stones were flying like a heavy rain from city walls. Most of the advancing troops stood in the water. Only those who managed to stand on stones that had been thrown stood dry above the water. They succeeded in setting the draw bridge and the draw equipment on fire, but the Poles managed to put the fire out before it reached the city gate. Daniel and Vasilko went on horseback around the city. The besieging forces fired many arrows into the city that wounded 160 defenders who stood on city walls.

When evening came, Rus forces returned to their camp. Stanislav Mikulich then said: "There was neither water nor high wall where we were." Daniel [immediately] mounted his horse in order to inspect city defenses and was convinced that [the story of Stanislav Mikulich] was correct. Then Daniel came to Konrad and told him that: "Had we known about this [vulnerable] spot, the city would have been captured." Konrad asked them to advance against the city next day. Next day Daniel and Vasilko led their men [against Kalusz] and started to clear the brush around the city. City inhabitants became frightened and did not throw any stones at them. Instead they requested that Konrad send Pakoslav and Mestiui to them. Pakoslav then said to Daniel: "Change your clothes and come with us." Daniel did not want to go along but his brother Vasilko told him: "Go ahead and listen to their suggestion." Konrad did not trust Mestiui. Daniel put on Pakoslav's helmet and stood behind him. The defenders who were at the city wall shouted to them: "Convey this to Grand Prince Konrad: Does not this city belong to you? We, the people, have suffered greatly in this city. We are not transients but your subjects and your brothers. Why don't you have mercy on us? If Rus soldiers take us prisoner, what kind of benefit will Konrad have? If the Rus emblem is posted on city walls, the honor will belong to the descendants of [Prince] Roman [Daniel's and Vasilko's father], while your [honor] will decline. Now we belong to your brother, but tomorrow we will belong to you. Do not grant glory to Rus! Do not dishonor this city!" They said many more words. Then Pakoslav replied. "Konrad would like to be merciful toward you; but Daniel is very mean. He does not want to depart without taking the city." At this point he started to laugh and said: "Here he is! Talk to him!" Prince Daniel jokingly hit Pakoslav with the wooden tip of his lance and then he removed his helmet. The besieged began to shout from the walls. "Accept our service, we beseech you. Sign peace with us." Daniel joked and talked with them for a long time. He then accepted from them two knights [as envoys] and rode back to Konrad's [camp]. Konrad concluded peace with them and took with him some hostages. Rus [soldiers] took many commoners and nobles into captivity. Then Rus and Polish [leaders] took an oath, pledging that if a war should develop between them [in the future], then Poles would not capture Rus commoners and Rus would not capture Polish commoners.

Then Daniel and Vasilko returned from Konrad's [homeland] safely to their land with honor. No other prince of Rus, except Vladimir the Great who brought Christianity to Rus, went so deep into Poland [as had Daniel and Vasilko].

Shortly after this, Vasilko went to Grand Prince Iurii of Suzdal to attend the wedding of his brother-in-law. He was accompanied there by Miroslav and others.

At about that time Prince Daniel was in [the town of] Uhrovsk. There he received envoys from Halych, who informed him that: "Sudislav has gone to

Ponizie [the lower basin of the Dniester River] and the son of the [Hungarian] king is in Halych alone. Come to us as quickly as can." Daniel hurriedly assembled his warriors and dispatched Demian against Sudislav, while he led a small army from Uhrovsk to Halych. They reached Halych on the third night. Sudislav did not wait for Demian and fled toward Halych. When Daniel arrived before Halych, the city shut itself in. Daniel then seized Sudislav's estate, where he found a great abundance of wine, fruits, food supplies, lances, and arrows. When he realized that his warriors were heavily loaded with the loot, Daniel decided not to camp close to the city; instead he went across the Dniester River [and camped there]. That night Sudislav sneaked back into the city. [Daniel's people] captured some of his men and they informed him [Daniel] that Sudislav was back in Halych. Daniel encamped in the town of Uholnytsi on the banks of the Dniester. The men of Halych and [their] Magyar [allies] came out and began to ready themselves for a fight on the ice [of the frozen Dniester River]. In the evening the ice broke, spilling the water over. Then, Semeon, the mean scoundrel, as red as a fox, set the bridge across the Dniester on fire. Then Demian arrived with his Halych *boyars*, Mstislav, Vladislav, and many others. Daniel was pleased with their arrival, but [nevertheless] expressed concern about the [condition] of the bridge and the problem of the crossing of the Dniester. Daniel approached the bridge and discovered that at the end of the bridge the fire had died out [without destroying it] and this situation pleased him very much. Early next morning Vladimir Ingvarovich joined Daniel's forces and they crossed the bridge and encamped on both banks of the Dniester. Next morning Daniel went around the city of Halych, gathered many men of Halych, and divided his forces around the city into four camps. His armies now included men from throughout [Galicia]—from the Bobrik River to Ushitsa and Prut. With this force he now laid siege to the city, and when the inhabitants became weakened they surrendered.

After he captured the city, Daniel, recalling the service of [the Magyar] King Andrew, released [Andrew's] son and accompanied him across the Dniester River. He was accompanied [on his way to Hungary] by Sudislav. [Because the latter angered] many people they threw stones at him, saying: "You traitor of the country! Leave the city!"

[The young] Andrew came to his father and his brother while Sudislav urged constantly that they "March against Halych and occupy the land of Rus, for if you will not they will advance against us."

The Magyar King Bela [IV, Andrew's brother] assembled a large army, saying: "Halych cannot remain independent; there is no one capable of taking it away from my control." Then he advanced to the Carpathian Mountains and God sent the Archangel Michael against him. A great rainstorm developed and many horses drowned while men sought dry land. Bela was determined to capture the city and the country [in spite of these losses]. Daniel prayed and God protected him from the crafty [king].

After he surrounded the city of Halych, Bela sent an envoy who shouted in a strong voice: "Listen to the words of the great Magyar king: 'Do not be deceived by Demian who is telling you that God will save you! Do not believe your [prince] Daniel who is telling you that God will not allow this town to go under the rule of the Magyar king! As king [of Hungary] I have marched [victoriously] against other countries on many occasions. Because of the strength of my armies, no one can save you from my rule!' " Demian was not frightened by these threats. He remained firm and God protected him.

Daniel attracted to his side the Poles and the Polovtsians of Kotian [a chieftain]; the king [was aided by] Polovtsians of [chieftain] Begobars.

God sent against the king a pharoah-type of punishment. The city increased its strength constantly while Bela's forces were weakened constantly. He decided to retreat from the city, leaving behind many dead horses and dead warriors with armor. The citizens of Halych attacked the retreating forces and many drowned in the river; others were killed, still others were wounded, and the rest were taken prisoner. . . . The Dniester played a dirty trick on the Magyars. The king retreated [from Halych] to Vasiliev and after he crossed the Dniester he advanced to Prut. Thanks to God's will, Daniel retained his city of Halych. But let us now turn to great treasons, deceits, and countless wars.

In the year 1230, the dishonest *boyars* of Halych developed a conspiracy [against Daniel]. They conspired with Prince Alexander, Daniel's cousin. Their aim was to murder Daniel and then to dispose of his land. The conspirators met and planned to start a fire. At that point the merciful God induced Vasilko to step out. He unsheathed his sword and engaged one of the conspirators, while another seized his shield. The God-praying *boyars* noticed this and became frightened. They said: "Our conspiracy has been uncovered." And they fled like the cursed Sviatopolk. They fled, but neither Prince Daniel nor Vasilko was aware of what happened. Vasilko left for Vladimir, while the godless [*boyar*] Filip invited Prince Daniel to [the town of] Vyshnia. He conceived another plot to kill Daniel with the aid of his cousin, Alexander. When Daniel reached the Branevich Shoal he was met there by a messenger [Constantine], sent by *tysiatskii* Demian, who warned [Daniel]: "The feast will end tragically for you because your godless *boyar*, Filip, and your cousin, Alexander, are planning to kill you. Now that you are aware of this, turn back and rule on the princely throne of your fathers."

When Constantine finished telling this, Daniel returned to the Dniester River and the godless *boyar* took another road in order not to encounter him.

When he reached Halych Daniel sent a messenger to his brother, Prince
Vasilko [saying]: "Proceed against Alexander." Alexander fled to Peremyshl
to his councillors and Vasilko seized [the town of] Belz. Daniel sent one of
his officials after the God-praying traitors and after Voldris, and Ivan Mikhailovich succeeded in capturing twenty-eight men. These men, however, were
not executed but were pardoned. Once when Daniel was feasting, one of the
ungrateful *boyars* even spilled wine over him and he [Daniel] tolerated this.
Let God punish them for this.

In 1231 Daniel called a meeting. There were present eighteen trusted
members of his *druzhina* and his *tysiatskii*, Demian. And Daniel told them:
"If you will be loyal to me I shall go against my enemies." And they replied:
"We are all loyal to God and to you our lord; go with God's blessing!" And
sotskii [a leader of a hundred] Mikula said: "Lord, if you don't kill the bees
you will not get any honey." After he prayed to God, and to Mary, and to
Archangel Michael, Daniel thought of leaving with a small number of warriors;
he was joined by Miroslav who brought several members of his *druzhina*.
The traitors came to Daniel's side, pretending they were loyal to him. They
again organized a conspiracy because they hated him. When Daniel reached
Peremyshl, Alexander fled. During this campaign Lev was wounded. He was
brave and died with honor. Traitor Volodislav Iurievich conceived the con-
spiracy. They pursued Alexander to Sanok and then to a pass across the
Carpathians. Alexander fled, leaving behind all of his property. He fled to
Hungary to join Sudislav, who was at that time in Hungary.

Sudislav took the matter up; came to the Magyar king, Andrew, and
persuaded him to start a war. King Andrew and his son, Bela, and another
son, Andrew, advanced to the city of Iaroslav. On orders of Prince Daniel,
boyars David Vyshatich and Vasilii Gavrilovich shut themselves up in Iaroslav.
The Hungarians fought till sunset. After they had repulsed the enemy, the
besieged forces held a council in the evening. David became frightened . . .
and told Vasilii: "You cannot defend this city." Vasilii told him, however:
"We shall not defame the honor of our prince; that army cannot capture this
town." Vasilii was a tried and brave warrior. But David did not listen to
him and wanted to surrender the city, even though Chak, who had deserted
from the Hungarian forces, told him that: "They cannot capture you because
their ranks have been greatly depleted." Vasilii fought hard against surrendering the city. David was very frightened and gave up. He marched out of
the town with his forces and the king seized Iaroslav and then marched to
Halych. Klymiata fled from the mountains, deserting Prince Daniel for the
king, and then all the *boyars* of Halych deserted [Daniel].

From here the [Magyar] king advanced on Vladimir. When he approached
Vladimir he observed: "I have not seen such a city, even in German lands."

Armed warriors stood guard atop the walls and their shields and armor glittered like the sun. Miroslav, once brave prince, who was now in the city, became mentally unbalanced—God only knows why—and concluded peace with the king without the consent of Prince Daniel and his brother Vasilko. By this agreement [Miroslav] relinquished to Alexander [the cities of] Belz and Cherven. The king placed in Halych his son, Andrew, on the advice of the Halych traitors. . . . Both brothers Daniel and Vasilko strongly reprimanded [Miroslav] for agreeing to such a peace, because he had many warriors. At the time when the king was in Vladimir, Prince Daniel captured many [Magyar] prisoners in campaigns around Buzhsk.

[After] the king returned home to Hungary, Daniel received a message from [Prince] Vladimir [of Kiev]. "Brother, come to my aid. [Prince] Michael [of Chernigov] is advancing against me." Daniel came and brought peace between them. Daniel took away from the Rus land the area of Torchesk and gave it to Mstislav's children, his brothers-in-law, saying: "Take and hold the city of Torchesk. [You deserve it] on account of the good deeds of your father."

Then the [Hungarian] king's son, Andrew, advanced with his armies against Daniel. He moved towards Belobereg. Vladislav [Daniel's commander] left Kiev with Daniel's advance guard and met the [Hungarian] armies near Belobereg. They fought near the Sluch River and drove the Magyars from the Devil's Forest to the Derevna River. Vladislav sent a message to Daniel and Vladimir in Kiev. Then Daniel said to Vladimir, "Brother, I know that they are advancing against both of us. Let me go and I shall attack them from the rear." When the Magyars learned of this they returned to Halych. . . .

This happened in the year 1233. [After a series of great military reverses] the young king [of Hungary] and Sudislav enlisted the service of Dionisius [a Magyar military expert] against Daniel. Daniel went to Kiev and brought against them the Polovtsians and [Prince] Iziaslav Mstislavich. He took an oath in the church with Iziaslav and Vladimir to march jointly against the Magyars, and they advanced against Dionisius. But Iziaslav committed treason; he ordered the plundering of Daniel's land, took [the town of] Tikhomil, and returned home. Only Vladimir and Kotian [a Polovtsian chieftan] remained with Daniel. . . . From here they advanced to Peremyshl. Young King Andrew, Dionisius, and the Magyars fought Vladimir and Daniel for control of a bridge, but were defeated. The Magyars left for Halych, leaving behind their battering rams. Vladimir and Daniel pursued them, and in Buzhsk were joined by Alexander and Vasilko. Here Vladimir, Kotian, and Iziaslav decided to go home.

This happened in the year 1234. Gleb Zeremeevich deserted the young king and joined Daniel. Daniel and Vasilko went to Halych alone and more than half of Halych came out to greet them, including Dobroslav, Gleb, and many other *boyars*. When they came [to Halych], Daniel and Vasilko halted on the bank of the Dniester, and Daniel thus gained control of the land of Halych and distributed cities to his *boyars* and *voevods*. They had plenty of supplies, while the young king, Dionisius, and Sudislav were starving inside the city. For nine weeks Daniel and Vasilko laid siege to the city, fought all the time, and waited for ice [on which] to cross the river. Sudislav sent a treasonous note to Alexander [saying]: "I'll give you Halych, if you desert your cousin [Daniel]!" He [Alexander] departed from Halych. But shortly after that the young king died, Sudislav went to Hungary, and the inhabitants of Halych sent Semeon Ryzhii to invite Daniel [to become their prince]. . . .

This happened in the year 1235. The [treacherous] men of Halych advanced to Kamenets. With them were all the princes of Bolokhov. They fought near Khomor; they they captured Kamenets, took many prisoners, and escaped. At that time Vladimir sent Torks and Daniel Nazhirovich to help [Prince] Daniel. Daniel's *boyars* joined the Torks near Kamenets, caught up with the traitors, defeated them and all the princes of Bolokhov, and Vladimir brought them before Prince Daniel. When summer came Michael and Iziaslav sent messengers threatening: "Release our brothers or we will fight you!" . . . Michael and Iziaslav even brought against Daniel the Poles, the Rus, and a multitude of Polovtsians. Konrad encamped where presently the city of Kholm is located, and from there he sent out plundering [detachments] to Cherven. Vasilko's men met them, fought them, took many Polish *boyars* prisoner, and brought them to Daniel in the city of Horodok. Michael was encamped at Podgorie, where he hoped to join Konrad and where he expected the arrival of Polovtsians led by Iziaslav. The Polovtsians came to Galicia, but they did not want to go against Daniel. Instead they plundered all Galicia and withdrew. When he learned about this Michael returned to [the city of] Halych and Konrad fled to Poland by night. Many of his warriors drowned in the Wieprz River. Later that summer Daniel and Vasilko joined forces and advanced against Michael and Rostislav to Halych, where they had locked themselves in with a multitude of Magyars. Daniel and Vasilko returned and warred around Zvenihorod until autumn. . . . In the spring they advanced against the Iatvigians and came as far as Brest, but because of floods caused by the overflowing rivers they could not advance further against the Iatvigians. . . .

That year [1236] Daniel advanced against Michael in Halych. [Michael] sued for peace and Daniel gave him Peremyshl. That same year Daniel sent Mindovg's Lithuanians and [Prince] Iziaslav of Novgorod against Konrad [of Poland]. Daniel and his brother [Vasilko] went at that time to Hungary to see the king, who had invited them in order to bestow honors on them. At that time Emperor Frederick [II] went to war against the [Austrian] Herzog

[Frederick]. Daniel and his brother Vasilko wanted to aid the Herzog, but the king dissuaded them. So they returned to their own country. Then Iaroslav of Suzdal seized Kiev from Vladimir but could not hold it and returned to Suzdal. Michael [of Chernigov] captured Kiev, leaving his son, Rostislav, in Halych, and took Peremyshl away from Daniel. War and peace between them alternated.

Then with God's aid, Daniel received the news while he was in Kholm that Rostislav had gone to Lithuania with all of his *boyars* and cavalry. When that happened Daniel left Kholm with his warriors and three days later he was in Halych. The citizens loved him. He approached the city and said: "Oh city inhabitants! How long will you continue to tolerate the rule of outside princes?" They responded: "There is our lord, whom God gave us." And they flocked to him like children to the father, like bees to the queen, like the thirsty to water. Bishop Artemii and *dvorskii* [a high-ranking courtier] Grigorii tried to stop them, but when they realized they could not control the town they came out like children, their eyes full of tears, their cheeks red, licking their lips, because they could not maintain the power of their prince. They were compelled to tell Daniel: "Prince Daniel, go ahead and take the town." Daniel entered into his city, went to the Cathedral of the Holy Mother of God, accepted the throne of his father, and as a sign of his victory he posted his emblem above the German [western] gate [of Halych].

⚔ *20* ⚔

A Treaty between Novgorod and the Hanseatic League, 1270

Next to Kiev, Novgorod was the most prosperous city along the route "from the Varangians to the Greeks." Its prosperity stemmed largely from both regional and international trade. Before the twelfth century Novgorod traded mainly with Constantinople, but also with the Scan-

---

From Ivan Andreevskii, ed., *O dogovore Novagoroda s nemetskimi gorodami i Gotlandom zak-liuchenom v* 1270 godu (On a Treaty Concluded in 1270 between Novgorod and German Cities and Gottland) (St. Petersburg: 1855), pp. 19–34. This edition includes Russian, Middle High German, and Modern German texts. Translation mine. Words in brackets are mine.

dinavian countries and with Central Asia and the Middle East via the Volga River. During the thirteenth and fourteenth centuries, Novgorod's commercial relations were closely tied to the fortunes of the Hanseatic League whose merchants had their own quarter, church, and guild in Novgorod. Relations with the Hanseatic merchants were based on treaties whose terms regulated the traffic, needs of merchants, claims, debts, loss of property, and similar problems.

I, Prince Iaroslav, the son of Prince Iaroslav, with *posadnik* [mayor] Pavlo, *tysiatsky* [police officer] *Gospodin* Ratibor, city elders, and all the Novgorodians [on the one hand], and German Ambassador Heinrich Wullenpund from Lübeck, and Ludolf Dobrücke and Jacob Kuring from Gottland [on the other hand], have reviewed, approved, and signed a treaty in your language, for you Germans and Gottlanders and for all the people of the Catholic faith.

Article 1

[We have approved] the old treaty concerning travel on the Neva River between Gottland and the island of Kotlin [in the Neva] and between Kotlin and Novgorod; according to this [treaty], should anything happen to a merchant coming to Novgorod during the summer, the prince and the Novgorodians will be responsible for it; those merchants who come [to Novgorod] during the winter shall receive protection from the prince, the mayor, and all the Novgorodians in accordance with a previous treaty and without any hindrances, and they shall, in accordance with the previous treaty, receive a Novgorodian commissioner and Novgorodian merchants. And should they not accept a Novgorodian commissioner then, in case something develops [on the way] between Novgorod and Kotlin, neither the prince nor the Novgorodians will be responsible for it; should the Novgorodians fail to dispatch a commissioner and should their merchants fail to go, then the Germans will leave without a commissioner and in that case they will travel directly to Kotlin in accordance with the previous treaty. Should a German or a Gottlander leave on a business venture to Karelia, and should something happen to him, the Novgorodians will not be responsible for it. Should any Novgorodian [hired by a German to go to Karelia] refuse to return by boat, then he must pay a fine of one-half of a silver *mark* for the trip.

Article 2

Whenever a merchant enters the Neva River and has need for either wood or a mast he has the right to cut down the necessary trees along both banks of the river wherever he wants.

Article 3

If a thief should be apprehended between Ketlingen and Aldagen, he should be taken to Aldagen and sentenced there according to the laws [of Aldagen]; but if a thief should be apprehended between Aldagen and Novgorod, he should be sentenced in Novgorod, according to the latter's laws.

Article 4

Whenever the Germans or the Gottlanders enter the Volkhov Rapids they must request, without delay, rapid pilots and take passengers on their vessels and collect from them only as much as in the past and not more.

Article 5

And when a merchant arrives at Gesteveld he should pay a tax in the amount that was customarily paid in the past and no more.

Article 6

And the pilot who is hired for the journey up and down the Neva River should receive food and five marks of *kuna,* or one *okorok*; if he is hired [for a journey] from Novgorod to Ladoga and back, he should receive food, three marks of *kuna,* or half of one *okorok.*

Article 7

Should a bark sent after goods or [loaded] with goods be destroyed, there is no need to pay for it; however, one should pay for the rent of that bark.

Article 8

Should the above mentioned pilots disagree with the merchants during their voyage up and down the river and then reconcile, let it thus be; however, should there be no reconciliation during the voyage, the entire matter should then be taken to the merchant court at Novgorod where the *tysiatsky* and other Novgorodians will try to resolve it.

Article 9

Drivers in Novgorod should be paid for every bark [load] brought from the river to Novgorod—those going to the German warehouse [should be paid] fifteen *kunas,* those to the Gottland warehouse ten *kunas,* and those leaving [Novgorod] half of one mark per bark.

Article 10

Should a Novgorodian merchant contract a debt in Gottland he should not be arrested. Equally the same treatment should apply to German and Gottland merchants in Novgorod; likewise no bailiff should be sent to them, nor clothes be collected from them, but each side should demand the presence of a city official.

Article 11
Should there develop a disagreement between the Germans and the Novgorodians, it ought to be settled at the Court of St. John with the *posadnik, tysiatsky,* and merchants present.

Article 12
Should someone come to either the German or the Gottland warehouse armed and wound anyone with the intent to steal a commodity and then be apprehended, he should be turned over to the court and be sentenced according to custom.

Article 13
Should anyone break a gate or a fence, he should be sentenced according to custom; if the fence was old, a new one should be installed and no additional charges made.

Article 14
Meadows that belong either to Germans or Gottlanders should be their property wherever they should decide them to be so.

Article 15
Should there develop a disagreement during the summer journey, it should not affect the winter journey; equally, disagreements on winter journeys should not affect summer journeys.

Article 16
In case summer or winter merchants should have court cases pending against them, they should settle these with city officials, the elders, or Novgorodians, and depart without delay on their journey. Should a new case develop, it should be resolved on the spot.

Article 17
Should there develop a dispute over the sequestration of property, it should be reported during the first year, but commodities should not be seized; this rule is also applicable for the second year; when the dispute is not settled by the third year, then commodities should be seized and the owner arrested.

Article 18

In case a war should develop between Novgorod and its neighboring territories, merchants are allowed [to travel] without hindrance by water and overland [routes] as far as the sovereignty of Novgorod extends. Accordingly, a merchant who travels along the Neva River should be allowed to proceed on the Neva, and those coming overland should be allowed to move along.

Article 19

In case a German and a Novgorodian should both produce witnesses, and should they both agree on the same individual, that individual's testimony should be accepted as final. But should they disagree and fail to produce a witness, then they should draw lots and he who draws the lot is the winner.

Article 20

Anyone who enters into a business transaction with either a German or a Gottlander and then either dissipates or damages his goods, must first compensate those merchants and then all those to whom he is obligated.

Article 21

In case a wife vouches for her husband, she is personally responsible with him for the debt they are unable to repay. If a wife did not vouch for her husband then she is not responsible for his debt.

Article 22

In case a Novgorodian ambassador is killed abroad, twenty marks of silver should be paid for his death; the same sum of money is to be paid for the death of a German ambassador [killed] in Novgorod or its territories.

Article 23

The above sum of twenty marks of silver should also be paid for the killing of a priest as well as for an elderman, while for a merchant the sum of ten marks of silver is to be paid.

Article 24

Whoever wounds a man with a sharp weapon or a lance should pay him a fine of one and one-half marks of silver.

Article 25

If someone strikes another on his ear or on his neck, he should pay him a fine of three *verdings* [one-half mark of silver].

Article 26

Weights and measures for silver and other goods measured on scales should be kept accurate. A *Kap* [a measure of some 417 kilograms] should contain eight Livonian pounds.

⚔ *21* ⚔

Life in Medieval Novgorod

Novgorod is a unique phenomenon in medieval Rus history. In theory it was a principality, but the powers of the prince were greatly limited so that in reality both the city and its possessions were governed by a merchant oligarchy. Life in the city of Novgorod was crowded, busy, exciting, and dangerous. The danger stemmed from multiple causes, of which fire, famine, foreign invasions, and bloody street fights between feuding factions of the populace were the most common.

A.D. 1124. On the 11th day of August before evening service the sun began to decrease and it totally perished; oh, there was great terror and darkness! there were stars and the moon; then it began to re-appear and came out quickly in full; then all the city rejoiced. . . .

A.D. 1128. . . . This year it was cruel; one *osminka* of rye cost a *grivna*; the people ate lime tree leaves, birch bark, pounded wood pulp mixed with husks and straw; some ate buttercups, moss, horse flesh; and thus many dropping down from hunger, their corpses were in the streets, in the market place, and on the roads, and everywhere. They hired hirelings to carry the dead out of the town; the serfs could not go out; woe and misery on all! fathers and mothers would put their children into boats in gift to [foreign] merchants, or else put them to death; and others dispersed over foreign lands. Thus did

---

From *The Chronicle of Novgorod* 1016–1471. Translated from the Russian by Robert Michell and Nevill Forbes. With an Introduction by C. Raymond Beazley, and an account of the Text by A. A. Shakhmatov. (Camden Third Series, vol. 25) (London: Royal Historical Society, 1914), pp. 10–11, 18, 22–23, 27, 31, 34–35, 37, 42, 52, 54, 58, 72, 74, 79–80, 84–87, 92–97, 110, 117–118, 137, 143–145, 153, 186–188, 204. Reprinted with permission of the publishers. Words in brackets are mine.

our country perish on account of our sins. This year, the water was high in the Volkhov, and carried away many houses. . . .

A.D. 1145. There were two whole weeks of great heat, like burning sparks, before harvest; then came rain, so that we saw not a clear day till winter; and a great quantity of corn and hay they were unable to harvest; and that autumn the water was higher than three years before; and in the winter there was not much snow, and no clear day, not till March. . . .

A.D. 1157. There was a bad tumult in the people, and they rose against *Knyaz* [Prince] Mstislav Gyurgevits, and began to drive him out of Novgorod; but the Mercantile Half [Eastern Half] stood up in arms for him; and brother quarrelled with brother; they seized the bridge over the Volkhov, and guards took their stand at the town gates, and [so did] the others on the other side; and they were within a little of shedding blood between them. And then Svyatoslav Rostislavits and David entered, and that night Mstislav fled out of the town. After three days Rostislav himself entered, and the brothers came together, and there was no harm at all. . . .

A.D. 1161. . . . The same year the sky stood clear all summer and all the corn was scorched, and in the autumn frost killed all the spring corn.

But furthermore for our sins the evil did not stop there, but again in the winter the whole winter stood with heat and rain, and there was thunder; and we bought a little barrel for seven *kunas*. Oh, there was great distress in the people and want! . . .

A.D. 1170. There was dearness in Novgorod; and they bought a barrel of rye at four *grivnas,* and bread at two *nogatas,* honey at ten *kunas* a *pud.* The men of Novgorod having taken counsel showed *Knyaz* Roman the road [that is, expelled him], and themselves sent to Andrew for peace with [guarantee of] full liberty. . . .

A.D. 1181. . . . The same year the men of Novgorod went to Dryutsk with Svyatoslav, Oleg's grandson; and at that time came Vsevolod with his whole force and with men of Murom and of Ryazan against Novitorg; and the men of Novitorg shut themselves in the town with *Knyaz* Yaropolk, and they beseiged the town, and sat [there] five weeks, and they became exhausted in the town: because there was no food for them, others of them ate even horse flesh; and they shot at *Knyaz* Yaropolk in the town, and there was great distress among them; and the men of Novitorg surrendered, and he led away Yaropolk with him, having fettered [him], and all the men of Novitorg with wives and children, and set fire to the town; and the men of Novgorod returned from Dryutsk, having set fire to the town. . . .

A.D. 1188. . . . The same winter things were dear, they bought bread for two *nogatas,* and one barrel of rye for six *grivnas;* but by God's mercy there were no ill effects among the people. The same year the men of Novgorod were plundered by the Varangians in Gothland and by the *Nemtsy* [Germans], in Khoruzhk and in Novitorg, and in the spring they let no man of their own go beyond sea from Novgorod, and gave no envoy to the Varangians, but they sent them away without peace. . . .

A.D. 1191. The men of Novgorod went in sailing vessels with the Korel people against the Yem people, and made war on their land and burned it, and cut to pieces the cattle. . . .

The same year *Knyaz* Yaroslav went to Luki, summoned by the *Knyazes* and people of Polotsk, and took with him the foremost *druzhina* of the men of Novgorod, and they met on the border and put love between each other, how in the winter they would all meet either against the Lithuanians or the Chud people. And *Knyaz* Yaroslav came to Novgorod with gifts. . . . And it was in the winter, *Knyaz* Yaroslav with the men of Novgorod, of Pleskov and of his own province went against the Chud people, took the town of Gyurgev, burned their country, and brought countless plunder; and themselves all came back well to Novgorod. . . .

A.D. 1194. A fire broke out in Novgorod on All Saints' Sunday during Fast, on going to early morning service; it started in Savko's Court in Yaryshev Street, and the fire was bad, three churches were burned; . . . and many good houses; and they subdued it at Luka Street. And for our sins evil did not stop here; but on the next day it started in Cheglov Lane, and about ten houses took fire. And then more arose; on Friday in the same week during market, it started from Khrevkov Street as far as the Stream in the Nerev end, and seven churches were burnt and large houses. Thence the evil grew: every day it would start unseen at six and more places, and people dared not feed in their houses, but lived a-field; and then the *Gorodishche* [Novgorod's suburb] took fire. The same year Ladoga took fire before Novgorod, and then, too, Russa took fire; and in the Lyudin end ten courts took fire; and thus wonders continued from All Saints up to Our Lady's Day. . . .

A.D. 1200. The Lithuanians took the Lovot [River] up to [the village of] Nalyuch from Belaya [village] as far as [the villages of] Svinort and Vorch and the men of Novgorod pursued them to [the village of] Tsernyany and fought with them and killed eighty men of the Lithuanians, and of the men of Novgorod fifteen [were killed]: . . . they [Novgorodians] recovered all the plunder and the rest escaped. The same year Nezdila Pekhtsinits went as *Voyevoda* to Luki; he went with a small *druzhina* from Luki into Lotygola [Livonia], and they found them [Livonians] in their bedrooms, killed forty men of them, took their wives and children, and themselves came all well to Luki; and from those who had not followed them from Molbovich with some of the *druzhina* they took money, having beaten them. . . .

A.D. 1212. Mstislav went with the men of Novgorod against the Chud people called Torma, and made many captives and brought back countless cattle. Later, in the winter, *Knyaz* Mstislav went with the men of Novgorod against the Chud town called Medvezhya Golova, and ruined their villages; and they came up to the town and the Chud people bowed down to the *Knyaz*, and he took tribute from them; and all came [back] well. . . .

A.D. 1214. On February 1, on Quinquagesima Sunday, there was thunder after morning service, and all heard it; and then at the same time they saw a flying snake. On the same day *Knyaz* Mstislav marched with the men of Novgorod against the Chud people to Ereva, through the land of the Chud people towards the sea, he ruined their villages and captured their forest fortresses. And he stayed with the men of Novgorod by the town of Vorobino and the Chud people bowed down to him, and *Knyaz* Mstislav took tribute from them; and gave two parts of the tribute to the men of Novgorod, and the third part to the courtiers. . . .

A.D. 1215. . . . The same autumn much harm was done; frost killed the corn crops, throughout the district; but at Torzhok all remained whole. The *Knyaz* seized all the corn in Torzhok, and would not let one cartload into the city; and they sent Semen Borisovits, Vyacheslav Klinyatits, for Zubets Yakun to fetch the *Knyaz* and he detained them; and he detained whomever you sent. And in Novgorod it was very bad, they bought one barrel of rye for ten *grivnas,* one of oats for three *grivnas,* a load of turnips for two *grivnas;* people ate pine bark and lime tree leaves and moss. O brothers, then was the trouble; they gave their children into slavery. They dug a public grave and filled it full. O, there was trouble! corpses in the market place, corpses in the street, corpses in the fields; the dogs could not eat up the men! The Vod people all died; the rest were scattered. And thus for our sins our power and our town went asunder. . . .

A.D. 1217. Mstislav went away to Kiev, leaving the *Knyaginya* [Princess] and his son Vasili in Novgorod. . . . Then, too, Volodimir went to Novgorod on his own business, and the Lithuanians made war in Shelon. The men of Novgorod went in pursuit of them but did not reach them; and they went with *Knyaz* Volodimir and *Posadnik* [Mayor] Tverdislav to Medvezhya-Golova, and halted before the town. And the Chud people began to send greetings deceitfully, but sent for the *Nemtsy*. And the men of Novgorod began to deliberate with the men of Pleskov about the message of the Chud people; going far away from their baggage, and the night guards had come in and the day guards had not gone out, and they [the Chud people] unexpectedly attacked the baggage, and the men of Novgorod ran from their *Veche* [meeting] to the baggage, and having taken up their arms, beat them off the baggage. And the *Nemtsy* fled to the town, and the men of Novgorod killed two *Voyevodas* [leaders] and took a third with their hands; and they took

700 horses, and returned all well. And *Knyaz* Mstislav came to Novgorod without them [while they were away], and took Stanimir Dirnovits with his son, Nezdila, and having put them in fetters, imprisoned them; and seized countless quantity of goods and let them go again. The same spring, on May 31, a bakery caught fire in the middle of the morning at Ivan Yarishevits's; by midday the whole side was burnt as far as the fishery, not a house was left; and all who had fled into the stone churches with their goods were all burnt there themselves together with their goods. And in the Varangian church all the countless Varangian merchandise was burnt; fifteen churches were burnt; and the tops and the porches of the stone churches were burned. . . .

A.D. 1229. *Knyaz* Mikhail came from Chernigov to Novgorod on Holy Day, at the close of St. Thomas's Week, and the men of Novgorod were glad at their choice; and he kissed the Cross [that is, took the oath of office] on the whole liberty of Novgorod and on all the charters of Yaroslav, and he granted the serfs freedom not to pay taxes for five years, who ever had fled to other folk's land, and those who live here he ordered to pay taxes as former *Knyazes* had fixed. And the men of Novgorod took much money from Yaroslav's favorites and the people of *Gorodishche;* they did not plunder their houses but made them give towards the building of the great bridge. The same year they began the foundation of a great bridge above the old bridge. They then took the *Posadnik*-ship from Ivanko Dmitrovits and gave it to Vnezd Vodovik; and they gave Torzhok to Ivanko; he went to Torzhok but the Novitorg people would not receive him, and thence he went to Yaroslav. . . .

A.D. 1230. . . . The same year, Stepan Tverdislavits quarrelled with Vodovik, Ivanko Timoshkinits siding with Stepan, and the *Posadnik's* servants beat Ivanko; this happened in the *Gorodishche*. And the next morning he called a *Veche* in Yaroslav's Court against the *Posadnik,* and went against his Court, and they plundered it. The *Posadnik* and Simon Borisovich again roused up the whole town against Ivanko and Yakim Vlunkovits and Proksha Lashnev; they went from the *Veche* and plundered many houses and they killed Volos Blutkinits at the *Veche*. The *Posadnik* said: "Thou didst try to set fire to my Court." Proksha's Court they set fire to, and Yakim fled to Yaroslav, while others hid themselves, but they made these take oath and then let them go. And Vodovik having caught Ivanko, later killed him, casting him into the Volkhov. . . .

A.D. 1234. *Knyaz* Yaroslav with the men of Novgorod and with the whole district, and with his own forces, went against the *Nemtsy* towards Yurev, and the *Knyaz* halted before he had reached the town with his forces, and he let his people ravage the land. But the *Nemtsy* issued out of the town, some staying to guard Medvezhya Golova, and fought with them right up to the main force. And God helped *Knyaz* Yaroslav with the men of Novgorod; and they drove them down to the river, and several of the best *Nemtsy* fell there; and when the *Nemtsy* were crossing the river Omovyzh they broke through and many were drowned; and some of the wounded escaped to Yurev, others to Medvezhya Golova. And they laid much of their land waste, and destroyed many of their crops about Yurev and Medvezhya Golova. And the *Nemtsy* did obeisance to the *Knyaz*, and Yaroslav took peace with them on his own terms, and the men of Novgorod returned all well, but some men of the Low country {area southeast of Moscow} fell. . . .

The same year the Lithuanians drove the men of Russa nearly as far as the market place and the men of Russa halted; and [there was] an ambuscade; and the citizens and body-guard and some of the merchants and traders drove them out of the town again, fighting in the field, and here they killed several of the Lithuanians, and four of the men of Russa. . . . And they pillaged the whole monastery of St. Saviour, and the whole church they stripped, the images and the altar, and four monks they killed, and retired to Klin. Then the news came to Novgorod to *Knyaz* Yaroslav, and the *Knyaz* with the men of Novgorod taking to the boats, and others on horse-back, went after them up the Lovot. And when they came to the village of Moravin the boatmen turned back thence to the town; and the *Knyaz* let them go because they had not enough bread, and he himself with the mounted men went after them and overtook them at Dubrovna, a village in the Toropets district, and there he fought with the accursed and godless {Lithuanians}. And there God and the Holy Cross and the Holy Sophia [Church], the Mighty Wisdom of God, helped *Knyaz* Yaroslav and the men of Novgorod over the pagans, and they took from them 300 of their horses with their goods and they fled into the woods, having thrown down their arms and shields and lances and everything from themselves; and others fell here dead. And of the men of Novgorod they killed there ten men. . . .

A.D. 1240. The Swedes came in great strength with the Murman, Sum, and Yem people in very many ships. The Swedes came with their *Knyaz* and with their bishops, and halted in the Neva at the mouth of the Izhera, wishing to take possession of Ladoga, or in one word, of Novgorod, and of the whole Novgorod province. But again the most kind and merciful God, lover of men, preserved and protected us from the foreigners since they labored in vain without the command of God. For the news came to Novgorod that the Swedes were going towards Ladoga, and *Knyaz* Alexander [Nevsky] with the men of Novgorod and of Ladoga did not delay at all; he went against them and defeated them by the power of St. Sophia and the prayers of our Sovereign Lady the Holy Mother of God. . . . And there was a great slaughter of Swedes. Their *Voyevoda,* by name Spiridon, was killed, and some thought that their bishop was also killed there; and a very great number of them fell. And having loaded two vessels with their best men got away first to sea; and the rest of them having dug a pit they threw into it without number; and many others were wounded; and the same night without waiting for the light of Monday they went away in shame. . . . And *Knyaz* Alexander with the men of Novgorod and of Ladoga all came back in health to their own country, preserved by God and St. Sophia, and through the prayers of all the saints.

The same year the *Nemtsy* with the men of Medvezhya [Golova], of Yurev, and of Velyad with *Knyaz* Yaroslav Volodimirich took Izborsk. And the news came to Pleskov that the *Nemtsy* had taken Izborsk and all the men of Pleskov went out and fought with them and the *Nemtsy* beat them. And there they killed the *Voyevoda* Gavrilo Gorislavich, and pursuing the men of Pleskov, killed many of them and others they caught with their hands. And having driven them up under the town, they burned the whole place, and there was much damage, churches, honorable ikons, books, and Gospels were burnt, and they devastated many villages around Pleskov. And they stayed near the town a week, but they did not take the town. But the children of good men they took as hostages, and went away and so they were without peace. . . .

A.D. 1242. *Knyaz* Alexander with the men of Novgorod and with his brother Andrei and the men of the Lower country went in the winter in great strength against the land of the Chud people, against the *Nemtsy,* that they might not boast, saying: "We will humble the Sloven race under us," for Pskov was already taken, and its *Tiuns* in prison. And *Knyaz* Alexander occupied all the roads right up to Pleskov; and he cleared Pleskov, seized the *Nemtsy* and Chud men, and having bound them in chains, sent them to be imprisoned in Novgorod, and himself went against the Chud people. And when they came to their land, he let loose his whole force to provide for themselves. And Domash Tverdislavich and Kerbet were scouring [the country] and the *Nemtsy* and Chud men met them by a bridge; and they fought there, and there they killed Domash, brother of the *Posadnik,* an honest man, and others with him, and others again they took with their hands, and others escaped to the troops of the *Knyaz*. And the *Knyaz* turned back to the lake and the *Nemtsy* and Chud men went after them. Seeing this, *Knyaz* Alexander and all the men of Novgorod drew up their forces by Lake Chud at Uzmen by the Raven's Rock; and the *Nemtsy* and Chud men rode at them driving themselves like a wedge through their army; and there was a great slaughter of *Nemtsy* and Chud men. And God and St. Sophia and the Holy Martyrs Boris and Gleb, for whose sake the men of Novgorod shed their blood, by the great prayers of those Saints, God helped *Knyaz* Alexander. And the *Nemtsy* fell there and the Chud men gave shoulder, and pursuing them fought with them on the ice, seven *versts* short of the Subol shore. And there fell of the Chud men a countless number; and of the *Nemtsy* 400, and fifty they took with their hands and brought to Novgorod. . . . The same year the *Nemtsy* sent with greeting, in the absence of the *Knyaz:* "The land of the Vod people, of Luga, Pleskov, and Lotygola, which we invaded with the sword, from all this we withdraw, and those of your men whom we have taken we will exchange, we will let go yours, and you let go ours," And they let go the Pleskov hostages, and made peace. . . .

A.D. 1245. . . . The Lithuanians made ravages about Torzhok and Bezhitsy, and the men of Novitorg with *Knyaz* Yaroslav Volodimirovich chased and fought them; and they took the horses from the men of Novitorg, and beat the men themselves and went away with their plunder. And Yavid and Erbet with the men of Tver and of Dmitrov, and Yaroslav with the men of Novitorg, pursued them and beat them near Toropets, and the sons of their *Knyaz* took refuge in Toropets.

The next morning Alexander came up with men of Novogorod and took away all the plunder, and slew more than eight of their *Knyaz's* sons. And from there the men of Novgorod turned back; but the *Knyaz* pursued them {Lithuanians} with his own court and defeated them near {the village of} Zizech, and did not let a single man go, and there he killed the rest of the *Knyaz's* sons. And he himself took his own son from Vitebsk and went with a small company and met another force at Lake Vosvyat; and there God helped him, and he destroyed those two and himself returned well and his company also. . . .

A.D. 1253. The Lithuanians ravaged the district of Novgorod and went off with captives, and the men of Novgorod with *Knyaz* Vasili overtook them at Toropets; and so Christian blood was avenged on them. And they defeated them and took back the captives from them, and returned well to Novgorod. The same year the *Nemtsy* came to Pleskov and burned the town, but the men of Pleskov killed many of them. And the men of Novgorod went out to them in arms from Novgorod, and they ran away, and the men of Novgorod having come to Novgorod, and having armed and prepared themselves, went beyond the Narova and laid waste their district; and the Korel people also did much harm to their districts. And the same year they went with the men of Pleskov to ravage them, and they put out a force against them; and the men of Novgorod with the men of Pleskov defeated them by the power of the honorable cross; for they began it against themselves, the accursed transgressors of right; and they sent to Pleskov and to Novgorod desiring peace on all the terms laid down by Novgorod and Pleskov. And so they made peace. . . .

A.D. 1257. Evil news came from Russia, and the Tartars desired the *tamga* {a customs tax} and tithe on Novgorod; and the people were agitated the whole year. And at Lady Day *Posadnik* Anani died, and in the winter the men of Novgorod killed *Posadnik* Mikhalko. If anyone does good to another, then good would come of it; but digging a pit under another, he falls into it himself.

The same winter Tartar envoys came with Alexander, and Vasili fled to Pleskov; and the envoys began to ask the tithe and the *tamga* and the men of Novgorod did not agree to this, and gave presents to the *Tsar* [the Tartar khan], and let the envoys go with peace.

And *Knyaz* Alexander drove his son out of Pleskov and sent him to the Low Country, and punished Alexander and his company. He cut off the noses of some, and took out the eyes of others, of those who had led Vasili to evil; for evil every man shall perish evilly!

The same winter they killed Misha. The same winter they gave the *Posadnik*-ship to Mikhail Fedorovich, having brought him out of Ladoga, and they gave the post of *Tysyatski* [commander of Novgorod's militia] to Zhirokha.

A.D. 1258. The Lithuanians with the men of Polotsk came to Smolensk and took [the town of] Voishchina by assault. The same autumn the Lithuanians came to Torzhok, and the men of Novitorg issued out. For our sins the Lithuanians ambushed them; some they killed, others they took with their hands, and others barely escaped, and there was much evil in Torzhok. The same winter the Tartars took the whole Lithuanian land, and killed the people.

A.D. 1259. There was a sign in the moon; such as no sign had ever been. The same winter Mikhail Pineshchinich came from the Low Country with a false mission, saying thus: "If you do not number yourselves for tribute there is already a force in the Low Country." And the men of Novgorod did number themselves for tribute. The same winter the accursed raw-eating Tartars, Berkai and Kasachik, came with their wives, and many others, and there was a great tumult in Novgorod, and they did much evil in the province, taking contribution for the accursed Tartars. And the accursed ones began to fear death; they said to Alexander: "Give us guards, lest they kill us." And the *Knyaz* ordered the son of the *Posadnik* and all the sons of the *boyars* to protect them by night. The Tartars said: "Give us your numbers for tribute or we will run away [and return in greater strength]." And the common people would not give their numbers for tribute but said: "Let us die honorably for St. Sophia and for the angelic houses." Then the people were divided: who was good stood by St. Sophia and by the True Faith; and they made opposition; the greater men bade the lesser be counted for tribute. And the accursed ones wanted to escape, driven by the Holy Spirit, and they devised an evil counsel how to strike at the town at the other side, and the others at this side by the lake; and Christ's power evidently forbade them, and they durst not. And becoming frightened they began to crowd to one point to St. Sophia, saying: "Let us lay our heads by St. Sophia." And it was on the morrow, the *Knyaz* rode down from the *Gorodishche* and the accursed Tartars with him, and by the counsel of the evil they numbered themselves for tribute; for the *Boyars* thought it would be easy for themselves, but fall hard on the lesser men. And the accursed ones began to ride through the streets, writing down the Christian houses; because for our sins God has brought wild beasts out of the desert to eat the flesh of the strong, and to drink the blood of *Boyars*. And having numbered them for tribute and taken it, the accursed ones went away, and *Knyaz* Alexander followed them, having set his son Dmitri on the throne. . . .

A.D. 1287. There was a great tumult in Novgorod against Semeon Mikhailovich; all Novgorod rose against him without just cause, they went out against him from all the quarters, like a strong army, every man armed, in great strength, a pitiful sight! and thus they went against his house and took his whole house with uproar. Semeon fled to the *Vladyka* [Bishop] and the *Vladyka* led him into St. Sophia; and thus God preserved him; and on the morrow they came together in love. . . .

A.D. 1311. The men of Novgorod went in war over sea to the country of the *Nemtsy* [in this case Finland], against the Yem people, with *Knyaz* Dmitri Romanovich, and having crossed the sea they first occupied the Kupets River, they burned villages, and captured people and destroyed the cattle. And there Konstantin, the son of Ilya Stanimirovich, was killed by a column that went in pursuit. They then took the whole of the Black River, and thus following along the Black River they reached the town of Vanai and they took the town and burned it. And the *Nemtsy* fell back into the Detinets [citadel]: for the place was very strong and firm, on a high rock, not having access from any side. And they sent with greeting, asking for peace, but the men of Novgorod did not grant peace, and they stood three days and three nights, wasting the district. They burned the large villages, laid waste all the cornfields, and did not leave a single horn of cattle; and going thence, they took the Kavgola River and the Perna River, and they came out on the sea and returned all well to Novgorod.

The same spring, on May 19, a fire broke out at night in Yanev Street, and forty less three houses were burnt and seven people. Then in the night of June 28 Glebov's house in Rozvazha Street caught fire, and the Nerev quarter was burnt, on one side so far as the fosse, and on the other beyond Borkov Street; and the Church of SS. Kuzma and Demyan was burnt, also that of St. Sava, and forty churches were damaged by fire and several good houses. Oh, woe, brethren, the conflagration was fierce, with wind and hurricane! And wicked and bad men having no fear of God, seeing people's ruin, plundered other men's property. Then on July 16 a fire broke out at night in the Ilya Street, and here likewise was a fierce conflagration with a high wind, and crashing noise; the market place was burnt, and houses up to Rogatitsa Street, and the churches burnt were—seven wooden churches. . . .

A.D. 1342. The same year the men of Pleskov gave themselves over to Lithuania, renouncing Novgorod, and the *Veliki Knyaz*. They fetched into their midst *Knyaz* Olgert from Lithuania, son of Gedymin, with the Lithuanians; they had first turned out Alexander Vsevolodits. And Olgert and his son baptised in the name of Andrei, and he set him in Pleskov, and himself departed to Lithuania.

The same year the men of Pleskov beat the *Nemtsy,* pursuing them up to their town Novogrodek on the border, killing about 300 of them. And the *Nemtsy* came in great strength to Izborsk with battering rams, and stood before the town eleven days and nearly took it; but they killed many *Nemtsy,* and there also they killed Voinev, son of the Lithuanian *Knyaz,* and several Lithuanians and men of Izborsk fell; and the *Nemtsy* withdrew.

The same year a fire broke out in Novgorod in Danislav Street, extending along the bank to the fosse, and up the hill to the Churches of the Forty Saints and SS. Kuzma and Demian, and three churches were burnt, St. Nikola and the stone Church of St. Yakov; and a watchman also was burnt there, and good man Esif Davidovich; the third was the Church of St. Georgi; and much evil was done. And the people took fright, and dared not dwell in the town, but over the fields, others settled on the water-meadows, others along the banks, in boats. And the whole town was to be seen in motion; the people wandered about for a week and longer; people endured much harm and loss at the hands of miscreants who fear not God. . . .

A.D. 1350. The men of Novgorod went to war against the *Nemtsy,* with Boris the son of the lieutenant, Ivan Fedorovich the *Tysyatski,* the *Voyevodas* Mikhail Danilovich, Yuri Ivanovich, and Yakov Khotov; and came to the town of Viborg on Monday the 21st day of March, and burned the whole of the town. On the next day the *Nemtsy* came out of the town and the men of Novgorod fell on them and the *Nemtsy* fled into the town, and there they killed several *Nemtsy,* and ravaged and burned the district near the town and killed many *Nemtsy,* both women and children, and took others alive; and they returned to Novgorod all well.

The same year the men of Novgorod went to Yurev, and made an exchange with the *Nemtsy* of the Swedish captives taken at Orekhov for Avraam and Kuzma, Alexander and Andrei and the company who had been over sea in the Swedish King Magnush's country. And they returned all well to Novgorod by the mercy of God, and by the power of the honorable Cross in which they trusted. . . .

The same year the men of Novgorod drove *Posadnik* Fedor out of Novgorod, together with his brother Mikhail, and Yuri and Ondreyan; their houses they pillaged, and they plundered the whole of Prussian Street. And Fedor, Mikhail, Yuri, and Ondreyan fled to Pskov, and after being there a short while they went to Koporya. . . .

A.D. 1352. . . . There was a great plague in Pleskov. The same year envoys arrived in Novgorod from Pleskov calling the *Vladyka* to Pleskov to bless the people. And the *Vladyka* heard their prayer and went and blessed the people of Pleskov, and on his way back to Novgorod going from Pleskov he was seized with a severe illness, and died at the Uza River on the third day of July. . . .

The same year there was a great plague [the Black Death] in Novgorod; it came on us by God's loving kindness, and in His righteous judgment, death came upon people, painful and sudden, it began from Lady Day till Easter; a countless number of good people died then. These were the symptoms of that death: a man would spit blood and after three days he was dead. But this death did not visit Novgorod alone; I believe it passed over the face of all the land. . . .

A.D. 1372. The men of Novgorod went to Torzhok to build up the town [that was completely burnt in 1371]; and they sent Mikhail's lieutenants away from Torzhok. And *Knyaz* Mikhail came with a force to Torzhok, and burned the whole town, and the Christians suffered great distress. Some were burnt with fire in their houses with their property; others took refuge in St. Saviour's, and were there suffocated; very many were burnt, others escaping from the fire were drowned in the Tvertsa River. And good women and girls, foreseeing their violation at the hands of the men of Tver, for they were stripping them to utter nakedness, as even the pagans did not do, from shame and grief drowned themselves in the river; monks and nuns were all stripped. First of all Alexander Obakunovich met them in the open, and there laid his bones for St. Saviour and for the wrongs of Novgorod; and with him they killed Ivan Shakhovich and another Ivan Timofeich, and Grigori Shchebelkov; and several others fell there, but some escaped. Others again were taken, and were led away captives to Tver, men and women, a countless number. They also took a great deal of property, what was left from the fire, and many of the silver frames from off the pictures. And who, my brethren, can help grieving over this? Those who remained alive, seeing how those others suffered violent and bitter death, the churches burnt and the town utterly laid waste: for such wrongdoing had never been suffered even from the pagans. And they filled five pits with dead bodies of the killed, drowned and burnt; and others were burnt so that nothing was left, and others drowned without being heard of, and floated down the river Tvertsa. . . .

A.D. 1418. The same month [April] this happened in Novgorod at the instigation of the devil: a certain man Stepanko seized hold of the *Boyar* Danilo Ivanovich, Bozha's grandson, and, holding him, cried out to the people: "Here, sirs! help me against this miscreant." And seeing his cry folk dragged him like a miscreant to the people, beating him with wounds nearly to death, and they led him from the *Veche* and hurled him from the bridge. And a certain man from the people, Lichko's son, wishing him well, caught him up into his boat; but the people, enraged against that fisherman, plundered his house. And the aforesaid *Boyar*, wishing to avenge his dishonor, caught the impostor and put him to torture, and wishing to cure the evil raised up still greater trouble; I will not recall the spoken words: "Vengeance is mine." And the people learning that Stepanko had been seized, began to summon a *Veche* in Yarslav's Court, and a multitude of people assembled, and they kept shouting and crying for many days: "Let us go against that *Boyar* and plunder his house." And they came armed and with a banner to Kuzma Demyan Street, sacked his house and many other houses, and ravaged the quay in Yanev Street. And the people of Kuzma Demyan Street became afraid at these robberies that worse would befall them, surrendered Stepanko, and coming to the *Vladyka* prayed him to send him to the meeting of the people. And the prelate heard their prayer and sent him with a priest and one of his own *Boyars*, and they received him. And again they became enraged like drunkards, against another *Boyar*, Ivan Yevlich, of Chudinets Street, and on his account pillaged a great many *Boyars'* houses, as well as the monastery of St. Nikola in the Field, crying out: "Here is the treasure house of the *Boyars*." And again the same morning they plundered many houses in the Lyudgoshcha Street, calling out: "They are our enemies." And they came to Prussian Street, but there they beat them off successfully. And from that hour the mischief began to increase. Returning to their own, the commercial side, they said: "The Sophia side is going to arm against us, and to plunder our houses." And they began to ring throughout the whole town, and armed men began to pour out from both sides as for war, fully armed, to the great bridge. And there was loss of life too. Some fell by arrows, others by arms, they died as in war, the whole town trembled at this terrible storm and great rebellion and a dread fell on the people on both sides. And *Vladyka* Simeon shed tears from his eyes on hearing of the internecine war between his children, and he ordered those under him to gather his congregation; and the *Vladyka,* having entered the Church of St. Sophia, began to pray with tears, and arraying himself in his vestments with his clergy he ordered them to take the Lord's Cross and the image of the Holy Mother of God, and went to the bridge, and there followed him the priests and servants of the church and all who called themselves Christians, and a great multitude, shedding tears and saying:

"O Lord, make it to cease by the prayers of our lord." And God-fearing people fell in tears at the feet of the prelate, saying: "Go, lord, and may the Lord cause this internecine war to cease, through thy blessing." And others said: "May this evil be on the heads of those who began the fighting." And on reaching the middle of the bridge the prelate raised the life-giving Cross and began to bless both sides. And those who looked at the honorable Cross wept. The opposite side, hearing of the prelate's arrival, *Posadnik* Fedor Timofeich came with other *Posadniks* and *Tysyatskis* and bowed to the *Vladyka*; and the *Vladyka* heard their prayer and sent the Archimandrite Varlam and his spiritual father, and an archdeacon to Yaroslav's Court to bestow the blessing on the acting *Posadnik* Vasili Esifovich and on the *Tysyatski* Kuzma Terenteyevich to go to their homes; and they dispersed through the prayers of the Holy Mother of God and with the blessing of *Vladyka* Simeon, and there was peace in the town. . . .

A.D. 1446. *Tsar* Mahmed let the *Veliki Knyaz* Vasili return to the Russian Land, taking a ransom of two hundred thousand *roubles*; and what else, God knows, and they.

That same year the people began to find fault with the silver coinage, till all the men of Novgorod looked one at the other, there was tumult and rebellion and animosity amongst them.

And the *Posadnik* and the *Tysyatski* and all Novgorod appointed five minters, and they began to remold the old coins and to mint new coins of the same value: of the same weight of four *pochki,* and half a *denga* was taken off the new *grivna.* There was much distress and loss among the Christians in the town and in the districts. And this will not be forgotten even in the last generations.

The same year, on January 3, there were heavy clouds with rain, and wheat and rye and corn were beaten down altogether [the autumn-sown crops], both in the fields, and in the forests, all round the town for five *versts* from the Volkhovets [river], and as far as the Msta river, for fifteen *versts*. The people bore into the town whatever they could gather up; and the townspeople collected to see this curious marvel, whence and how it came.

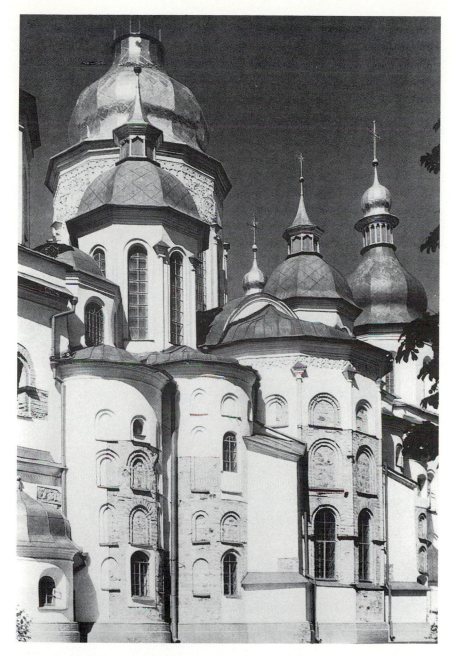

Kiev. Cathedral of St. Sophia. View from the southeast, 1017–1037.

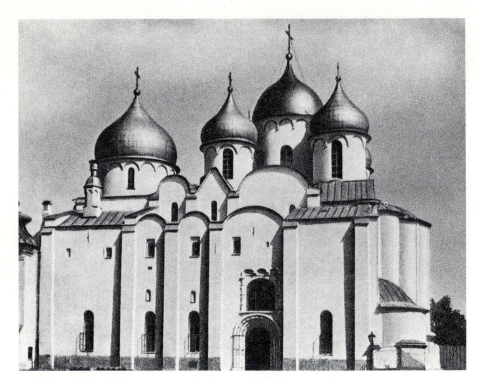

Cathedral of St. Sophia in Novgorod, 11th century.

Smolensk. Church of SS. Peter and Paul, 1146.

The Crown of Monomakh.

Iuriev Monastery. Cathedral of St. George. 1119–1130.

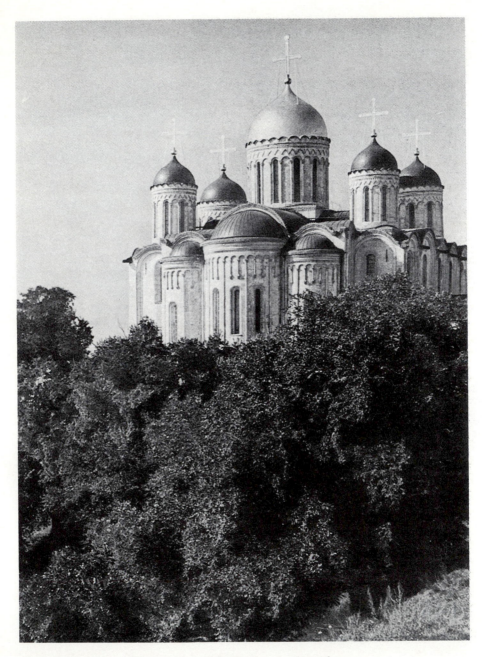

Cathedral of the Assumption in Vladimir, 1158–1161.

Church of the Intercession of the Virgin-on-Nerl. 1165.

The Virgin of Orans. Painting by Unknown Artist. 12th century.

Church of the Sign of the Virgin at Dubrovitsy, 1690–1704.

*Pskov. Ivanovskii Monastery. Cathedral of St. John the Baptist. First half of
the 13th century.*

PART II

Mongol Yoke

✠ 22 ✠

Mongol Conquest
of Northern Rus
in 1237–1238

The Mongol conquest of Northern Rus in 1237–1238 was part of a larger scheme—the conquest of Europe—devised by Genghis Khan's successors at a Great *Kuriltai*, or Council, in 1235. Led by Batu Khan, the Mongols, using Chinese technicians and Turkic manpower, encountered little or no opposition from the feuding princes of Rus. They captured and devastated the cities of Riazan, Moscow, Suzdal, Vladimir, and Tver. They took some of the inhabitants captive, massacred others, and forced those who survived to pay tribute. This conquest inaugurated a period in Russian history known as the "Mongol Yoke" that technically was to last until 1480.

It happened in 1237. That winter, the godless Tatars, under the leadership of Batu, came to the Riazan principality from the East through the forests. Upon arriving they encamped at Onuza, which they took and burned. From here they despatched their emissaries—a woman witch and two men—to the princes of Riazan demanding a tithe from the princes and complete armor and horses from the people. The princes of Riazan, Iurii Igorevich and his brother Oleg, did not allow the emissaries to enter the city, and [together with] the Murom and Pronsk princes [they] moved against the Tatars in the direction of Voronezh. The princes replied: "When we are gone, everything will be yours." . . . The princes of Riazan sent a plea to Prince Iurii of Vladimir, begging him to send aid or to come in person. Prince Iurii, however, did not go; neither did he listen to the plea of the princes of Riazan, as he wanted to fight the Tatars alone. . . .

The princes of Riazan, Murom, and Pronsk moved against the godless and engaged them in a battle. The struggle was fierce, but the godless Mohammedans* emerged victorious with each prince fleeing toward his own city. Thus angered, the Tatars now began the conquest of the Riazan land with

---

great fury. They destroyed cities, killed people, burned, and took [people] into slavery. On December 6, [1237] the cursed strangers approached the capital city of Riazan, besieged it, and surrounded it with a stockade. The princes of Riazan shut themselves up with the people of the city, fought bravely, but succumbed. On December 21, [1237] the Tatars took the city of Riazan, burned it completely, killed Prince Iurii Igorevich, his wife, slaughtered other princes, and of the captured men, women, and children, some they killed with their swords, others they killed with arrows and [then] threw them into the fire; while some of the captured they bound, cut, and disemboweled their bodies. The Tatars burned many holy churches, monasteries, and villages, and took their property.

Then the Tatars went toward Kolomna. From Vladimir, Grand Prince Iurii Vsevolodovich sent his son, Prince Vsevolod, against them; with him also went Prince Roman Igorevich of Riazan with his armies. Grand Prince Iurii sent his military commander, Eremei Glebovich, ahead with a patrol. This group joined Vsevolod's and Roman Igorevich's forces at Kolomna. There they were surrounded by the Tatars. The struggle was very fierce and the Russians were driven away to a hill. And there they [the Tatars] killed Prince Roman Igorevich Riazanskii, and Eremei Glebovich, the military commander of Vsevolod Iurievich, and they slaughtered many other men. Prince Vsevolod, with a small detachment, fled to Vladimir. The Tatars [then] went toward Moscow. They took Moscow and killed the military commander Philip Nianka, and captured Vladimir, the son of Prince Iurii; they slaughtered people old and young alike, some they took with them into captivity; they departed with a great amount of wealth.

When Grand Prince Iurii Vsevolodovich heard about this . . . he entrusted the rule of Vladimir to a bishop, Princes Vsevolod and Mstislav, and his own military leader Peter Osliadiukovich, while he himself went toward the Volga with his nephews—Vasilko Konstantinovich, Vsevolod Konstantinovich, and Vladimir Konstantinovich. They made their camp on the Siti. There the Grand Prince awaited the arrival of his brothers—Prince Iaroslav Vsevolodovich and Prince Sviatoslav Vsevolodovich—with their soldiers, and he himself began to collect an army; while he appointed Zhiroslav Mikhailovich his military commander.

On Tuesday February 3, [1238] . . . the Tatars approached Vladimir. The inhabitants of Vladimir, with their princes and military commander, Peter Osliadiukovich, shut themselves up in the city. The Tatars came to the Golden Gates, brought with them Prince Vladimir, the son of the Grand Prince Iurii Vsevolodovich, and inquired: "Is the Grand Prince Iurii in the city?" But the inhabitants of Vladimir began to shoot at them. They, however, shouted: "Do not shoot!" And, having approached very close to the gates, they showed the inhabitants of Vladimir their young Prince Vladimir, son of Iurii, and asked: "Do you recognize your young Prince?" As a result of privation and misfortune, his face was sad and he looked weak. Vsevolod and Mstislav stood atop the Golden Gates and recognized their brother Vladimir. Oh, how sad and tearful it is to see one's brother in such a condition! Vsevolod and Mstislav, with their *boyars* and all the inhabitants, wept as they looked at Vladimir. And the Tatars departed from the Golden Gates, circled the entire city, examined it, and encamped at Zremany in front of the Golden Gates and about the entire city; and there were many of them. . . .

After they made camp around Vladimir, the Tatars went and occupied the city of Suzdal. . . . They brought a multitude of prisoners into their camp, approached the city of Vladimir on Saturday, and from early morning till evening they built scaffolds and set up rams, and during the night they surrounded the entire city with a fence. In the morning, the princes, Bishop Mitrophan, military leader Peter Osliadiukovich, and all the *boyars* and the people realized that their city would be taken and they all began to weep. . . . On Sunday, February 8, {1238} . . . early in the morning the Tatars approached the city from all sides and began to hit the city {walls} with rams, and began to pour great stones into the center of the city from far away, as if by God's will, as if it rained inside the city; many people were killed inside the city and all were greatly frightened and trembled. The Tatars broke through the wall at the Golden Gates, also from the Lybed {side] at the Oriniiny and the Copper Gates, and from the Kliazma [direction] at the Volga Gates, and in other places; they destroyed the whole city, threw stones inside, and . . . entered it from all sides like demons. Before dinner they took the new city which they set on fire; and there they killed Prince Vsevolod with his brother, many *boyars* and people, while other princes and all the people fled into the middle city. Bishop Mitrophan and the Grand Duchess with her sons and daughters, daughters-in-law, grandchildren, *boyars,* and their wives, and many people fled into a church, locked the church gates, and climbed inside the church to the choir loft. The Tatars took this city too, and began to search after the princes and their mother, and found that they were inside the church. . . . The Tatars broke the gates of the church and slaughtered those who were inside and resisted. And they began to ask the whereabouts of the princes and their mother and found they were in the choir loft. They began to entice them to come down. But they did not listen to them. The Tatars then brought many fire logs inside the church and set it on fire. Those present in the choir loft, praying, gave their souls to God; they were burned and joined the list of martyrs. And the Tatars pillaged the holy church, and they tore the miracle-making icon of the Mother of God.

From here the Tatars advanced against Grand Prince Iurii; some went toward Rostov, while others went toward Iaroslavl, which they took; some went along the Volga and toward Gorodets and burned everything along the Volga up to Merski Golich. Some went toward Pereiaslavl and took that city and slaughtered the people. And from there they set the entire countryside and many cities on fire: Iuriev, Dmitrov, Volok, Tver, where they also killed Iaroslav's son; and there was not a town till Torzhok which was not occupied by the Tatars. In February [1238], in the Rostov and Suzdal principalities alone, they took fourteen cities in addition to villages and churchyards.

At the end of February [1238], a messenger brought the news to Grand Prince Iurii Vsevolodovich, his brother Sviatoslav Vsevolodovich, and their nephews Vasilko, Vsevolod, and Vladimir Konstantinovich, that the city of Vladimir had been captured, the bishop, grand dukes, princes, and all the inhabitants had been burned and some slaughtered. "And they killed your eldest son Vsevolod, and his brothers, inside the city and now they go toward you." . . . Iurii waited for his brother Iaroslav, but he did not come. And the prince ordered that his military leader strengthen his people and prepare them to fight, and sent a brave man, Dorofei Semeonovich, with 3000 men, to gather information about the Tatars. But hardly had he left when he returned with these words: "Lord! The Tatars have surrounded us."

When he heard this, Prince Iurii with his brother Sviatoslav and his nephews—Vasilko, Vsevolod, and Vladimir—and with their men, mounted their horses and advanced against the heathens. Grand Prince Iurii Vsevolodovich began to organize his regiments when suddenly the Tatars arrived at Siti. Prince Iurii forgot all about fear and advanced to meet them. Regiments met and there ensued a major battle and fierce slaughter; blood flowed like water. Because of God's will, the Tatars defeated the Russian princes. Grand Prince of Vladimir, Iurii Vsevolodovich, was killed then as were many of his military leaders and *boyars* and soldiers. The Tatars took his nephew, Vasilko Konstantinovich of Rostov, into captivity and brought him to the Sherenskii Forest. They also encamped there.

THE MONGOL-TATAR INVASIONS OF THE THIRTEENTH CENTURY

Domain of the Golden Horde

Routes and dates of Mongol-Tatar conquests

Boundaries of Rus principalities

Area of Rus principalities paying tribute to the Golden Horde

SCALE OF MILES

0   200

ADRIATIC SEA

HOLY ROMAN EMPIRE

HUNGARY

Budapest

Liegnitz

Cracow

POLAND

1241

1241

1241

TEUTONIC ORDER

LITHUANIA

LIVONIAN ORDER

Minsk

Pskov

Novgorod

Galich

Lvov

Vladimir

Kiev

Chernigov

Smolensk

Novgorod-Seversk

Tver

Moscow

Rostov

Belozero

Riazan

Vladimir

Suzdal

Galich

SEA OF AZOV

GOLDEN HORDE

1238

1239

1237

1237

Sarai

CASPIAN SEA

⚔ *23* ⚔

Mongol Capture of Kiev
in 1240

The Mongol conquest of Northern Rus removed a possible threat to their westward progress. In 1240, after two years of rest, Batu Khan ordered his forces west. Employing tactics of siege and massive assault, the Mongols overran Pereiaslavl and Chernigov and took Kiev in December of 1240. Mongol capture of Kiev was important for two basic reasons: it cleared the road through Galicia and Poland to central and western Europe, though actually they reached only the city of Liegnitz, near Breslau; and it symbolized the end of the Kievan state, which had been on the decline for quite some time.

In this year [1240] Batu Khan approached and surrounded the city of Kiev with a great multitude of soldiers. The Tatar force besieged it and it was impossible for any one either to leave the city or to enter it. Squeaking of wagons, bellowing of camels, sounds of trumpets and organs, neighing of horses, and cry and sobs of an innumerable multitude of people made it impossible to hear one another in the city. The entire country was overflowing with Tatars. The Kievans then captured a Tatar by the name of Tavrul, and he named all the great princes who were with Batu, and spoke of his innumerable strength. And he had with him the following of his brothers and of his strong military leaders: Urdiuy, Baydar, Biriuy, Kaydar, Bechar, Mengay, Kailug, [and] Kuiuk; but he [Kuiuk] returned [to Mongolia] when he learned of the death of the [Great] Khan. [The Great] Khan did not belong to the Batu family, but was his first and great leader. Batu Khan mourned him because the latter liked him very much. Other military leaders [of Batu Khan at Kiev] and great princes included: Butar, Aydar, Kilemet, Burunday, Batyr, who captured the Bulgar and Suzdal lands, and a great number, countless, other military leaders. Batu ordered that many wall-destroying rams be brought to Kiev and placed near the Polish Gate, because that part was wooded. Many rams hammered the walls without interruption day and night and the inhabitants were frightened, and there were many killed and blood

---

From *Polnoe Sobranie Russkikh Letopisei* (Complete Collection of Russian Chronicles) (St. Petersburg: 1885), vol. 10, pp. 115–117. Translation mine. Words in brackets are mine.

flowed like water. And Batu sent the following message to the inhabitants of Kiev: "If you surrender to me, you will be forgiven; if, however, you are going to resist you will suffer greatly and will perish cruelly." The inhabitants of Kiev, however, did not listen to him, but calumniated and cursed him. This angered Batu very much and he ordered [his men] to attack the city with great fury. And thus with the aid of many rams they broke through the city walls and entered the city, and the inhabitants ran to meet them. It was possible to hear and see a great crash of lances and clatter of shields; the arrows obscured the light and because of this it was impossible to see the sky, but there was darkness from the multitude of Tatar arrows, and there were dead everywhere and everywhere blood flowed like water. [Kiev's] military leader Dmitrii was severely wounded and many strong men were killed. The inhabitants [of Kiev] were defeated, and the Tatars climbed on the walls and because of great exhaustion they remained there. The night came. During the night the inhabitants [of Kiev] built a new fortification around the Church of the Virgin Mary. When morning came the Tatars attacked them and there was a bitter slaughter. Some people fainted and [some] fled to the church steeple with their possessions; and the church walls collapsed from the weight and the Tatars took the city of Kiev on St. Nicholas Day, December 6, [1240]. They brought the wounded military leader Dmitrii before Batu, and Batu ordered that he not be killed because of his bravery. And Batu began to inquire about Prince Daniel [of Galicia], and they told him that the Prince had fled to Hungary. Batu left his own military leader in Kiev and he himself went toward Vladimir in Volyn.

☙ *24* ☙

John of Pian de Carpine's Journey to Mongolia in 1246

The Mongol conquest of all of northern and central Asia and of eastern Europe made a very strong impression in western Europe. In 1245 Pope Innocent IV sent a monk, John of Pian de Carpine, on a mission to Mongolia to determine whether the Mongols could be converted to Christianity. Brother John set out from Lyons on April 16, 1245 via Prague, Galicia, and Kiev, and delivered the Pope's letter to Emperor Kuiuk Khan near the Mongol capital of Karakorum. Although the mission failed to accomplish its main purpose, Brother John left an interesting description of his efforts to reach his destination. As the first west European to travel to the capital of the Mongol Empire at its peak, unfamiliar with the language and geography of the area, Brother John's account is vague and unclear in several places. Taken as a whole, however, the story of his journey is rich in description of medieval travel hazards, of the vastness of the Mongol Empire, and of customs and practices of Mongol officials. Some of these practices were later adopted by Russian princes and thus became an integral part of Russia's cultural heritage.

When therefore we had arranged, as has been already stated elsewhere, to set out for the (land of the) Tatars we (left Lyons on the 16th April, 1245, and after travelling through Germany) came to the King of Bohemia. And having asked his advice, for we were personally acquainted with this lord [Wenceslaw I] from of old, which was the best road for us to go by, he answered that it were best, it seemed to him, to go by Poland and Rus [Galicia]; for he had relatives in Poland, with whose aid we could enter Rus; so having given us his letters and a good escort to take us through Poland, he caused also money to be given us to defray our travelling expenses through his lands and cities

---

Reprinted with permission of the Cambridge University Press from *The Journey of William Rubruck to the Eastern Parts of the World, 1253–55, as Narrated by Himself, With Two Accounts of the Earlier Journey of John of Pian de Carpine.* Translated from the Latin, and Edited, with an Introductory Notice by William Woodville Rockhill (London: Published for the Hakluyt Society, 1900), pp. 1–32. See original source for footnote references. Spellings of certain proper names have been modernized. Words in brackets are mine.

as far as (the court of) Boleslaw, Duke of Silesia, his nephew, with whom also we were personally acquainted.

The latter also gave us his letters and an escort and money for our expenses in his towns and cities, as far as Conrad, Duke of Lenczy [Cracow]. At that time, through God's special grace, the Lord Vasilko, Duke of Rus [Volyn and Vladimir], had come there, from whom we learnt more accurately of the Tatars; for he had sent his ambassadors to them, who had come back to him and to his brother Daniel [Duke of Galicia], bearing to the lord Daniel a safe conduct to go to Batu. And he told us that if we wanted to go to them we must have rich presents to give them, for they were in the habit of asking for them most importunately, and if they were not given them (and this is quite true), an ambassador could not conduct his business satisfactorily with them; and that furthermore he was looked upon as a mere nothing. Not wishing that the affairs of the Lord Pope and of the Church should be obstructed on this account, with some of that which had been given us in charity, so that we should not be in want and for use on our journey, we bought some skins of beavers and of some other animals. Duke Conrad, the Duchess of Cracow, some knights and the Bishop of Cracow, hearing of this, gave us some more of these skins. Furthermore, Duke Conrad, his son, and the Bishop of Cracow besought most earnestly Duke Vasilko to help us as much as he could in reaching the Tatars; and he replied that he would do so willingly.

So he took us with him to his country; and as he kept us for some days as his guests that we might rest a little, and had called thither his bishops at our request, we read them the letters of the Lord Pope, in which he admonished them to return to the unity of holy mother Church; we also advised and urged them as much as we could, as well the Duke as the Bishops, and all those who had met there, to that same end. But as at the very time when this duke had come to Poland, his brother, Duke Daniel, had gone to Batu and was not present, they could not give a final answer, but must wait his return before being able to give a full reply.

After that the Duke sent one of his servants with us as far as Kiev. Nevertheless we travelled ever in danger of our lives on account of the Lithuanians, who often committed undiscovered outrages as much as possible in the country of Rus [Volyn] and particularly in these places through which we had to pass. And as the greater part of the men of Rus [Volyn] had been killed by the Tatars or taken off into captivity, they were unable to offer them the least resistance. We were safe, however, from the Ruthenians on account of this servant. Thence then, by the grace of God, having been saved from the enemies of the Cross of Christ, we came to Kiev, which is the metropolis of Rus. And when we came there, we took counsel with the Millenarius

[Mongol official] and the other nobles who were there, as to our route. They told us that if we took into Tatary the horses which we had, they would all die, for the snows were deep, and they did not know how to dig out the grass from under the snow like Tatar horses, nor could anything else be found (on the way) for them to eat, for the Tatars had neither straw nor hay nor fodder. So, on their advice, we decided to leave our horses there with two servants to keep them; and we had to give the Millenarius presents, that he might be pleased to give us pack-horses and an escort. Before we reached Kiev, when in Danilov I was ill to the point of death; but I had myself carried along in a cart in the intense cold through the deep snow, so as not to interfere with the affairs of Christendom.

Having settled then all these matters at Kiev, on the second day after the feast of the Purification of Our Lady (February 4, 1246), we started out from Kiev for other barbarous peoples, with the horses of the Millenarius and an escort. We came to a certain town which was under the direct rule of the Tatars and is called Canov. The prefect of the town gave us horses and an escort as far as another town in which was a certain Alan prefect who was called Michaes, a man full of all malice and iniquity, for he had sent to us to Kiev some of his bodyguard, who lyingly said to us, as from the part of Corenza, that we being ambassadors were to come to him; and this he did, though it was not true, in order that he might extort presents from us. When, however, we reached him, he made himself most disagreeable, and unless we promised him presents, would in no wise agree to help us. Seeing that we would not otherwise be able to go farther, we promised to give him some presents, but when we gave him what appeared to us suitable, he refused to receive them unless we gave more; and so we had to add to them according to his will, and something besides he subtracted from us deceitfully and maliciously.

After that we left with him on the second day of Quinquagesima (February 19), and he led us as far as the first camp of the Tatars, and on the first Friday after Ash Wednesday (February 23), while we were stopping for the night as the sun went down, the Tatars broke in on us in arms in horrible fashion asking who we were. We answered them that we were envoys of the Lord Pope, and then, having accepted some food from us, they left at once. Starting again at morn, we had only gone a little way when their chiefs who were in the camp came to us, and inquired of us why we came to them, and what was our business. We answered them that we were the envoys of the Lord Pope, who was the lord and father of Christians; that he had sent us to the King as well as to the princes and all the Tatars, because he desired that all Christians should be friends of the Tatars and at peace with them. Moreover, as he wished that they should be mighty with God in heaven, he, the Lord Pope, advised them as well through us as by his letters, that they should become Christians and receive the faith of Our Lord Jesus Christ, for otherwise they could not be saved. He told them furthermore that he was astonished at the slaying of human beings done by the Tatars, and especially of Christians and above all of Hungarians, Moravians, and Poles, who were his subjects, when they had injured them in nothing nor attempted to injure them; and as the Lord God was gravely offended at this, he cautioned them to abstain henceforth from such acts, and to repent them of those they had done. Furthermore, we said that the Lord Pope requested that they should write to him what they would do and what was their intention; and that they would give answer to him to all the above points in their letters. Having heard our motives, and understood and noted them down, they said that, in view of what we had said, they would give us pack-horses as far as Corenza [a Mongol general], and supply a guide. At once they asked for presents, which we gave them, for we must needs to their will.

Having given them the presents, and taken as pack-horses some from which they got off, we started under their guidance for Corenza; but they sent ahead a swift messenger to this chief with what we had told them. This chief is lord of all those (Tatars) who are encamped facing the peoples of the West, lest they suddenly and unexpectedly attack them. This chief has under him, we were told, sixty thousand armed men. When we reached him, he made us put our tents far from him, and sent us his slave stewards who asked us with what we wanted to bow to him, that is to say whether we would make him presents. We replied that the Lord Pope had not sent any presents, for he was not sure we could reach them; and that furthermore we had to pass through very dangerous places, exposed to the Lithuanians, who make raids along the roads from Poland to near the Tatars, over which we had had to travel; but nevertheless with what we were carrying with us, by the grace of God and of our Lord the Pope, and for our personal use, we would show him our respect as well as we could. But when we had given him a number of things, they were not enough for him, and he asked for more through intermediaries, promising to have us conducted most honorably if we complied with his request, which we had to do since we wished to live and carry out satisfactorily the order of the Lord Pope.

Having received the presents, they led us to his *orda* or tent, and we were instructed to bend three times the left knee before the door of his dwelling, and to be very careful not to put our feet on the threshold of the door; and this we were attentive to observe, for sentence of death is on those who knowingly tread upon the threshold of a chief's dwelling. After we had entered we were obliged to repeat on bended knee before the chief and all the other nobles, who had specially been convened there for that purpose, what has been previously said. We presented to him also the letters of the Lord Pope; but as our interpreter, whom we had brought with us from Kiev, was not able to translate them for him, nor was there any one else competent to do so, they could not be interpreted. After this, horses were given to us, and three Tatars, two of whom were chiefs over ten, and the other a man of Batu, guided us with all speed to that latter chief. This Batu is more powerful than all the other Tatar princes save the Emperor, whom he is held to obey.

We started (for Batu's camp) on the Monday after the first Sunday of Quadragesima (February 26), and riding as fast as horses could go trotting, for we had fresh horses three or four times nearly every day, we rode from morning to night, and very often even at night, and it was not before Wednesday in Holy Week (April 4) that we could get to him. We crossed the whole country of the Comans [that is, Polovtsians], which is all a plain, and has four great rivers. The first is called Dnieper, along which, on the side of Rus [Western side] roams Corenza, and on the other side through those plains, Mauci, who is mightier than Corenza. The second is the Don, along which roams a certain prince called Catan, who has as wife Batu's sister. The third is the Volga, a very big river, along which goes Batu. The fourth is called Yaik [Ural], along which go two Millenarii, one along one side of the river, the other along the other. All these (chiefs) descend in winter time to the sea, and in summer go up the courses of these rivers to the mountains. Now this sea is the Mare-Magnum [Black Sea] from which goes out the arm of Saint George which goes to Constantinople. We went along for many days on the ice of the Dnieper. These rivers are big, very full of fish, especially the Volga, and they fall into the sea of Greece which is called Mare-Magnum. We went for many days along the shore of this sea, which on account of the ice was very dangerous in several places; for it freezes along the coast quite three leagues out. But before we came to Batu, two of our Tatars went ahead to tell him all we had said at Corenza's.

When then we came to Batu on the borders of the Coman's country, we were made to camp a good league from their tents, and before we were taken to his court we were told we would have to pass between two fires, which we refused to do under any consideration. But they told us: "Fear not, we only make you pass between these two fires lest perchance you think something injurious to our lord, or if you carry some poison, for the fire will remove all harm." We answered them: "Since it is thus we will pass through, so that we may not be suspected of such things." When we came to the *orda* we were questioned by his procurator, who is called Eldegai, as to what we wanted to make our obeisance with, that is to say, what gifts we desired to give him; we answered him as we had previously answered Corenza, that the Lord Pope had sent no presents, but that we ourselves, of those things which we had by the grace of God and the Lord Pope for our expenses, desired to show him our respect as best we could. Presents having been given and accepted, the procurator called Eldegai questioned us as to our coming; and to him we gave the same reasons as we had previously given to Corenza.

Having been informed of our reasons, they led us into the dwelling, after having made a bow, and heard the caution about the threshold, which has been mentioned. Having entered then we said what we had to say on bended knees, and then we presented him the letters (of the Pope), and requested that interpreters be given us able to translate them. These were given us on Good Friday (April 6), and we carefully translated the letters into the Ruthenian, Saracenic, and Tatar languages, and this latter interpretation was given to Batu, who read it and noted it carefully. After that we were taken back to our dwelling, but no food was given us, save once on the night of our arrival a little millet in a bowl.

This Batu holds his court right magnificently, for he has doorkeepers and all the other officials like unto their Emperor. He sits also in a raised place, as on a throne, with one of his wives; but every one else (of his family), as well as his brothers and his sons as others of lesser degree, sit lower down on a bench in the middle (of the tent). All the other people sit behind them on the ground, the men to the right, the women to the left. He has tents made of linen. They are large and quite handsome, and used to belong to the King of Hungary. And no outsider save a servant dare enter the tent, no matter how great and mighty he may be, unless he is called, unless perchance he knows he is wanted. When we had stated our object, we took a seat to the left, for thus do all ambassadors in going, but on coming back from the Emperor they always placed us on the right. In the middle of the dwelling near the door is a table, on which is placed drink in gold and silver vases; and Batu never drinks, nor does any prince of the Tatars, especially when they are in public, without there being singing and guitar playing. And when he rides out, there is always carried over his head on a pole an umbrella or little awning; and all the very great princes of the Tatars do likewise. This Batu is kind enough to his own people, but he is greatly feared by them. He is, however, most cruel in fight; he is very shrewd and extremely crafty in warfare, for he has been waging war for a long time.

On Holy Saturday (April 7) we were called to his tent and that same procurator of Batu's came out to us and told us from him that we were to go to the Emperor Kuiuk in their country, and that some of our party would be kept there (with Batu) in the expectation that they would want to send them back to the Lord Pope. We gave them letters concerning all we had done to carry back (to the Pope), but when they had got as far as Mauci, he detained them until our return. As for ourselves, on the day of the Resurrection of the Lord (April 8), having said mass and settled everything, accompanied by the two Tatars who had been detailed to us at Corenza's, we started out most tearfully, not knowing whether we were going to life or death. We were furthermore so feeble that we could hardly ride; during the whole of that lent our only food had been millet with salt and water; and likewise on the other fast days; nor had we anything else to drink but snow melted in the kettle. . . .

After that we entered the country of the Cangitae, which in many places suffers from a great scarcity of water, and in which but few people remain on account of this deficiency of water. And so it happened that the men of Iaroslav, Duke of Rus, who were going to join him in the country of the Tatars, lost some of their number who died of thirst in this desert. In this country and also in Comania, we found many human skulls and bones scattered about on the ground like cattle-dung. We travelled through this country (of the Cangitae) from the eighth day after Easter to nearly the Ascension of the Lord (May 17). These people are pagans, and the Comans as well as the Cangitae do not till the soil, but only live on the produce of their animals; nor do they build houses, but live in tents. The Tatars have also annihilated them, and now occupy their country; those of them who were left they have reduced to slavery.

Leaving the country of the Cangitae we entered that of the Bisermins. These people used to speak the Coman language, and do still speak it; but they hold the religion of the Saracens. We found in that country innumerable ruined cities, overthrown villages, and many deserted towns. There is a great river in that country whose name I do not know,* and on which stands a city called Ianckint, and also another called Barchin, and still another called Ornas [also known as Ortar], and many more whose names I do not know. This country used to have a lord who was called the Great Sultan, and he was put to death by the Tatars with all his progeny, but I am ignorant of his name. The country has very high mountains; to the south of it is Jerusalem, Baghdad, and the whole country of the Saracens. Near its borders are stationed the chiefs Burin and Cadan, who are uterine brothers. To the north of it is a part of the country of the Black Kitayans and an Ocean, and in that quarter is stationed Sitan, a brother of Batu. We travelled through this country from the feast of the Ascension (May 17) to about eight days before the feast of Saint John the Baptist (June 24).

After that we entered the country of the Black Kitayans, in which they (the Mongols) have built anew, as it were, a city called Omyl, in which the Emperor has erected a house where we were invited to drink; and he who was there on the part of the Emperor made the nobles of the town and also

*Syr Daria.

his own two sons clap their hands before us (when we drank). Leaving this place we found a not very large lake, and as we did not ask its name, we do not know it. On the shore of this lake was a little hill, in where there is said to be an opening, whence in winter there issue out such great tempests of wind that people can barely and at great danger pass by. In summer, however, though one always hears the sound of the winds, but little comes out of the opening, according to what the inhabitants told us. We travelled along the shore of this lake for several days; it has several islands on it, and it lay upon our left hand. This country has great abundance of streams, not large ones, however; on either bank of these rivers are woods, but of no great width. Ordu lives in this country; he is older than Batu, in fact older than any of the other chiefs of the Tatars, and the *orda* or court is that of one of his wives who rules over it. For it is a custom among the Tatars that the courts of their princes and nobles are not broken up (on their death), but some women are always appointed who govern them, and the same proportion of presents are given them that their lord had been in the habit (during his life) of allowing them. After this we came to the first *orda* of the Emperor [Ogodai], in which was one of his wives; but as we had not yet seen the Emperor they would not invite us nor let us come into her *orda*, though they had us well served in our own tent, according to Tatar fashion; and they kept us there for a whole day, so that we might rest.

Proceeding thence on the eve of the feast of Saint Peter (June 28), we entered the country of the Naiman, who are pagans. On the day of the feast of the apostles Peter and Paul (June 29) there fell in that place a great snow, and we experienced great cold. This country is exceptionally mountainous and cold, and there is very little plain in it. These two nations {Black Kitayans and Naimans] do not till the soil, but like the Tatars live in tents. These latter have nearly exterminated them. We travelled through this country many days.

After that we entered the country of the Mongols, whom we call Tatars. And we journeyed through that country for three weeks, I think riding hard, and on the day of the feast of blessed Mary Magdalen (July 22) we arrived at Kuiuk's, the present Emperor. Along all this (part of the) route we travelled very fast, for our Tatars had been ordered to take us quickly to the solemn court which had already been convened for several years for the election of an emperor, so that we might be present at it. So we had to rise at dawn and travel till night without a stop; often we arrived so late that we did not eat at night, but that which we should have eaten at night was given us in the morning; and we went as fast as the horses could trot, for there was no lack of horses, having usually fresh horses during the day, those which we left being sent back, as I have stated previously; and in this fashion we rode rapidly along without interruption.

When we reached Kuiuk's camp, he caused us to be given a tent and allowances such as the Tatars are in the habit of giving; but they treated us better than they did the other ambassadors. We were not called (before Kuiuk) however, for he had not yet been elected, nor had they settled about the succession; the translation of the letters of the Lord Pope, and what else we had said (to Corenza and Batu) had been sent him by Batu. And when we had been there five or six days, he sent us to his mother, where the solemn court was being held. When we got there they had already erected a great tent made of white purple, which in our opinion was large enough to hold more than two thousand persons; and around it a wooden paling had been made, and it was ornamented with diverse designs.

On the second or third day we went with the Tatars who had been assigned to guard us (to this tent); and all the chiefs met there, and each one was riding around in a circle over hill and dale with his men. On the first day they were all dressed in white purple; on the second day, and then it was that Kuiuk came to the tent, they were dressed in red (purple); on the third day they were all in blue purple, and on the fourth day in the finest *baldakins*. In the paling near the tent were two big gates: one through which only the Emperor could pass, and at which there was no guard though it was open, for no one would dare to go in or out by it; and the other way by which all those who had admittance went in, and at this one were guards with swords, bows and arrows, and if anyone came near the tent outside of the set bounds, he was beaten if caught, or shot at with headless arrows if he ran away. The horses were kept at about two arrow-flights, I should say, from the tent. The chiefs went about everywhere with a number of their men all armed; but nobody, unless a chief, could go to the horses, without getting badly beaten for trying to do so. And many (of the horses) there were which had on their bits, breastplates, saddles, and cruppers quite twenty marks worth of gold I would think. And so the chiefs held counsel beyond the tent, and discussed the election, while all the rest of the people were far away from the tent. And there they remained till about noon, when they began drinking mare's milk, and they drank till evening so plentifully that it was a rare sight.

They called us inside (the tent), and gave us mead, for we would not drink mare's milk at all. This was a great honor they showed us; and they kept on urging us to drink, but not being in the habit of it, we could not do so, and we let them see that it was distasteful to us, so they stopped pressing us. In the great square was the Duke Iaroslav of Suzdal in Rus, and several princes of the Kitayans and Solanges, also two sons of the King of Georgia, a sultan, the ambassador of the Caliph of Baghdad, and more than ten other sultans of the Saracens, I believe, and as we were told by the procurators. For there were more than four thousand envoys, as well those bringing tribute as those offering presents, sultans and other chiefs who had come to present themselves in person, those who had been sent by their (rulers), and those who were governors of countries. All these were put together outside the paling, and drink was given to them at the same time; as for ourselves and the Duke Iaroslav, whenever we were outside with them they always gave us a higher place. I think, if I remember rightly, that we were at that place for a good four weeks; and I am under the impression that the election was made there, though it was not proclaimed. It was for the following reason that it was generally believed (that Kuiuk had been chosen): whenever Kuiuk came out of the tent, they sang to him, and as long as he remained outside of it they inclined before him certain fine staffs on the ends of which were (tufts of) red wool, which was done to no other chief. They call this tent or court the Sira-Orda.

Coming out of the tent, we all rode together to another place some three or four leagues distant, where there was a fine large plain near a river flowing between mountains, where another tent was set up, and it is called by them the Golden Orda: and here it was that Kuiuk was to have been placed on the throne on the day of the Assumption of our Lady (August 15); but it was deferred on account of the hail which fell, to which I have referred previously. This tent rested on pillars covered with gold plates, fastened with gold nails and other woods, and the top and sides of it were covered with *baldakins;* the outside, however, being of other kinds of stuff. Here we remained until the feast of Saint Bartholomew (August 24), when there assembled a great multitude, and they all stood with their faces turned to the south, some of them a stone's throw from others, going ever farther and farther away, making genuflections towards the south. As for us, not knowing whether they were making incantations or bending their knees to God or what else, we would not make any genuflections. After doing this for a long while they went back to the tent, and placed Kuiuk on the imperial seat, and the chiefs knelt before him; and after that the whole people did likewise, except ourselves who were not his subjects. They then began drinking, and as is their custom, they kept on drinking till evening. After that they brought in carts of cooked meat, without salt, and to each four or five they gave a quarter. To those who were inside (the tent) they gave meat and salted broth for sauce; and in this fashion they passed days in feasting.

It was at this place (the Golden Orda) that we were called into the Emperor's presence; after that Chingay the *prothonotary* had written down our names and the names of those who had sent us, and also those of the chief of the Solanges and of the others, he repeated them all, shouting with a loud voice before the Emperor and all the chiefs. When this had been done each of us had to bend the left knee four times, and they cautioned us not to touch the threshold, and having searched us carefully for knives, and not having found any, we entered the door on the east side, for no one dare enter that on the west side save the Emperor; and the same rule applies if it is the tent of a chief; but those of low rank pay little attention to such matters. And when we entered his tent, it was the first occasion since he had been made Emperor (that he had given an audience). He received likewise the ambassadors, but very few persons entered his tent. Here also such quantities of presents were given him by the ambassadors, silks, *samites*, purples, *baldakins*, silk girdles worked in gold, splendid furs, and other things, that it was a marvel to see. Here also it was that a kind of umbrella or awning that is carried over the Emperor's head was presented to him, and it was all covered with precious stones. Here also a certain governor of a province brought to him many camels covered with *baldakin* and with saddles on them, and a kind of arrangement inside of which people could sit, I think there were forty or fifty of them; and (he also gave him) many horses and mules covered with armor, some of hide, others of iron. They asked us if we wished to make any presents; but we had already used up nearly everything we had, so we had nothing at all to give him. It was while here that on a hill some distance from the tent there were more than five hundred carts, all full of gold and silver and silken gowns, all of which was divided up between the Emperor and the chiefs; and the various chiefs divided their shares among their men as they saw fit.

Leaving this place, we came to another where there was a wonderful tent, all of red purple, a present of the Kitayans. We were taken into it also, and here again when we entered they gave us mead or wine to drink, and offered us cooked meat, if we wanted it. There was a high platform of boards on it, on which was the Emperor's throne; and the throne was of ebony, wonderfully sculptured, and there were also (on it) gold, and precious stones, and, if I remember rightly, pearls; and one went up to it by steps, and it was rounded behind. There were benches placed around the throne, on which the ladies sat in rows on the left side; on the right side no one sat on raised seats, but the chiefs sat on seats of lesser height placed in the middle (of the tent), and the other people sat behind them, and the whole day there came there a great concourse of ladies. These three tents of which I have spoken were very big; but his wives had other tents of white felt, and they were quite large and handsome. It was here also that they separated. The mother of the Emperor went in one direction, the Emperor in another, for the purpose of rendering justice. The paternal aunt of the Emperor was in prison, for she had killed his father in the time when their army was in Hungary, and it was for this that the army had retreated from those countries. She and a number of others were tried for this, and put to death.

At this same time Iaroslav, Grand Duke in a part of Rus called Suzdal, died at the Emperor's *orda*. It happened that he was invited by the mother of the Emperor (to her tent), and she gave him to eat and drink with her own hand, as if to honor him; and he went back to his lodgings straightway and felt ill, and after seven days he was dead, and all his body became livid in strange fashion; so that everyone believed that he had been poisoned, that they might get free and full possession of his lands. As an argument in favor of this (supposition, the Empress) sent at once, without the knowledge of any of her people who were there, an envoy in all haste to his son Alexander in Rus to come to her, for she wished to give him his father's lands; but he would not go, but remained there (at home); in the meanwhile (the Empress) sent also letters for him to come and receive his father's lands. It was believed by all that he would be put to death if he should come, or imprisoned perpetually.

It was after this death (of Iaroslav) that our Tatars took us to the Emperor, if I remember correctly the time; and when the Emperor heard from our Tatars that we had come to him, he ordered us to go back to his mother, for he wanted two days after that to unfurl his standard against the whole of the western world, as was emphatically told us by those who knew, as has been previously stated, and he wished us not to know it. When we had returned (to the Empress), we remained there a few days, when we were sent back again to him; and we remained with him for quite a month, in such hunger and thirst that we were barely able to keep alive, for the allowances which they gave the four of us were scarcely enough for one; and we could find nothing to buy, the market being too far away. Had not the Lord sent us a certain Ruthenian called Kuzma, a goldsmith, and a great favorite of the Emperor, who helped us a little, I verily believe we should have died, unless the Lord had helped us in some other way. He showed us before putting it in place the throne of the Emperor which he himself had made, and also the seal he had manufactured for him, and he told us the superscription on his seal [God in Heaven, and Kuiuk Khan on Earth, Might of God. The Seal of the Emperor of All Men]. We also learned many private details about the Emperor, from those who had come with other chiefs, several Ruthenians and Hungarians who knew Latin and French, also Ruthenian clerks and others who had been with them, some as long as thirty years, in war and in other events, and who knew all about them as they understood the language, having been continually with them some twenty, others ten years, more or less. From these we were able to learn about everything: they told us most freely of all things without our having to question them, for they knew of our desire

After these things had happened the Emperor sent his *prothonotary* Chingay to tell us to write down what we had to say and our business, and to give it to him; this we did, writing down all we had previously said at Batu's, as has been stated above. After an interval of several days, he had us again called, and told us, through Kadak, the procurator of the whole Empire, and in the presence of the *prothonotaries* Bala and Chingay, and of many others of his secretaries, to say all we had to say; and this we did right willingly. Our interpreter on that occasion as well as on the other, was Temer, a knight of Iaroslav's, now a clerk with him, and another clerk of the Emperor's. And he (Kadak) asked us on the latter occasion if there were any persons with the Lord Pope who understood the written languages of the Ruthenians or Saracens or Tatars. We replied that we did not use either the Ruthenian, Tatar, or Saracenic writing, and that though there were Saracens in the country, they were far distant from the Lord Pope. We added that it appeared to us the best plan for them to write in Tatar, and to have it translated to us, and that we would carefully write it down in our language, taking both the (original) letter and the translation to the Lord Pope. On this they left us and went back to the Emperor.

On the feast of Saint Martin (November 11) we were again summoned, and Kadak, Chingay, Bala, and several others of the secretaries came to us, and the letter was translated to us word for word; and as we translated it into Latin, they made us explain each phrase, wishing to ascertain if we had made a mistake in any word; and when the two letters were written they made us read them together and separately for fear we had left out anything, and they said to us: "Be sure you understand it all, for it must not be that you do not understand everything, when you have reached such very distant lands." And having told them: "We understand it all," they re-wrote the letter in Saracenic, so that it might be read to the Lord Pope if he could find any one in our part of the world able to do so.

It is the custom of the Emperor of the Tatars never to address in person a stranger, no matter how great he may be; he only listens, and then answers through the medium of someone, as I have explained. Whenever they explain any business to Kadak, or listen to an answer of the Emperor, those who are under him (that is, his own subjects), remain on their knees until the end of the speech, no matter how great they may be. One may not, for it is not the custom, say anything more about any question after it is disposed of by the Emperor. This Emperor has a procurator, *prothonotaries*, and secretaries, and also all the other officers for public as well as private affairs, except advocates, for they carry out without a murmur all judgments according to the Emperor's decision. The other princes of the Tatars do in like manner as regards those things which pertain to their offices.

This Emperor may be forty or forty-five years or more old; he is of medium stature, very prudent and extremely shrewd, and serious and sedate in his manners; and he has never been seen to laugh lightly or show any levity, and of this we were assured by Christians who were constantly with him. We were also assured by Christians who were of his household that they firmly believed that he was about to become a Christian. As signal evidence of this he keeps Christian clerks and gives them allowances, and he has always the chapel of the Christians in front of his great tent, and (these priests) chant publicly and openly and beat (a tablet) according to the fashion of the Greeks at appointed hours, just like other Christians, and though there may be ever so great a multitude of Tatars and of other people. And the other chiefs do not have this.

Our Tatars who were to come back with us told us that the Emperor proposed sending his ambassadors with us. He wished, however, I think, that we should ask him to do so, for one of our Tatars, the elder of the two, told us to ask it; but it not seeming to us good that they should come, we replied that it was not for us to ask it, but that if the Emperor of his own will sent them, we would with God's help guide them safely. There were various reasons, however, for which it seemed to us inexpedient that they should come. The first reason was that we feared they would see the dissensions and wars among us, and that it would encourage them to march against us. The second reason was that we feared they were intended to be spies. The third reason was that we feared lest they be put to death, as our people for the most part are arrogant and hasty; thus it was that when the servants who were with us at the request of the Cardinal Legate in Germany were going back to him in Tatar dress, they came near being stoned by the Germans on the road, and were forced to leave off that dress. And it is the custom of the Tatars never to make peace with those who have killed their envoys till they have wreaked vengeance upon them. The fourth reason was that we feared they would carry us off, as was once done with a Saracen prince, who is still a captive, unless he is dead. The fifth reason was that there was no need for their coming, for they had no other order or authority than to bring the letters of the Emperor to the Lord Pope and the other princes (of Christendom), which we (already) had, and we believed that evil might come of it. Therefore it pleased us not that they should come. The third day after this, which was the feast of Saint Brice (November 13), they gave us permission to leave and a letter of the Emperor with his seal, and then they sent us to the Emperor's mother, who gave to each of us a fox-skin gown with the fur outside and wadding inside, and also a piece of purple—of which our Tatars stole a palm's length from each, and also more than half of another piece which was given to our servant; but though it was no secret to us, we did not choose to make any ado over it.

So we started on our way back, and we were travelling the whole winter, resting most of the time in the snow in the desert, save when in the open plain where there were no trees we could scrape a bare place with our feet; and often when the wind drifted it we would find (on waking) our bodies all covered with snow. And so we travelled along till we came to Batu, on the Ascension of our Lord (May 9, 1247), and to him we told what (the Emperor) had answered the Lord Pope. He replied that he had nothing to ask other than what the Emperor had written; but he said that we must carefully tell the Lord Pope and the other lords everything the Emperor had written. Safe conducts having been given us we left him, and reached Mauci on the Saturday after the octave of Pentecost (June 2), where were our companions and servants who had been detained, and whom we caused to be brought back to us. Thence we went to Corenza, who again begged presents of us, but not having (anything) we gave nothing. He gave us two Comans, who were accounted of the Tatars, as far as Kiev in Rus. Our own Tatar did not leave us till we had left the last Tatar camp. The others who had been given us by Corenza led us in six days from the last camp to Kiev.

We reached (Kiev) fifteen days before the feast of Saint John the Baptist (June 9). The Kievans who had heard of our arrival all came out to meet us rejoicing, and congratulated us as if we had risen from the dead, and so they did to us throughout Rus, Poland, and Bohemia. Daniel and Vasilko, his brother, received us with great rejoicing, and kept us, against our will, for quite eight days; during which time they held counsel between themselves and the bishops and other notables about those things on which we had spoken to them when on our way to the Tatars. And they answered us jointly, saying, that they wished to have the Lord Pope for their particular lord and father, and the holy Roman Church as their lady and mistress, and confirming likewise all they had previously transmitted on the matter through their abbot; and after that they sent with us to the Lord Pope their letters and ambassadors.

☙ *25* ☙

The Court of Batu Khan in 1253

The Mongol appearance in eastern Europe aroused the interest of the political as well as the religious leaders of western Europe. In 1253, the French king, Louis IX, sent a Franciscan monk, William of Rubruck, on a mission to Mongolia to seek an alliance against the followers of Islam in the Near East and North Africa. The assignment took Brother William to the Mongol capital of Karakorum. This mission, like that of John of Pian de Carpine, was a failure in its main task, but Brother William left an interesting account of his impressions of the Court of Batu Khan and his audience with the ruler of the Golden Horde. The account of Brother William, like that of Brother John, ranks as high as Marco Polo's report in the literature of medieval travel.

When I saw the *ordu* of Batu, I was astonished, for it seemed like a great city stretched out about his dwelling, with people scattered all about for three or four leagues. And as among the people of Israel, where each one knew in which quarter from the tabernacle he had to pitch his tents, so these know on which side of the *ordu* they must place themselves when they set down their dwellings. A court is *orda* in their language, and it means "middle," for it is always in the middle of the people, with the exception, however, that no one places himself right to the south, for in that direction the doors of the court open. But to the right and left they may spread out as they wish, according to the lay of the land, so long as they do not bring the line of tents down right before or behind the court.

We were first taken to a certain Saracen, who gave us no food. The next day we were taken to the court, and they had a great awning spread, for the dwelling could not hold all the men and women who had come thither. Our guide cautioned us to say nothing until Batu should have bid us to speak,

---

Reprinted with permission of the Cambridge University Press from *The Journey of William Rubruck to the Eastern Parts of the World, 1253–55, as Narrated by Himself, With Two Accounts of the Earlier Journey of John of Pian de Carpine*. Translated from the Latin, and Edited, with an Introductory Notice by William Woodville Rockhill (London: Published for the Hakluyt Society, 1900), pp. 122–126. See original source for footnote references. Spellings of certain proper names have been modernized. Words in brackets are mine.

and then to speak briefly. He asked also whether you had already sent ambassadors to the Tatars. I said that you had sent to Keu Khan [that is, the mission of Friar Andrew in 1249], but that you would not even have sent envoys to him and letters to Sartach if you had not believed that they were Christians. Then they led us before the pavilion, and we were warned not to touch the ropes of the tent, for they are held to represent the threshold of the door. So we stood there in our robes and barefooted, with uncovered heads, and we were a great spectacle unto ourselves. (Friar John of Pian de Carpine) had been there; but he had changed his gown, fearing lest he should be slighted, being the envoy of the Lord Pope. Then we were led into the middle of the tent, and they did not require us to make any reverence by bending the knee, as they are used to do of envoys. We stood before him the time to say: *"Miserere mei, Deus,"* and all kept profound silence. He was seated on a long seat as broad as a couch, all gilded, and with three steps leading up to it, and a lady was beside him. Men were seated about on his right, and ladies on his left; and where the room on the women's side was not taken up by them, for there were only present the wives of Batu, men occupied it. A bench with *cosmos* and big cups of gold and silver, ornamented with precious stones, was in the entry of the tent. He looked at us intently, and we at him, and he seemed to me to be about the height of my lord John de Beaumont, may his soul rest in peace. And his face was all covered at that time with reddish spots. Finally he bid me speak, and our guide told us to bend the knee and speak. I bent one knee as to a man, but he made sign to me to bend both, which I did, not wishing to dispute over it. Then he bid me to speak, and I, thinking I was praying to God, having both knees bent, began my speech by saying: "Oh lord, we pray God from whom proceedeth all good things, and who gave you these worldly goods, to give you hereafter celestial ones, for the former without the latter are vain." And as he listened attentively, I added: "You must know for certain that you shall not have the celestial goods unless you have been a Christian; for God saith: 'He who shall have believed and have been baptized, shall be saved, but he who shall not have believed shall be condemned!' " At this he quietly smiled, and the other Moal began clapping their hands, laughing at us, and my interpreter stood dumbfounded, and I had to reassure him that he be not afraid. Then silence being reestablished, I said: "I came to your son, because we had heard that he was a Christian, and I brought him letters from the lord King of the French. He (Sartach) it is who has sent me here to you. You must know the reason why." Then he caused me to rise, and asked your name and mine, and that of my companion and of the interpreter, and he had it all written down, and he also asked against whom you were waging war, for he had heard that you had left your country with an army. I replied: "Against the

Saracens who are profaning Jerusalem, the house of God." He also asked whether you had ever sent envoys to him. "To you," I said, "never." Then he made us sit down, and had us given of his milk to drink, and they hold it to be a great honor when anyone drinks *cosmos* with him in his dwelling. While sitting there I was looking down, but he bid me turn my face up, either wishing to see me better, or on account of their sorcery, for they hold it to be a bad omen or sign, or as portending evil, if one sits before them with face turned down as if in sorrow, and especially so if he rest his chin or his cheek in his hand. Then we went out, and after a little while our guide came to us, and while conducting us to our lodging said to me: "The lord King requests that you remain in this country, but Batu may not do this without the permission of Mangu Khan. So you and your interpreter must go to Mangu Khan. As to your companion and the other man, they will go back to Sartach, where they will await your return." Then the interpreter Homo Dei began to lament, deeming himself lost, and my companion to declare that they might sooner cut off his head than separate him from me; and I said that without a companion I could not go, and moreover that we really required two servants, for should one happen to fall ill, I could not be left alone. So he went back to the court and told Batu what I had said. Then he commanded: "Let the two priests and the interpreter go, and the clerk return to Sartach." He came back and told us the decision; but when I wanted to speak about the clerk, that he might come with us, he said: "Say no more about it, for Batu has settled it, and I dare not go again to the court." The clerk Gosset had twenty-six *yperpera** of your alms and no more; of these he kept ten for himself and the boy [a slave boy called Nicholas, bought at Constantinople], and he gave the sixteen others to Homo Dei for us; and so we parted from each other with tears, he going back to Sartach, and we remaining there.

*According to Mr. Rockhill's calculations, 24 *yperpera* equalled £14 and 12s. in 1900.

⚔ 26 ⚔

Prince Daniel of Galicia's Relations with the Mongols

Mongol conquest had a devastating effect on all principalities of Kievan Rus. Yet it should be remembered that the conquest affected each principality differently. Because it was located on the western periphery of Mongol domains, the principality of Galicia-Volyn enjoyed some degree of freedom, and Mongol rulers treated it as a vassal state.

This indirect control offered its princes, Daniel and Vasilko, an opportunity to take full advantage of their new status. In their respective principalities they tried to fortify their cities and they also founded new towns, including Lvov/Lviv, to serve both as defensive outposts against possible renewed Mongol attacks and as centers of urban trade, craft, and commerce. Abroad, both Daniel and Vasilko established good relations with Hungary, Poland, Lithuania, and the Teutonic Order. Daniel also established friendly contact with Pope Innocent IV, who, in 1253, bestowed on him the title and crown of King of Galicia-Volyn. Obviously, those changes did not escape the notice of the Mongol masters. They forced Daniel and his brother Vasilko to tear down their fortifications and to break up their new alliances.

In 1250 the mighty Khan [Batu] sent his envoy to [Prince] Daniel [of Galicia] and [to his brother] Vasilko [of Volyn]. At the time both princes were in the town of Dorogovsk. [Batu's envoy said:] "Surrender Galicia!" [Prince Daniel] was in grave danger because he had failed to fortify his towns. He conferred with his brother [Vasilko] and left for Batu's camp saying: "I will not surrender half of my patrimony. Instead I will go to Batu in person. . . ."

He arrived in Pereiaslav where he was met by Tatar [officials]. From there Daniel travelled to [the camp of one of Batu's military leaders named] Kuremsa. He did not see much that was worthwhile among the Tatars. . . . From there he reached Batu's [camp] along the Volga [River] in order to pay homage to him. There Daniel encountered a man named Songur, [an alleged] confidant

From V. I. Lebedev, et al., eds. *Khrestomatiia po istorii SSSR. S drevneishikh vremen do kontsa XVII veka.* (A Source Book on the History of the USSR. From Ancient Times to The End of the XVII Century), 3rd ed. (Moscow: Ministry of Education, 1949), vol. I, pp. 142–146. Translation mine. Words in brackets are mine.

of Prince Iaroslav [of Vladimir-Suzdal] who told him: "Your brother Iaroslav has bowed to an idol and you must do the same." Daniel replied: "The devil is speaking through you. May God silence you so that no one can again hear your voice."

At that moment Daniel was requested to appear before Batu and God saved the prince from Mongol evil magic and sorcery. In accordance with their custom, he [Daniel] bowed and was received in their tent. The Khan said: "Daniel! Why did you not come here earlier? I am pleased that you are here now. Do you drink black milk, our drink, mare's *kumys*?" To this Daniel responded: "Until now I have never drunk it, but since you have offered it to me now I will drink it." The Khan then said: "Now you are one of us! You are a Tatar. Drink our drink." After Daniel finished his drink, he bowed [to the Khan and] in accordance with their custom, delivered his speech, and, [in conclusion] said: "I would like to pay my respects to Grand Princess Barakchina [Batu's favored wife]." The Khan said: "Go ahead."

When [Daniel approached Barakchina's quarters], he bowed according to Mongol custom and the princess sent him a jug of wine, saying: "You are not accustomed to drinking [mare's] milk; drink then this wine." Oh, Tatar honor is evil! Daniel Romanovich was Grand Prince, who, together with his brother [Vasilko] ruled over such Rus principalities as Kiev, Vladimir [in Volyn], and Galicia, as well as other principalities. Now he sits [on Batu Khan's] knees and has identified himself as his servant. Moreover, the Mongols are asking tribute. There is very little hope for a better life. There are constant threats. Tatar honor is evil.

In 1261 there was peace throughout the land. In that year Prince Vasilko celebrated a marriage in the city of Vladimir [in Volyn]. He approved the marriage of his daughter Olga to Prince Andrei Vsevolodovich of Chernigov. Present at the wedding were Vasilko's brother Daniel, and Daniel's two sons, Lev and Shvarn, as well as many princes and *boyars*. The wedding in Vladimir experienced unexpected excitement when Princes Daniel and Vasilko were informed that the damned and cursed Burundai [Batu's principal military commander] would attend the wedding. Both princes [Daniel and Vasilko] expressed concern about it. Burundai sent the following message: "If you are in peace with me then invite me. Otherwise I will consider your silence a belligerent act."

Prince Vasilko and his nephew Lev went to meet Burundai. Prince Daniel did not accompany his brother. Instead, he sent Ivan, his bishop of Kholm. Prince Vasilko, his nephew Lev, and the bishop went on to meet Burundai. They took with them many gifts and drink, and met him near the town of Shumsk [in Volyn]. Vasilko, Lev, and the bishop went with the gifts before Burundai. Burundai, however, gave Vasilko and Lev a very hostile reception, while the bishop was left in great fear. Burundai told Vasilko: "If you wish to have peace with me, then destroy [all fortifications of] your towns." Accordingly, Lev destroyed Danilov Istozhek and then Lvov, while Vasilko destroyed Kremenetsk and Lutsk. From Shumsk Prince Vasilko sent the bishop to his brother [Daniel] informing him of everything that had transpired and about Burundai's displeasure. Daniel became very concerned and fled first to Poland and then to Hungary.

Accompanied by Vasilko, Burundai approached the town of Vladimir [in Volyn]. He decided to stay for the night in Zhitania. Burundai then talked about Vladimir. "Vasilko"! [he said], "destroy this city." Prince Vasilko then began to think about the fate of the city. Because its size made it impossible to destroy it at once, he ordered that it be burned. And so that night the entire city was set on fire. When next day Burundai entered the city of Vladimir he saw with his own eyes that the entire city was burned down. He stopped at Vasilko's mansion to dine and to drink. After the feast he stopped at a resort called Piatidna. Next day he sent [to Vasilko] a Tatar messenger named Baimur. Baimur came to the prince and said: "Vasilko! Burundai has sent me and has authorized me to destroy the city." And Vasilko replied: "Do as you have been instructed." And so, as a sign of triumph, he [the Tatar] began to destroy the city.

Then, along with Vasilko, his *boyars* and servants, Burundai went to Kholm. When they approached Kholm the city was closed. When they came closer they could do nothing because inside were *boyars* and other good people and, moreover, the city was well fortified and stocked with necessities and crossbows. When Burundai realized that the city was well fortified and it would be impossible to capture it, he told Prince Vasilko: "Vasilko! This city belongs to your brother [Daniel]. Go ahead and tell its inhabitants that they should surrender!" He then dispatched with Vasilko three Tatars named Kuichii, Ashik, and Buliui and an interpreter who knew the Rus language.

What do you think Vasilko did when he approached the city walls? When Vasilko approached the city, he picked up a rock and when he came near the city wall he told its inhabitants, so the Tatars who accompanied him could hear, the following: "Servant Constantine, and you, Luka Ivankovich, another servant! This city, which belongs to me and to my brother [Daniel], should surrender!" When he said these words he threw the rock to the ground, indicating thereby that they [should] fight and not surrender. Indeed, he repeated these words three times and three times he threw the rock to the ground.

By using this sign, as if sent by God, Prince Vasilko helped the citizens of [Kholm] and gave them the necessary encouragement. [A town official named] Constantine, who was at the wall, understood the signal Vasilko gave him and responded to Vasilko [as follows]: "Go away! You are not related to your brother [Daniel] as you claim. You are his enemy." The Tatars who heard these words went away and reported them to Burundai. They also informed him of what Vasilko told Kholm citizens and what they said to him.

⚔ *27* ⚔

Mongol Rule and the Orthodox Church

The Mongol or Tatar Yoke (1237–1480) had a profound impact on all Rus principalities. Initially, the most visible feature of that yoke was savage physical destruction. Except for Novgorod, Pskov, Polotsk, and Smolensk, most cities lay in smoldering ruins. So, too, did the countryside. Subsequently, Mongol treatment of Rus principalities was never uniform. It varied from one principality to another and from one *khan* to another. The most fortunate in treatment received was the distant northwest region (Novgorod-Pskov), followed by the southwest (Galicia-Volyn). The most unfortunate was the central region (Kiev-Pereiaslav-Chernigov), followed by the northeast (Vladimir-Suzdal-Riazan-Tver). These principalities suffered tremendously because of their geographic proximity to Sarai, capital of the Golden Horde.

But while Mongol-Tatar masters subjected towns and the countryside of Rus to countless abuses (such as the payment of tribute, recruit levies, obligatory work assignments, and the like), the Orthodox Church fared rather well during that period. Its good fortune came in 1267, when Khan Mangu-Temir granted the church an immunity *iarlyk* (charter). By its terms the church was exempted from the Mongol census (and associated obligations) in return for offering prayers for the ruling *khan* and his family. Also all church and monastery estates, and all people who worked for them, were freed from the payment of taxes and from performing military service. Moreover, Mongol and Rus tax agents were forbidden, under penalty of death, to seize church property or to demand

---

From L. V. Cherepnin, ed. *Pamiatniki prava perioda obrazovaniia russkogo tsentralizovannogo gosudarstva, XIV–XV vv.* (Legal Documents From the Period of the Formation of the Russian Centralized State, XIV–XV Centuries) (Moscow: Gosizdat Iuridicheskoi Literatury, 1955), pp. 467–470. Translation mine. Words in brackets are mine.

services from church people. Those who did not heed this injunction, or who defamed or vilified the Orthodox faith were liable to capital punishment. In 1357, Khan Berdibek reaffirmed these privileges to Metropolitan Alexei.

The iarlyk *[Charter] of Khan Mengu-Temir to Metropolitan Theognostos, August 1, 1267*

By the power of Eternal Heaven and by the Will of Eternal Heaven! [Khan] Temir hereby issues the following instruction to all of his people, officials, princes and high-ranking military commanders as well as to all tax collectors, office secretaries, circuit envoys, falconers, and officials in charge of hunting.

Emperor Ghengis Khan had once decreed that there be no collection of tribute or of food provisions from those [subjects of the Mongol rule] who genuinely prayed to God for us and for our nation and who gave us their genuine blessings. Subsequent [Mongol] emperors have respected this injunction and have bestowed favors on priests and monks [of all other faiths]. [This injunction applies to the collection of] tribute as well as anything else, including a tax on trade goods, a tax on ploughshares, postal fees, recruit levies, and whatever may be requested. We have agreed to reconfirm these original benefits [to the Orthodox Church] and hereby are making them known to everyone. And, invoking God's name, we are not amending any former existing charters.

Consequently, regardless of his position or status [no Mongol official] may request or collect from them [that is, officials of the Orthodox Church], any tribute, or ploughshare tax, or transport obligation, or food provisions. The same rule applies to the collection of postal fees, recruit levies, and a tax on trade goods. Likewise, no one should appropriate anything that belongs to the Orthodox Church, such as their buildings, land holdings, water resources, orchards, flour mills, winter homes [and forests], and summer lodges [and pastures]. And those who may do so are hereby required to return it back [to the church]. Also no church craftsman, or a falconer, or any other church employee may be either taken away [by local Mongol official] or be subjected to a close supervision. Moreover, whatever legally belongs to the Orthodox Church and is duly registered in their records, should be neither occupied, expropriated, alienated, or destroyed. And anyone who would dare to blaspheme their [Orthodox] faith will be guilty of committing a crime and will be executed.

Priests [of the Orthodox faith] who may live in the same home or whose brothers or sons have committed themselves to priesthood are entitled to the same [existing] benefits and protection as long as they are actively involved in it. However, once they leave the profession, they must pay the required tribute and do whatever is requested from them. Priests, who have received benefits from our earlier *iarlyks*, and who pray for us and bless us are to continue to enjoy their rights. Those, however, who fail to say prayers or who do not express their genuine feelings are hereby considered sinners and they will be punished accordingly. Finally, those individuals who are not priests, but who pray to God in our behalf, will also enjoy these benefits.

We have granted this charter to Metropolitan [Theognostos]. Those who may see or hear the content of this charter are hereby prohibited from collecting any tribute or anything else from priests or monks [of the Orthodox Church]. Consequently, any Mongol official, or a secretary of the prince, or a tribute collector, or a collector of trade dues, or any one who may try to collect or requisition anything that is contrary to the intent or the letter of this imperial *iarlyk*, which is based on Ghengis Khan's original injunction, will be guilty of a very serious crime and will be executed.

This *iarlyk* was issued in the steppe on the first day of the hunting season [August 1, 1267].

The iarlyk [Charter] of Khan Berdibek to Metropolitan Alexei, November, 1357

By the Might of Eternal Heaven, by the Will of Eternal Heaven, and in accordance with the terms of the [*iarlyks*] that have been previously issued by the father and the grandfather of [Khan] Berdibek, [the following] instruction is hereby given to all Tatar officials of the Golden Horde, all military commanders, all princes, all local customs officials, all office secretaries, tax collectors, frontier guards, and all other officials, falconers, officials in charge of hunting, provisioning, river transport, and those responsible for all other activities—indeed to all officials and people [of the Golden Horde].

Emperor Ghengis Khan and his successors, our forefathers, have received prayers from the entire priestly community [of the Orthodox Church]. As a result [of their prayers], they [Orthodox Church officials] are hereby freed from all tribute, taxes and all other obligations as long as they offer their prayers. [In accordance with this long established policy] we are granting them this [beneficial] *iarlyk*. All of our predecessors have also granted them the same kind of *iarlyks*. Moreover, in no way have we altered the content of the *iarlyks* of our previous *khans*. As long as he occupies the Metropolitan See of Vladimir and prays to God for us and for our nation, we have granted Metropolitan Alexei the following privileges:

We hereby decree that no tribute or taxes be collected from them [that is, the Orthodox Church], that no transport obligations be imposed on them, that neither food, drink, nor any special provisions be requisitioned from them, and that they not be subjected to any abuse or humiliation. Furthermore, no one should expropriate any church structure, estates, waters [that is, lakes and rivers], gardens, orchards or flour mills, nor do any damage to them. Whoever has in the past or would try to expropriate [these church properties] in the future must return them [to the church]. Moreover, regardless of their status, all people [belonging to the Orthodox] church should not be required to perform any obligation [that are performed by all non-church people] and in no way should they be abused. And whoever will compel them to do these things or violate [these provisions] commits a sin and therefore is liable to receive a death sentence.

And you, Metropolitan Alexei, and your entire ecclesiastical personnel, are hereby informed what benefits we have granted you regarding church buildings, estates, waters, gardens, orchards, and people belonging to the church. You also are hereby authorized to issue any [internal] regulations regarding taxes and other matters. Finally, you have full authority to punish anyone who may cause violence or theft, or who may tell a lie or commit any crime [on church property or its jurisdictions. In return for these privileges] we only ask that you pray for us and for all of our ancestors. . . .

� 28 ✻

The Anti-Mongol Uprising in Tver in 1327

The "Mongol Yoke" describes the period from 1238 to 1480 in Medieval Rus history. It was a bitter experience for the population. The most depressing immediate feature of this "Yoke" was the physical destruction of the country. Subsequently the burden of tribute, and the abuses and arrogance of Mongol officials, emerged as prime factors in popular discontent. How the people felt about the Mongols is very difficult to ascertain because contemporary records are incomplete and references to or descriptions of discontent are few. An exception to this generalization is

---

From *Polnoe Sobranie Russkikh Letopisei* (Complete Collection of Russian Chronicles) 2d edition (Petrograd: 1922), vol. XV, cols. 42–43. Translation mine. Words in brackets are mine.

the Chronicle's description of a violent anti-Mongol riot that took place
in Tver in 1327. The importance of this riot lies not in the slaughter of
Mongol officials but in the fact that this action eliminated Tver's chances
to become the leader in Northeastern Rus—the position that went to
Tver's chief rival, Moscow.

This happened in the year 6835 [1327]. On September 15, two princes [of
Rus], Prince Dmitrii Mikhailovich of Tver and Prince Alexander Novoselskii,
were killed in the [Golden] Horde. [Both were killed] on the same day and
in the same place—on the banks of the Kondrakliia River. That same year
the foundations of the Uspenskii Cathedral in Moscow [that subsequently was
completed in the reign of Ivan III (1462–1505)] were laid. That same year
Prince Alexander Mikhailovich [of Tver] received [from the Tatars] the title
of Grand Prince [of Rus], and when he returned from the [Golden] Horde
he began to rule as Grand Prince [of Rus]. Then a few days later, on account
of a multitude of our sins, God allowed the devil to instill evil thoughts into
the [minds of] godless Tatars and to counsel their lawless Tsar [Khan Uzbek]
in the following manner: "Unless you destroy Prince Alexander [of Tver] and
all other Princes of Rus you shall never be able to rule them." The leader of
this evil was the cursed and lawless Shevkal [Chol-khan, first cousin of the
ruling Khan Uzbek], the destroyer of Christianity. He opened his foul mouth
and began to speak in a devil-like manner: "Tsar, my Lord, allow me to go
to Rus to destroy their Christian faith, to kill their princes and to bring you
their wives and their children." And Tsar [Uzbek] allowed him to do this.

The lawless Shevkal, the destroyer of Christianity, went to Rus with many
Tatars. He came to Tver, drove the Grand Prince from his court and entrenched himself there with great haughtiness and violence. He inaugurated
great persecution of the Christians, [using] force, pillage, torture, and abuse.
Constantly offended by the infidels, city inhabitants complained repeatedly to
their [deposed] Grand Prince, asking that he protect them. While he saw
the injustice done to his people, he could not defend them and only counseled
them to be patient. The suffering people of Tver waited patiently for an
opportune time [to strike against the Tatars].

As the fair opened in the morning of August 14 [1327], a certain deacon
of Tver, named Dudko, led a young mare to the Volga to water her there.
When the Tatars saw her [the mare], they took her away from him. The
deacon complained [at first] and [when that failed] he began to shout [for
help] crying: "Oh, men of Tver, do not forsake me!" And soon fighting
developed between them [the Tatars and the Tverians]. Using their full authority, the Tatars started beating up [everybody]. The people [of Tver] came
out to the streets and great confusion emerged. Some rang the [church] bell

and a *veche* was called [into session by this action]. The entire city assembled and the uprising was in the making. The Tverians cried out and began to kill the Tatars wherever they found them until they killed Shevkal and the rest [of his men]. They missed killing the messengers who were with the horses that grazed in the meadows [outside the city]. They [the messengers] saddled their best horses and swiftly galloped to Moscow and from there to the [Golden] Horde, where they brought the news of the death of Shevkal.

⚔ *29* ⚔

Moscow's First Successful Challenge of the Mongols, 1380

Until about the middle of the fourteenth century Moscow's princes were, outwardly at least, the most loyal subjects of the Golden Horde. The major by-product of this "loyalty" was the rise of Moscow's military power. The strength of the principality became so formidable that by 1380 Moscow was in a position to challenge openly the military might of the Golden Horde. The challenge took place at Kulikovo Pole near the headwaters of the Don River. Led by Prince Dmitrii Donskoi (1359-1389), Moscow's armies inflicted a major defeat upon the once invincible Mongol forces. While this victory proved to be a short lived affair (since the Mongols recovered, regrouped, and overwhelmed Moscow's armies in 1382), the successful challenge of the Mongols in 1380 nevertheless elevated Moscow to the leading principality in northeastern Rus and to prime "gatherer of Russian lands."

That year [1380] Prince Mamai of the [Golden] Horde, accompanied by other princes and all the Tatar and Polovtsi forces, and joined by such mercenaries as: the Turks, Armenians, Genoese, Cherkessians, Burtasians, and supported by [Grand Prince] of Lithuania Iagello and [Prince] Oleg of Riazan, advanced against Grand Prince Dmitrii, and on September 1, made a camp

---

From *Polnoe Sobranie Russkikh Letopisei* (Complete Collection of Russian Chronicles) (St. Petersburg: 1885), vol. XXIII, pp. 124–127. Translation mine. Words in brackets are mine.

on the bank of the Oka River. Oleg supplied everything to Mamai and to Iagello through Epiphan Koreev. Grand Prince [Dmitrii] was informed about all this in August [1380]. Following this, Oleg, like Judas, informed the Grand Prince about Mamai's preparation against him. Having learned this, the Grand Prince went to the Church of the Mother of God, where he prayed for a long time; after he had finished he sent for all the Russian princes, *voevodas*, and all the people, and having collected his own force of 100,000, excluding those of the Russian princes and local *voevodas*, he went to Kolomna. There never was such a mighty Russian army, for all forces combined numbered some 200,000. With him, [Dmitrii] was Andrei Olgerdovich [Prince of Pskov] with his people and [Andrei's brother] Dmitrii [Prince of Briansk] with his people. Mamai's camp was in a meadow, not far from the Don where, with all of his forces he awaited for about three weeks the arrival of Iagello. To the Grand Prince, Mamai sent [a message] demanding the tribute which had existed during the reign of Dzhanibek Khan [1342–1357]. The Grand Prince wanted to give him a tribute from the Christian force, but this he did not want to accept. Oleg, however, paid him a tribute and also sent to him some of his forces. Grand Prince Dmitrii offered a prayer at the Church of the Holy Virgin, received a blessing from Bishop Herasim, left Kolomna on August 20, and upon arriving at the mouth of the Lopastra River [left tributary of the Oka] he received information about the heathens. There at last he also received Prince Vladimir Andreevich [his half-brother] and Timofei [a *voevoda* from Vladimir]; here they crossed the river a week before St. Simeon's Day and a week later, on September 6, they reached the River Don. Then he [Dmitrii] received a letter from the Reverend Abbot Sergei [founder of the Troitsk Monastery] urging him to fight the Tatars; Dmitrii, however, ordered his troops to put on their native garments while he himself waited for a long time, contemplating. Some said, "Let us go beyond the Don"; but others opposed it saying, "If we do, our enemies will increase, from the Tatars to the Lithuanians and to the people of Riazan." When Mamai learned of the arrival of the Grand Prince at the Don . . . he said, "Let us move toward the Don before Iagello arrives there." The Grand Prince ordered bridges built across the Don and a search by night for fords, and early Saturday morning, on September 8, he told his troops to cross the river and go to the meadow. At first there was a heavy fog but when it later disappeared everyone crossed the Don; there was a real multitude of troops as far as one could see, extending all the way to the mouth of the Nepriadva River. At six o'clock in the morning, the godless Tatars appeared in the field and faced the Christians. There was a great multitude of both; and when these two great forces met they covered an area thirteen *versts* long. And there was such a great massacre and bitter warfare and great noise, such as there never had been in Russian principalities;

and they fought from six to nine, and blood flowed like a heavy rain and there were many killed on both sides. At nine o'clock God took mercy on the Christians; many saw an angel and saintly martyrs helping the Christians; even the godless [that is, the Tatars] saw regiments moving in the air and hitting mercilessly. Shortly thereafter the godless fled and the Christians pursued them, hitting them until they reached the Mecha River; regiments of the Prince pursued the Tatars to their camp, where they took all of their wealth and their cattle, killing many and trampling others. It was here that many Russians lost their lives. . . .

The Grand Prince himself was very fortunate, for, although he had fought the Tatars from the very beginning, he received no wounds to his body. His *voevodas* told the Prince, "Lord, do not stay at the front; go either to the rear or to the side, or to a safe place." He, however, replied: "I will neither protect my face nor hide in the rear, but let us all brothers fight together. I want to die for Christianity ahead of anyone else, with deed as well as word, so that all others who see it will become bold." He did what he said. He fought ahead of everyone else, striking to the right and to the left, killing many; he himself was surrounded by many [Tatars] and was hit many times on his head and his body but God protected him from everything. Lithuanian Prince Iagello came to Mamai's aid with all of his Lithuanian and Latvian forces one day too late; when he heard what had happened to the Tatars and that Mamai had fled, he [Iagello] fled back with all of his force. The Grand Prince remained overnight at the Tatar-deserted camp, which was full of their bodies, where he, together with his troops, thanked God [for victory]; in the morning he departed for his land. There he was informed that Prince Oleg of Riazan had sent his force to aid Mamai, that he had destroyed bridges across the rivers and that he had robbed and stripped of everything all those subjects of the Grand Prince who crossed his land [Riazan]. The Grand Prince wanted to send an army [against Riazan]. But at about that time the *boyars* from Riazan came to him and told him that Prince Oleg had fled from his principality with his wife and children; and the *boyars* paid homage and prayed him not to attack them. He accepted them and sent his governors to Riazan.

Mamai, angered, arrived in his territory with his few remnants and began collecting a new force in an effort to undertake a new expedition against Rus. He received news, however, that Khan Tokhtamysh from the Ak-Orde was advancing against him from the east. Mamai went to meet him and both forces met at the River Kalka and began to fight. Mamai's princes dismounted from their horses and joined Tokhtamysh. When Mamai saw this he fled, but Tokhtamysh ordered a pursuit. He fled to Kafa [in Crimea], where he asked protection, which he received. He took much gold, wealth, and silver with him, and after a period of flattery ended, the people of Kafa killed him.

Khan Tokhtamysh advanced, took his [Mamai's] camp and his wives, and divided his treasury among his troops. He sent his ambassadors to Rus, to the Grand Prince, and to all Russian princes, informing them that, having defeated Mamai, he had ascended the Khanate of the Golden Horde. They received his ambassadors with dignity, and in the spring they sent to him their own ambassadors with many gifts.

⚐ *30* ⚐

A Letter from a Tatar Leader, Edigei, to Moscow's Grand Prince Vasilii I, 1409

Technically, Mongol domination of northeastern Rus principalities lasted from 1237 to 1480. Actually, the domination ended in 1380 when, assisted by other Rus princes, the armies of Moscow's Grand Prince Dmitrii Donskoi defeated the forces of Khan Mamai of the Golden Horde. That victory at Kulikovo Pole, immortalized in an epic poem *Zadonshchina* (Beyond the Don), elevated Muscovy to the foremost power among the northeastern principalities of Rus and set in motion the dis-integration process of the once mighty Empire of the Golden Horde into several warring units. And while these units, individually or collectively, were still capable of inflicting severe damage on Rus principalities (and they often did), the former power and threat of the Golden Horde was never the same. It was further weakened by spectacular victories of Ta-murlane, who inflicted near-total destruction of the Horde's economic foundation.

    After Tamurlane's death in 1405, the fortunes of his empire, which now included former domains of the Golden Horde, fell into the hands of Edigei, one of the most capable of Tamurlane's military commanders. In a series of spectacular campaigns, Edigei brought all of Central Asia under his control and then turned to and laid siege to Moscow. Although

From *Polnoe Sobranie Russkikh Letopisei* (Complete Collection of Russian Chronicles), vol. 11, pp. 209–210, translated and published in *Source Book for Russian History from Early Times to 1917*, vol. I, *Early Times to the Late Seventeenth Century*. Edited by George Vernadsky, et al. (New Haven: Yale University Press, 1972), p. 113. Reprinted with permission of Yale University Press.

his armies devastated the countryside, they failed to capture the city. Muscovy's ruler Vasilii I (1389–1425) successfully defied Edigei's claim to suzerainty and, to annoy him, granted political asylum to rivals of Edigei.

[A.D. 1409,] The prince of the [Golden] Horde, Edigei, sent [a letter] to Grand Prince Vasilii Dmitrievich, saying thus: "We have heard that the children of Tokhtamysh are with you, and for this reason we have come in war; and we have also heard that you act wrongfully in the towns: the tsar's [*khan's*] envoys and merchants come from the Horde to you, and you ridicule the envoys and merchants, and moreover they are subjected to great injury and persecution from you. This is not good; for in the past this was the tsar's [*khan's*] domain [*ulus*] and he held power; you respected the ancient customs and the tsar's envoys, and merchants were treated without persecution and without injury; and you should ask the old men how this was done in the past. Now you do not do this; but is this [change] good? Temir-Kutlui became tsar, and you became sovereign of your domain, and since that time you have not visited the tsar in the Horde; you have not seen the tsar with your own eyes, nor have you dispatched any princes, or elder *boyars*, or younger [*boyars*], or anyone else, nor have you sent a son or a brother with any message. Then Shadibeg ruled for eight years, and you did not visit him either, or send anyone with any message. And the reign of Shadibeg likewise came to an end, and now Tsar Bulat-Saltan [Pulad] has become tsar, and this is already the third year of his rule, and you have likewise failed to visit him yourself, or to send a son, or brother, or elder *boyar*. You are the eldest, the grand prince, over such a great domain, but all your deeds are evil and wrongful. . . . It would be well for you . . . to observe the ancient customs, and then you will live safely and rule in your domain. Whenever you suffer any harm, either from Russian princes or from Lithuania, each year you send complaints to us against them, and you ask us for charters of protection from them, and you give us no respite on this account; and you say that your domain is destitute and that there is no means of paying tribute. Heretofore we have never seen your domain with our own eyes, but only heard reports of it; but as for your messages and letters which you have sent to us in the Horde, you have lied to us everywhere; and as for the [tribute of] one *ruble* per two *sokhi* ["plows" taxation units] which you have collected from each region of your realm, where is that silver? It would be well for you to acknowledge this, [to give over] what was given over honestly in the past, lest evil befall your domain, and Christians meet their final doom, and our anger and war be upon you."

⚔ *31* ⚔

*Ending
of the Mongol Yoke
in 1480*

The reign of Ivan the Great (1462–1505) is remembered for such significant developments in domestic and foreign policy as energetic annex-
ation of territories to Moscovy, conquest of Novgorod, establishment of
contacts with western Europe, efforts to gain an outlet on the Baltic for
Moscovy, the emergence of the concept of "Moscow, the third Rome,"
and the overthrow of the Mongol yoke, to name only a few. The last
achievement, as the following Chronicle account indicates, came in 1480.
It was far from a spectacular victory, for the once powerful Golden Horde
had, by this time, disintegrated into several independent, feuding *khan-
ates* (Kazan, Crimean, Nogai, and others), which were incapable and
unwilling to challenge the rapidly rising might of Moscow.

In the year [1480] the Grand Prince [Ivan III] received news that Khan
Akhmat was advancing with the entire Horde, with his sons and feudal lords
and princes, in accordance with an agreement reached with King Casimir [of
Poland], whereby the King incited him against the Grand Prince in order to
destroy [Orthodox] Christianity. The Grand Prince went to Kolomna, where
he remained, and sent his son, Grand Prince Ivan, to Serpukhov, while Prince
Andrei Vasilevich Menshoi [brother of Ivan III] was in Tarusa; the remaining
princes and *voevodas* were in other places on the Oka River. Khan Akhmat,
upon learning that the Grand Prince was along the [Oka] river with all his
forces, advanced toward Lithuania, around the Oka River, where he expected
the arrival of the King [Casimir] and his armies, but his guides led him to
the ford on the Ugra River. The Grand Prince dispatched his son and his
brother and *voevodas* with all of their forces to the Ugra River. Upon reaching
the Ugra, their destination, they occupied the ford and ferries. The Grand
Prince himself left Kolomna for Moscow to attend a council and get advice
from his [spiritual] father, Metropolitan Gerontii, his mother, Grand Princess
Maria, his uncle, Prince Michael Andreevich [of Mozhaisk], and his [spiritual]

From *Polnoe Sobranie Russkikh Letopisei* (Complete Collection of Russian Chronicles) (St.
Petersburg: 1885), vol. 8, pp. 205–207. Translation mine. Words in brackets are mine.

father, Archbishop Vassian Rostovskii, and all of his *boyars*, inasmuch as they
were all in Moscow preparing for a siege. And they pleaded with the Grand
Prince to remain firm against Islam on behalf of Orthodox Christianity. The
Grand Prince took note of these pleas, received a blessing, and went to the
Ugra, where he encamped himself at Kremnets with a small group of people,
sending others to Ugra. Back in Moscow, the mother of the Grand Prince,
Metropolitan Gerontii, Archbishop Vassian, and the Abbot of the Troitsk
Monastery, Paisii, pleaded that the Grand Prince request the help of his
brothers [Andrei the Elder, and Boris, with whom Ivan III was not on speaking
terms]. The Grand Prince consented to their pleas and allowed his mother to
send for them, promising to reward them. The Grand Princess sent after them,
instructing them to go immediately to the aid of the Grand Prince.

Khan Akhmat went to Lithuania near Mtsensk and Liubutsk and Odoev
with his Tatars, and camped at Vorotinsk, where he expected the royal aid.
The King [of Poland], however, did not come to his aid; neither did he send
any army, because he was engaged in another war [with the Crimean Tatars].
At that time Khan Mengligirei of the Crimean Tatars pillaged the royal lands
of Podolie, thereby helping the Grand Prince.

Akhmat arrived at the Ugra with all of his forces, with the intent of crossing
the river. When the Tatars came they began to shoot at our [forces], and our
[forces] shot at them. Some Tatars advanced against Prince Andrei; others
against the Grand Prince; while still others unexpectedly advanced against the
voevodas. Our forces, using arrows and harquebusses, killed many Tatars; their
arrows were falling among our forces but did not hurt anyone. They pushed
the Tatars away from the river, though they tried to advance for many days;
as they could not cross the river they stopped and waited until it should
freeze.

The brothers Prince Andrei and Prince Boris came to Kremenets to the
Grand Prince, who greeted them cordially. When the river froze, the Grand
Prince, afraid of Tatar invasion, ordered his son, Grand Prince Ivan, and his
brother Andrei, and his *voevodas* to join him at Kremenets with all of their
forces in order to unite their forces in the struggle with the enemy. In Moscow
itself everyone was afraid. When our forces left the bank of the river, then
the Tatars were frightened and fled, thinking that the Russians were letting
them across the river in order to fight them, while our forces thought that
the Tatars had crossed the river and were pursuing them, and so they came
to Kremenets.

The Grand Prince with his son and brothers and with all his *voevodas* went
to Borovsk, saying that he would fight them there.

Khan [Akhmat] fled to the Horde, and Khan Ivak of the Nogai Tatars
advanced against him, killed him, and took the Horde; one of the Tatar

Khans wanted to occupy some frontier lands beyond the Oka River, but the Grand Prince sent his two brothers against him, and when the Tatars heard about it they fled.

O, brave and courageous Russian sons, try to defend your country, Russian land, from the Tatars! Make all necessary sacrifices in order to put an end to the burning and pillaging of your homes, the killing of your children, the abusing of your wives and your daughters—things that other great lands are now suffering from the Turks, such as Bulgaria, Serbia, Greece, Trapezund, Peloponnesus, Albania, Croatia, Bosnia, Mankup, Kafa, and many other lands. They did not defend themselves courageously and were defeated, and lost the countries, lands, and states, and now they move through foreign lands poor and homeless, . . . because they were not courageous enough. Those who fled to foreign lands with wealth and gold, wives and children, have lost their soul and body and think that those who died during the initial conquest are better off than they who wander homeless through foreign lands.

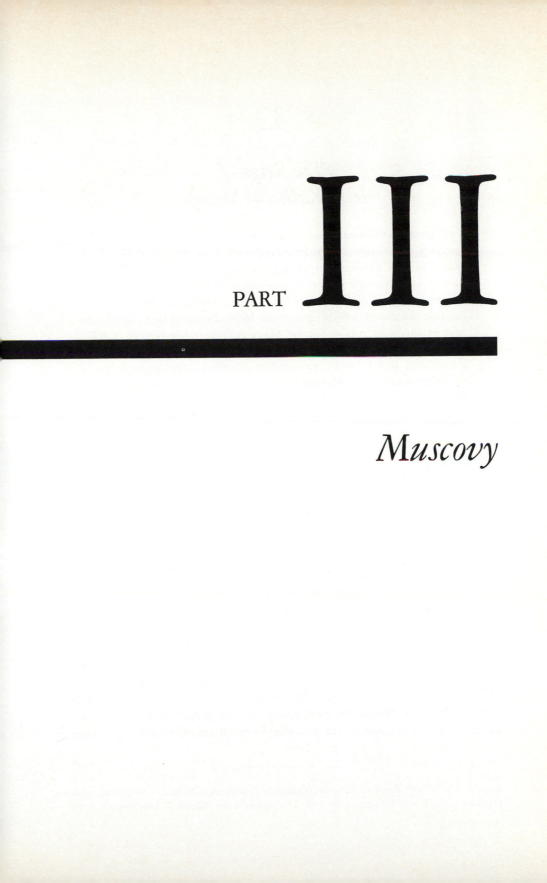

PART III

Muscovy

32

The Reign of
Ivan Kalita of Moscow

Two factors seem to stand out in Moscow's ascendancy among the north-eastern principalities of Rus: its exceptionally favorable geographical location, and the cleverness of its early rulers combined with their ability to take full advantage of every opportunity. The founder of the opportunistic trend was Grand Prince Ivan Danilovich Kalita. Thanks to his pretense of extreme subservience to the Mongol masters he received permission to collect tribute for the Mongols from other princes of Rus. With this powerful leverage Ivan accumulated great wealth, strengthened the military posture of his principality, attracted other opportunists to his side (including the Metropolitan), and forced others to acknowledge his preeminence. By these actions Ivan elevated Moscow principality into a major power among the northeastern principalities of Rus and provided everyone who joined him a safe place to live.

This happened in the year 6836 [1328]. The reign of Ivan Danilovich as Grand Prince [of Rus] began. When Grand Prince Ivan Danilovich assumed power in the Grand Principality [of Moscow], for many years there was peace to all Christians throughout the land of Rus. That same year Greek Metropolitan Theognostos arrived in Rus [from Constantinople]. That same year the entire city of Iuriev went up in flames. Many churches and stone palaces were destroyed and 2530 Germans and four Rus men lost their lives. That same year Prince Constantine Vasilievich of Rostov married a daughter of Prince Ivan Danilovich [of Moscow]. [That same year] Grand Prince Ivan Danilovich journeyed with Prince Constantine Mikhailovich [of Tver] to the Tsar of the [Golden] Horde [Khan Uzbek]. The Novgorodians sent Feodor Kolesnitsa [to the Golden Horde]. Tsar Uzbek allowed everyone to return home safely but ordered a search for Prince Alexander [of Tver who, after the anti-Tatar uprising of 1327, had escaped to Pskov]. Grand Prince Ivan Danilovich sent to Pskov his envoys and the Novgorodians sent their bishop Moisei and their *tysiatskii* Avram to urge Prince Alexander [of Tver] to journey

From *Polnoe Sobranie Russkikh Letopisei* (Complete Collection of Russian Chronicles) 2d series (Moscow: 1949), vol. XV, pp. 168–172. Translation mine. Words in brackets are mine.

to the [Golden] Horde. He did not listen to their advice. That autumn, on September 8, Bishop Prokopii of Rostov died, and in his place Bishop Antonii was appointed.

This happened in the year 6837 [1329]: On March 26, Grand Prince Ivan Danilovich came to Novgorod, together with the Princes of Tver, Prince Constantine and his brother Vasilii Mikhailovich, and Prince Alexander of Suzdal, and many other princes of Rus. At the same time Metropolitan Theognostos arrived in Great Novgorod. That same year, on May 21, the foundations were laid out in Moscow for the church of John Climacus and it was completed and consecrated in the same year, on September 1. Another church, dedicated to the Apostle Peter, was started on August 13, and was completed on October 14.

This happened in the year 6838 [1330]. On May 10, the Orthodox Grand Prince Ivan Danilovich founded a stone church in Moscow near his court to commemorate the Transfiguration of Our Lord Jesus Christ. And he also founded there a monastery and assembled monks in it. And he was respected on account of the monasteries [he helped to organize] and prayers were offered there in his behalf. And he gave much food, drink, clothing, tax money, and all other necessities of life to the monks living there. And he also granted them protection so they would not be abused by anyone. He adorned this church with ikons, books, chalices, and all sorts of other splendid ornaments. And he appointed Ivan as its first archimandrite. [Ivan was] an honest man, very knowledgeable, wise, literate, and dignified. Because of his great benef- icence he was later appointed Bishop of Rostov, where he guided his flock very well. . . . That same year the Grand Prince sent from Novgorod an embassy to Prince Alexander Mikhailovich in Pskov. It was headed by Luka Protasiev. The Novgorodians sent their archbishop and their *posadnik,* who told [Prince Alexander]: "Go to the [Golden] Horde in order to save the Christians from a massacre by the heathens." Prince Alexander felt guilty, agreed to go the Horde, and declared: "I alone shall die so that Christianity may live." The Pskovians, however, urged him not to go. "Do not go to the Horde, and if they come after you we shall all die [fighting] with you." Grand Prince Ivan Danilovich marched with his armies against Pskov. With him were two princes of Tver, Constantine and Vasilii Mikhailovich [brothers of Alexander], Prince Alexander of Suzdal, and other princes of Rus and of Novgorod. They encamped at Opoka, and the people of Pskov gave very strong support to their Prince Alexander. When Grand Prince Ivan realized that he could neither capture nor expel Prince Alexander from Pskov, he ordered Metropolitan Theognostos to excommunicate Prince Alexander and the people of Pskov. Then Prince Alexander told the Pskovians: "Dear Broth- ers! I do not wish to be the cause of your excommunication. I am leaving

your city. I am releasing you from your oath to me, and you release me from
my oath to you." [After he said this] he departed to Lithuania. The Pskovians
then sent an embassy with a petition to the Grand Prince [Ivan] at Opoka,
and he granted them peace. . . . On March 28 of that year, Prince Feodor of
Rostov died. That year, too, Grand Prince Ivan and other princes [of Rus]
departed from Novgorod, each going to his own patrimony. Metropolitan
Theognostos left for Volyn. That year [the Archbishop of Novgorod] Moisei
left his bishopric and went to Kolomna.

This happened in the year 6839 [1331]. On May 3, a great fire engulfed
Moscow and the Kremlin went up in flames. A week before Easter [Sunday]
envoys from Metropolitan Theognostos came from Volyn to Novgorod and
they invited Vasilii to become [Novgorod's] archbishop. On June 24 he left
for Volyn and he was accompanied there by the following *boyars*: Kuzma
Tverdyslav and Ofremii Ostafiev, son of [Novgorod's] *tysiatskii*. As they
travelled through Lithuania they were seized by Prince Gedymin. In prison
they were forced to grant to his son, Narimont, and to the latter's descendants
as their patrimonies the following territories of Novgorod: Ladoga, the towns
of Orekh and Korel, the district of Korel and half of Koporie. And when
they reached Vladimir-Volynskii, Metropolitan Theognostos invested Vasilii
as the new archbishop of Novgorod. The ceremony took place on August 25
in the Church of the Holy Mary. At that time a bright star appeared above
the church and it glittered there for a day. During this time the Metropolitan
of Kiev and All Rus received envoys from Prince Alexander Mikhailovich of
Pskov, and from Gedymin and from all Lithuanian princes. They brought
with them Arsenii, whom they wanted to consecrate as bishop of Pskov. Their
efforts, however, were not successful. . . .

This happened in the year 6840 [1332]. Grand Princess Elena Ivanova
died in a nunnery as a nun, and was buried on March 1 in the Church of
Our Savior. That year the entire land of Rus experienced an acute drought.
That year Grand Prince Ivan Danilovich returned from the Horde and became
very angry at Novgorod. He demanded from them silver from the Trans-
Kama region and [when they refused he] occupied the towns of Torzhok and
Bezhetsk Verkh. That same year Prince Alexander Vasilievich of Suzdal died.

This happened in the year 6841 [1333]. Vasilii, the Archbishop of Novgorod went to Pskov to baptize Michael, son of Prince Alexander. That same
year Gedymin's son, Narimont, named Gleb at his baptism, came to Novgorod to seek [political] asylum. He declared that he did not care to live in
Lithuania any more and took an oath of allegiance to Novgorod. Metropolitan
Theognostos arrived in Moscow, having previously visited Constantinople and
the Horde. That year Grand Prince Ivan Danilovich ordered the construction
of a church in Moscow in honor of Archangel Michael. The structure was

completed in one year and was dedicated by Metropolitan Theognostos. That winter Prince Semeon Ivanovich [son of the Grand Prince] was married in Moscow. His bride was a Lithuanian princess, Augusta, who at baptism took the name of Anastasia. Prince Semeon was seventeen years old. That winter Grand Prince Ivan Danilovich came to Torzhok [a southeastern outpost of Novgorod] with all the princes of Nizovie [that is, Moscow, Iaroslavl, Suzdal, and Nizhnii Novgorod]. He dispatched his *namestniks* to Novgorod while he himself remained in Torzhok, whose surroundings he plundered. The Novgorodians sent to him the following envoys: Archimandrite Lavrentii, Feodor Tverdislavich and Luka Ofromeev. They petitioned him to assume rule in Novgorod. Grand Prince Ivan Danilovich, however, rejected their offer and returned to Moscow without agreeing to peace. . . .

This happened in the year 6843 [1335]. Grand Prince Ivan Danilovich came to wage a war against Lithuania over the *volost* of Novotorzhok. The Grand Prince sent his armies [to Lithuania] and they burned Osechen, Riasna, and other Lithuanian towns.

This happened in the year 6844 [1336]. Grand Prince Ivan Danilovich went to the Horde and returned the same winter with a charter to his patrimony. That same year Prince Feodor Alexandrovich [of Tver] returned from the Horde. That year Bishop Antonii of Rostov died and was succeeded by Bishop Gavriil. . . .

That year [1337] Prince Alexander Mikhailovich [of Tver] journeyed to the [Golden] Horde from Pskov, where he stayed for ten years. A son was born to Prince Semeon Ivanovich. There was a major fire in Moscow that consumed eighteen churches. That fall there was a great flood [in Moscow].

This happened in the year 6846 [1338]. The Novgorodians sent [envoys] to Lithuania to Prince Narimont, but he did not return. He even withdrew his son, Prince Alexander, from Orekhov, leaving there only his lieutenant. That same year Prince Alexander Mikhailovich [of Tver] returned from the Horde, where Tsar Uzbek granted him back his patrimony of Tver. [Prince Alexander] sent [envoys] to Pskov and they accompanied his wife and his children to Tver. [Young] Prince Vasilii, son of Prince Semeon, died.

This happened in the year 6847 [1339]. Grand Prince Ivan Danilovich went to the [Golden] Horde. He was accompanied there by his [two] sons, Semeon and Ivan. He sent his third son, Andrei, to Novgorod. At his [Ivan's] suggestion, Tsar Uzbek ordered that Prince Alexander Mikhailovich [of Tver] and Prince Vasilii Davidovich of Iaroslavl and all other princes of Rus [come to the Horde]. Prince Alexander sent first to the Horde his son, Feodor, from whom he expected to hear the news. Tsar [Uzbek], however, requested his own presence. Prince Alexander was accompanied there by Prince Vasilii of Iaroslavl. [When they arrived at the Horde] Grand Prince Ivan Danilovich was departing from the Horde with his sons. The Novgorodians sent to him two envoys: Sylvester Voloshevich and Feodor Avramovich. They brought him the tribute [which he was to transmit to the Horde]. Grand Prince Ivan Danilovich dispatched to Novgorod his own envoys who demanded additional tribute, saying: "Give me the Tsar's demand—what the Tsar has demanded from me." The Novgorodians replied, however: "That has never happened before. Besides, sir, you took an oath to Novgorod to abide by the terms of the old Novgorodian dues and by the terms of the Charter of your ancestor, Grand Prince Iaroslav Volodimirovich [that is, Iaroslav the Wise, who ruled Kiev from 1018 to 1054].

On July 23 of that year, Prince Andrew Mstislavich of Kozelsk was killed by his nephew, son of the impious Vasilii Panteleev. That autumn Prince Ivan Danilovich sent his sons, Semeon, Ivan, and Andrei, to the Horde. On October 29 of that year the godless Tatars murdered Prince Alexander Mikhailovich [of Tver] and his son Feodor in the Horde, on orders of the godless Tsar Uzbek, who had summoned him there deceitfully. . . . That winter [Princes] Semeon, Ivan, and Andrei, sons of Grand Prince Ivan Danilovich, were affectionately released from the Horde with the charter. That same winter, on November 25, the wall around the city of Moscow was started, and [the work] was completed that same winter before Lent. That same winter, Grand Prince Ivan Danilovich withdrew his lieutenants from Novgorod, and he was not at peace with the Novgorodians.

This happened in the year 6848 [1340]. Tovlu Bei arrived from the Horde. Tsar [Uzbek] sent him and his armies against the city of Smolensk. With him [Tovlu Bei] was Prince Ivan Korotopol of Riazan. They first came to Riazan. At that time Prince Alexander Mikhailovich of Pronsk went to the Tsar with tribute. When Korotopol met him [Alexander] he had him seized, robbed him, brought him to Pereiaslavl-Riazanskii, and ordered him to be killed. From Pereiaslavl, Toblu Bei went with his armies to Smolensk. In accordance with the Tsar's [Uzbek's] orders, Prince Ivan Danilovich sent his armies with Toblu Bei. [They were led by] Prince Constantine Vasilievich of Suzdal, Prince Constantine of Rostov, Prince Ivan Iaroslavich of Iuriev, Prince Ivan of Driutsk, Prince Feodor of Fomin, and [two] *voevods* of the Grand Prince: Alexander Ivanovich and Feodor Okinfovich. They besieged the town [of Smolensk] for about eight days, but left without gaining anything. That winter, on December 6, the people of Briansk killed their prince, Gleb Sviatoslavich, as he left the Church of St. Nicholas. Metropolitan Theognostos was at that time in Briansk, but he could not restrain them.

This happened in the year 6849 [1341]. On March 31, Grand Prince Ivan Danilovich died. He died as a monk in a monastery and was buried on April 1 in Moscow in the Church of the Archangel Michael. All princes of Rus went to the Horde [to seek the Grand Princely title]: Prince Semeon Ivanovich with his brothers [Ivan and Andrei], Prince Vasilii Davidovich of Iaroslavl, Prince Constantine of Tver, Prince Constantine Vasilievich of Suzdal, and all other princes of Rus.

⚜ *33* ⚜

The Last Will of Ivan Kalita, or "Money Bag," ca. 1339

Ivan Kalita (1325–1340) was one of the most Machiavellian princes of Muscovy. Little is known of his early life except that as a young man he spent some time in Sarai, the capital of the Golden Horde, where he artfully ingratiated himself with the ruling Khan Uzbek, and where he worked hard to bring about the downfall of his brother Iurii. For his apparent loyalty and blind obedience, Khan Uzbek appointed Ivan as the ruling prince of Moscow in 1325, and later bestowed on him the title of Grand Prince of Rus. In that capacity Ivan became the sole collector of Mongol tribute throughout northeastern Rus. That new position reduced Mongol incursions into Rus principalities, enabled Ivan to dabble in Rus affairs, and gave him an opportunity to acquire considerable estates and other riches.

The inventory of his wealth, as evident from his last will, was substantial. He distributed his possessions among his children, his wife, and the church. The role of the church was important in his reign because, in return for relative safety and security, the Church hierarchy moved its "See of Kiev and all Rus" from Vladimir to Moscow in 1328, and it has been there ever since. That move enhanced Ivan's prestige and importance and made Moscow both a political and a religious center.

In the name of the Father, and of the Son, and of the Holy Spirit. I, Ivan, sinful and humble servant of God, on leaving for the [Golden] Horde, and being of sound mind and body, write this my last free will. Should God

---

From V. I. Lebedev, et al., eds. *Khrestomatiia po istorii SSSR. S drevneishikh vremen to kontsa XVII veka* (A Source Book on the History of the USSR. From Ancient Times to the End of the XVIIth Century), third ed. (Moscow: Ministry of Education, 1949), vol. I, pp. 202–205. Translation mine. Words in brackets are mine.

decide something about my life, I bequeath all of my possessions set forth in this will to my sons and to my princess.

I bequeath my Moscow patrimony to my sons and have arranged the following distribution of it. To my oldest son Semeon, I bequeath Mozhaisk with all of its *volosti* [districts] and Kolomna, with all of its *volosti*, Gorodenka, Meziniia, Posochina, Seredokhorodna, Pokhriane, Ust-Merska, Broshevaia, Gvozdnaia and Ivani; the hamlets of Mokovets, Levichin, Skulnev, Kanev, Gzhel, Goretov, Gorki, the village Astafskoe, the village on the Seversk [River] in Pokhriane *uezd* [county], the village Konstantiovskoe, the village Orinin-skoe, the village Ostrovskoe, the village Kopotenskoe, the small village Mik-ulskoe, the village Malakhovskoe, [and] the village Naprudskoe near the city. Also, during my lifetime, I have given my son Semeon: four gold chains, three gold belts, two gold cups with pearls, one small gold plate with pearls and precious stones, [and] two large gold ladles. And of the silver vessels, I have given him three silver plates.

To my son Ivan I give [the following]: Zvenigorod, Kremichna, Ruza, Fominskoe, Sukhodol, Velikaia *sloboda* [settlement], Skirminovskoe, Trostna, [and] Neguchaia. And [to my son Ivan I give] the [following] villages: the village Riukhovskoe, the village Kamenetskoe, the village Ruzskoe, the village Belzhinskoe, the village Maksimovskoe, the village Andreevskoe, the village Viazemskoe, the village Domontovskoe, the village in Zamoshskaia *sloboda*, [and] the village Semchinskoe. Also, to my son Ivan I have given [the following] gold items: four gold chains, one large gold belt with pearls and precious stones, one gold belt with clasps, one carnelian belt mounted with gold, two gold ladles, two round gold cups, one silver plate from [the Persian town of] Ezd, and two small [silver] plates.

To my son Andrei I have [already] given [the following]: Lopasna, Sev-erskaia, Naruzhinskoe, Serpukhov, Nivna, Temna, Golichikhi, Shchitov, Per-emyshl, Rostovets, [and] Tukhachev. Also [the following] villages: the village Talezhskoe, the village Serpukhovskoe, the village Kolbasinskoe, the village Narskoe, the village Peremyshlskoe, the village Bitiagovskoe, the village Tru-fonovskoe, the village Iasinovskoe, the village Kolomenskoe, [and] the village Nogatinskoe. Also to my son Andrei I have given [the following] gold items: four gold chains, one gold Italian belt with pearls and precious stones, one gold belt with a clasp on purple silk, one gold belt from the Golden Horde, two gold cups, [and] two small gold ladles. And of [silver] dishes, [I have given him] one silver plate and two small [silver] plates.

And to my princess with small children I give [the following]: Surozhik, Mushkina Gora, Radonezhskoe, Beli, Voria, Chernogolovl, Sofronskaia *sloboda* on the Voria [River], Vokhnia, Deikovo, Ramenie, Danilishcheva *sloboda*, Mashev, Selna, Guslitsa, [and] Ramenie that [already] belonged to the princess. Also [to my princess I give the following] villages: the village Mikhai-lovskoe, the village Lutsinskoe, the village by the lake, the village Rado-nezhskoe, the village Deiguninskoe, the village Tylovskoe, Rogozh, the village Protasevskoe, the village Aristovskoe, the village Lopastenskoe, the village Mikhailovskoe on the Iauza [River, and] Kolomna villages. Also from town revenues I give my princess the *osmichee* [one-eighth], while my sons will share the *tamga* [taxes on trade] and other city revenues. My sons will also share revenues levied on transit trade which is collected in their respective countries. Likewise, my sons will share city taxes collected by the office of Vasilii [Veliaminov]. And concerning my beekeepers and purchased *obrok* [quitrent] tenants, these will belong to each of my sons on whose rolls they are listed. And if, because of my sins, the Tatars should demand certain *volosti*, and if they should take them away from you, my sons, and from my princess, then you will divide the remaining *volosti* in place of these [that have been taken away]. And my sons will jointly take care of the people listed [on Tatar tax rolls] and will divide among themselves my purchased people who are registered in the Great Roll.

To my daughter Fetinia I have given the [following] gold items that belonged to my princess Elena: fourteen rings and her mother's necklace [and] a new necklace which I [ordered to be] made. Also I gave her a headband and a neckchain. And gold which I have acquired, and that which God has given me, as well as a small gold box—these I have given to my princess and the small children.

And concerning my clothing [I divide it as follows]: to my son Semeon [I give] the crimson mantle with pearls and the gold crown; to my son Ivan [I give] the mantle of yellow silk and the large cloak with shoulder pieces; to my son Andrei [I give] the sable pelisse with a turned-down collar with large pearls and precious stones and woolen vestments with shoulder pieces.

And the two mantles with breastplates and pearls, which recently I have ordered to be made, I have given, along with a necklace, to my younger children, Mariia and Fedosiia. And my silver belts should be distributed among the priests. And my 100 *rubles* which Eska has should be distributed among the churches. And my remaining silver vessels should be divided among my sons and my princess. And my remaining clothes should be distributed among the priests and in Moscow. I give the larger platter with four rings to the [Cathedral of the] Holy Mother of God in Vladimir.

I have given a herd of livestock to my son Andrei and another one to [my son] Ivan. My other sons and my princess should divide my remaining livestock among themselves.

To my son Semeon, in addition to Moscow villages, I give [the following] villages which I purchased: the village Avakovskoe in Novgorod on the Ulala

[River] and another [village], Borisovskoe in Vladimir. To my son Ivan, I give [the following] villages which I purchased: Petrovskoe, Aleksinskoe, Vsedobrich, and Pavlovskoe on the Mas [River], half of which I purchased and half of which I acquired through exchange from the metropolitan, as well as the small villages on the Mas [River] which I purchased from Afenii. To my son Andrei I give [the following villages] which I purchased: Varvarskoe and Melovskoe near Iuriev, which I acquired in exchange for the Matveishchevskoe village. To my princess I give the village Pavlovskoe (which our grandmother purchased), a new little village which I purchased, and [the Monastery of] St. Alexander on the Kostroma [River].

And the village Bogoroditskoe, which I purchased in Rostov and gave to Boris Vorkov—that village should be his as long as he serves one of my sons. But if he should fail to serve my children, then they should take that village away from him.

And the little village on the Kerzhach [River], which I purchased from Abbot Prokofii, and another [village] Leontievskoe and a third [village] Sharapovskoe I give to [the Monastery of] St. Alexander for the memory of my soul.

My son Semeon! I charge you to be the guardian of your younger brothers and of my princess with small children. You will care for them in accordance with God's [commandments].

And may God judge him whomever violates this my last will. [The following] are the witnesses of this [will]: my spiritual father Efrem; my spiritual father Feodosii; and my spiritual father, the priest Davyd.

⚔ 34 ⚔

A Brief Biography of Prince Dmitrii Donskoi

The fame of Prince Dmitrii Ivanovich Donskoi rests on two achievements: his imposition, with the help of Moscow's church hierarchy, of authority over such Rus principalities as Suzdal, Vladimir, Riazan, and Tver; and

From *Polnoe Sobranie Russkikh Letopisei* (Complete Collection of Russian Chronicles), vol. 4, Part 1, as reprinted in *Anthology of Old Russian Literature*, edited by Ad. Stender-Petersen in Collaboration with Stefan Congrat-Butlar. (New York: Columbia University Press, 1954), pp. 231–234. Translation mine. Words in brackets are mine. Reprinted by permission of Columbia University Press.

his defeat, with the generous assistance of other Rus principalities, of Mongol-Tatar forces at Kulikovo Pole in September, 1380. With these two accomplishments Dmitrii established Moscow's hegemony over the northern and central principalities of Rus and thus it became the obvious center of national unification and consolidation. And his triumph over Mongol-Tatar forces set in motion the disintegration process of the once mighty Empire of the Golden Horde.

No one knows for certain who wrote this brief biography of Dmitrii Donskoi, although some scholars believe that it was Epifanii the Sage, author of two hagiographies of Muscovite saints: Stefan of Perm and Sergei of Radonezh. Some internal evidence indicates that in the beginning of the fifteenth century Moscow's rulers commissioned Dmitrii's biography in order to commemorate his triumph over Mongol-Tatar forces, glorify his ascetic virtues, and to reemphasize Moscow's leadership and hegemony over other Rus principalities.

This story concerns the life of Grand Prince Dmitrii [Donskoi, 1350–1389], son of an honorable and pious father, Grand Prince Ivan Ivanovich [II, 1353–1359] and his mother, Grand Princess Alexandra; grandson of Grand Prince Ivan Danilovich [Kalita, 1328–1341], the gatherer of Rus lands; and direct descendant of the saintly, God-appointed, and wonderful Prince Vladimir [the Great, 979–1015], the new Constantine, who baptized Rus. He [Dmitrii] also was a relative of Boris and Gleb in piety, glory, and all other activities which the Church has imposed and God has endorsed.

His father, Grand Prince Ivan Ivanovich, died when the young prince was nine years old. His younger brother, Prince Ivan Ivanovich [died in 1364]. His mother, Grand Princess Alexandra, served as Regent [until Dmitrii reached maturity]. Then she turned over to him the scepter of power over Rus, the burden of government of the Grand Principality which was his by God's grace, honor, and glory.

In his youth Dmitrii was very religious, never talked foolishly about trivia, and never used profane language. He stayed away from dishonest people and always tried to associate himself with well-meaning individuals. He always read the Holy Scriptures, listened to sermons, expressed deep concern for the well-being of churches, and had a high interest in the security of Rus. Intellectually, he was very astute. In battle he was greatly feared by the enemy and triumphed over many enemies who challenged him. [In 1365] he surrounded his famous city of Moscow with an unusual wall. He was well-known throughout the world and his influence grew like the cedars of Lebanon and flourished like date palm trees.

When he was sixteen years old he married Princess Evdokiia of Suzdal, daughter of Grand Prince Dmitrii Constantinovich [1306–1363] and Grand

Princess Anna. All Rus rejoiced over this marriage. After the marriage Dmitrii led a wise life, and, with genuine feelings, searched for salvation. He governed his earthly tsardom with a clear conscience and firm conviction. He also pledged full allegiance to the heavenly kingdom. In short, he was like a captain who sails his ship against a strong current being guided solely by the interests of higher authority. Like a prophet guarding God's plan, Dmitrii took care of his tsardom.

The fame of his name spread similarly, as did that of St. Vladimir the Great. During Dmitrii's reign, Rus territories increased the same way as did those of ancient Israel. He protected the entire territory of Rus by the resoluteness of his rule. His name was praised from East to West, from sea to sea, and from rivers to all corners of the world.

Other worldly rulers respected him whenever they heard his name. His enemies, and especially those who lived along the borders of Rus, were envious and feared him. They incited the mean Mamai [Khan of the Golden Horde] against him using the following argument: "Moscow's Grand Prince now calls himself Tsar of all Rus and claims that he is more famous than you and that his realm is greater than yours."

After he was advised by his cunning counselors on how to destroy the Christian faith and on how to create all sorts of hardships for Christians, Mamai gathered his princes and warriors and addressed them as follows: "I intend to conquer Rus, destroy their Christian churches, force them to adopt my faith, and compel them to owe allegiance to our Mohammed! And wherever their churches now stand I will erect mosques, will appoint my tax collectors in all cities of Rus, and will destroy all Rus princes. . . .

Before he advanced against Rus with his armies, the heathen Mamai dispatched there his *voevoda* [military commander], the damned [Murza] Begich, in charge of a large force that included many princes of the Orda [that is, Mamai's empire]. When Grand Prince Dmitrii Ivanovich learned about this invasion, he assembled a large and powerful force of Rus warriors, met the enemy in the Riazan territory and fought the pagans along the Vozha River. God and His Holy Mother helped Grand Prince Dmitrii Ivanovich, and the pagan descendants of Ishmael, son of Hagar, were humiliated. Some were killed; the rest fled. Grand Prince Dmitrii Ivanovich returned to [Moscow] in triumph after defending his Rus patrimony against pagan attacks.

The hideous Mamai was overwhelmed by shame because he gained dishonor instead of gaining glory. Consequently, [in 1380] he decided to invade Rus itself and although he congratulated Grand Prince Dmitrii Ivanovich [on his recent victory], his heart was filled with evil venom. When Grand Prince Dmitrii Ivanovich learned about Mamai's intentions, from the bottom of his heart, he appealed to God and to His Virgin Mother, saying: "Oh, Most

Holy Virgin Lady, Mother of God, Ruler, Protector, and Promoter of Peace! . . . The Most Holy Lady! Help us build defenses to protect us from this vicious enemy. Elevate your Christians above the heathen descendants of the son of Hagar and humiliate them forever."

Then he called upon his nobles and all princes of Rus who were under his jurisdiction. [And when they assembled in Moscow] he told them as follows: "Brothers! It would be better if all of us died for our Orthodox faith rather than allow pagans to occupy our cities, desecrate our holy churches, and permit them to scatter us throughout the world. We must not allow these pagans to take our wives and our children into slavery. The Virgin Mother of God will intercede with Her Son in our behalf."

The assembled Rus princes and nobles responded to this plea as follows: "Sovereign Tsar of Rus! We have resolved to sacrifice our lives in your service. We are prepared to shed our blood and, in this way, are ready to accept our second baptism!" Then they received Abraham [?], prayed to God and His assistant, St. Metropolitan Peter, the miracle worker and protector of Rus, and marched to meet the vicious pagan Mamai, similarly as the ancient Grand Prince Iaroslav Volodimirovich marched against [his brother] Sviatopolk [in 1015].

Dmitrii encountered Mamai in the Tatar-held territory along the Don River [that is, Kulikovo Pole]. They engaged in battle like two powerful storms, their shining weapons glittering like lightning during a storm. Warriors cut each other and many locked arms. Blood flowed down the valley and the water of the Don was mixed with blood. Tatar heads rolled around like boulders and the corpses of these heathens lay down like cut-down forest. Many faithful [Orthodox] warriors saw God's angels helping Christians. God and his saintly martyrs, Boris and Gleb, also assisted Grand Prince Dmitrii Ivanovich. The cursed Mamai escaped . . . and perished without a trace.

Grand Prince Dmitrii Ivanovich returned [to Moscow] in great triumph. . . . Thereafter peace prevailed throughout Rus. Dmitrii humiliated his enemy, and upon hearing of his victory, which God had granted him, other neighboring countries consented to come under his rule. Dmitrii punished dissenters and rebels [that is, those princes and nobles of Rus who had declined to join him].

* * *

I would like to add the following information about Dmitrii's life. Until his marriage he kept his body pure. He was fully dedicated to the church and the Holy Spirit. He always stared at the earth and the earth received him. In his soul and thoughts, however, he always believed in heaven, where doubtless he now has a pleasant place. Even after his marriage he continued to keep his body pure and did not live in sin. . . . He held the tsar's title with great dignity, led the life of an angel, fasted and prayed regularly, often stayed up the entire night, slept very little, said his prayers early in the morning and always tried to do good things without asking anything in return. He governed Rus well, sat on the tsarist throne with dignity and in his heart he kept it like a precious treasure. He carried his purple robe and crown well, even though he frequently wanted to dress in the attire of a monk. He received many honors from other worldly leaders, always wore a little cross around his neck, fasted on all holidays, received communion every Sunday, and in every way tried to preserve his pure soul for God. In short, he was an angel on earth as well as a man from heaven.

He spent twenty years with his Princess Evdokiia, two of those years in chastity. He had sons and daughters whom he brought up in piety. He ruled his patrimony, the Grand Principality, for twenty-nine years and six months. He died at the age of thirty-eight years and five months. He worked very hard and achieved many victories in behalf of the Orthodox faith. Few individuals can match his record.

Then he became ill and was very distressed. Subsequently, his health improved and the Grand Princess and their sons as well as his nobles rejoiced over his recovery. But then he suffered a relapse and became the victim of a greater affliction. His heart [beat] became irregular; it burst and he died. . . .

35

Zadonshchina

One of the most remarkable literary pieces of the early history of Muscovy is the narrative called *Zadonshchina*, or "Beyond the Don." The story commemorates a military victory of the forces of Muscovy and other principalities of Rus over their Mongol-Tatar overlords at Kulikovo Pole in September 1380. The Moscow-led forces were under the command

---

From S. Šambinago, *Povesti o Mamaevom poboishche* (Stories About Mamai's Defeat), (St. Petersburg: 1906), as reprinted in *Anthology of Old Russian Literature*, edited by Ad. Stender-Petersen in Collaboration with Stefan Congrat-Butlar. (New York: Columbia University Press, 1954), pp. 177–186. Translation mine. Words in brackets are mine. Reprinted by permission of Columbia University Press.

of Prince Dmitrii Ivanovich (1359–1389), subsequently known as Donskoi. The Mongol-Tatar armies were led by Mamai, Khan of the Golden Horde. Each side lost many men in the battle. Dmitrii triumphed because Mamai fled the battlefield, leaving behind all of his personal possessions, and because Dmitrii was ably assisted by many other Rus princes.

The battle of Kulikovo Pole, which forms the central theme of *Zadonshchina*, was important for two reasons. It was the first decisive triumph by Rus forces over their Mongol-Tatar overlords. And the victory proved that, if united, Rus forces were capable of defeating their hitherto invincible masters. There is no doubt that this victory propelled Muscovy to a hegemonic position over other principalities of Rus, leading the Muscovite author of *Zadonshchina* to extol the triumph. The author of this glorification was a certain Sofonii of Riazan who used the example of *The Tale of the Host of Igor* to create poetic imagery, metaphors, symbolic parallelisms, and lamentations, and to deplore the cruelty of war. Because *Zadonshchina* was an instant success, several versions of it appeared.

Brothers! Friends! Sons of Russia! Let us gather and compose a poem. Let us enliven the Russian land and inflict a major humiliation on an oriental country! Let us triumph over the mean Tsar Mamai [ruler of the Golden Horde]. And let us bring glory to our Grand Prince Dmitrii Ivanovich [1359-1389] and to his cousin [Prince] Vladimir [of Serpukhov].

We also should say as follows: Brothers! It would be best if we could begin our panegyric by focusing on contemporary events, on the military exploits of Grand Prince Dmitrii Ivanovich and his cousin Prince Vladimir Ivanovich, descendants of [Prince] Vladimir of Kiev. We will base our story on facts and on the *byliny* [legends]. Still in our thoughts we will soar over our land and will recall our beginnings and will praise Kiev's prophetic *boian* [the mythical bard of *The Tale of Igor*]. That prophetic *boian* placed his golden fingers on the live strings and sang glory to such Russian princes as: Riurik, Igor Riurikovich, Vladimir Sviatoslavich, and Iaroslav Vladimirovich.

In this story we must mention Grand Prince Dmitrii Ivanovich and his cousin [Prince] Vladimir Andreevich, descendants of St. Vladimir, Prince of Kiev. We will glorify and praise all of them in song and in boisterous musical compositions, because they were brave and because they defended the Russian land and [Orthodox] Christianity [from foreign enemies].

Grand Prince Dmitrii Ivanovich and his cousin Prince Vladimir Andreevich resolved to meet the challenge. They emboldened their hearts, excited the military spirit, appointed brave *voevody* [military commanders] throughout Russian territories, and recalled their great ancestor Grand Prince Vladimir of Kiev. On a beautiful day they also released a sky lark to soar underneath the blue heavens to sing glory to Grand Prince Dmitrii Ivanovich and his cousin Vladimir Andreevich. A storm brought the sky lark from the Principality of Zalesk to the Polovtsian prairie.

Horses neigh in Moscow, drums beat in Kolomna, trumpets sound in Serpukhov! Glory resounds throughout the Russian land! . . . Warriors of Novgorod have gathered in St. Sophia and have declared: "Brothers! The time has come for us to go and help Grand Prince Dmitrii Ivanovich however we can!" It appeared that all the eagles had descended from the north. But these were not eagles. They were Russian princes who came to assist Grand Prince Dmitrii Ivanovich. And they said: "Lord! Grand Prince! The heathen Tatars are attacking our territories and are seizing our patrimonies. They are encamped between the Don and the Dnieper Rivers, along the Mecha River, which they want to ford. We are ready to sacrifice our lives for our glory!"

Then Grand Prince Dmitrii Ivanovich said to his cousin Prince Vladimir Andreevich: "Cousin! Let us advance beyond the swift Don. Let us quickly seize the territory, revive the old story, do something for the young to remember, test our brave men and shed our blood for Russian land beyond the Don, and for the Christian faith."

Then Grand Prince Dmitrii Ivanovich addressed his brothers, the Russian princes: "My dear brothers! Russian princes! Our common roots go to Prince Vladimir of Kiev. We were not born to be abused either by the eagle, or the hawk, or a black raven, or that mean dog Mamai. You, noble birds! Praise the two brothers, two sons of Olgert [Grand Prince of Lithuania, 1341–1377], Andrei of Polotsk [brother-in-law of Prince Vladimir of Serpukhov] and Dmitrii of Briansk [Andrei's brother]. These two men are brave. They were born nobles, were swaddled under trumpets, were brought up in chivalry, and were nourished by the tips of their lances and the sharp blades of their Lithuanian-made swords."

Then Andrei said to his cousin Dmitrii: "Yes, we are brothers, sons of Olgert, grandsons of Gedymin [1316–1341], and great-grandsons of Skoldimir [a mythical prince of Lithuania]. Brother [Cousin]! Let us gather a good military force. Let us then mount our quick horses, watch the swift flowing Don, use our helmets to taste its waters, and test our Lithuanian swords on Tatar helmets and our German-made lances on the chain armor of the Mohammedan foe!"

Then Dmitrii responded as follows: "Brother [Cousin]! Let us sacrifice our lives for the Russian land and for the Christian faith! Let us avenge the insult directed against Grand Prince Dmitrii Ivanovich! Brother [Cousin]! Let us not forget a sound is being heard and thunder is resounding in the famed city of Moscow. The mighty force of Grand Prince Dmitrii Ivanovich is restless. Valiant Russian men are pounding on their helmets and shields, anxious to gain new victories. Cousin Andrei! Ready your swift horses! Mine are ready. They were saddled ahead of yours. Cousin! Let us ride out to the wide steppe and review our forces.

* * *

Then a strong wind began to blow from the sea and brought with it a great storm to the mouth of the Dnieper River and to the Russian land. From that storm emerged blood-covered stars, and around them flashed lightning. Great noise and thunder resounded between the Don and the Dnieper. Many humans fell on the plain of Kulikovo Pole. Much blood was shed on the Nepriadva River. Tatar wagons moved between the Don and the Dnieper. The Huns [actually the Tatars] advanced against the Russian land. Gray wolves sneaked from the estuaries of the Don and the Dnieper rivers. But they were not gray wolves. They were pagan Tatars who wanted to conquer the entire Russian land. Then wild geese hissed and swans flapped their wings. But those geese were not hissing nor were those swans flapping their wings. Those were pagan warriors whom Mamai had brought to Rus. Before any misfortune, birds fly to the clouds, crows frequently caw, daws chatter in their way, eagles shriek, wolves howl, and foxes bark for prey. Oh, land! Russian land! A roof has fallen in on you!

Then from their golden perches, hawks, eagles, and white gerfalcons flew away. They shattered their cages made of silk, flew beneath the blue heavens and, above the swift-flowing Don; using their golden bells they sounded an alarm in order to strike the many flocks of geese and swans. Russian warriors, too, would like to challenge the mighty forces of the mean Tsar Mamai.

Then Grand Prince Dmitrii Ivanovich mounted his horse, put a sword in his right hand, and said a prayer to God and to His Virgin Mother. The sun radiated on him from the east and showed him the way, while Boris and Gleb prayed for their descendants. What is that noise? What is that thunder about, so early in the morning? Prince Vladimir Andreevich is reviewing his forces and is leading them to the swift-flowing Don saying: "My Lord, Prince Dmitrii! Do not yield to the pagan Tatars even though they are advancing."

Then Prince Dmitrii Ivanovich said to his cousin Prince Vladimir Andreevich: "Dear cousin! We are cousins and have descended from Grand Prince Ivan Danilovich [Kalita, 1325–1341]. . . . Our *voevody* are very firm and their forces are experienced. They have swift horses and they are veterans of many successful campaigns. Moreover, they have breast plates made of steel chain, Cherkessian helmets, Muscovite-made shields, Frankish lances, and Syrian daggers. They are familiar with the terrain and their transport and supplies are in place. They want only to sacrifice their lives for the Russian land and for Christianity. These living banners are waving and are seeking honor and due respect."

* * *

And so the hawks, the eagles and the white gerfalcons swiftly flew beyond the Don to attack the many flocks of [invading] geese and swans. Actually, they were neither eagles nor gerfalcons. They were the advancing Russian princes and the courageous Lithuanian warriors, who moved the powerful Tatar forces and struck their steel lances against Tatar armor. Then [Russian] steel swords struck the helmets of the Khan's warriors at Kulikovo Pole along the Nepriadva River.

Violent storms have gathered at Kulikovo Pole along the Nepriadva River and have produced strong lightning flashes and loud thunder. Under those conditions you, Russian sons, have encountered mean Tatars, have gained a great victory and have avenged past humiliations. The Russians' gilded armor glittered and their steel swords resounded as they struck the helmets of the Khan's warriors.

* * *

Early in the morning the powerful Rus *voevody* did not see any aurochs in the meadow of Kulikovo Pole, near the mighty Don. Instead they saw dead warriors of Grand Prince Dmitrii Ivanovich who had been killed by the vile Tatars. Russian authorities brought in a monk named [Alexander] Peresvet, a former *boyar* from Briansk. And Peresvet told Grand Prince Dmitrii Ivanovich: "It would be better for all of us to perish than to be captives of the vile Tatars." Then the brave Peresvet galloped across the meadow on his magic white horse telling everyone: "Brothers! Now is the time for all old men to get young and for all young men to gain honor and to test their backs!"

Then [Roman] Oslab [a *boyar* from Briansk who, with Peresvet resided at the Trinity Monastery near Moscow] told his brother Peresvet: "Brother! I see serious wounds on your body. Lay your head on the grass of the gray soil of this steppe so that a descendant of Jacob can be buried in the steppe at Kulikovo Pole along the Nepriadva River, having died for the Russian land and to avenge the affront directed against Grand Prince Dmitrii Ivanovich."

At that time no one heard any trumpets sound or plowmen shout any alarm in the Principality of Riazan. Only the crows cawed and the cuckoos cuckooed in the expectation of human corpses. It was very painful and sad to witness this, especially since the grass was covered with blood and since even the trees were bent down as if overwhelmed by grief.

* * *

Then all birds sang a sorrowful song and all princesses, and the wives of *boyars* and *voevody* [cried for their husbands who had been killed]. Mariia, wife of *voevoda* Mikula Vasilevich, cried early in the morning on the ramparts of Moscow, saying: "Oh, Don! You swift Don! You, who have cut through rocky mountains; you who have pierced through iron banks; you who have crossed the Polovtsian territory, [please] bring my lord, Mikula Vasilevich, back to me!"

And Feodosiia, wife of Timofei Valuevich, as well as Mariia, wife of Dmitrii Vsevolozhskii, also lamented, saying: "Our good life in the great city of Moscow has come to a sudden end and we will never see again our masters alive!" And Mariia, wife of Andrei, and Xenia, wife of Michael, also lamented saying: "The sun has set for both of us in the famous city of Moscow. Sad news has come from the swift River Don about our relatives, and has brought us great sorrow. Our knights have dismounted [for the last time] from their swift horses on the fateful plain of Kulikovo Pole along the swift Don." . . .

On the ramparts of the city of Kolomna, their women too lamented for their dead and, looking at the swift-flowing and glorious Moscow River, said: "Moscow! Swift River Moscow! Why have you taken our husbands away to the Polovtsian territory? Sovereign Grand Prince Dmitrii Ivanovich! Why can't you close the Dnieper River with your fleet? Why can't you dam the Don, using Tatar corpses? Sovereign! Also dam the Oka River so that henceforth the vile Tatars will never come or bother us on behalf of their rulers, since now our military strength is formidable."

On Saturday [September 8, 1380], the anniversary commemorating the birth of the Holy Mother of God, Christian forces defeated vile Tatar forces at Kulikovo Pole along the Nepriadva River. Wearing his gilded helmet as he galloped through the defeated mean Tatar forces, Prince Vladimir Andreevich exhorted [his warriors] to strike their steel swords against the helmets of the *khan's* men.

Prince Dmitrii [Mikhailovich of Bobrok] in Volyn [who, with his emigre forces joined Grand Prince Dmitrii of Moscow and thus helped to turn the tide of the battle] praised Prince Vladimir Andreevich in these words: "You were a shield of iron in this critical time of peril." Prince Vladimir Andreevich responded to Prince Dmitrii of Volyn as follows: "Do not leave your forces because mean Tatars are on the move again and have already killed many of our brave men. . . ."

Then Dmitrii of Volyn said: "Brothers! Russian princes, *boyars* and *voevody*. Here is the place and the time for all old men to become young and for the young to gain fame and glory! This is not the place to sample Moscow's sweet honey. It is a place to gain honor and fame!" And after he had said these words it seemed that all the falcons flew away. Then Prince Dmitrii of Volyn charged with all of his forces, saying: "Cousin! Prince Vladimir Andreevich! Now is the time to drink a cup of mead! Cousin! Let our strong forces attack the vile Tatar armies!"

And then Prince Vladimir Andreevich attacked a strong Tatar force. Steel swords struck the helmets of the Khan's warriors. Dirty Moslems used their hands to cover their faces [in shame]. Russian forces surrounded the wide meadow and attained a glorious victory. It appeared that even the aurochs participated in the battle.

Under the horses' hooves the black earth was covered with Tatar corpses and was drenched with their blood. Powerful [Russian] units moved into position and occupied the adjacent hills and meadows. Even rivers, their tributaries and near-by lakes were affected. The Div [demon bird] informed all animals of the world, including the vicious ones, to hear the news. The news of the victory spread quickly to the sea shore, to the Iron Gate [on the Danube], to Rome, to Tirnovo [capital of Medieval Bulgaria], to Kaffa [the ancient name of Theodosia, center of Italian trade in Crimea], and to Tsargrad [Constantinople], that Rus had defeated the vile Tatars. Then the vile Tatars fled. Some took the untrodden trails to the sea shore, while others, grinding their teeth and covering their faces with their hands, said: "Brothers! We will never return to our homes, will never [again] see our wives and our children and will never [again] attack Rus with our military forces or ask Russian princes to pay tribute to us."

Currently the Tatar state is experiencing great misfortune and grief. Their rulers will never [again] be able to gain fame and glory by attacking Russian land. Now, Russian sons have plundered Tatar wealth. They have brought home [Tatar] horses, camels, damask, satin, silver, gold, strong armor, and select pearls. Now Russian women can display Tatar gold. Throughout the Russian land there is both celebration and bewilderment in glorifying Russian triumph over the heathens. The firm rule of Grand Prince has now spread over the entire land. When Russian princes and strong *voevody* drove away the nasty enemy forces, the enemy threw down their weapons and bowed their heads to Russian swords.

* * *

Grand Prince Dmitrii Ivanovich, his cousin Prince Vladimir Andreevich, and other *voevody* stopped and surveyed battle casualties at Kulikovo Pole along the Nepriadva River. Brothers! It is both terrible and sad to view these casualties! Here along the mighty Don lie Christian corpses like blue hay stacks. For three days the Don flowed with blood.

Then Grand Prince Dmitrii Ivanovich said: "Brothers! Princes! *Boyars* and *deti boyarskie* [petty nobles]! Fate has destined for you a place between the Don and the Dnieper at Kulikovo Pole along the Nepriadva River. You have sacrificed your lives for the Holy Church, for the Russian land, and for Christianity! Brothers! Forgive me now and in the future. My cousin, Prince Vladimir Andreevich! Let us go now to your principality of Zalesk and to my illustrious Moscow and let us resume our reigns in our respective principalities. My Cousin! We have gained honor and fame for ourselves. Glory be to our God!''

☩ 36 ☩

A Journey from Moscow to Constantinople in 1389

Mongol conquest of Rus forced many principalities into the political and economic "orbit" of the Great Mongol Empire. Only Novgorod, Pskov, and several lesser principalities in western regions of the former Kievan realm escaped the new orientation. Culturally, however, all principalities continued to maintain their association with Constantinople. The prime link of this association was the Orthodox Church, which periodically sent its metropolitans first to Kiev, then to Vladimir, and, from the reign of Ivan Kalita on, to Moscow. Since Vladimir and Moscow were close to the Don, that river served as the main avenue of travel in the long and hazardous journey to and from Constantinople.

That spring [1389] Metropolitan Pimin journeyed to Constantinople for the third time to see the Patriarch. He was accompanied by Michael, the Bishop of Smolensk, Sergei, the Archimandrite of the Church of Our Savior, monks, servants, an archpriest, and archdeacon, and other priests and deacons. The journey originated in Moscow on April 13, which was Tuesday of the Holy Week. Grand Prince Dmitrii Ivanovich [Donskoi] was angry with the Metropolitan because the latter left [Moscow] without his knowledge. There was some sort of disagreement between them.

And so commenced the journey. Metropolitan Pimin suggested to Michael, the Bishop of Smolensk, and to Sergei, the Archimandrite of the Church of Our Savior, and to everyone [who accompanied him to Constantinople] that they describe the journey—how we travelled, what happened and where, and who would or who would not return. And so, I, [Ignatii] decided to describe [our journey].

From *Polnoe Sobranie Russkikh Letopisei* (Complete Collection of Russian Chronicles) (St. Petersburg: 1897), vol. XI, pp. 95–101. Translation mine. Words in brackets are mine.

As noted above, we departed from Moscow [on April 13] and we reached Kolomna on Holy Saturday [April 17]. On Easter [Sunday] we departed for Riazan along the Oka River and reached the city of Perevitsk. When we approached the city of Pereiaslavl [-Riazanskii] we were met there by the sons of Grand Prince Oleg Ivanovich of Riazan. And when they had departed and we had travelled a bit further, Grand Prince Oleg Ivanovich himself, his children, and his *boyars*, met us with great joy. When we approached the city of Pereiaslavl [-Riazanskii] a solemn procession carrying crosses met us. The Metropolitan went straight to the Cathedral to celebrate the *Te Deum* and then we feasted at [the court of] the Grand Prince, where we were treated with great respect. He [the Grand Prince] and his bishop, Jeremiah the Greek, honored us constantly. When we resumed our journey, Grand Prince Oleg Ivanovich of Riazan, his children, and his *boyars*, accompanied us for a while with great honor and respect. Then when we parted we kissed each other. He [Grand Prince Oleg] returned to his capital and we continued on our journey. The Prince of Riazan sent Stanislav, one of his *boyars*, with sufficient military retinue to accompany us to the Don River on account of the great danger from [highway] robbers. We also were accompanied by many bishops: Feodor of Rostov, Efrosin of Suzdal, Jeremiah the Greek, the Bishop of Zvenigorod, the archimandrites, the *igumens,* and monks.

We left Pereiaslavl-Riazanskii on Sunday [April 25, 1389]. They gave us three small river boats that were carried overland on wheel carts. We reached the Don River on Thursday [April 29] and put the boats onto the water. Next day we reached the Mikhailov Chiur [the boundary of Riazan Principality], where once had stood a town. Here we comforted one another, kissed each other, and with great emotion and feeling we parted with the bishops, the archimandrites, the *igumens,* the priests, the monks, and the *boyars* of Prince Oleg Ivanovich of Riazan. We all kissed the Holy Bible and they returned to their homes.

We resumed our journey on Sunday [May 2]. . . . The journey was mournful and dismal. Everywhere prevailed a desert-type [environment]. We did not see anything—neither cities nor villages. Yet, in the years gone by beautiful and well-populated towns had been located there. Now everything was deserted. No people could be seen anywhere—just one empty space. There were many animals, however, such as goats, elks, wolves, foxes, martens, bears, [and] beavers [and such] birds as eagles, swans, cranes, and others. But emptiness reigned everywhere.

On the second day of our journey on the [Don] River we passed two of its tributaries, the Mecha and the Sosna, while on the third day we sailed by the Ostraia Luka. On the fourth day, we passed the Krivoi Bor and on the sixth day we reached the mouth of the Voronezh River. The next day, which was a Sunday [May 9], Prince Iurii of Elets, his *boyars,* and many of his people, met us. Prince Oleg Ivanovich of Riazan had informed him through a messenger of our coming. He fulfilled the request by welcoming us and by creating for us great joy and happiness.

From here we sailed to Tikhaia Sosna, where we saw the white stone pillars. They stand there in a row mysteriously and beautifully. The small pillars on the Sosna River were white and very bright. We then passed the Chervlenyi Iar, the Betiuk, and the Porokh Rivers. On the fifth Sunday [since our departure from Moscow] we passed the Medveditsa and the Belyi Iar Rivers.

On Monday [May 17] we sailed between very beautiful stone hills and on Tuesday we passed the city of Terkli. Now it is not a city but a small town. Then we passed the Perevoz, where for the first time we saw the Tatars. There was a great multitude of them—like foxes and dogs.

On Wednesday [May 19] we sailed by the Velikaia Luka and the *ulus* [a nomad village] belonging to the reigning *khan.* Here for the first time we became frightened because we entered into the Tatar domains. There was a multitude of Tatars on both banks of the Don River—like dogs. On Thursday [May 20] we passed by the *ulus* belonging to Bek-Bulatov [Bulat Bei]. There we saw such great herds of Tatar livestock that it is very difficult to comprehend: sheep, goats, oxen, camels, and horses. Then, on Friday [May 21] we passed the Chervlenye Hills and on the sixth Sunday [since the departure from Moscow] we sailed past the *ulus* of Ak-Bushinov, where we saw a great many Tatars and their countless livestock. The Tatars did not bother us; they only asked us where we were going, and when we answered to their satisfaction they caused us no harm. They gave us milk and we sailed on in peace and solitude.

On Monday [May 24] we passed the Buzan River, and in the evening, in our attempt to reach the sea, we arrived at the city of Azov. On Sunday [May 30], just below the city of Azov we boarded a ship at the mouth of the Don River. At that time Italians lived in and controlled the city of Azov. We sailed out to the Sea [of Azov]. It was about midnight. The ship was [then] anchored. Someone in town spread rumors about us among the Italians. The Italians sailed in boats, caught up with us, and swiftly boarded our ship. There was a noisy stamping on the deck of our ship. I did not know what it was. I went to the deck and I saw there a great commotion. The bishop then said to me: "Brother Ignatii, how can you stand there without showing any grief?" I replied: "What is this all about, my reverend Lord?" And he told me. "These are the Italians who came here from the city of Azov. They arrested our Lord Metropolitan Pimin, put him in chains, and they did the same to Archpriest Ivan, Archdeacons Grigorii and Ghermann, and Secretary Michael. All these [people] contracted some debts with them and we will have to suffer with them even though we are innocent." We then asked an elder of these Italians what they were going to do with us. And he replied: "Do not fear; what belongs to you, you can take with you." Subsequently Metropolitan Pimin satisfied their [the Italians'] demands, and when they had received sufficient payment in money they released everybody without any harm. There we spent one day, and on the following day we put to sea.

At first the wind was very favorable and we sailed happily and were quite jubilant. Then, on the third day of our journey a strong head wind began to blow and because the ship rocked very heavily we all became sea sick. [The storm was so severe that] even the ship's crew could not stand up. The wind blew some of the men down [on the deck] and some walked as if they were drunk. Then we crossed the mouth of the Sea of Azov [the Straits of Kerch] and sailed into the great sea [the Black Sea]. On the sixth day, which was Saturday, we sailed past the Bay of Kaffa [present-day Theodosia], and Surozh [Sudak]. We sailed peacefully for the next four days: Sunday, Monday, Tuesday, and Wednesday. On Thursday a strong head wind began to blow again and forced us to sail to our left in the direction of the city of Sinope. [Actually] we anchored in a bay near Sinope. Some people in Sinope saw our distress; they came to meet us, brought us food and wine and treated us very well. We stayed there for two days. Then a favorable sailing wind began to blow again; we put to the sea but sailed close to the shore. Along the way we saw high mountains, half of which were covered by clouds. From here we sailed a short distance toward the city of Amastris and ate meat for the last time before the fast of St. John the Baptist [June 14]. On Tuesday we sailed past [the town of] Pandoraclia and on the following day we again encountered a strong head wind that forced us to anchor in Pandoraclia. There we stayed for nine days. . . .

We resumed our journey to Constantinople on St. John the Baptist's Day [June 24]. On the following day, Friday, we sailed past the city of Diopolis; on Saturday we ate our dinner at the mouth of the Sakhara [Sangarius] River; on Sunday we passed the fortresses of Daphnusium and Karfa. Then we came to the city of Astrava, where we stopped and where we learned that the Turkish Tsar Murad [I, (1359–1389)] had gone to war against Lazar, the Tsar of Serbia. . . .

Fearing an [anti-Christian] insurrection [in the aftermath of the battle of Kosovo], Metropolitan Pimin allowed the Monk Michael to proceed to Constantinople. Michael, the Bishop of Smolensk, gave me, Ignatii, permission; while the Archimandrite Sergei Azakov permitted one of his monks to go along. We left the city of Astrava on Sunday [June 27]. Next day we sailed past Phila and Riva and reached the Straits of Bosphorus. We then passed the Lighthouse and with a very favorable wind we reached Constantinople on the eve of St. Peter's Day [June 29]. Our joy was boundless. At Vespers the Rus people who live there [in Constantinople] visited us and both they as we were very happy. . . .

Then, the Most Reverend Metropolitan Pimin became ill and on September 11 [1389] died in [the city of] Chalcedon. They brought his remains to Constantinople and laid them to [eternal] rest in the Church of St. John the Baptist, located along the shores of the sea in the section [of Constantinople] called Galata. At that time the Metropolitan of Kiev, Kiprian, was in Constantinople to resolve [with the Patriarch] who should head the Rus See. When he was still alive Metropolitan Pimin had visited Patriarch Antony [1388–1390] for the same purpose. God helped to resolve the problem. As noted above, Metropolitan Pimin died and Patriarch Antony consecrated Kiprian as Metropolitan of Kiev and of all Rus and sent him [to his new post] with great honors.

He left Constantinople on October 1 [1389]. He was accompanied by Michael, the Bishop of Smolensk, Iona, the Bishop of Volyn, two Greek Metropolitans, and Feodor, the Archimandrite of Simonov and the Confessor of the Grand Prince [Dmitrii Donskoi]. Shortly after they departed, news came to the effect that "the Rus party sank at sea and only one ship carrying the Metropolitan was saved; the ship carrying the bishops disappeared without any trace." Some [people] said that they all drowned; others thought that they were killed by pirates; still others thought that the heavy storm tossed them to Amastris; and some thought that they were in Daphnusium. Then, a few days later a message came from Kiprian, the Metropolitan of all Rus. In it he spoke of great suffering from sea travel, of a tortuous trip, of thunder and noise, of lightning and of great sea waves that brought their souls perilously close to death. The great winds and the storm had separated their ships and they did not know of each other's whereabouts. [Kiprian's message concluded] "Thanks to God's grace the storm subsided, the sea became very calm, and slowly we all gathered in Belgorod [Akkerman] safe and sound."

⚔ *37* ⚔

Nestor-Iskander's
Tale *of the Capture*
of Constantinople, 1453

Turkish capture of Constantinople in 1453 was a momentous historical event. It terminated the millennium-old Byzantine Empire. It finalized Turkish control of the Balkan peninsula, the Black and the Aegean Seas, and the Eastern Mediterranean. It forced many Byzantine and Balkan refugees to seek asylum in Italy (where they contributed to the growth of the Renaissance) and in Muscovy (where they helped to strengthen its autocracy). Finally, Constantinople's fall to the Turks made it possible for Moscow to claim that it was the political and religious heir of Byzantium and Rome.

The earliest sign of that claim appeared in *Tale,* which was written by a certain Nestor-Iskander shortly after the Turkish capture of Constantinople. All evidence indicates that he was of Slavic, Orthodox background but, for whatever reasons, became a convert to Islam and took an active part in the capture of Constantinople. His account provides a lengthy historical background of the city and a colorful description of its final days as the imperial capital and the center of Orthodox Christianity.

At the conclusion of his story, Nestor-Iskander cites an old Byzantine "prophesy" which held that one day in the future the *rhusios* people would become masters of Constantinople. In Greek the term *rhusios* means "red-haired." The Russians interpreted it differently. To them it was *russkii,* that is, Russian. This "prophesy" soon led to development of the idea that Moscow was the Third Rome and hence the legitimate heir not only to Byzantine but to Roman traditions and greatness. Indeed, Moscow's rulers soon listed among their many titles that they were "descendants of Caesar Augustus, ruler of the entire universe."

The godless [Sultan] Mohammed [II, 1451–1481], son of Murad [II,

---

From Archimandrite Leonid, ed., *Pamiatniki drevnei pismennosti i iskustva* (Sources on Ancient Literature and Art) (St. Petersburg: 1886), vol. LXII, as reprinted in *Anthology of Old Russian Literature,* edited by Ad. Stender-Petersen in Collaboration with Stefan Congrat-Butlar. (New York: Columbia University Press, 1954), pp. 243–249. Translation mine. Words in brackets are mine. Reprinted by permission of Columbia University Press.

1421–1451], who at that time ruled the Turks, took note of all the problems [that plagued Constantinople]. And, although he professed peace, he wanted to put an end to Emperor Constantine [XI, 1449–1453]. Towards that end he assembled a large army and, by land and by sea, suddenly appeared with that large force before the city [of Constantinople] and laid siege to it. The Emperor, his nobles, and the rest of the population did not know what to do at first, because no public meeting was called and because the Emperor's brothers were not present. [The Emperor], therefore, sent his envoys to Sultan Mohammed in order to discuss peace and past [relations]. But Mohammed did not trust them, and as soon as the envoys departed, he ordered cannons and guns to fire at the city. Others were commanded to make ready wall-scaling equipment and build assault structures. Such city inhabitants as Greek, Venetian, and Genoese [mercenaries] left because they did not want to fight the Turks. . . .

When the Emperor saw this [exodus], he ordered his nobles and high officials to assign the remaining soldiers to each sector of the city's wall, to main gates, and to windows. The entire population was mobilized and alarm bells were hoisted throughout the city. Each person was informed of his assignment and each was told to defend his country. All were organized into a fighting force to battle the Turks from city walls and no one was allowed to leave the city. They also placed cannons and guns in strategic places to defend city walls. The Emperor, the Patriarch, bishops, priests, and the entire church council, as well as a multitude of women and children, attended church service, where they prayed, cried, and lamented. . . . The Emperor frequently travelled around the city, encouraging his military leaders, soldiers, and all inhabitants, telling them to have faith, not to allow themselves to be disheartened by enemy pressure, and to trust Almighty God, their Savior and Protector. He also implored them to pray. Meanwhile, day and night, the Turks bombarded all parts of the city without stopping, and gave its defenders no time to rest. They also made preparations for the final assault. This activity went on for thirteen days.

On the fourteenth day, after they had said their heathen prayers, the Turks sounded trumpets, beat their drums, and played on all other of their musical instruments. Then they brought many cannons and guns [closer to the walls] and began to bombard the city. They also fired their muskets and thousands of arrows. Because of continued heavy shooting, city defenders could not stand safely on the wall. Some crouched down awaiting the attack; others fired their cannons and guns as much as they could, killing many Turks. The Patriarch, bishops, and all clergy prayed constantly, pleading for God's mercy and for [His help in] saving the city.

When the Turks surmised that they had killed all the defenders on the wall, they ordered their forces to give a loud shout [before the assault]. Some soldiers carried incendiary devices, others ladders, still others wall-destroying equipment, and the rest many other instruments of destruction. They were ordered to attack and capture the city. City defenders, too, cried out and shouted back and engaged them in a fierce battle. The Emperor toured the city, encouraging his people, promising them God's help and ordering the ringing of church bells so as to summon all the inhabitants [to defend their city]. When the Turks heard the ringing of church bells, they ordered their trumpets, flutes, and thousands of other musical instruments to sound out. And there was a great and terrible slaughter! . . .

When Mohammed saw such a multitude of his men killed, and when he was told of Emperor's bravery, he could not sleep. [On May 27, 1453] he called in his Council and informed them that he wanted to lift the siege that night, before a large [Papal] fleet arrived in the city to reinforce [its defenses]. But then there appeared an unexpected miracle of God! The anticipated [Papal] help failed to materialize. Instead, at 7:00 p.m. that evening the entire city was suddenly engulfed by a great darkness. The air suddenly thickened and, in a moaning way, it hovered above the city. Then, big black drops of rain, as large as the eye of a buffalo, began to fall. People were shocked and horrified by this unusual occurrence. Patriarch Athanasius gathered all of his clergy and members of the Imperial Council, went to the Emperor, and told him the following: "Your Illustrious Majesty! All citizens of the city believe in its vitality. But they also think that the Holy Spirit has abandoned it. Now every living creature is foretelling the demise of this city. We beseech you to leave the city. All of us will perish here. For God's sake, please leave!". . . The Emperor did not listen to them. He replied instead: "Let God's will be done!"

When he saw that the great darkness engulfed the city, the impious Mohammed called in his learned men and dignitaries and asked them to explain: "What is the meaning of the sudden darkness that descended upon the city?" And they replied: "This is an important sign portending the demise of the city." Being a godless person, he then ordered that his entire force be ready for a new attack and informed his military commanders that the attack [was to] be spearheaded by thousands of foot soldiers, followed by cannons, guns, and the rest of his army.

Deploying all of these forces they [the Turks] concentrated their assault on the Poloe Mesto [the Lycus Valley?]. When city defenders retreated from the Poloe Mesto, Turkish foot soldiers hurriedly cleared the way for other units to advance [inside the city]. Turkish units broke through and their light cavalry units overwhelmed city defenders. All city inhabitants came to the rescue of city commanders, dignitaries, and the regular forces, and they [inhabitants] engaged the Turks. The Emperor joined the battle with all of his nobles, his special cavalry units, and his foot soldiers. They attacked the invading Turks inside the city, engaged them in fierce hand-to-hand combat, and drove them away from the Poloe Mesto.

[At that moment] a Turkish military governor, whose large force was deployed on the eastern flank, attacked the Greeks. His action divided Greek forces and forced them to retreat. He even captured their standards and advanced against the Emperor. The Emperor positioned his shield in a defensive position, knocked out [the Turk's] lance, and struck and cut off the enemy's head with his sword. When Turkish soldiers saw this they were shocked and carried away the corpse of their dead leader. Meanwhile, the Emperor encouraged all city inhabitants to join the battle, which they did, and they fought and drove the enemy from the city.

But then Pasha Karach-bey assembled a very large force with which he advanced towards the Poloe Mesto. His forces entered the city and compelled the Emperor and all defenders to retreat. The Emperor thanked his military commanders, officials, and nobles, as well as his people [for their sacrifices]. He also gave them additional encouragement. Then he attacked the Turks and, disregarding his personal safety, drove them away from the city. . . .

When Mohammed learned about the death of his eastern military commander, he wept profusely because he admired the commander's bravery and wisdom. He also became very angry and led all of his forces to the Sublime Porte. He ordered that the Emperor's positions be bombarded with cannons and guns, being concerned that the Emperor's forces might attack him. Then, the godless [Mohammed] appeared opposite the Poloe Mesto and ordered his forces to fire cannons and guns at defenders in order to induce them to retreat. He also instructed [Turkish Admiral] Balta-Oghlu, in charge of many regiments and a select force of 3000, to capture the Emperor dead or alive.

When they noticed the determination of the godless [Mohammed], [the Byzantine] military commanders, officials, and nobles joined the battle and implored the Emperor to leave in order to escape death. He wept bitterly and told them: "Remember the words I said earlier! Do not try to protect me! I want to die with you!" And they replied: "All of us will die for God's church and for you!"

Then they escorted him to [relative] safety and many people told him to leave the city. After they pledged their allegiance to him, they lamented and cried and returned to their posts. Meanwhile, Balta-Oghlu approached the city with a large force. [Byzantine] military commanders met him at the Poloe Mesto but were unable to stop him. His units entered the city and attacked the inhabitants. There was fierce fighting, more vicious than all previous encounters. Many [Byzantine] military commanders, officials, and nobles perished and the few who survived went to the Emperor to report to him about the disaster. There is no way to give an accurate number of Byzantine and Turkish casualties. The select Turkish force of 3000, like wild animals, dispersed and searched all corners of the city in an effort to capture the Emperor.

The impious Mohammed then ordered all of his forces to occupy all city streets and gates in order to capture the Emperor. In his camp he retained only the Janissaries, who readied their cannons and guns in fear of a sudden attack by the Emperor. Sensing God's command, the Emperor went to the Great Church [St. Sophia?], where he fell to the ground pleading for God's mercy and forgiveness for his sins. Then he bade farewell to the Patriarch, the clergy, and the Empress, bowed to those who were present and left the church. Then all the clergy, indeed the entire people, countless women and children, cried and moaned, hoping that their plea would reach heaven. As he left the church the Emperor said: "If you want to suffer for God's church and for the Orthodox faith, then follow me!"

Then he mounted his horse and went to the Golden Gate, hoping to encounter there the godless. He was able to attract some 3000 [Byzantine] soldiers. Near the Gate they met a multitude of Turks whom they defeated. The Emperor wanted to reach the Gate but could not on account of many corpses. Then he encountered another large Turkish force and they fought till darkness. In this manner the Orthodox Emperor Constantine suffered for God's churches and for the Orthodox faith. On May 29 [1453], according to eyewitnesses, he killed more than 600 Turks with his own hand. And the saying was fulfilled. *It started with Constantine and it ended with Constantine.* . . .

The Emperor sent a farewell message to the Empress, and she resolved to enter a nunnery. The surviving military commanders and nobles put the Empress, imperial young ladies and many young women aboard ships commanded by [Giovanni] Giustiniani [the Genoese admiral in charge of Constantinople's defenses] for safety with their relatives in Morea. City inhabitants in streets and courtyards refused to surrender to the Turks. They fought them and on that day [May 29] many died, including women and children. Others were taken into captivity. Brave soldiers stationed themselves in windows and refused to surrender and give up their posts. They fought the Turks inside and outside the city. During daylight they ran and hid themselves in various abysses and at night they came out and fought the Turks. Others, especially women and children, threw bricks, tiles, and burning pieces of wood at them and thereby caused them great trouble.

[This form of resistance] stunned the *pashas* and *sanjak-beys*. Because they did not know what to do, they sent a messenger to the Sultan with the following information: "The city will not be pacified until you enter it!" He ordered that a search be made for the Emperor and the Empress. He [the Sultan] himself was afraid to enter the city and that fact troubled him greatly. He then called in [Byzantine] nobles and military commanders who had been captured in the battle and were held as war prisoners by the *pashas*. He gave them his resolute word and some gifts, and sent them, together with the *pashas* and *sanjak-beys*, to deliver the following message to [the defiant] city inhabitants in streets and courtyards: "All fighting must stop! There should be neither fear, nor killings nor taking people into captivity! If you disobey this order, all of you, including your wives and children, will be put to the sword!" And so it was. The fighting stopped. All resisters surrendered to [Byzantine] nobles, military commanders and to [Turkish] *pashas*.

When he heard this the Sultan was pleased. He then ordered that city streets and fields be cleared [of corpses and abandoned war equipment]. On [June] 11, [1453] he dispatched *sanjak-beys* and many of his people throughout city streets to guard traitors. Accompanied by his high officials he [the Sultan] himself went from the Sublime Porte to the Gate of St. Romanus to a church where the Patriarch, his clergy, and a multitude of people, including women and children, were assembled. He came to the square before the church, dismounted his horse, prostrated himself on the ground, put a handful of dust on his head, and thanked God. And, as he admired the wonderful structure, he said: "Truly no one can transcend the people who are here and who were here before!"

Then he went inside the church. The holy place resembled a wasteland. He stopped at a place reserved for highest dignitaries. The Patriarch, his clergy, and all who were present there cried, sobbed, and knelt before him. With his hands he motioned for them to rise and then said: "Athanasius! I am telling you, your suite and all of your people: From now on, do not fear my anger. Henceforth neither killing nor enslavement will be permitted!" Then he turned to his *pashas* and *sanjak-beys* and said: "I hereby decree that all of my soldiers and all of my officials stop abusing city inhabitants, killing women and children, enslaving them, and perpetrating other crimes! If anyone disobeys my order he will be executed!"

Then he told everyone to leave the church and go home, while he examined the organization and the church's treasures. . . . He was overwhelmed by the presence of so many people in one church as they left it and crowded the square and the adjacent streets. Then he went to the Imperial Palace. There he met a certain Serb who handed him the Emperor's [Constantine's] head. Mohammed was pleased with it and called [Byzantine] nobles and military commanders and asked them to verify whether or not the head was really Emperor's. Because they were afraid, they all said: "It is the Emperor's head!"

He examined it and said: "It is clear that God is the creator of all, including emperors. Why then does everyone have to die?"

Then he sent the head to the Patriarch, instructing him to inlay it with gold and silver and to preserve it the best he knew how. The Patriarch placed it in a silver chest, gilded it, and hid it under the altar of the great church. I have heard from others that the survivors [of the battle] at the Golden Gate [where the Emperor was killed] took the Emperor's corpse that night and buried it in Galati.

There also was a great inquiry into the whereabouts of the Empress. They informed the Sultan that the Grand Duke and other members of the imperial family and of the administration had left the Empress aboard the boat. The Sultan ordered that a thorough inquiry be made into the matter.

All of this happened as a consequence of our sins, that the godless Mohammed ascended the imperial throne. . . . Yet, those who know [history] also know that all of this was prophesied by Methodius of Patera [a third-century martyred Church Father] and by Leo the Wise [author of several prophetic works] concerning the destiny of this city. Its past has been fulfilled and so will be its future. For it is written: "*A nation of Rus, as has been prophesied in the vision of St. Daniel, will triumph. And they will inherit the traditions of the seven hills [namely, Rome], as well as its laws, and will disseminate them among five or six nations that comprise Rus, and they will implant seeds among them and will harvest many benefits.*"

⚜ 38 ⚜

Restrictions on Peasant Movement

In general, serfdom in Russia developed slowly from two basic sources: obligations which princes and nobles imposed upon free peasants; and government decrees which sought to limit free movement of the peasantry. The following two decrees, dating from about 1450 and 1463–1468, are the earliest known official documents which paved the way to serfdom in Russia. By the terms of these decrees, Russian peasants were allowed to leave or change their masters only during a designated time, that is, about November 26, after the harvest and the fulfillment of other annual obligations toward their masters. This freedom was of little real value, for by late November the full fury of the Russian winter would have a hampering effect.

[An instruction] from Prince Michael Aleksandrovich [1432–1486] of Beloozero to [my] governor, all *boyars,* lesser nobility, inhabitants of the region, administrators of my *votchinas,* and everyone without exception. My [spiritual] father, Abbot Kasian of the Kirilov Monastery, has petitioned me, and has informed me that you entice his financial debtors, sharecroppers, and persons hired for a given task as well as those hired for the entire year; [he has informed me that] you entice these people not during the period of St. George's Day [November 26], but around Christmas and some on St. Peter's Day [June 29]. Do not entice financial debtors, sharecroppers, and monastery peasants. You may entice financial debtors and sharecroppers on St. George's Day only if they have paid their debt; after St. George's Day do not entice financial debtors; when he pays his debt, yes. I have instructed the Abbot not to release debtors after St. George's Day. Whoever shall disobey this decree shall be fined.

From *Akty, sobrannye v arkhivakh Rossiiskoi imperii Arkheograficheskoiu ekspeditsieiu imp. Akademii nauk* (Documents Collected in Libraries and Archives of the Russian Empire by the Archeographic Expedition of the Imperial Academy of Sciences) (St. Petersburg, 1836), vol. 1, no. 48 and *Akty sotsialnoekonomicheskoi istorii Severo-Vostochnoi Rusi kontsa XIV i nachala XVI v.* (Documents on Socio-Economic History of North Eastern Rus from the End of the 14th to the Beginning of the 16th Century), (Moscow: Akademiia Nauk, 1952), vol. 1, no. 338, p. 245. Translation mine. Words in brackets are mine.

* * *

[An instruction] from Grand Prince Ivan Vasilevich to Prince Ivan Vasilevich, my *boyar* and *namestnik* in Iaroslavl, to your *volost* administrative assistants, and to your steward.

The Abbot of the Troitsk-Sergeev Monastery, with his brothers, has informed me that you accept people from his villages of Fedorovsk and Nerekhta as well as other [villages] during the entire year and that you then dispatch them to my possessions in Iaroslavl. As his Grand Prince I have granted his petition [and am instructing you] not to accept [in the future] any people from his village of Fedorovsk as well as other villages into the Iaroslavl district during any other time than St. George's Day [November 26]. And whoever should leave [monastery estates] on other than St. George's Day, I am ordering you to return him. Do not accept any people during the rest of the year; whoever wants to come from monastery estates to my estate in Iaroslavl, you may accept him only during two weeks of the year—one week before and one week after St. George's Day. But do not, in accordance with this instruction, accept anyone during any other time of the year. Read this instruction [to the people who will come to you] and send them back and he [the Abbot] will keep them thereafter.

Grand Prince

⚔ *39* ⚔

Ivan III's Conquest of Novgorod in 1471

One of the most startling successes of Ivan III's reign (1462–1505) was the relatively easy absorption of the city and territories of Novgorod. The underlying causes of Moscow's triumph were fourfold: the rise of Moscovy's ambition to "gather Russian lands"; Novgorod's lack of adequate

---

Reprinted with permission of the Royal Historical Society from *The Chronicle of Novgorod*, 1016–1471, translated from the Russian by Robert Michell and Nevill Forbes. With an Introduction by C. Raymond Beazley, and an account of the Text by A. A. Shakhmatov. (Camden Third Series, vol. 25) (London: Royal Historical Society, 1914), pp. 205–220. Words in brackets are mine.

defenses; constant feuds between the members of the ruling oligarchy; and Ivan's effective control of Novgorod's food supplies. However, the immediate factor was the decision of Novgorod's ruling group to seek aid and protection from a Catholic Lithuanian Prince. This action was interpreted as treason to Orthodox Christianity, both by Ivan and by the lower strata of Novgorod's population. Ivan conquered the city in 1471 and absorbed it fully into his state by 1475. The following account of the suppression of Novgorod's independence was edited by Ivan the Terrible in the sixteenth century.

A.D. 1471. The *Veliki Knyaz* Ioan Vasilievich marched with a force against Novgorod the Great because of its wrong doing and lapsing into Latinism.

Concerning these [people of Novgorod] this is a copy of the introductory words to the narrative of the first taking [of Novgorod] by the *Veliki Knyaz* Ioan Vasilievich of all Russia [Ivan III], the grandfather of the *Veliki Knyaz* Ioan Vasilievich [Ivan the Terrible] of all Russia, when there were dissensions in Great Novgorod.

King of kings, and Lord of lords, God supreme and ruling and strong, Owner and Creator of all, our Lord Jesus Christ, keep everlasting kingdom, having neither beginning nor end. That one only is all powerful whom the Creator of Heaven and earth and all else may create of His own will; power and glory he is pleased to give to him, the sceptres of empire. He entrusts him with, and by His mercifulness establishes all virtue, and pours His grace on all who fear him. It is written in the old books as it was said: "A country wishing to be ruled in the face of God sets up a prince who is pious and just, regardful of his kingdom and of the governing the land, and loving justice and truth." Of those, it is said, who in goodness build earthly [kingdoms] receive also a heavenly one. Truly has the Lord God of His unspeakable mercy with His lifebearing right hand raised a chief over the God-loved Russian Land, who maintains it in truth and piety, whose honorable head is filled with wisdom, who has organized it like to a lamp of illumination of piety, a promoter of truth, a guardian of godly law, a strong champion of Orthodoxy, the honorable, pious and trusty *Veliki Knyaz* Ioan Vasilievich [Ivan III] of all Russia. The Lord God and the most pure Mother of God by their unspeakable mercy have committed to him the prosperity and the strengthening of all; extending their godly mercy through shedding the light of religion over Russian Lands.

Likewise it is written. Length of days, and long life and peace shall be added to thee, and he found favor and was beloved for his righteous acts, the *Veliki Knyaz* of all Russia, Ioan Vasilievich; yet the deceitful people would not submit to him; stirred by a savage pride, the men of Novgorod would not obey their sovereign *Veliki Knyaz,* until they were reminded of the great

piety of old times told to them. For that reason did their fame abate, and
their face was covered with shame: by reason of the men of Novgorod leaving
the light and giving themselves over in their pride to the darkness of ignorance,
saying that they would draw away and attach themselves to the Latins.

Thus have these inclined away from their sovereign the *Veliki Knyaz,*
wishing to give themselves over to the Latin king, bringing evil to all Orthodoxy. The pious sovereign and *Veliki Knyaz* of all Russia, Ioan Vasilievich,
has frequently sent his messengers to them, calling on them to keep his
patrimony from all harm, to improve themselves in all things within his
ancestral estates, and to live according to old custom. He suffered much in
these things from their vexatious ways and contumacy within his paternal
domains, while he expected from them a thorough amendment of their conduct towards himself and a respectful submission.

And again when the Novgorod *Posadnik* Vasili Ananin came as envoy from
Great Novgorod, the patrimony of the *Veliki Knyaz,* laying before him all
the affairs of Novgorod, he did not say a single word of the ill-behavior of
the men of Novgorod and of their failure to amend their ways, but in reply
to the *boyars* of the *Veliki Knyaz* Vasili he said: "Under that head I have no
instructions from Great Novgorod, and I have no orders to speak." The
sovereign *Veliki Knyaz* was sorely aggrieved by their churlishness, who, while
sending to him men from his patrimonial domains to implore favors, bear
themselves with insolence and are unmindful of their misbehavior. There has
the *Veliki Knyaz* laid his anger upon them, upon the land of his inheritance,
upon Great Novgorod, and he has commanded Vasili, the Novgorod envoy,
to tell Great Novgorod: "Mend your ways towards me, my patrimony, and
recognize us; encroach not on my lands and my waters, and keep my name
of *Veliki Knyaz* in strictness and in honor as of old; and send to me, the
Veliki Knyaz, representatives to do homage and to make settlement. I desire
to keep you, my patrimony, in good favor, on the old conditions." With that
he dismissed him, informing his patrimony that his power of endurance was
exhausted, and that he would not suffer their misbehavior and contumacy
any longer.

The *Veliki Knyaz* sent also to Pskov, his patrimony, repeating the same
words and with commands to acquaint Pskov with the opposition to him of
his patrimony Great Novgorod, and to say: "If you send to me, the *Veliki
Knyaz,* with due homage, then I will hold them in my favor; but if my
patrimony, Great Novgorod, fails in so doing, then must you be ready to act
against them with me." And after this the *Vladyka* [bishop] Ioan of Great
Novgorod and of Pskov died amongst them, and the men of Novgorod chose
the monk Feofil [Theophilus] as their father to occupy his place, without
reference to the *Veliki Knyaz* Ivan Vasilievich of all Russia. And it was after

this selection that they sent their *Boyar*, Nikita Savin, to the *Veliki Knyaz* Ivan Vasilievich of all Russia to ask on behalf of Great Novgorod, the patrimony of the *Veliki Knyaz,* for letters of safe conduct; and Nikita in the name also of all Great Novgorod prayed Filip the Metropolitan of all Russia and the spiritual father of the *Veliki Knyaz,* as well as the *Knyaginya* Marya, the mother of the *Veliki Knyaz,* to intercede for them with the *Veliki Knyaz,* in obtaining guarantee of security in submitting their petition for Feofil whom the men of Novgorod had nominated, for the *Posadniks* and *Tysyatskis* and *Boyars* who would come to Moscow to do homage to the *Veliki Knyaz* and to obtain confirmation of Feofil as *Vladyka* of Novgorod the Great and of Pskov, with the white hood, that they might all depart again in freedom. The *Veliki Knyaz* acceding to the solicitations of his spiritual father the Metropolitan and of his mother the *Knyaginya* Marya, granted letters of security and withdrew his displeasure from his patrimony Great Novgorod. Yet the men of Novgorod, gone mentally astray, and forgetful of this, went not in fear of God's words spoken to the whole congregation of the children of Israel.

Those ancient Israelites hearkened not to the words of God, and they did not obey his commandments; they were therefore deprived of the promised land and were scattered over many countries. Thus also the people of Novgorod, enraged by the pride in them, followed in the ways of the old desertion and have been false to their sovereign the *Veliki Knyaz,* choosing to have a Latin ruler as their sovereign, and having before that accepted from him in Great Novgorod the *Knyaz* Mikhail Alexandrovich of Kiev, keeping him a long time in Novgorod, doing offense in this wise to their sovereign Ivan Vasilievich the *Veliki Knyaz* of all Russia. By their artful devices they won over evilly inclined men, who were thus caught in the nets of the snarer and destroyer of the soul of man, the many-headed beast and cunning enemy, the devil; like a living hell has he devoured them by his evil counsel.

That tempter the devil entered in their midst into the wily Marfa [Martha] Boretskaya, widow of Isaak Boretski, and that accursed [woman] entangled herself in words of guile with the Lithuanian *Knyaz* Mikhail. On his persuasion she intended to marry a Lithuanian *Boyar*, to become Queen, meaning to bring him to Great Novgorod and to rule with him under the suzerainty of the King over the whole of the Novgorod region.

This accursed Marfa like to them beguiled the people, diverting them from the right way to Latinism, for the dark deceits of Latinism blinded her soul's eyes through the wiles of the cunning devil and the wicked imaginings of the Lithuanian *Knyaz.* And being of one mind with her, prompted to evil by the proud devil Satan, Pimin the monk and the almoner of the old *Vladyka,* the cunning [man], engaged with her in secret whispering and helped her in every wickedness, seeking to take the place of his lord as *Vladyka* of Great Novgorod during his life, having suffered much punishment for his rogueries; his desire had not been gratified, inasmuch as the Lord God had not favored him in the drawing of the lot, and he was not, therefore, accepted by the people for the high office. That wicked man is like Peter the Stammerer, the first perverter of the faith, or like the ancient *Farmos,* those originators of the Latin heresies; and they were followed in our time by the apostate Metropolitan Isidor who attended the eighth *Veche* of Rome at Florence [*i.e.,* Council of Florence, 1438–1439], tempted by the Pope's gold and coveting a cardinal-ship, seceding to Latinism. Among these is also Grigori, his apostate pupil who is now in Kiev called Metropolitan; but he is not received into our great Orthodox church of the Russian Land, but excluded.

This cunning monk Pimin sought his appointment by the apostate Grigori, spreading it among the people that he should be sent to Kiev where he would receive his confirmation, being unmindful of the words in the Holy Gospels spoken by the lips of our Lord: "He that entereth not by the door into the sheep-fold, but climbeth up some other way, the same is a thief and a robber." Now this cunning man not only sought like a wolf to climb over the fence into the sheep-fold of the house of Israel, but to scatter and to destroy God's church; and he in this wise ruined the whole of the Novgorod land, the accursed one. According to the Prophet: "He made not God his strength, but trusted in the abundance of his riches and strengthened himself in his wickedness." This Pimin did similarly trust in the abundance of his riches, giving of them also to the crafty woman Marfa, and ordering many people to give money to her to buy over the people to their will; and this accursed wicked serpent fearing not God and having no shame before man, has spread destruction throughout all the Novgorod land and destroyed many souls.

The most venerable priest-monk Feofil, their spiritual father, nominated to the *Vladyka*-ship, exhorted them to refrain from their wicked ways, but they would not hearken to him, and he tried many times to withdraw to his cell in his own monastery, but they would not let him go, while they persevered in their wicked design.

The *Veliki Knyaz* Ioan Vasilievich, hearing of what was doing in his patrimony, Novgorod the Great, of the uncurbed outrages of his people who were like the waves of the sea, bethought him of these occurrences in the goodness of his heart, yet he did not hasten to show his wrath, but quieted his most honest soul with a goodly patience, filled, like the Apostle, with the fear of God, and in remembrance of the holy light of the righteous Son, of Christ's merciful long-suffering, when the word of God came down from heaven and humbling himself, he descended to the earth, taking the form of a servant for the salvation of mankind; the *Veliki Knyaz* allowed them sufficient time, saying to himself: "Thou art just, O Lord, and Thy judgments are correct; and as the Lord is just, so may I, loving justice, be just in His sight." Thinking thus, being favorably inclined towards his patrimony, and not being desirous of witnessing the shedding of Christian blood, he said to himself: "Even as the waves dash into foam against the rocks and come to naught, so also our people the men of Novgorod have more than once acted treasonably towards us, and the Lord God will subdue them." With this view he commanded his [spiritual] father Filip, the Metropolitan of all Russia, to write to them in his name, admonishing them, and instructing them not to draw away from the light of piety, to abandon their evil designs, and to withstand the darkness of the Latin allurements. The Metropolitan of all Russia did repeatedly write to Novgorod the Great, sending his blessing and writing instructions from the sacred Book: "It has come to my hearing, my sons, that some among you are endeavoring to cause a great rebellion and to produce dissent in God's holy church, to renounce the Orthodox Christian faith, and to pass over to the Latins. You must disadvise those wicked people among you from their evil inclinations, for, my sons, theirs is false and godless work; for by abandoning the light of piety they will unwittingly bring down upon themselves the future judgment of God and many eternal torments; let them be guided by a godly wisdom and by God's commandments. Stand in fear of the wrath of God, and in dread of the awful scythe which was seen by the great prophet Zachariah descending from heaven upon the unruly; you must punish those who make tumult and sow dissension among you, and teach them to walk in the old ways of their fathers and to dwell in the former ways of peace and piety. Cruel and irremediable will be the effects of these beginnings, if you neglect the new law of piety and salvation of the testament of the living God, and adhere to Latinism. The Lord God will call to account all the godless perverters of the faithful, so that you must restrain the evildoers according to the words: 'Fly from sin as from a foe; fly from deceit as from the face of a serpent, that it may not sting thy soul with the barb of eternal perdition.' You know, my sons, how many cities, countries and places of mighty kingdoms have been ruined and desolated in former times for breaking the law and for disobeying the Prophets and for not following the teachings of the Apostles and the holy Fathers; that countries and cities which did not submit to God and to their sovereign were destroyed. The once pious and great Imperial city of Constantinople perished because of that same Latinism; it fell through impiety, and is now possessed by the heathen Turk. Fear the wrath of God, ye sons of God's world, it is not only one or two among you who are working to depart from the truth and to turn from the right way, forgetting your past greatness and the laws of your fore-fathers; but the whole multitude of your people are in commotion. Submit yourselves, my sons, to him under whose strong arm God has placed you and the God-serving land of Russia, the *Veliki Knyaz* Ioan Vasilievich our hereditary ruler, according to the direction of Christ's Apostle Paul the teacher of the universe, who said: 'Whosoever submits to the power of God, obeys His ordinances, but whosoever resisteth the power, resisteth the ordinance of God'; and again: 'Fear God and obey the king.' The minister of God beareth not the sword in vain as an avenger, but also in defense of the godly. Ponder, therefore, my children, over these things, and humble yourselves, and may the God of peace be with you."

They remained, however, not only implacable, but also stone-hearted, and gave no attention to the above writing, and were as deaf as adders, closing their ears to the voice, as it were, of the charmers. So these men of Novgorod giving no heed to the writing, nor accepting the benediction, and continuing in their evil courses, could not be compacted [in the right]. The pious sovereign and *Veliki Knyaz* of all Russia Ioan Vasilievich being still gracious to them, sent to Great Novgorod, his patrimony, his servant Ioan Fedorovich Tovarkov with fair words, saying: "His patrimony should not abandon the Orthodox faith, but cast the evil thought from off their hearts, and should not adhere to Latinism; that the great sovereign holds the men of Novgorod in favor and in his regards as of old." But the wicked people minded him not, and clung to the intention of abandoning Orthodoxy and giving themselves over to the king. We will state the accusation against them.

The *Veliki Knyaz* being informed of the unceasing evil doings of the men of Novgorod, dispatched to Novgorod the Great a challenge in writing exposing the malpractices of the people and their treason, and announcing that he was himself marching with a force against them. The *Veliki Knyaz* had first sent his *Voyevodas* Vasili Fedorovich Obrazets and Boris Matveyevich Tyushtev with his men of Ustyug, of Vyatka, and of the Vologda district, to the Dvina and the country beyond the *Volok,* and into all the territories of Novgorod in those parts. In advance of his own force the *Veliki Knyaz* sent an army under his *Voyevodas, Knyaz* Danilo Dmitrievich Kholmski and his *Boyar* Fedor Davidovich, accompanied by many others of his court; they were ordered to scour the country around Novgorod, towards Russa beyond the Ilmen lake and to burn all places of habitation. To his patrimony Pskov the *Veliki Knyaz* sent to say that the men of Pskov should release themselves from their engagement on oath to Great Novgorod, and take to horse in his service against Novgorod which had abjured Orthodoxy and was giving itself to the Latin king. They issued forth at once with all the men of the country of Pskov, and at the instance of the *Veliki Knyaz* they revoked their oath on the Cross to Novgorod the Great.

The pious sovereign and *Veliki Knyaz* Ioan Vasilievich prayed to God and

Map: NORTHEASTERN RUS, LATE FOURTEENTH CENTURY

Legend:
- Boundary of Northeastern Rus
- Territory of the Grand Duchy of Moscovy
- Other frontiers
- Capitol cities of the grand duchies
- Autonomous principalities

SCALE OF MILES 0 150

to the most pure Mother of God, shedding many tears before them, beseeching their mercy for the pacification of the world, and for the well-being of God's holy churches and the Orthodox faith. His heart filled with sorrow, he said to himself: "It is known to Thee, Almighty God and everlasting King, who knowest the secrets of all men's hearts, it is not of my own desire and will that I dare to do this which may cause much shedding of Christian blood upon this earth. I stand by the godly laws of the holy Apostles and holy Fathers and for the true Orthodox faith of the Russian Land, also for my patrimony and against their renunciation of the true faith and adoption of Latinism." And praying thus, the pious worker invoked to his aid the great defender and speedy helper in war, the *Voyevoda* of the celestial forces, the *Archistrategos* Mikhail, and the great unconquerable sufferers for Christ, Dmitri of Selun [Salonika], Georgi the Brave and Feodor Stratilat [Theodore

Stratelates], also his saintly and Orthodox ancestors St. Vladimir and his two sons Boris and Gleb; and putting his trust in the prayers of the Saints, of the great sanctifier Ioan Zlatoust [John Chrysostom], the Bishop of Tsargrad [Constantinople], the miracle-worker Nikola, Peter the Russian Metropolitan, Alexis the miracle-worker and Russian Metropolitan, St. Leonti the miracle-worker and Bishop of Rostov, and the Saints and miracle-workers Sergei, Varlam, and Kiril, and Nikita the almoner of the miracle-worker of Pereyaslavl. By their prayers might he be strengthened and established for many years by the Lord God with His help from on high.

And so putting his trust in God, the *Veliki Knyaz* mounted his horse; and in the house of the Most Pure Mother of God and of the great Sanctifier Peter the miracle-worker, he left his son the faithful and pious *Veliki Knyaz* Ioan Ioanovich to sit in his throne in Moscow in guard of his patrimony and to govern the land of Russia; he left his younger brother *Knyaz* Andrei Vasilievich with him, and he commanded his son to retain by him the *Tsarevich* Murtasa, the son of *Tsar* Mustafa, with his *Knyazes* and *Kazaks* [Bodyguard], to serve him on any emergency.

The *Veliki Knyaz* took along with him his younger brother *Knyaz* Yuri Vasilievich and his youngest brothers Andrei and Boris Vasilievich, also *Knyaz* Mikhail Andreyevich with his son Vasili, with a large number of other *Knyazes* in his service, and *Boyars* and *Voyevodas;* he took with him also the son of *Tsar* Aldayaras Kasimovich of the Meshcher country with his *Kazaks* and retinue. The men of Pskov joined their forces from the borders of their country.

Thus did the *Veliki Knyaz* advance with all his host against his patrimonial domain Novgorod the Great because of the rebellious spirit of the people, their pride and their conversion to Latinism. With a numerous and overpowering force he occupied the entire Novgorod country from border to border, visiting every part of it with the dread powers of his fire and sword. As in ancient times Jeremiah prophesied of Nebuchadnezzar, King of Jerusalem: "From the rumbling and thunder of his chariots and from the neighing of his horses the earth shall tremble"; and so by the mercy and aid of God, shall the same prophecy be fulfilled in our time over the wicked men of the Novgorod country, through the pious sovereign *Veliki Knyaz* Ioan Vasilievich of all Russia, for their abjuration of the faith and for their wrong-doing.

The Novgorod country is filled with lakes and swamps, for which reason mounted forces were never employed against Novgorod by former *Veliki Knyazes* and the wicked people in their wonted contumacy dwelled in security during the summer after, following their own evil ways from the autumn to the winter, and even up to spring time, by reason of the inundation of the lands.

By the beneficence of God, vouchsafed by God from on high to the *Veliki*

Knyaz Ioan Vasilievich of all Russia to the detriment of the Novgorod land, not a drop of rain had fallen during the summer. From the month of May to the month of September the land was dry and the heart of the sun had dried up all the swamps. The troops of the *Veliki Knyaz* found no impediments and could ride in every direction over the country, driving the cattle over dried ground; thus did the Lord God through this desiccation punish the men of Novgorod for their evildoing and subject them to the strong hand of the pious sovereign and *Veliki Knyaz* Ioan Vasilievich of all Russia. When the men of Novgorod heard that the *Veliki Knyaz* was marching upon them with a large army, those cunning men sent to him professions of duty and again asked for guarantees of security while proceeding with their evildoing. At the same time they sent forces from Novgorod the Great by the Ilmen lake in boats against the advancing columns of the *Veliki Knyaz,* and fought them; but God aided the *Voyevodas* of the *Veliki Knyaz,* and 500 men of Novgorod were killed and others were captured or drowned, while others fled back to the town informing the townsmen that they had been defeated by the *Voyevodas* of the *Veliki Knyaz.* Thrown into great agitation, the men of Novgorod, after deliberation, dispatched another messenger to the *Veliki Knyaz, Posadnik* Luka Klementievich, doing homage and again asking for guarantee of security and ignoring the defeated force which had passed down in boats, declared that as yet no men from the town had fought with those of the *Veliki Knyaz.*

Without waiting for the return of their venturesome envoy the crafty people conceived a great wicked design; the rebel *Posadniks* and *Tysyatskis,* the *Boyars,* well-to-do-men, the merchants and the whole of Great Novgorod collected together, forming a fighting body of fully 30,000 men, being unaware that the sword of God was sharpened against them, and mounting their horses, rode quickly out of the town to fall upon the advance force of the *Veliki Knyaz,* which was led by *Knyaz* Danilo Dmitrievich and by Fedor Davidovich. Here befell what was said by David the Prophet: "By the morning shall all the wicked of the earth be slain; I shall destroy all the lawless of the city." When the watchers and the scouts informed the *Voyevodas* that a large force of mounted men was advancing from Novgorod, and that an auxiliary force was coming in boats into the Shelon river, then the *Voyevodas* of the *Veliki Knyaz* began to acknowledge the justice of the *Knyaz's* cause and the perfidy of the men of Novgorod and, praying to the Lord God and to the most pure Mother of God, and reposing their trust in God, they said to their company: "It is our duty, brothers, to serve our sovereign the *Veliki Knyaz* Ioan Vasilievich of all Russia, and were they 300,000 strong we should all the same lay down our lives in fighting for the cause of our sovereign *Veliki Knyaz;*

and God and the holy Mother of God know that the cause of the *Veliki Knyaz* is a just cause."

Early on the morning of July 14, the day of the Apostle St. Kuld, the entire force of the men of Novgorod was ranged on the Shelon river, and the opposing armies faced each other across the river.

When they saw the forces of the men of Novgorod the troops of the *Veliki Knyaz* precipitated themselves into the river on their horses, not one of their horses stumbling in descending the steep bank, nor floundering in the water, and closing up they rushed upon the whole body of the men of Novgorod and they joined in battle. And here was fulfilled what was said by the Prophet: "Like drunken men did they stagger and fall into confusion, and all their understanding was swallowed up"; and again: "As in drowsiness they mounted their horses, terrible art Thou, O Lord; who can stand against Thee?"

Thus was God's favor bestowed on the troops of the *Veliki Knyaz,* maintaining his just cause; even as God helped Gideon against the Midianites, and Abraham against the King Hodologomor of Sodom, so did he aid the *Voyevodas* of the *Veliki Knyaz* against these unrighteous backsliders, the men of Novgorod. Although they rebelled and arrayed themselves against the troops of the *Veliki Knyaz,* yet they could not raise strong hands against them, but themselves fell into confusion from the stretching of their arrowed bows, and from the weapons of their hands. Thus likewise did God in his goodness turn their faces in an hour's time, as they threw down their arms and fled back whence they had come; they ran in disgrace, casting away their armor to relieve their horses of weight, and a great number of them fell dead, for their lawlessness and for their rebellion against their sovereign the *Veliki Knyaz.* It did not appear to them that they were stricken by men's hands, but by the invisible power of the Living God and by the aid of the great *Archistrategos* Mikhail, the leader of the heavenly forces. All were in great terror and many fell dead with their faces to the earth, while others throwing themselves off their horses ran into the forests, where they strayed like cattle in their separate ways—being there were no married men amongst them—but hearing on all sides the shout of "Moskva" [Moscow] from the troops of the *Veliki Knyaz.*

So did the Lord fill their wicked souls with dread that they strayed in the forests not knowing their own country. The troops of the righteous sovereign and *Veliki Knyaz* triumphing over them by God's mercy, chased the wicked men of Novgorod twenty *poprishche* [about twenty *versts*] killing many and taking others alive, while others were drowned in their boats in the Shelon river.

The troops on the field of battle proclaimed their victory by trumpet sound and kissed the sacred images, glorifying God for their victory over their presumptuous enemies.

And searching in the transport they found a writing which was the draft of an agreement between Novgorod and the king [of Poland]. This was a surprise, and it caused astonishment, and the papers were forthwith sent to the *Veliki Knyaz* Ioan Vasilievich by the hand of the *Boyar* Ivan Vasilievich Zamyatin; he was to report that a large army of Novgorod men had advanced against them with banners with the best men among them, and had fought desperately, but that God had aided the *Voyevodas* of the *Veliki Knyaz,* that the great Novgorod army was completely defeated, that many Novgorod men had fallen, and many had been captured, to the number of 1700; that here were the copies of a treaty with the King of Poland, and with these they sent a prisoner, the man who had written out the draft, to serve the *Veliki Knyaz* in his accusation of the crafty men of Novgorod.

The pious *Veliki Knyaz* was gladdened by the unspeakable mercy of God in the aid given to him from on high against his cunning enemies. Praising God and the most pure Mother of God for having frustrated their wicked design of corrupting the sacred churches of God, of causing agitations and of producing hostilities between great sovereigns to the utter discomfiture of all Orthodoxy. He found among the documents the draft of a treaty with the king, by the terms of which the men of Novgorod agreed to surrender all the towns and districts of the *Veliki Knyaz,* with his lands and waters and with all the taxes of Novgorod the Great, setting forth the names of the envoys to be sent to the king—Panfili Selifontov and Kurila Ivanov, son of Makar—and naming him "our honorable king and sovereign." It is written, that their sickness shall turn upon their heads and their untruth shall descend upon them. So may it be with them for their craftiness and evil counsels.

The pious *Veliki Knyaz* of all Russia Ioan Vasilievich, having prayed to God and to the most pure Mother of God, went forward in his great work to Novgorod the Great, with his younger brothers *Knyaz* Yuri Vasilievich and *Knyaz* Boris Vasilievich, with the [Tatar] *Tsarevich* with all his *Knyazes* and *Voyevodas* and with all the people of his lands, hastening to his *Voyevodas* and to his advance army.

When the men of Novgorod were brought before the *Veliki Knyaz,* he, the pious one, with a godly wisdom accused the crafty men of their cunning and dishonorable proceedings, of departing from the light of true worship and giving themselves up to Latinism, of surrendering themselves to the Latin king while being the patrimony of him the *Veliki Knyaz;* and of surrendering to the Latin king according to the draft of a treaty with him all the towns, districts, lands, and waters which belonged to him the *Veliki Knyaz* of Moscow, together with the taxes. Having found them guilty of all this, and being thus stirred against the men of Novgorod, he ordered them to execution by the sword, the chief *Posadniks,* among whom was Dmitri the eldest son of the

charming Marfa, the town *Posadnik;* and she was also to lose her life by
decapitation; together with these Vasili Seleznev Guba, Kiprian Arzubiev,
and Iremia were also beheaded for their conspiracy and crime in seeking to
take to Latinism. Many other *Posadniks, Tysyatskis, Boyars,* and men of substance of Novgorod were sent away to various towns or thrown into prisons,
while others were retained in the fortress under charge to bide their time.

When God's aid came down from on high, with the leader of the heavenly
host, the great *Archistrategos* Mikhail, in that hour Great Novgorod trembled
before the wrath of God, and the *Posadniks,* the *Tysyatskis,* the men of
substance, the *Boyars*, the merchants, and all the land of Novgorod turned
their hearts towards good.

So did those men of Novgorod come unanimously to one decision; taking
with them the priest-hermit Feofil, nominated *Vladyka* of Novgorod the Great
and of Pskov, the Archimandrites, and *Igumens,* the worthy fathers and hermits, the priests from all the seven cathedral churches, and a great number
of the best men of the town, they went to the pious sovereign and *Veliki
Knyaz* of all Russia Ioan Vasilievich, and all of them prostrating themselves
before him, they repented them with tears and in great sorrow of their crimes,
praying: "Merciful lord and *Veliki Knyaz* of all Russia Ioan Vasilievich, for
the Lord's sake pardon us guilty men of Novgorod the Great your patrimony;
grant us, Lord, your favor, withdraw your anger, hold back your sword and
extinguish your fires, silence your thunders, spare the land from ruin, be
merciful and let your irresponsible people see the light."

And they all came on many days to his brothers, *Knyaz* Yuri Vasilievich,
Knyaz Andrei Vasilievich, and to *Knyaz* Boris Vasilievich, humbling themselves before them and praying them to plead for them to their elder brother,
the *Veliki Knyaz* Ioan Vasilievich; and on many days they likewise visited
the *Boyars*, the *Knyazes,* and *Voyevodas,* beseeching them because of the
sorrows of all Great Novgorod to plead for them, before the *Veliki Knyaz*.
The gracious brothers of the *Veliki Knyaz, Knyaz* Yuri Vasilievich, *Knyaz*
Andrei Vasilievich, and *Knyaz* Boris Vasilievich, favored them as of their
patrimony, and compassionating them, and together with all the *Knyazes* and
Boyars, did plead for them before their brother the *Veliki Knyaz* of all Russia,
praying him to have regard for them of his patrimony and to lay aside the
wrath in his heart. The gracious and intelligent sovereign *Veliki Knyaz* of all
Russia, Ioan Vasilievich, seeing before him such a multitude of penitent
people, and among them his own priests, the hermit priest Feofil, the *Vladyka*-
elect of Novgorod the Great and of Pskov, who had grieved sore many days,
as also his brothers and the *Boyars* and *Knyazes* in supplication before him,
and the righteous *Veliki Knyaz,* being also mindful of the writing he had
received from his spiritual father Filip, Metropolitan of all Russia in which

as pastor and teacher of Christ's flock the Metropolitan entreated the *Veliki Knyaz,* with his blessing, to be merciful to the people of his patrimony, those many Orthodox Christians for whose souls he grieved, and for the sake of Christian peace to accept their petitions, and remembering also the words which came from the mouth of our Lord: "Be merciful even as our Father in heaven, forgive man's trespasses as your Father will forgive yours," and again: "Blessed is the merciful," so because of these words spoken by God, and of all these intercessions, the *Veliki Knyaz* granted grace to his patrimony, to Feofil the *Vladyka*-elect of Novgorod the Great and of Pskov, to the *Posadniks, Tysyatskis,* merchants and to the whole of Novgorod the Great: he withdrew from them the anger of his heart, withheld his sword and his menace over the land, and commanded that all the captives should be freed without ransom. He put a termination to the war and to plunder; and as to taxes and tribute, he settled them all in writing, on oath, after which the *Veliki Knyaz* withdrew from his patrimonal domains of Novgorod peacefully with his brothers, his *Boyars,* with the *Knyazes* and *Voyevodas* and with all his armed forces.

From his *Voyevodas* operating on the Dvina the *Veliki Knyaz* received communications to the effect that they had defeated *Knyaz* Vasili Shuiski, the servant of Great Novgorod, who with men from the country beyond the *Volok,* from the Dvina country and from the Korel region had advanced in large numbers and had fought with them great battles from morning to night on land and on water, but that God had aided the forces of the *Veliki Knyaz* under *Voyevoda* Vasili Fedorovich and his comrades, that a large number of the men of Novgorod were slain and others captured; so were the men of Novgorod overcome with fatigue and staggered in battle that they could not move their hands or turn their heads; that their *Knyaz* was wounded by an arrow and was taken away in a boat by his men, being barely alive, and that the towns on the Dvina had been burned and demolished. Thus did God's grace and mercy descend from on high in aid of the right of our sovereign the righteous and pious *Veliki Knyaz* Ioan Vasilievich of all Russia. On receipt of this intelligence the pious *Veliki Knyaz* gave praise to God and to the most pure Mother of God for those great mercies, and returned to his throne in the God-protected city of Moscow on the first day of September of the new year 6980 (1472).

Having received their liberty from their sovereign Ioan Vasilievich the *Veliki Knyaz* of all Russia, the men of Novgorod at once dispersed from out of the town to their several homes. A large number of people proceeded to Russa in big vessels, and to the Volkhov river with their wives and children and possessions; their cattle and with their movable houses, going to the places of their residence by the Ilmen Lake, or by way of Russa Lake, the breadth from shore to shore on all sides being sixty *poprishche* [about forty miles]. When their numerous big vessels reached the middle of the lake, a storm with a hurricane of wind broke suddenly upon them, and tore their sails; there was terrible thunder and heavy rain with hail, and waves of mountain height, and dreadful, broke up their barges and all their big vessels in the middle of that frightful lake. There was in that hour an overwhelming terror and a raging storm, with shrieking and crying, many people clinging to each other, bitterly bewailing their peril, and in their agony tearing their clothes; mothers embracing their infants, fathers their sons, while shedding many tears and praying: "Lord save us, in the hour of our destruction and of our separation from the evils of this world." Sadness and woe to those who take to evil! This was not within sight of their friends, and they got no help from them; unless it came from on high, because of the straits of the great city and the angry spirit pervading it; the while that the big vessels were being shattered and wrecked, and all the men and women with their children were perishing in the deep waters separating from each other and tumbling about at the will of the waves which left nothing living in the waters, but all drowned and put to death. It was heard afterwards that the number of drowned in the lake was 7000. Thus did God punish his people of the Novgorod country for their wicked imaginings, those evil-minded men, even for relinquishing their faith and inclining to Latinism. When it came to the ears of Great Novgorod that on the Dvina the *Voyevodas* of the *Veliki Knyaz* had beaten *Knyaz* Vasili Shuiski and the Novgorod men, while a large multitude had been drowned in the lake, then tears were added to tears, and wailings to wailings, realizing that the whole of the Novgorod country was by the wrath of the *Veliki Knyaz* of all Russia, Ioan Vasilievich, burned and laid waste by war, with its best men driven out, which had never happened to them before. But all this evil and ruin they had brought upon themselves by their cunning and faithlessness and for their going to Latinism, having allowed themselves to be misled by cunning people and rebels; and that civic disaster and human blood shall they be made to account for by the Almighty God, according to the writing: "Lord! destroy the provokers of strife; and let the consequences fall on the heads of the traitors and on their souls in this world and in the next, amen."

☙ *40* ☙

Contarini's Impression of Muscovy in 1476

The Italians were the first west Europeans to notice the rising power of Muscovy. Their perception stemmed partly from contacts they established with Moscow following the marriage, in 1472, of Ivan III to Sophia Paleologue (the niece of the last Byzantine Emperor), who was brought up in Florence. Sophia attracted many Italian Renaissance artists and architects to Moscow, including Aristotle Fioraventi, Marco Ruffo, Pietro Solario, and Marco Bruno, who built and decorated several palaces and cathedrals within the Kremlin walls. Italians also sought contacts with Muscovy to establish an alliance against the growing menace of the Ottoman Turks. In 1476, Venetian ambassador Ambrosio Contarini (n.d.–1499) stopped in Moscow on his journey home from Persia, where he had unsuccessfully sought aid against the Turks. In Moscow, Contarini had an audience with Ivan III which resulted in the following impression of Ivan and of conditions in his state.

On September 22, 1476, it pleased God that we should enter Russia. There were a few little Russian villages in the middle of the woods, and when it was known that Marco [Russian guide] was with the caravan, the people came forth—with great timidity, however, on account of the Tatars—and brought him a little honey in the combs. Of this he gave me a portion, and I was certainly in want of it, as all our provisions were exhausted, and we were reduced to such a state that we could scarcely mount our horses. We left here, and reached a city called Resan [Riazan], belonging to a lord whose wife is sister to the Duke of Muscovy, the houses, as well as the castle of which, are all of wood. Here we obtained bread and meat in abundance, as well as their beverage of apples, by which we were much restored. After leaving here, we travelled through extensive forests, and at night we all lodged in Russian villages, and were able to take some repose, as by the aid of God we appeared to have reached a place of security. We then came to another

---

Reprinted with permission of the Cambridge University Press from *Travels to Tana and Persia* by Josafa Barbaro and Ambrogio Contarini. Translated from the Italian by William Thomas and S. A. Roy, and Edited, with an Introduction by Lord Stanley of Alderly (London: Published for the Hakluyt Society, 1873), pp. 158–166. Words in brackets are mine.

city named Colonna [Kolomna], which is situated in a branch of the Volga, called Mosco, over which there is a large bridge. We left here, and I was sent in advance by Marco, as the caravan would not go so quickly.

On the 26th, praising and thanking God, who had taken pity on us in so many dangers and extremities, we entered Moscow, which belongs to Duke Zuanne [Ivan III], the sovereign of Great White Russia. I should state that, during the greater part of the time we occupied in passing the desert, which was from August 18, when we left Citracan [Astrakhan], until we reached Moscow on September 25, as we had no wood, we cooked our food with the dung of the cattle. Having reached here, then, in safety, Marco provided lodgings for myself and my people, and stables for the horses, which, although small and cheerless, seemed to me a grand palace in comparison with what I had had to put up with.

On the 27th, Marco entered Moscow, and came in the evening to see me, bringing with him some provisions, which are very abundant in this city, as I shall describe hereafter. He exhorted me in the name of his sovereign to be of good cheer, as I might consider myself at home; for which I thanked him as well as I was able.

On the 28th, I went to visit Marco, and, as I was desirous of returning home, I requested him to be pleased to procure me an audience of the Duke. This he did, as the Duke shortly afterwards sent for me. After the usual salutations I thanked his lordship for the good offices I had experienced at the hands of Marco, his ambassador, as I could certainly say, with truth, that by his means I had escaped many dangers. And, although I had benefited by these services personally, they might be considered as having been rendered to my Illustrious Seignory, whose ambassador I was. The Duke scarcely allowed me to finish my speech, but, with a severe look, complained of Zuan Battista Trivisano. I will not enter into this subject, as it is beside the purpose; but when, after a long conversation, I requested to be allowed to take my departure, he said that I should receive an answer on that subject at another time; and with this I was dismissed by the Duke, who was about to leave the city. It is his custom to visit the various parts of his dominions every year. He especially looks after a Tatar, in his pay, who commands, it is said, five-hundred horsemen, to guard the frontiers of his territory from the incursions of the Tatars.

Being desirous, as I have said, of leaving, I endeavored to obtain an answer to my request, and was again summoned to the palace, before three of the Duke's principal barons. They informed me, in the Duke's name, that I was welcome, and repeated everything that the Duke himself had said, complaining at the same time about the above-mentioned Zuan Battista. In conclusion, they told me that I might go or stay, as I pleased; and with this they dismissed me.

As I was indebted to Marco for the amount of my ransom with the interest, as well as for some other expenses which he had incurred on my account, I begged him to have the goodness to allow me to leave, and that as soon as I had reached Venice I would send him all that I owed him. He would not, however, consent to this, as he said that the Tatars and Russians whom I had promised to pay, wanted the money; and, as I was unable, after various attempts, to influence either the Duke or Marco in this matter, I determined to send Stephano to Venice to advise the Illustrious Seignory of all that had occurred, that they might with their accustomed clemency and good nature provide against my ending my days in this country.

On October 7, 1476, I dispatched Priest Stephano in company with a certain Nicolo da Leopoli, who was well acquainted with the road, while I remained in Moscow. I found here Maestro Trifoso, a goldsmith from Catharo, who had made, and was engaged in making, many beautiful vases and other articles for the Duke. There was also a Maestro Aristotele da Bologna, an engineer, who was building a church in the Piazza, besides many Greeks from Constantinople, who had come in the suite of Despina [Sophia], with all of whom I was on terms of great friendship. The room which Marco had given me was small and unpleasant, and made an uncomfortable dwelling-place; but, by the influence of Marco, I obtained a lodging in the house of Maestro Aristotele, which was situated close to the Duke's palace, and was very convenient. A few days afterwards, however (for what reason I never heard), I was ordered, in the Duke's name, to leave this house, and I was, with difficulty, provided with two little chambers outside the castle, where I remained until my departure, one of which I occupied myself, while the other served for my attendants.

The city of Moscow is situated on a little hill, and is built entirely of wood, as is the castle. It is traversed by a river called Moscow, on one side of which stands the castle and part of the city, and on the other the remaining portion. The river is crossed by numerous bridges. Moscow is the principal city, and the residence of the Duke. It is surrounded by forests, with which, indeed, the greater part of the country is covered. The country abounds in all kinds of corn; and when I was there, you might have bought more than ten of our *stare* of wheat for a *ducat,* and other corn in proportion. The meat principally eaten is that of cows and pigs, of which you can procure, I believe, more than three pounds for a *soldo.* They give a hundred fowls or forty ducks for a *ducat,* and geese are little more than three *soldi* each. A great number of hares are brought to market, but other game is very scarce, because, I imagine, they do not know how to catch them. There are small birds of all kinds, and very

cheap. They do not make wine of any kind, nor have they any fruit, with
the exception of a few water melons and wild apples. The climate is so
excessively cold, that the people stay nine months of the year indoors. As it
is difficult to travel in the summer time, on account of the thick forests and
the great quantity of mud caused by the melting of the ice, they are obliged
to get in all their provisions in the spring, for which purpose they use their
sani or sledges on which they stow everything, and which are easily drawn
by one horse. By the end of October the river which passes through the city
is frozen over, and shops and bazaars for the sale of all sorts of things are
erected on it, scacely anything being sold in the town. They do this, as the
river, from being surrounded on all sides by the city, and so protected from
the wind, is less cold than anywhere else. On this frozen river may be seen,
daily, numbers of cows and pigs, great quantities of corn, wood, hay, and
every other necessary, nor does the supply fail during the whole winter. At
the end of November, all those who have cows or pigs, kill and bring them,
from time to time, to the city market. They are frozen whole, and it is curious
to see so many skinned cows standing upright on their feet. The meat that
you eat has sometimes been killed three months or more. Fish, fowls, and all
other provisions are treated in the same way. Horses run on this river when
it is frozen, and a good deal of amusement takes place. Sometimes, also a
neck is broken. Both the men and women are handsome, but they are a brutal
race. They have a pope of their own, appointed by their sovereign, and hold
ours in little esteem, saying that we are doomed to perdition. They boast of
being great drunkards, and despise those who are not. They have no wine of
any kind, but drink a beverage made of honey and the leaves of the hop,
which is certainly not a bad drink, especially when old. The sovereign, however,
will not grant permission to every one to make it; for, if they had that
permission, they would be constantly intoxicated, and would murder each
other like brutes. Their custom is to remain from morning till midday in the
bazaars and to spend the remainder of the day in the taverns in eating and
drinking. After midday you cannot obtain any service of them whatever. A
great many merchants frequent this city from Germany and Poland during
the winter, for the sole purpose of buying peltries, such as the furs of young
goats, foxes, ermines, squirrels, wolves, and other animals; and, although these
furs are procured at places many days' journey from Moscow—towards the
north-north-east, or the north-west—they are all brought here where the merchants buy them. A great many, also, go to a town called Novogardia [Nov-
gorod], on the confines of *Francia* and Upper Germany, and eight days'
journey west of Moscow. This town, although it has a republican government,
is subject to the Duke, to whom it pays a yearly tribute. This prince, from
what I have heard, possesses a large territory, and might raise a large army,

but the men are worthless. The country is bounded by that part of Germany which belongs to the King of Poland. Towards the north-north-west there is said to be a certain nation of idolaters, without any sovereign, but who, when so inclined, pay obedience to the Duke of Muscovy. There are some who are said to adore the first thing they see, and others who sacrifice an *animal* at the foot of a tree, and afterwards worship it. Many other things are told, which I shall not repeat, as I have not witnessed them myself, nor are they credible. The Duke may be thirty-five years of age; he is tall and thin, and handsome. He has two brothers, and his mother is still alive. Besides two daughters by Despina, who is said to be *enceinte,* he has, by another woman, a son who is not in great favor, on account of his bad conduct. I might mention other things, but it would take too long. I remained in Moscow from September 25 until January 21, and I certainly received good treatment from everyone. After visiting his dominions, the Duke returned to Moscow about the end of December. I had sent Priest Stephano for my ransom, and was certain that it would be forthcoming, yet wishing very much to hasten my return home, as the way of living of the country did not agree with me, I spoke to some gentlemen who were favorable to my desire of leaving; and a few days afterwards received an invitation to dine with the Duke. He then told me that he was willing that I should depart, and that he should be happy to serve our Illustrious Seignory, and pay whatever was due to the Tatars and Russians for my ransom. The banquet to which I was invited was certainly served in good style, not only with regard to the numerous dishes, but in every other respect. As soon as the dinner was over, according to the custom of the country, I returned to my apartments. A few days afterwards the Duke invited me to dine with him again, and he ordered his treasurer to give me what money I required to pay the Tatars and the Russians. I then went to his palace, where I was made to put on a dress of ermine (that is, the skin only), and received also a thousand squirrel skins, with which I returned home. I also, at the Duke's request, paid a visit to Despina, with whom, after the usual salutations and compliments, I had a long conversation. She treated me with great kindness and courtesy, and entreated me earnestly to recommend her to my Illustrious Seignory.

The following day I was invited to the palace to dine with the Duke. Before sitting down to table, we entered a chamber where I was received by His Highness Marco, and one of the secretaries in a most courteous manner. The Duke entreated me to signify to my Illustrious Seignory that he was their good friend, and wished to remain so; that he willingly allowed me to depart, and that if I required anything more I should have it. When the Duke spoke to me I retired from him, but he approached me with great kindness. I answered all his questions, and thanked him appropriately, and we conversed for more than an hour. He showed me, with great good nature, some of his dresses of cloth of gold, lined with ermine, which were most beautiful. We then left this chamber, and soon after sat down to table. The dinner was longer than usual; the dishes more numerous; and many of his barons were present. When the banquet was over, I rose from table and presented myself before His Highness, who, with a loud voice, that everyone might hear, took leave of me in courteous terms, and with great demonstration of good-will towards our Illustrious Seignory; and I replied in a becoming manner. I was, afterwards, presented with a large cup of silver filled with their beverage made of honey, and was told to drink the contents, and keep the cup. This custom is observed when they wish to show very great honor either to ambassadors or others. But as there appeared to me too much to drink at once, I drank about a quarter of it, and His Highness, who was aware of my habits, seeing that I could not drink more, ordered the cup to be emptied and given back to me. I kissed His Highness's hands, and took leave of him. I was accompanied to the staircase by many of his barons, who embraced me with great demonstrations of friendship. I then went home, and had prepared everything for my departure; but Marco wished that I should previously dine with him.

On January 21, 1476, after partaking of a good dinner with Marco and my own people, I took leave of him, and we entered our *sani* and departed. These *sani,* which are only used on the ice, somewhat resemble little houses, and are drawn by one horse. Each person has his own. You sit inside with as much clothing as you require and drive the horse. They go very fast and are made to contain all the provisions and everything that is necessary. The Patriarch of Antioch, or Brother Ludovico, who had been detained by the Duke on the representation of Marco, was, after great efforts on my part, released, and was to have accompanied us; but, seeing that he appeared to have no desire to do so, I started alone with my people, and a man was sent by the Duke to accompany me, with orders that I should be provided with other guides from place to place throughout the whole of his territories. In the evening we lodged at a very strange village; and, although I was aware that we should have to undergo many discomforts and hardships, on account of the intense cold of those countries, and from having to travel continually through forests, I welcomed every discomfort and was intent on nothing but travelling day and night; nor had I any fear, so great was my desire to escape from those places and ways of living.

We left this village on the 22d, and travelled continually through forests, in extreme cold, until the 27th, when we reached a little town called Viesemo [Viazma]. Leaving here, we took guides from place to place, and reached another little town called Smolencho [Smolensk], from which we departed with another guide, leaving the dominions of the Duke of Muscovy to enter

Lithuania, which belongs to Casimir, King of Poland. We then proceeded to a small town called Trochi, where we found His Majesty, the said King.

Be it observed that, from January 21, when we left Moscovy, until February 12, when we reached Trochi, we travelled continually through forests. The country was generally flat, with a few hills. Sometimes we found a village where we rested, but usually slept in the forest. At midday we took our meals at places where we found that fires had been made, and the ice had been broken to water the horses by persons who had preceded us. We then added wood to the fire, and sat around it to partake of what little provision we had with us. We certainly underwent great suffering; for when we were warm on one side, we had to turn the other to the fire, and I slept in my *sano* rather than on the ground. We travelled three days and slept two nights on a frozen river; and we were said to have travelled three hundred miles, which is a great distance. . . .

ᛘ *41* ᛘ

The Sudebnik *[Code of Law] of Ivan III, 1497*

The reign of Ivan III (1462–1505) was quite memorable for a number of reasons. He reinforced the foundation of Moscow's autocracy. Through his marriage in 1472 to Zoe Paleologa, a Byzantine Princess, he established a claim to Byzantine and Roman heritage. Between 1471 and 1478 he destroyed the Republic of Novgorod and brought its vast territories under Moscow's control. In 1480 he formally terminated the 240-year-long Mongol domination of northern Rus principalities, and shortly thereafter he precipitated a conflict with the Polish-Lithuanian commonwealth for control of territories east of the Dnieper River, and with Sweden and the Livonian Knights over control of the eastern shores of

From R. P. Muller and L. V. Cherepin, eds., *Sudebniki XV-XVI vekov* (Judicial Charters of XV-XVI Centuries) (Moscow, Akademiia Nauk, Institut Istirii, 1952), pp. 19–29, in *Muscovite Judicial Texts, 1488–1556*. Compiled, translated, and edited, with annotations and selected glossary, by H. W. Dewey. (Ann Arbor: Michigan Slavic Materials, 1966), pp. 9–21. Reprinted with permission of Department of Slavic Languages and Literature, University of Michigan.

the Baltic. During the same period, Ivan also established friendly ties with the Crimean Tatars and, in 1497, as a sign of his strength and permanency he promulgated a new code of law, the *Sudebnik*.

Patterned after Kiev's *Ruskaia pravda* (The Rus Code of Law) and some provisions of Pskov's charters, the *Sudebnik* of 1497 introduced uniformity in judicial procedures throughout expanded Muscovy, attempted to curb the widespread corruption of officials, prescribed detailed punishments for offenders, placed control on *boyar* activities, fixed nationwide limits on peasant mobility, authorized capital punishment for armed rebellion or conspiracy against the sovereign, and designated Ivan not simply Grand Prince of Moscovy, but Grand Prince of all Rus principalities. That new title was a dramatic demonstration of the growth of power of Muscovy's princes and of Moscow as the center of all activities.

In the year 1497, in the month of September, the Grand Prince of all Rus' Ivan Vasilievič, with his children and *boyars*, compiled a code of law on how *boyars* and major-domos (*okolničie*) are to administer justice.

I

Boyars and major-domos are to administer justice. And secretaries (*djaki*) shall be present at the court of *boyars* and major-domos. And the *boyars*, major-domos and secretaries are not to receive bribes for judging or participation in deciding a case. Likewise no judge is to receive a bribe for judging. And no one is to use the court for purposes of [personal] revenge or favor.

2

And if a plaintiff shall come to a *boyar*, he is not to dismiss the plaintiffs [*sic*], but shall give hearing in all matters to all plaintiffs for whom it is proper. But whenever there is a plaintiff whom it is not proper for him to hear, he shall inform the Grand Prince or send him (the plaintiff) to him who has been ordered to administer such people.

3

And the *boyar* and secretary are to take from the guilty party, whether plaintiff or defendant, out of a *ruble* case: the *boyar* two *altyns,* the secretary eight *dengi*. And if the case involves more than a *ruble* or less, the *boyar* shall take [fees] in the same proportion.

4. Concerning Fees for Judicial Duels

And if a case is to be tried by judicial duel but the parties become reconciled without having stood in the dueling field, the *boyar* and the secretary are to take [fees] in the same proportion: the *boyar* two *altyns* per *ruble*, the secretary eight *dengi;* but the major-domo and secretary and the bailiffs (*nedel'ščiki*) shall be paid no judicial-duel fees.

5

And should the parties, having stood in the dueling field, become reconciled, the *boyar* and secretary are to take their fees in the same proportion; the major-domo [shall receive] one quarter-*ruble* and the secretary four *altyns* and one *denga;* the bailiff one quarter-*ruble* and a *viaščee*-fee[1] of two *altyns*.

6

And if they fight a judicial duel over a question of loan or physical violence, the *boyar* and secretary shall take from the losing party a *protiven'*-fee based on plaintiff's damages; and the major-domo [shall take] one half-*ruble*, and his secretary one quarter-*ruble*, and the bailiff one half-*ruble* plus a *viaščee*-fee of four *altyns*.

7

And if they shall fight in the field about arson, or murder, or brigandage, or theft, then the sum at issue is to be levied from the loser; and the major-domo is to get from the loser one half-*ruble* and the [loser's] armor; the secretary [gets] one quarter-*ruble*; the bailiff one half-*ruble* and a *viaščee*-fee of four *altyns;* and the loser himself is to be given over to the *boyar* and secretary for punishment and fine.

8. Concerning Theft

And if evidence is brought against anyone of theft, or brigandage, or murder, or false accusation or any other such evil deed, and he is a notorious criminal [lit., is known as evil], then the *boyar* is to order him executed and the sum at issue paid from his property, and whatever remains of this property shall be taken by the *boyar* and his secretary for themselves. And the fee and fine are to be divided between the *boyar* and his secretary: to the *boyar* two *altyns,* to his secretary eight *dengi*. And if a criminal has no such property with which to pay the sum at issue, the *boyar* shall [nevertheless] not give him up to the plaintiff to make good plaintiff's loss, but shall order the Moscow Grand Prince's deputy and steward to have him executed.

9

And the murderer of his master, or a conspirator, temple robber or kidnapper, or *podymščik*[2] or arsonist, such a notorious criminal shall not be allowed to live, but shall be put to death.

10. Concerning Thieves

And if a thief be caught stealing in any way for the first time, except [in the case of] temple robbery and kidnapping [or theft accompanied by murder?] and there has been no previous accusation of other theft made against him, then he shall be punished on the market place, flogged with the knout and made to pay plaintiff's damages, and the judge shall sell him/impose a fine upon him. And if the thief has no property with which to pay the sum at issue, then, after flogging him with the knout, they shall give him over to the plaintiff in slavery to make good plaintiff's loss, and the judge shall take nothing from him.

I I

And if a thief be caught a second time stealing, then he shall be executed and the sum at issue paid from his property, the remainder of his property going to the judge. And if he has no property sufficient for the satisfaction of the plaintiff's loss, he shall [nevertheless] not be given up to plaintiff [in slavery] to cover his damages, but shall be put to death.

I 2

And if a person be accused as a thief by five or six reputable petty nobles, after kissing the Grand Prince's cross, or by five reputable common peasant cross-kissers [wardens?], and if there be no evidence against him in a previous case that he had stolen from anyone or had paid damages for theft to anyone, then plaintiff's loss shall be taken from him without court proceedings.

13. Concerning Stolen Goods

If defendant be brought with stolen goods (*poličnoe*) for the first time, and five or six men swear, after kissing the Grand Prince's cross, that the defendant is a known thief and has stolen more than once before, then he shall be executed and the sum at issue/plaintiff's loss paid from his property.

14. Concerning Testimony of Thieves

And whomever a thief shall accuse, he shall be interrogated; if the accused has in the past been charged with theft, and supporting evidence given, he shall be tortured on accusation of theft; if there has been no previous charge, supported by evidence, of any sort against him, then the thief's accusations shall not be given [full] credence and he (the accused) shall be let out on bail pending further investigation.

15. Concerning the Written Court Decision
(pravaja gramota)

For affixing a seal on a court decision the fee shall be nine *dengi* per *ruble*, and the secretary, for signing it, shall receive one *altyn* per *ruble*, and the scribe who writes up the decision shall receive three *dengi* per *ruble*.

16. Concerning the Record of Trial (dokladnyj spisok)
[referred up to the boyar *judge]*

And the *boyar* shall affix his seal to the trial record, and the secretary shall sign it. And for [each] record the *boyar* shall take one *altyn* per *ruble*; the secretary, for signing it, four *dengi* per *ruble*; and the scribe, who writes up the record, two *dengi* per *ruble*.

17. Concerning Court Decisions on Slaves

And for a written court decision and for a manumission (*otpustnye*) of a male or female slave the *boyar* shall receive, for affixing his seal, nine *dengi* a head; the secretary, for signing, one *altyn* a head, and the scribe, who writes up the decision or manumission, three *dengi* a head.

18. Concerning the Slave Manumission

And if anyone presents a manumission without reporting to the *boyar* and without the secretary's signature, or, in towns, without reporting to the *vicegerent* who is a *boyar* holding full jurisdictional grant, then such manumission is not valid, except when the master (*gosudar'*) with his own hand shall write it, and then said manumission is valid.

19. Concerning Unjust Court Procedure

And whomever a *boyar* without [proper] trial declares in the wrong, and, with the secretary, issues a written court decision against him, then that decision shall be invalid, and that which was taken [shall be] returned. But the *boyar* and secretary shall pay no fine, and the parties shall commence proceedings anew.

20. Concerning the Decree to Vicegerents

And city *vicegerents* and rural *vicegerents* who hold limited jurisdictional grants shall not release a male or female slave without formal report [to higher authorities], nor issue documents returning runaway slaves to their masters. Likewise they shall not issue to a male or female slave a court decision against the master without reference up, nor issue a manumission to a male or female slave.

21. Concerning the Grand Prince

And for the administration of justice by the Grand Prince and his children the same shall be taken from the guilty party as for the *boyar* court, [to wit,] two *altyns* per *ruble*, to whomever the Grand Prince shall order.

22. Concerning the Written Court Decision

For a written court decision the seal-keeper of the Grand Prince and of the Grand Prince's children shall receive nine *dengi* per *ruble* for [affixing his] seal; the secretary shall receive an *altyn* per *ruble* for signing; the scribe, who writes up the decision, three *dengi* per *ruble*.

23
And from a male or female slave the seal-keeper shall take, for a written court decision, nine *dengi* a head; the secretary shall take, for signing, an *altyn* a head; the scribe, who writes up the decision, three *dengi* a head.

24. Concerning the Record of Trial
And the record of trial for reporting up to the Grand Prince and to his children shall be stamped by the seal-keeper of the Grand Prince and by the seal-keeper of his children. For affixing the seal upon such record he shall take nine *dengi* per *ruble*; the secretary, for signing, shall take an *altyn* per *ruble*; and the scribe, who writes it up, shall receive two *dengi* per *ruble*.

25. Concerning Record(s) of Default Judgments
And for [recording] a default judgment the seal-keeper shall receive an *altyn* per *ruble*; the secretary, for signing it, also an *altyn* per *ruble*; and the scribe shall take two *dengi* per *ruble*.

26. Concerning Court Summons
And for summonses the secretary shall take, for his signature, two *dengi* apiece. And for postponements the secretary shall take, for his signature, three *dengi* per *ruble*. And the scribes shall take two *dengi* per *ruble* for writing it up. And if the plaintiff [or] defendant both desire a postponement, each shall pay one half the cost of signing and writing it up, plus a service fee, (literally, walking-distance fee—*xoženoe*), to the bailiff. And if a plaintiff or defendant does not answer a summons, and sends for a postponement, he alone shall bear the costs of both the summons and the postponement, and the service fee. And the secretaries shall keep the summonses in their possession.

27. Concerning Default Judgments
And when time comes to issue default judgments, the secretaries shall themselves gather together the summonses, and, having themselves sorted them out, they shall order the scribes to issue default judgments and write out postponements. And the scribes [on their own initiative] shall issue no summons. And the default judgments shall be issued the eighth day [after the date set in the summons and the failure of a party to appear in court].

28. Concerning Bailiff Warrants
And for a bailiff's warrant the seal-keeper is to be paid from [and according to] the bailiff's riding-distance fee. When, according to the warrant, the bailiff

is paid one *ruble*, the secretary takes an *altyn* from the bailiff's *ruble* for signing, and the seal-keeper also takes an *altyn* from it for affixing the seal. If the riding-distance fee to any city is more than a *ruble*, or less, the secretary and the seal-keeper shall take [fees] in the same proportion. And if the sum in dispute is less than the riding-distance fee, the secretary shall not sign such warrant; and without bailiffs the secretaries shall likewise not sign warrants. And no matter how many parties there are to a suit (literally, how many portions [into which the total fee is divided] there are in the warrant), the bailiff shall have a single riding-distance fee to that city for which the warrant is drawn.

29

And the walking-distance fee for the bailiff shall be ten *dengi* in Moscow and double this sum for an investigation; they shall take no additional fee for [placing parties on] bond. And the bailiff shall have a riding-distance fee for any other city [besides Moscow], and double this sum for an investigation.

30. Decree on Riding-Distance Fee

And the riding-distance fee from Moscow to Kolomna is one half-*ruble*; to Kašira one half-*ruble*; to Xotun' ten *altyns*; to Serpuxov one half-*ruble*; to Tarusa twenty *altyns;* to Aleksin twenty-five *altyns;* to Kaluga one *ruble*; to Jaroslavec one half-*ruble*; to Vereja one half-*ruble*; to Borovsk a half-*ruble*; to Vyšegorod a half-*ruble*; to Kremensk twenty *altyns;* to Možaisk one half-*ruble*, and to Medyn' twenty-five *altyns;* to Vjazma one and one-half *rubles*; to Zvenigorod one-fifth of a *ruble* (two *grivny*); to Vorotynsk forty *altyns;* to Odoev forty *altyns;* to Kozel'sk one *ruble* and a quarter-*ruble*; to Belev the same; to Mezeck forty *altyns;* to Obolensk one half-*ruble*; to Dmitrov ten *altyns;* to Radonež one quarter-*ruble*; to Perejaslavl' twenty *altyns;* to Rostov one *ruble*; to Jaroslavl' one *ruble* and one quarter-*ruble*; to Vologda two and one-half *rubles*; to Beloozero two and one-half *rubles*; to Ustjug five *rubles*; to Vyčegda seven *rubles*; to Dvina and to Xolmogory eight Moscow *rubles*; to Vladimir one *ruble* and one quarter-*ruble*; to Kostroma one and one-half *rubles*; to Jurev one *ruble*; to Suzdal' one *ruble* and one quarter-*ruble*; to Galič two and one-half *rubles*; to Murom one and one-half *rubles*; to the patrimonial estate of the Starodub princes, one and one-half *rubles*; to Meščera two *rubles*; to Nižnij-Novgorod two and one-half *rubles*; to Uglič one *ruble*; to Bežickij Verx one and one-half *rubles*; to Romanov one *ruble* and one quarter-*ruble*; to Klin one half-*ruble*; to Kašin one *ruble*; to Tver' one *ruble*; to Zubcev and Opki one *ruble*; to Xlepnja forty *altyns;* to Rževa one *ruble* and one quarter-*ruble*; to Velikij Novgorod two and one-half Moscow *rubles*.

31

And the bailiffs themselves shall travel with warrants and put them [defend-
ants] on bond, or shall send their relatives or servants with warrants. No men
hired especially for the job shall be sent by them with warrants. And riding
with warrants, they are not to take anything for placing a defendant on bond.
Decree concerning bailiffs. And in whatever city a bailiff shall reside, he shall
not ride in that city with warrants nor send [anyone else] with warrants to
his home city in any matter.

32

And whosoever shall send a bailiff after someone in a matter, whatever loss
shall occur to him in this matter through deliberate delay, or whatever he
shall spend as a result of a summons and a written court decision and a default
judgment, the loser shall pay all [such costs] to the one adjudged right.

33

And bailiffs shall not ask for or take bribes for the *boyar* or major-domo or
for the secretary, nor shall they themselves take any bribes for putting on
bond.

34

And to whomever they shall deliver up a thief and order him interrogated,[3]
he (the bailiff) shall interrogate the thief zealously. And whomever a thief
shall [in turn] accuse of something, he (the bailiff) shall tell the Grand Prince
or judge who has handed the thief over to him, and shall order the thief not
to accuse any person falsely. And if they send a bailiff out after thieves he
shall apprehend them in lawful fashion, and he shall not favor anyone. And
having taken custody of the thief he shall not release him nor shall he accept
bribes, and he shall not apprehend other people (that is, people other than
those he was specifically commissioned to seize).

35

And whenever a bailiff has thieves in his charge, he shall not release them
on bond without report, nor is he to sell the thieves.

36

And if a thief be released on bond in any case whatsoever, they (the bailiffs)
shall not put off the plaintiffs and defendants, but shall bring them before
the judges. They shall draw up postponements and issue default decrees to
peasants (Christians?) without delay and they shall take nothing from peasants
(Christians?) for default judgments. And if a postponement is issued for both

the parties together, he (the bailiff) shall take one walking-distance fee from both parties and besides this he shall take nothing. And in respect to his riding-distance fee, he is to be given guarantee of payment prior to the enquiry [pertaining to theft] and he is to take his riding-distance fee from the party adjudged guilty. And if a plaintiff or defendant does not appear in answer [to a summons] but sends [someone else] in his place for a postponement, the bailiffs shall take their fees from him alone who comes in his place to have the case postponed.

37. Decree to City Vicegerents about Justice
And into whatever city or *canton* there shall come a bailiff or his agent with warrant, he shall show the warrant to the local city *vicegerent* or rural *vicegerent* or their deputies. And if both litigants are of that city or *canton,* then he shall place them both before the city *vicegerent* or rural *vicegerent* or their deputies.

38
And those *boyars* and petty *boyars* to whom are given grants with full jurisdiction shall administer justice, and at their court there must be [present]: a steward (*dvorskij*), an elder (*starosta*) and outstanding citizens (*lučšie ljudi*). And without a steward, elder and outstanding citizens the city and rural *vicegerents* shall not hold court; and they are to take no bribes for administering justice, nor shall their deputies or agents take bribes for administering justice, either for their lord or for their deputy, and the tax-collectors shall also not ask for bribes in connection with judicial administration. And he (the *vicegerent*) is to receive [a fee] for the trial if the plaintiff wins; and he (the *vicegerent*) and his deputy are to receive from the loser a *protiven'*-fee in accordance with the charters, and where there is no charter he shall have them in proportion to the sum at issue. And if plaintiff does not win his case, but is [instead] found guilty, he (the *vicegerent*) shall collect two *altyns* per *ruble* from the plaintiff, and his deputy shall have eight *dengi* per *ruble*. And if the case involves more than one *ruble*, or less than one *ruble*, then the fee shall be collected from the plaintiff in the same proportion. And the criminal-investigator (*dovodčik*) shall take his walking-distance fee and riding-distance fee and investigation expenses according to the charter. And if the case proceeds to the point of a judicial duel and the parties become reconciled [prior to the duel], he (the judge) shall have his fees according to the charter. And if they fight it out on the field, [the *vicegerent*] shall have his *vina*-fee[4] and *protiven'*-fee according to the charter. And where there is no charter, and they become reconciled, he (the *vicegerent*) and his deputy shall be given a *protiven'*-fee of half the sum sought by the plaintiff. And if the parties fight it out on the [dueling] field in a case involving a loan or assault and battery, he shall have

a fee equal to the sum sought by plaintiff. And if they fight it out on the [dueling] field in a case of arson, murder, brigandage or theft, then he shall exact the sum at issue from the defeated party, and the defeated party himself shall be subject to punishment and fine at the hands of the *vicegerent* and his deputy.

39. Decree Concerning Thieves

And if evidence be brought against a person of theft or brigandage or murder or defamation (false accusation), or any other such evil deed, and he is a known criminal, then he (the *vicegerent* or judge) shall order him put to death, and shall exact the sum at issue from his estate, and what is left over of his property the *vicegerent* and his deputy shall take for themselves. And if the known criminal has no property with which to pay the sum at issue, then [nevertheless] he (the *vicegerent*) shall not hand him over to plaintiff to make up plaintiff's loss, [but] shall order him put to death.

40. Concerning Written Court Decisions

And for a written court decision the *boyar* or petty *boyar* who holds a full-jurisdictional grant shall receive, together with his deputy, two and one-half *altyns* per *ruble* for affixing the seal; the secretary, who writes the court decision, shall take three *dengi* per *ruble* for writing. And if the deputy issues a written court decision he shall receive, for affixing a seal to it, two and one-half *altyns* per *ruble* for his lord and himself, and his secretary shall be paid three *dengi* per *ruble* [for each copy]. And the *boyar* and petty *boyar* with a full-jurisdictional grant shall receive for a written court decision or manumission for a male or female slave, two and one-half *atlyns* a head, from the male or female slave, for affixing the seal. And his secretary shall have three *dengi* a head for writing it up.

41

And his deputy in local administration (*na kormlenie*) shall not issue a slave a written court decision without reporting to his master, nor shall he issue a manumission.

42. Concerning the Slave's Manumission

And if anyone presents a manumission without report to the *boyar* and without the secretary's signature, or from the cities without report to the *vicegerent* who has the status of a petty *boyar* with full-jurisdictional grant, then such manumission shall be invalid unless the (slave's) master shall have written it with his own hand, [in which case] the manumission is valid.

43

City and rural *vicegerents* who hold limited-jurisdictional grants, and deputies of the Grand Prince and of *boyars* who hold full-jurisdictional grants, shall not release a male or female slave without report [to the Grand Prince or higher *boyar*] and shall not issue a manumission; and they are not to release a thief or murderer, nor sell, punish or release any other felon without report [to the higher authorities].

44. Concerning Bailiffs

And a *vicegerent's* bailiffs shall, according to the charter, receive walking-distance fees and riding-distance fees. And where no charter exists, such bailiff shall take walking-distance fees of four *dengi,* and one *denga* per *verst* riding-distance fees [outside the city], and twice this sum for investigative duties in the city and rural *canton.*

45

And if one sends a bailiff after a city *vicegerent,* a rural *vicegerent,* or a *boyar,* or petty *boyar,* or their deputies, or the deputies of the Grand Prince, then the city *vicegerent* and the rural *vicegerent* and their deputies and the Grand Prince's deputies and criminal-investigators shall answer [the warrant or summons] and appear [at the designated time]; and if [the summoned person] does not himself appear at the designated time he shall send [someone to appear] in his place at the designated time.

46. Concerning Tradespeople

And if a person buys something new, except a horse, not knowing the vendor, and if [the transaction] be known to two or three good men (*dobrye ljudi,* who represent the community in court), and if [subsequently those objects] are seized from him [as stolen goods], those good men shall testify in accordance with the law that defendant bought the goods at the market in their presence, then the person in whose possession [those objects] were seized is without fault and need not kiss [the cross].

47

And if a person purchases [something] on foreign soil and those objects are seized [as stolen goods], and if he has as witness two or three good men who shall testify according to law that he purchased the goods in their presence at a market, then the person in whose possession [those objects] were seized is without fault and need not kiss [the cross]; and if he has no witnesses he must be made to give oath.

48. *Concerning Witnesses' Testimony*

And when a witness shall give testimony in a case of assault or robbery or loans, then the trial procedure shall be left to the choice of the defendant; if he wishes, he may go to the [dueling] field with the witness, or, having stood on the field, he may place that for which he is being sued at the cross; [in the latter case] the plaintiff shall take what he claims as his, without kissing the cross, and the defendant shall pay the duel fees but not the loser fees. And if he does not go out on the [dueling] field but places [the sum or property demanded by plaintiff] at the cross, he shall pay the judges a fee according to the list, but shall pay no duel fees.

49

And if the defendant be too old [himself to fight] against a witness, or too small, or a cripple, or a priest or a monk or a nun, or a woman, then [he or she] shall be allowed to hire a fighter against the witness, but the witness may not hire such a fighter. And whatever losses accrue to the party who wins the case, or to his witness, such losses [shall be charged] against the loser.

50

And if a witness fails to appear before the judge, whether or not he has any testimony to give, then from such witness shall the sum at issue and all dues be taken. And concerning time of appearance, this witness shall deal with the sergeant-at-arms.

51

And if a witness refuses to testify before the judge in [support of] the plaintiff's allegations, then the plaintiff is at fault.

52

And if a woman, or small child, or an old person, or a sick person, or cripple, or priest, or monk, or nun shall bring suit against anyone or if any of these shall serve as a witness for anyone, then he is allowed to hire a substitute [for dueling]. And the litigants or witness must kiss [the cross] but the hired fighters must fight. Against these hired fighters the plaintiff or defendant [may hire] fighters [of his own, or], if he so desires, he may himself fight in the [dueling] field.

53

If any person shall have another seized by a bailiff in connection with a fight or verbal insult, or a loan, and they shall not desire to go to court, and if, reporting to the judge, they become reconciled, then the judge shall take no fees from them except the [bailiff's] riding-distance or walking-distance fees.

54

And if a hired worker does not serve out his period and goes away, he shall be deprived of his wages.

55. *Concerning Loans*

And whatever merchant, departing on a business trip, shall take money or goods from another [for purposes of commerce], and on the way these goods shall, through no fault of his, be lost, for instance, shall be sunk, or burned, or seized by troops, the *boyar* [judge], after investigating the matter, shall order the Grand Prince's secretary to issue him a document entitling him to pay back the debt by installment, [which document shall bear] the seal of the Grand Prince, and [which document shall allow defendant] to pay plaintiff the principal without interest. But if [a merchant] shall take something to trade and then go and drink it up or through some other foolishness lose it in non-accidental fashion, such person shall be handed over to the plaintiff in slavery to make up the loss.

56

And if a slave be captured by Tatar enemy troops and escapes from captivity, he shall be free and no longer the slave of his former master.

57. *Concerning the Peasant Quitting-Time*

And peasants may leave a canton [to go to another *canton*], or [go] from village to village, once a year, for a week before and a week after St. George's Day in the autumn. For field living quarters they shall pay one *ruble*, for forest quarters a half-*ruble*. And whatsoever peasant shall live one year under a given master and then leave, he shall pay one-fourth of the living-quarters' value, or if he lives two years and leaves, he shall pay one-half; if he lives three years and leaves, he shall pay three-fourths of the living-quarters' value, and if he lives four years he shall pay the full amount of living-quarters' value.

58. *Concerning Foreigners*

And whatsoever foreigner shall bring suit against another foreigner, the defendant is free to take an oath [with cross kissing] that he is innocent, or he can lay at the cross that for which he is being sued, and plaintiff, after kissing the cross, shall take it.

59

And a priest, and a deacon, and a monk, and a nun, and a sexton, and a widow, who are sustained by God's church, are to be judged by a bishop or his judge. And if a layman {is in litigation] with a church man, then a joint court shall decide the case. And if a widow is not supported by the church, but lives in her own home, then she shall not be under ecclesiastical jurisdiction.

60

And if a person dies without a will and has no son, then all his personal property and lands [shall pass] to the daughter; and if he has no daughter, then his closest of kin shall take.

61. *Concerning Fences*

And between villages and hamlets fences are to be erected by halves (that is, each side putting up half the fencing), and through whose fence there shall occur damage by cattle, he whose fence it is shall pay the damages. And when meadowlands are far from villages or hamlets, then the owner of such lands shall not erect a fence, but he whose lands are ploughed fields next to the meadow shall erect the entire enclosure.

62. *Concerning Boundaries*

And whoever shall plough up a boundary or cut down markers, be he from the lands of the Grand Prince [and trespass on those of] a *boyar* or a monastery, or from *boyar* and monastery holdings [and trespass] on the lands of the Grand Prince, or from *boyar* and monastery lands [and trespass] on [lands of another] *boyar*, or from *boyar* lands [and trespass] on monastery land, whosoever has ploughed up a boundary or cut down markers shall be flogged with the knout and the plaintiff shall take a *ruble* [fine] from him. And if peasants among themselves in a *canton* or village shall plough across or mow beyond a boundary, then the rural *vicegerents* or the estate manager shall take from him (the guilty one) two *altyns* in place of a ram and for bodily injury they will fine according to the person, the injury and the circumstances (lit., reasonings).

63. *Concerning Land Litigation*

And if a *boyar* shall start proceedings against [another] *boyar*, or a monastery shall sue a monastery, or a *boyar* sue a monastery, or a monastery a *boyar*, then the case must be tried (trial must begin?) within three years and after three years action will not lie. And if a free peasant brings suit against another free peasant, or a *pomeščik* (holder of land on service tenure) sues another *pomeščik* who holds lands belonging to the Grand Prince, or if a free peasant or landlord's peasant sues a *pomeščik,* or if a *pomeščik* sues a free peasant or landlord's peasant, then the suit shall be brought within three years, and after three years action will not lie. And if a *boyar* or monastery are sued for lands belonging to the Grand Prince, then the case must be tried within six years, not more. And when lands are held by a bailiff pending litigation, the court shall complete the case.

64

And judges reviewing a case shall have a review fee of two *grivny* from the party found guilty, and there shall be no review fee [for cases involving] less than one *ruble*. And for court records [sent up for review], and for cases dealing with land or slaves, there shall be no review fee. A review fee (an amount equal to a review fee?) shall be collected for all cases in which a judicial duel has occurred. And if a party shall declare the court record false and demands an investigation, then there shall be a review fee. And the bailiffs (*podvojskim*) shall receive an investigation-fee or four *dengi,* and it shall be collected from the loser.

65

And whenever there are two city *vicegerents* in a city or two rural *vicegerents* in a canton, they shall have fees in accordance with this document, both [jointly receiving the fee] for a single *vicegerent,* and their deputies the fees of a single deputy, and they shall share the fees equally.

66. Concerning the Full-Slavery Document

By a full-slavery document [one becomes] a slave. By taking the position of a deputy or village steward, one becomes a slave whether with formal report [to higher authorities] or without it, along with one's wife and one's children, provided they live under the same master; and those children who shall have begun living under another master, or by themselves, shall not become slaves; and by being a city steward [one does not become] a slave. Whoever marries a female slave becomes himself a slave; a woman marrying a slave becomes herself a slave. Slaves may pass by dowry and by will.

67. Concerning Bribes and Testimony of Witnesses

And it shall be ordered proclaimed in the markets in Moscow and all cities of the Moscow and Novgorod territories, and decreed in all *cantons* that the plaintiff and defendant shall not offer bribes to judges and bailiffs and that witnesses shall not testify to what they have not seen, and shall tell only the truth concerning what they have seen. And if a witness falsely testifies concerning something he has not seen, and this is later discovered, then this witness shall pay the sum at issue and damages.

68. Fees for Judicial Duels

And to the dueling field there shall ride a major-domo and a secretary, and the major-domo and secretary shall enquire of the litigants, plaintiff and defendant, who [of the people present] are their backers and sureties; and whoever are designated as backers and sureties shall be ordered to stand [on the sidelines], and backers and sureties shall have no armor, oak clubs or sticks in their possession. And if any outsider stand at the field, the major-domo and his secretary shall send them away. And if such outsiders do not go away, the major-domo and secretary shall order the sum at issue and fees paid by them and order them placed on bond, seized and brought before the Grand Prince.

Notes

1. Although this fee has generally mystified Russian legal historians, it is translated as a fee for arranging the duel in *Pamjatniki russkogo prava,* III, p. 358.

2. This is another work which has mystified scholars. Commentaries on it have generally been based on Herberstein's version, which defines a *podmetčik* (a different word altogether!) as one who secretly carries off property to another's house in order to make that person appear as the thief of the property; see original Latin text of Herberstein in *Sudebniki XV-XVI vekov,* pp. 31–32. Čerepnin believes the word *podmetčik* may refer to a spy or person disclosing secret information; *Pamjatniki russkogo prava,* III, p. 383. If, however, we relate the word *podymščik* to the verb *pod'jat'sja,* the code may be considered as referring to some sort of raising of arms against lawful authority, or uprising; I. I. Sreznevskij translates *pod'jat'sja* as "to gather; to arm oneself; to set off on campaign"; *Materialy dlja slovarja drevne-russkogo jazyka* (St. Petersburg, 1893), II, column 1074. A German scholar believes that the *podmetčik* was "der Anstifter vielleicht eines Aufruhrs"; A. von Reutz, *Versuch über die geschichtliche Ausbildung der russischen Staats- und Rechts-verfassung* (Mitau, 1829), p. 307.

3. It is possible that the word *pytati* in this sentence should be translated as "to torture"; Sreznevskij, *op. cit.,* II, columns 1759–1760. Torture was unquestionably used in the *Sudebnik* era. A modern specialist suggests, however, the *pytati* did not acquire the connotation of "torture" until later, in the sixteenth century; M. A. Bricyn, *Iz istorii vostočnoslavjanskoj leksiki* (Kiev, 1965), p. 135.

4. This *vina*-fee has been translated as a "charge for law proceedings" in *Pamjatniki russkogo prava,* III, p. 367.

⚔ *42* ⚔

Filofei's Concept of the "Third Rome"

In the second half of the fifteenth century, Muscovy's secular and ecclesiastical leaders were profoundly influenced by three events. The first was the Turkish capture of Constantinople in 1453 and their subsequent absorption into the Ottoman Empire of all Christian states of the Balkan peninsula. The second was the break-up of the once-mighty empire of the Golden Horde into several small, quarreling units. And the third was the emergence of Muscovy as a major power in northeastern Europe. Some Muscovy spokesmen interpreted these far-reaching geopolitical changes as the work of Providence, and they soon formulated a new theory to explain these events.

The articulator of the new theory was a monk named Filofei who, between 1515 and 1521, submitted it to Moscow's Grand Prince Vasilii III (1505–1533). The central theme of Filofei's theory was simple. Ancient Rome, he argued, collapsed because its people subscribed to heresies. Constantinople, the second Rome, fell to the Turks because its people were not true Christians. The burden of carrying on the true Christian faith had fallen now on Moscow, the Third Rome, selected by God for that role, as evident in recent Moscow triumphs. And there would be no fourth Rome!

Soon this simplistic argument produced an interesting imposture. It said that Moscow's rulers—who descended from Riurik, who had in turn descended from a close relative of the Roman Caesar Octavian Augustus—were the descendants of and, hence, rightful heirs to Roman heritage and greatness. Before too long, in their official correspondence (with non-European rulers), Moscow's *tsars* referred to themselves as "the Great Sovereign Tsar and Grand Prince and Autocrat of all Russia, descendant of Caesar Augustus, ruler of the entire universe, descendent of the Great Prince Riurik and of all other great monarchs."

To you who have been selected to rule, by the highest, the all-powerful and

---

From V. I. Lebedev, et al., eds., *Khrestomatiia po istorii SSSR. S drevneishikh vremen do kontsa XVII veka* (A Source Book on the History of the USSR. From Ancient Times to the End of the XVIIth Century), Third ed. (Moscow: Ministry of Education, 1949), vol. I, pp. 277–279. Translation mine. Words in brackets are mine.

almighty hand of God, by Whose will all rulers on earth govern and Whom all great people praise and about Whom the powerful write the truth, [I address these words] to you, the illustrious sovereign, Grand Prince [of Muscovy], occupier of the high throne, the Orthodox Christian Tsar and lord of all, the administrator of all Holy Churches of God and of the Holy Universal and Apostolic Church and of the Church of the Holy Mother of God, that has made such honest and illustrious progress that it has been enabled to triumph over the Church of Rome as well as over the Church of Constantinople.

The Apollinarian heresy caused the downfall of old Rome. The Turks used their axes to shatter the doors of all churches of the Second Rome, the city of Constantinople. Now [in Moscow], the new Third Rome, the Holy Ecumenical Apostolic Church of your sovereign state shines brighter than the sun in the universal Orthodox Christian faith throughout the world. Pious Tsar! Let [people of] your state know that all states of the Orthodox faith have now merged into one, your state. You are the only true Christian ruler under the sky!

Tsar! As long as you hold that position, be mindful always of God. Fear God who has bestowed so much on you. Do not rely on gold, wealth, or glory! All of that is collected here and it will remain here on earth. Tsar! Remember the Blissful who held the scepter in His hand and the imperial crown on His head and said: "Do not turn your heart to wealth that is running away from you." The wise Solomon said: "Wealth and gold are valued not when they are hidden, but when people offer help to those in need. . . ." Tsar! During your rule remember [an additional] two commandments. . . . [The first is]: Do not violate the order which was chosen by your great predecessor [Emperor] Constantine, the beatific Vladimir, the great and God-selected Iaroslav, and all other blissful and saintly [rulers] from whom you have descended. [And second]: Tsar! Do not harm the Holy churches of God and honest monasteries. [Do not expropriate] that which has been given to God in return for eternal blessing of the memory of a family. The Fifth Great and Holy Ecumenical Council issued a very strict injunction [against such action]. . . .

Now I beg you and beg you again, please remember what I have said. For God's sake, please also remember that now all [Orthodox] Christian kingdoms have merged into your tsardom. Henceforth we can expect only one kingdom to come. That kingdom is eternal. I have written this because, admiring you as I do, I have appealed and have prayed to God that He may bless you. Change your stinginess to generosity and your inclemency to kindness. Comfort those who cry and moan day and night. Protect the innocent from their tormentors.

I repeat here what I have written above. Pious Tsar! Listen and remember that all Christian kingdoms have now merged into one, your [tsardom]. Two Romes have fallen. The third stands [firm]. And there will not be a fourth. No one will replace your Christian tsardom. . . .

❧ *43* ❧

Herberstein's Observations of Muscovy

Beginning with the reign of Ivan the Great (1462–1505), the military might of Moscow was elevated and Russia was exposed to west European travelers, who in turn left many interesting descriptions of the country and its people. The foremost of these observations is that of Baron Sigismund von Herberstein, who visited Russia in 1517 and again in 1526 as Ambassador of the Holy Roman Empire. Herberstein's observations are vital for two basic reasons: first, they are based upon the personal experience and sixteen months' residence in the country of a man familiar with the history and language of the people; and second, they represent the first authentic and detailed account of sixteenth century Moscovy, the power of its rulers, the customs of its people, and the climate and resources of the country.

In thus entering upon the description of Moscow, which is the capital of Russia, and which extends its sway far and wide through Scythia, it will be indispensable, candid reader, that I should in this work touch upon many parts of the north, which have not been sufficiently known either to ancient authors or those of our own day, and it will follow that I shall sometimes be compelled to differ from the accounts they give. And in order that my opinion in this matter may not be looked upon with suspicion, or considered presumptuous, I assert with all honesty, that not once only, but repeatedly, while engaged as ambassador for the Emperor Maximilian, and his grandson Fer-

---

Reprinted with permission of the Cambridge University Press from Sigismund von Herberstein, *Notes Upon Russia: Being a Translation of the Earliest Account of that Country, Entitled Rerum Moscoviticarum Commentarii.* Translated and edited by R. H. Major (London: Published for the Hakluyt Society, 1851), vol. 1, pp. 3–6, 24–25, 30–38, 55–59, 84–85, 91–95, 101–102, 105–107, and vol. 2, pp. 1–7. Words in brackets are mine. Spellings of some proper names have been modernized.

dinand king of the Romans, I have seen and investigated Moscow, as it were under my very eyes (as the saying is); that I made myself acquainted with the greater part of the talented and trustworthy men of the place, and did not rely upon this or that man's account, but trusted only to the unvarying statements of the many; and having the advantage of knowing the Slavonic language, which is identical with the Russian and Moscovite, I have written these things and handed them down to the memory of posterity, not only as an ear, but as an eyewitness, and that not with any disguise in my description, but openly and freely. . . .

[There follows an outline of Russian history from the Varangians to Ivan the Great and his son Vasili, 1505–1533]

This Ivan Vasilievich was so successful, that he overcame the people of Novgorod in battle at the river Scholona, and reduced them to acknowledge him as their lord and prince, on certain proposed conditions. He granted them a large sum of money and then left them, after having first appointed a representative to supply his place; then again returning after the lapse of seven years, he entered the city with the cooperation of the Archbishop Theophilus, reduced the inhabitants to the most abject servitude, and seizing the gold and silver and all the goods of the citizens, carried off more than three hundred wagons full of booty.

He himself was only once engaged in war, when the principalities of Novgorod and Tver were taken possession of; at other times he never used to go to battle, but nevertheless always carried off the palm of victory; so that Stephen the Great Palatine of Moldavia would often say, when speaking of him at his banquets: "That he increased his dominion while sitting at home and sleeping, while he himself could scarcely defend his own boundaries by fighting every day." He even appointed and deposed the kings of Kazan at his own pleasure; sometimes he threw them into prison, but at length, in his old age, received a severe defeat at their hands. He was the first who fortified his ducal residence at Moscow with a wall, as it is seen at this day. Moreover he was so hostile to women, that if any women met him by chance, they almost always fainted with terror at the sight of him. No access was allowed to him for poor men, who were oppressed by the more powerful or unjustly treated; he generally drank so excessively at dinner as to fall asleep, and while his guests were all struck with terror and sitting in silence, he would awake, rub his eyes, and then first begin to joke and make merry with them. But although this Grand Duke was so powerful a prince, he was nevertheless compelled to acknowledge the sway of the Tatars, for when the Tatar ambassadors were approaching, he would go forth from the city to meet them, and make them be seated while he stood to receive their addresses, a circumstance which so annoyed his Greek wife, that she would daily tell him she had married a slave of the Tatars, and to induce her husband to throw off this servile habit would sometimes persuade him to feign sickness on the approach of the Tatars. There was within the citadel of Moscow a house in which the Tatars lodged for the purpose of learning what was going on at Moscow, and as this also gave great offense to his wife, she sent messengers with liberal presents to the queen of the Tatars, begging her to give up that house to her; for that she had been admonished in a dream from heavens to build a temple upon that spot; at the same time she promised to allot another house to the Tatars. The queen granted her request; the house was destroyed and a temple was built on its site, and the Tatars thus driven out of the citadel have never been able to obtain a house from any subsequent Duke. . . .

At that time also the grand duke attacked the kingdom of Kazan both with a naval and military force, but returned unsuccessful, and with the loss of a large number of his soldiers. Although, however, the Prince Vasiley is thus most unsuccessful in war, he is, nevertheless, constantly being praised by his courtiers as if he had brought things to a happy issue; and on occasions when scarcely half his army has returned home, they have told him that not a man was lost in battle. In the sway which he holds over his people, he surpasses all the monarchs of the whole world, and has carried out his father's plan of ejecting all princes and others from the garrisons and fortified places. He certainly grants no fortresses to his relations, nor even puts them in charge of any, but oppresses nearly all of them with close confinement; and whoever receives his orders to attend at court, or to go to war, or upon any embassy, is compelled to undertake whatever it may be at his own expense, with the exception of the younger sons of nobles of slender fortune, whom he sends for every year, and maintains with a fixed but inadequate stipend. But such of these as receive six gold pieces yearly, forfeit the stipend every third year; and those who receive twelve gold pieces every year, are compelled to hold themselves in readiness, and fully equipped, for the performance of any duty, at their own expense, and with their own horses; and to the more distinguished among them, namely, such as undertake an embassy, or any office of a more weighty character, are assigned districts, or towns, or villages, which are allotted to them according to their respective dignity, or the task performed. From each of these governments, however, certain annual tributes are paid to the prince: the fines extorted from the poor who may chance to be guilty of any delinquencies, and some other perquisites, are all that these nobles receive. The Grand Duke grants tenures of this kind generally for a year and a half; but if he regards any one with unusual favor or goodwill, he adds a few months to the period, but when that time is elapsed, all favor ceases, and the service must be performed six years gratuitously. There was one Vasiley Tretyack Dolmatov, a favorite of the prince, and one of his private secretaries, who, when appointed ambassador to the Emperor Maximilian, and receiving orders to make his preparations, declared that he had not the means and appurtenances necessary for such a journey; upon which he was immediately seized in Bielosero [Beloozero], and thrown into prison for life. After his death, which was most miserable, his property, both real and personal, was seized by the prince for himself; and although he thus acquired three thousand *florins* in ready money, he did not give even a *farthing* to the brothers and heirs of the deceased. Independent of common report, one Ivan, a scribe, who was appointed by the prince to supply me with the daily necessaries of life, confessed that this was the case, and that he had him in his custody at the time that he was taken. The two brothers of Vasiley likewise, Feodore and Zacharias, who were appointed my purveyors on my return from Moscow to Smolensko [Smolensk], confirmed his statement.

Whatever articles of value ambassadors who have been sent to foreign princes bring back with them, the prince places in his own treasury, saying, that he will recompense them in some other manner, which manner is as I have described above. For when the ambassador, Prince Ivan Posetzen Ya-roslavski, was sent with Semen (that is, Simeon) Trofimov as his secretary, to the court of Charles V, they were presented by the emperor with heavy torques and chains of gold, and with Spanish money, and that in gold; and also by my master, the emperor's brother Ferdinand, Archduke of Austria, with cups of silver and baskets of gold and silver, and German money in gold; but when they returned with us to Moscow, the prince immediately on their arrival took away from them the chains and cups, and the greater part of the Spanish gold pieces. When I enquired of the ambassadors respecting the truth of this matter, one of them constantly denied it, from fear of compromising his prince; the other said, that the prince had ordered the royal presents to be sent to him that he might see them: as I alluded to the matter on frequent subsequent occasions, one of them, in order to avoid falsehood on the one side if he denied, or danger on the other if he were to confess the truth, ceased to visit me. The courtiers did not deny that it was the fact, but replied, "What then, if the prince repays them in some other kind?"

He uses his authority as much over ecclesiastics as laymen, and holds unlimited control over the lives and property of all his subjects: not one of his counsellors has sufficient authority to dare to oppose him, or even differ from him on any subject. They openly confess that the will of the prince is the will of God, and that whatever the prince does he does by the will of God; on this account they call him God's key-bearer and chamberlain, and in short, they believe that he is the executor of the divine will. Thus if at any time petitions are presented on behalf of any captive, or with reference to any important business, the prince himself is accustomed to reply, "when God commands, he shall be liberated." In like manner also, if any one enquires respecting some doubtful and uncertain matter, the common answer is, "God and the great prince know." It is a matter of doubt whether the brutality of the people has made the prince a tyrant, or whether the people themselves have become thus brutal and cruel through the tyranny of their prince. . . .

As Russia began, so to the present day it continues to observe the Christian faith according to the Greek ritual. The metropolitan formerly resided in Kiev, afterwards in Vladimir, but now in Moscow. It was a custom of the metropolitans to pay a visit every seven years to that part of Russia which was subject to the Lithuanians, and to return after exacting sums of money from them; but Witold* fearing that his territories would become exhausted of coin, would no longer permit this. He therefore called a convocation of bishops, and appointed a special metropolitan, who at this day holds his seat at Wilna, the metropolis of Lithuania, a city which though observing the Roman ritual, has more Russian than Roman churches in it. The Russian metropolitans hold their authority from the Patriarch of Constantinople. . . .

Metropolitans and bishops were formerly chosen at an assembly of all the archbishops, bishops, abbots, and priors of monasteries; a man remarkable for sanctity was sought for through monasteries and deserts, and was selected. But they say that it is the custom of the present prince to summon certain ecclesiastics to him, and choose one of their number according to his own judgment. . . .

There are also two other archbishops in the Russian monarch's dominions in Novgorod, namely, the archbishop of Magrici and of Rostov'; also, the bishops of Tver, Resan [Riazan], Smolensko, Permia [Perm], Suzdal, Columna [Kolomna], Tczernigov [Chernigov], and Sari. All these are subject to the metropolitan of Moscow; but they have certain revenues of their own out of estates and other extraordinary accidentals (as they call them); they have, however, no forts, cities, or other secular administration (as they call it). They abstain constantly from meats. I only found two abbots in Russia, but very many priors of monasteries, all of whom are chosen at the will of the prince himself, whom no one dares resist.

The mode of electing the priors is described in the letters of one Varlamus, prior of the monastery of Hutten, established in the year 7034 [1525], from which I have only selected the leading particulars. In the first place, the brothers of any monastery beseech the Grand Duke to choose a fitting prior to instruct them in divine precepts. After the election, he is compelled, before he is

*Grand Duke of Lithuania (n.d.–1430)

confirmed by the prince, to bind himself by an oath and a bond, that he will live a pious and holy life in that monastery, according to the appointment of the holy fathers—to appoint all officers with the consent of the elder brothers, according to the custom of their predecessors—to advance such as are faithful in performing their duties, and to give diligent attention to the welfare of the monastery—to consult three or four of the elders on important questions of business, and after deliberation to refer the matter to the whole fraternity, and to decide and settle according to their general opinion; not daintily to live in private, but constantly to be at the same table and eat in common with the monks; diligently to collect all the registers and annual returns, and deposit them faithfully in the treasury of the monastery. All these things he promises to observe under a heavy penalty, which the prince can inflict on him even to the deprivation of his office. The senior monks also bind themselves by an oath that they will observe all the aforesaid rules, and faithfully and diligently obey the prior who shall be appointed.

Those who are consecrated secular priests are for the most part such as have served a long time in the churches as deacons. But no one is consecrated deacon unless he be married, hence they are very often married and ordained deacons at the same time. But if the betrothed of any deacon is in bad repute, he is not ordained deacon: it is necessary that he should have a wife of unblemished character.

When the wife of a priest is dead he is immediately suspended from officiating, but if he lives in chastity, he may be present in the choir as a minister with the other minister of the church, at the offices and other divine engagements. Indeed it was the custom formerly for widowers who lived in chastity to administer the sacraments without blame, but now the custom is introduced that no widower be permitted to perform the sacraments, unless he enter some monastery and live according to rule. If any priest who is a widower enter on a second marriage, which he is free to do, he has nothing in common with the clergy, nor does any priest whatever dare either to administer the sacrament, to baptize, or to perform any other duty, unless a deacon be present.

Priests hold the first place in the churches, and if any one of them on any account were to do that which is contrary to religion and the priestly office, he is brought to a spiritual tribunal; but if he be accused of theft or drunkenness, or fall into any other vice of that sort, he is punished by the *secular* magistrate as they call him. I saw some drunken priests publicly whipped at Moscow, whose only complaint was, that they were beaten by slaves, and not be a gentleman. A few years ago, one of the prince's deputies caused a priest who had been caught in theft to be strangled, at which the metropolitan was very displeased, and laid the matter before the prince. When the deputy was summoned to the prince, he replied, that "according to the ancient custom of the country a thief who was not a priest was hanged"; and so he was sent away unblamed. If a priest complain before a lay judge that he has been struck by a layman (for all kinds of assaults and injuries apply to the secular law), then the judge, if he happen to learn that the layman was provoked by the priest, or previously injured in any way by him, punishes the priest.

Priests are generally maintained from the contribution of the people connected with the court, and have some small tenements allotted to them with fields and meadows, whence they derive their support by their own and their families' industry, like their neighbors. They have very slender offerings. Sometimes the church money is put out at interest at ten percent, and they give the interest to the priest from fear of being compelled to maintain him at their own expense. There are some also who live by the liberality of the princes. Certainly, not many parishes are found endowed with estates and possessions, except the bishoprics and some monasteries. No parish or priesthood is conferred on any one but a priest. In every church there is only one altar, and they do not think it right that the service should be performed more than once a day. A church is seldom found without a priest, who is bound only to perform the services three times a week.

They wear nearly the same dress as the laity, with the addition of a small round skull cap to cover the tonsure, and a broad hat to keep off the heat and rain, or they use an oblong beaver hat of a grey color. They all carry staves to lean upon, called Possoch [*Posokh*].

Abbots and priors, as we have said, preside over monasteries—the latter are called *Igumens*, the former Archimandrites. Their laws and regulations are very severe, but are gradually falling into disuse, and becoming obsolete. They dare not indulge in any sort of amusement. If any one is found to have a harp or any musical instrument, he is most severely punished. They constantly abstain from meat. They all obey, not only the commands of the prince, but all the *boyars* sent by the prince. I was present when my purveyor requested something at the hands of a certain prior, and finding that he persisted in refusing to comply with his request, he threatened to have him beaten, the hearing which immediately produced the desired effect. There are many who leave the monasteries and betake themselves into wildernesses and there built huts, in which they live sometimes alone and sometimes with companions. They seek their livelihood from the earth and the trees, eating roots and the fruits of the trees. These are called Stolpniki; for *Stolp* means a column, and their narrow little dwellings are raised up high in the air and supported on columns.

The metropolitan, the bishops, and archbishops, constantly abstain from all kinds of meat; but when they invite laymen or priests at seasons when meat is eaten, they have the prerogative of being permitted to place meat before them at their entertainment; but this is prohibited to abbots and priors.

The archbishops, bishops, and abbots, wear round black *mitres*; but the bishop of Novgorod alone wears a white two-horned *mitre* after our fashion. The daily garments of the bishops are like those of other monks, except that sometimes they have them of silk, especially the black *pallium*, which has three white strips waving, like the flowing of a river, from the breast in every direction, to signify that from their mouth and heart flow streams of the doctrine of faith and good works. They carry a staff in the form of a cross, on which they lean, which in the common language is called Possoch. The bishop of Novgorod wears a white *pallium*. The bishops confine their attention entirely to matters of divinity and to the pious promotion and advancement or religion itself, and intrust the management of both private and public affairs to their officials. . . .

The principal care of the monks is to convert all men whatsoever to their own creed. The hermit monks have already brought over to the faith of Christ a great part of those who were idolaters through daily and industriously disseminating the word of God amongst them. Even now they go to various countries in the north and east, which they can only reach by the greatest toll, at the risk of both fame and life, and without hope of the least personal advantage; nor do they seek it, for they have an eye to this one thing only, namely, that they may be able to do an acceptable service to God, and to recall into the right path the souls of many who have gone astray (sometimes confirming the doctrine of Christ by death), and to bring them in as gain to Christ. . . .

The Moscovites boast that they are the only true Christians, and condemn us as deserters from the Primitive Church and from the old sacred institutions. But if any one of our religion of his own accord goes over to the Muscovites, or even flees to them against the will of his master, as though for the sake of learning and embracing their religion, they say that he ought not to be let go or restored to his master, even if he should demand him back, a fact which came to my knowledge in a certain instance. . . .

They do not contract marriages within the fourth degree of consanguinity or relationship. They think it heretical for brothers to marry their sisters. Also, no one dare take to wife the sister of his kinsman. They likewise most rigidly observe that no marriage take place between those who are connected by the spiritual relationship of baptism. If any one marry a second wife, and become a bigamist, they allow it indeed, but scarcely think it a lawful marriage. They do not permit a third marriage, except for some weighty cause; but a fourth they allow to nobody, and do not even consider it Christian. They admit divorces, and grant a writ of repudiation, but they mostly conceal it, because they know it to be contrary to religion and the statutes. . . .

They do not call it adultery unless one have the wife of another. Love between those that are married is for the most part lukewarm, especially among the nobles and princes, because they marry girls whom they have never seen before; and being engaged in the service of the prince, they are compelled to desert them, and become corrupted with disgraceful connections with others.

The condition of the women is most miserable; for they consider no woman virtuous unless she live shut up at home, and be so closely guarded that she go out nowhere. They give a woman, I say, little credit for modesty, if she be seen by strangers or people out of doors. But shut up at home they do nothing but spin and sew, and have literally no authority or influence in the house. All the domestic work is done by the servants. Whatever is strangled by the hands of a woman, whether it be a fowl, or any other kind of animal, they abominate as unclean. The wives, however, of the poorer classes do the household work and cook. But if their husbands and the men-servants happen to be away, and they wish to strangle a fowl, they stand at the door holding the fowl, or whatever other animal it may be, and a knife, and generally beg the men that pass by to kill it. They are often seldom admitted into the churches, and still less frequently to friendly meetings, unless they be very old and free from all suspicion. On certain holidays, however, men allow their wives and daughters, as a special gratification, to meet in very pleasant meadows, where they seat themselves on a sort of wheel of fortune, and are moved alternately up and down, or they fasten a rope somewhere, with a seat to it, in which they sit, and are swung backwards and forwards; or they otherwise make merry with clapping their hands and singing songs, but they have no dances whatever.

There is at Moscow a certain German, a blacksmith, named Jordan, who married a Russian woman. After she had lived some time with her husband, she one day thus lovingly addressed him: "Why is it, my dearest husband, that you do not love me?" The husband replied, "I do love you passionately." "I have as yet," said she, "received no proofs of your love." The husband inquired what proofs she desired. Her reply was: "You have never beaten me." "Really," said the husband, "I did not think that blows were proofs of love; but, however, I will not fail even in this respect." And so not long after he beat her most cruelly; and confessed to me that after that process his wife showed much greater affection towards him. So he repeated the exercise frequently; and finally, while I was still at Moscow, cut off her head and her legs.

All confess themselves to be Chlopos [*Kholops*], that is, serfs of the prince. Almost all of the upper classes also have serfs, who either have been taken prisoners, or purchased; and those whom they keep in free service are not at liberty to quit at their own pleasure. If any one goes away without his master's consent, no one receives him. If a master does not treat a good and useful servant well, he by some means gets a bad name amongst others, and after that he can procure no more domestics.

This people enjoy slavery more than freedom; for persons on the point of death very often manumit some of their serfs, but they immediately sell themselves for money to other families. If the father should sell the son, which is the custom, and he by any means become free or be manumitted, the father can sell him again and again, by right of his paternal authority. But after the fourth sale, the father has no more right over his son. The prince alone can inflict capital punishment on serfs or others. . . .

Justice is carried out very strictly against thieves; when they are caught, the order is, that they shall first have their heels broken, and then rest two or three days while they swell, and then while they are yet broken and swollen they make them walk again. They employ no other method of torturing malefactors to confess robberies or to inform against their accomplices. But if a man, when brought up for examination, be found to deserve death, he is hanged. Criminals are seldom punished with any other kind of punishment, unless they have committed some uncommonly heinous crimes. Thefts, and even murders, unless they have been committed for the sake of gain, are seldom visited with capital punishment. If, indeed, a man catch a thief in the act and kill him, he can do so with impunity, always provided, however, that he bring the man that he has killed to the prince's palace, and explain how the matter occurred. . . .

Few magistrates have authority to inflict capital punishment. No subject dares to put another to the torture. Most malefactors are brought to Moscow or the other principal cities, but convicts are generally punished in winter time, for in summer military pursuits preclude the opportunity of attending to these matters. . . .

The testimony of one nobleman is worth more than that of a multitude of low condition. Attorneys are very seldom allowed: every one explains his own case. Although the prince is very severe, nevertheless all justice is venal, and that without much concealment. I heard of a certain counsellor who presided over the judgments being apprehended, because in a certain case he had received bribes from both parties, and had given judgment in the favor of the one who had made him the largest presents: when he was brought to the prince he did not deny the charge, but stated that the man in whose favor he had given judgment was rich, and held an honorable position in life, and therefore more to be believed than the other, who was poor and abject. The prince revoked the sentence, but at length sent him away with a laugh unpunished. It may be that poverty itself is the cause of so much avarice and injustice, and that the prince knowing his people are poor, connives at such misdeeds and dishonesty as by a predetermined concession of impunity to them.

The poor have no access to the prince, but only to the counsellors themselves; and indeed that is very difficult. Ocolnick holds the place of a *praetor* or judge appointed by the prince, otherwise the chief counsellor, who is always near the prince's person, is so called. *Nedelsnick* is the post of those who summon men to justice, seize malefactors and cast them into prison; and these are reckoned amongst the nobility.

Laborers work six days in the week for their master, but the seventh day is allowed for their private work. They have some fields and meadows of their own allowed them by their masters, from which they derived their livelihood: all the rest is their master's. They are, moreover, in a very wretched condition, for their goods are exposed to plunder from the nobility and soldiery, who call them Christians and black rascals by way of insult.

A nobleman, however poor he might be, would think it ignominious and disgraceful to labor with his own hands; but he does not think it disgraceful to pick up from the ground and eat the rind or peeling of fruits that have been thrown away by us and our servants, especially the skins of melons, garlic, and onions; but whenever occasion offers, they drink as immoderately as they eat sparingly. They are nearly all slow to anger, but proud in their poverty, whose irksome companion they consider slavery. They wear oblong dresses and white peaked hats of felt (of which we see coarse mantles made) rough from the shop.

The halls of their houses are indeed large and lofty enough, but the doors are so low, that in entering, one must stoop and bend one's self.

They who live by manual labor and work for hire, receive a *deng* and a half as one day's pay; a mechanic receives two *dengs*, but these do not work very industriously unless they are well beaten. I have heard some servants complain that they had not received their fair amount of beating from their masters. They think that they have displeased their master, and that it is a sign of his anger if they are not beaten. . . .

The city of Moscow then, the capital and metropolis of Russia, together with the province itself, and the river which flows by it, have but one and the same name, and in the vernacular language of the people are called Mosqwa [Moskva]. Which of the three gave its name to the other two is uncertain; but it is likely that the name was derived from the river. For although the city itself was not formerly the capital of the nation, yet it is evident that the name of Moscovites was not unknown to the ancients. The river Mosqwa, moreover, has its source in the province of Tver, nearly seventy *wersts* [*versts*] above Mosaisko [Mozhaisk] (a *werst* is nearly the length of an Italian mile), not far from a place called Oleskno, and measuring thence a distance of ninety *wersts*, flows down to the city of Moscow, and having received some streams into itself, flows eastward into the river Occa [Oka]. It begins, however, to be navigable six miles above Mosaisko, at which place materials for building houses and other purposes are placed on rafts and brought down to Moscow. Below the city the merchandise, imported by foreigners, is brought up in ships. The navigation is, however, slow and difficult on account of the numerous turnings and windings with which the river is indented, especially between Moscow and the city of Columna [Kolomna], situated on the bank of the river about three miles from its mouth, where, by its many long windings, it increases the length of the passage by 270 *wersts*. The river is not very abundant in fish, for indeed, with the exception of mean and common sorts, it has none at all. The province of Moscow also is not over extensive or fertile, for the sandy soil which covers it and which kills the corn with the least excess of dryness or moisture, is a very great obstacle to fertility. To this must be added the immoderate and excessive inclemency of the atmosphere, for as the severity of the winter overpowers the heat of the sun, the seed which is sown cannot in some places reach maturity. For the cold is sometimes so intense there that in the same manner as with us in summer time the earth splits into clefts with too much heat, so with them it does so from the extreme cold, and water thrown into the air, or saliva spit from the mouth, freezes before it reaches the ground. We ourselves, when we arrived there in the year 1526, saw some boughs of fruitbearing trees that had entirely perished with the rigor of the preceding winter, which had been so severe that year, that many couriers (whom they call *gonecz*) were found frozen in their carriages. There were some men driving cattle tied together with ropes from the neighboring districts to Moscow, who, overpowered by the excessive cold, perished together with the cattle. Several itinerants also, who were accustomed to wander about the country with bears taught to dance, were found dead in the roads. The bears also, stimulated by hunger, left the woods and ran about hither and thither through the neighboring villages and rushed into the houses, while the rustic multitude, terrified at their aspect and strength, fled and perished miserably out of doors with the cold. This excess of cold is sometimes equalled by the too great heat, as in A.D. 1525, when nearly everything that had been sown was burnt up by the immoderate heat of the sun; and such a want of provision followed that drought, that what could previously be bought for three *dengs*, would afterwards cost twenty or thirty. A great many districts, and woods, and cornfields, were seen burnt up by the excessive heat. The smoke of this so filled the country, that the eyes of those who walked out were severely injured by it; and besides the smoke, a certain darkness supervened, which blinded many.

It is evident from the trunks of large trees which still exist, that the whole country was not long since very woody; but although the husbandmen give care and labor to the cultivation of trees, all except such as grow in the fields are brought hither from the neighboring provinces. There is abundance of corn and common vegetables, but none of the sweeter kinds of cherries or nuts (except filberts) are found in the whole country. They have indeed the fruits of other trees, but they are insipid. They cultivate melons with particular care and industry. They put earth mixed with manure into beds of a good depth, and set the seed in them, by which plan it is equally protected against immoderate cold or heat; for if the heat should happen to be too great, they prevent it from suffocating the seed by making little spiral chinks in the earth, which has been thus mixed with manure, while in excessively cold weather the warmth of the manure itself affords protection to the buried seed.

There is no honey in the province of Moscow, nor is there any game, except hares. Their cattle are much smaller than ours, but not without horns, as a certain person has written, for I have seen there oxen, cows, goats, and rams, all horned. The city of Moscow has a very eastward position among the other cities of the north, which we easily perceived in our journey thither; for when we left Vienna, we proceeded direct to Cracow, and thence travelled nearly a hundred German miles northward; at length the road turning eastward, we reached Moscow, situated, if not in Asia, at any rate on the very extreme confines of Europe, where it joins Asia, of which circumstance I shall say more hereafter in my description of the Don.

The city itself is built of wood, and tolerably large, and at a distance appears larger than it really is, for the gardens and spacious court-yards in every house make a great addition to the size of the city, which is again greatly increased by the houses of smiths and other artificers who employ fires. These houses extend in a long row at the end of the city, interspersed with fields and meadows. Moreover, not far from the city, are some small houses, and the other side of the river some villas, where, a few years ago, the Prince Vasiley built a new city for his courtiers, called Nali (which in their language means "pour in"), because other Russians were forbidden to drink mead and beer, except on a few days in the year, and the privilege of drinking was granted by the prince to these alone; and for this reason they separated themselves from intercourse with the rest of the inhabitants to prevent their being corrupted by their mode of living. Not far from the city are some monasteries, which alone appear like a great city to persons looking from a distance. Moreover, in consequence of the great extent of the city, it is confined by no settled boundary, nor has it any useful defenses in the shape of walls, fosses, or ramparts. The streets are, however, blocked up in some places by beams thrown across them, and are guarded by watchmen placed there at early nightfall, so that no one is allowed access by that way after a stated hour; and any who are taken after that by the watchmen are either beaten, stripped, or thrown into prison, unless they happen to be persons of distinction or respectability: and even these are generally accompanied home by the watchmen. Such watches are generally set wherever there is an open entrance into the city, for the Mosqwa flows by one side of the city, and the river Jausa [Iauza], which flows into it under the city itself, has such steep banks, that it scarcely admits of being forded. In this latter river many mills have been erected for the public use of the city, which seems to be mainly defended by these rivers; with the exception of a few stone houses, churches, and monasteries, it is entirely a city of wood. The number of houses which it is said to contain is scarcely credible. For they say, that six years before my arrival at Moscow, the houses were counted by an order of the prince, and that the number exceeded 41,500. This city is so broad and spacious, and so very dirty, that bridges have been constructed here and there in the highways and streets and in the other more distinguished parts. There is a fortress in it built of burnt tiles which on one side is washed by the Mosqwa and on the other by the River Neglima [Neglinaia]. The Neglima flows from certain marshes, but is so blocked up before the city around the upper part of the fortress, that it comes out like stagnant water, and running down thence, it fills the moats of the fortress, in which are some mills, and at length, as I have said, is joined by the Mosqwa under the fortress itself. The fortress is so large that it not only contains the very extensive and magnificently built stone palace of the prince, but the metropolitan bishop, the brothers of the prince, the peers, and a great many others, have spacious houses of wood within it. Besides these, it contains many churches, so that from its size it might itself almost be taken for a city. This fortress was at first surrounded only by oaks, and up to the time of the Grand Duke Ivan Danielovich was small and mean in appearance. It was he, who, by the persuasion of Peter the metropolitan, first transferred the imperial residence to this place. Peter had originally selected that place from love of one Alexius, who was buried there, and who is said to have been famous for miracles; and after his death, being buried in this place, miracles were likewise done at his tomb, so that the place itself acquired such a celebrity, from a certain notion of its sacredness and religious character, that all the princes who succeeded Ivan thought that the seat of empire ought to be held there. For on the death of Ivan, his son of the same name retained his seat there; and after him, Dimitry; and after Dimitry, that Vasiley, who married the daughter of Witold, and left behind him Vasiley the Blind. Of him was born Ivan, the father of that prince, at whose court I was ambassador, and who first surrounded the fortress with a wall; and his descendants, nearly thirty years after, have brought the work to completion. The ramparts and battlements of this fortress, as well as the prince's palace, were built of brick, in the Italian style, by Italians, whom the prince had sent for from Italy with the offer of large remuneration. There are also, as I have said, many churches in it, nearly all of wood, except the two handsomest, which are built of brick. One of these is consecrated to the Blessed Virgin, the other to St. Michael. In the church of the Blessed Virgin are buried the bodies of the two archbishops who were the cause of the prince's transferring thither the seat of empire and the metropolis; and principally on that account they have been enrolled among the number of saints. The other church is used as a burial-place for the princes. There were also many churches, being built of stone, at the time that I was there.

The climate of the country is so wholesome, that, from the sources of the Don, especially northwards, and a great way towards the east, no plague has raged there in the memory of man. They sometimes, however, have a disorder of the bowels and head, not unlike the plague, which they call "the heat": those who are seized with it die in a few days. That disorder was very prevalent when I was at Moscow, and took off one of my servants; but from the people being accustomed to live in so wholesome a climate, if the plague at any time be raging in Novgorod, Smolensko, or Plescow [Pskov], from fear of contagion they exclude from their own country any people who come thence to them.

The people of Moscow are more cunning and deceitful than all others, their honor being especially slack in business contracts—of which fact they themselves are by no means ignorant, for whenever they traffic with foreigners, they pretend, in order to attain greater credit, that they are not men of Moscow, but strangers.

The longest day in Moscow in the summer solstice, is said to be seventeen hours and three quarters. I could not, at that time, ascertain from anybody the exact elevation of the pole, although one man told me, but upon uncertain authority, that he had heard it was fifty-eight degrees. At length I myself made a venture with the astrolabe, and on the ninth day of June, at noon, observed that the sun was at fifty-eight degrees. From which observation it was deduced, by the reckoning of men skilled in these things, that the elevation of the pole was fifty degrees, and that the longest day was seventeen hours and one quarter.

⚡ *44* ⚡

Ivan the Terrible's Own Account of His Early Life

The childhood of Ivan the Terrible (1530–1584) was not a pleasant one. His father, Vasili III (1505–1533), died when Ivan was three years old; his mother, Helena Glinskaia, when he was seven. The regency period was marked by the absence of a strong central government and offered Russian *boyars* an opportunity for intrigue, corruption, violence, and neglect of and lack of respect for the young Prince. During his youth Ivan concealed his feelings of revenge, but when he assumed full power in 1547, upon his formal coronation, his reign spelled the end for many *boyars*. Ivan forced some of the *boyars* into exile, but other perished during the reign of terror known as *oprichnina*. Ivan's policies strengthened the power of the Tsars at the expense of the nobility.

. . . I will prove in the greatest detail what evil I have suffered from my youth even unto the present day. For this is clear (even if you were young in those years, yet none the less this you can know): when, by the decree(s) of God, our father, the great sovereign, Vasiley, having exchanged the purple for the angel's form, had left all that was perishable and the fleeting earthly kingdom and come to the heavenly [realm], to that everlasting eternity, to stand before the Tsar of Tsars and the Lord of Lords, I remained with my only (begotten) brother Georgiy, who has departed this life in sanctity. I was then three years old and my brother was one, and our mother, the pious Tsaritsa Elena, was left in such miserable widowhood—as though in the midst of flames, she suffered on all sides not unmitigated strife stirred up against her by all peoples—by the foreign peoples encircling [our realm], Lithuanians, Poles, Perikopians, Nadchitarkhan, and Nogais, and Kazan',—now manifold misfortune(s) and suffering(s) [inflicted by] you traitors; for, like unto you, you mad dog, Prince Semen Bel'sky and Ivan Lyatsky ran away to Lithuania;

Reprinted with permission of the Cambridge University Press from J. L. I. Fennell, ed., *The Correspondence between Prince A. M. Kurbsky and Tsar Ivan IV of Russia 1564–1579* (Cambridge, England: Cambridge University Press, 1955), pp. 69–101, alternate. See original source for footnote references.

[from there] whither did they not run like men possessed? To Tsargrad and to Crimea and to the Nogai [Tatars] and on all sides they raised strife against the Orthodox. But they had no success. Thanks to the intervention of God and the most pure Mother of God and the great miracle workers, and because of the prayers and the blessing of our parents, all these things, like the counsel of Ahitophel, were scattered. In like manner later did the traitors raise up our uncle, Prince Andrey Ivanovich, against us, and with those traitors did he go to Novgorod, (so, these are they whom you praise! You call them our "well-wishers" and "those that lay down their lives for us"!). And at that time did these [traitors] secede from us and adhere to our uncle, Prince Andrey, and at their head was your brother [that is, cousin], Prince Ivan, the son of Prince Semen, the son of Prince Petr Romanovich Lvov, and many others. And likewise with the help of God did this plot miscarry [literally, this counsel was not achieved]. Well then, is that the "well-wishing" of those whom you praise? Thus do they "lay down their lives for us" by wishing to destroy us and raise our uncle to the throne? But later, in their treacherous manner, they began to hand over our patrimony to our Lithuanian enemy—the towns of Radogoshch, Starodub, Gomel'—thus do they "wish us well'? When there is no one in the land with whom to wreak destruction at home [literally, from the land] and to turn glory to deceit, then do they cast in their lot with [literally, join in love with] foreigners, only so that they may wreak destruction of which no memory shall remain!

Thus by God's will did it come to pass that our mother, the pious Tsaritsa Elena, went from the earthly kingdom to the heavenly; and we and our brother Georgiy, who has departed this life in sanctity, remained as orphans, [having lost] our parents and receiving no human care from any quarter; and hoping only for the mercy of God, we put our trust in the mercy of the most pure Mother of God and the prayers of all the Saints and the blessing of our parents. But when I had entered upon my eighth year of life [literally, from birth] and when thus our subjects had achieved their desire, namely to have the kingdom without a ruler, then did they not deem us, their sovereigns, worthy of any loving care, but themselves ran after wealth and glory, and so leapt on one another [in conflict]. And what did they [not] do then! How many *boyars* and well-wishers of our father and *voevodas* did they massacre! And the courts and the villages and the possessions of our uncles did they seize and they set themselves up in them! And [the majority of] my mother's treasure did they transfer to the Great Treasury, furiously kicking out [at each other] and stabbing with sharp implements; but the remainder they shared amongst themselves. Your grandfather, Mikhailo Tuchkov, did this. And so Prince Vasily and Prince Ivan Shuisky of their own accord did appoint themselves my guardians and thus did they raise themselves to the throne; and all those who had been our father's and our mother's main traitors did they release, one after the other, from imprisonment and win over [literally, reconcile] to their side. And Prince Vasily Shuisky began to live in the court of our uncle, Prince Andrey Ivanovich, and in that court—as it were in a Jewish synagogue—they seized Fedor Mishurin, the private *d'yak* of our father and of us, and having put him to shame they murdered him. And they banished Prince Ivan Fedorovich Bel'sky and many others to various places and rose up in arms against the Church and, deposing the Metropolitan Daniel from the metropolitanate, they sent him into banishment; thus did they achieve their desire in all things and themselves began to rule. But as for us, together with our only (-begotten) brother Georgiy, who has departed this life in sanctity—they began to feed us as though we were foreigners or the most wretched menials. What sufferings did I [not] endure through [lack of] clothing and through hunger! For in all things my will was not my own [literally, I had no will]; everything was contrary to my will and unbefitting my tender years. I (will) recall one thing: whilst we were playing childish games in our infancy Prince Ivan Vasil'evich Shuisky is sitting on a bench, leaning with his elbows on our father's bed and with his leg up on a chair; and he did not even incline his head towards us, either in parental manner, or even as a master—nor was there any element of servility to be found [in his attitude to us]. And who can endure such arrogance? How can I enumerate such countless sore sufferings as I put up with in my youth? Many a time did I eat late, not in accordance with my will. But what of the treasures inherited by me from my father [literally, of my parental heritage]? With their cunning scheming they seized it all, as though it were pay for the *boyar* children; but from them they took it all for themselves for their own profit, rewarding them [the *boyar* children] not according to their service and recompensing them not according to their merits; and they appropriated the incalculable treasure of our grandfather and of our father; and so from this treasure did they forge for themselves golden and silver vessels and upon them they inscribed the names of their parents as though they had been the possession of their parents. Now all people know that during the rule of our mother Prince Ivan Shuisky had a marten fur coat [lined] with green mohair and the skins were shabby [literally, ancient]; now supposing this was a [genuinely] ancient possession of the Shuiskys, surely it would have been better, rather than to forge those vessels [as they did], to have exchanged the fur coat and with the surplus [money accruing from the sale of the new coat] to have forged the vessels? But what shall I say concerning the treasure of my uncles? They seized it all for themselves and after this they fell upon [literally, jumped on] the towns and villages and thus with the bitterest torment in divers ways did they plunder without mercy the properties of those living there. Who can enumerate the attacks [carried out] by them on their neighbors? All my subjects did they make as servants unto themselves; but their own servants did they set up like grandees; and thinking they were ruling and organizing—instead of this they brought to pass much injustice and disorganization, making immeasurable profit from all and doing and saying everything for gain.

And when they had lived thus for a long time and when I was growing up physically, I did not wish to remain in servile submission [literally, under servile power] and for this reason I sent away (from myself) Prince Ivan Vasil'evich Shuisky to service and ordered my *boyar*, Prince Ivan Fedorovich Bel'sky, to be beside me. And Prince Ivan Shuisky, having united all the people beneath his banner and led them to the oath of allegiance [literally, to the kissing of the Cross], marched in arms on Moscow and his advisers, Kubensky and others, before his arrival seized our *boyar*, Prince Ivan Fedorovich Bel'sky, and other *boyars* and *dvoryane* one after the other and exiled them to Beloozero and murdered them; yea, and they drove Metropolitan Ioasaf with great indignity from the metropolitanate. Then Prince Andrey Shuisky, together with his partisans, came into our refectory and in frenzied manner having seized and put to shame before us our *boyar*, Fedor Semenovich Vorontsov, they bore him out from our refectory and intended to kill him. And we sent unto them Metropolitan Makary and our *boyars*, Ivan and Vasily Grigor'evich Morozov, with our order not to kill him, and they, barely [hearkening] unto our order, exiled him to Kostroma; and they afflicted the metropolitan with indignity and they tore his cloak upon him to shreds together with the *istochniki* and they pushed our *boyars* in the back. Well then, is that their "well-wishing"—that they, opposing our commands, seized our *boyars* and those who are pleasing to us, and murdered and tortured them with various torments and persecutions? Is it thus that they "lay down their lives" for their sovereigns, waging war against our state and in a mob seizing [*boyars*] before our very eyes, and [is it right] for a servant to have intercourse with us, [his] sovereign, or for a sovereign to beg [favors] from his servant? Is it right to call this "faithful service"? Indeed the whole universe will mock, seeing such "faithfulness"! And what of the persecutions inflicted by them, which occurred at that time? From the death of our mother unto that time for six-and-a-half years they ceased not to practice these evil things!

But when we reached the fifteenth year of our life, then did we take it upon ourselves to put our kingdom in order and thanks to the mercy of God our rule began favorably. But since human sin ever acerbates the Grace of God, it came to pass that—because of our sins and the intensification of God's wrath—a fiery flame burned the ruling city of Moscow, and our treacherous *boyars*, who are called martyrs by you (their names will I intentionally pass over), seized the moment which appeared [literally, as it were] favorable to their treacherous wickedness [and] incited the feeblest-witted of the people [by saying] that the mother of our mother, Princess Anna Glinsky, together with her children and her retinue extracted human hearts and with such magic set fire to Moscow and that we had knowledge of this their counsel; and owing to the incitement of those traitors, the people, raising a cry and having seized in frenzied manner our *boyar*, Prince Yury Vasil'evitch Glinsky, in the chapel of the holy martyr Dimitry of Salonica, and having dragged him out, inhumanely slew him in the apostolic cathedral of the Assumption of the most Holy Mother of God opposite the throne of the metropolitan, and filled the church with his blood; and they dragged his dead body into the porch of the church and laid him, like one condemned [to death], in the market place. And this his murder in the church is known to all, and not as you lyingly assert, you cur! (Now) while we were living in our village of Vorob'evo these traitors stirred up the people to kill us too, on the grounds that we were hiding from them the mother of Prince Yury [Glinsky], Princess Anna, and his brother Prince Mikhail. How can one help but deride such sophistries! For what reason, pray, should we ourselves be the incendiary of our own kingdom? Indeed, so many possessions—the legacy [literally, blessing] of our forefathers—did we lose as could not be found again in the whole universe. Who could be so insensate or wild as to destroy his own possessions when in anger with his servants? He would burn down their [houses], but would preserve himself. In everything is your currish treachery brought to light. And how could one sprinkle water to such a height as [the church of] St. John? This is indeed clear madness. And with such "well-wishing" is it befitting for our *boyars* and *voevodas* to serve us, (namely) by assembling like a pack of hounds without our knowledge and slaughtering our *boyars*—yea, and even those in blood relationship [literally, in blood line] with us? And thus do they lay down their lives for us, desiring at all times to despatch our soul from this world into the world to come? For us they deem the law to be sacrosanct, but themselves wish not the travel the [same] path with us! Why too in your pride do you boast, you cur, of your warlike bravery and likewise [of that] of other hounds and traitors? For our Lord Jesus Christ says [literally, saying. Dat. absolute] "if a kingdom can be divided against itself, that kingdom cannot stand"; and how can one conduct military operations against an enemy if the kingdom be torn by fratricidal struggles? For how can a tree flower if its roots are dry? Likewise [is] this [the case] too: if there is not good order in the kingdom beforehand, how can wars be fought with bravery? For if a commander does not sufficiently strengthen his army, then he is conquered rather than conqueror. But you, disregarding all these things, praise bravery alone; and as for what bravery consists in, this you consider of no importance and you show yourself to be a man who not only does [not] strengthen bravery, but rather destroys it, for you are [as] nought: at home a traitor, in the field—bereft of reasoning; for you wish by fratricidal strife and by wilfulness to strengthen your bravery, which is impossible.

Now at this time that cur, Aleksey, your chief, was in the court of our kingdom during our youth, and I knew not by what means he was promoted from *batozhnik*; but we, having seen such treachery on the part of our grandees, hoping for faithful [literally, straight] service from him. What honors and riches did I not heap upon him—[and] not only upon him, but also upon his family! Yet what true service did I get from him? Listen further. Afterwards, for the sake of spiritual counsel and the salvation of my soul, I took [into my service] the priest Sylvester, thinking that he, because of his ministry at the altar of the Lord, would have care for his soul; but he, having trampled under foot his priesthood vows and his ordination [and] all that [appertains] to service with the angels at the altar of the Lord, "which things the angels desire to look into," where the Lamb of God is ever sacrificed for the salvation of the world and is never consumed—he, indeed, whilst still in the flesh, was deemed worthy [to perform] the Seraphic service with his own hands; and all this he trampled down in his cunning way; yet at first it seemed as though he had begun in a righteous manner, following the Holy Scriptures; [and] when I saw in the Holy Scriptures that it is right to submit to good perceptors without any consideration, then, willingly, but through ignorance, did I obey even him for the sake of spiritual counsel. But he was carried away by power like Eli the priest [and] began to form friendships as laymen do. Then we assembled all the archbishops and bishops and all the holy synod of the Russian metropolitanate, and as for what befell us in our youth, the disgraces inflicted by us [literally, our disgraces] upon you, our *boyars*, and likewise too the hostility towards us and the misdemeanors committed by you, our *boyars*—for all these things did we ourselves publicly ask forgiveness before our father and interceder, Makary, Metropolitan of All Russia. And [to] you, our *boyars*, and to all our people did I grant [forgiveness] for your misdemeanors and [decreed] that henceforth all memory of them be obliterated; and so then did we begin to treat you all as [though you were] good men.

But you did not abandon your first cunning habit[s], but returned again to your former ways and thus began to serve us with cunning counsel and false, and to do all things with scheming and not with simplicity. And so the priest Sylvester joined Aleksey too in friendship and they began to hold counsel in secret and without our knowledge, deeming us to be incapable of judgment; and thus did they begin to give worldly counsel in the place of spiritual, and thus did they begin little by little to lead all the *boyars* into contumacy, taking the splendor of our power from us and leading you into opposition, and in honor almost levelling you with us, while they made the young *boyar* children your equals in honor. And so did this evil little by little become confirmed; and he [Sylvester] began to allocate to you patrimonies and villages—such patrimonies which by the decree of our grandfather, the Grand Prince, had either been taken from you or might not be disposed of by you—even these patrimonies did he scatter in the wind in an unbefitting manner and [thus] did he destroy that decree of our grandfather and win the friendship of [literally, reconcile to himself] those many people. And then he admitted his confederate, Prince Dimitry Kurlyatev, into our council; and taking precedence over us in such manner by means of [literally, for the sake of] spiritual advice he thus acts as it were for the sake of [my] soul and not from cunning; and thus did he and that confederate of his begin to establish their evil counsel; not one position [literally, power] did they neglect in which they did not appoint their favorites, and so in all things did they achieve their desire. And after this did he and that confederate of his take from us the power given to us by our forefathers so that you, [who are] our *boyars* [only] by our grace [alone], might be honored with the dignity of precedence. And all these things did they place in their hands [literally, power] and in your hands, as it suited you and as anyone of you desired; for that reason, then, did they strengthen [their positions] with friendships and when they had all things in their power entirely according to their will, then, without asking us aught, as though we did not exist, did they make regulations and take measures according to their will and to the desire of their advisers. Whenever we gave any good advice, they did not avail themselves of it; but if *they* were to give any refractory or corrupt advice, then were they acting for the common weal!

And so neither in external affairs nor in internal affairs, nor in the smallest and prettiest things (and [I refer to such things as] footwear and sleeping)— was anything according to my will; but everything was done according to their desire, while we remained, as it were, a child. Now is this "contrary to reason" that, I, having reached man's estate, did not desire to be a little child? Likewise afterwards this too became a habit [literally, was established]: if we had at that time to contradict even one of the most insignificant counsellors, then all these [my words] were interpreted as impious, as is written in your calumnious epistle; but if any of his most inferior advisers were in their madness to utter haughty words to us, not as to a master or as to a brother, but as to the most inferior thing, then all these things too were reckoned to be pious; and whoever provided us with a little obedience or peace, to his lot fell persecution and torment. And should anyone annoy us in aught or cause us to suffer [literally, bring to us] any oppression, to his lot fell wealth, glory and honor. And if I did not acquiesce [literally, if it were not so], then [they said,] this [would lead] to the downfall of my soul and the destruction of the kingdom. And so, while we continued to suffer such persecution and oppression, such evils increased, not from day to day, but from hour [to hour]; and all that was repugnant to us increased, while as for obedience and peace [being] afforded to us—these things decreased. Such then was the Orthodox Faith at that time! Who indeed can recount in detail both the persecutions and oppressions [I suffered] in my ways of life, in my movements and in repose, and likewise in my attendance at church and in all my manner of life? And so it was then; they imposed these things upon us in God's name, deeming that they were inflicting such persecutions upon us for the good of our soul and not through cunning.

Likewise, when by God's will we set out against the godless people of Kazan' with the banner inscribed with the Cross, the banner of all the Orthodox Christian host, to defend Orthodox Christianity, and [when] thus by the inexpressible mercy of God, who gave [us] victory over that Mussulman people, we returned home safe and sound with all the host of Orthodox Christianity—what shall I say of the "well-wishing" towards me of those who are called martyrs by you? This then [will I say]: having placed me like a prisoner on a ship they conveyed me with very few people through the godless and most unbelieving land! Had not the all-powerful right hand of the Almighty protected my humility, then in any case would I have lost my life. Such is the "well-wishing" of those men in whose defence you speak, and thus do they "lay down their lives for us" by striving to deliver our soul into the hands of foreigners!

Likewise, when we had arrived in the ruling city of Moscow God increased his mercy towards us and gave us at that time an heir, our son Dimitry. But after a short time had passed [it fell to our lot]—as indeed it falls to the lot of [all] men—to be afflicted with sickness and to be sorely ill; and then did those who are called by you "well-wishers" rise up like drunken men with the priest Sylvester and with your chief Aleksey, thinking that we were no longer alive, having forgotten our good deeds and even their own souls too, and [having forgotten] that they had kissed the Cross [in allegiance] to our father and to us, [vowing] to seek no other sovereign but our children. Yet they desired to raise to the throne Prince Vladimir, who is far removed from us in the line of succession [literally, generation]; while our infant, given to us by God, did they, like Herod, desire to destroy (and how could they fail to destroy him!), having raised Prince Vladimir to the throne. For even though it was said in the ancient secular writings, yet none the less is [the following] fitting: "Tsar does not bow down to tsar; but when one dies, the other rules." [If] then we, while still alive, enjoyed such "well-wishing" from our subjects, what will it be like after our death! But again, thanks to God's mercy, we recovered, and thus was this counsel scattered. But the priest Sylvester and

Aleksey ceased not from that time forth to counsel all that was evil and to inflict [on me] still harsher oppression, conceiving persecutions of various kinds against our [true] well-wishers, while indulging every whim of Prince Vladimir; and likewise they stirred up great hatred against our tsaritsa Anastasia and likened her to all the impious tsaritsas; as for our children, they were not able even to call them to mind.

Likewise did that cur, that traitor, Prince Semen Rostovsky, who, because of our grace and not according to his merits, was honored by us with [the dignity of] counsellorship, revile our counsel in his treacherous manner before the Lithuanian ambassadors, Pan Stanislas Dowojna and his suite, censuring us and our tsaritsa and our children. And when we had investigated this wickedness of his we none the less inflicted a merciful punishment upon him [literally, mercifully inflicted . . .]. And after that the priest Sylvester with you, his evil counsellors, began to surround that dog with every protection [literally, to keep him in great protection] and to help him with every [possible] favor—and not only him, but all his kin. And so from that time forth a period of prosperity fell to the lot of all traitors; while we from that time forth suffered great oppression. And even you too were at one with them: it is well known that you and Kurlyatev (the son) intended to judge the Sitsky case.

Likewise, when the war began, that is, the war against the Germans—but more will be said about this in greater detail later on—the Priest Sylvester together with you, his counsellors, attacked us fiercely on this score, and as for the sickness which, because of our sins, had been visited upon us and upon our tsaritsa and upon our children—they claimed that these things happened because of them—that is, because of our disobedience to them. How shall I recall the hard [literally, merciless] journey to the ruling city from Mozhaisk with our ailing tsaritsa Anastasia? Owing to one single little word did she rank as worthless [in their eyes]. But as for prayers and journeys to desert places [that is, hermitages], gifts and vows to the saints [literally, sanctity] for the salvation of our soul, for our bodily health and for all our well-being and for that of our tsaritsa and of our children—all these things were taken completely from us by your cunning scheming. And as for medical skill, for our health's sake, there was no mention of it at that time.

And as we remained thus in such dire afflictions and as we were not able to endure such oppression as you inhumanly inflicted [upon us], for this reason did we investigate the treacherous deeds of that dog Aleksey Adashev and all his advisers, and [yet] we exercised our wrath with mercy; the death penalty we did not inflict, but we banished them to various places. But the Priest Sylvester, seeing his advisers set at naught, for this reason left of his own will; but we, having given him our blessing, did not dismiss him, not because we were ashamed [of anything], but because we did not wish to judge him here

[on earth], but in the world to come, before the Lamb of God, for the evil
he has done to me while ever serving me and [yet] in his cunning manner
overlooking me. There will I accept judgment for as much as I have suffered,
spiritually and bodily, at his hands. For this reason I have allowed his son to
remain unmolested even to the present day—and only from our presence is
he debarred. And should anyone like you say that it is ridiculous to give way
to [literally, obey] a priest, [then my reply would be that,] seeing you know
not thoroughly the Christian monastic rule [wherein we are told] that it is
right to submit to one's teachers, and seeing you were dull of hearing, needing
a teacher for the time and now you are become such as have need of milk
and not of strong meat—for these reasons would [such a person like you] say
these things. And for the reason I have mentioned above did I do Sylvester
no harm. But as for the laymen who are under our power, with them did
we deal according to their treachery; at first we punished [literally, touched]
no one with the death penalty; but we ordered everyone—whoever had adhered
to them—to keep away from them and not to adhere to them [further]; and
when we had laid down this decree we confirmed it by [exacting] the oath
on the Cross. But since our decree was disregarded by those whom you call
martyrs and their accomplices and since they transgressed the oath on the
Cross, they not only did not keep away from those traitors, but they began
to help them still more and to scheme in all manner of ways in order to
return them to their former dignity and to plot all the more fiercely against
us; and since their malice showed itself to be unquenchable and their will
[literally, understanding] was revealed as inflexible—for this reason the guilty
ones received such a judgment according to their guilt.

☒ 45 ☒

Domostroi

One of the most fascinating of documents to come to light from the
early reign of Ivan the Terrible (1547–1584) is *Domostroi*, or Rules
Governing Household Management. Composed by Archpriest Sylvester,

From Leo Wiener, ed., *Anthology of Russian Literature From the Earliest Period to the Present
Time*, (In two Parts), Part I, *From the Tenth Century to the Close of the Eighteenth Century*,
(New York-London: G. P. Putnam's Sons, 1902), pp. 126–130.

an advisor to the tsar, the document consists of three parts. The first is a guide regarding faith. The second treats government administrative matters. And the third deals with successful management of a well-to-do household.

Two themes permeate the *Domostroi*. The first advocates unconditional obedience to God and to the tsar, God's representative and the leader of the nation. The second stresses obedience of the family to the father, as its head and as a representative of the tsar. These two themes have led scholars to conclude that the first originated in Moscow, the center of religious and political power; the second in Novgorod, the center of economic activity. Both themes heavily emphasize obedience to hierarchal authority.

The *Domostroi* not only obligates but also empowers the head of the family to educate and punish his wife, his children, and his servants, and enumerates a whole galaxy of skills each member of the household should acquire—from preparing food to sewing clothes. It also offers numerous suggestions to the head of the family on how to treat all members of the household and how to handle purchases, loans, taxes, and other daily problems. Finally, the *Domostroi* embodies a great amount of folkish wisdom and stresses that education is the main factor in human progress.

How to Educate Children and Bring Them Up in the Fear of God

If God send children, sons or daughters, father and mother must take care of these their children. Provide for them and bring them up in good instruction. Teach them the fear of God and politeness and propriety, and teach them some handicraft, according to the time and age of the children: the mother instructing her daughters, and the father his sons, as best he knows and God counsels him. Love them and watch them and save them through fear. Teaching and instructing them and reasoning with them, punish them. Teach your children in their youth, and you will have a quiet old age. Look after their bodily cleanliness, and keep them from all sin, like the apple of your eye and your own souls. If the children transgress through the neglect of their parents, the parents will answer for these sins on the day of the terrible judgment. If the children are not taken care of and transgress through lack of the parents' instruction, or do some evil, there will be both to the parents and children a sin before God, scorn and ridicule before men, a loss to the house, grief to oneself, and cost and shame from the judges. If by God-fearing, wise and sensible people the children be brought up in the fear of God, and in good instruction and sensible teaching, in wisdom and politeness and work and handicraft, such children and their parents are loved by God, blessed by the clerical vocation, and praised by good people; and when they are of the proper age, good people will gladly and thankfully marry off their sons, according to their possessions and the will of God, and will give their daughters in marriage to their sons. And if God take away one of their children, after the confession and extreme unction, the parents bring a pure offering to God, to take up an abode in the eternal mansion; and the child is bold to beg for God's mercy and forgiveness of his parents' sins.

How to Teach Children and Save Them Through Fear

Punish your son in his youth, and he will give you a quiet old age, and restfulness to your soul. Weaken not beating the boy, for he will not die from your striking him with the rod, but will be in better health: for while you strike his body, you save his soul from death. If you love your son, punish him frequently, that you may rejoice later. Chide your son in his childhood, and you will be glad in his manhood, and you will boast among evil persons, and your enemies will be envious. Bring up your child with much prohibition, and you will have peace and blessing from him. Do not smile at him, or play with him, for though that will diminish your grief while he is a child, it will increase it when he is older, and you will cause much bitterness to your soul. Give him no power in his youth, but crush his ribs while he is growing and does not in his wilfulness obey you, lest there be an aggravation and suffering to your soul, a loss to your house, destruction to your property, scorn from your neighbors and ridicule from your enemies, and cost and worriment from the authorities.

How Christians Are to Cure Diseases and all Kinds of Ailments

If God send any disease or ailment down upon a person let him cure himself through the grace of God, through tears, prayer, fasting, charity to the poor, and true repentance. Let him thank the Lord and beg His forgiveness, and show mercy and undisguised charity to everybody. Have the clergy pray to the Lord for you, and sing the mass. Sanctify the water with the holy crosses and holy relics and miracle-working images, and be anointed with the holy oil. Frequent the miracle-working and holy places, and pray there with a pure conscience. In that way you will receive from God a cure for all your ailments. But you must henceforth abstain from sin, and in the future do no wrong, and keep the commands of the spiritual fathers, and do penance. Thus you will be purified from sin, and your spiritual and bodily ailment will be cured, and God will be gracious to you.

The Wife Is Always and in All Things to Take Counsel with Her Husband

In all affairs of everyday life, the wife is to take counsel with her husband, and to ask him, if she needs anything. Let her be sure that her husband wants her to keep company with the guests she invites, or the people she calls upon. Let her put on the best garment, if she receives a guest, or herself is invited somewhere to dinner. By all means let her abstain from drinking liquor, for a drunk man is bad enough, but a drunk woman has no place in the world. A woman ought to talk with her lady-friends of handwork and housekeeping. She must pay attention to any good word that is said in her own house, or in that of her friend: how good women live, how they keep house, manage their household, instruct their children and servants, obey their husbands, and ask their advice in everything, and submit to them. And if there be aught she does not know, let her politely inquire about it. . . . It is good to meet such good women, not for the sake of eating and drinking with them, but for the sake of good converse and information, for it is profitable to listen to them. Let not a woman rail at anyone, or gossip about others. If she should be asked something about a person, let her answer: "I know nothing about it, and have heard nothing of it; I do not inquire about things that do not concern me; nor do I sit in judgment over the wives of princes, *boyars*, or my neighbors."

How to Instruct Servants

Enjoin your servants not to talk about other people. If they have been among strangers, and have noticed anything bad there, let them not repeat it at home; nor should they bruit about what is going on at home. A servant must remember what he has been sent for, and he must not know, nor answer any other questions that are put to him. The moment he has carried out his commission, he should return home and report to his master in regard to the matter he has been sent for; let him not gossip of things he has not been ordered to report, lest he cause quarrel and coldness between the masters.

If you send your servant, or son, to tell, or do something, or buy a thing, ask him twice: "What have I ordered you to do? What are you to say, or do, or buy?" If he repeats to you as you have ordered him, all is well. . . . If you send anywhere some eatables or liquids, send full measures, so that they cannot lie about them. Send your wares after having measured or weighed them, and count the money, before you send it out. Best of all, dispatch under seal. Carefully instruct the servant whether he is to leave the things at the house, if the master be absent, or if he is to bring them back home. . . .

When a servant is sent to genteel people, let him knock at the door softly. If anyone should ask him, as he passes through the courtyard: "What business brings you here?" let him not give him any satisfaction, but say: "I have not been sent to you; I shall tell to him to whom I have been sent." Let him clean his dirty feet before the antechamber, or house, or cell, wipe his nose, clear his throat, and correctly say his prayer; and if he does not receive an "amen" in response, he should repeat the prayer in a louder voice, twice or three times. If he still receives no answer, he must softly knock at the door. When he is admitted, he should bow before the holy images, give his master's respects, and tell his message. While doing so, let him not put his finger in his nose, nor cough, nor clean his nose, nor clear his throat, nor spit. If he absolutely must do so, let him step aside. He must stand straight and not look to either side when reporting the message; nor should he relate any matter not relevant to the message. Having done his duty, he should forthwith return home, to report to his master.

46

Moscow and the Court of Ivan the Terrible in 1553

In 1553, three English ships set out to find a northern passage to China. Two of the ships were lost in the Arctic and the third, under Captain Richard Chancellor, sailed to the mouth of the Northern Dvina. Chancellor made his way to Moscow, where he was well received by Ivan the Terrible, who encouraged him to return. This journey is important for two reasons: it inaugurated lively commercial relations between England and Russia, carried on by the Muscovy Company, which was organized in London for that purpose and endowed with extensive privileges by Ivan the Terrible (see Chapter 27); and it resulted in Chancellor's interesting description of Moscow and of his reception at the court of Ivan the Terrible.

The [city of] Moscow is from Iaroslav 200 miles. The country between them is very well replenished with small villages, which are so well filled with people that it is wonder to see them: the ground is well stored with corn which they

---

Reprinted with permission of the Cambridge University Press from Richard Hakluyt, *The Principal Navigations, Voyages, Traffiques, & Discoveries of the English Nation* (Glasgow: James MacLehose and Sons, 1903), vol. 2, pp. 225–230, 234–236. Spellings have been modernized to facilitate reading. Words in brackets are mine.

carry to the city of Moscow in such abundance that it is wonder to see it. You shall meet in a morning 700 or 800 sleds coming or going thither, that carry corn, and some carry fish. You shall have some that carry corn to Moscow, and some that fetch corn from thence, that at the least dwell a thousand miles off; and all their carriage is on sleds. Those which come so far dwell in the North parts of the Duke's dominions, where the cold will suffer no corn to grow, it is so extreme. They bring thither fish, furs, and beasts' skins. In those parts they have but small store of cattle.

The [city of] Moscow itself is great: I take the whole town to be greater than London with the suburbs: but it is very rude, and stands without all order. Their houses are all of timber, very dangerous for fire. There is a fair castle, the walls whereof are of brick, and very high: they say they are eighteen feet thick, but I do not believe it, it does not so seem, notwithstanding I do not certainly know it: for no stranger may come to view it. The one side is ditched, and on the other side runs a river called Moscow which turns into Tatary and so into the sea called Mare Caspium: and on the North side there is a base town, which has also a brick wall about it, and so it joins with the castle wall. The Emperor lies in the castle, wherein are nine fair Churches, and therein are religious men. Also there is a Metropolitan with diverse Bishops. I will not stand in description of their buildings nor of the strength thereof because we have better in all points in England. They are well furnished with ordinance of all sorts.

The Emperor's or Duke's house neither in building nor in the outward show, nor yet within the house is so sumptuous as I have seen. It is very low built in eight square, much like the old building of England, with small windows, and so in other points.

Now to declare my coming before his Majesty: After I had remained twelve days, the Secretary which has the hearing of strangers did send for me, advertising me that the Duke's pleasure was to have me to come before his Majesty with the king's my master's letters: whereof I was right glad, and so I have my attendance. And when the Duke was in his place appointed, the interpreter came for me into the outer chamber, where sat one hundred or more gentleman, all in cloth of gold very sumptuous, and from thence I came into the Council chamber, where sat the Duke himself with his nobles, which were a fair company: they sat round about the chamber on high, yet so that he himself sat much higher than any of his nobles in a chair gilt, and in a long garment of beaten gold, with an imperial crown upon his head, and a staff of crystal and gold in his right hand, and his other hand half leaning on his chair. The Chancellor stood up with the Secretary before the Duke. After my duty done and my letter delivered, he bade me welcome, and inquired of me the health of the King my master, and I answered that he was in good health at my departure from his court, and that my trust was that he was now in the same. Upon the which he bade me to dinner. The Chancellor presented my present unto his Grace bareheaded (for before they were all covered) and when his Grace had received my letter, I was required to depart, for I had charge not to speak to the Duke, but when he spoke to me. So I departed unto the Secretary's chamber, where I remained two hours, and then I was sent for again unto another palace which is called the golden palace, but I saw no cause why it should be so called; for I have seen many fairer than it in all points. And so I came into the hall, which was small and not great as is the King's Majesties' of England, and the table was covered with a tablecloth. The Marshal sat at the end of the table with a little white rod in his hand, which board was full of vessel of gold; and on the other side of the hall did stand a fair cupboard of plate. From thence I came into the dining chamber, where the Duke himself sat at his table without cloth of estate, in a gown of silver, with a crown imperial upon his head, he sat in a chair somewhat high. There sat none near him by a great way. There were long tables set round about the chamber, which were full set with such as the Duke had at dinner; they were all in white. Also the places where the tables stood were higher by two steps than the rest of the house. In the midst of the chamber stood a table or cupboard to set plate on; which stood full of cups of gold, and amongst all the rest there stood four marvelous great pots or crudences as they call them, of gold and silver. I think they were a good yard and a half high. By the cupboard stood two gentlemen with napkins on their shoulders, and in their hands each of them had a cup of gold set with pearls and precious stones, which were the Duke's own drinking cups; when he was disposed, he drunk them off at a draught. And for his service at meat it came in without order, yet it was very rich service, for all were served in gold, not only he himself, but also all the rest of us, and it was very massive. The cups also were of gold and very massive. The number that dined there that day was 200 persons, and all were served in golden vessel. The gentlemen that waited were all in cloth of gold, and they served him with their caps on their heads. Before the service came in, the Duke sent to every man a great shiver of bread, and the bearer called the party so sent to by his name aloud, and said, John Basilevich Emperor of Russia and great Duke of Moscovy does reward you with bread; then must all men stand up, and do at all times when these words are spoken. And then last of all he gave the Marshal bread, whereof he ate before the Duke's Grace, and so did reverence and departed. Then came the Duke's service of the Swans all in pieces, and every one in a different dish, which the Duke sent as he did the bread, and the bearer said the same words as he said before. And as I said before, the service of his meat is in no order, but comes in dish by dish; and then after that the Duke sends drink, with the like saying as before is told. Also before dinner he changed his crown, and in dinner time two crowns; so that I saw three different crowns upon his head in one day. And thus when his service was all come in he gave to every one of his gentlemen waiters meat with his own hand, and so likewise drink. His intent thereby is, as I have heard, that every man shall know perfectly his servants. Thus when dinner is done he calls his nobles before him name by name, that it is wonder to hear how he could name them, having so many as he has. Thus when dinner was done I departed to my lodging, which was an hour within night. I will leave this, and speak no more of him nor his household, but I will somewhat declare of his land and people, with their nature and power in the wars. This Duke is Lord and Emperor of many countries, and his power is marvelous great. For he is able to bring into the field 200,000 or 300,000 men: he never goes into the field himself with under 200,000 men: And when he goes himself he furnishes his borders all with men of war, which are no small number. He leaves on the borders of Liefland 40,000 men, and upon the borders of Lithuania 60,000 men, and toward the Nogay Tatars 60,000, which is wonder to hear of; yet never does he take to his wars neither husbandman nor merchant. All his men are horsemen: he uses no footmen, but such as go with the ordinance and laborers, which are 30,000. The horsemen are all archers, with such bows as the Turks have, and they ride short as do the Turks. Their armor is a coat of plate, with a skull on their heads. Some of their coats are covered with velvet or cloth of gold; their desire is to be sumptuous in the field, and especially the nobles and gentlemen, as I have heard their trimming is very costly, and partly I have seen it, or else I would scarcely have believed it. The Duke himself is richly attired above all measure; his pavilion is covered either with cloth of gold or silver, and so set with stones that it is wonderful to see it. I have seen the King's Majesties' of England and the French King's pavilions, which are fair, yet not like unto his. And when they are sent into far or foreign countries, or foreigners come to them, they are very gorgeous. Else the Duke himself goes but meanly in apparel, and when he goes between one place and another he is but reasonably apparelled over other times. In the while that I was in Moscow the Duke sent two ambassadors to the King of Poland, which had at the least 500 horses; their sumptuousness was above measure, not only in themselves, but also in their horses, as velvet, cloth of gold, and cloth of silver set with pearls and not scant. What shall I farther say? I never heard of nor saw men so sumptuous; but it is no daily guise for when they have not occasion, as I said before, all their doing is but mean. . . .

The Duke gives sentence himself upon all matters in the law. It is very commendable, that such a Prince will take pains to see ministration of justice.

Yet notwithstanding, it is wonderfully abused, and thereby the Duke is much deceived. But if it fall out that the officers be espied in cloaking the truth, they have most condign punishment. And if the plantiff can nothing prove, then the defendant must take his oath upon the Crucifix whether he is in the right or no. Then is demanded if the plaintiff be any thing able further to make proof; if he be not, then sometimes he will say, I am able to prove it by my body and hands, or by my champion's body, so requiring the contest. After the other has his oath, it is granted as well to the one as to the other. So when they go to the field, they swear upon the Crucifix, that they are both in the right, and that the one shall make the other to confess the truth before they depart forth of the field. And so they go both to the battle armed with such weapons as they use in that country: they fight all on foot, and seldom the parties themselves do fight, except they be Gentlemen, for they stand much upon their reputation, for they will not fight, but with such as are come of as good a house as themselves. So that if either party require the combat, it is granted unto them, and no champion is to serve in his place: wherein is no deceit; but otherwise by champions there is. For although they take great oaths upon them to do battle truly, yet is the contrary often seen, because the common champions have none other living. And as soon as the one party has gotten the victory, he demands the debt, and the other is carried to prison, and there is shamefully used till he take order. There is also another order in the law, that the plaintiff may swear in some causes of debt. And if the party defendant be poor, he shall be set under the Crucifix, and the party plaintiff must swear over his head, and when he has taken his oath, the Duke takes the party defendant home to his house, and uses him as his bond-man, and puts him to labor, or lets him for hire to any such as need him, until such time as his friends make provision for his redemption, or else he remains in bondage all the days of his life. Again there are many that will sell themselves to Gentlemen or Merchants to be their bond-men, to have during their life meat, drink, and clothes, and at their coming to have a piece of money. Yes, and some will sell their wives and children to be bawdes and drudges to the buyer. Also they have a law for felons and pickers contrary to the laws of England. For by their law they can hang no man for his first offense; but may keep him long in prison, and oftentimes beat him with whips and other punishment: and there he shall remain until his friends are able to bail him. If he be a picker or a cut-purse, as there are very many, the second time he is taken, he has a piece of his nose cut off, and is burned in the forehead, and kept in prison till he find sureties for his good behavior. And if he be taken the third time, he is hanged. And at the first time he is extremely punished and not released, except he have very good friends, or that some Gentleman require to have him to the wars. And in so doing, he shall enter into great bonds for him; by which means the country is brought into good quietness. But they are naturally given to great deceit, except extreme beating did bridle them. They are naturally given to hard living as well in fare as in lodging. I heard a Russian say, that it was a great deal merrier living in prison than forth, but for the great beating. For they have drink and meat without any labor, and get the charity of well-disposed people. But being at liberty, they get nothing. The poor are very innumerable, and live most miserably, for I have seen them eat the pickle of herring and other stinking fish. Nor the fish cannot be so stinking nor rotten, but they will eat it and praise it to be more wholesome than other fish or fresh meat. In my opinion there are no such people under the sun for their hardness of living.

𝄞 47 𝄞

First Privileges Granted
by Ivan the Terrible
to English Merchants, 1555

The immediate result of Chancellor's unintended voyage to Moscow was the chartering of the Muscovy Company in London in 1555 in order to establish trade relations with Moscow. Because Ivan the Terrible was interested in west European commercial and military relations, the Muscovy Company had no difficulty in acquiring many rights and privileges. Its representatives set up trading depots in many Russian cities and traveled extensively through most of the possessions of Moscovy.

Ivan Vasilevich, by the grace of God Emperor of Russia, Great Duke of Novgorod, Moscow, etc. To all people that shall see, read, hear, or understand these presents, greeting. Foreasmuch as God has planted all realms and dominions in the whole world with sundry commodities, so as the one has need of the amity and commodities of the other, and by means thereof traffic is

---

Reprinted with permission of the Cambridge University Press from Richard Hakluyt, *The Principal Navigations, Voyages, Traffiques, & Discoveries of the English Nation* (Glasgow: James MacLehose and Sons, 1903), vol. 2, pp. 297–303. Spellings have been modernized to facilitate reading.

used from one to another, and amity thereby increased: and for that as amongst men nothing is more to be desired than amity, without the which no creature being of a natural good disposition can live in quietness, so that it is as troublesome to be utterly wanting, as it is perceived to be grievous to the body to lack air, fire, or any other necessities most requisite for the conservation and maintenance thereof in health: considering also how needful merchandise is, which furnishes men of all that which is convenient for their living and nourishment, for their clothing, trimming, the satisfying of their delights, and all other things convenient and profitable for them, and that merchandise brings the same commodities from diverse quarters in so great abundance, as by means thereof nothing is lacking in any part, and that all things be in every place (where intercourse of merchandise is received and embraced) generally in such sort, as amity thereby is entered into, and planted to continue, and the enjoyers thereof be as men living in a golden world: Upon these respects and other weighty and good considerations, us hereunto moving, and chiefly upon the contemplation of the gracious letters, directed from the right high, right excellent, and right mighty Queen Mary, by the grace of God Queen of England, France, and so forth, in the favor of her subjects, merchants, the governor, consuls, assistants, and community of merchants, adventurers for the discovery of lands, and so forth.

Know ye therefore, that we are of our grace special, mere motion, and certain knowledge, have given and granted, and by these presents for us, our heirs and successors, do give and grant as much as in us is and lies, unto Sebastian Cabot, Governor, Sir George Barnes, Knight, and so forth, Consuls: Sir John Gresham, etc., Assistants, and to the community of the aforenamed fellowship, and to their successors forever, and to the successors of every of them, these articles, grants, immunities, franchises, liberties, and privileges, and every of them hereafter following, expressed and declared. Videlicet:

1. First, we for us, our heirs and successors, do by these presents give and grant free license, faculty, authority, and power unto the said Governor, Consuls, Assistants, and community of the said fellowship, and to their successors for ever, that all and singular the merchants of the same company, their agents, factors, doers of their business, attorneys, servants, and ministers, and every of them may at all times hereafter for ever more surely, freely, and safely with their ships, merchandises, goods, and things whatsoever sail, come and enter into all and singular our lands, countries, dominions, cities, towns, villages, castles, ports, jurisdictions, and districts by sea, land, or fresh waters, and there tarry, abide, and sojourn, and buy, sell, barter, and change all kind of merchandises with all manner of merchants and people, of whatsoever nation, rite, condition, state, or degrees they be, and with the same or other ships, wares, merchandises, goods, and things whatsoever they be, unto other

empires, kingdoms, dukedoms, parts, and to any other place or places at their pleasure and liberty by sea, land, or fresh waters may depart, and exercise all kind of merchandises in our empire and dominions, and every part thereof freely and quietly without any restraint, impeachment, price exaction, pressure, straight custom, toll, imposition, or subsidy to be demanded, taxed, or paid, or at any time hereafter to be demanded, taxed, set, levied, or inferred upon them or any of them, or upon their goods, ships, wares, merchandises, and things, of, for or upon any part or parcel thereof, or upon the goods, ships, wares, merchandises, and things of any of them, so that they shall not need any other safe conduct or license general, or special, of us, our heirs or successors, neither shall be bound to ask any safe conduct or license in any of the aforesaid places subject unto us.

2. Item, we give and grant to the said merchants this power and liberty, that they, neither any of them, nor their goods, wares, merchandises, or things, nor any part thereof, shall be by any means within our dominions, lands, countries, castles, towns, villages, or other place or places of our jurisdiction, at any time hereafter attached, stayed, arrested, nor disturbed for any debt, duty, or other thing, for the which they be not principal debtors or sureties, nor also, for any offense or trespass committed, or that shall be committed, but only for such as they or any of them shall actually commit, and the same offenses (if any such happen), shall be by us only heard, and determined.

3. Item, we give and grant, that the said merchants shall and may have free liberty, power, and authority to name, choose, and assign brokers, shippers, packers, weighers, measurers, wagoners, and all other meet and necessary laborers for to serve them in their feat of merchandises, and minister and give unto them and every of them a corporal oath, to serve them well and truly in their offices, and finding them or any of them doing contrary to his or their oath, may punish and dismiss them, and from time to time choose, swear, and admit other in their place or places, without contradiction, let, vexation or disturbance, either of us, our heirs, or successors, or of any other of our justices, officers, ministers, or subjects whatsoever.

4. Item, we give and grant unto the said merchants and their successors, that such person as is, or shall be commended unto us, our heirs or successors by the Governor, Consuls, and Assistants of the said fellowship resident within the city of London within the realm of England, to be their chief factor within this our empire and dominions, may and shall have full power and authority to govern and rule all Englishmen that have had, or shall have access, or repair in or to this said Empire and jurisdictions, or any part thereof, and shall and may minister unto them, and every of them good justice in all their causes, plaints, quarrels, and disorders between them moved, and to be moved, and assemble, deliberate, consult, conclude, define, determine, and make such acts,

and ordinances, as he so commended with his Assistants shall think good and meet for the good order, government, and rule of the said merchants, and all other Englishmen repairing to this our said empire and dominions, or any part thereof, and to set and levy upon all, and every Englishmen, offender or offenders, of such their acts and ordinances made, and to be made, penalties and mulcts by fine or imprisonment.

5. Item, if it happen that any of the said merchants, or other Englishmen, as one or more do rebel against such chief factor or factors, or his or their deputies and will not dispose him or themselves to obey them and every of them as shall appertain, if the said rebels or disobedients do come, and be found in our said empire and jurisdictions, or any part and place thereof, then we promise and grant, that all and every our officers, ministers, and subjects shall effectually aid and assist the said chief factor or factors, and their deputies, and for their power shall really work, to bring such rebel or disobedient rebels, or disobedients to due obedience: And to that intent shall lend unto the same factor or factors, and their deputies upon request therefore to be made, prisons, and instruments for punishments from time to time.

6. Item, we promise unto the said merchants, and their successors upon their request to exhibit and do unto them good, exact and favorable justice, with expedition in all their causes, and that when they or any of them shall have access, or come to or before any of our justices, for any their plaints moved, and to be moved between any of our subjects or other foreigner, and them, or any of them, that then they shall be first and forthwith heard, as soon as the party which they shall find before our justices shall be depeached, which party being heard forthwith, and as soon as may be, the said English merchants shall be rid and dispatched: And if any action shall be moved by or against any of the said merchants being absent out of our said empire and dominions, then such merchants may substitute an attorney in all and singular his causes to be followed as need shall require, and as shall seem to him expedient.

7. Item, we grant and promise to the said merchants, and to their successors, that if the same merchants or any of them shall be wounded, or (which God forbid) slain in any part or place of our empire or dominions, then good information thereof given, we and our justices and other officers shall execute due correction and punishment without delay, according to the exigence of the case: so that it shall be an example to all other not to commit the like. And if it shall chance the factors, servants, or ministers of the said merchants or any of them to trespass or offend, whereby they or any of them shall incur the danger of death or punishment, the goods, wares, merchandises, and things of their masters shall not therefore be forfeited, confiscated, spoiled, nor seized by any means by us, our heirs or successors, or by any of our

officers, ministers, or subjects, but shall remain to their use, frank, free, and discharged from all punishment and loss.

8. Item, we grant that if any of the English nation be arrested for any debt, he shall not be laid in prison, so far as he can put in sufficient surety and pawn: neither shall any sergeant, or officer lead them or any of them to prison, before he shall have known whether the chief factor or factors, or their deputies, shall be sureties, or bring in pawn for such arrested: then the officers shall release the party, and shall set him or them at liberty.

9. Moreover, we give, grant, and promise to the said merchants, that if any of their ships or other vessels shall be spoiled, robbed, or damnified in sailing, anchoring or returning to or from our said empires and dominions, or any part thereof, by any pirates, merchants, or other person, whatsoever he or they be, that then and in such case, we will do all that in us is to cause restitution, reparation, and satisfaction to be duly made to the said English merchants by our letters and otherwise, as shall stand with our honor, and be consonant to equity and justice.

10. Item, for us, our heirs and successors, we do promise and grant to perform, maintain, corroborate, authenticate, and observe all and singular the aforesaid liberties, franchises, and privileges, like as presently we firmly do intend, and will corroborate, authenticate, and perform the same by all mean and way that we can, as much as may be to the commodity and profit of the said English merchants, and their successors forever.

And to the intent that all and singular the said gifts, grants, and promises may be inviolably observed and performed, we the said Ivan Vasilevich by the grace of God Emperor of Russia, Great Duke of Novgorod, Moscow, and so forth, for us, our heirs and successors, by our Imperial and lordly word in stead of an oath have and do promise by these presents, inviolably to maintain and observe, and cause to be inviolably observed and maintained all and singular the aforesaid gifts, grants, and promises from time to time, and at all and every time and times hereafter. And for the more corroboration hereof have caused our seal hereunto to be put.

�üÑ *48* ⚜

A Letter from King Sigismund of Poland to Elizabeth I, 1559

The establishment of commercial relations, followed by Ivan the Terrible's search for closer ties with England, was ill received in some European countries. At first the French feared that Ivan might be persuaded by Mary Tudor and her husband Philip II of Spain to join the anti-French and anti-Ottoman struggle then in progress. When Ivan the Terrible started his drive to establish Moscow's control in the Baltic Sea, the Poles became chief opponents of English rapprochement with Moscow and, through their King, pleaded for termination of English trade with Moscow.

Sigismund Augustus by the grace of God King of Poland, Great Duke of Lithuania, Russia, Prussia, Masovia and Samogetia, etc. Lord and heir etc., to the most Noble Princess Lady Elizabeth, by the same grace of God Queen of England, France and Ireland, and so forth, our dear sister and kinswoman, greeting and increase of all felicity. Whereas your Majesty writes to us that you have received two of our letters, we have looked that you should have answered to them both. First to the one, in which we intreated more at large in forbidding the voyage to Narva, which if it had been done, we had been unburdened of so often writing of one matter: and might have answered your Majesty much better to the purpose. Now we thus answer to your Majesty to those matters of which you write to us October 3 [1559] from Windsor. First, forasmuch as your Majesty at the request of our letters has discharged the arrest of merchants' goods, and of the names of the men of Denmark our subjects, which was set upon them by the commandment of Your Majesty: and also have restored the old and ancient liberty of traffic, we acknowledge great pleasure done unto us in the same: and also think it to be done according to common agreement made in times past. Neither were we ever at any time of any other opinion touching your Majesty, but that we should obtain right

---

Reprinted with permission of the Cambridge University Press from Richard Hakluyt, *The Principal Navigations, Voyages, Traffiques, & Discoveries of the English Nation* (Glasgow: James MacLehose and Sons, 1903), vol. 2, pp. 485–487. Spellings have been modernized to facilitate reading.

and reason at your hands. Forasmuch as we likewise shall at all times be ready
to grant to your Majesty, making any request for your subjects, so far as shall
stand with justice, yet neither will we yield anything to your Majesty in
contention of love, benevolence, and mutual office, but that we judge every
good turn of yours to be recompensed by us to the uttermost: and that shall
we prove as occasion shall serve. Therefore we shall command the arrests, if
any be made by our subjects (as it is unknown to us) of merchants' goods
and English names to be discharged: and shall conserve the old liberty of
traffic, and all other things which shall seem to appertain to neighborhood
between us and your Majesty, so that none of the subjects of your Majesty
hereafter presume to use the navigation to the Narva forbidden by us and
full of danger not only to our parts, but also to the open destruction of all
Christian and liberal nations. The which as we have written afore, so we now
write again to your Majesty that we know and feel of a surety, the Moscovite,
enemy of all liberty under the heavens, daily to grow mightier by the increase
of such things as be brought to the Narva, while not only wares but also
weapons heretofore unknown to him, and artifices and arts be brought unto
him: by means whereof he makes himself strong to vanquish all others. Which
things, as long as this voyage to Narva is used, cannot be stopped. And we
perfectly know your Majesty cannot be ignorant how great the cruelty is of
the said enemy, of what force he is, what tyranny he uses on his subjects,
and in what servile sort they be under him. We seemed hitherto to vanquish
him only in this that he was rude of arts and ignorant of policies. If so be
that this navigation to the Narva continue, what shall be unknown to him?
Therefore we that know best, and border upon him, do admonish other
Christian princes in time, that they do not betray their dignity, liberty, and
life of them and their subjects to a most barbarous and cruel enemy, as we
can no less do by the duty of a Christian prince. For now we do foresee,
except other princes take this admonition, the Moscovite puffed up in pride
with those things that be brought to the Narva, and made more perfect in
warlike affairs with engines of war and ships, will make assault this way on
Christendom, to slay or make bound all that shall withstand him: which God
defend. With which our admonition diverse princes already content themselves
and abstain from the Narva. The others that will not abstain from the said
voyage shall be impeached by our navy and incure the danger of loss of life,
liberty, wife, and children. Now therefore if the subjects of your Majesty will
forbear this voyage to Narva there shall be nothing denied to them of us.
Let your Majesty well weigh and consider the reasons and occasions of our
stopping of ships going to the Narva. In which stopping our subjects of
Denmark be in no fault, as we have already written to your Majesty, neither
use we their counsel in the same. In any other matter, if there be any fault

in them against your Majesty or your subjects, we will gladly do justice upon them, that your Majesty may well understand that we be careful of you and your subjects. Neither think we it meet to take Hamburg, or any other place to judge the matter; for we have our council and judgment seat at Rie, where your Majesty and your subjects, or any other shall have justice administered unto them, with whom we have had ancient league and amity. And thus much we have thought good to let your Majesty understand. Fare you well. Dated the sixth of December, the 39th year of our reign.

Sigismund Augustus Rex

⚔ *49* ⚔

A Letter
from Ivan the Terrible
to Elizabeth I, 1570

Ivan the Terrible sought to establish closer ties with the English government after he granted privileges to their merchants. He sent several diplomatic missions and in 1567, through Anthony Jenkinson, a representative of the Muscovy Company, he even proposed a military alliance between England and Muscovy "against all of our mutual enemies." British failure to respond to Ivan's plans resulted in a substantial reduction of privileges and a series of rather bitter letters from Ivan to Elizabeth.

For that before time certain subjects of your brother King Edward, namely Richard Chancellor and others, being sent for some occasion to all people and places and having writings to all kings, emperors, dukes, lords, and rulers (but namely unto us not one word was written), and those your brother's subjects, Richard and his fellows, we know not after what sort, whether it were willingly or unwillingly, came and anchored in our haven, by the sea side, and to our town of Dvina, and we, as it behooved a Christian prince,

From Iurii Tolstoy, ed., *Pervyia sorok let snoshenii mezhdu Rossieiu i Anglieiu. 1555–1593* (The First Forty Years of Relations between Russia and England, 1553–1593) (St. Petersburg: 1875), pp. 110–115. Spellings have been modernized to facilitate reading.

showed them so much favor that we received them with honor, and at our princely and appointed dinners, we of our goodness sent for them; and we sent them back again unto your brother. And after that it pleased your brother to send the said Richard Chancellor and one Richard Gray unto us, and we in like cause showed our goodness unto them and sent them back again. And after that your brother sent the said Richard to us the third time, and thereupon we sent unto your brother our messenger Osip Grigorevich Nepeia. And to your brother's merchants and to all Englishmen we gave our letters of privilege so large as the like was given to our nation, never thinking to have had received friendship of your brother and of you and service of Englishmen. And in the meantime that we sent our messenger the same time your brother died, and your sister Mary* succeeded his place; and so married with Philip, king of Spain, the which king and your sister received our messenger honorably, and so sent him back again unto us; but they sent no word to us. And at that time your merchants did work much deceit against our merchants, and began to sell their wares dear, taking for all things more than things were worth. And since that time the Queen, your sister, died, and that the King Philip was sent away and that you were crowned Queen of England; and we all that time did your merchants no harm, but willed them to traffic, as they had done before time.

And how many letters have been brought to us hither, and not one letter that has been sealed with one seal, but every letter has had a contrary seal, which is no princely fashion, and such letters in all places be not credited, but every prince has in his realm one proper seal; but we did give credit to these letters, and according to your letters we wrought.

And after that you sent unto us your messenger Anthony Jenkinson about the affairs of merchants, and we, thinking him to have had credit with you, we had therefore sworn him, and also your merchant Ralph Ruttar, because of interpreting for that in such weighty affairs, we stood need of true interpreting, and we sent you by word of mouth of our great and secret meaning desiring friendship of you and that you would have sent over to us some near and trusty servant of yours and Anthony to have come with him, or else Anthony alone for that we know not whether Anthony did tell you all our words or no, for we heard not of him in a year and a half after, and here came not from you neither messenger neither ambassador. And therefore we of our goodness gave unto your merchants another privilege, thinking how to have been in good credit with you and therefore our goodness was the greater to them.

And after that we had news, that a subject of yours was come to the Narva,

---

*Mary Tudor, 1553–1558.

by name Edward Goodman, which had many letters. But we sent to him to inquire of Anthony but he told us nothing of him, and [we] commanded him to be searched for letters and we found many letters; and in those letters were written words not allowable against our princely state and empire, how that in our empire were many unlawful things done, and he gave evil language to our messengers, which were sent to him, but we of our goodness caused him to be stayed honorably till such time as we should have answer from you of those affairs that we sent of to you by Anthony.

And after that there came from you a messenger to the Narva about merchants' affairs, namely George Midelton, and we sent to him to know whether Anthony were come to you or no, and when he should come from you to us. But your messenger George would tell us nothing of this matter, but did miscall our messengers and Anthony also, and we commanded him to be kept, till such time as we had and knew of the matter, that we committed to Anthony.

And not long after that we were informed that your ambassador Thomas Randall was come to our port of Dvina, and we of our goodness sent to meet him, the son of a gentleman, and we commanded the said gentleman to be his guide, and we did entreat him with great honor and we commanded our said gentleman to inquire of him whether Anthony were with him or no, but he told our gentleman nothing; for Anthony was not with him, but all his talk was of bourses and affairs of merchants. And when he was come to our empire we sent unto him many times, that he would come and confer with our counsel that we might have had knowledge of those great affairs that we sent you word of by Anthony, but he after a rude manner denied to come; but he wrote supplications against Glover and Rutter and upon affairs of merchandise he wrote, but of our princely affairs he made them of none effect and therefore your ambassador was kept the longer from our presence, and after that our city was stricken by the hand of God with the plague, so that it was not possible for us to give him presence, but so soon as it pleased God to withdraw from us the plague of sickness, we gave him presence, and all his talk was upon merchants' affairs; and then we sent unto him our counsellor and captain of Vologda Duke Athanasius Ivanovich Viazemskii, and our seal keeper Ivan Mikhailov, and our secretary Andrei Vasilev. We willed them to inquire of him if he had commission of those affairs, which we sent you word of by Anthony, and he told them that he had commission for those affairs also; thereupon we did augment our goodness unto him after that he was diverse times with us and ever he spoke about bourses and affairs of merchandise and very seldom would talk with us of our princely affairs, and at that time we had occasion for to ride to our inheritance of Vologda, and we gave commandment to our gentlemen that they should conduct him thither, and he being arrived thither we sent unto him our presaid counsellor and our secretary Peter Grigoriev, and willed them to treat with him how those affairs of amity might be between us, but the talk which your ambassador had was to establish merchants, and we willed him to talk with us of our affairs, and we talked of them and we did agree how those affairs should pass between us, and then we wrote our letters, and to our letters we set our seal and then if they had pleased you, that then you would have caused your letters to have been written and to have sent some trusty ambassador, and that Anthony Jenkinson might have been sent with him. The cause which we were so desirous to have had Anthony Jenkinson to have come, was that we would have known of him whether he did declare unto you the words which we commanded him to tell you by mouth, and to have known of him whether the words did please you, or no, and how you were minded of that matter. And so we sent in company with your ambassador our ambassador, Andrei Gregorievich Savin.

And you have sent us our ambassador back, but you have not sent your ambassador to us, and you have not ended our affairs according as your ambassador did agree upon, and your letters be not thereto agreeable, for such weighty affairs be not ended without confirmation by oath, or without ambassadors, but you have set aside those great affairs, and your counsel does deal with our ambassador about merchants' affairs; and your merchants Sir William Garrard and Sir William Chester did rule all business. And we had thought that you had been ruler over your land and had sought honor to your self and profit to your country, and therefore we did pretend those weighty affairs between you and us. But now we perceive that there be other men that do rule, and not men but boursers and merchants, the which seek not the wealth and honor of our majesties, but they seek their own profit of merchandise: and you flower in your maidenly estate like a maiden. And whosoever was trusted in our affairs, and did deceive us, it were not meet that you should credit them.

And now seeing it is so, we do set aside these affairs. And those bourser merchants, that have been the occasion that the pretended wealths and honors of our majesties has not come [to] pass, but do seek their own wealth, they shall see what traffic they shall have here, for our city of Moscow, before their traffic to it, has not greatly wanted English commodities. And the privileges that we gave to your merchants and sent to you, that you would send it [to] us again, and whether it be sent or no, we will give commandment that nothing shall be done by it, and all those privileges which we have given aforetime be from this day of none effect.

Written at our honor of Moscow since the foundation of the world 7079 [1570] years, the twenty-fourth day of October.

⚔ *50* ⚔

Ivan the Terrible's Punishment of Novgorod in 1570

The reign of Ivan the Terrible (1547–1584) is usually remembered for its conquest of the Volga Basin and Siberia, its establishment of commercial ties with England, its struggle with Poland for access to the Baltic Sea, and its perfection of an autocratic, brutal rule in Russia. The latter achievement, in fact, gave him the descriptive title by which he is most commonly known, "the Terrible." The validity of this description is evidenced by Ivan's utter devastation of Novgorod in 1570, when tens of thousands of Novgorodians were butchered in a week-long orgy because of Ivan's unfounded suspicion that Novgorod's Archbishop contemplated placing the city under Polish-Lithuanian protection.

On Monday the second day of January, in the year 7079 [1570], after the creation of the world, the day of commemoration of the Holy Father and Roman Pope Silvester, the illustrious Tsar and Grand Prince Ivan Vasilevich, lord of All Russia, sent an advance guard of the army in forced march toward Great Novgorod. The army units consisted of *boyars*, army commanders, princes, nobles, courtiers, and an uncountable multitude of other troops.

When these troops had arrived before Great Novgorod, according to the order of the illustrious Tsar and Grand Prince Ivan Vasilevich, lord of All Russia, they established a great camp in the environs of the city, surrounded by strong posts with fortifications of every kind. They erected sentinel towers near the posts and decreed that the inhabitants of the city be closely watched in order that not one human being could escape from the city.

And other princes and nobles of the Tsar from the same advance guard rode in all directions in the area around Great Novgorod and sealed all the monasteries and money boxes of the Church. They captured the abbots, the black clergy, the deacons, and the elders from the monasteries, and took them, perhaps 500 or more persons, to Great Novgorod. They were brought to the place of execution, where they were to wait until the arrival of the Tsar.

And other nobles of the Tsar from the same advance guard seized the priests and deacons of all the churches in Novgorod and also brought them to the execution site. Every ten prisoners were assigned a police officer. And

---

From *Polnoe Sobranie Russkikh Letopisei* (Complete Collection of Russian Chronicles) (St. Petersburg: 1885), vol. 3, pp. 254–262. Translation mine. Words in brackets are mine.

these officers received orders to keep the prisoners in iron chains and to beat them mercilessly from morning to evening at the place of execution until ransom was obtained. The Tsar ordered that each prisoner pay twenty *rubles* in the currency of Novgorod for ransom.

And other nobles of the Tsar from the same advance guard dispersed over all streets in Great Novgorod and among all the parishes, whereupon they sealed up all the manors of the distinguished people of Great Novgorod, along with their wealth, and erected numerous guard posts for the purpose of keeping watch until the arrival of the Tsar.

By order of the monarch, other nobles of the same advance guard arrested all the administrative officials and all the important merchants of Great Novgorod and placed them under guard. They were chained, their houses were sealed up with all their wealth, and their wives and children were ordered closely watched until the arrival of the sovereign.

On January 6 of the same year, 1570, the festival of our Lord and Savior Jesus Christ's baptism, the illustrious Tsar and Grand Prince Ivan Vasilevich, lord of All Russia, arrived in Great Novgorod. He was accompanied by his son, the rightful heir to the throne, Prince Ivan Ivanovich, and an uncountable host of princes, *boyars*, courtiers and other troops, including 1500 *streltsy* [musketeers]. . . .

On Saturday, the day after his arrival, the illustrious Tsar and Grand Prince Ivan Vasilevich, lord of All Russia, gave the order that the abbots, clergy, and monks who had previously been brought to the place of execution should be beaten to death with clubs. After they had all been killed, he ordered that each be buried at the monastery where he had resided. . . .

On Sunday, January 8, the Tsar went the Church of St. Sophia with his troops to attend High Mass. At the great Volkhov bridge, near the Black Cross, the Tsar was welcomed, according to custom, by Pimen, the Archbishop of Great Novgorod, with crosses and miraculous ikons. When, according to old custom, Archbishop Pimen wanted to bless the Tsar and Grand Prince Ivan Vasilevich, as well as his rightful heir to the throne, Prince Ivan Ivanovich, with the crucifix, the Tsar and Grand Prince Ivan Vasilevich and his son and heir to the throne, Prince Ivan, refused to receive the Archbishop's blessing. The Tsar said to Archbishop Pimen, "You villain, you do not hold a lifegiving cross in your hand, but rather a weapon. And with this weapon you want to wound the Tsar's heart, for you are malicious and you are devising plots with traitors among the inhabitants of this city. You want to give the great, holy city of Novgorod, which is a part of our inherited dominion, to the enemies, to the aliens, the Lithuanian King Sigismund Augustus. Although you call yourself the shepherd, the teacher, the ecclesiastical prince of the great apostolic cathedral of divine wisdom and of St. Sophia, you are only a wolf, a thief,

a murderer, a traitor. You attempt to damage our sceptre and crown." After
the Tsar had revealed his anger through such words, he ordered the Archbishop
to go into the Church of St. Sophia and to perform the holy liturgy in its
entirety. And the Orthodox Tsar and Grand Prince Ivan Vasilevich himself,
accompanied by the rightful heir to the throne, Prince Ivan Ivanovich, and
all his retinue, walked behind the holy, lifegiving crucifix and the sacred,
miraculous ikons, and entered the Church of St. Sophia where he heard the
divine liturgy. After the divine service the Tsar, accompanied by his courtiers,
princes, and warriors, went to Archbishop Pimen's palace for dinner. The Tsar
sat at the table and began to eat. Soon afterwards, he stopped and turned to
his princes and *boyars*. As was his custom, he shouted an order in a loud
voice shaking with anger. The Tsar commanded his men to plunder the
Archbishop's money box, his entire court with all the neighboring buildings,
cells, and rooms, and to seize his courtiers and attendants and place them
under guard until further orders. The Tsar ordered that the Archbishop himself
be placed under close surveillance after his property had been confiscated, but
the Tsar sent two *dengas* each day from the treasury for his maintenance.

The Tsar ordered his steward, Lev Andreevich Saltykov, as well as his high
priest, Eustachius, together with several *boyars*, to go into the Church of St.
Sophia and to confiscate the treasures in the vestry as well as costly, sacred
vessels, the holy and miraculous ikons from Korsun, and paintings by Greek
artists. In addition, the Tsar decreed that all holy church treasures, the holy,
divine, costly, and wondrous ikons, and the chasubles used in celebrating
mass, and the bells in all of Great Novgorod's churches be confiscated. . . .
(The Tsar had similar confiscations carried out in the monasteries in the
environs of Novgorod.)

Thereupon, the Orthodox Tsar and Grand Prince Ivan Vasilevich, lord of
All Russia, and his son, the rightful heir to the throne, Prince Ivan Ivanovich,
held court in the suburbs of Gorodishche where he had encamped upon his
arrival. The Tsar commanded that the powerful *boyars*, the important merchants, the administrative officials, and the citizens of every rank be brought
before him, together with their wives and children. The Tsar ordered that
they be tortured in his presence in various spiteful, horrible, and inhuman
ways. After many various unspeakable and bitter tortures, the Tsar ordered
that their bodies be tormented and roasted with fire in refined ways. And the
Tsar commanded his nobles to bind the hands and feet and heads of these
tortured and roasted human beings with fine ropes in various ways. He ordered
that each man be tied to a sled, be dragged to the Volkhov bridge behind
the fast-moving sleds, and be thrown into the Volkhov River from the bridge.
The Tsar ordered that their wives and children be brought to the Volkhov
bridge, where a high platform had been erected. He commanded that they

be chained on the arms and legs and that the children be tied to their mothers and then be thrown from the platform into the waters of the Volkhov River. Meanwhile, the Tsar's men, the nobles and soldiers, moved about in small boats on the Volkhov River, armed with spears, lances, hooks, and axes. When the people, men and women of all ages, surfaced, they were stabbed by the soldiers with hooks, lances, and spears, or they were struck with axes. In a horrible manner they were submerged without mercy in the depths of the river, and abandoned to a terrible and bitter death.

Because of our sins, this unspeakable shedding of Christian blood, caused by the excessive anger of the Tsar, continued uninterrupted each day for five weeks or more. And every day perhaps a thousand human beings of all ages were thrown into the water and drowned; occasionally there were fifteen hundred, and if perchance only five or six hundred people were thrown into the water, the day in question was considered an easy day, one deserving of thanks.

After the end of the punishment, the Orthodox Tsar and Grand Prince Ivan Vasilevich, lord of All Russia, went to the renowned and important monasteries in the environs of Great Novgorod. He decreed that the churches, the monasteries, the cells, and the buildings be plundered. He ordered that the grain in the barns and the fields be burned, and that the livestock of every kind, horses and cows, be slaughtered.

Thereupon, the Orthodox Tsar and Grand Prince Ivan Vasilevich, lord of All Russia, returned to Great Novgorod. He ordered that the merchant's stores in all the city, in the alleys and streets, be robbed of their goods and that the warehouses and shops be destroyed. Afterwards, the Orthodox Tsar and Grand Prince rode with all of his people and warriors through all of Novgorod and its suburbs, pitilessly robbing all the inhabitants, including the women, breaking windows and doors, and demolishing the houses and manors. (For several weeks similar treatment was given the region under control of Great Novgorod. The surviving citizens of Novgorod were pardoned, with the exception of those whom the Tsar had transported to Moscow and ordered beheaded.)

❧ *51* ❧

Muscovy at the End of the Sixteenth Century

The establishment of commercial relations between England and Moscovy enabled many Englishmen to travel to and report on Russia. One of the most interesting of these reports is *The Russe Commonwealth*, by Dr. Giles Fletcher, who visited Russia in 1588 as an ambassador of Queen Elizabeth I. Like all European visitors, Fletcher paid special attention to the resources of the country, and customs, manners, and behavior of the people. This should not be surprising, for, to a sixteenth century European, Russia was as distant and mysterious as is perhaps Tibet to the western world today. Scholars regard Fletcher's work as an excellent source on Russia at the close of the sixteenth century.

The State or Form of Their Government

The manner of their government is much after the Turkish fashion: which they seem to imitate as near as the country, and reach of their capacities in politic affairs, will give them leave to do.

The state and form of their government is plain tyrannical, as applying all to the behoof of the prince, and that after a most open and barbarous manner: as may appear by the *sophismata* or secrets of their government afterwards set down, as well for the keeping of the nobility and commons in an under proportion, and far uneven balance in their several degrees, as also in their impositions and exactions, wherein they exceed all just measure, without any regard of nobility or people: farther then it gives the nobility a kind of unjust and unmeasured liberty to command and exact upon the commons and baser sort of people in all parts of the realm where so ever they come, specially in the place where their lands lie, or where they are appointed by the emperor to govern under him; also to the commons some small contentment, in that they pass over their lands by descent of inheritance to whither son they will;

Reprinted with permission of the Cambridge University Press from Edward A. Bond, ed., *Russia at the Close of the Sixteenth Century. Comprising the Treatise "Of the Russe Common Wealth,"* by Dr. Giles Fletcher; and the *Travels of Sir Jerome Horsey.* . . . (London, Published for the Hakluyt Society, 1856), pp. 26–45, 146–152. Spellings have been modernized to facilitate reading. Words in brackets are mine.

which commonly they do after our gavelkind; and dispose of their goods by gifts or testament without any control. Wherein notwithstanding both nobility and commons are but storers for the prince, all running in the end into the emperor's coffers: as may appear by the practice of enriching his treasury, and the manner of exactions set down in the title of his customs and revenues.

Concerning the principal points and matters of state, wherein the sovereignty consists (as the making and annulling of public laws, the making of magistrates, power to make war or league with any foreign state, to execute or to pardon life, with the right of appeal in all matters, both civil and criminal) they do so wholly and absolutely pertain to the emperor, and his counsel under him, as that he may be said to be both the sovereign commander, and the executioner of all these. For as touching any law or public order of the realm, it is ever determined of before any public assembly or parliament be summoned. Where, besides his council, he has none other to consult with him of such matters as are concluded before hand, but only a few bishops, abbots, and friars: to no other end than to make advantage of the people's superstitions, even against themselves, which think all to be holy and just, that passes with the consent of their bishops and clergy men, whatsoever it be. For which purpose the emperors are content to make much of the corrupt state of the Church, as now it is among them, and to nourish the same by extraordinary favors, and immunities to the bishops' sees, abbeys, and friaries: as knowing superstition and false religion best to agree with a tyrannical state, and to be a special means to uphold and maintain the same.

Secondly, as touching the public offices and magistracies of the realm, there is none hereditary, neither any so great nor so little in that country, but the bestowing of it is done immediately by the emperor himself. Insomuch that the very *diaks* or clerks in every head town, are for the most part assigned by himself. Notwithstanding, the emperor that now is (the better to intend his devotions) refers all such matters pertaining to the state, wholly to the ordering of his wife's brother, the L[ord] Boris Fedorovich Godunov.

Thirdly, the like is to be said of the jurisdiction concerning matters judicial, specially such as concern life and death. Wherein there is none that has any authority or public jurisdiction that goes by descent, or is held by charter, but all at the appointment and pleasure of the emperor, and the same practiced by the judges with such awe and restraint, as that they dare not determine upon any special matter, but must refer the same wholly up to Moscow to the emperor's council. To show his sovereignty over the lives of his subjects, the late emperor Ivan Vasilevich [Ivan the Terrible], in his walks or progresses, if he had misliked the face or person of any man whom he met by the way, or that looked upon him, would command his head to be struck off. Which was presently done, and the head cast before him.

Fourthly, for the sovereign appeal, and giving of pardons in criminal matters to such as are convicted, it is wholly at the pleasure and grace of the emperor. Wherein also the empress that now is, being a woman of great clemency, and withal delighting to deal in public affairs of the realm (the rather to supply the defect of her husband), does behave herself after an absolute manner, giving out pardon (specially on her birthday and other solemn times) in her own name, by open proclamation, without any mention at all of the emperor. Some there have been of late of the ancient nobility, that have held diverse provinces by right of inheritance, with an absolute authority and jurisdiction over them, to order and determine all matters within their own precinct without all appeal or control of the emperor. But this was all annulled and wrung clean from them by Ivan Vasilevich, father to this emperor. . . .

The Manner of Holding Their Parliaments

Their highest court of public consultation for matters of state is called the [*Zemskii*] *Sobor*, that is, the public assembly. The states and degrees of persons that are present at their parliaments, are these in order. (1) The emperor himself. (2) Some of his nobility, about the number of twenty, being all of his council. (3) Certain of the clergy men, etc., about the same number. As for burghers or others to represent the community, they have no place there: the people being of no better account with them than as servants or bond slaves that are to obey, not to make laws, nor to know any thing of public matters before they are concluded.

The court of parliament (called *Sobor*) is held in this manner. The emperor causes to be summoned such of his nobility as himself thinks meet, being (as was said) all of his council, together with the patriarch, who calls his clergy, to wit, the two metropolitans, the two archbishops, with such bishops, abbots, and friars as are of best account and reputation among them. When they are all assembled at the emperor's court, the day is intimated when the session shall begin. Which commonly is upon some Friday, for the religion of that day.

When the day is come, the clergy men assemble before at the time and place appointed, which is called *stol*. And when the emperor comes attended by his nobility, they arise all, and meet him in an out room, following their patriarch, who blesses the emperor with his two forefingers, laying them on his forehead and the sides of his face, and then kisses him on the right side of his breast. So they pass on into their parliament house, where they sit in this order. The emperor is enthroned on the one side of the chamber. In the next place, not far from him, at a small square table (that gives room to twelve persons or thereabouts), sits the patriarch with the metropolitans and bishops, and certain of the principal nobility of the emperor's council, together with two *diaks* or secretaries (called *dumnyi diaks*), that enact that which passes. The rest place themselves on benches round about the room, every man in his rank after his degree. Then is there propounded by one of the secretaries (who represents the speaker) the cause of their assembly, and the principal matters that they are to consider of. For to propound bills what every man thinks good for the public benefit (as the manner is in England), the Russian parliament knows no such custom nor liberty to subjects.

The points being opened, the patriarch with his clergy men have the prerogative to be first asked their vote, or opinion, what they think of the points propounded by the secretary. Whereto they answer in order, according to their degrees, but all in one form without any discourse: as having learned their lesson before, that serves their turns at all parliaments alike, whatsoever is propounded. Commonly it is to this effect:

> That the emperor and his council are of great wisdom, and experience, touching the policies and public affairs of the realm, and far better able to judge what is profitable for the common wealth than they are, which attend upon the service of God only, and matters of religion. And therefore it may please them to proceed. That instead of their advice, they will aid them with their prayers, as their duties and vocations do require, and so forth.

To this or like effect having made their answers every man in his course, up stands some abbot or friar more bold than the rest (yet appointed before hand as a matter of form), and desires the emperor it would please his majesty to command to be delivered unto them what his majesty's own judgment and determinate pleasure is, as touching those matters propounded by his *diak*.

Whereto is replied by the said secretary in the emperor's name:

> That his highness, with those of his noble council, upon good and sound advice have found the matters proposed to be very good and necessary for the common wealth of his realm. Notwithstanding, forasmuch as they are religious men, and so forth, know what is right, his majesty requires their godly opinions, yea and their censures too, for the approving or correcting of the said propositions. And therefore desires them again to speak their minds freely. And if they shall like to give their consents, that then the matters may pass to a full conclusion.

Hereunto, when the clergy men have given their consents (which they used to do without any great pausing), they take their leaves with blessing of the emperor: who brings the patriarch on his way so far as the next room, and so returns to his seat, till all be made ready for his return homeward. The acts that thus are passed by the *Sobor* or parliament, the *diaks* or secretaries draw into a form of proclamation, which they send abroad into every province and head town of the realm, to be published there by the dukes and *diaks* or secretaries of those places. The session of parliament being fully ended, the emperor invites the clergy men to a solemn dinner. And so they depart every man to his home. . . .

Of the Nobility, and by What Means It Is Kept in an Under Proportion Agreeable to That State

The degrees of persons or estates of Russia (besides the sovereign state or emperor himself), are these in their order.

1. The nobility, which is of four sorts. Whereof the chief for birth, authority, and revenue are called the *udelnye kniazia*, that is, the exempted or privileged dukes. These hold sometimes a several jurisdiction, and absolute authority within their precincts, much like unto the states or nobles of Germany. . . . But the late Emperor Ivan Vasilevich, father to this prince, being a man of high spirit, and subtle in his kind, meaning to reduce his government into a more strict form, began by degrees to clip off their greatness, and to bring it down to lesser proportion: till in the end he made them not only his vassals, but his *kholops*, that is, his very villains or bond slaves. For so they term and write themselves in any public instrument or private petition which they make to the emperor. So that now they hold their authorities, lands, lives, and all at the emperor's pleasure, as the rest do.

The means and practice whereby he wrought this to effect against those and other of the nobility (so well as I could note out of the report of his doings) were these, and such like. First, he cast private emulations among them about prerogatives of their titles and dignities. Wherein he used to set on the inferiors, to prefer or equal themselves to those that were accounted to be of the nobler houses. Where he made his advantage of their malice and contentions, the one against the other, by receiving devised matter, and accusations of secret practice and conspiracies to be intended against his person and state. And so having singled out the greatest of them, and cut them off with the good liking of the rest, he fell at last to open practice, by forcing of the other to yield their rights unto him.

2. He divided his subjects into two parts or factions by a general schism. The one part he called the *oprichniki* or select men. These were such of the nobility and gentry as he took to his own part, to protect and maintain them as his faithful subjects. The other he called *zemskii*, or the commons. The *zemskii* contained the base and vulgar sort, with such noblemen and gentlemen as he meant to cut off, as suspected to mislike his government, and to have a meaning to practice against him. Wherein he provided that the *oprichniki* for number and quality of valor, money, armor, etc., far exceeded the other

of the *zemskii* side, whom he put (as it were) from under his protection: so that if any of them were spoiled or killed by those of the *oprichniki* (which he accounted of his own part), there was no amends to be sought for by way of public justice, or by complaint to the emperor.

The whole number of both parts was orderly registered and kept in a book: so that every man knew who was a *zemskii* man and who of the *oprichniki*. And this liberty of the one part to spoil and kill the other, without any help of magistrate or law (that continued seven years), enriched that side and the emperor's treasury, and wrought that withal which he intended by this practice, namely, to take out of the way such of the nobility as [he] himself misliked: whereof were slain within one week to the number of three hundred within the city of Moscow. This tyrannical practice of making a general schism and public division among the subjects of his whole realm, proceeded (as should seem) from an extreme doubt and desperate fear which he had conceived of most of his nobility and gentlemen of his realm, in his wars with the Poles and Crimean Tatars. What time he grew into a vehement suspicion (conceived of the ill success of his affairs), that they practiced treason with the Poles and Crimeans. Whereupon he executed some, and devised his way to be rid of the rest.

And this wicked policy and tyrannous practice (though now it be ceased) has so troubled the country, and filled it so full of grudge and mortal hatred ever since, that it will not be quenched (as it seems now) till it burn again into a civil flame.

3. Having thus pulled them, and ceased all their inheritance, lands, privileges, etc., save some very small part which he left to their name, he gave them other lands of tenure of *pomestie* (as they call it), that are held at the emperor's pleasure, lying far off in an other country; and so removed them into other of his provinces, where they might have neither favor nor authority, not being native nor well known there. So that now these of the chief nobility (called *udelnye kniazia*) are equalled with the rest: save that in the opinion and favor of the people they are of more account, and keep still the prerogative of their place in all their public meetings.

Their practice to keep down these houses from rising again and recovering their dignities, are these and such like. First, many of their heirs are kept unmarried perforce, that the stock may die with them. Some are sent into Siberia, Kazan, and Astrakhan, under pretense of service, and there either made away or else fast clapped up. Some are put into abbeys, and shire themselves friars by pretense of a vow, to be made voluntary and of their own accord; but, indeed, forced unto it by fear, upon some pretended crime objected against them. Where they are so guarded by some of special trust, and the convent itself (upon whose head it stands that they make no escape), as that they have no hope but to end their lives there. Of this kind there are many of very great nobility. These and such like ways, begun by the Emperor Ivan Vasilevich, are still practiced by the Godunovs, who, being advanced by the marriage of the empress their kinswoman, rule both the emperor and his realm (specially Boris Fedorovich Godunov, brother to the empress), and endeavor by all means to cut off or keep down all of the best and most ancient nobility. Whereof diverse already they have taken away, whom they thought likeliest to make head against them and to hinder their purpose, as *Kniaz* Andreas Petrovich Kurakin, a man of great birth and authority in the country. The like they have done with Peter Golovin [?] (whom they put into a dungeon where he ended his life), with *Kniaz* Vasilii Iurievich Golitsyn, with Andrei Ivanovich Shuiskii, accounted among them for a man of a great wisdom. So this last year was killed in a monastery (whither they had thrust him) one *Kniaz* Ivan Petrovich Shuiskii, a man of great valor and service in that country: who, about five or six years since, bore out the siege of the city of Pskov, made by Stefan Batory, King of Poland, with 100,000 men, and repulsed him very valiantly, with great honor to himself and his country and disgrace to the Pole. Also Nikita Romanov, uncle to the emperor by the mother's side, was supposed to have died of poison or some like practice. . . .

The second degree of nobility is of the *boyars*. These are such as the emperor honors (besides their nobility) with the title of counsellors. The revenue of these two sorts of their nobles, that rises out of their lands assigned them by the emperor, and held at his pleasure (for of their own inheritance there is little left them, as was said before) is about a thousand *marks* a year: besides pension which they receive of the emperor for their service in his wars, to the sum of 700 *rubles* a year, and none above that sum. . . .

In the third rank are the *voevodas*, or such nobles as are of have been generals in the emperor's wars. Which deliver the honor of their title to their posterities also: who take their place above the other dukes and nobles that are not of the two former sorts, namely, of the *udelnye kniazia* nor of the *boyars*.

These three degrees of their nobility, (to wit) the *udelnye kniazia*, the *boyars*, and the *voevodas*, have the addition of *vich* put unto their surname, as Boris Fedorovich, and so forth: which is a note of honor that the rest may not usurp. And in case it be not added in the naming of them, they may sue the *beschest* or penalty of dishonor upon them that otherwise shall term them.

The fourth and lowest degree of nobility with them is of such as bear the name of *kniazia* or dukes, but come of the younger brothers of those chief houses, through many descents, and have no inheritance of their own, save the bare name or title of duke only. For their order is to deliver their names and titles of their dignities over to all their children alike, what so ever else they leave them. So that the sons of a *voevoda*, or general in the field, are called *voevodas* though they never saw the field, and the sons of a *kniaz* or duke are called *kniazia*, though they have not one groat of inheritance or livelihood to maintain themselves withal. Of this sort there are so many that the plenty makes them cheap: so that you shall see dukes glad to serve a mean man for five or six *rubles* or *marks* a year, and yet they will stand highly upon their *beschest* or reputation of their honors. And these are their several degrees of nobility.

The second degree of persons is of their *syny boyarskie*, or the sons of gentlemen: which all are preferred, and hold that name by their service in the emperor's wars, being soldiers by their very stock and birth. To which order are referred their *diaks* or secretaries, that serve the emperor in every head town, being joined in commission with the dukes of that place.

The last are their commons, whom they called *muzhiks*. In which number they reckon their merchants and their common artificers. The very lowest and basest sort of this kind (which are held in no degree) are their country people, whom they call *krestiane.* . . .

Of the Government of Their Provinces and Shires

The whole country of Russia . . . is divided into four parts, which they call *chetverts* or tetrarchies. Every *chetvert* contains diverse shires, and is annexed to a several office, whereof it takes the name. The first *chetvert* or tetrarchy bears the name of *Posolskii chetvert*, or the jurisdiction of the office of the ambassages, and at this time is under the chief secretary and officer of the ambassages, called Andrei Shuvalov [?]. The standing fee or stipend that he receives yearly of the emperor for this service, is 100 *rubles* or *marks*.

The second is called the *Razriadnii chetvert*, because it is proper to the *razriad* or high constable. At this time it pertains by virtue of office to Basil Shuvalov [?], brother to the chancellor, but it is executed by one Zapon Abramov. His pension is a hundred *rubles* yearly.

The third is the *chetvert of Pomestie*, as pertaining to that office. This keeps a register of all lands given by the emperor for service to his noblemen, gentlemen, and others, gives out and takes in all assurances for them. The officer at this time is called Lazar Belushkin [?]. His stipend is 500 *rubles* a year.

The fourth is called *Kazanskii dvorets*, as being appropriate to the office that has the jurisdiction of the kingdoms of Kazan and Astrakhan, with the other towns lying upon the Volga, now ordered by one Druzhinin Penteleev

[?], a man of very special account among them, for his wisdom and promptness in matters of policy. His pension is 150 *rubles* a year.

From these *chetverts* or tetrarchies is exempted the emperor's inheritance or *votchina* (as they call it), for that it pertained from ancient time to the house of Belsky [?], which is the surname of the imperial blood. This stands of 36 towns with their bounds or territories. Besides diverse peculiar jurisdictions, which are likewise deducted out of those *chetverts*, as the shire of Vagha [?] (belonging to the Lord Boris Fedorovich Godunov), and such like.

These are the chief governors or officers of the provinces, not resident at their charge abroad, but attending the emperor whether soever he goes, and carrying their offices about with them, which for the most part they hold at Moscow, as the emperor's chief seat.

The parts and practices of these four offices, is to receive all complaints and actions what soever that are brought out of their several *chetverts* and quarters, and to inform them to the emperor's council. Likewise to send direction again to those that are under them in their said provinces, for all matters given in charge by the emperor and his council, to be done or put into execution within their precincts.

For the ordering of every particular province of these four *chetverts* there is appointed one of these dukes, which were reckoned before in the lowest degree of their nobility, which are resident in the head towns of the said provinces. Whereof every one has joined with him in commission a *diak* or secretary to assist him, or rather to direct him. For in the executing of their commission the *diak* does all.

The parts of their commission are these in effect. First, to hear and determine in all civil matters within their precinct. To which purpose they have under them certain officers, as *gubnii starets* or coroners, who, besides the trial of self murders, are to attach felons: and the *sudia* or under justices, who themselves also may hear and determine in all matters of the same nature, among the country people of their own wards or bailiwicks: but so that in case either party dissent, they may appeal and go farther to the duke and *diak* that reside within the head town. From whom also they may remove the matter to the higher court at Moscow of the emperor's council, where lie all appeals. They have under them also *sotskii starets*, that is aldermen, or bailiffs of the hundreds.

Secondly, in all criminal matters, as theft, murder, treason, and so forth, they have authority to apprehend, to examine, and to imprison the malefactor, and so having received perfect evidence and information of the cause, they are to send it ready drawn and orderly digested up to Moscow, to the officer of the *chetvert* whereunto that province is annexed: by whom it is referred and propounded to the emperor's council. But to determine in any matter criminal, or to do execution upon the party offending, is more than their commission will allow them to do.

Thirdly, if there be any public service to be done within that province (as the publishing of any law or common order by way of proclamation, collecting of taxes and impositions for the emperor, mustering of soldiers, and sending them forth at the day and to the place assigned by the emperor or his council), all these and such like pertain to their charge.

These dukes and *diaks* are appointed to their place by the emperor himself, and are changed ordinarily at every year's end, except upon some special liking or suit the time be prorogued for a year or two more. They are men of themselves of no credit nor favor with the people where they govern, being neither born nor brought up among them, nor yet having inheritance of their own there or else where. Only of the emperor they have for that service 100 *marks* a year, he that has most, some fifty, some but thirty. Which makes them more suspected and odious to the people, because being so bare, and coming fresh and hungry upon them lightly every year, they rack and spoil them without all regard of justice or conscience. Which is easily tolerated by the chief officers of the *chetverts*, to the end they may rob them again, and have a better booty when they call them to account: which commonly they do at the end of their service, making an advantage by their injustice and oppression over the poor people. There are few of them but they come to the *pudki* or whip when their time is ended, which themselves for the most part do make account of. And therefore they furnish themselves with all the spoil they can for the time of their government, that they may have for both turns, as well for the emperor and lord of the *chetvert*, as to reserve some good part for themselves.

They that are appointed to govern abroad are men of this quality: save that in the four border towns that are of greatest importance, are set men of more special valor and trust, two in every town. Whereof one is ever of the emperor's privy council. These four border towns are Smolensk, Pskov, Novgorod, and Kazan, whereof three lie towards Poland and Sweden, one borders far off upon the Crimean Tatar. These have larger commission than the other dukes of the provinces that I spoke of before, and may do execution in criminal matters. Which is thought behoofull for the commonwealth: for incident occasions that may happen upon the borders that are far off, and may not stay for direction about every occurrence and particular matter from the emperor and his council. They are changed every year (except as before), and have for their stipend 700 *rubles* a year he that has most: some have but 400. Many of these places that are of greatest importance, and almost the whole country, is managed at this time by the Godunovs and their clients.

The city of Moscow (that is the emperor's seat) is governed altogether by the emperor's council. All matters there, both civil and criminal, are heard and determined in the several courts held by some of the said council, that reside there all the year long.

Only for their ordinary matters (as buildings, reparations, keeping of their streets decent and clean, collections, levying of taxes, impositions, and such like) are appointed two gentlemen and two *diaks* or secretaries, who hold a court together for the ordering of such matters. This is called the *zemskii* house. If any townsman suspect his servant of theft or like matter, hither he may bring him to have him examined upon the *pudki* or other torture. Besides these two gentlemen and secretaries that order the whole city, there are the *starostas*, or aldermen, for every several company. The alderman has his *sotskii* or constable, and the constable has certain *desiatskii* or decurions under him, which have the oversight of ten households apiece, whereby every disorder is sooner spied, and the common service has the quicker dispatch. The whole number of citizens, poor and rich, are reduced into companies. The chief officers (as the *diaks* and gentlemen) are appointed by the emperor himself, the *starosta* by the gentlemen and *diaks*, the *sotskii* by the *starosta* or alderman, and the *desiatskii* by the constables.

This manner of government of their provinces and towns, if it were as well set for the giving of justice indifferently to all sorts, as it is to prevent innovations by keeping of the nobility within order and the commons in subjection, it might seem in that kind to be no bad nor unpolitic way for the containing of so large a commonwealth, of that breadth and length as is the kingdom of Russia. But the oppression and slavery is so open and so great, that a man would marvel how the nobility and people should suffer themselves to be brought under it, while they had any means to avoid and repulse it: or being so strengthened as it is at the present, how the emperors themselves can be content to practice the same, with so open injustice and oppression of their subjects, being themselves of a Christian profession.

By this it appears how hard a matter it were to alter the state of the Russian government as now it stands. First, because they have none of the nobility able to make head. As for the lords of the four *chetverts* or tetrarchies, they are men of no nobility, but *diaks* advanced by the emperor depending on his favor, and attending only about his own person. And for the dukes that are appointed to govern under them, they are but men of a titular dignity (as was said before), of no power, authority, nor credit, save that which they have out of the office for the time they enjoy it. Which does purchase them no favor, but rather hatred of the people, for as much as they see that they are set over them, not so much for any care to do them right and justice, as to keep them under in a miserable subjection and to take the fleece from them, not once in the year (as the owner from his sheep), but to poll and

SWEDEN

FINLAND

LIVONIAN
ORDER

Archangel

TEUTONIC
ORDER

BALTIC SEA

Novgorod

Pskov

Tver

Dvina R.

GRAND
PRINCIPALITY
OF
LITHUANIA

Smolensk

Moscow

Tobolsk

POLAND

Kiev

Kursk

Kazan

Ufa

UKRANIAN (OR
ZAPOROZHIE)
COSSAKS

Dnieper R.

Volga R.

OTTOMAN

*Don
R.*

CRIMEAN
TATARS

Astrakhan

BLACK SEA

EMPIRE

CASPIAN SEA

**GROWTH OF THE
MOSCOVITE STATE
FROM THE FOURTEENTH
TO SEVENTEENTH CENTURIES**

Moscow Principality in 1300

Moscow Grand Principality and
colonies in 1462

Annexations 1462-1533

Boundaries in 1533

Annexations in 1533-1600

Boundaries in 1600
Boundaries of the Lithuanian
Grand Principality and the Polish
Kingdom in 1462
Boundaries of Ottoman Empire at the
end of the sixteenth century

0   300

SCALE OF MILES

clip them all the year long. Besides, the authority and rule which they bear
is rent and divided into many small pieces, being diverse of them in every
great shire, limited besides with a very short time: which gives them no scope
to make any strength, nor to contrive such an enterprise, if happily they
intended any matter of innovation. As for the common people (as may better
appear in the description of their state and quality afterwards set down) besides
their want of armor and practice of war (which they are kept from of purpose)
they are robbed continually both of their hearts and money, (besides other
means) sometimes by pretense of some service to be done for the common
defense, sometimes without any show at all of any necessity of commonwealth
or prince. So that there is no means, either for nobility or people, to attempt
any innovation, so long as the military forces of the emperor (which are the
number of 8000 at the least in continual pay) hold themselves fast and sure

unto him and to the present state. Which needs they must do, being of the quality of soldiers, and enjoying withal that free liberty of wronging and spoiling of the commons at their pleasure, which is permitted them of purpose, and to make them have a liking of the present state. As for the agreement of the soldiers and commons, it is a thing not to be feared, being of so opposite and contrary practice much one to the other. This desperate state of things at home, makes the people for the most part to wish for some foreign invasion, which they suppose to be the only means to rid them of the heavy yoke of this tyrannous government. . . .

Of the Private Behavior, or Quality of the Russian People

The private behavior and quality of the Russian people, may partly be understood by that which has been said concerning the public state and usage of the country. As touching the natural habit of their bodies, they are for the most part of a large size and of very fleshly bodies, accounting it a grace to be somewhat gross and burly, and therefore they nourish and spread their beards to have them long and broad. But, for the most part, they are very unwieldy and unactive withal. Which may be thought to come partly of the climate, and the numbness which they get by the cold in winter, and partly of their diet, that stands most of roots, onions, garlic, cabbage, and such like things that breed gross humors, which they use to eat alone and with their other meats.

Their diet is rather much than curious. At their meals they begin commonly with a *charka*, or small cup, of *aqua vitae* (which they call Russian wine) and then drink not till towards the end of their meals, taking it in largely and all together, with kissing one another at every pledge. And therefore after dinner there is no talking with them, but every man goes to his bench to take his afternoon's sleep, which is as ordinary with them as their night's rest. When they exceed and have variety of dishes, the first are their baked meats (for roast meats they use little) and then their broths or pottage. To drink drunk, is an ordinary matter with them every day in the week. Their common drink is mead; the poorer sort use water, and thin drink called *kvas*, which is nothing else (as we say) but water turned out of his wits, with a little bran mashed with it.

This diet would breed in them many diseases, but that they use bathstoves or hot houses instead of all physic, commonly twice or thrice every week. All the winter time, and almost the whole summer, they heat their *peches*, which are made like the German bathstoves, and their *potlads*, like ovens, that so warm the house, that a stranger at the first shall hardly like of it. These two extremities, specially in the winter, of heat within their houses and of extreme cold without, together with their diet, makes them of a dark and sallow complexion, their skins being tanned and parched both with cold and with heat, specially the women, that for the greater part are of far worse complexions than the man. Whereof the cause I take to be, their keeping within the hot houses, and busying themselves about the heating and using of their bathstoves and *peches*.

The Russian, because that he is used to both these extremities of heat and cold, can bear them both a great deal more patiently than strangers can do. You shall see them sometimes (to season their bodies) come out of their bathstoves all on a froth, and fuming as hot almost as a pig at a spit, and presently to leap into the river stark naked, or to pour cold water all over their bodies, and that in the coldest of all the winter time. The women, to mend the bad hue of their skins, used to paint their faces with white and red colors, so visibly that every man may perceive it. Which is made no matter, because it is common and liked well by their husbands, who make their wives and daughters an ordinary allowance to buy them colors to paint their faces withal, and delight themselves much to see them of foul women to become such fair images. This parches the skin, and helps to deform them when their painting is off.

They apparel themselves after the Greek manner. The nobleman's attire is on this fashion. First, a *tafta*, or little night cap, on his head, that covers little more than his crown, commonly very rich wrought of silk and gold thread, and set with pearl and precious stone. His head he keeps shaven close to the very skin, except he be in some displeasure with the emperor. Then he suffers his hair to grow and hang down upon his shoulders, covering his face as ugly and deformedly as he can. Over the *tafta* he wears a wide cap of black fox (which they account for the best fur) with a tiara or long bonnet put within it, standing up like a Persian or Babylonian hat. About his neck (which is seen all bare) is a collar set with pearl and precious stone, about three or four fingers broad. Next over his shirt (which is curiously wrought, because he strips himself into it in the summer time while he is within the house) is a *zhupan*, or light garment of silk, made down to the knees, buttoned before; and then a *caftan*, or a close coat buttoned and girt to him with a Persian girdle, whereat he hangs his knives and spoon. This commonly is of cloth of gold, and hangs down as low as his ankles. Over that he wears a loose garment of some rich silk, furred and faced about with some gold lace, called a *ferris*. Another over that of chamlet or like stuff, called an *alkaben*, sleeved and hanging low, and the cape commonly brooched and set all with pearl. When he goes abroad he casts over all these (which are but slight, though they seem to be many) another garment, called an *honoratka*, like to the *alkaben*, save that it is made without a collar for the neck. And this is commonly of fine cloth or camel's hair. His buskins (which he wears instead of hose, with linen folds under them instead of boot hose) are made of a Persian leather called *saphian*, embroidered with pearl. His upper stocks commonly are of cloth of gold. When he goes abroad he mounts on horseback, though it be but to the next door, which is the manner also of the *boyars* or gentlemen.

The *boyar's* or gentleman's attire is of the same fashion, but differs in stuff; and yet he will have his *caftan* or undercoat sometimes of cloth of gold, the rest of cloth of silk.

The noblewoman (called *chyna boyarshina*) wears on her head, first, a calotte of some soft silk (which is commonly red) and over it a frontlet, called *poviazka*, of white color. Over that, her cap (made after the coif fashion of cloth of gold) called *shapka zemskaia*, edged with some rich fur, and set with pearl and stone. Though they have of late begun to disdain embroidery with pearl about their caps, because the *diaks'* and some merchants' wives have taken up the fashion. In their ears they wear earrings (which they call *sarzha*) of two inches or more compasse, the matter of gold set with rubies, or sapphires, or some like precious stone. In summer, they go often with kerchiefs of fine white lawn or cambric fashioned under the chin, with two long tassels pendant. The kerchief is spotted and set thick with rich pearl. When they ride or go abroad in rainy weather, they wear white hats with colored bands (called *shapka zemskaia*). About their necks they wear collars of three or four fingers broad, set with rich pearl and precious stone. Their upper garment is a loose gown, called *rubashka*, commonly of scarlet, with wide loose sleeves hanging down to the ground, buttoned before with great gold buttons, or, at least, silver and gilt, nigh as big as a walnut. Which has hanging over it, fastened under the cap, a large broad cape of some rich fur, that hangs down almost to the midst of their backs. Next under the *rubashka* or upper garment they wear another, called a *letnik*, that is made close before with great wide sleeves, the cuff or half sleeve up to the elbows, commonly of cloth of gold; and under that a *ferris zemskii*, which hangs loose, buttoned throughout to the very foot. On the hand wrists they wear very fair bracelets, about two fingers broad, of pearl and precious stone. They go all in buskins of white, yellow, blue, or some other colored leather, embroidered with pearl. This is the attire of the noblewoman of Russia, when she makes the best show of herself. The gentlewoman's apparel may differ in the stuff, but is all one for the making or fashion.

As for the poor *muzhik* and his wife, they go poorly clad. The man, with his *odnoratka*, or loose gown, to the small of the leg, tied together with a lace before, of coarse white or blue cloth, with some *shuba*, or long waistcoat, of fur or of sheepskin under it, and his furred cap and buskins. The poorer sort of them have the *odnoratka*, or upper garment, made of cow's hair. This is their winter habit. In the summer time, commonly they wear nothing but their shirts on their backs and buskins on their legs. The woman goes in a red or blue gown when she makes the best show, and with some warm *shuba* of fur under it in the winter time. But in the summer nothing but her two shirts (for so they call them) one over the other, whether they be within doors or without. On their heads they wear caps of some colored stuff, many of velvet or of cloth of gold; but for the most part kerchiefs. Without earrings of silver or some other metal, and her cross about her neck, you shall see no Russian woman, be she wife or maid.

As touching their behavior and quality otherwise, they are of reasonable capacities, if they had those means that some other nations have to train up their wits in good nurture and learning. Which they might borrow of the Poles and other [of] their neighbors, but that they refuse it of a very self pride, as accounting their own fashions to be far the best. Partly also (as I said before) for that their manner of bringing up (void of all good learning and civil behavior) is thought by their governors most agreeable to that state and their manner of government. Which the people would hardly bear, if they were once civilled and brought to more understanding of God and good policy. This causes the emperors to keep out all means of making it better, and to be very wary for excluding of all peregrinity that might alter their fashions. Which were less to be disliked, if it set not a print into the very minds of his people. For as themselves are very hardly and cruelly dealt withal by their chief magistrates and other superiors, so are they as cruel one against another, specially over their inferiors and such as are under them. So that the basest and wretchedest *krestianin* (as they call him) that stoops and crouches like a dog to the gentleman, and licks up the dust that lies at his feet, is an intolerable tyrant where he has the advantage. By this means the whole country is filled with rapine and murder. They make no account of the life of a man. You shall have a man robbed sometime in the very streets of their towns, if he go late in the evening, and yet no man to come forth out of his doors to rescue him, though he hear him cry out. I will not speak of the strangeness of the murders and other cruelties committed among them, that would scarcely be believed to be done among men, specially such as profess themselves Christians.

The number of their vagrant and begging poor is almost infinite, that are so pinched with famine and extreme need, as that they beg after a violent and desperate manner, with "give me and cut me, give me and kill me," and such like phrases. Whereby it may be guessed what they are towards strangers, that are so unnatural and cruel towards their own. And yet it may be doubted whither is the greater, the cruelty or intemperancy that is used in that country. I will not speak of it, because it is so foul and not to be named. The whole country overflows with all sin of that kind. And no marvel, as having no law to restrain whoredomes, adulteries, and like uncleanness of life.

As for the truth of his word, the Russian for the most part makes small regard of it, so he may gain by a lie and breach of his promise. And it may be said truly (as they know best that have traded most with them) that from the great to the small (except some few that will scarcely be found) the Russian neither believes anything that another man speaks, nor speaks anything himself worthy to be believed. These qualities make them very odious to all their neighbors, specially to the Tatars, that account themselves to be honest and just in comparison of the Russian. It is supposed by some that do well consider of the state of both countries, that the offense they take at the Russian government and their manner of behavior, has been a great cause to keep the Tatar still heathenish, and to mislike (as he does) the Christian profession.

⚶ *52* ⚶

Possevino's Observations of Muscovy and Its People

Although Moscow claimed to be "the third Rome," and in the seventeenth century its rulers officially referred to themselves as descendants of the Roman Emperor Augustus, there were few contacts between Moscow and Rome, a situation that contributed to mutual ignorance and suspicion. The two centers were further alienated by the long-standing division between the Orthodox East and the Catholic West, as well as by prolonged wars between the Orthodox state of Muscovy and the Catholic Polish-Lithuanian Commonwealth. Relations between Moscow and Rome were also affected by Orthodox refugees from the Balkans who brought with them to Moscow not only anti-Turkish but anti-Rome and anti-West European attitudes. Finally, after the triumph of the Protestant Reformation, the Muscovites absorbed a good dose of anti-Rome feelings from Protestant English and Dutch visitors. So negative, indeed,

---

Reprinted from *The Moscovia of Antonio Possevino, S. J.* Translated with Critical Introduction and Notes by Hugh F. Graham. (Pittsburgh: University Center for International Studies, 1977), pp. 4–11. With permission of the University of Pittsburgh Press. ©1977 by University Center for International Studies, University of Pittsburgh. See original source for footnote reference.

was the Muscovite view of Catholic Rome that the government imposed a number of restrictions aimed at preventing any Catholics from entering Muscovy.

It should be noted, however, that in spite of long-standing hostility between Moscow and Rome there were a few brief official contacts. One came in 1438–1439, when a large delegation of Muscovite clergy attended the Rome-sponsored Ferrara-Florence Church Council, in an effort to reconcile differences between the Orthodox and Catholic churches. Another contact took place in 1581–1582, when Tsar Ivan the Terrible, pressed by successes of the Polish-Lithuanian armed forces, requested Papal assistance in mediating the so-called Livonian War. The task of mediation was undertaken by Jesuit scholar and diplomat Antonio Possevino (1533–1611). His mission to Moscow was a success in two ways. It helped to terminate the war. And it produced a most memorable account of Possevino's impressions of Muscovy and of his encounters and discussions with Ivan the Terrible.

There is no doubt that the Prince's capital, which, as I have said, is Moscow, now contains less than 30,000 inhabitants, including women and children. Although Moscow appears large as one approaches it, when one draws closer (to say nothing of entering it) one notices that the houses themselves take up a great deal of space. This impression is strengthened by the great wide streets, the numerous large squares, and all the big churches, which seem to have been built more for show than worship, as most of them are closed during the bulk of the year. Moscow was a handsomer and more populous place during the earlier part of this Prince's reign, but in 1570 the Tatars destroyed it; many of its inhabitants perished in the fire, and the city was reduced to its present and smaller confines. Traces of the older and larger city remain. It probably used to be eight or nine miles in circumference, whereas now it can scarcely be five. The people keep oxen, cows and other such animals in their homes with them, and lead them out to pasture every day. Most of the houses are enclosed by wattle fences; they are reminiscent of the homes of our peasants. There is, however, a degree of elegance in the two citadels of Moscow, which are interconnected. One of them contains the Prince's palace and some fine brick churches (the other churches in the city are made of wood), while the other is filled with new shops, each trade with a street of its own. The shops are tiny; a single enterprise in Venice would do more business than a whole street in Moscow. Very few of the artisans live on the premises. They have homes in town, and show clearly how highly they value this privilege.

I should be inclined to estimate the number of inhabitants in Smolensk, Novgorod, and Pskov as approximately the same: that is, in times of peace each one of them would contain 20,000 people at most. They allege that their populations are somewhat larger, but I would not put the numbers higher, for the reasons I have already given, and because the houses and buildings take up so much space. On the approach of envoys the Prince orders the peasants living in the villages and the countryside to come to town and create an appearance of large numbers, as I have already noted. The population of Tver' is much smaller today, although from a distance it gives the impression of a large and beautiful city. It is not surrounded by walls, and a considerable number of houses lie scattered around and about, because it has not seriously experienced war or enemy attack, which is also the reason why Vologda, Kazan', and above all the regions further north still have large populations. However this may be, and in spite of the fact that the territory belonging to the Grand Prince of Muscovy, which extends from Lithuania and Livonia as far as the Caspian Sea, and from the Lapps to the Cheremis, consists of more land than people, there is general agreement that the Prince can field forces of two or three hundred thousand cavalry, or an innumerable multitude of Tatars, whenever he wishes.

Fortifications and Defense Against Assault

The fortresses and other means of defense the Muscovites possess today are quite different from those they had before, and not all their centers are protected in the same way. Some fortresses are built of brick and stone, like the two in Moscow, the ones in Novgorod, Pskov, Porkhov, Startisa, and Aleksandrovskaia Sloboda, a partial construction at Iaroslavl', the one in Beloozero, and some others. Other places are fortified with ramparts held together by vines and tamped down till the earth within them becomes hard, as at Smolensk, and like the new wall put up around Moscow itself after the Tatar sack. The rest of the towns are protected by piles of tree trunks placed in squares, which are packed with earth or sand. They will not collapse under attack, but they are susceptible to fire and are often smeared with mud to guard against it. In general the experience of the past two centuries has failed to impress the Muscovites with the need for high towers and comparable fortifications.

Muscovy lacks the architectural tradition of this nature that prevails among us, although Vasilii, the father of the present Prince, did have the two citadels of Moscow constructed by an architect from Milan and Italian workmen. A Latin inscription, preserved over the entrance beneath a pious ikon of the Virgin Mary, is a memorial to their work. With its high walls and towers set in a circle, the place conveys a majestic appearance. A similar fortification is found in Novgorod, but the citadel contains scarcely any houses besides the church and the adjacent manse inhabited by the Archbishop and his clergy. This structure was built a long time ago in a kind of circle; last year another Italian architect surrounded it with a rampart and included a nearby monastery within the new fortification. At appropriate positions on the rampart he placed platforms capable of sustaining the weight of heavy artillery to ward off enemy attacks.

Pskov's first line of fortifications consists of a stone wall with towers standing before a river bed; next a second wall approximately the shape of an oblong triangle runs through the center of town; three forts are located near it, one after the other, and the whole complex presents a formidable appearance. Such a system of fortifications encourages the besieged while causing besiegers great concern and anxiety, as we were made constantly aware when we were in the Polish camp. The Poles succeeded in knocking down battlements, but they failed to sap the underground foundations of the wall with their axes and mattocks to cause its collapse. As a result, even though they managed with great effort to scale the high wall, they had still to climb down, in constant danger of being dislodged by the Muscovites. Those who tried to jump found themselves cut off from the rest of the army by the city wall and perished to a man. Even if a charge was at first completely successful and the attackers got down from the walls they would eventually find themselves driven inside the wooden houses in which the city abounds; the Muscovites then set fire to them, and thus the enemy was bound to be destroyed, while the Muscovites withdrew to the safety of their enclosed turrets. Furthermore, within the walled turrets the Commander had ordered wooden platforms capable of sustaining the weight of heavy cannon placed in a circle, and the cannon kept up a continuous fire.

Similarly, at Polotsk the Muscovites had built a large tower out of beams, from which they kept such a close watch on the enemy camp and all the rest of the terrain that it was virtually impossible for anyone to approach. However, the tower was struck so frequently by barrages from the Polish artillery that it actually appeared to be leaning over to one side and the fortress of Polotsk was finally captured by the valor of King Stefan and a bold assault by his troops. Porkhov has but one tower, located above the single entrance gate; hence, it is possible to set ladders and mount anywhere. In the absence of other towers from which to assail an approaching enemy the issue can only be settled by hand-to-hand combat at close quarters on the wall or by hurling down javelins and rocks. The fortifications of other towns are constructed in a similar manner. However, the ramparts of Smolensk abut on one side upon the waters of the river Dniepr and form protective layers three deep, and the fortress and the church are built high on a hill. This alone would render the task of any attacker extremely difficult, but, in addition the rampart itself is honeycombed with tiny apertures set very close to one another, which permits intensive small-arms fire to be directed against an enemy seeking to penetrate the defenses. Those observations should convey some idea of Muscovite fortifications.

Although the Muscovite soldiers do not oppose the Poles vigorously on the regular field of battle, they give an extraordinarily fine account of themselves when defending their fortresses and cities; even the women often perform military duties—bringing water to put out fires, piling up stones and pushing them down from the walls, or hurling stakes which they hold in their hand for this purpose—and their actions are of great help to their side and dangerous to the enemy. Whenever one soldier is killed in a barrage during an attack another takes his place, and so on down the line; in short, no one spares his energy or his life. They are inured to cold; often their only shelter against it, or rain, snow, or wind is a heap of branches, or their cloaks hung up on stakes thrust into the ground. They can subsist on most meager rations, content to drink a bitter and tasteless mixture of water and oat dust and to eat nothing but bread. The Polish King told me that he had found Muscovite soldiers in Livonian fortresses who had subsisted on such a diet for a long time. Most were dead, but those who had managed to survive, although scarcely breathing, were still fearful that their surrender would constitute a betrayal of their oath to serve their Prince to the death. This characteristic endows them with great strength; all concentrate simultaneously upon the same goal, and if often happens that the more robust of them are able to survive numerous engagements, or at least their stubborn endurance and dedication wear down an enemy. However, other writers have noted this on other occasions.

Other Resources of the Prince

The Prince alone controls everything. Cities, towns, villages, houses, fields, estates, forests, lakes, rivers, rank, and position: everything in this huge country bears witness to the enormous power and resources he possesses. It is believed that these were formerly even more substantial; when war did not hamper commerce, Livonia was prosperous, and navigation on the Baltic Sea was more extensive. When these favorable conditions ceased or diminished, an inevitable decline in the general level of prosperity took place, but the ostentation of the Prince's court has remained unchanged and he is thought still to possess enormous treasure. He acquires as much of the gold coin and bullion brought into Muscovy as he can, and he scarcely ever allows the export of gold. The Prince rarely exports silver either, except to ransom prisoners or hire foreign mercenaries, things which he does only very sparingly. The Muscovites often use skins and hides instead of coins for money, and when they go on a journey they generally take their own food with them. They convert *thalers* (a German currency) into *dengas* and *moskovkas*, as their monetary units are called. At the present time the Muscovite coinage contains a higher percentage of adulterated silver than it did formerly because they have abandoned their previous caution and indiscriminately allow any artificer to strike coins. Any gifts of gold and silver brought back by envoys returning from a mission the Prince adds to his stocks of treasure; he takes all the silver money the envoys have received, and even confiscates any personal gifts that may have been made to them. It is general knowledge that his relative seized all the works of art, bullion, gold and silver vessels, chalices and many other such objects in the cities and churches of Livonia he could, loaded them on wagons and carted them off. In this way the Prince acquired an enormous plunder, which, after the great Tatar invasion and sack of Moscow, he distributed among the three fortresses of Moscow, Iaroslavl', and Beloozero.

The cities and districts of Muscovy are no longer ruled by the kind of petty princes we are accustomed to calling Dukes. Although the Muscovites use this title to enhance their own dignity, to curry favor with the Prince, or to designate an official position, they lack all the realities of power. A certain Tatar, who had proven his loyalty to the Prince during the capture of Kazan' and by accepting the schismatic Muscovite religion, relinquished some of his own land and was given the town of Kolomna and certain other territory, but virtually all the real power remained in the hands of the Prince, who even juggled the revenues just as he pleases. Lands and villages assigned to individuals cannot be bequeathed by them to their descendants without the Prince's approval, and the peasants pay a tithe to and perform labor for the Prince in addition to the services they render their masters. They use for their own sustenance or sell the small surplus they manage to produce. The result of this policy is that no one can really say what actually belongs to him, and every man, whether he wishes it or not, exists in a state of dependency upon the Prince. The more a person has, the more he recognizes this dependency; the richer he is, the more he is afraid, for the Prince often takes back everything he has given. Prudence and caution constrain men to hold their tongues, for any attempt at conspiracy is cut short by uprooting entire families or by exiling (not assigning) men to different outposts. When the Prince believes a conspiracy to exist he frequently orders the death of those he suspects, including their sons, daughters, and peasants, even though the latter are entirely innocent. A nobleman of the Prince's court told me that he had acquired several estates, but for a number of years he was not allowed to thatch the wooden huts or even to repair them, because the peasants he needed for the work were so heavily burdened with the duties they had to perform for the Prince that they did not even have time to breathe.

Forty kindred families were among those forcibly removed from Livonia and put to work in the factories of Moscow on the Prince's orders; many others were sent to Kazan', and elsewhere, and all of them have to pay an annual tribute. Manifesting their displeasure, they referred to the Pope in the most respectful terms and showed me every possible deference. They reminded me of how much Livonia had once contributed to the Apostolic See and recalled how peaceful it had been when that country, known as a bulwark of the Christian Commonwealth, had born the title of Province under its own legitimate Catholic rulers, particularly at the time when it was under the protection of the Pope. When the Pope's paternal rule was overthrown, the Livonians became the prey of the Teutonic Knights when the latter were in revolt against the Church. With their country in danger of partition their appeals for aid to numerous quarters proved in vain, and they were finally brought under the yoke of heretics. Now they are living a most wretched life in Muscovy, if indeed an existence among heretics can be called living at all.

The best specimens from the huge amounts of valuable skins and fish that are taken from the forests, lake, and rivers are reserved for the Prince's own use as gifts or for sale. Some of the fish are dried and sent to be used as food for the garrisons. The consignments destined for the Prince are set aside and given preference over all the rest; no one may dispose of his own wares until the Prince's goods have been sold.

The Muscovites call their Scribes, or Secretaries, by the title of *D'iaki*, which is a corruption of the Greek word for Deacon, or Minister. These officials maintain very careful records and accounts at the Prince's palace, keep accurate records of all developments in each province, and send in reports to the Royal Treasurer.

Revenues are low. Ambassadors may bring any number of merchants with them, who ply their trade, pay no taxes, and receive maintenance at the Prince's expense. At one time fairs were frequently held in Astrakhan' which attracted traders from the Caspian Sea littoral and even from Persia, but now that the Tatars have been largely expelled from the region, and the war with Persia has been dragging on for some time, these fairs are held but rarely. I heard nothing about gold and silver mines. A few iron mines exist, but the miners do not work efficiently, and they are not effectively utilized.

The deference universally accorded the Prince is something the mind can scarcely comprehend. Even if the Muscovites do not really believe it, they incessantly declare that they owe their lives, their health, and all their worldly possessions to him and convey the impression that they attribute everything to the Grace of God and the Mercy of the Great Tsar (the title they use to address the Prince, which means King, or Emperor). Even when beaten to the point of death they will sometimes say that the Prince has done them a favor by chastising them. One would assume that the Muscovites were a people born more to slavery than achievement were it not for the fact that most of them fully realize the nature of their servitude and know that if they should flee the country their children would be killed on the spot and all their property would be immediately confiscated. They have grown accustomed to this sort of life from childhood and it has become second nature, as it were, for them to praise the Prince extravagantly, to declare that they can only live and prosper when the Prince lives and prospers, and to denigrate everything else in comparison, although if those of better understanding did not fear informers and had an opportunity to visit foreign countries, they would have no difficulty discerning the resources and strength possessed by other peoples.

The Entombment. Painting of the early 15th century.

The Prophet Elijah. Painting by unknown artist. Early 15th century.

Moscow. Cathedral of the Assumption, 1475–79.

The Intercession of the Virgin. Painting by Dionisius, late 15th century.

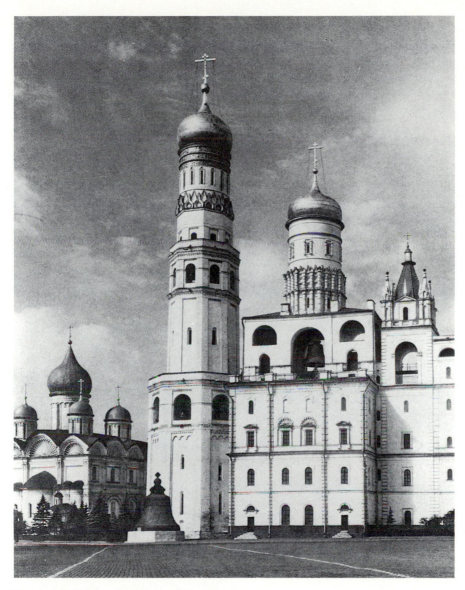

Moscow. Bell Tower of Ivan III. 1505.

Moscow. Church of the Trinity in Nikitinki.

Donskoi Monastery. "Old" Cathedral of the Virgin of the Don, 1593.

Chernigov. Church of St. Paraskeva Piatnitsa. Late 12th-early 13th century.

Boyarina Morozova on her way to prison. A painting by V. I. Surikov.

☙ *53* ❧

Russian Conquest and Exploitation of Siberia

Between 1580 and 1650, the Russians took control of all northern Asia from the Urals to the Pacific. The conquest of this vast territory, rich in resources and inhabited by primitive tribes, transformed the hitherto East European, Orthodox, Slavic Muscovite state into a huge multinational and multicultural Eurasian Russian colonial empire. In the process, many Asians became Russianized and many Russians became Asianized.

Like contemporary West European colonial expansions, the Russian drive was propelled by many forces and pressures, varying in purpose, skill, intensity, and duration. While the conquerors were few in number and mostly illiterate, they were audacious men, driven by ambition, sheer nerve, and energy. They succeeded, thanks to the existence of large riverine systems that enabled great distances to be covered in a relatively short time; the absence of significant, organized, and sustained native resistance; superiority of Russian weapons and fortifications; artful use of native guides and interpreters; and the absence of European competitors.

The Russians derived four basic benefits from their new colony. They extracted great wealth from the collection of tribute imposed on native inhabitants. They utilized it as a place to exile malcontents. They made it a base from which to launch new conquests. And they took advantage of its location to establish contacts with China and Japan and North America. Yet, as evident from the following selections, the Russians encountered many problems in their attempt to administer the new colony.

The following selections on Russian conquest and administration of Siberia come from diverse original documents and are reprinted here with permission of the Oregon Historical Society Press from Basil Dmytryshyn, E. A. P. Crownhart-Vaughan and Thomas Vaughan, eds., *Russian Conquest of Siberia: A Documentary Record,* 1558–1700. (Portland: Oregon Historical Society Press, 1985), pp. 53–54, 175–176, 198–199, 237–244, 348–351, 356, and 492–494.

A Report from the Voevoda of Tobolsk, to the Voevoda of Pelym, Concerning Unrest Among the Natives, June 21, 1606

Roman Troekurov reports to Ivan Mikhailovich [Godunov] and Petr Danilovich. Gospodin, on June 21, 1606, word reached us that the Ostiak prince, Okseit Boiarov, has joined forces with the *iasak* people from the Pelym *volost* of Kondinsk and the *iasak* Ostiak, Amalyk Grigorev, from Niazymsk *volost*. They are assembling a large force and plan to attack Prince Ivan and Prince Mikhail, the sons of Igicheev Alachev. They now have some 300 men. In Tobolsk we questioned the Ostiak prince Okseit about this in detail. Under questioning, he told us he had not been plotting with the Kondin people and that there is no unrest in his *volost*, but that there is great unrest among the *iasak* people of Pelym *uezd* in the Kondin *volost*. They are gathering, and plan to attack Prince Ivan and Prince Mikhail in force. When they reach the settlement of Ketsk, they plan to kill these men because they are the ones who collect *iasak* from them. At the present time, Prince Ivan and Prince Mikhail are under siege from these Pelym *iasak* people in the settlement.

Gospodin, if there is unrest among the *iasak* people in the Kondin *volost*, and you learn of it but do not inform us of it, this will be a serious matter. Gospodin, upon receipt of this *gramota*, you are to send a detailed written report about this by rapid courier to us in Tobolsk. If you do not know anything of this, Gospodin, then you are immediately to send all available servitors from Pelym to the Kondinsk *volost*, and order that five or six of the Kondinsk *volost* leaders be brought to you in Pelym immediately so that you can interrogate them about this.

They have given their oath to the Sovereign not to commit treason, nor to assemble warriors, nor to launch an attack. If they know of any rebels, they are to bring them to you in Pelym. You are to find out from them why there is unrest among the *iasak* people of the Kondinsk *volost*, why they plan to attack Prince Ivan and Prince Mikhail, the sons of Igicheev, and what oppressions and hardships they have suffered because of them. They may send a petition to the Sovereign about these problems, but they are not to assemble for the purpose of an attack. If there are insurgents, they must be apprehended and brought to you. The Sovereign will give generous rewards to any persons who hand over traitors. And if the plotters personally plead their guilt to the Sovereign, he will pardon them.

Gospodin, whatever you learn from these persons during the questioning, why there is unrest and who is responsible for it, you are to write down all the details immediately, and send the report to us post haste, without losing a minute. Send the report with the first available courier and order him to travel day and night to Tobolsk.

If the unrest in Kondinsk *volost* becomes any worse, you are not to release any of these suspects from Pelym until you have an *ukaz* from the Sovereign. Give them as much food as they need. Send to Kondinsk *volost* two or three *iasak*-paying people who are well known and well regarded in that *volost*. Also send Pelym servitors with them and three or four interpreters. Instruct them to speak firmly with the *iasak* people of Kondinsk *volost* so that they will disperse back to their settlements, and will not come together to make an unwarranted attack on anyone. They are not to assemble for any reason. They are not to cause any unrest or disturbance. If their dwellings or hunting grounds have been violated, or if they have suffered any other oppression or harm, they are to go to Pelym to file a complaint with you.

The Sovereign Tsar and Grand Prince Dmitrii Ivanovich [The False Dmitrii] of all Russia will issue his Tsarist *ukaz* against any persons guilty of violence and of inflicting injury.

In addition to investigating unrest in the Kondinsk *volost*, you are also to make inquiries into other matters there and in other *volosts* which pay *iasak* to Pelym. You are immediately to report to Tobolsk any information you may secure from these *iasak* people and from the servitors you send to them.

A Petition from the Merchant Guselnikov to Tsar Mikhail Fedorovich Protesting Excessive Regulation of the Fur Trade in Siberia, 1639

To Tsar Mikhail Fedorovich, Sovereign and Grand Prince of all Russia, a petition from Vasilii Fedotov [Guselnikov], a humble servant in your *gostinnaia sotnia* [merchant guild].

I, your humble servant, send my people Grigorii Ivanov and Afanasii Andreev and their *prikashchiks* [agents] to the towns of Siberia, to Eniseisk *ostrog*, to the mighty Lena River, and to Mangazeia; they carry all manner of Russian goods and supplies used to prepare sable pelts.

It is impossible to take any Russian provisions except for fresh honey to the Lena and Tunguska rivers because of the vast distances involved.

Sovereign, the *voevodas* and other servitors in the towns in Siberia stop our rafts and boats and collect taxes on both equipment and vessels from our contract trappers and hired people. On the winter route from Verkhotur'e they will not issue permits to go into other Siberian towns to prepare rafts and boats and the necessary equipment for the sable hunt; rather, they force us to stay in Verkhotur'e until spring. Neither will they let us travel from Eniseisk *ostrog* to the Turukhansk *zimov'e* with provisions and equipment, nor from that *zimov'e* to the sable hunting grounds and the Lena River. Instead, they keep us here for their own profit.

Because the *voevodas* and servitors impose these halts, the hunters cannot travel the entire distance to the sable hunting grounds in one season, and the result is that they freeze to death in barren places. Furthermore, Sovereign, when I, your humble servant, send my *prikashchiks* and hired people into Siberia by way of Kamen and Obdor, the officials there stop them and collect a transit fee of ten percent, in Russian goods or in cash, just as they do at Verkhotur'e. This is contrary to your *ukaz*, Sovereign. Those persons who come to Obdor from Mangazeia with furs have to pay, in Mangazeia and other towns, an impost of one *denga* per *ruble*, based on the customs officials' assessments. These men issue transit papers with your Sovereign seal. Then in Obdor there are officials who stop the fur traders and collect another tax of one *denga* per *ruble* on the same furs. The officials there reissue the transit documents, and they stop everyone, causing great losses thereby.

Merciful Sovereign, Tsar Mikhail Fedorovich, Grand Prince of all Russia, have mercy on me, your humble servant. Sovereign, allow my men and my *prikashchiks* in the sable trade to carry 150 *pud* of fresh honey with them, free of duty. Allow them to buy provisions in all Siberian towns. Permit them to leave Verkhotur'e by the winter route, so they can procure boats and provisions in any Siberian town. Let them leave Eniseisk *ostrog* and Turukhansk *zimov'e* with their rafts, boats, and dugouts without hindrance.

Sovereign, decree that in Obdor your officials are to collect your taxes only in accordance with your decree which pertains to collection in Verkhotur'e. Sovereign, do not allow tax collectors to impose a reissue fee on furs, and do not permit them to reissue transit documents.

Sovereign, please send your Sovereign decree on this matter to all Siberian towns.

Tsar, Sovereign, have mercy and grant my petition.

The Oath of Allegiance which Russians Administered to Bratsk Native Leaders, 1642–1645

I, Bului, a man of the Bratsk tribe, hereby give my firm oath of allegiance to my Sovereign Tsar and Grand Prince Mikhail Fedorovich, Autocrat of all Russia, and to his Sovereign Lordship, the Tsarevich and Grand Prince Aleksei Mikhailovich. I, Bului, and my brother Bura and our other brothers and tribesmen, and all my *ulus* people, swear on our faith, by the sun, by the earth, by fire, by the Russian sword, and by guns, that we will come under His Tsarist Majesty's mighty authority, in eternal servitude, without treason, undeviatingly, for all time. I will serve my Sovereign in every way, loyally and gladly.

I will not commit any treason against his Sovereign servitors or against any other Russians or against his Sovereign people in the Verkholensk *ostrozhek*, or against agricultural settlers, in any places where the Sovereign's servitors and Russians may be working, nor will I come in war or in secret to kill them or harm them or commit treason against them. Neither I, Bului, personally, nor my brother, nor any of my *ulus* people will incite other hostile Bratsk people to commit treason against the Sovereign's people, nor incite them or guide them to come to kill.

Likewise, I, Bului, will encourage other Bratsk leaders and their *ulus* people to come under His Tsarist Majesty's mighty hand in eternal servitude and to pay *iasak* and *pominki* to the Sovereign, in large amounts and in full every year, for themselves and for their brothers, and in every way to be in complete concord with the Sovereign's people.

When the Sovereign's men come to collect *iasak* in my *ulus*, I will protect them, and will not allow them to be killed. If any Bratsk leaders and their *ulus* people become disloyal to the Sovereign, then I, Bului, will report about these disloyal persons to the Sovereign's *prikashchiks* in Verkholensk *ostrog*, and I will join the Sovereign's forces in war against these disloyal people, and will try to pacify them by means of war and bring them back under your Sovereign Tsarist mighty hand, and will collect *iasak* from them for the Sovereign.

If I, Bului, do not carry out all these promises for my Sovereign Tsar, the Grand Prince Mikhail Fedorovich of all Russia, and for the Lord Tsarevich and Grand Prince Aleksei Mikhailovich, as written in this document, and if I do not serve loyally for all time, and gladly, or if I commit any treason against the Sovereign's servitors and go to war against the Russian people near Verkholensk *ostrog*, or against the agricultural settlers, or in other places where the Sovereign's people may come, or if I commit murder, or do not pay *iasak* in full for myself and for all my *ulus* people, or if I commit some foolish act, then, in accordance with my faith, the sun will not shine on me, Bului, I will not walk on the earth, I will not eat bread, the Russian sword will cut me down, the gun will kill me, and fire will destroy all our *uluses* on our lands.

And if I commit treason, the final punishment will be that the Sovereign's anger will be loosed on me and I will be put to death without mercy and without pity.

Instructions from the Voevoda of Iakutsk, Frantsbekov, to the Explorer Khabarov, Regarding His Expedition into the Land of the Daurs, 1649–1651

On March 6, 1649, the veteran explorer, Erofei P. Khabarov, reported to the Sovereign Tsar and Grand Prince Aleksei Mikhailovich of all Russia. In his report he stated that in accordance with the Sovereign's *ukaz*, during the past years he had been sent on government service against [princes] Lavkai and Botogo, under the administration of the *stolnik* and *voevoda* Petr Petrovich Golovin, and the *pismennaia golova* Enalei Bakhteiarov. Seventy servitors were sent with him, but they did not reach these princes. They went along the Vitim, not along the Olekma, because they were not familiar with the direct route. From the government warehouse they received money and provisions of food, powder, shot, and firearms.

He now asks that the Sovereign again grant him, Erofei, permission to go, together with volunteer servitors and *promyshlenniks*, however many may choose to go, and this time without being given government supplies. He wants about 150 men, or as many as possible, and he would provision them himself. He would provide their food and all supplies, including boats and equipment, and, the Sovereign's luck permitting, he would bring Lavkai and Botogo under the Sovereign Tsar's mighty hand as well as any other *transmontane* non-*iasak* people, from whom the Sovereign would receive considerable benefit from the collection of *iasak*.

In accordance with the *ukaz* of the Sovereign Tsar and Grand Prince Aleksei Mikhailovich of all Russia, the *voevoda* Dmitrii Andreevich Frantsbekov and the *diak* Osip Stepanov have given Erofei permission to proceed, together with volunteer servitors and *promyshlenniks* numbering about 150 in all, or as many as he can gather, who will be willing to go without receiving government provisions. They will go along the Olekma and Tugur rivers to the Shilka portage and thence along the Shilka; they will put down any indigenous people who are disobedient and disloyal and will not pay *iasak* either for themselves or on behalf of their *ulus* inhabitants. They are also to force Lavkai and Botogo and their *ulus* people and other *transmontane* non-*iasak* people to submit, on behalf of the Sovereign Tsar and Grand Prince Aleksei Mikhailovich of all Russia. They will collect *iasak* and explore new territories. They are instructed to proceed with care, taking due precautions; they are to post sentries wherever they stop so the natives will not harm them in any way.

They are to follow the Olekma River and the Tugur River to the portage, or to the Shilka; they are to ascertain where it would be most advantageous to build an *ostrozhek*, and then they are to build it and protect it with all possible fortifications so this *ostrozhek* can provide complete safety and security against attack by hostile non-*iasak* people for persons who may be sent there in the future to collect the Sovereign's *iasak*.

Erofei is to go out from this *ostrog* with the volunteer servitors and *promyshlenniks* who go with him, against Lavkai and Botogo and other non-*iasak transmontane* people who are disobedient and insubordinate to His

Imperial Majesty. He is to persuade them to submit in eternal *iasak* servitude under the mighty hand of the Sovereign Tsar and Grand Prince Aleksei Mikhailovich of all Russia, and to pay *iasak* for themselves, Lavkai, and Botogo, and for all their *ulus* subjects. Erofei is to take guides selected from the Tungus *iasak*-paying natives and go against those disobedient non-*iasak*-paying Lavkai and Botogo, and their *ulus* subjects, and other non-*iasak*-paying *transmontane* people. The guides are to be knowledgeable, reliable men, and he is to take as many as he needs, and they are to know where to lead him, and be able to point out to the Russian troops the places where the non-*iasak*-paying people live, and where their settlements are.

If these newly contacted people, Lavkai and Botogo, and their *ulus* subjects, and other non-*iasak transmontane* people are obedient and submissive and willing to come under the mighty hand of the Sovereign Tsar and Grand Prince Aleksei Mikhailovich of all Russia, and pay *iasak* from themselves and from their *ulus* subjects, for all eternity, then Lavkai and Botogo and their *ulus* people can live in their previous nomadic grounds, without fear, and the Sovereign will order that his government troops protect them.

Lavkai and Botogo and other leaders are to be induced to take the oath, according to their religious faith, so that henceforth they and all of their relatives and their *ulus* subjects will be forever, undeviatingly, in direct *iasak* servitude, under the mighty hand of the Sovereign Tsar and Grand Prince Aleksei Mikhailovich of all Russia. They are to pay *iasak* to the Sovereign from themselves and from all of their tribesmen, as much as circumstances allow, forever, without interruption. [Erofei] is to induce the tribesmen of the new non-*iasak* people to swear allegiance. The names of the leaders are to be written down in the books. And when he persuades them to take the oath of allegiance, he is to take their leaders as hostages, so that in the future these tribes will pay the Sovereign's *iasak* and *pominki* for all time to come.

Lavkai and Botogo and their *ulus* subjects and other *transmontane* non-*iasak*-paying people are to be given firm orders and threatened with punishment from the Sovereign, including death, if they steal from the merchants and *promyshlenniks* or kill them or harm them. If these new non-*iasak* people become rebellious, and decide not to pay the Sovereign's *iasak*, or to give hostages, then Erofei and his servitors and the *promyshlenniks* are to invoke God's mercy and then find them and attack them, using all the servitor and *promyshlennik* volunteers, so that the hostile non-*iasak* people, Lavkai and Botogo and their *ulus* subjects and other *transmontane* non-*iasak* people, will be pacified by military means (that is, by war) and hostages are to be taken from their leaders, so that in the future, the Sovereign's *iasak* will be collected from them. Depending on the situation at the time, all measures are to be used to establish complete control over the inhabitants of new territories,

Lavkai and Botogo and other non-*iasak* people; and every effort is to be made, and no mistakes are to be committed, in order to bring substantial profit to the Sovereign's *iasak* treasury, so that it will be stable and constant in the future. In return for this service they are to receive compensation from the Sovereign.

You, Erofei, are personally entrusted with the government assignment to pacify and bring under the suzerainty of the Sovereign both Lavkai and Botogo as well as non-*iasak* people who are not paying *iasak* to the Sovereign. Invoke God's aid, and use force, either war or surprise attacks.

You are to collect *iasak* for the Sovereign from them, which is to be made up of sables, sable *shubas*, neck pieces, sable backs, sable bellies, black foxes, black-brown foxes, brown foxes, cross foxes, red foxes, ermine *shubas*, beavers, and otters. Since there are no sables, foxes, beavers, or otters in the steppe, then from those non-*iasak* people who live in the steppe rather than in the forest, you are to collect any other kind of animal pelt, or whatever precious goods the land may offer, such as gold, silver, silk, or precious stones, depending on what is available. They must not think that because there is a scarcity of animals for *iasak*, they will not come under the Sovereign's mighty hand.

They are not to be fearful for themselves because of this, but rather, they should believe that in the future the Sovereign will have firm and solid control and that the new people will not be oppressed or overburdened; otherwise they may be turned away from the mighty Tsarist hand.

If Lavkai and Botogo will not pay *iasak* from themselves and from their *ulus* people, and will not willingly come under the mighty hand of the Sovereign Tsar and Grand Prince Aleksei Mikhailovich of all Russia, in eternal servitude, then invoking God's aid, the *voevoda* Dmitrii Andreevich Frantsbekov and the *diak* Osip Stepanov will personally assemble and head a large force and will attack Lavkai and Botogo and all the other non-*iasak* people.

Some will be hanged, and others will be ruined. After they have totally destroyed them, they will take their wives and children into captivity. But if the non-*iasak* people bow down and are in every way obedient to the Sovereign, then in accordance with their religious practices, these people are to be brought to swear allegiance so that they will be personally under the Sovereign Tsar's mighty hand in eternal *iasak* servitude, for all time, undeviatingly, and pay *iasak* for themselves and for their *ulus* subjects without interruption.

You, Erofei, are to settle any disputes among the servitors and *promyshlenniks* who go with you as volunteers, depending on what the problem is. Try to avoid trouble. If any of the servitors and *promyshlenniks* petition you on matters of service, Erofei, or if they seek to bring legal action, accept their petition or the suit regarding service, and record it, but do not give judgment.

Record who is the plaintiff and who the defendant. Send these petitions and reports to the *Prikaz* office in Iakutsk *ostrog* and make a written report to the *voevoda* Dmitrii Andreevich Frantsbekov and to the *diak* Osip Stepanov. Then, God willing, and with God's mercy and the luck of the Tsar, when you cross the Shilka River and go down the Olekma and Tugur rivers you will bring those new people, Lavkai and Botogo and other such non-*iasak* people, under the Tsar's mighty hand and collect *iasak* from them for the year 1650, and take hostages.

Erofei, you are to send as many men as possible with the government *iasak* treasury and the *pominki* to Iakutsk *ostrog*, and you are also to enter the names of the *iasak* people into the *iasak* books. Prepare a chart of the rivers, noting where there are large numbers of persons living along the rivers and to what tribes they belong. Send this information in writing to the *Prikaz* office at Iakutsk *ostrog*, to the *voevoda* Dmitrii Andreevich Frantsbekov and the *diak* Osip Stepanov.

Erofei, you are to make a thorough investigation of any merchants or *promyshlenniks* who are on the Olekma for their own trade and hunting. Look into their belongings, and if you find any furs which they have acquired from the Tungus, make a record of that fact, and send those persons under guard to Iakutsk *ostrog* so that they will not pass through into any other towns. Order them to appear before the *voevoda* Dmitrii Andreevich Frantsbekov and the *diak* Osip Stepanov in the *Prikaz* office in Iakutsk *ostrog*.

However, if these people do not appear to have acquired any furs from the Tungus, then you are to let them proceed to Iakutsk *ostrog* without detaining them. Do not bring any false charges. Report on all of this to the *Prikaz* office in Iakutsk *ostrog*.

Three Petitions to Tsar Alexei Mikhailovich from Iakut Natives Protesting Inequitable and Ruinous Iasak *Impositions, 1659–1664*

[A petition from the Iakuts of Bordonsk *volost*.]

To the Sovereign Tsar and Grand Prince Aleksei Mikhailovich, Autocrat of all Great, Little, and White Russia, we, your orphans of the Bordonsk *volost*, the *iasak*-paying Iakuts Ketyrei and Ochei, sons of Mygiev, submit this petition.

Sovereign, ever since 1652 we, your orphans, have had great difficulty in paying *iasak* for you, Great Sovereign, and *pominki* for the *voevoda* and the *diak*. We are assessed both for ourselves and for our dead father. This added burdensome *iasak* obligation for our dead father's past years' arrears has been imposed on us, your orphans. But, Sovereign, our father was poor. There is no livestock left. Our father lived on the lake and ate fish. When he died he had a cow, but Iakuts stole that cow. Our father was assigned to pay your Great Sovereign's *iasak* of eighteen sable pelts per year, but he could not pay all of that because he was so poor. Now we, your orphans, have no way to pay this enormous extra *iasak* for you, Great Sovereign, because, Sovereign, we, your orphans, do not have any livestock. All the livestock we had, Sovereign, we have already sold in order to pay your *iasak*, Great Sovereign. And now, Sovereign, we, your orphans are ruined, and poor right down to the bone. Now, Sovereign, if you order that this extra *iasak* be collected from us, your orphans, for you, Sovereign, for our father's past years' arrears, we, your orphans, will certainly perish.

Merciful Sovereign Tsar and Grand Prince Aleksei Mikhailovich, Autocrat of all Great, Little and White Russia, have mercy on us your orphans; Sovereign, do not order that your Great Sovereign's extra *iasak* for our father for the past years be collected from us, lest we, your orphans, perish. Tsar, Sovereign, have mercy, we beg you.

[A petition from the Iakuts of the Baturusk *volost*.]

To the Sovereign Tsar and Grand Prince Aleksei Mikhailovich, Autocrat of all Great, Little, and White Russia, your orphans, your *iasak*-paying Iakutus . . . [seventeen names follow] submit this petition.

Sovereign, for the past years, since 1642, we your orphans have had great difficulty in paying *iasak* and *pominki* to you, Great Sovereign, and *pominki* for the *voevoda* and *diaks*. We pay both current assessments and past arrears for ourselves and for our dead fathers and brothers. And your additional heavy *iasak* for years past is now also due for those who are dead, Great Sovereign. Great Sovereign, we your orphans cannot pay this enormous extra *iasak* for our dead fathers and brothers, and in the future, Sovereign, we your orphans will not be able to pay *iasak* and *pominki* to you and *pominki* to the *voevoda* and *diaks* because we do not have any livestock, Sovereign. Sovereign, we sold all the livestock we had to the Tungus in exchange for sables in order to pay your Sovereign's *iasak*. We sold one cow for two sables, and a mare for three or four, so that now, Sovereign, we, your orphans, are ruined, and impoverished right down to the bone.

Now, Sovereign if you order your great additional *iasak* for our dead fathers and brothers for the past years to be collected from us your orphans for you, Great Sovereign, we will perish. Sovereign, how can we pay your Great Sovereign's *iasak* for ourselves and also for our dead fathers and brothers, especially since they have been dead for twenty years?

Merciful Sovereign Tsar and Grand Prince Aleksei Mikhailovich, Autocrat of all Great, Little, and White Russia, have mercy on us, your orphans. Sovereign, do not order that his huge additional *iasak* for past years for our fathers and brothers be collected, lest we, your orphans, perish, and not be able to pay our current assessment of *iasak* and *pominki*, as well as *pominki* for the *voevoda* and *diaks*.

Sovereign Tsar, be merciful.

[A petition from Iakuts of various *volosts*.]

To the Sovereign Tsar and Grand Prince Aleksei Mikhailovich, Autocrat of all Great, Little, and White Russia, your orphans, *iasak*-paying natives from various *volosts*, submit this petition. . . . [Names of thirty-six petitioners from eleven *volosts* and other *uluses* follow.]

For the past years, Great Sovereign, they have been collecting *iasak* for your Great Sovereign's Treasury from us, your orphans and slaves, who do not hunt foxes. Instead of each fox pelt they have collected money from us, twenty *altyns*. But now, in this year of 1664, Great Sovereign, your Great Sovereign's *stolnik* and *voevoda* Ivan Fedorovich Bolshoi Golenishchev-Kutuzov wants to collect *iasak* from us, your slaves, who do not hunt [foxes], in the amount of one *ruble* for each fox pelt not presented. Great Sovereign, we your orphans will surely be ruined from this burdensome imposition, and then we will not be able to obtain any furs for *iasak*. We travel to far-off places now, in every direction, because all the animals have been killed or driven away, and it is only with great difficulty and great hardship that we can trap.

Merciful Sovereign Tsar and Grand Prince Aleksei Mikhailovich, Autocrat of all Great, Little, and White Russia, have mercy on us your orphans, and decree, Great Sovereign, that your Sovereign's *stolnik* and *voevoda* Ivan Fedorovich Bolshoi Golenishchev-Kutuzov collect only as much *iasak* from us, your orphans and slaves, for your Great Sovereign's Treasury, as was collected in previous years, that is, twenty *altyns* in place of each fox pelt. Otherwise we your orphans and slaves will suffer ruin and eventual death as a result of the heavy impositions of *iasak*, and from the additional payments of money in place of fox pelts.

Sovereign Tsar, be merciful.

Instructions from Voevoda of Iakutsk, Golenishchev-Kutuzov, to Prison Officials about Procedures for Guarding Prisoners, June 3, 1663

You are to be present in the prison compound, and exercise extreme caution and vigilance with the prisoners day and night, so they cannot tunnel out from prison and escape. When you go outside the prison grounds, out of kindness you may take prisoners with you who are there for minor offenses; however, any prisoners who have committed serious offenses are not to be allowed out of the prison without permission from the *voevoda* and *stolnik* Ivan Fedorovich Bolshoi Golenishchev-Kutuzov. If they are let out, they are either to be in chains or to have their legs shackled. Guards are to walk behind them. No one is to be allowed to enter the prison secretly either day or night. If anyone brings a gift to the prison as a kindness, or if someone wants to bring food into the prison for one of the prisoners, then such persons are to appear before the *tselovalnik* and the guards when they enter the prison.

If any persons try to enter the prison secretly, without appearing before the *tselovalnik* and the guards, such persons are to be seized and brought to the *Prikaz* office. In accordance with this instruction, prisoners are to be guarded very cautiously and with great vigilance. If anyone escapes from prison because of your inattention and lack of vigilance, you *tselovalniks* and guards will be severely punished by order of the Great Sovereign, and may be put to death.

You are also to be very careful that no prisoner sends any written message out of prison. No letters, ink, or paper are to be brought into the prison. You *tselovalniks* are to keep paper and ink in your quarters. If anyone wishes to write a petition, then it is to be written in your presence. No petition is to be written unless you are present. If any unauthorized communications come out of prison, or if ink and paper are found inside the prison, then you will be severely punished by order of the Great Sovereign.

The Sentences Imposed by the Voevoda of Iakutsk, Petr Zinovev, on the Participants in a Cossack Rebellion, July 14, 1690

In accordance with the *ukaz* of the Great Sovereigns, the *stolnik* and *voevoda* Petr Petrovich Zinovev questioned all of the rebels in great detail, and then interrogated them under torture. This was done in accordance with the instructions of the Great Sovereigns, the articles of the *Sobornoe Ulozhenie* [1649 Code of Laws], the letters of the Great Sovereigns and the articles of the New Code. He sentenced the outlaw rebels Filip Shcherbakov and Ivan Palamoshnoi who admitted and confessed under torture that they had plotted to pillage the Great Sovereigns' supplies of gunpowder and shot in Iakutsk, and had plotted to kill the *stolnik* and *voevoda* Petr Petrovich Zinovev and the townsmen and make off with their possessions, and to steal goods from the merchants and *promyshlenniks* at the *gostinnyi dvor*,* and then flee beyond the cape to the Anadyr and Kamchatka rivers.

---

*The *gostinnyi dvor* was a large covered structure that housed numerous retail shops in some Russian towns that enabled authorities to keep a close eye on all transactions.

Zinovev ordered that the *syn boiarskii* Mikhail Ontipin be executed along with his comrade, the *desiatnik* Ivan Golygin. The cossacks Sofronii Ilin, Ivan Ondronov, Nikita Grebenshchikov, Ignatii Shishev, and the townsman Onufrii Balushkin, all of them had taken part in the banditry and rebellion, and who had confessed their guilt under torture, were not put to death but were knouted and then exiled with their wives and children to Nerchinsk *ostrog*. The townsman Onufrii Balushkin and his wife and children were permanently exiled to the Omolonsk *zimov'e* beyond the rivers that flow to the sea. The accomplices, *ataman* Stepan Poluekhtov and the cossacks Nikita Karmolin and Nikita Popov were exiled with their wives and children to Irkutsk *ostrog*. The cossack Sergei Mukhoplev was sent into permanent exile with his wife and children to the sea at the mouth of the Iana River.

The wives and children of the dead outlaws Filip Shcherbakov, and those of Mikhail Ontipin and Ivan Palomoshnoi were exiled to Nerchinsk *ostrog* in order to teach them not to steal in the future or plot rebellion or kill townsmen or rob anyone else.

The *stolnik* and *voevoda* Petr Petrovich Zinovev authorized these sentences to be carried out in accordance with the *ukaz* of the Great Sovereigns. The sentences were read to the thieves and rebels Mikhail Ontipin and his comrades. A decree of the Great Sovereigns was issued authorizing the sentences ordered by the *stolnik* and *voevoda* Petr Petrovich Zinovev to be carried out.

The *syn boiarskii* Mikhail Ontipin was sentenced to death, and his wife and children and his unmarried brother Ivan were exiled; but his wife remained in Iakutsk with her young children because she is ill and near death.

The *piatidesiatnik* Filip Shcherbakov and Ivan Palamoshnoi, in accordance with the *ukaz* of the Great Sovereigns, died under torture in prison. Filip's wife and children were exiled, but Ivan Palamoshnoi's wife was not exiled because she is very ill, close to death, and has no children.

The *desiatnik* Ivan Golygin and the line cossacks Ivan Ondronov, Sofronii Ilin, Nikita Grebenshchikov, Ignatii Shishev, and the townsman Onufrii Balushkin were manacled and knouted without mercy and then sent into exile.

The other outlaws and rebels, and their wives and children, are listed below, with their places of exile.

Exiled to Irkutsh *ostrog*:

The cossack *ataman* Stepan Poluekhtov and his wive Irena, and their children Anfilofeva, Ivan, Onufrei, Petr, and Oleg.

The cossack Nikita Karmalin and his son Petr.

The cossack Nikita Spiridonov Popov and his sons Fedor, Ivan, and Vasilii, and his daughter Evdokiia.

Exiled to Nerchinsk *ostrog*:

The *desiatnik* Ivan Golygin and his wife Irena and their daughters Efimiia, Marta, and Anastasiia.

The unmarried line cossack Sofronii Ilin, Ivan Ondronov, Nikita Grebenshchikov, and Ignatii Shishev.

The outlaw and rebel Mikhail Ontipin's son Filip, his wife Mariia, and Ivan's three brothers.

The outlaw and rebel Filip Shcherbakov's wife Evdokiia Vasileva and their sons Stepan and Ivar and their daughters Anna and Paraskeviia.

The cossack Sergei Mukhoplev and his wife Marina Osipova and their son Ivan and daughter Anna were sent into permanent exile to the sea at the mouth of the Iana River.

The townsman Onufrii Balushkin and his wife Dariia Ofanaseva and their daughter Anna were sent into permanent exile to Omolonsk *zimov'e* beyond the rivers which flow to the sea.

⚔ *54* ⚔

Bussow's Account of the Famine in Moscow, *1601–1604*

The reign of Boris Godunov (1598–1605) is noted for its energetic policy of expansion across Siberia, for interest in west European contacts, and above all, for setting the stage for the chaos known as "Time of Troubles." Many factors contributed to Russia's troubles; however, some contemporary observers thought that famine and social unrest were "the beginning of the calamity." The following is an eyewitness account of the famine by a German merchant, Konrad Bussow, who lived in Moscow from 1584 to 1613.

In 1601 the high price of bread began, and continued until 1604. The price of a barrel of rye rose to ten to twelve *florins*; whereas earlier it cost no more than twelve to fifteen *groschen*. The famine in the country was more severe than the famine in besieged Jerusalem which is described by Joseph. According

---

From Konrad Bussow, *Moskovskaia Khronika, 1584–1613* (Moscow Chronicle, 1584–1613) (Moscow-Leningrad: Akademiia Nauk, 1961), pp. 97–98. Translation mine. Words in brackets are mine.

to Joseph, the Jews ate dogs, cats, rats, mice, and even leather from old saddles, shields, and boots, as well as pigeon dung. One wellborn woman, tormented by the famine, killed her only child, cooked it, and ate it. This is one of the most depressing situations that one finds in Joseph's account. But I swear by God that in Moscow I saw, with my own eyes, people who rolled in the streets and, like animals, ate grass during the summer and hay during the winter. Some of those who died had hay as well as human excrement in their mouths. Parents killed, prepared, and cooked many of their children; children did the same with their parents; hosts with visitors; and visitors with hosts. Human flesh, finely ground, baked in pies (a kind of pastry), was sold and consumed like beef. A traveler, then, was forced to be careful in his selection of an inn. When Tsar Boris [Godunov] was informed of these horrible, inhuman killings, which the famine and high cost of living brought about, and of the great number of the famine's casualties, he proposed to alleviate this poverty and God's punishment with the help of his treasury. He ordered four large enclosures to be constructed within the outside walls [of the city of Moscow] (which were about four German miles long), where every morning the poor of the city of Moscow assembled and where they received one *denga* per person. When poor peasants near Moscow heard of this mercy, they left their homes and jobs and ran to Moscow with their wives and children in order to receive money. As a result, there assembled so many people in Moscow that they were forced to distribute as much as 500,000 *dengas* daily. This [distribution of aid] continued for a long time but did not decrease the cost of living at all. Daily, on the Tsar's orders, they collected hundreds of corpses and carried them outside the city in wagons—an undertaking which was awesome to observe. Specially appointed people washed the dead, wrapped them in a white cloth, put red shoes on them, and wheeled them to the church to be buried. During those four years of the high cost of bread, as a result of the Tsar's mercy in feeding the poor, clothing them, and burying them, the state treasury was drained of many hundreds of thousands of *rubles*. How depleted the treasury became during this time can be easily ascertained. I have been told by trustworthy individuals—government clerks and merchants—that during the high cost of bread, in Moscow alone, more than 500,000 people whom the Tsar fed, died from hunger, and he ordered them to be buried in red shoes and wrapped in cloth. And this occurred in one city only. [No one knows] how many people in the countryside and other cities perished from starvation and diseases and were buried at the expense of the tsarist treasury. . . . Woe to a country or people subjected to God's anger. Boris, however, was embittered, blind, and did not humble before these horrible misfortunes, but hoped to ease the misery with the aid of a rich treasury. By the will of the merciful God, several ships from German seaports arrived in Narva with a cargo of wheat, which could have made possible the feeding of hundreds of thousands of people. Boris, however, did not wish this kind of humiliation, that is, buying and selling foreign food in a country rich in food. The ships were ordered to leave without selling the grain because the Russians were forbidden to buy it under threat of the death penalty. Boris ordered the food reserves of the entire country to be surveyed. They discovered large grain stacks, one hundred or more *sazhens* [one *sazhen* equals seven feet] long, which had stood there unthreshed, for about fifty years and which were covered with weeds and other growth. Boris ordered that these be threshed and that the grain be sent to Moscow and other cities. He also ordered that his warehouses be opened in all cities, and many thousands of barrels of grain were sold daily at half price. He decreed that poor widows, orphans, and especially foreigners, receive a number of barrels of flour in their homes without charge in order to prevent their suffering.

He called upon princes, *boyars*, and monasteries to take notice of the country's plight and to offer their grain reserves and sell these at a low price.

Princes, *boyars*, and monasteries fulfilled the Tsar's will. But the devil . . . suggested to rich grain merchants of Moscow to buy the princely, *boyar*, and monastery grain through the poor at a low price and sell it back to the poor at a high price. With the decline of the high cost of bread, which caused the death of hundreds of thousands and drained Boris' treasury, a new punishment appeared—war and bloodshed.

❦ 55 ❦

A Letter from the False Dmitrii to Boris Godunov, 1604

In Russian history, the period from 1601 to 1613 is commonly known as the "Time of Troubles." One of its basic characteristics was the appearance of several pretenders to the Russian throne, the earliest of whom was Dmitrii, who claimed to be a son of Ivan the Terrible. Dmitrii made

---

From S. M. Soloviev, *Istoriia Rossii s drevneishikh vremen* (History of Russia since Ancient Times) (Moscow: Izdatelstvo sotsialnoekonomicheskoi literatury, 1960), vol. 8, pp. 413–414. Translation mine.

a favorable impression on many Russians, and with their support he came
to Moscow, only to be assassinated shortly thereafter.

It grieves us that you have desecrated your soul—created in the image of
God—to such a degree, and that you are preparing its destruction through
your tenacity. Do you not know that you are a mortal? You should have been
satisfied, Boris, with the position which God accorded you; but you, our
subject, have stolen our state, against the will of God and with the help of
the devil. Your sister, our brother's wife, secured power of government over
the entire state for you; and you exploited the fact that our brother dedicated
himself for the most part to the service of God, by murdering, under various
pretexts, several of the most respected princes, such as the Princes Ivan and
Andrei Shuiskii, then the best people of our capital, and partisans of the
Shuiskii family. You blinded Tsar Simeon and had his son Ivan poisoned.
You have not even spared the clergy: you banished Metropolitan Dionisius
into a monastery, but you nevertheless told our brother Feodor that he had
suddenly died; we know, however, that he is still alive today and that you
eased his lot after our brother's death; you have also ruined others whose
names we cannot remember, because we were still in our childhood at that
time. Although we were just a child, you will still recollect how often we
admonished you not to murder the subjects. You will recall how we dispatched
your partisan Andrei Kleshnin, whom our brother Feodor had sent to us in
Uglich. Your partisan, after delivery of the commissioned message, and count-
ing on your protection, did not show us proper deference. You were dissatisfied
with this, and we were an obstacle to you in the path leading to the throne.
After you murdered our dignitaries you began to sharpen your knife for us
also; you persuaded our official Michael Bitiagovskii, together with twelve
chamberlains, Nikita Kachalov, and Osip Volokhov, to assassinate us; you
though that our physician, Simeon, was part of the plot, but thanks to his
efforts we were saved from the death which you prepared for us. You told
our brother that we had fatally wounded ourselves in a fit of epilepsy. You
know how deeply our brother mourned the news. He ordered that our body
be brought to Moscow; you, however, influenced the patriarch, who ruled
that it would be improper to place the body of a suicide victim beside those
who died in Jesus Christ. Thereupon our brother wanted to travel personally
to Uglich for the funeral; you told him, however, that a dangerous epidemic
was raging in Uglich, and at the same time you challenged the Khan of the
Crimean Tatars. You had at your disposal an army twice as large as that of
the enemy, but you pitched camp before Moscow and forbade your troops
to attack the enemy under penalty of death. For three days you lay encamped
across from them, and then you let them withdraw unmolested; the Khan

left our kingdom without being punished. And you returned home, and only three days later did you begin to pursue the enemy. When Andrei Klobukov apprehended the incendiaries and they explained that you had incited them to set Moscow in flames, you instructed them to accuse Klobukov of the guilt, and you had him seized and tortured to death on the rack. After the death of our brother (whose passing you hastened), you began to bribe beggars, cripples, and blind men with great sums of money, so that they loudly cried out everywhere that you should be Tsar. After you had assumed the throne, however, the families of the Romanovs, Cherkasskiis, and Shuiskiis were given the opportunity to become acquainted with your kindness. Come to your senses and do not incite us to great anger with your evil. Give back to us what is ours. And we will forgive you all your guilt and allot to you a peaceful place. It is better for you to suffer somewhat in this world than to burn eternally in hell for the sake of the numerous souls whom you have murdered.

⚜ *56* ⚜

Massa's Account of Events Surrounding the Death of the False Dmitrii in 1606

Although Isaac Massa (1586–1643) is a shadowy Dutch figure, his name is very important in the history of the Time of Troubles. This is because the Dutch merchant and diplomatic agent lived in Moscow during that turbulent period, knew the language, and had close contact with many high-ranking officials of Moscow's bureaucracy, including Tsar Boris Godunov and his son Feodor. From his Muscovite contacts Massa received valuable information on all major developments in Moscow and Muscovy, including its new Siberian colony. He carefully recorded that information and, upon returning to Holland, published it in his *History*.

Massa's experience in and knowledge of Muscovy transformed him into a Dutch "Kremlinologist." To counter the growing English influence,

---

From Isaac Massa, *A Short History of the Beginnings and Origins of these Present Wars in Moscow under the Reign of Various Sovereigns down to the Year 1610*. Translated and with an Introduction by G. Edward Orchard. (Toronto: University of Toronto Press, 1982), pp. 136–149. Reprinted with permission of University of Toronto Press and G. Edward Orchard. See original source for footnote reference.

the Dutch Estates-General dispatched Massa to Moscow in 1615 to represent Dutch commercial interests. During that assignment he met and was well received by the newly elected Tsar Michael Romanov. In short, while Massa's observations contain some biases (especially anti-English) and lacunae, they are a very important contemporary source for the understanding of the Time of Troubles.

Dmitry Is Killed in Moscow with about Seven Hundred Poles

On Saturday morning, May 17, towards the second hour of the day, a fearful pealing of bells resounded, first in the Kremlin and then through all the town. At the same time there was a tumult of horsemen riding armed and at a gallop towards the castle, and the cry the heralds of the conspiracy sounded in all the streets: "Brothers, the Poles want to assassinate the tsar! Do not let them into the Kremlin!" By this ruse, the Poles, seized with terror and armed in their houses, were pinned down by the multitude outside, eager to pillage and murder all of them. Even those found on the street in Polish garments were massacred relentlessly. When a patrol of Polish cavalry appeared in a street, they were barricaded at once by the closing of the barriers, where there were such, so that the horses could not get out. In streets without barriers, they made barricades of beams, the same that are used in this town to pave all the roads. Thus, there was a terrible massacre of all the Poles who could be found. The crowd also broke into a great number of Polish houses. Anyone trying to defend himself was run through with the sword. As for those who surrendered, almost all were spared, but they were so thoroughly plundered that they were not even left with shirts. The riot spread through the town; the entire population, including young boys and children, began running through the streets with bows, muskets, axes, sabres, pikes, and clubs, crying out and howling: "Death to the Poles! Let us take all they have!"

It was then that the conspirators killed the tsar in his apartments. Here is how this event took place. They had bribed a chancellor who was a saint in their eyes. He was very zealous in their religion, drank no strong liquor, and ate very sparingly; he was called Timofei Osipov. On that day—it was the day of the solemn oath with the kissing of the cross, which was sworn to the tsarina as sovereign lady of Moscow—this person was to present himself to the people and speak against this inauguration. The conspirators were to profit from this incident to attack the person of Dmitry. This Timofei had taken the sacrament twice, and receiving absolution from the priest or confessor, he had also been blessed in a great ceremony as a hero going to his death for his country and the well-being of his fellow citizens. In the morning, he had said his last farewell to his wife and children, who understood nothing about it, though his wife believed that he wanted to enter a monastery.

After he had done all this, Timofei went resolutely to the palace and entered the hall where the oath was to be administered. There, he cried that he recognized Dmitry, not as the tsar's son, but as an unfrocked monk named Grishka Otrepiev who had won the throne of Moscow only through the agency of the Devil; he held this throne unjustly. As for the tsarina, he refused to swear her allegiance. She was a lady Jesuit, a pagan whose presence had profaned the sanctuaries of Moscow, and it was she who was the cause of the country's ruin. He would have said more had he not been struck dead on the spot and thrown through a window. Thereupon, the conspirators began sounding the tocsin and mounted hurriedly, their muskets loaded, by all the staircases at the same time. These conspirators were for the most part Muscovite lords and merchants. A great number came from Novgorod, Pskov, and other towns. For a long time, they had been coming secretly to Moscow to forward their design. The first thing they did was attack the *halberdiers* guarding the entrance hall of the palace. They disarmed them and took them prisoner. They were all shut in a room on the ground floor and threatened with death if they dared utter a single sound. At that moment, precisely half the guard were absent from their posts. Half the men had gone one way, half the other. In the end, God let all this happen to them through their own fault, for they could have kept a close watch. The conspirators spread out everywhere, killing anyone who resisted, and moved on the tsar's apartments firing musket shots.

Meanwhile, Dmitry had come out of his apartments, demanding to know what was happening and what was the cause of the tocsin and uproar. Those he questioned were seized with such terror that they did not know what to reply. Then he called for his sword, but he who was responsible for presenting it to him had already managed to escape, taking the sword with him. Sensing danger, the tsar seized a *halberd* and rushed into his apartments, closing and barring the doors. Hearing shots being fired through the windows and axe blows striking the door, he fled from room to room by secret passages, and finally leapt into a small room which was on a lower floor than the other apartments. While jumping, he was caught in the arms of a Livonian gentleman called Fürstenberger who was trying to save him, for he was already spitting blood, but this gentleman was killed. Dmitry succeeded in reaching a bathhouse through an alley. He hoped from there to gain the outside by a hidden door and lose himself in the crowd, which was already rushing in hundreds up the back stairs. If he had been able to get himself into the crowd he would doubtless have escaped, and the townspeople would have massacred the lords and conspirators; but, knowing nothing of the affair, the people believed that the tsar was being attacked by the Poles, and that the conspirators were trying to save him. That was what they had been told so that they would pin the Poles down in the city. The conspirators pursued Dmitry into the secret passage, where he was trapped. They laid hold of him and quickly dragged him out, firing on him and striking him with their sabres and axes, for fear that he might escape again.

It is said that the lords who held him still questioned him on certain matters; but that was impossible, because they did not have time to pause. As soon as Dmitry saw the people, he cried: "Bring me on to the square, and listen to me! I will tell you who I am!" Then the conspirators, for fear of the people pressing about them, killed him in haste, shouting: "It is a renegade monk, and not Dmitry! He has admitted it himself!" They tied a strap to the corpse's feet, dragged it naked as a dog out of the Kremlin, and threw it on the square. Some conspirators went behind and ahead of this sorry procession, carrying masks, and calling to the people: "Here are the gods whom he adored!" Now these masks had been taken from the apartments of the tsarina, where they had been prepared for the masquerade that was to have been held for the tsar's entertainment. Not knowing what these objects were, the Muscovites believed, and still believe today, that these masks were really Dmitry's gods.

Various Opinions Concerning His Death

Some claim that he was still in bed, and that he was killed fleeing in his night shirt; but this version cannot be believed, for why would they have slit that chancellor's throat? They would have said that the chancellor was killed during the evening, but that is false, because I have the facts as I have reported them from eyewitnesses who were with the conspirators.

Meanwhile, the tsarina was half dead of fright. A crowd of people surrounded her apartments, breaking and pillaging everything they could find. A gentleman, one of the conspirators, came to her and conducted her to a vaulted chamber built of solid walls, where he placed a strong guard around her and some of her companions. As for the maids of honor, they underwent the most extreme outrages. They were all stripped naked, each of the conspirators taking from them his part of the booty, and having one of them as his share. They were led through the streets of the city like lambs by wolves, suffering all manner of humiliation. Some were even sold by their enraged ravishers, many of whom killed one another over the spoils.

It was amazing to see the mob carrying off what they had pillaged from the Poles—beds, bedding, mattresses, clothing, horses, harness, saddles, and furniture. It looked like the salvage from a conflagration.

At the beginning of the uprising, Basmanov was still in his bath. It is said that he had spent the night with two women, and, according to the Russian custom, was purifying himself in the bathhouse.

As soon he heard the tocsin, he hastily dressed only in his undergarments, jumped on his horse, and, telling ten or twelve armed servants with loaded muskets to follow him, went off at the gallop towards the Kremlin. He believed that conflict had erupted between the Poles and the Muscovite lords, and had no suspicion of what was really going on. Reaching the palace, he came to the apartments, where a gentleman from Novgorod began to abuse him, calling him a traitor and the tsar a renegade monk. He made ready to reply, but was not given the chance. Ten swords struck him at once, and he fell. His body was thrown outside next to a wall, and dragged on the square. There, he was laid on a bench at the feet of the body of the Renegade Monk, or Dmitry, which lay on a table, and they were left there exposed to the view of the entire populace.

The house of the palatine of Sandomierz was guarded all round by soldiers and safeguarded along with those within. The same was done with the palace of the king's ambassador. The palatine of Sandomierz had sent a messenger to the ambassador, warning him to remain calm, and gave the same advice to his own son, who was in his lodgings surrounded by three hundred armed cavalrymen.

After Dmitry's death, the principal lords went about the town on horseback, urging the people to cease their murdering and looting. It was by their efforts that the three aforesaid dwellings were saved. They exhorted the Poles, who in some houses were under arms, to lay them down so that they would not be massacred. The majority followed this advice. In the street called the Pokrovka there was one house with a great number of armed Poles putting up a vigorous defense. The chief of the conspirators, Vasily Shuisky, went and begged them to cease fighting so that the people's fury and bloodletting could abate; but before obeying, they insisted that he guarantee their lives by oath, and he did so. They were still not reassured, so they sent one of their number through the door to parley with him. Shuisky threw himself around his neck, embraced him, and swore that nobody would do him any harm. Then peace was made, and the populace went elsewhere.

All houses offering resistance were sacked and their defenders massacred. Those who surrendered saved their lives, but they were completely despoiled. Nearly all the musicians were killed; a Polish lord who had been present at the wedding feast given in Poland by the Muscovite ambassador perished with all his family; many other lords and gentlemen lost their lives.

In the palace where the lord Wisniowiecki resided, they fought valiantly to the end. It was there that this lord and his people had assembled after the invasion of the Kremlin by the conspirators. This palace was situated in a vast meadow close to the Neglinnaia river. It was quickly surrounded by thousands of besiegers, who began to fire, pillage, and loot the kitchens, the stables, and the apartments on the ground floor. The Poles, who occupied the upper stories, put up a stiff resistance, and fired on the Muscovites from the upper windows, killing a great number of them. From time to time, they threw precious garments and fistfuls of gold from the windows. The besiegers would fall in masses upon these spoils, and then the Poles would let fly with terrible volleys into the middle of these crowds, slaughtering them like flocks of birds or wild beasts. Three times, they pretended to be on the verge of surrender. Deceived by this feint, the Russians rushed in hundreds on to the staircases to begin the pillage, and crowded together in the vestibule of the upper story, which the Poles had opened. As soon as the room was filled, forty or fifty muskets were discharged all at once into the crowd of besiegers, who fell and rushed down the stairs like rats being chased from a granary. Such was the ardor of the assailants, inspired by hope of pillage, that they went to fetch artillery from the ramparts. They trained cannon on the building and fired at their own people, who were still blocking the staircase. The fight lasted a long time.

At length the lords arrived, and by their entreaties and supplications persuaded both sides to lay down their arms. More than three hundred Muscovites had lost their lives there, and a great number had been wounded. The Poles suffered no more than two or three fatalities. Thus, after this great frenzy in Moscow, the killing and pillaging ceased. Several persons became wealthy by buying up articles looted by the rioters, who were for the most part the scum of the earth, scoundrels and thieves, a class quite numerous in this country. Orders were given at once that all the objects were to be brought to the treasury in the Kremlin so that they could be divided up, but very few paid any attention to that order. The horses were nearly all returned, however, probably because nobody knew how to conceal them and they would have been recognized straight away. Some carriages were also returned. As for jewels, money, clothing, or furniture, the looters had hidden all these safely away, and they did not reappear.

Towards the afternoon, the people's frenzy abated, thanks to the lords' intervention. The people were satisfied; they had wreaked their vengeance on the Poles, whom they regarded as their enemies. They were in great ecstasy at the revolution, and considered its authors to be the saviors of the country and the sanctuaries of Moscow. Strong guards were set everywhere, the tranquillity reigned in the capital once again. The corpses were gathered up; there were about eight hundred on the Muscovite side and fifteen hundred on the Polish side. Among the latter were a number of lords and young gentlemen; their bodies, pierced by blows and despoiled, were left in the streets three days, along with those of Dmitry and Basmanov. The Russians milled around these cadavers and flung insults and anathemas at them as if they could have heard. Among the Poles, the most prominent to lose their lives were Sklinski, Wonsowicz, Pomecki, Lipnicki, Iwanicki, Bal Jan Pologowski, and many other noblemen, several of whom had jumped from the Kremlin walls into the river, where they were pierced by arrows. Buczynski had hidden under the plants and trees of a garden behind the tsar's palace. He was discovered there and saved, along with several others in the ambassador's house.

Innocent People Killed in the Massacre

Most to be pitied were those who come to Moscow for the sole purpose of selling their merchandise, several of whom were taken for Poles simply because they were dressed in the Polish style. Thus were Nemiecki [Neueskij], Volsky, Andreas Nathan, Nicholas Demist, of whom I have already spoken, and who had brought with them such precious treasures, despoiled of everything, and lost thousands of *florins*. When they went to the Shuisky regime to claim payment for objects they had sold to the tsar, they were told that they should claim their money from the Renegade Monk with whom they had been dealing. They added that the treasury was empty; Dmitry had drained it completely to send to Poland. This was the only answer they were prepared to give. A number of merchants from other countries suffered similar misfortunes. The people of Philip Holbein of Augsburg were mortally wounded, having first been plundered of everything they had. A Milanese, Ambrogio Cellari, utterly looted by these scoundrels, still gave them all the gold, silver, and effects he possessed. He was left with only a shirt to cover his nakedness, but the brigands insisted that he take off this last garment, and when he refused, they stuck a knife in his belly. He fell dead to the ground, but was not found among the dead, however diligently they sought him.

A Brabançon named Jacques Marot was also murdered, but his body was found. He could then he buried, with a number of others, by permission of the new court, after the riot ended.

Dmitry's Appearance

Dmitry was a strong and well-built man. He was clean-shaven, with solid shoulders and a large nose, beside which a small blue mole was noticeable. His face was broad, his tint brownish, and his mouth large. He was endowed with extraordinary strength in his hands. Brave and hardy, he loved to see blood flow, but did not let this tendency show very much. There was not a lord or chancellor in Moscow who had not seen proof of the violence of his character. He had strange caprices. Thus, he wanted to launch an attack on Narva in midwinter. And he would have done so had the lords not restrained him, arguing the unseasonableness of the venture. We have seen that in his life he sent great quantities of munitions and provisions to a town named Elets, allegedly to prepare a campaign against Tatary; but his secret design was really to attack Poland, conquer it, and drive out its king, or else capture him by treachery, and make Poland subject to Muscovy.

His Undertaking and Great Designs: His Plan to Change the Religion of Muscovy and Destroy all the Noble Families

In this, he was following the advice of a number of Poles—Sandomierski, Wisniowiecki, and others. He also contemplated some ambitious and extraordinary enterprises. He had at first resolved to kill all the Muscovite lords and great families. Having fixed a day for the execution of this plan, he secretly brought a large quantity of artillery to a place outside the town, with the aim, he said, of staging a mock battle after the marriage celebrations in the presence of all the lords, in the guise of a military parade; but he had given secret instructions to the Polish lords, his army commanders, Basmanov, and his other adherents. Each of them knew where he was to be, either in the town or in the Kremlin, and exactly whom he was responsible for killing. He himself was to be outside the city with all the artillery, Polish troops, and his supporters. If this attempt had gone according to plan, who would have been able to offer him any resistance in Moscow, since all the means for defending the town were in his possession? But God would not permit it, and gave the Muscovites the strength to destroy him who had conceived it.

Only Buczynski had the courage to dissuade Dmitry from his project, pointing out to him how contrary to God's will it would be, and advising him to draw the magnates to him by tokens of favor, giving them functions in which they could not become too powerful. With the aid of time, he would thus be reconciled with all hearts; but he, who knew the Muscovite character better, relied that these people could not be governed by gentle methods; rather, the most rigorous means had to be used with them. This is true, for a Muscovite must be held by fear and led by force. As soon as he is allowed his own will a little, he does no good. Dmitry thought it best to dispose of the magnates first so that he could the reign uncontrolled over a wicked and ignorant people, doing anything he desired with them.

This proved to be ample justification for the Muscovites' actions as far as all the foreign rulers were concerned, for after Dmitry's death, written evidence of his plans was found—lists of those who were to be killed and the names of the Poles who would replace them in their offices. These documents were read out to the people, who thereby felt all the more joy and security in what they had just accomplished. Copies were sent to Poland and other foreign powers in order to make these facts known to all.

There is no doubt that if these plans of Dmitry and the Jesuits had succeeded, much harm would have befallen the country. Much harm would also have been done to the whole world through the machinations of the court of Rome, of which Dmitry had been the mere instrument. But God, who rules all, overturned their designs, for which all true believers should render him thanks.

Although he was a hero and a warrior, Dmitry was a very dissolute man. He abused innocent young girls every day, and got a number of young nuns with child. He also had a shameful passion for a young gentleman of the powerful family of Khvorostinin [Guorostinin]. He conferred great honors on this conceited young man, who was full of arrogance because he was allowed to do anything he pleased.

Some Persons Flee; Others Are Arrested

After the tsar's assassination, when the tidings of it spread, Mikhail Molchanov, one of his secret counsellors in both his acts of tyranny and his debauches, took flight and went to Poland. After his departure, the disappearance of a sceptre and a golden crown was noticed, and there was no doubt that he had taken these objects with him.

Another of these intimate counsellors, named Yury Mikulin, fled on one of the tsar's horses but was captured at Viazma, about six miles from Moscow on the road to Poland. Several Polish servants, appropriating their masters' horses, took flight as the rioting began. They had only their bare sabres to defend them, and as they did not know the roads, they were lost in the countryside. Some of the nobles set out in pursuit and attacked them vigorously. Nearly all these unfortunates were left on the road, because the nobles, being armed with pistols, killed them from a distance. The latter still lost eleven men, even though they were very numerous.

The English merchants, and we also, were not without anxiety in the midst of a riot in which the tsar's very doctors were despoiled; but God surrounded us with his protection, and we emerged safe and sound.

When the fury had died down, I ventured out to see the corpses, on which the conspirators were still testing their sabres. The bodies of Dmitry and Basmanov, his favorite, were stretched out on a table where the crowd came to rain insults for three days. However, some people wept on seeing these examples of the inconstancy of human affairs. As for myself, I looked at him with great interest and was able to convince myself that what I saw before me was the same tsar whom I had seen many times, the same who had reigned for a year. It was indeed he, despite the assertions of those who, in this new war, claimed that the true tsar was not assassinated, but another in his place.

Dmitry's Corpse is Cast into a Ditch

I counted his wounds. They were to the number of twenty-one. His skull had been stove in from above, and his brain lay beside him. The following Thursday, the body was thrown into a ditch. As for Basmanov, he was buried by his brother with the permission of the court.

We have said enough about the character of this tsar; but there are those who claim that he was none other than Satan himself—who later, using the same mask and the same name, caused yet further evil, and continues to cause evils that are ten times more terrible than those of the past. Is it not extraordinary, in fact, that they are always occasioned by the same name—Dmitry's? God's justice appears in such diverse and astonishing ways to punish nations and cities. Did not the divine Homer rightly say: "God looks upon mortal things and punishes justice, and the just deeds of men. Jupiter sees all the actions of men, and punishes the wicked. The immortal gods detest crimes; they love justice and the men who practice it."

Dmitry the Unfrocked Monk

Tell me your name, hero of this tragedy
Which covered Muscovy with blood and ruin.
You did not expect that cruel treatment
That you made so many others suffer unjustly.
But once more your name will serve as a banner
In a struggle, alas! even more murderous.
And as your name is raised, it seems
That of your country is daily abased.
But God, whose puissant eye
O'ersees men, space and earth,
Will never permit against his will
A land to be diminished or o'erthrown.

Dmitry's Body Is Burned

There was a great prodigy the same night Dmitry's body was thrown out. Within a radius of twenty miles from Moscow, all the plants, from blades of grass to trees, were dried up at their tops, as if a fire had passed by. The pine trees, which are always green, winter and summer, had their crowns and sprouts burnt. It was a sad spectacle, and on seeing this prodigy the Muscovites commented that the late tsar had yet again, with Satan's help, sent his spirit on the earth to do evil. To put an end to this, they saw fit to burn his body. They went to dig him up, and at the same time seized the wooden castle he had built on the ice during the winter, called the "Monster of Hell" by the Russians. They carried it out of the city to the small stream of Kotly, and enclosing the body inside it, burned it completely, and the wind dispersed its ashes.

Vasily Ivanovich Shuisky Becomes Emperor in Moscow

After that, the Muscovites believed they had done everything possible and won a complete victory, and could live thereafter without fear or care. The magnates elected a tsar from their own number; their choice fell upon Shuisky. They led him on to the square before the assembled people, and their orator cried out that they had just chosen Vasily Ivanovich Shuisky as tsar; that they had not been able to find a better or more worthy man among them. He was a man who many times risked his life for the public good and the country's well-being. Then the orator, addressing the community, asked if they approved the choice they had just made, seeing that the land could not long remain without a sovereign. With one voice, the community shouted that they were completely satisfied, that nobody was more worthy of the throne. Everybody submitted to the newly elected, and they prostrated themselves at his feet, saying: "Health and prosperity to Vasily Ivanovich, tsar and Grand Prince of all the Russias!" Then the magnates led him to the church, where thanksgiving was offered to God for the deliverance of the empire.

A great frost came to grip all the country, and destroyed the greater part of the crops. All the Muscovites were full of consternation. Having burned Dmitry's body, they did not know whom to blame for this scourge, and stared at each other, seized with the greatest astonishment.

Tsar Vasily Ivanovich was crowned as his predecessors had been, according to the Muscovite usages, and gold was also strewn under his feet.

On May 30, the entire community was summoned on to the square. Most of the magnates came, and there ordered the reading of the motives which they thought justified depriving a crowned tsar, the previous sovereign, of his life. These were their arguments.

Accusations Against Dmitry

First, he was accused of not having been born of the imperial blood, of being, not the son of Tsar Ivan Vasilievich of blessed memory, but merely a scoundrel and an impostor inspired by Satan. His real name was Grigory Otrepiev, and he had been born at Galich, where his father and mother still lived. His parents were poor people. They had been ordered to appear and had admitted that he was truly their son. They had said, moreover, that after gaining control of the country he had sent emissaries to Galich to seize all the members of his family and throw them in prison, where they were narrowly guarded so that they might not divulge the secret of his identity. These unfortunates were about sixty in number. They added also that after his arrival in Russia he had bribed a worthless person, who then claimed to be Grigory Otrepiev and feigned insanity, wandering around in a monk's cowl. After Dmitry's death, this false monk also confessed that he had been paid to play this role. Dmitry had truly been in a monastery in Moscow, and the lords repeated in their proclamation everything I have already reported about his flight into Poland with stolen papers and documents, and the manner in which he said he was the true Dmitry.

Furthermore, some said he was Satan himself, while others said that he was a Pole sent by the machinations of the Jesuits into Muscovy, whose language he had learned, and that he had travelled throughout the land to gather information about the state of the country, learning at the same time, through reading, the peculiarities of its history. After this journey he had returned to Poland, where the Jesuits and their supporters, backed by the pope, had him play the part of the person whose adventures we have recounted. This opinion is very plausible, and a number of people hold it to be the truth.

They also accused him of having been a sorcerer in communication with the Devil. His tutor, a Pole, came to affirm that he was devoted to magic and other occult sciences, and the Muscovites supported this opinion with various conjectures, such as the "Monster of Hell" he had built, and other fables of the same sort.

Thirdly, they accused him of having been a heretic, because he had not observed their days of rest or their feasts, and did not go to church.

For the fourth charge, they showed the letters addressed by the pope to Dmitry during his reign, letters in which he was warned that it was time to begin work on the reform of the country, building schools for children similar to those in Poland and purging the churches of altars and images of the Greek religion in order to sanctify them by Roman Catholic images with the help of people sent for that purpose, and other such abominations.

For the fifth charge, they brought forward the agreement made in Poland between Dmitry and the palatine of Sandomierz, whereby the latter was to obtain the principality of Pskov with all its dependencies, and also the land of Novgorod; and his son, the tsarina's brother, the whole land of Siberia and the Samoyed, with all the adjacent territory. Dmitry had also promised to cede the principality of Smolensk to some Polish lords who would have governed it jointly with the Jesuits, but to do this he had to begin by ridding himself of the magnates of the country, as we have related.

Sixthly, they accused him of not having had the least regard for them, and allowing them to be the butt of the injuries and insults of the Poles without being able to obtain justice. On the contrary, he himself had added to these slights, raining blows on the magnates of the country and sending them to die in exile.

Their seventh complaint was directed against his extravagances and excessive expenditures, made without taking the slightest account of the country's resources. He had had a throne erected that was far greater than those of any of the preceding tsars, and had a sceptre, crown, and orb borne before him, and also a great sword. He rewarded his *halberdiers*, life guards, and captains as richly as lords, without at all considering that he might drain the treasury dry.

They accused him under the eighth heading of having been the most corrupt and debauched of men. He did not even respect the sacred character of virgins consecrated to God, and dishonored a great number of them in the convents. He also indulged in unnatural vice. He celebrated his wedding on one of the feasts of St. Nicholas in the springtime; that was a great crime in their eyes, for they hold this saint to be almost as important as Christ, and honor him ten times as much. He often borrowed thousands of crowns from the treasuries of the holy monasteries without giving any of them back. Many times, he had caused priests, monks, and other holy persons to be beaten with rods. Now this was a treatment to which they had never been subjected. He had dismissed and sent into exile the venerable patriarch of Moscow, replacing him with a wicked and impious man, and this with no regard for the rights of election of the bishops and clergy.

Under the ninth heading, they accused him of having provoked the appearance of an impostor who was to come and lend him assistance in case of danger. This impostor, with a large party of Cossacks, had descended on to the banks of the Volga, where he wrought great depredations, plundering loaded boats which came from Astrakhan and causing millions in losses. He claimed to be Peter Fyodorovich, a natural son of Tsar Fyodor Ivanovich, even though it was quite certain that this tsar, who had lived like a saint, as we have already said, would never have strayed away from his wife to get bastards by other women.

The tenth heading of the accusation was the invasion of the Poles, and the insolence of these strangers whom he had summoned. They took objects from all the shops without payment, did not tolerate one word from the Russians, and answered them with their swords. If a Russian lodged a complaint he could be certain that he would not obtain justice, but would instead be treated and repulsed like a dog by the wicked judges appointed by Dmitry's will. These Poles pushed their audacity beyond all bounds. In the evenings, in the open streets, they dared attack carriages, and, despite the escorts of footmen, seize the ladies in them, even if they were princesses or *boyars'* wives. Intolerable affrays often arose from these incidents.

To conclude this catalogue of crimes, the lords affirmed that no matter what person he had been in reality, Dmitry would still have been their tsar had he wished to reign in peace, marry a Muscovite princess, and observe their religion and their laws; but, alas, they did not see that it was all a punishment inflicted on them by heaven for their manifold sins and their willful hardness of heart, which increased daily.

⚔ *57* ⚔

Shuiskii's Decree against Runaway Peasants, March 9, 1607

The "Time of Troubles" (1601–1613) saw major political and social chaos. It witnessed the appearance of a number of pretenders to the vacant throne of Russia, invited foreign intervention, and, above all, presented the peasants with an opportunity to seek better working conditions. The nobles who disapproved of peasant flights, forced the newly elected Tsar Shuiskii (1606–1610) to issue a decree that allowed them an extended period of time to search for their runaway peasants. This decree was a significant milestone in the growth of Russian serfdom.

On March 9, 1607, Vasilii Shuiskii (1606–1610), Tsar and Grand Prince of All Russia, together with Patriarch Ermogen, the Holy *Sobor* and the tsar's own council, heard a report of the *pomestie prikaz* [Estates Department] [prepared by] the *boyars* and clerks, which complained that peasant changes from one place of work to another created great difficulties, extremes, and violence

---

From *Vosstanie Bolotnikova, Dokumenty i materiialy* (Bolotnikov's Uprising: Documents and Sources) (Moscow, Sotsekgis, 1959), pp. 211–214. Translation mine. Words in brackets are mine.

against the weak by the strong—something that was absent during the reign of Ivan Vasilevich, when peasants had freedom of movement. At Boris Godunov's suggestion, discarding the advice of old *boyars*, Tsar Feodor Ivanovich [1584–1598] prohibited the [free] movement of peasants and forced everyone to report how many peasants he had, an action which soon thereafter led to many animosities, extremes, and litigations. When Tsar Boris Feodorovich [Godunov] saw the great commotion among the people, he set aside the law and allowed the peasants a limited freedom of movement, an action which judges did not know how to interpret in passing sentences. Consequently, now we are witnessing many quarrels and violence; many are ruined and there are many murders, banditries, and highway robberies.

As a result, with the aid of the Holy Synod and in accordance with the rule of the Holy Fathers, we have prepared [the following law]:

Those peasants who were registered in 1601 should, within the next fifteen years, return to those with whom they were originally registered; and should these peasants now be working for someone else, and if there is a search warrant for them, as well as [a complaint] against those who harbor them now, even if the litigation is incomplete, or should former owners start legal proceedings by September 1, [1607] those people who have such peasants on their estates should return them by 1616, together with their wives, children, and their livestock without any charge to those to whom they originally belonged; and whoever shall not return them by the said time as provided in this *ukaz* [decree], he will be forced to pay a fine as well as a rental. Those peasants for whom there will be no search warrant by September 1, [1607] should not be returned, but should be registered with those to whom they currently belong.

And those peasants who will henceforth leave their owners and join other [owners], regardless of whom they may be, and if [the new owners] accept them, this will be contrary to our *ukaz*. When such a peasant is found he will be returned, together with all the fruits of his labor, to the original owner from whom he fled; and if that peasant had built a home, that home should not be transferred, but a fair price must be paid for it; he should also be fined ten *rubles* for violating the tsar's *ukaz*; do not accept any strangers; if you do you will pay a rental of three *rubles* per year to the owner of the runaway peasant; annual rental for a runaway slave is also three *rubles*.

And should a peasant without a family come to anyone and hire himself for a seasonal summer's or winter's work or for the entire year, he who hires him for a year does not violate this *ukaz* and cannot be fined for accepting him because his real master knows where he lives.

And should a woman or a widow or a maid run away into someone's estate and marry there, the peasant who marries a strange woman should be given to the owner of the woman, with all of his livestock and [all of his] children born of this marriage; and should this peasant have children from his former wife, they are not affected; the stepmother should not take them; those under fifteen years old, however, should be allowed to go with their father.

Those individuals who have a slave girl under eighteen years old, or a widow of two years' widowhood, or a young single man under twenty, and allow them neither to marry nor be free, such maids, widows, and young men should go and complain to the state treasury; and if the treasury, upon investigating the complaint, should prove that these individuals are grown and their master does not allow them to marry, they should be set free, in Moscow by the treasury, and in other cities by a local state official and courts; and should their master then complain that these individuals had stolen or taken away something, he should not be heard nor [should] the matter [be] allowed to be brought before the court. Do not detain unmarried persons since it is contrary to the Divine law and the teachings of the Holy Fathers; moreover such practice will not cause the population to increase.

Those peasants, slave men, and slave women, who will run away from their masters following the issuing of this *ukaz*, and should they be harbored by other masters, their owner has permission to search for his peasants, male slaves, and women slaves, for fifteen years following their flight; after fifteen years they should neither be sought after nor punished.

In cities, *namestniks* [administrators], *voevodas* [appointed officials], judges, clerks, and all state officials should know [of all developments] in their cities and learn of all happenings in territories under their respective jurisdiction from the elders, [land] captains, and priests whether there are any newcomers; and if they be informed of their whereabouts they should apprehend them and ask to whom they belong, where they are from, from whom they ran away, how long and where they have lived. And should anyone attempt to bribe him [the official] and should he reveal it and report it, the would-be briber should be fined by the treasury and be forced to deposit a guarantee that he will transport the fugitive to his master. The treasury should collect a fine of ten *rubles* from him, while those who harbor fugitives more than seven days should be fined ten *rubles* per household for every runaway man, and three *rubles* for harboring a fugitive woman or a girl.

And should someone's slave, or a peasant, or a woman be accepted on the lands or villages of the Tsar and the Grand Prince, or on monastery lands, or in villages of the Patriarch, the Church, or a monastery, the responsibility for accepting these fugitives should be placed on the stewards and elders of those villages or lands. This *ukaz* permits searches for the fugitives in all those villages, lands, cities, and settlements.

And those *namestniks*, judges, clerks, and all other officials who will neither investigate nor inquire about the newcomers but will accept bribes, and should this be reported, then such officials should be fined twice the amount of their gain, dismissed from their position, and never accepted into the state service again.

☙ *58* ☙

Conditions for Wladislaw's Ascension to the Throne of Muscovy, 1610

One of the candidates for the Russian throne during the "Time of Troubles" was Prince Wladislaw, the son of an ambitious Polish King, Sigismund III. For a time it appeared that Wladislaw had a strong chance to become tsar of Russia, but the obstinacy of his father, who actually wanted the Russian throne for himself, upset Wladislaw's chance. As the following excerpts indicate, Wladislaw would have been a "constitutional" tsar of Russia.

A reply of the most illustrious Sigismund III, by the grace of God, King of Poland and Grand Prince of Lithuania, on articles and petitions of the *boyars*, courtiers, nobles, officials, and counsellors of the Muscovite state.

1. You have requested: that with God's blessing the great lord, his grace the King [of Poland] permit his son Wladislaw to become the great Tsar and Grand Prince of the state of Moscovy and of all famed and great Russian states; that his majesty the great Tsar and Grand Prince be crowned on the Muscovite throne with the tsarist crown and diadem in Moscow by the Patriarch of Moscow in accordance with ancient custom, in the same fashion as all past rulers of Moscow and of the famed Muscovite state were crowned. To this his royal grace consents and hopes that providence will in time send real peace to this state [of Moscovy].

2. [You have requested] that the Holy Orthodox Greek faith and the Holy Apostolic Church be preserved, that it retain its former beauty as well as the

---

From *Akty otnosiashchiesia k istorii Zapadnoi Rossii, sobranye in izdannye arkheograficheskoiu Kommissieiu* . . . (Documents Pertaining to the History of Western Russia, Collected and Published by the Archeographic Commission) (St. Petersburg: 1846–1853), vol. 4, pp. 314–317. Translation mine. Words in brackets are mine.

content of the teachings of the apostles and the Church fathers, and that Roman Catholic, Lutheran, and other teachers cause no religious schism. And that those Roman Catholics who wish to attend Greek Church service must come there in humility, as befits true Christians, and not with pride, or with their hats on, or with their dogs, or at times when it is not appropriate. To this [request] his royal grace would like to state the following: Roman Catholics must have their own church, a problem which was negotiated during the reign of Boris [Godunov], and in that Church they must have priests or Polish clergy, government, and all important *boyars*, for there is a need for at least one Roman Catholic church in the capital city of Moscow to serve Poles and Lithuanians; and should a Russian happen to go to a [Roman Catholic] church he should conduct himself in the same appropriate manner as is done in Russian churches. Neither his grace, the King, nor his royal grace, the son, will allow conversions from Greek to Roman or any other faith, inasmuch as faith is God's gift and no one should be forced to renounce his belief; a Russian should have free worship in the Russian faith, and a Pole or a Lithuanian in the Polish faith.

3. His grace, the King, as a great Christian sovereign, with his son, will have great respect for holy shrines and remains of the saints. The Patriarch of Moscow, as well as metropolitans, archbishops, bishops, and all the clergy will be protected and respected [by us] similarly as we protect and respect Roman Catholic servants of God, that is, archbishops, bishops, and all priests. We will neither interfere in Church affairs nor do we wish to comment on matters relative to the teachings of the Holy Fathers and of the Apostolic Church; and his grace, the lord, will not approve as bishop anyone who does not deserve that position. . . .

5. His grace, the lord, would like to be kind to the *boyars*, courtiers, and all important government officials, as was the custom earlier, and he would also like to preserve all ancient customs; those who had grants, or monetary rewards, or owned either *pomesties* [estates of service nobles], or *votchinas* [hereditary estates], will have them as of old; his grace, the lord, from his own grace and generosity and in return for service, will increase and add to their wealth.

6. In accordance with the ancient custom, his grace, the lord, will make his gracious grants to the service people, nobles [*dvorianom*] and lesser nobility early each year; and should something be acquired not from the sovereign and not according to their dignity, or should someone suffer unjustly, then his grace, the sovereign, will consult with the *boyars*, and whatever their judgment will be, his sovereign grace will approve; he will also follow the advice of the *boyars* on the means to improve devastated *pomesties* and *votch-inas*; those nobles and petty nobility who receive the sovereign's grants [of

tax proceeds] from cities, his grace, the lord, will continue to grant them in return for services, as was the custom earlier.

7. His grace, the lord, will pay, as of old, from the government treasury, monetary and grain salaries to the gunners and hoopers in Moscow and other cities, who were in the service of previous sovereigns.

8. Courts must be conducted by custom and in accordance with the Code of Law [*Sudebnik*]; and should anyone wish to introduce changes aimed at improving the justice of the courts, this change is reserved to the *boyars* of the whole country; and his grace, the lord, will not interfere with improvements in the court system. . . .

11. Should anyone commit a crime deserving of punishment, his grace, the lord, will punish him, regardless of his rank, on the basis of his crime, but with prior just consultation with the *boyars* and other important people; wives, children, and brothers who neither took part in the crime nor knew of it, should not be punished and may remain on their *votchinas* or *pomesties*; and no one should be punished or deprived of his honor, or imprisoned or deprived of his *pomestie* or *votchina* without first being found guilty by the court and by all the *boyars*. Individuals of high rank should not be unjustly demerited while lesser officials should be promoted according to their service only. *Votchinas* and other property should not be confiscated; property of those who die without heirs should pass on to their next of kin. And his grace, the lord, will do all this only in consultation with the *boyars* and with agreement of influential *boyars*, and without their consent he will do nothing. His grace, the lord, will not exile anyone to prison in Lithuania or Poland. For learning purposes, citizens of Moscow are free to travel abroad in every Christian country, except pagan or Islamic, and his grace, the lord, will not confiscate their estates or properties for this. . . .

14. His grace, the lord, will collect goods and all state revenues from cities and villages, and money from taverns, and from customs as of old; that is, as was done similarly by his predecessors; his grace, the lord, will add no new taxes to the existing ones. To cities destroyed by the war, his grace, the lord, will send officials to assess the damage. Taxes from those who remained there will be collected on the basis of this assessment. And his grace, the lord, may increase the taxes in cities that were not damaged [only] with the consent of the *boyars* and other influential people.

15. Polish and Lithuanian merchants are free to trade in the Muscovite state, and Russian-Muscovite merchants are free to trade in Poland and Lithuania. This freedom is applicable to all commodities. His royal grace allows Russian merchants to travel freely through Poland and Lithuania to other countries; his royal grace will collect dues from them in Moscow and in all

cities of Moscovy as well as in Poland and Lithuania on the basis of the old customs, neither adding anything new to these nor collecting anything illegally.

16. His royal grace will not allow peasants to go from Russian to Lithuania or from Lithuania to Russia; while in Russia he will not permit mixing between various layers of Russian society.

17. His royal highness will allow the *boyars* to retain their slaves on the basis of the old custom so that they will serve their *boyars* or their lords as of old; and his grace will not grant them [the slaves] any freedom.

18. Should his grace, the lord, wish to station cossacks along the Volga, Don, Ural, and Terek Rivers, he may have them, upon prior consultation concerning it with *boyars* and important people. When, with God's permission, his royal grace [Wladislaw] shall reach Moscow, the Patriarch, the Holy Synod, *boyars*, nobles, and people of other social layers may petition for items not included in these articles; then his grace will approve these according to the custom of the Muscovite state with [the consent of] the Patriarch, the Holy *Sobor*, *boyars*, and all the country.

Written in our camp near Smolensk, February 4, 1610.

Sigismund rex.

⚜ *59* ⚜

A French View of Seventeenth Century Muscovy

There is a perception among some western historians of Russia that sixteenth and seventeenth century Muscovy was discovered by Scandinavian, German, English, and Dutch merchants and travellers. This perception is apparently based on the publication of a number of accounts by visitors from these countries. This perception is, of course, wrong. For many years, for example, Muscovy had contacts with a number of Italian

---

Reprinted from *The Russian Empire and Grand Duchy of Muscovy. A 17th Century French Account*, by Jacques Margeret. Translated and Edited by Chester S. L. Dunning. (Pittsburgh: University of Pittsburgh Press, 1983), pp. 11–15 and 27–51. Reprinted by permission of the University of Pittsburgh Press. ©1983 by University of Pittsburgh Press. See original source for footnote reference.

states, including the Vatican. And in the sixteenth and the seventeenth centuries it had numerous French connections. Indeed, during the second half of the sixteenth century many French merchants visited Moscow, and in 1587 a French company was granted a number of privileges by the government of Muscovy.

One of the most interesting Frenchmen to visit Moscow was Jacques Margeret (1560s–1620s). A soldier of fortune, Margeret entered Muscovy's service in 1600, was well received by Tsar Boris Godunov and, in return for his military service, was granted a large estate. After Godunov's death, Margeret briefly served Tsar Vasilii Shuiskii, but in 1606 he returned to France and a year later published his *Estat de l'Empire de Russi et Gran de Duche de Muscouie* (The Russian Empire and the Grand Duchy of Muscovy). Margeret's account is superior to most other west European descriptions because it presents an intelligent assessment of Muscovy, and provides a clear picture of the country's possessions, resources, peoples, officials, and rulers. In short, Margeret's work is one of the most important historical sources on Muscovy for the early part of the seventeenth century.

This country is very cold—I mean in the more settled parts, the north and west mentioned above. Although in the plains of Tatary, along the Volga, in Kazan and Astrakhan, and on the eastern side of the Ob River are very temperate regions; in the said cold provinces there are six months of winter. During winter there is always snow up to one's waist, and one can cross entire rivers on ice. Nonetheless, the land there is very fertile, yielding an abundance of all kinds of grains which we have in France. Rye is sown at the beginning or middle of August, wheat and oats, according to the length of winter, in April or May, and barley at the end of May. There are fruits such as huge melons (better than I have eaten elsewhere), plenty of cucumbers, good apples, cherries, but few pears and plums. There is also a great quantity of nuts, strawberries, and such fruit. There is little rain in the summer and none in the winter.

In Kholmogory, Archangel, and Saint Nicholas, likewise in some other places in the north, in summer one can always see the sun, day and night, for the space of a month or six weeks; at midnight one can see it two or three *brasses* above the horizon. In winter, for the space of a month, there is hardly any daylight, because the sun is not visible at all.

Moreover, there are in Russia all sorts of wild game and animals which are found in France, except wild boars. Stags, hinds, and wild goats are found in large numbers to the east and south, in the plains of Tatary and between Kazan and Astrakhan. Everywhere in Russia are to be found a great many elk, called the "great beast." Rabbits are very scarce there. Pheasants, partridges, thrushes, blackbirds, quail, and larks are found there in great abundance, besides infinite other fowl. However, very few woodcocks are seen. In August and September there are great numbers of cranes. Swans, geese, and wild ducks are found there in winter. I saw only one stork, which was entirely black. The carnivorous beasts of Russia include black and white bears in great quantity, five kinds of foxes, and plenty of wolves, which live in the large forests and do great damage to livestock. Besides this, reindeer are found in some places in the north. They are smaller than stags and have large, beautiful antlers. Their coat is gray, almost white. Their hooves are more cloven than stags' hooves. These reindeer serve as food, clothing, and horses for the people of that region. They harness one of them to a sleigh built especially for the purpose and go more quickly than any horses can. Most of the time the reindeer feed on what they find under the snow. In the winter all the hares in Russia turn white, and in the summer they are the same color as in France. In summer and winter white partridges are found there, as well as falcons, hawks, and other birds of prey. In all of Europe there are no better nor more diverse kinds of freshwater fish than the Russians have in great abundance. These include sturgeon, beluga, *belaia ryba* (which means "white fish" and is larger than a salmon), sterlet, and all the varieties of fish which we have in France, except trout.

Fish and every other type of foodstuff is cheap, for, notwithstanding the great famine (of which I will speak below) which depopulated nearly all the country of livestock, I bought on my departure from Russia a lamb as big as one of our sheep in France, or almost as big, for ten *dengi*, which is worth about thirteens *sols*, four *deniers*. (I also bought a chicken for seven *deniers tournois*; there are no capons in Russia, except among the foreigners.) The reason that lambs are so cheap is that each ewe ordinarily has two or three of them, and these lambs the following year become themselves mothers of just as many lambs. As for beef and cows, they also increase in numbers extraordinarily, for they do not eat any veal at all in Russia, since it is against their religion. Moreover, they observe fifteen weeks of fasting each year, besides Wednesday and Friday of each week. That makes nearly a half year of fasting, which causes meat to be cheap. Given that grains (of which there are a great many varieties) are not exported, they too are cheap. The land itself is so rich and fertile that, except for a few places, it is never manured. And thus, a child of twelve to fifteen years and a small horse will plow an arpent or two of land each day.

Although there is a great abundance of food, and at low cost, the common people content themselves with very little. They cannot afford the cost, having no industry, and being very lazy. They do not apply themselves to work; rather, they are given to drunkenness more than to anything else. Their principal drink when they make merry is *aqua vitae* and mead, which they make from honey (which comes to them without labor and in great abundance, as one can judge by the great quantity of wax which is taken out of the country annually). They also have beer and other beverages of little value. All, without distinction (men as well as women, girls and boys, and the ecclesiastics as much or more than the others), are addicted to this vice of excessive drinking. Whenever there is liquor (which they are permitted to make for the principal festival days of the year) they can be expected to keep drinking day and night until it is gone. Here I am speaking of the common people, for the gentlemen have liberty to make such liquor as they wish and to drink whenever they want.

It is maintained that the grand dukes are descended from three brothers who came from Denmark. According to the *Russian Chronicles*, they invaded Russia, Lithuania, and Podolia about eight hundred years ago. Riurik, the eldest brother, had himself called grand duke of Vladimir. From him are descended all the grand dukes in the male line up to Ivan Vasil'evich, who was the first to receive the title of emperor from the [Holy] Roman Emperor Maximilian, after the conquests of Kazan, Astrakhan, and Siberia.

Now, concerning the title which the grand dukes hold, they think that there could be no title greater than their own, having themselves called *tsar'*. They call the [Holy] Roman emperor, or *tsesar'*, which they derive from Caesar, and they call kings *korol'* in imitation of the Poles. They call the king of Persia *kizilbasha* and the Turkish sultan *velikii gospodar' turskoi*, which means "great lord of Turkey," in imitation of *grand seigneur*. But this word *tsar'*, they say, is found in the Holy Scripture. Everywhere mention is made of David or of Solomon or of other kings, they are called *Tsar'* David, *Tsar'* Solomon, which is, as we interpret, King David, King Solomon, etc. Thus they keep for themselves the more authentic name of *tsar'* with which God was pleased to honor David, Solomon, and others ruling over the house of Judah and Israel in olden times. They say that the words *tsesar'* and *korol'* are only human inventions, which names someone acquired by great feats of arms. For that purpose, after Fedor Ivanovich, tsar of Russia, raised the siege of Narva (which he had besieged), and when the deputies and ambassadors of both sides were assembled to conclude peace between Russia and Sweden, they debated for more than two days on the title of emperor which Fedor wanted to have, the Swedes not wanting to recognize him as such. The Russians say that the word *tsar'* is even greater than emperor, so the accord was made that the Swedes would always call Fedor "Tsar and Grand Duke of Muscovy," each of the parties thinking the other had been outwitted in the use of the word *tsar'*. The king of Poland writes to [the grand duke] in the same way. The [Holy] Roman emperor gives him the title of emperor, as did the late Queen Elizabeth and as do the king of Great Britain, the king of Denmark, the grand duke of Tuscany, and the king of Persia. All [the sovereigns] of Asia give him the titles that he claims. As for the Turkish sultan, given that there has been neither correspondence nor ambassadors between them in my time, I do not know what title he gives him. . . .

All the routes out of Russia are so closed that it is impossible to leave without the permission of the emperor. They have not allowed any of those who carry arms to leave the country in our times; for I was the first. Even if there is a war against the Poles, they do not cast out any Poles although they have a goodly number of them. Instead, they send them to the frontiers of Tatary. They do likewise with the other non-Russian peoples among them, out of fear that these foreigners will run away or surrender to the enemy, for this is the most distrustful and suspicious nation in the world.

All their castles or fortresses are of wood, except Smolensk, the castle of Ivangorod or Narva, the castle of Tula, Kazan, Astrakhan, the castle of Kolomna, and the castle of Putivl on the frontiers of Podolia, and the city of Moscow.

Moscow is a large city, through which flows a river larger than the Seine. The city is enclosed by a wall of wood which has a circumference, as I estimate, greater than Paris. Inside there is a big wall which has a circumference half that of the wooden wall, but which does not extend across the river. Inside this there is a third made of brick which encloses all the stone shops of the merchants. Then there is the castle, which is large and was built by an Italian in the time of Vasilii Ivanovich, father of Ivan Vasil'evich. In the castle there are several stone churches, among which are four covered with gilded copper. The city is full of wooden buildings, each building having only two stories. There is a large yard around each dwelling because of fires, to which they have been very subject lately. They have built many stone churches; there is also an infinite number of wooden ones there. Even the streets are paved or planked with wood.

The high nobility always reside in Moscow. There are the *kniaz'ia* (that is, the dukes), then those of the council who are called *dumnye boiare*, then the *okol'nichie* (who are marshals), then the *dumnye dvoriane*, and other *moskovskie dvoriane*. From these are chosen the principal officers and governors of the towns. There is in the council no fixed number, for it is up to the emperor to appoint as many as he deems proper. I have known there to be as many as thirty-two [in the council]. The privy council is customarily made up of those closely related by blood to the emperor and meets in matters of great consequence. One takes (as a matter of form) the advice of the clergy, summoning the patriarch with some bishops to the council. Strictly speaking, however, there is no law or council save the will of the emperor, be it good or bad. He has the power to put all to fire and sword, be they innocent or guilty. I consider him to be one of the most absolute princes in existence, for everyone in the land, whether noble or commoner, even the brothers of the emperor, call themselves *kholopy gosudaria*, which means "slaves of the emperor." Moreover, they admit to the council two *dumnye d'iaki*, whom I take more for secretaries than chancellors, however they may interpret their function. One of them holds the office from which all ambassadors are dispatched and foreign relations are conducted. The other holds the office from which all troops receive their orders, including lieutenants general, governors of towns, and others, except for the *strel'tsy*, the best Russian infantry (who are *harquebusiers*) who have an office of their own.

Beyond this, each province of the land has an office in Moscow where a member of the council or an *okol'nichii*, together with a *d'iak*, judge all differences among those who serve the emperor. It must be noted that no judges or officers dare to take any gifts from those who have business with them. If they are accused by their own servants or by those who gave them gifts (which happens often when things do not come out as the gift-giver wished) or by anyone else, and if they are convicted, all their possessions are confiscated. After restitution of the gifts, the guilty ones are placed on the *pravezh* (of which we will speak below) to make them pay a fine of five hundred, a thousand, or two thousand *rubles*, more or less, as ordered by the emperor according to the rank of the individual concerned. If the guilty one is a *d'iak* who is not well favored by the emperor, he is whipped through the streets. If it is money which he has taken, a purse full of money is hung around his neck. And it is the same with all the other things, for if they have taken furs, pearls, or anything whatsoever, including salted fish, this is usually hung around the guilty one's neck when he is beaten. This is done not with canes, but rather with a whip. Then the guilty are sent into exile. In this they are looking not only to the present, but to the future as well. Notwithstanding this punishment, these officials do not stop taking [gifts]. They have found a new trick, which is that one offers [the gift] to the [ikon] of whomever he has business with. (Everyone has a large number of these [ikons] in his house, which the more simple people call *Bog*, which means "God," and the others call *obraz*, which means "image" or "representation.") The gift is hung on the [ikon]. This does not always excuse the official if the gift surpasses seven or eight *rubles* in value and if the emperor is informed of it. It is also somewhat permissible for them during the week after Easter to accept some little thing when they meet, kiss each other, and exchange eggs. However, they may not take any gift it if be presented to them in hope thereby of gaining favor, for they are not exempted should they be accused by parties from whom they have received [a gift] at Eastertime, inasmuch as [accusers] can testify to having given them [a gift] for such and such a reason; otherwise they are exempt during this time from all other accusations. Thus all judges and officials must be content with their annual salaries and the lands which they possess from the emperor.

There is no appeal from a given sentence. Except for inhabitants of towns, everyone, including those from faraway provinces, must come to be judged in Moscow. As for the inhabitants of towns, they have in each town a *gubnoi starosta* who judges all cases. His decisions may be appealed to Moscow. These subaltern judges also have the power to search out and imprison all murderers, robbers, and thieves; to interrogate and torture them; and, after their confession, to forward this information to a special office in Moscow which they call *Razboinyi Prikaz*. Nowhere in Russia can a man be executed without express order from the sovereign court of Moscow. Their laws provide that everyone plead his own case or have some kinsman or servant of his assigned to do this, for they have no lawyers at all. All differences, except those which one may judge on sight, end with an oath which one of the parties swears against the other. To do this he must kiss a cross with some ceremony in a church designated for this purpose. It must be noted that those who serve the emperor on horse are exempt from making this oath in person. They can have a servant kiss the cross for them, except when they swear an oath of homage to princes.

Those who are indebted to the emperor or to someone else, and who cannot or do not wish to pay, are put on the *pravezh*. This is a place where they must go at sunrise on weekdays to be beaten and lashed on the calves of the legs with a rod or switch by men appointed for this, who are called *nedel'-shchiki*. [The punishment] lasts until ten or eleven A.M. I have seen several brought back on wagons to their homes after they have been beaten. This continues until the debt is fully repaid. Those who serve the emperor on horse are exempt from this, putting one of their men in their place.

The nobility, by which I mean all those receiving an annual salary and possessing lands from the emperor, maintain this regimen: During the summer they ordinarily get up at sunrise and go to the castle (if they are in Moscow), where the council meets [from five A.M. until ten A.M.]. Then the emperor, attended by the council, goes to hear the church service. This lasts from eleven until noon. After the emperor leaves the church, the nobles go home to eat dinner, and after dinner they lie down and sleep for two or three hours. At about [six P.M.] a bell rings, and all the lords return to the castle, where they remain until two or three hours after sunset. Then they retire, eat supper, and go to bed.

Now one should mention that all the nobles go on horseback in the summer and in winter on sleighs, so that they get no exercise. This makes them stout and obese. They even hold in honor those who have the biggest bellies, using the name *dorodnyi chelovek*, which signifies "a brave man." The nobles dress very simply except on festival days or when the emperor goes out in public or some ambassador is due to have an audience.

Noblewomen ride in a carriage in summer and in a sleigh in winter. However, when the empress goes into the country there are a number of women who follow her carriage riding on horseback like men. These ladies all wear white felt hoods, similar to those that the bishops and abbots wear in the countryside, except that the hoods of the latter are dark gray or black. These women are dressed in [long gowns], as wide at the shoulders as at the bottom. These gowns are ordinarily of scarlet or some other beautiful red cloth. Under this gown they have another dress of silk, with great sleeves more than an *ell* of Paris wide. The cuffs of these sleeves are of some cloth of gold a third of an *ell* long. If she is a woman she wears a cap embroidered with pearls; but if she is a girl she wears a tall hat of black fox fur, as do the nobles when audience is given to an ambassador. A woman who has not had any children may wear the same hat as a girl. They all wear a collar of pearls a good four fingers in width and earrings which are very long. They wear boots made of red and yellow moroccan leather, with heels three fingers high. These boots are hobnailed like the boots of the Poles or Hungarians. They all paint themselves, but very crudely. They consider it to be a disgrace not to paint oneself, whether old or young, rich or poor.

Russian women are held under close supervision and have their living quarters separate from that of their husbands. One never sees them, for to present their wives is the greatest favor that Russian men extend to one another (except to close kin). Even if someone wants to marry, he must talk to the kinsmen of the girl, who, if they are content to enter into alliance with the prospective bridegroom, allow one of the suitor's most loyal kinsmen or friends to go see the girl and to make his report. On the basis of this report the marriage is contracted. If either party backs out, a sum of money mutually agreed upon must be paid. After the contract has been signed, the prospective bridegroom may go to see his intended wife.

On the day of the marriage the bride is led to the church with a veil on her face (like Rebecca, when she was informed that it was Isaac that she saw coming from far away) so that she can see no one and no one can see her face. After the ceremony she is brought back in the same fashion and seated at the table. She continues so veiled until the marriage is consummated. Then the husband and wife go to the baths; or, if they do not go, they have a bucket of water poured over their heads, for they consider themselves to be unclean until that moment, following in this the Jews and the Turks. They must receive a blessing from a priest or monk before entering their church

or even before presenting themselves before any [ikons], of which each house
has a good number. They do the same every time that they have sexual
intercourse. The entire dowry and everything else given for the marriage are
evaluated at double or triple [their real worth], and, should she die without
children, the husband pays the full amount to her closest kin according to
the evaluation.

The wealth of one and all is measured by the number of men and women
servants that one has and not by the money that one possesses. They have
retained this practice from the Ancients. The servants, of whom they have a
great number, are slaves; and they, along with their children, remain serfs
belonging to the heirs of their first master. They follow several other practices
from antiquity, as in their writing. Their registers, reports, and requests or
petitions are rolled in parchment and not registered in books or folded as
among us. So it is with all their other writings. In this they imitate the
Ancients, and even the Holy Scripture, as we read from the Prophet Ezekiel,
chapter 3. They also imitate the Ancients in the way in which they invite a
man to a banquet or to dinner. Even the emperor, inviting ambassadors, does
not say anything but *Khleba esh' so mnoi,* which means "Eat some bread with
me." Their greatest reproach to someone who appears ungrateful is to say,
"Thou hast forgotten my bread and my salt." Even if the emperor makes
some journey, or when he is crowned or marries or [when there is an imperial]
baptism, the common people individually come to offer him, among other
presents, a loaf of bread and some salt.

The Russian way of showing reverence is to remove one's hat and to bow
low. This is not done in the fashion of the Turks or the Persians and other
Mohammedans, who put their hand on their head or on their chest; rather
it is done by lowering the right hand to the ground, or not so low, according
to the respect which they wish to show. However, if an inferior wishes to
entreat something from his superior, he will prostrate himself before his master,
with his face against the ground as they do in their prayers before some
[ikons]. They know no other signs of respect. They do not regard kneeling
as such, because the Mohammedans (they say) customarily kneel merely to
sit down on the ground. The Russian women show respect in the same way
[as the men].

There are among the Russians many people aged from 80, 100, to 120
years. They are not so subject to illness as in these parts. Except for the emperor
and some principal lords, they do not know about physicians. They even
consider to be unclean several things which one uses in medicine. Among
other things, they do not take pills voluntarily. As for enemas, they abhor
them, along with musk, civet, and other such things. If the common people
are sick, they usually take a good draught of *aqua vitae,* place in it a charge

of *harquebus* powder or a peeled clove of garlic, stir this, and drink it. Then they go immediately to a hot-house which is so hot as to be almost unendurable, and remain there until they have sweated an hour or two. They do the same for all sorts of maladies.

Now let us consider the revenue of the empire. First, the *demesne* of the emperor comes under an office which is called the *Dvorets*. The master of the house has superintendence over this office and, along with two *d'iaki*, judges matters related to it. Beyond this, the country is divided into five offices, which they call *chetverti*, to which offices are brought the ordinary revenues. In addition, there is another office which they call the *Bol'shoi Prikhod*, which supervises these *chetverti*. If there are any extraordinary taxes, they are all brought to the *Bol'shoi Prikhod*.

The revenue of the emperor, beyond his *demesne*, consists in direct property taxes, which not only the towns must pay, but also all the peasants, including even those on the hereditary lands of the emperor's kinsmen. Then there are imposts and excise taxes on all sorts of merchandise and on the drinking houses where *aqua vitae*, mead, *hydromel*, and beer are sold. None dare sell those beverages anywhere in Russia except those who have leased the drinking houses in each town or village. There is also revenue from furs, wax, and other merchandise.

The revenue from the emperor's *demesne* consists for the most part in food, such as grains, *aqua vitae*, honey, wild game, meat, poultry, fruits, and other things necessary for the kitchen and larder. This notwithstanding, everything is taxed at a particularly high rate, and those who are a little distant from the city pay in money instead of in kind. There are even many who are taxed in money for each *vyt'*, which contains seven or eight *desiatiny* of tilled land, depending on where it is located. A *desiatina* is a piece of land on which one may sow two *chetverti* of grain. (A *chetvert'* is also what one would call an arpent of land [in France].) They pay an annual tax on each *vyt'* of ten, twelve, fifteen, even up to twenty *rubles*, according to the fertility of the land, each *ruble* making about six *livres* and twelve *sols*. This tax adds up every year to a great amount, so that there is found in the [*Dvorets*] the clear sum of up to one hundred twenty thousand, indeed up to one hundred fifty thousand *rubles* each year. The actual total depends on the costs and expenses of the foreign ambassadors and other extraordinary expenditures which are incurred by this office.

Some of the five *chetverti*, such as that of Kazan and the *Novaia Chetvert'*, yield each year a clear sum of eighty or one hundred thousand *rubles*, after all costs are met (for these are the offices from which all pensions and salaries of most of the soldiers are paid). Beyond this, the *Bol'shoi Prikhod* receives, in addition to the extraordinary levies made on all the land by the command of the emperor, the income from casual forfeitures, such as the confiscated possessions of those who fall into disgrace.

Furs and wax come to an office called the *Kazna*, which is where the treasury is located. The returns from the government seal are also contained in this office. For each sealed document the government receives a quarter of a *ruble*. All sorts of merchandise taken for the emperor are paid for out of the *Kazna*.

Moreover, each office of the provinces yields a good sum of money at the end of the year, for the emperor has the tenth part of all penalties and judgments in legal disputes. Besides that, there are two more offices. One handles the land grants and is called the *Pomestnyi Prikaz*. For each grant the recipient must give two, three, or four *rubles*, according to the extent of the land of which he takes possession. Then if one of these landholders falls into disgrace, the revenue from said land returns to the *Pomestnyi Prikaz* until the emperor grants the land to someone else. The other office is called the *Koniushenyi Prikaz*, which is the office of the equerry. This office also has several sources of revenue and casual income. All horses which are sold in the country, except by the peasants, must be registered (at a cost of twenty *sols* each) by the purchasers to avoid any danger of someone claiming that the horse had been stolen. Then there are great revenues from horses that the Nogai Tatars bring to sell in Russia. First, the emperor takes the choice tenth part of these horses. Then, for each horse which they sell he takes from either the seller or buyer, as agreed upon by them, five percent of the price. Now after being raised for two or three years, the emperor's tenth part of the Tatar horses, which are young horses or colts when received, are sold. This amounts to a great sum of money, for I have seen the Nogai Tatars lead at one time nearly forty thousand horses into the country. They come two or three times a year and bring more or less each time, so that one cannot be exactly certain of the revenue of the emperor.

Nevertheless, Russia is a very rich land, for no money leaves it, while there is a good amount coming in every year. All payments are made with merchandise, of which they have a great quantity, including all sorts of pelts, wax, tallow, hides of cows and elk, other hides dyed red, flax, hemp, all sorts of cordage, caviar (which are salted eggs of fish, of which a great quantity is sent to Italy), salted salmon, plenty of fish oil, and other merchandise. Although there is a great abundance of grain in Russia, they do not dare to transport it out of the country through Livonia. Beyond this, they have much potash, linseed, thread, and other merchandise which they barter or sell. The Russians, including the emperor, buy nothing from foreigners with ready money. If the emperor owes a sum such as four or five thousand *rubles*, he will make the payment in furs or wax.

By his thrift the emperor has a treasury which he never touches and which he adds to, more or less, every year. Besides this, there is the *Raskhodnaia Kazna*, which is the treasury where money is taken for extraordinary expenditures. It is full of all sorts of jewels in great number, but principally pearls—for they wear more of them in Russia than in all the rest of Europe. I saw in the treasury at least fifty of the imperial robes, around which were jewels instead of lacing; also, robes entirely [embroidered] with pearls, and others bordered all around with about a foot, a half-foot, or four fingers of pearls. I saw bedspreads by the half dozen, all bordered with pearls, and diverse other things. There are also costly jewels, for they buy them every year. These remain in the treasury, along with those that the emperor receives from ambassadors. There are four crowns: three of the emperor and a fourth with which the grand dukes were crowned in former times. This does not include the crown that Dmitrii had made for his wife, the empress, which was left unfinished, for it is not the custom of the country to crown the wives of emperors or grand dukes. Dmitrii was the first. There are at least two scepters and two golden orbs. All this I saw, having the honor several times of accompanying Dmitrii Ivanovich to the vaults in which the treasury is located. The Russians maintain that everything belongs to the treasury, be it clothes, jewels, cloth, or money.

Also in the treasury there are two intact unicorn horns and a crosier which the emperors carry, the entire length of which is made of one piece of unicorn [horn]. The transverse part of the crosier, on which one leans, is made of another piece of unicorn [horn]. There is also another half unicorn [horn] which is for everyday use in medicines. I have seen there yet another crosier, this one of gold, but a little hollowed inside because of the weight. There are a great number of gold dishes large and small, and cups to drink from. Beyond this, there are innumerable vessels of silver, gilded and plain, as one can judge by this account: After the election of Boris Fedorovich, when he had assembled the army at Serpukhov as we have mentioned above, he held a feast six weeks long, entertaining ten thousand men at a time nearly every day. They dined under tents, and all ate from silver dishes, according to the word of those who were there. I have seen in the treasury a half dozen casks made of silver which Ivan Vasil'evich had made from silver vessels which he found in Livonia when he conquered that country. One of these casks is nearly the size of a half *muid*; the others are not so large. There are also a great number of silver basins, very large and very deep, with handles on the side to carry them. Four men customarily bring to each table these basins full of mead, three or four, more or less, according to the length of the table. There are large silver cups to draw the mead from these basins because two or three hundred men would not suffice to pour drinks for those invited to the emperor's banquet. All these vessels are works of Russia. Moreover, there are a great number of silver vessels from Germany, England, and Poland, which are either presents of princes sent by ambassadors, or which have been purchased for the rarity of the workmanship.

There is in this treasury an abundance of all sorts of fabric—cloth of gold and of silver from Persia and from Turkey, all sorts of velvets, satin, damask, taffeta, and other silk cloth. In truth they need a great quantity of fabrics, for all those who come to serve the emperor have their "welcome" as they call it, which consists of money and, according to the quality of the man, a robe of cloth of gold or enough velvet, satin, damask, or taffeta to make him a garment. Moreover, when the emperor recompenses someone, be it for service done in war or in some other matter, he gives him fine cloth. Also, all ambassadors coming from the Nogai Tatars, the Crimean Tatars, or of some other nation of Asia receive, along with their attendants, robes of silk cloth, each according to his quality. To keep the treasury perpetually supplied, all merchants, foreigners as well as Russians, are obliged to bring all fine cloth and other things of value to the treasury, where some are chosen for the emperor. If it is found that a merchant sold or concealed, for example, ten or twelve *écus* worth of merchandise before bringing it to the treasury, all the rest of his merchandise would be confiscated, even though the merchant had paid the excise tax and all imposts.

They have no minerals except iron, which is very soft. However, I do not doubt that in such a large country there are other metals, but they have no person knowledgeable in such matters.

There is no other coin among them but *dengi* or *kopeks*, which are worth about sixteen *deniers tournois*, and some *moskovskie dengi*, which are worth eight *deniers tournois*. There are a few *polushki*, which are worth four *deniers*. This money is of silver, a little finer than the *reals de ocho*. They pay all sums with these coins, for there are no others in all of Russia. They convert all their sums into *rubles*, which are equal to one hundred *dengi*. (A *ruble* is worth, as we have already mentioned, six *livres* and twelve *sols*.) They also convert sums into half *rubles* or quarter *rubles*, then into *grivny*, which are ten *dengi*, and into *altyny*, which are three *dengi* (which is worth four *sols*).

Foreign merchants bring to Russia plenty of *reals* and *reichstalers* on which they make a profit. Russians buy them for twelve *altyny* apiece (thirty-six *dengi* or about forty-eight *sols*). Then they resell them to the mint at which, after just a little refining takes place, what we call a *real* of forty *sols* [thirty *dengi*] is restruck as forty-two *dengi*. Beyond this, these merchants bring to Russia a great number of *ducats*, which are bought and sold like other merchandise, and on which they often make a considerable profit. I have seen *ducats* bought for up to twenty-four *altyny* apiece, which makes about four *livres* and sixteen *sols*. I have also seen them sold for sixteen *altyny* or half a *ruble* apiece; but the most common price is from eighteen to twenty-one *altyny*. *Ducats* become very valuable when an emperor is crowned or marries and [when there is an imperial] baptism, for everyone comes to offer him presents. The common people join together in groups which vie with one another in offering rich presents. Among these presents there are customarily a number of *ducats*, be they in goblets or silver cups, or in plates covered with taffeta. *Ducats* also increase in value some days before Easter, because for a week after Easter the custom is to visit one another, to kiss, and to present red eggs (as was mentioned above). However, when one goes to visit the great nobles and those with whom one has some business, one offers them, along with the egg, some jewels, pearls, or some *ducats*. This is the only season of the year in which they dare to take gifts. Yet it is necessary that this be done secretly, for this season does not excuse anyone from taking something of greater value than ten or twelve *rubles*.

The greatest office of Russia is of grand master of the stable, called by them, *boiarin koniushii*. After him comes the one who supervises the doctors and apothecaries, and who is called *aptechnyi boiarin*. Then there is the master of the household; and after him, the emperor's taster. These four offices are the principal ones of the council. After them there are various offices, such as *stol'niki*, *chashniki*, *striapchie*, pages, and others, in great number.

The guard of the emperor is composed of ten thousand *strel'tsy*, who reside in the city of Moscow. These are *harquebusiers*. They have only one general. The *strel'tsy* are divided into *prikazy*, which are companies of five hundred. Each *prikaz* is commanded by a *golova*, whom we shall call a captain. Each hundred men is commanded by a centurion, and each ten men a *desiatnik*, whom we shall call a corporal. They do not have lieutenants or ensigns. Each captain, according to the services which he has done, receives a salary of thirty, forty, up to sixty *rubles*, annually, and he receives up to three, four, or five hundred *chetverti* of land. (Each *chetvert'* is comparable to an arpent of land and is to be understood as such throughout this work.) Most of the centurions have lands, and they receive from twelve to twenty *rubles* annually. The corporals receive up to ten *rubles* and the *strel'tsy* four or five *rubles* each year. Beyond this, each one receives twelve *chetverti* of rye and as much of oats every year. When the emperor goes into the countryside, even if it is only six or seven *versts* from the city, most of the *strel'tsy* go with him, receiving horses from the stables of the emperor. If the *strel'tsy* are sent somewhere with the army or are garrisoned somewhere, they are given horses. There are men designated to feed them, and every ten *strel'tsy* have a wagon to carry their provisions.

Besides these soldiers who reside in Moscow, those called *dvoriane vybornye* are selected from the principal gentlemen of each town within the jurisdiction of which they hold their lands. According to the size of the town, sixteen, eighteen, up to twenty or, indeed, thirty *vybornye dvoriane* are chosen, who reside in the city of Moscow for three full years. Then others are chosen, and those in Moscow are dismissed. This means that there is always a multitude of cavalry, so that the emperors seldom go out without eighteen or twenty thousand riders with them. All those attached to the court ride horses. Most of them sleep in turns at the castle, without any weapons.

In receiving some ambassador whom the prince wishes to honor, he sends some of his *strel'tsy* with their *harquebuses* to place themselves in rows on each side of the road up to the ambassador's lodging, starting from the entry gate of the wooden or stone wall of the city, depending on the emperor's orders. Then a number of his *moskovskie dvoriane* and *vybornye dvoriane* go to meet the ambassador, accompanied by the principal merchants, who are very richly dressed if necessary. This depends on the degree of respect one wishes to show the ambassador. Everyone has three of four changes of clothes for this purpose. Sometimes the emperor has them dress in his cloth of gold and silver from Persia, with the tall hat of black fox. Sometimes he has them dress with the *tsvetnoe plat'e* (which are robes of *tabis* or camlet of silk, or of scarlet, or some other beautiful fine cloth of light color, laced with gold) and with the black tall hat. Otherwise, they wear what they call *chistoe plat'e*, which is simpler, but comely attire. The number of men of quality meeting the ambassador is increased or diminished according to the honor that one wishes to show. They go to receive the ambassador at an arrow's flight from the city, or sometimes a quarter of a league away. To this meeting place one brings horses from the stable of the emperor for the ambassador and his attendants to ride into the city. Thus the ambassador is conducted all the way to his lodging, before which are placed guards. These guards do not permit anyone to enter the ambassador's residence except those who are assigned to do so. Nor, for that matter, do they allow anyone to leave who does not have a guard with him to see where he goes, what he will do, and what he will say. There are men appointed for this task and others who supply the ambassador's party with all kinds of necessary victuals at the emperor's expense. This service is provided from the time the ambassador crosses the border. Not only ambassadors, but all foreigners who come to serve the emperor are provided with all food necessary for themselves as well as for their horses, both in the city of Moscow and on the journey—each according to his quality. This is called *korm*, [the amount of which] given to the ambassadors is augmented or diminished according to the emperor's orders. All this is furnished from the office called *Dvorets*, as has been mentioned above.

Concerning the military, we must first speak of the *voevody*, who are the generals of the army. They are chosen customarily from the *dumnye boiare* and *okol'nichie*—that is to say, if some enemies appear. Otherwise, they are chosen annually from the *dumnye dvoriane* and *moskovskie dvoriane*, who are sent to the frontiers of Tatary to stop the incursions of any assembled forces of Tatars, who come sometimes to steal the grazing horses of some garrisons. If they were to meet no resistance, they would ravage all the more. The *voevody* separate their army into five units: the advance guard, which is near some town close to the confines of Tatary; the right wing, which is near some other town; the left wing; then the main force of the army; and the rear guard— all separated one from another. However, the generals must be ready at a moment's notice to join the main force. There are no other officers in the army but these generals. However, all the men-at-arms, both cavalry and infantry, are led by captains, without lieutenants, ensigns, trumpets, or drums. Each general has his own banner, which is identifiable by some saint who is painted on it. These banners are blessed by the patriarch, just as other images of saints. There are two or three men designated to hold the banner upright. Moreover, each general has his own *nabat*, as it is called. These are the brass drums which are carried on horseback. They each have ten or twelve of them, as many trumpets and some shawms. These are never sounded except when they are about to give battle or during a skirmish. One of the drums is used to signal the cavalry to dismount or to mount up.

The method they use to discover the enemy in these great plains of Tatary is as follows: There are routes which they call the road of the emperor, the Crimean road, and the road of the great *khan*. In addition, there are some oaks scattered here and there on the plains, eight, ten, up to forty *versts* from one another. Under most of these trees there are certain sentinels—that is to say, two men, each with a fresh horse. One of them keeps watch while perched in the tree, and the other one feeds the horses, which are kept saddled. They exchange places every four days. In case the sentinel in the tree spots some thick dust rising in the air, he has orders to descend, without saying a word until he is in the saddle, and to ride as fast as he can until he comes to the next tree, shouting from afar and making signs that he has seen men. The sentinel who guards the horses of this second tree mounts a horse on the command of the sentinel in the tree, who sees the first rider while he is still far off. As soon as they are able to hear or discern in what direction the approaching rider indicates that he has seen the cloud of dust, this second rider gives his horse free reign and rides as fast as he can to a third tree. Here they do the same thing, and so on, from one to the next, up to the first fortress. From there a message is sent to Moscow, without any other news except that men have been sighted. It turns out often to be only a herd of wild horses or of some other wild animals. But if the sentinel who remained in the first tree comes and continues the news, and in this manner further word is relayed, then they take to arms and the above-mentioned generals join together.

They send men to try to reconnoiter the forces of the enemy. Also, those sentinels scattered from the route which they are taking spread out on both sides, waiting for the enemy to pass. Then they come to their trail and reconnoiter the approximate size of their forces by the width of the path which they make across the grass. The prairie grass is taller than a horse, but in this region the Russians put fire to it every spring, so that the land is desolate. This is done so that the Tatars cannot find pasture so soon and in order to make the grass grow even taller. If the Tatars come by any of the above-named roads, the Russians survey their approximate strength by exact measurement of the depth of the path which they make. They also know the approximate size of the Tatar force by the dust which they see rising into the air, for the Tatars do not go voluntarily across the grass for fear of putting their horses out of breath.

These sentinels come by some secret paths which they know to bring news of the enemy's forces. To resist these forces, the generals withdraw toward some rivers and woods to block their passage. However, the Tatar is an enemy so nimble and so skillful that, knowing this, he will divert the Russian army with twenty or thirty thousand horses, while he sends some force to ransack the country by some other route. This they will effect with such swiftness that they will strike their blow before the Russian army receives any warning of it. Now the Tatars do not burden themselves with any booty except prisoners. They carry no baggage with them, although each one of them has a change or two of horse, which are so well trained that they are no trouble at all. Tatars are so skillful that they can descend from a trotting horse and leap onto another. They carry no arms except a bow, arrows, and a scimitar. They shoot much more steadily and more surely in retreat than otherwise. The provision which they carry is a little sun-dried meat, which is sliced very small. Moreover, they have plenty of rope attached to their pommel. In short, a hundred Tatars will always put to flight two hundred Russians, unless the latter are elite troops.

The Russian infantry or *harquebusiers*, being on the bank of a river or in some woods, make the Tatars retreat exceedingly fast, although in truth they are more adept at frightening them than they are at inflicting any damage to their forces. If any [Tatar] battalion of fifteen or twenty thousand horses should move against them a little, no more than three or four thousand come within cannon range, the rest seeming more like phantoms on asses than horsemen. So the Tatars retreat without ever sustaining great loss—unless one holds the passage in some woods or on a river, waiting for their return, which does not often happen.

The Russian forces consist mostly of cavalry. Besides the *dvoriane* mentioned above, one must add here the rest of the *dvoriane—vybornye dvoriane, gorodovye dvoriane*, and the *deti boiarskie*, who together constitute a great number. The companies call themselves by the name of the towns under which they have their lands. Some cities have three, four, up to eight or twelve hundred men, such as Smolensk, Novgorod, and others. There are a great number of towns furnishing a great multitude of men. Now each of these men must provide, beyond himself, a man on horse and a foot soldier for each one hundred *cheverti* of land which he possesses; but this is only in times of necessity. Normally, there is need for only the *dvoriane* themselves. This makes an incredible number of shadows rather than men.

The stipend of the lords of the council ranges from 500 *rubles* up to 1200 *rubles*. The latter amount is the salary of prince Fedor Ivanovich Mstislavskii, who has always had the first place during the lives of four emperors. The *okol'nichie* receive from 200 up to 400 *rubles* and from 1000 to 2000 *chetverti* of land; I have know there to be fifteen *okol'nichie* at the same time. The *dumnye dvoriane*, who customarily do not exceed six in number, receive from 100 *rubles* to 200 *rubles* and from 800 up to 1200 *chetverti* of land. The *moskovski dvoriane* receive from 20 up to 100 *rubles* and from 500 up to 1000 *chetverti* of land. The *vybornye dvoriane* receive from 8 up to 15 *rubles*; the *gorodovye dvoriane*, from 5 up to 12 *rubles*. Each receives up to 500 *chetverti* of land. All of these are paid annually out of the *chetverti* [or fiscal departments] and must furnish two men for each one hundred *chetverti* [of land], as mentioned above. As for the *deti boiarskie*, their pay is from 4 to 6 *rubles*, paid for six or seven years at a time. They all hold from 100 to 300 *chetverti* of land from the emperor. Their service, which is more to fill out the number [of troops] than anything else, customarily corresponds to their salary.

The important nobles mentioned above must have a shirt of mail, a helmet, a lance, bow, and arrows. So must each of their servitors, along with a good mount. The *dvoriane* must have fairly good horses, a bow, arrows, and a scimitar. So must their servitors. This makes a multitude of men badly mounted, without order, courage, or discipline. Many often do more damage to the army than good. Beyond this, there are the forces of Kazan, which, joined together with the Cheremissians, are said to make nearly twenty thousand horses. Then there are the Tatars who serve the emperor. These, along with the Mordvinians, will make seven or eight thousand horses. Their annual pay is from 8 up to 30 *rubles*. Then there are the Cherkasy, who are from three to four thousand. The foreigners, as many Germans and Poles as Greeks, number two thousand five hundred. They draw a salary of from 12 to 60 *rubles*. Some captains have up to 120 *rubles* and from 600 up to 1000 *chetverti* of land.

Finally, there are the *datochnye liudi* that the patriarch, bishops, abbots, and all other ecclesiastics who possess lands must furnish. As mentioned above, they must provide a man on horse and one on foot for each one hundred *chetverti* of land they hold. Depending on the army's needs, one sometimes takes from these ecclesiastics a great number of horses in place of men. These horses transport the artillery and other munitions of war, and they serve as mounts for the *strel'tsy* and others to whom horses must be furnished. That is all that need be said about the calvary.

Most of their horses come from the Nogai Tatars, which horses they call *koni*. They are of a middling size, very good for work, and they can run for seven or eight hours without being winded. However, if they become tired and winded, they need four or five months to recover completely. They are very wild and are greatly terrified by the noise of a *harquebus*. They are never shod; nor, for that matter, are the horses which come from Russia. They eat little or no oats, and they must be made accustomed little by little to that feed if one wants to give it to them. They also have jennets from the Georgians; but these are not common. They are very beautiful and good horses, but they do not compare to the *koni* for long wind or speed, unless it is just for a short run. Then they have some Turkish horses and some from Poland, which they call *argamaks*. There are some good ones among them. These horses are all geldings. Beyond this, there are found a few very good ponies among the Nogai Tatars. These are all white and spotted with black, like a tiger or leopard, so that one might think them to be painted. The horses native to the land are called *merina*. They are usually small and good, especially those which come from Vologda and that region. They are quicker to train than the horses of Tatary. A very beautiful and good horse of Tatary or of Russia can be bought for twenty *rubles*. This horse will do more service than a Turkish *argamak* horse, which costs fifty, sixty, up to a hundred *rubles*.

All their horses are subject to greater illnesses than in France. They are very subject to a malady which they call *maritsa*. This disease first appears in the chest; and if one does not cure it quickly, it goes into the legs and nothing more can be done about it. However, as soon as they perceive this malady, they pierce the skin of the horse's chest, almost between the legs, and push through this hole a cord made of hemp and of bark (which one rubs with tar). The horse is made to run two or three times a day, until it is all in a lather, and the cord is moved around often. At the end of three or four days the pus comes to maturity and leaves through the hole. This process continues up to two or three weeks. Then they withdraw the cord, the hole closes itself, and the horse is very sound after that. To avoid this malady they send all the horses into a river after the ice is melted. There they are kept in the water up to their necks for one or two hours, until they are almost unable to stand upright because of their shivering. This makes the horses very thin, for they continue this remedy for two weeks. Afterward, the horses are very agile. These horses are also very subject to short-windedness.

They do not think a horse of Tatary or of Russia to be fit for work until it is seven or eight years old, and these horses continue to work until they are twenty years old. I saw horses twenty-five to thirty years of age still render good service. They consider horses to be young at ten or twelve years, and they find very good pacers among these.

The best infantry consists of the above-mentioned *strel'tsy* and of Cossacks, of whom we have not yet spoken. Besides the ten thousand *harquebusiers* of Moscow, there are *strel'tsy* in each town within a hundred *versts* of the frontiers of Tatary. According to the size of the castles located there, sixty, eighty, up to a hundred fifty *strel'tsy* may be in each town. The towns on the actual frontier are well garrisoned.

There are Cossacks who are sent in winter to the towns in the vicinity of the Oka River. They receive pay equal to that of the *strel'tsy*, with grain; moreover, they are furnished with powder and lead by the emperor. There are other Cossacks in arms, numbering perhaps from five to six thousand, who possess lands and do not leave their garrisons. Then there are the true Cossacks who maintain themselves along the rivers in the plains of Tatary, like the Volga, the Don, the Dnieper, and others. They often do much more damage to the Tatars than the whole Russian army. They do not have large stipends from the emperor, but they do have liberty, it is said, to do the worst they can against the Tatars. They are permitted to withdraw sometimes to the frontier towns, there to sell their booty and to buy what they need. When the emperor wishes to make use of them, he sends them powder, lead, and some seven, eight, or ten thousand *rubles*. It is the Cossacks who usually bring in the first Tatar prisoners, from whom one learns the designs of the enemies. The custom is to give to whoever captures and brings in some prisoner enough good cloth and damask to make a garment from each, forty martens, a silver cup, and twenty or thirty *rubles*. On these rivers there are found up to eight to ten thousand Cossacks who will join the army on the command of the emperor, which happens in time of need. However, those Cossacks from above the Dnieper support themselves most often in Podolia.

In time of need a man from each hundred *chetverti* of land is added to the army. These recruits are all peasants, more fit to handle a plow than a *harquebus*, although one cannot tell them by their dress for they must be dressed like Cossacks. This means that each one wears a robe which comes

to below the knees, is close to the body like a doublet, and which has a large
turned-back collar descending to the waist. Half of these peasants must have
harquebuses, two pounds of powder, four pounds of lead, and scimitar. The
others, at the discretion of those who send them, carry a bow, arrows, and
scimitar or a kind of spear more proper to pierce a bear coming from its den
than for any military service they might perform with it. Moreover, in times
of necessity the merchants must furnish men according to their means, be it
three or four, more or less.

Now, as noted above, at about the beginning of Lent the Cossacks bring
in prisoners from whom one learns if the Tatars are assembling. According
to this information, orders are issued throughout the country, while the snow
is still on the ground, that each member of the military send his provisions
into the towns near which it had been resolved to await the enemy. These
provisions are brought on sleighs to these towns. They consist of *sukhari*,
which is bread cut in little pieces and dried in an oven like a biscuit. Then
there is *krupa*, which is made of millet and hulled barley, but principally of
oats. Then they have *tolokno*, which is made of oats scalded, dried, and ground
to flour. This they use in various ways, in both food and drink, putting two
or three spoonfuls of that flour in a good draught of water, along with two
or three grains of salt, stirring it, and drinking it; they consider this to be a
good and wholesome beverage. Then they have pork, beef, and mutton, salted
and dried in smoke. There is also butter and dried cheese, pounded fine like
sand. With a spoonful or two of this they make good soup. Then there is
plenty of *aqua vitae* and some dried and salted fish which they eat without
cooking. This is the provision of the most important persons; as for the others,
they content themselves with biscuit, some *krupa* of oats, and *tolokno*, with
a little salt.

The Russians seldom place themselves in the field against the Tatars until
they begin to see grass underfoot. As for other enemies, if they do not come
unexpectedly, the same plan of defense is used against them. In this way the
emperor spends little more for the army in wartime than during times of
peace, apart from recompense for those who have performed some service,
such as taking a prisoner or killing one of the enemies, receiving a wound,
or other such things. They are given money; and, depending upon the quality
of the person, each one receives a piece of cloth of gold or other silk cloth to
make a garment for himself.

⚶ *60* ⚶

Olearius' Commentaries on Muscovy in the 1630s and 1640s

Commercial, diplomatic, and cultural contacts between Muscovy and Europe attained a lively tempo in the seventeenth century. Not only did Europeans come to Moscow in greater numbers than ever before, but they also left more accurate accounts of their impressions of Muscovite politics, customs, habits, and related matters. The best of these accounts is that of Adam Olearius (1599–1671), a German scholar who, as an official of the Duke of Holstein, visited Moscow on four occasions—1634, 1636, 1639, and 1643. Olearius, who had studied at the University of Leipzig, spoke Russian, mingled with the Muscovites, and observed and recorded their virtues and follies as no foreigner had done before. Olearius' descriptions and sketches are considered a major work on the seventeenth century history of Russia, and his analysis is so penetrating and so richly rewarding for the reader that it is presented here at considerable length.

But it is time we returned to our Muscovites, whom we shall consider, first, in relation to their habit and stature, then to their humor and manner of life.

They are for the most part corpulent, fat, and strong, and of the same color as other Europeans. They much esteem great beards (when the mustaches hide the mouth) as also great bellies; so that those who are well furnished about the mouth, and have good fat pouches, are very considerable among them. The *gostis*, or the Great Duke's merchants, whom we found in the antechamber, when we were brought to our public audience, had been chosen particularly for those two perfections, for the greater honor of their prince.

The great lords shave their heads; persons of lower condition cut their hair, and priests and others belonging to the church, wear their hair so long, that it hangs down over their shoulders to half their backs. Those lords who are

---

From Adam Olearius, *Voyages and Travells of the Ambassadors Sent by Frederick Duke of Holstein to the Great Duke of Muscovy and the King of Persia . . . Containing a Complete History of Muscovy, Tatary, Persia, and Other Adjacent Countries . . .* The Second Edition Corrected. (London: 1669), pp. 56–73, 88–98, 100–108. Spelling has been modernized to facilitate reading. Words in brackets are mine.

out of favor at Court, let their hair grow and hang negligently about their heads, thereby expressing their affliction; no doubt after the example of the ancient Greeks, whom the Muscovites are apt to imitate in all their actions.

The women are well proportioned; neither too big, nor too little: having possible good faces, but they paint so palpably, that if they laid it on with a brush, and had a handful of meal cast in their faces when they had done, they could not disfigure themselves as much as the paint does. But the custom is so general, that the most handsome must comply, lest they should discredit the artificial beauty of others; whereof we saw an example in the wife of Prince Ivan Borisovich Cherkasskii, who was the handsomest lady of all Muscovy, and was loath to spoil with painting what the rest of her sex took so much pains to preserve thereby: but the other women informed against her, and would not be quiet, till their husbands had forced that prince to give way that his wife might daub her face after the ordinary manner. So that painting is so common in Muscovy, that when any are to be married, the bridegroom, that is to be, sends among other presents some paint to his bride, as we shall see when we come to speak of their marriages.

Married women put up their hair within their caps or coifs, but the maids let theirs hang down their backs in two tresses, and tie it at the ends with a piece of crimson silk. Children under ten years of age, as well girls as boys, have their hair cut, all except two mustaches, which are left over the temples; so that there being no difference in their habits, that of their sex is discovered only by the brass or silver rings, which the girls wear in their ears. . . .

If a man consider the natures and manner of life of the Muscovites, he will be forced to avow, that there cannot be anything more barbarous than that people. Their boast is that they are descended from the ancient Greeks, but, to do them no injustice, there is no more comparison between the brutality of these barbarians and the civility of the Greeks, to whom all other parts of the world are obliged for all their literature and civilization, than there is between day and night. They never learn any art or science, nor apply themselves to any kind of study: on the contrary, they are so ignorant, as to think, a man cannot make an almanac unless he be a sorcerer, nor foretell the revolutions of the moon and eclipses, unless he have some communication with devils. Upon this account it was, that the Muscovite generally grumbled when the Great Duke would have entertained me into his service, in the quality of his astronomer and mathematician, as we returned from our voyage into Persia, and raised a report that their prince was going to bring a magician into his Court. This aversion I discovered in the Muscovites, took off that little inclination I sometimes had to embrace that employment, which was offered me, not so much upon the account of my abilities in astronomy, as to engage me to continue in the country, because they knew that I had exactly observed and drawn into a map the whole course of the river Volga whereof they were unwilling that strangers should have any knowledge. When I came to Muscovy, upon the affairs of the Duke of Holstein, my master, in the year 1643, I showed them upon a wall of an obscure chamber, through a little hole I had made in the shutter of the window, by the means of a piece of glass polished and cut for optics, all that was done in the street, and men walking upon their heads. This wrought such an effect in them, that they could never after be otherwise persuaded than that I held a correspondence with the devil.

They esteem physicians, and medicine, but will not permit that people should make use of the same means as is done elsewhere to gain the perfection of that science. They will not suffer the body to be opened, so that the causes of diseases may be found out, and they have a strange aversion for skeletons. . . .

Their industry and subtlety is chiefly seen in their traffic, in which there is no craft or cheat but they make use of, rather to circumvent others, than to prevent being deceived themselves. I wondered to see them sell cloth at three crowns and a half the *ell*, which they had bought of the English at four, and yet I was told they made a good profit thereby; for buying the cloth at twelve months time per payment, and selling it for ready money, though at a lower rate, they made use of the money, and employed it in other things, which brought in more profit than they would have made by selling the cloth upon time, though they sold it much dearer than it cost them. They make a conscience to retain what is paid them more their due, and are so honest as to return what they have received by mistake: but they think it no sin, in their dealings, to surprise those who trade with them, giving this reason, that the merchant is to make his advantage of the wit and industry God has bestowed on him, or never meddle with traffic. According to this principle, a certain Dutch merchant having notoriously over-reached several Muscovites, these gentlemen were so far from being troubled at it, that they spoke of him, as of an excellent ingenious man, and desired they might go partners with him, out of a hope they conceived, that he would discover some great secrets to them.

And whereas cheating cannot be exercised without treachery, lying, and distrust, which are its constant attendants, they are marvelously well versed in these qualities as also in the features of calumny, which they commonly make use of against those on whom they would be revenged for theft, which among them is the most enormous of all crimes, and the most severely punished. To this end, they are so cunning, as to pawn at, or get secretly conveyed into their lodgings, whom they would accuse, those things which they would have believed were stolen from them, or they thrust them into their enemy's boots; for in them the Muscovites commonly carry their money and letters. To make some provisions against these abuses, the Great Duke made an edict in the year 1634, enjoining that for the future, all promises or obligations, whether for borrowing of money or pawning, though it were between father and son, should be set down in writing and signed by both parties, else the debt to be lost. Heretofore, especially in the reign of the tyrant Ivan Vasilevich, there needed no more to procure a man's death or banishment, than to accuse him of high treason, without any process, evidence, or defense allowed, all that were charged being punished, without any distinction of sex, age, or quality. Calumnies and false suggestions were so common under that prince, that many strangers, even public persons, many times fell into those misfortunes, the tyrant never regarding their character as ambassadors, nor that of the princes by whom they were sent. He banished into Siberia, the Emperor's ambassador, and caused him to be so ill-treated, that the poor man resolved at last to change his religion, hoping by his apostasy to alleviate his misery. The Great Duke Michael Feodorovich, showed no more respect for the late king of France, when he sent the Marquis of Exidueil into Siberia where, by the artifices of his colleague, James Russel, he was a prisoner three years. . . .

But now they proceed with more caution, and no man is condemned without an exact information of the crime laid to his charge. And for the utter taking away of all calumny, the accuser must be content to endure the torture first; and if, while he is in the torment, he persists in his accusation, the accused person is also put to it, nay many times he is condemned without so much as being heard. We saw an example of this in the wife of one of the Great Duke's farriers, who desirous to be rid of her husband, charged him that he would have poisoned the horses, and had he the opportunity, even the Great Duke himself. She endured the torture without varying in her accusation, and her husband was sent to prison into Siberia. We were shown this woman, who was still paid the one-half of her husband's pension. From this kind of demeanor among the Muscovites and their infidelity one to another, it may be judged what foreigners are to expect from them, and how far they are to be trusted. They never profess their friendship, nor contract any with others, but for their own interest and advantage. The ill-education they have when young, never learning anything beyond reading and writing, and certain vulgar prayers, makes them blindly follow that which in beasts is called instinct; so that nature being in them depraved and corrupted, their whole life must needs be a constant course of viciousness. Thence it comes they are brutish, doing all things according to their unbridled passions and appetites.

The fierceness of all other nations, some islanders excepted, argues something of spirit and generosity; but the opinion the Muscovites have of themselves and their abilities, is sottish, gross, and impertinent; and the pride and vain glory of those who are even so little advanced in honors or estates, is insupportable. They dissemble it not, but all their behavior, words, and actions, discover what they really are. Upon this principle they ground the fond conceit they have of the greatness, power, and wealth of their prince, whom they prefer before all the other monarchs of Europe. Thence it is also, that they would not have other princes assume those qualities which may denote their competition with him. They sottishly and insolently command ambassadors to be uncovered first, and by force take all advantages over them, imagining it were a great injury to themselves and their prince, to treat foreigners with any civility. Private persons write and speak in unhandsome terms, but such as give the less offense, in that they bear with the same treatment from others. 'Tis true, they began to learn a little civility, since they became sensible of the advantages arising to them from the commerce they have with foreigners, and there are some who use them with discretion: but of these there are very few. . . .

They are all much given to quarrelling, insomuch that in the streets they will rail at, and abuse one another like fish-wives, and that with such animosity, that those who are not acquainted with their humor think they will not part without fighting; but they seldom come to those extremities, or if they fight, it is with their fists, or switches, and the height of their rage is kicking, as much as they can, in the belly and about the sides. 'Twas never yet known that any Muscovite fought with sword or pistol, or that they are sensible of that gallantry wherein many would unjustly place true courage. The great lords, princes, and *boyars*, fight on horseback, but the weapon is a good whip, and so they soon decide what differences happen between them.

When they quarrel, they forbear cursing, swearing, and blaspheming, but rail at one another in such bitter and horrid expressions, as no country being able to parallel them, 'tis but discretion to forbear defiling this relation therewith. The language of fathers and mothers to their children, and of the children to them again, is such as cannot be expressed without horror, much beyond what the most debauched persons elsewhere are guilty of. Some year since the Great Duke prohibited these insolences upon pain of whipping, and the magistrate was ordered to send *streltsy* and sergeants among the people to surprise offenders and to see them immediately punished. But it was found by experience that the remedy came too late, and that the mischief was so deeply rooted, and so generally spread, that it was not only hard but absolutely impossible to put those prohibitions into execution. So that, for the vindication of persons of high quality an order was made, that he who affronts any such, or any of the Great Duke's officers, either by word or deed, should be fined, which fine they call *beschestie*, and sometimes amounts to 2000 crowns, according to the quality of the person injured. If an officer of the Great Duke's makes his complaint of injury done him, his reparation will be according to his relation to the Court; to a lady, 'tis doubled, to a son, 'tis augmented by a third part; to a daughter, there is an abatement of a third part: and the penalty is paid as many times as there are persons injured, though they were dead many years before. If the offender has not to pay, he is put into his adversary's hands, who disposes of him so as to make him his slave, or cause him to be whipped by the common executioner. . . .

There is nothing polite in their conversation; on the contrary, they are not ashamed to yawn, belch, and stretch themselves wherever they are, their belching being the more offensive, by reason of the abundance of onions and garlic they use in all their meat, which make their breaths strong enough without those exaltations. This they are so accustomed to, that they stick not to do it in any company, the Great Duke's presence only excepted.

They do not apply themselves to the study of any art or science, nor inquire into the affairs of other countries, and consequently never discourse of any thing: but it were well on the other side, if they could forbear talking of their uncleannesses and brutalities, which they make their divertissement in their debauches. I speak not of the entertainments of great lords, but of the ordinary company keeping of the Muscovites, where all of their discourse is of the abominations which they themselves have done, or seen committed by others, making ostentation of crimes which here would be expiated by fire, and the memory thereof buried in their ashes. But as they are wholly given up to all licentiousness, even to sins against nature, not only with men, but also with beasts, he who can tell most stories of that kind, and set them out in most gestures, is accounted the bravest man. Their fiddlers put them into songs, and their mountebanks make public representations of them, and stick not to show their breeches, and sometimes all they have to their spectators. Those who lead bears about, jugglers, and puppet players, who erect a stage in a moment, by the means of a coverlet, which, being tied about their waist, is brought up over their heads, and within it they show their puppets, representing their brutalities and sodomies, make sport to the children, who are thereby induced to quit all sentiments of shame and honesty.

Nay these are quite discarded by the Muscovites. The posture of their dancing, and the insolence of their women, are infallible marks of their bad inclinations. We have seen at Moscow both men and women come out of the public brothel-houses stark naked, and incite some young people of our retinue to naughtiness by filthy and lascivious expressions. Idleness, which is the mother of all vices, and seems to have been bestowed on these barbarous people as their portion, is that which makes them run into these excesses, whereto their drunkenness does also contribute; inasmuch as being naturally inclined to luxury, when they are once got into their wine they mind nothing else. I have to this purpose a story, which the Great Duke's interpreter told me when we were at Novgorod: how that in the said city, there is an anniversary devotion, to which come abundance of pilgrims. He who is allowed to keep a tippling-house, gets a permission from the Metropolitan, to pitch several tents, for the accommodation of the pilgrims of both sexes, who are sure to be there betimes in the morning before service, and to take some cups of strong water. Nay some of them, instead of minding their devotions, spend the day in drinking, whence arise such strange disorders, that he told me he saw a woman so drunk there, that coming out of a tent she fell down; and fell asleep, naked as she was, in the street in the daytime. Which gave occasion to a Muscovite, who was also drunk to lie down by her, and, having made use of her, to fall also asleep in sight of many people, who having made a ring about them, only laughed at the posture they were in, till at last an old man, conceiving a horror at the spectacle, covered them with his own garment.

There is no place in the world where drunkenness is more common than in Muscovy. All, of all conditions, ecclesiastics and lay, men and women, old and young, will drink strong water at any time, before, at, and after their meals. They call it *tsarkovino*, and fail not to offer it to those who visit them. The lowest sort of people, peasants and slaves, refuse not cups which are given them by some persons of quality, but will drink of it till they lie down, and many times die in the place. Nay their great ones are not free from this vice, as for example, the Muscovite ambassador, sent to Charles, King of Sweden, in the year 1608, who, forgetting his quality and the affairs his master had entrusted him with, took so much strong water the night before he was to have audience, that the next day being found dead in his bed, they were forced to carry him to his grave, instead of conducting him to audience.

The meaner sort of people think it not enough to stay in the tippling-house till they have not a *kopeck* left in their purses, but many times pawn their clothes there even to their shirts, which is no more than what is seen daily during our abode in Moscow. Being lodged at Lubeckhouse, as I went to Novgorod, in my voyage to Moscow in 1643, I saw coming out of an alehouse not far thence, several of those drunkards, some without caps, other without shoes or stockings, some without waistcoats, and only their shirts. . . .

Being in the same city of Novgorod at the time of our second embassy, I saw a priest coming out of the tippling-house, who coming by our lodging would needs give the benediction to the *strelets*, who stood sentinel at the door, but as lifted up his hands, going to make the inclination used in that ceremony, the head, fraught with the vapors of the wine, was so heavy, that weighing down the whole body, the priest fell down in the dirt. Our *strelets* took him up with much respect, and received his daggled benediction; it being, it seems, a thing very ordinary among them.

The Great Duke Michael Feodorovich [1613–1645], who was a sober person, and hated drunkenness, considering with himself that it was impossible absolutely to prevent these excesses, made in his time several orders for the moderating of them, causing the tippling-houses to be shut up, and prohibition the selling of strong water, or *hydromel* without his permission, and that those places where they were sold, should sell only by the quart and pint, and not by cups. This had some effect, in that there were no more Adamites seen in the streets, but hindered not their being strewed with drunkards, the neighbors and such of their friends, as had a design to be merry, sending to the tavern for several bottles of strong water which they would be sure to turn off ere they parted.

The women are no less given to drink than the men. I saw a pleasant example of it at Narva, in the house where I lodged, whither many Muscovite women came one day to their husbands, sat down with them, and took off their cups as smartly as they did. The men being got drunk, would have gone home, but the women thought it was not yet time to draw off, though invited thereto by a good number of boxes o' th' ear, and got their husbands to sit down again, and to drink roundly as before, till such time as that the men being fallen down asleep upon the ground, the women sat upon them, as upon benches, and drunk on till they also were forced to lie down by them. . . .

Tobacco was heretofore so common there, that it was generally taken, both in smoke and powder. To prevent the mischiefs occasioned by the use of it, which were not only that the poorer sort of people ruined themselves thereby, in as much as if they had but a penny, they would rather bestow it in tobacco than bread, but also because many times it set houses on fire and those that took it presented themselves with their stinking and infectious breaths before their images, the Great Duke and the Patriarch thought fit in the year 1634 absolutely to forbid the sale and use of it. Those who are convicted of having either taken or sold any, are very rigorously punished. They have their nostrils split or are whipped, as we have often seen done; of the manner of which punishment we shall speak when we come to treat of the administration of justice in that country.

The perverse disposition of the Muscovites, the baseness of their education, and the slavery they seem born to, cause them to be treated like beasts, rather than people endowed with reason. They are naturally so much inclined to idleness, that it were impossible to bring them to take any pains, but by the whip, and the cudgel, which yet they are not much troubled at, as being hardened to blows, by the custom which the younger sort have to meet on holidays, and to divert themselves by cuffing or fighting with staves, never being angry at what happens. Those who are free born, but poor, do so little value that advantage, that they sell themselves with their family for a small matter; nay, they are so mindless of their liberty, that they will sell themselves a second time, after they have recovered it, by the death of their master, or some other occasion.

Their submission to their superiors discovers the lowness of their spirits, and their slavery. They never come before persons of quality, but they bow down to the ground, which they touch and smite with their forehead, nay, there are some who will cast themselves at their lords' feet, to give them thanks after they have been sufficiently beaten by them. No Muscovite, what quality soever be he of, but makes his brag to be the Great Duke's *kholop* [slave], and to express their humility or abjection, even in the least things, they put their names into diminutives, and neither speak nor write to him, but instead of Ivan, they say Ivaniushka, that is the diminutive; and sign thus, *Petrushka tvoi kholop*, Peter, your slave. The Great Duke speaking to them uses the same expression, treating them in all things like slaves, as far as whips and cudgels can do it, which is but consonant to their own acknowledgment, that their persons and estates are God's and the Great Duke's. . . .

As for slaves, their number is not regulated; some lords have above a hundred of them in their country houses and farms; those they entertain for their service in the city do not diet in their houses, but have board wages, their allowance so small, that it is as much as they can do to live upon it. And this is one of the chiefest causes of the many disorders and mischiefs done at Moscow, there passing hardly a night but violences and murders are committed. Great lords and rich merchants have a guard in their courts, who watch all night, and are obliged to express their vigilance by the noise they make upon boards with a stick, much after the manner of playing upon the timbrels, which done, they give as many knocks as the clock has struck hours. But these guards watching many times more for the advantage of house breakers than of their masters, there is none used now, and no servant is taken into a house, but upon good city security of his truth.

This great number of slaves makes it unsafe to walk the streets of Moscow in the night time unarmed and without company. We had the experience of it in some of our servants upon several occasions. Our master cook, who had been employed at a person's of quality, where the ambassadors had dined, was killed as he came home in the night; which misfortune happened also to the steward belonging to the Swedish ambassador Spiring. The lieutenant, who had commanded our German and Scottish musketeers in our voyage into Persia, was in like manner killed in the night, having been with some

others at the wedding of a German merchant's daughter. And as there passed
no night almost without murder, so these disorders increased towards great
festivals, especially on flesh days, which they call *maslenitsa*. On St. Martin's
Eve, we counted fifteen dead bodies in the court of *zemskii*, a place where
they are exposed that their kins and friends may know them, and take order
for their burial. If nobody owns them, they are dragged thence like carrion
and thrown into a ditch without any ceremony.

The insolence of these villains is so great, that they stuck not to set upon
the Great Duke's principal physician in the day time. They stopped him in
the street as he was going home, struck him off his horse, and would have
cut off his finger, on which he had a gold seal-ring, had he not been relieved
by some sent to his rescue, by a prince of his acquaintance, who living near
thereabouts had seen him set upon. The misery is, that no citizen will so
much as look out of his window, much less come out of his house to relieve
those that are affronted, so much are they afraid to come into the same
misfortune they see others engaged in. Since our being there, some course has
been taken herein. Watches being set, who stop those who go in the night
without a torch or lantern and carry them to the *streletskii prikaz*, where they
are punished the next day.

At hay-making time the road between Moscow and Tver is very dangerous
to travel, by reason of the great number of slaves employed in that work,
making their advantage of a mountain whence they discover those that pass,
whom they rob and kill, without any reparation to be expected from their
masters, who, not allowing their slaves what to subsist upon, are forced to
connive at their crimes.

Masters dispose of their slaves, as they do of any other movable; nay, a
father may sell his son, and alienate him for his own advantage. But the
Muscovite have this piece of vain glory, that not only they seldom come to
those extremities, but also had rather see their children starve at home, than
suffer them to go out anywhere to service. 'Tis only debt that sometimes
engages them to make over their children to their creditors, the boys at ten,
the girls at eight crowns, a year, the children being no less obliged to satisfy
the debt than their fathers, as also to endure that cruel treatment which
desperate debtors are to expect, or to sell themselves to their creditors. . . .

The Muscovites spend not much in housekeeping, nor the *boyars*, as well
as those of a lower condition. It is not above thirty years, that their lords and
chiefest merchants have built their houses of stone: for before they were no
better lodged than the meaner sort, in very poor wooden buildings. Their
household stuff is suitable to their lodgings, and commonly consist in three
or four pots, and as many wooden or earthen dishes. Some have pewter, but
very few, and unless it be some few drinking cups and goblets, there is not

any of silver. They know not what scouring means, insomuch that the Great Duke's plate looks little better than the tavern pots, which are made clean but once a year. The better sort hang their rooms but with mat; and to set them out yet a little better, they have only two or three images wretchedly painted. They have few feather beds, but are content with mattresses, nay with chaff or straw, and if not that to be had, they lay upon their cloths, which in summer they lay upon a bench or table; in the winter, upon their stoves which are flat as in Livonia. In this country it is that master and mistress, men and maids, are shuffled all together into the same room; nay in some places in the country, I have seen the poultry and the pigs had ordinarily the same lodging with the master of the house. . .

No Muscovite, what condition or quality soever he be of, but sleeps after dinner; whence it is that about noon most shops are shut up, and the merchants or their apprentices sleeping at the door: so that about that time there is no more speaking with persons of quality or merchants, than there is at midnight.

This was one sign whereby they discovered the imposture of the pretender Dmitrii. We shall find in the ensuing story of him, that the imposter slept not after dinner, and that the Muscovites inferred thence that he was a foreigner; as also by his aversion to baths, which are so common in Muscovy, that there is neither town nor village, but has very many of them, both public and private. This is all they have gentle among them, as a thing they conceive necessary upon several occasions, especially at marriages, after the first coition.

At Astrakhan I had the curiosity to go unknown into one of them, which by a division of board was contrived into two rooms. But besides that it was easier to look out of one into the other, by reason of the distance there was between the boards, both men and women went out at the same door, those of either sex who would express a greater modesty hiding what they would not have seen with a handful of leaves, which being dried in summer, they for this purpose put a-soaking into warm water; but some were stark naked, and the women were not shy to come in that posture and speak with their husbands, even while other men stood by.

'Tis almost a miracle to see how their bodies, accustomed to, and hardened by cold, can endure so intense a heat, and how that, when they are not able to endure it any longer, they come out of the stoves, naked as the back of a man's hand, both men and women, and go into the cold water, or cause it to be poured upon them, and in winter, how they wallow in the snow. Some of our young men would often walk before these public stoves, to see the several postures of the women that came out, and diverted themselves in the water, and were so far from being ashamed, that they would talk wantonly with them, and were not troubled when any of our people came into the water to them. And this we saw not only in Muscovy, but also in Livonia, where the inhabitants, especially the Finns, who are settled there, going out of these stoves, in the coldest of the winter, run into the snow, and rub their bodies with it, as if it were soap, then return into the stoves to take advantage of a more moderate heat: and all this so as that this change of contrary qualities does not in any way prejudice their health. The reason then of it must be custom, in as much as being thus used from their childhood, and that habit being as it were converted into a second nature, they are indifferently enured to both heat and cold. . . .

The Muscovites are of a healthy and strong constitution, long lived and seldom sick; which when they are, their ordinary remedies, even in burning fevers, are only garlic and strong waters. Persons of quality make use of physicians, though but within these few years, and are persuaded that remedies may do them good.

Fornication is very common among them, and yet they permit not public stews, which diverse other Christian princes not only permit, but authorize, and have an advantage arising out of them for their protection. Marriage is thought honorable among them, and polygamy forbidden. A widower or widow may marry twice or thrice, but must not offer at a fourth marriage, which if they should, the priest that should bless them would be cast off.

They observe in their marriages the degrees of consanguinity, and do not willingly marry such as are near to them either by kindred or alliance. Nor do they permit two brothers to marry two sisters; and they observe also a spiritual alliance, not suffering that godfathers and godmothers of the same person should intermarry. The celebration of marriage among them is thus.

Young men and maids are not suffered to see one another, much less to have any discourse of marriage, or to make any promise one to another, by word or writing. But when those who have children marriageable, especially daughters, have found out a match they like, they speak to the young man's parents, and declare the desire they have to make an alliance with them. If they approve of what is proposed, and the young man desire to see the maid, yet is it absolutely denied. If she be handsome, they will be content the mother or some other woman of the kindred, should see her, and if she be no way defective, that is, neither blind nor lame, the friends on both sides treat about the marriage, and conclude all things, the intended young couple not so much as being allowed to see one another. For they bring up their daughters in very private chambers (especially persons of quality) where they keep them locked up, so as that the bridegroom does not see his bride till she is brought into his chamber. And thus it comes to pass, that he who thinks he has married a handsome maid, has some crooked piece put upon him; nay, instead of the man's daughter he was to have, some kinswoman or servant maid is thrust upon him; of which I have several examples. So that it is not to be wondered at, that matrimonial discontents are so frequent among them. . . .

As soon as the wedding is over, the women must resolve to live a retired life, and not to go out of the house but very seldom, receiving the visit of their kindred and friends oftener than they give any. The daughters of great persons, and rich merchants, as they are not much brought up to housekeeping, so they trouble themselves but little with it, when they are married. Their chief employment is sewing, or embroidering handkerchiefs of white taffeta or cloth, or making little purses or some such toys. The clothes they wear within doors are made of some common stuff of little value; but when they go to the church, or that their husbands would honor a friend with their presence, they are magnificently clad, and forget not to paint their faces, necks, and arms. . . .

It is not to be much wondered that they are so hardly treated by their husbands, for they have lewd tongues, are given to wine, and will not let slip the opportunity to pleasure a friend. So that having all these three excellent qualities, they cannot take much unkindly the cudgellings, which they from time to time receive from their husbands: but they take comfort from the example of their friends and neighbors, who, behaving themselves after the same manner, are accordingly no better treated. Yet I cannot believe what Barclay says in his *Icon Ammorum*, that the Muscovite women are not persuaded their husbands love them, if they are not beaten by them; at least I can say this, I never met with any who were glad when they were beaten. They have the same passions and inclinations as other women have. They are sensible of good and bad usage, and it is not likely they should take the effects of anger and displeasure for expressions of kindness and friendship.

It is possible some foolish women might tell her husband so in jest, or that one distracted might desire to be beaten, such as she of whom Petrejus in his *Chronicle of Moscovy* speaks of, who having lived many years in good correspondence with her husband (who was an Italian, as he says, though the Baron of Herberstein affirms he was a German, and by profession a blacksmith, named Jordan) told him one day that she could not believe he loved her, since he had not yet beaten her. The husband willing to assure her of his real affection gave her a good cudgelling, and perceiving that she took a certain pleasure in it, made use of that exercise so often, till at last she died. But were it granted that this is but a story, as it seems to be no other, yet ought we not to judge of all the Muscovite women by this particular example.

They think that adultery is not committed but when one man marries another man's wife: whatever else may be done amounts but to fornication, and when a married man is taken in it, his punishment is whipping, and some days imprisonment, or happily he is sentenced to live some time on bread and water. Then he is set at liberty, and may resent the complaints made by his wife against him upon that occasion. A husband who can convince his wife of a miscarriage of this nature, may have her shaved and put her into a monastery. Those who are weary of their wives often make use of this pretense, accuse their wives of adultery, and suborn false witnesses, upon whose depositions they are condemned without being heard. Religious women are sent to her lodgings, who put her into their habit, shave her, and carry her away by force into the monastery, whence she never comes out, having once suffered the razor to come upon her head.

The most ordinary cause of divorce, at least the most plausible pretense, is devotion. They say they love God better than their wives, when the humor takes them to go into a monastery: which they do without their consent, or making any provision for the children they have had between them. And yet this kind of retiring out of this world is so much approved among them (though St. Paul says that such are worse than heathens and infidels) that if the woman marries again they make no difficulty to confer priesthood on this new proselyte, though before he had been but a tailor, or shoemaker. Barrenness is also another cause of divorce in Muscovy: for he who has no children by his wife may put her into a monastery, and marry again within six weeks. . . .

The Muscovites are extremely venereous, yet will not have to do with a woman, but they must first take off the little cross which is hanged about her neck when she is christened; nor would they do it in a place where there are any images of their saints, till they have covered them. They go not to church the day they have dealt with a woman till they have washed themselves and changed their shirts. Those that are more devout go not into it at all, but say their prayers at the door. Priests are permitted to come into the church the same day, provided they have washed themselves above and below the navel, but dare not approach the altar. The women are considered more impure than the men, and therefore they ordinarily stay at the church door all service time. He who lies with his wife in Lent may not communicate that year; and if a priest commits that offense he is suspended for a year; but if one that pretends to priesthood be so unhappy as to fall into it, he can never recover himself, but must quit his pretension.

Their remedy against this kind of uncleanness is rather bathing than repentance, which is the reason they use the former upon all occasions. Dmitrii, who impersonated the son of the Great Duke Ivan Vasilevich, who had been killed long before at Uglich, never bathed himself, upon which the Muscovites suspected him to be a foreigner. For perceiving he would not make use of a bath made ready for him eight days after his marriage, they conceived a horror against him, as a heathen and profane person, sought diverse other pretenses, set upon him in the castle, and killed him the nineteenth day after his wedding. . . .

The politic government of Muscovy is monarchial and despotical. The Great Duke is the hereditary sovereign of it, and so absolute that no prince or lord in all his dominions but thinks it an honor to assume the quality of his majesty's *kholop*, or slave. No master has more power over his slaves than the Great Duke has over his subjects, what condition or quality soever they be of. So that Muscovy may be numbered among those states whereof Aristotle speaks when he says there is a kind of monarchy among the barbarians which comes near tyranny. For since there is no other difference between a legitimate government and tyranny than that in the one the welfare of the subjects is of greatest consideration, in the other the particular profit and advantages of the prince, we must allow that Muscovy inclines much to tyranny. We said before that the greatest lords think it is not below them to put their names in the diminutive; nor is it long since that for a small matter they were whipped like slaves, but now their lesser miscarriages are punished with two or three days imprisonment. . . .

No people in the world have a greater veneration for their prince than the Muscovites, who from their infancy are taught to speak of the Tsar as of God Himself, not only in their acts and public assemblies, but also in their entertainments and ordinary discourse. Thence proceed their submissive forms of speaking: The honor to see the brightness of the eyes of his Tsarist Majesty; only God and the Tsar know it; all they have belongs to God and the Tsar. The Great Duke Ivan Vasilevich [Ivan IV] reduced them to these submissions. . . .

When we said the state of Muscovy was monarchial were presupposed that the prince is a monarch and has alone all the prerogatives of sovereignty. He is not subject to the laws; he only makes them and all the Muscovites obey him with so great submission, that they are so far from opposing his will that they say: the justice and word of their prince is sacred and inviolable.

He only creates magistrates and deposes them, ejects them, and orders them to be punished with such absolute power that we may say of the Great Duke what the Prophet Daniel says of the king of Babylon, that he put to death whom he would and saved whom he would. He appoints governors and lieutenants for the provinces for the disposal of the ancient *demesne* and administration of justice, who have with them a *diak*, or secretary, and these take cognizance of all matters, give final and absolute judgment in all cases and cause their sentences to be put in execution without any appeal. . . .

He alone has the power to make war and peace with other princes. For though he takes the advice of his princes and *boyars*, yet he does not always follow it, but makes them know that notwithstanding the freedom he gives them to advise him, he reserves to himself the power of doing what he thinks fit.

He only confers honors and rewards the services that are done him with the qualities of princes, *boyars*, dukes; and whereas the Muscovites have heard that it is a mark of sovereignty in Germany to make doctors, the Great Duke meddles with that also and grants letters patents to physicians and surgeons who are foreigners. . . .

He only levies taxes and impositions and regulates them according to his pleasure, so as that he takes five in the hundred upon all merchandise upon the frontiers of his dominions, both coming and going out.

It is his prerogative to send ambassadors to the Emperor, the kings of Poland, Denmark, Sweden, and other princes, his neighbors. These ministers are either *Velikii posol*, Great Ambassador, or *poslannik*, or Envoy. Heretofore, especially in the time of Ivan Vasilevich, they treated foreigners, even the public ministers of princes, with much disrespect; but now it is otherwise. Ambassadors are entertained with great civility; and their charges defrayed from the day of their entrance into the Great Duke's dominions, to that of their departure thence, they are treated at great feasts and have very rich presents bestowed upon them. Whence it comes that other European princes make no difficulty to send their ambassadors thither, nay some have their ordinary residents there, as the kings of England and Sweden. All the presents made by the Great Duke consist in furs, and he never sends any solemn embassy but it carries such as are very considerable for the prince to whom it is sent. . . .

Heretofore the Muscovites had but few laws and few customs according to which all cases were decided. They concerned only attempts against the Great Duke's person; treason against the state; adulteries; thefts; and debts between private persons. The decision of all other affairs depended on the breast of the judge. But in the year 1647, the Great Duke assembled together the most famous men of the kingdom, and caused to be set down in writing, and to be published, several laws and ordinances, whereby the judges are to regulate themselves. They were printed in folio under the title of *Sobornoe Ulozhenie*, that is to say, universal and general right for the direction of the *boyars*.

Heretofore their proceedings were thus. In those cases where the parties were not agreed as to the matter of fact, and had no evidence of either side, the judge asked the defendant whether he would take his oath, that the matter was as he alleged, or refer it to the plaintiff's oath. He who proffered to take his oath was once a week for three weeks one after another brought before the judge, who every time pressed into him the importance of an oath and the sin he would burden his conscience withal, if he swore falsely. If, notwithstanding these remonstrances, he still persisted in his readiness to take his oath, though he swore nothing but the truth, yet people looked on him as an infamous person, would spit in his face and turn him out of the church, into which he was never received afterwards, much less was he admitted to the communion, unless it were at the point of death. Now they do not proceed with so much rigor, but only bring him, who is to take his oath, before an image of one of his saints where he is asked whether he will take his oath upon the salvation of his soul. If he persists, they give him a little Crucifix to kiss, and afterwards the saint's image, which for that purpose is taken down from the wall. If the oath be good, the party who took it is not to be admitted to the communion for three years, and though he be not treated as an infamous person, yet those of any quality will not easily suffer him in their company; but a perjured person is severely punished, first cruelly whipped, then banished. Whence it comes that the Muscovites endeavor all they can to avoid it, though upon any trivial occasion, especially in their dealings, they stick not to swear at every word, and have incessantly in their mouths their *po Khristu*, by Christ, making the sign of the cross at the same time; but there is little credit to be given to these kinds of oaths, as proceeding from deceit and passion. They permit foreigners to take their oaths according to the rules of their several religions.

No invention but they make use of to force people to confess the truth by torture. One of the most cruel, in my opinion, is the *strapado*, which is given in this manner. The malefactor, having his hands tied behind him, is wound up into the air and so hangs, having fastened to his feet a great beam upon which the executioner ever and again gets up to augment the pain and further the dislocation of the members, while the smoke and fire which are made under his feet, burns and stifles him. Sometimes they cause the malefactor's head to be shaven, and as he is so hanging they pour cold water drop by drop, upon the crown, which is such a torment as no other comes near, not even that of whipping (which they many times give those in that condition), though they at the same time clap a red-hot iron upon the stripes.

In ordinary quarrels, he who gives the first blow gets the worst. Murder committed without any necessity of defense is punished with death. The guilty person is kept six weeks in a very close prison, and fed only with bread and water, after which he receives the communion and has his head cut off.

Thieves are tortured that they may discover their accomplices, and confess their other crimes. If it be the first offense, they are whipped from the castle gate to the great market place, where the offender has an ear cut off, and is put into prison for two years. If he offends the second time, he is punished in the same manner, and is kept in prison till he has company, to be banished to Siberia. Theft is never punished with death in Muscovy; but the concealers and receivers fare no better, which is the best course that could be taken to bridle the lewd inclinations of that people.

The ordinary punishments are slitting the nostrils, whipping, and the *batovki*. The last is not always infamous and public; yet is there not any master of a family, but gives it his children and servants. He who is to receive this chastisement puts off his *kaftan*, and having only his shirt on, lays himself down upon his belly, and then two men set themselves cross upon him, one upon his neck, the other upon his feet, having each of them a little wand or switch in his hand, wherewith they beat him upon the back, much after the manner that feltmongers beat their furs to get out the worms. They ordinarily have their nostrils slit who have taken tobacco, in snuff, contrary to the Great Duke's prohibition.

Whipping, as it is given in Muscovy, is one of the most barbarous punishments that ever were heard of. September 24, 1634, I saw eight men and one woman whipped for selling of *aqua vitae* and tobacco. The executioner's man took them up one after another upon his back, being stripped down to the waist, and having their feet tied together with a cord, which passing between his legs that held them up, was held by another servant of the executioner's, so fast that they were not able to stir. The executioner stood three paces off with a bull's pizzle, having fastened to the end of it three straps or thongs of an elk's skin, not tanned, and consequently as sharp as a razor, with which he laid on their backs with all his strength, so that the blood gushed out at every lash. The men had each of them twenty-five or twenty-six till the clerk, who had in a note what number of lashes they were to receive, cried *dovolno*, that is to say, enough. The woman had but sixteen yet did she fall into a swoon. Being thus disciplined, so as their backs were in a manner sliced and slashed all over, yet were they all tied by the arms, two and two together—those who had sold tobacco, having a little horn full of it, and those who had sold *aqua vitae*, a little bottle about their necks— and whipped through the city. And after they had walked them about half a league about, they were brought back to the place of their first execution and dismissed. This is so cruel a punishment that some die of it. . . . Some after they are thus punished wrap themselves up in the skin of a sheep newly killed.

Heretofore these punishments were not infamous, and those who had passed through the executioner's hands were admitted into the best companies, as was also the executioner himself, whose profession was considered so honorable that sometimes even merchants quit theirs, to serve the magistrate at executions, and would buy the employment, and after certain years sell it again to others. The advantage of it is in this, that the executioner is not only paid by the judge, but gets money also out of the criminal to be more gently treated, though indeed the greatest profit he makes comes from the *aqua vitae*, which he sells underhand to the prisoners. But now this employment is not much courted since the Muscovites have begun to learn somewhat of civility from their neighbors. Nor is the executioner permitted to sell his office, but it must continue in his family, which failing, the butchers are obliged to recommend to the place one of their body.

All we said of the cruelty of their punishments is yet below what they inflict on such as cannot pay their debts. He who pays not at his time, mentioned in the bond, is put into a sergeant's house, having a certain further time to make satisfaction. If he fail, he is carried to prison, whence he is every day brought out to the place before the Chancery, where the common executioner beats him upon the shin bone with a wand about the bigness of a man's little finger for a whole hour. That done, he is returned to prison, unless he can put in security to be forthcoming the next day at the same hour, to be treated in the same manner, till he has made satisfaction. And this is executed with such rigor upon all sorts of persons, what conditions or quality soever they be of, subjects or foreigners, men or women, priests or lay persons. . . .

As to the religion of the Muscovites, before we enter into the discourse of it, we shall say that there have been Lutheran doctors in Sweden and Livonia, who have made it a problematical question whether the Muscovites were Christians or not. They might as well have made it disputable in their acts whether the Muscovites are men; since there is not so great a difference between their religion and that of other Christians as there is between their morality and manner of life and that of many other men; but as laughter and speech makes them men, so baptism and their external profession of the Christian religion denominates them Christians. If a man would take their word for it, they are the only true Christians in the world, since they only have been baptized, whereas others have been only sprinkled. . . .

'Tis true, their religion is full of abundance of chaffy superstitions; in that they consider the Virgin Mary, the Evangelists, the Apostles, and an infinite number of other saints, not only as simple intercessors, as the most intelligent affirm, but also as causes and cooperators of their salvation. There is no Muscovite but gives his saints and their images the honor due only to God, who is so jealous thereof, that He treats the false worship as spiritual whoredom. The ignorance of the meaner sort of people is so gross that they place all religion in the honors and veneration they give their images. It is also the instructions they give their children, who in order to devotion, learn only to stand with great respect before those images to say their prayers. Their good works (which they believe meritorious) are building of monasteries and churches, and giving alms; besides which they do nothing whereby a man might judge of their faith by their works. . . .

The Muscovites in their schools learn only to read and write in their own language, and care not for the learning of any other; but within these few years they have, with the Patriarch's consent, opened a school where Greek and Latin are taught under the direction of a native Greek, named Arsenius. It is not yet known what may be expected from it, but certain it is that there are among the Muscovites those that want neither ingenuity nor an inclination to study, and would learn anything did they but meet with anybody to teach them. . . .

Those who are to profess the Muscovite religion are obliged to go for six weeks into a monastery, where the monks instruct them and teach them their prayers, the manner of honoring the saints, of doing reverence to their images, the making the sign of the cross. Then they are brought to the place where they are to be baptized, where they are obliged to adjure their former religion, to detest it as heretical and to spit as often as it is named. After their baptism they are clad in Muscovite habits, being presented with a noble vestment from the Great Duke, who also allows them a pension suitable to their quality.

There is a great number of apostates in Moscow, where many foreign soldiers, especially French, were rebaptized after the War of Smolensk, about twenty-five years since, though they were not acquainted with the language of the country, nor had any knowledge of the Muscovite religion. Which may in some measure be excusable in common soldiers who mind not what they are to expect in the other world; but my wonder is, how persons of quality, such as want neither ingenuity nor judgment, should be inclined to apostatize and embrace a contrary religion, merely for subsistence sake. . . .

Those Muscovites who change their religion in other countries, and would return to their communion, must be first rebaptized; which is the more observable in that the Greek religion, though she approves not the baptism of the Latin church, yet seems to be satisfied with the former which they might have received in their church so as not to oblige converts to rebaptization upon their change of religion. . . .

[They] have images painted with oil upon wood, wretchedly colored and ill-proportioned, about a foot in breadth, somewhat more in length. They will not meddle with them if they are not made by one of their religion, though they came from the best painter's hand in Europe. At Moscow there is a particular market place for images where nothing else is sold, though they call that kind of commerce bartering or trucking with money, out of a belief they have that the names of buying and selling carry not enough respect in them for sacred things. Heretofore they obliged foreigners to have of them in their houses that their Muscovite servants might be thereby excited to the exercise of their devotion; but the present Patriarch permits not, they should be profaned by the Germans; insomuch that Charles du Moulin, having bought a stone house, the seller scraped the wall where an image had been painted and carried away what he had scraped off. The peasants would not permit us to touch them, not to turn our feet toward them when we lay down. Nay, some were at the charge of incense to purify them after we had left their houses.

The walls of their churches are full of them, and they represent for the most part our Savior, the Virgin Mary, St. Nicholas, Patron of Moscow, or the particular saints they make choice of for the principal object of their devotions. Those who commit sins deserving excommunication are obliged to cause their saint to be taken away, who is not to be suffered in their churches no more than their persons. Great persons and rich merchants adorn their images with pearls and other precious stones. All Muscovites look upon them as things so necessary as that without images they could not say their prayers, which whenever they do they always set wax candles before their saint and look very steadfastly upon him as long as the devotion lasts. . . .

The Muscovites respect their images as if there were somewhat of divinity in them, and they attribute unto them the virtue of miracles, whereof we had this example in the year 1643, that an old image began to change color and to turn a little reddish, they immediately cried out a miracle. The Great Duke and the Patriarch were frightened thereat, as if that red color presaged some misfortune to either the Prince or the people; nay they sent out orders for extraordinary fasts and public prayers to be made all over the kingdom, if the painters who were sent for to have their advice in this affair had not all assured them that there was nothing they should be troubled at, since there was nothing extraordinary, but that time, having consumed and eaten out the paint, had only discovered the first color of the wood, which was red.

Their monks and priests have nevertheless the art to make them do miracles, or to observe such things in them as oblige the people to extraordinary devotions, which must not want their offerings, that the priest may not want his advantage. The city of Archangel furnishes us with a good example to this purpose, of two priests there, who, having got together a vast sum of money by their impostures, must needs fall out at the parting of it, and upbraid one another of their cheats so loudly that the magistrate coming to hear of it, they had thirty lashes apiece with the executioner's good will, after the manner we have before described their whipping. These jugglers put the people into continuous frights, and besought them with so strange a veneration for their images that in their greatest dangers their recourse is only to them. . . .

As to their churches, we said, there were about 2000 churches and chapels in the city and suburbs of Moscow. Those which are of stone are round and vaulted, because God's houses ought to represent heaven, which is his throne. They have neither seats nor benches, by reason none sit down, but all say their prayers either standing or kneeling. The late Great Duke, who was much given to devotion, lay all along upon the ground when he said his prayers. They have no organs or other musical instruments in their churches, not using any out of this persuasion, that things inanimate cannot glorify God; that they were allowed in the pedagogy of the Law, but that under the New Testament, they were no more to be used than any other of the Jewish ceremonies. The Patriarch that now is has shown his enmity to music, yet greater, in prohibiting the use of all those musical instruments which the Muscovites were wont to make use of at their merry meetings. Some four or five years ago, he caused all private houses to be searched for instruments, and having loaded five wagons with them, he sent them over the River of Moscow, where they were all burnt. Only the Germans kept theirs, nor could the Patriarch, with all his authority, oblige the *boyar* Boris Nikita Ivanovich Romanov to put away his musicians. . . . They hold the [churches] are profaned by foreigners such as are not of their communion; upon which account it was that, when at the beginning of our travels, we entered into them, they came out and thrust us out, and many times they swept after us. If it chance a dog gets in, they think it not enough to sweep the church, but they also incense it, and purify it with holy water. They also have much respect for their church yards, and suffer not that any should make their water in them. . . .

The ecclesiastical government consists of a Patriarch, several Metropolitans, Archbishops, Bishops, Arch-deacons, Protopops, and Priests. The Patriarch among them has the same authority as the Pope has in the Latin Church. The Patriarch at Constantinople had heretofore the nomination of him. In time he came to have only the confirmation of him; but now of late he has lost both. Filaret Nikitich, the late Great Duke's father, was the last that desired confirmation from the Patriarch of Constantinople. At present the Patriarch of Moscow is chosen by the other prelates who meet in the great church within the castle, called *sobor*, and name two or three prelates of the most eminent for learning and good life and present them to the Great Duke, who, after some conference with the prelates proceeds jointly with them to the election; unless those that are named be all of such eminence that they are at a loss which to make choice of, and so forced to it by lot, which course they took at the election of this last Patriarch. He was a prelate of the second order, and had been named with two other Metropolitans, upon the reputation of his good life. The lot falling upon him, all those of the first order were discontented thereat, so that they put it to the lot a second time, in which also it fell again to him: but the ambition of the other competitors appearing still in their countenances, the Great Duke was pleased to comply with them and to put it to the lot a third time, which fell in like manner to the same person, upon which all acquiesced. His name is Nikon, and he had been before Metropolitan of Rostov and Iaroslav, and is now about forty-five years of age. He lives within the palace, where he has built him a house of stone. He keeps a good table, and is a person of so pleasant a disposition that he discovers it in those actions that require the greatest gravity. For a handsome gentlewoman being presented to him for his benediction after she had been rebaptized with several others of her friends, he told her that he was in some doubt whether he should begin with the kiss, which is given to proselytes after their baptism, or with the benediction.

The Patriarch's authority is so great that he in manner divides the sovereignty with the Great Duke. He is the supreme judge of all the ecclesiastical cases, and absolutely disposes of whatever concerns religion, with such power that in things relating to the political government, he reforms what he conceives prejudicial to Christian simplicity and good manners without giving the Great Duke any account of it, who, without any contestation commands the orders made by the Patriarch to be executed. . . .

They have a great number of monasteries, both for men and women, as well in cities as up and down the country, and they all in a manner follow the rule of Great St. Basil. Indigence, age, infirmities, domestic discontents, and violence fill their convents, rather than devotion. When any embrace that kind of life of their own accord, if they are of ability, they are permitted to carry some part of their estates along with them into the monastery, but are obliged to leave the remainder to their heirs. Heretofore, the more superstitious sort made over all they had, and the extravagance had so far prevailed on many, that in time, the monks would have been masters of the best part of Muscovy, if a course had not been taken to prevent it. They have set hours for their service, and they say most of their prayers by beads. Their austerity of life is very great in as much as they live only on salted fish, honey, milk, cheese, herbs, and pulse, especially cucumbers, fresh and pickled, which they mince very small and eat with a spoon in some of their *kvas*. They have this common with all the other Muscovites, that they can hardly write and read. Not one in ten can say the Lord's Prayer, much fewer that are acquainted with the Creed and the Ten Commandments. These monks live not so retired a life, but that they are seen in great numbers, both in cities and all over the country, where their employment is the same with that of the peasants from whom they are distinguished only by their habit. It is also true there are abundance of *anchorets*, who build chapels upon the highways, and live in woods like hermits, subsisting only by the alms given them by travellers. . . .

Their interments are accompanied by abundance of ceremonies, as indeed are all their public actions. As soon as the sick person is departed, they send for all his kindred and friends, who being come into the house stand about the body, excite one another to bemoan him, as it were to heighten the lamentations of the women, and ask the deceased why he would die. Whether his affairs were in good condition? Whether he wanted meat and drink? Whether his wife were not handsome and young enough? Whether she had been unconstant to him? etc. Then they send a present of beer, *aqua vitae*, and *hydromel* to the priest, that he may pray for the soul of the deceased party. The body is well washed, and after they have put a clean shirt or a shroud about him, they put on his feet a pair of new shoes of a very thin Russian leather, and so they lay him into the coffin with his arms across the breast. Their coffins are made of the trunk of a tree and are to be sold everywhere. It is covered with a cloth, or haply with some coat of the deceased, and carried to the church. If it be a rich man, and that the season of the year permit it, he is not buried so soon, but kept above ground eight or ten days during which the priest comes to incense the corpse and cast holy water on it every day.

The funeral solemnity is after this manner. First there goes a priest, carrying the image of the saint which had been assigned the deceased at his baptism for his patron. Next go four virgins of the next of kin to the deceased, who are to go as mourners, and who fill the air with their horrid cries and lamentations, keeping such exact time, that they both give over and then begin all together. Then follows the body carried by six men upon their shoulders; and if it be a monk or a nun, some of their own profession do them that office. The priests go all about the body, and incense it all the way to keep off evil spirits, and withal sing certain psalms. The kindred and friends follow the body, but without any order, having every one a wax candle in his hand.

Being come to the grave, the coffin is uncovered, and the image of the deceased party's saint is held over him, while the priest says certain prayers, in which there come often these words: Lord look upon this soul in righteousness, as also some passages of their liturgy, during which the widow continues her lamentations, and makes the same questions she had done before. Then the kindred and friends take leave of the deceased, kissing either him or the coffin, and at last the priest comes up to him, and puts between his fingers a piece of paper, which is a kind of testimonial of his behavior in this world, signed by the Patriarch, or the Metropolitan of the place, and the confessor, who sell those papers dear or cheap, according to their abilities who buy them. This testimonial, which is a kind of pass for his admittance into the other world, runs thus: We whose names are hereunto subscribed, the Patriarch, or Metropolitan, and Priest of the city of _____, do make known and certify, by these presents, that the bearer of these our letters has always lived among us like a good Christian, professing the Greek religion; and though he has committed some sins, yet that he has confessed the same, and that thereupon he has received absolution, and taken the communion, for the remission of his sins: That he has honored God and his saints; that he has said his prayers, and that he has fasted on the hours and days appointed by the church, and that he has carried himself so well toward me, who am his confessor, that I have no reason to complain of him, nor to deny him the absolution of his sins. In witness whereof, we have given him the present testimonial to the end that upon sight thereof, St. Peter may open unto him the gate of eternal bliss. As soon as he has this passport given him, the coffin is shut up and put into the grave, with the face of the deceased turned toward the East. Those who accompanied him thither do their devotion to the images, and return to the house of the deceased, where they find dinner ready, and where many times they drown their affliction with all other sentiments of mortality in *hydromel* and *aqua vitae*. Their mourning lasts forty days, during which they make three feasts for the kindred and friends of the deceased, to wit, the third, the ninth, and the twentieth day after the burial. . . .

Some build huts over their graves which they cover with mats for the convenience of the priest, who, morning and evening for the space of six weeks, is to make prayers there for the deceased. For though the Muscovites do not believe there is any purgatory, yet they say there are two several places to which the souls retire after their departure out of the body, where they expect the day of judgment; some in a pleasant and delightful place, having conversation with angels; others in a sad and dark valley, having the society of devils. That the souls being yet in their way, may be diverted out of the evil way by the prayers of priests and monks, nay, that these have so great an interest with God as to obtain a certain ease and alleviation of their misery, for those souls which are with the devils, and to appease him against the day of judgment. Such as are of ability give alms daily during the six weeks; which may indeed be ordinary among the Muscovites who made no difficulty to enrich themselves any way, and believe that sin is to be expiated by alms. Whence it comes that no Muscovite almost, but, as he goes to church, or about his occasions, buys bread, which he afterwards distributes among the poor, who, though very numerous, yet get so much, that being not able to consume all themselves, they dry up the rest in an oven and make it a kind of biscuit, which they call *sukhar* and sell it in the market to travelers.

The Muscovites tolerate all sorts of religions and suffer all nations to live among them, as Calvinists, Lutherans, Armenians, Tatars, Turks, and Persians, excepting none, but Jews and Roman Catholics. There is a great number of Protestants all over Muscovy, and in the city of Moscow itself there are about a thousand who have the free exercise of their religion. Those of the Reformed religion and the Lutherans had their churches heretofore in the quarter of *Tsargorod*; but it is about twenty years since that the Lutherans lost theirs by the imprudence of their wives; because those of merchants would not give place to the officers' wives, who indeed for the most part were but servant-maids, dressed up a little finer than they had gone before. The contest grew so high that they came from words to blows in the very church, with so much scandal that the Patriarch, then accidentally passing by, having understood the occasion of their falling out, commanded the church to be demolished, which was immediately done. But they were permitted to build another in the quarter *Bolshoi gorod*. They took away their church from those of the Reformed religion because, not content with the wooden chapel which had been given them within the white wall, they would needs build there an edifice of stone, which was in a manner finished, when the Patriarch, who had not given him consent for the doing of it, caused both to be pulled down. Now foreigners have neither church nor houses within the city. For the Germans, finding themselves exposed to the decision of the Muscovites, after the Patriarch had ordered them to go in a habit distinct from that of the inhabitants of the country, to free themselves out of that persecution, petitioned the Tsar to protect them against the outrages and affronts they daily received. On the other side the priests complained that foreigners built on their foundations, and lessened the revenue of the livings; so that the Great Duke, to please both sides assigned them without the city, near the gate called *Pokrovi*, a place big enough to contain all the houses of foreigners, who immediately demolished those they had in the city, and in a short time made up that part of the suburbs, which is called *Novaia innozemskaia sloboda* [New Foreign Quarter], where the Lutherans have two churches, and those of the Reformation two more, one for the Dutch and the other for the English; and where they have this further satisfaction that they converse but little with the Muscovites, and are out of all danger of those frequent fires which commonly begin in the houses of those barbarous Christians.

The Lutherans, and those of the Reformed religion live very quietly together, and the Muscovites trade indifferently with either; but they have so great an aversion for the Roman Catholics that they would never grant them a toleration of their religion in Muscovy. In the year 1627, the late king of France proposed, by Louis des Hayes, a treaty for the regulation of commerce with the French, and at the same time for a church where they might have Mass said, but it was denied. And in the first war of Smolensk, they would not entertain Catholic soldiers. Nay in the treaty they made with us for our passage into Persia, it is an express article that we should not take any Roman Catholics into our retinue. So that it is much to be admired that they should call to the crown Wladislaw, Prince of Poland and Sweden; though that election came to nothing, for reasons into which it is beside the subject of our relation to inquire, as it is also into those which may be given of the animosity of the Muscovites against the Roman Catholics, whereof the grounds are to be searched for in ecclesiastical history, which has nothing common with the relation of our travels. . . .

☙ *61* ❧

The Code of Law of 1649

One of the most important documents of seventeenth century Russia is the *Ulozhenie*, or Code of Law, of 1649. Prepared by a landed assembly (*zemskii sobor*), the *Ulozhenie* represents the first serious Russian attempt at codification. It consists of 968 articles grouped into twenty-five chapters of unequal length. The complete Table of Contents and Chapters I, II, IV, V, and VI are included here.

The *Ulozhenie*, among the other things, legalized the complete enserfment of the peasantry, granted the nobles broad privileges, furthered the consolidation of absolutism, and prohibited the further expansion of church and monastery estates. The *Ulozhenie*, in other words, provided the direction for Russia's development, and many of its basic provisions remained in force until 1833. This fact, however, should not be interpreted as a testimonial to the *Ulozhenie*'s merits, but rather, in the words of historian V. O. Kliuchevskii, as an indication that "Russia could do without a decent collection of laws."

From M. N. Tikhomirov and P. P. Epifanov, eds., *Sobornoe Ulozhenie 1649 g.* (The Code of Law of the 1649 Assembly) (Moscow: Izdatelstvo Moskovskogo Universiteta, 1961), pp. 70–75, 78–81. Translation mine. Words in brackets are mine.

Chapter
    I.   Blasphemers and Heretics (9 articles)
   II.   The Sovereign's Honor and How to Guard His Health (22 articles)
  III. The Sovereign's Court, so That There Will be no Outrages or Disorders at the Sovereign's Court (9 articles)
  IV. Forgers of Documents, Signatures, and Seals (4 articles)
   V. Mint Masters Who May Counterfeit Money (2 articles)
  VI. Permits to Travel into Other Countries (6 articles)
 VII. The Service of Diverse Military People of the Muscovite State (32 articles)
VIII. The Redemption of Captives (7 articles)
  IX. Tolls, Ferries, and Bridges (20 articles)
   X. Legal Procedure (287 articles)
  XI. Legal Procedure Concerning the Peasants (34 articles)
 XII. Legal Procedure Concerning All Subjects of the Patriarchal Department, the Court, and Peasants (3 articles)
XIII. The Monastery Department (7 articles)
XIV. The Oath (10 articles)
 XV. Contracts (5 articles)
XVI. *Pomestie* [Service] Estates (69 articles)
XVII. *Votchina* [Hereditary] Estates (55 articles)
XVIII. Seal Taxes (71 articles)
XIX. *Posadskie liudi* [Townsmen] (40 articles)
 XX. Legal Procedure Concerning *Kholops* [Bondmen] (119 articles)
XXI. Robbery and Theft Cases (104 articles)
XXII. An Instruction Regarding Offenses That Deserve Capital Punishment and Those That Do Not, but Which Should Be Punished (26 articles)
XXIII. The *Streltsy* [Professional Soldiers] (3 articles)
XXIV. The Atamans and the Cossacks (3 articles)
 XXV. Illegal Taverns (21 articles)

Chapter I
Blasphemers and Heretics

   1. If a member of another faith, regardless of which faith, or a Russian, should blaspheme our Lord and Savior Jesus Christ, or His Mother the Holy Queen, Mary, the Virgin Mother of God, or the honorable cross, or its holy servants, each such case should be investigated thoroughly, using all possible means. An inquiry about it should be organized, and the blasphemer of God should be burned at the stake.

2. And should some scoundrel come into God's church during the holy liturgy and should he in some way try to prevent its completion, he should be seized, his action investigated, and he should be condemned to death without mercy.

3. And should someone, upon entering God's church during the holy liturgy or during church singing, start directing insults against Patriarch, or Metropolitan, or Archbishop, or Bishop, or Archimandrite, or *Igumen*, or the ecclesiastical order [in general], and thereby disrupt holy singing in that church, the Sovereign should be informed of this, an investigation should be inaugurated, and for his action the scoundrel should be whipped at the market place.

4. And should anyone, upon entering God's church, start a fight with another person and kill that person, the murderer should be sentenced to death.

5. And should he only wound and not kill, he [the guilty one] should be mercilessly whipped at the market place, put in prison for a month, and made to compensate the injured person twice for the insult.

6. And if a scoundrel should strike anyone in God's church but inflict no wound, he should be whipped with a cane for this insult and [be] made to compensate the injured person.

7. If someone should insult another person verbally but should not harm him [bodily], the guilty person should be put into prison for a month. And whoever was insulted should be compensated in order to prevent the occurrence of any outrages in God's churches in the future.

8. In church during the singing, no one can present a personal petition to the Sovereign Tsar and Grand Prince Aleksei Mikhailovich of All Russia, nor to the Great Lord, His Eminence Joseph, Patriarch of Moscow and of All Russia, nor to Metropolitans, Archbishops, and Bishops, in order to prevent confusion in the church during the church singing, because God's church was created for prayer [not for business]. All Orthodox Christian should stand and pray in God's churches with fear and should not think of worldly matters.

9. And whoever should forget the fear of God and disregard the Tsar's decree and petition either the Sovereign, or the Patriarch, or other officials about a personal matter in God's church during church singing, such petitioner should be thrown into prison for a term to be determined by the Sovereign.

Chapter II
The Sovereign's Honor, and How to Guard His Health

1. Should anyone think maliciously about the Sovereign's health, and should another person report him concerning this malicious thought, there should

be made an inquiry into his malicious thought and intended action against his Tsarist Majesty, and such person, upon investigation, should be executed.

2. Likewise, should a member of his Tsarist Majesty's government wish to seize control of the Muscovite state and become Sovereign, and should he, to attain this evil goal, organize an army or conspire with the enemies of his Tsarist Majesty, issue out charters, or aid them in any way, in order to seize control of the Muscovite state or do some other foolish thing with the aid of those enemies of the Sovereign, and should someone report him, there should be organized a proper inquiry into his treason, and such traitor should be sentenced to death.

3. And should anyone give away a city of his Tsarist Majesty to an enemy through treason, or accept foreigners into cities of his Tsarist Majesty for treasonous purposes, and then investigation be conducted into it, such traitors should be executed.

4. And should anyone consciously and treacherously burn either a city or manors, and then be apprehended during his act or afterwards, and an inquiry be conducted into his evil act, such person should be burned mercilessly.

5. Service estates, hereditary estates, and livestock of all traitors should be transferred to the possession of the Sovereign.

6. Wives and children of traitors, if they were aware of their treasons, should be executed.

7. If a wife knew nothing of the treason of her husband, or children of the treason of their father, and if this be verified by an investigation, such persons should be neither executed not punished; the Sovereign will determine how much of the service and hereditary estates they should be allowed to retain for their livelihood.

8. If a traitor had children, but they, prior to his treason, were separated from him, did not live with him, and hence knew nothing of his treason, and if they had their own livestock and their own hereditary estates, from such children neither livestock nor hereditary estates should be confiscated.

9. And if someone should commit treason and leave [as survivors] in the Muscovite state either his father, or his mother, or his brothers, or his cousins, or his uncles, or any other member of his family, and if he lived with them and they jointly owned their livestock and their hereditary estates, such traitor should be thoroughly investigated in order to determine whether his father, or his mother, or his relatives knew of his treason. Should an investigation determine that they knew of his treason, they should be executed and their livestock and hereditary and service estates transferred to the Sovereign.

10. If, however, an investigation should determine that they knew nothing of the treason of the traitor, they should not be executed and their livestock and their service and hereditary estates should not be confiscated.

11. If a traitor should return from a foreign country to the Muscovite state,

and if the Sovereign should pardon him and forgive his guilty action, and then if he should obtain a new service estate through service, the Sovereign may return his old hereditary estate to him, but he cannot grant him his old service estate.

12. If someone should report that another person has revealed a great state secret, but he does not have witnesses to substantiate his report, does not convince anyone [with his arguments], and no evidence exists to aid in the investigation into the revelation of state secrets, a decree should be issued on this problem, following an inquiry, as the Sovereign should direct.

13. And if someone should reveal the state of the Sovereign's health, or if they should disclose information about people whom they serve, or, if they be peasants, to whom they belong, and if such reports are not convincing, they should not be believed. After they have been severely punished for spreading lies, through merciless whipping with a knout, such individuals should then be returned to those persons to whom they belong. Such informers should not be believed or listened to in the future on anything except matters of great importance.

14. And should anyone, regardless of his status, say that he is a government official, and then should it be determined that he is not, such person should be knouted for impersonating a government official, and afterwards he should be returned to those persons to whom he belongs.

15. And if someone apprehends a traitor on the road, and either kills him or captures him and returns him to the Sovereign, that traitor should [in the latter case] be executed, and the person who apprehended or killed him should be given the livestock of the traitor as the Sovereign should decree.

16. And whoever should report that another person had revealed state secrets or was about to commit treason, and the person who had been reported on is absent at the time, that person must be found and he must confront the accuser face to face. If a thorough investigation should verify the validity of the charge, a decree should be issued as stipulated above.

17. If a person should report that another is about to reveal state secrets or to commit treason, and then fail to prove it, and if an investigation should determine that he fabricated his evidence, such informer should be punished in the same manner that the person who had been reported upon would have been punished if he had been found guilty.

18. Should a person in the Muscovite state, regardless of his social status, learn of the existence of mass discontent, or conspiracy, or any other evil design, [in Moscow] the existence of such plots should be reported either to Aleksei Mikhailovich, the Sovereign Tsar and Grand Prince of All Russia, or to his *boyars* or his high assistants, or [in the provinces], to local *voevodas* or other officials of the central government.

19. If someone should know or hear of the existence of mass discontent or a conspiracy or any other evil design against his Tsarist Majesty, but fails to report it either to the Sovereign, or his *boyars*, or his high assistants, or *voevodas*, or other officials of the central government in provincial cities, and then the Sovereign should find out that that person was aware of the existence of such action but failed to report it, and an inquiry be conducted into it, such persons should be sentenced to death without mercy.

20. During an insurrection, mass discontent, or conspiracy, no one should break into, or rob, or inflict bodily harm on his Tsarist Majesty, his *boyars*, his high assistants, members of the *boyarskaia duma* [Council of Notables], his advisers, his *voevodas* in regiments, and other officials in provincial cities.

21. Whoever should initiate mass discontent or a conspiracy against his Tsarist Majesty or his *boyars*, or his high assistants, or members of the *boyarskaia duma* or his advisers, or *voevodas* in regiments, or other officials of the central government in provincial cities, and pillage or inflict bodily harm on them, those persons who initiate it should be condemned to death without mercy.

22. Should *voevodas* of regiments or officials of the central government in provincial cities inform the Sovereign that either service people or people of other classes had approached them in numbers resembling mass discontent or a conspiracy and threatened to kill them, and if those people who had been reported on should petition the Sovereign to investigate those *voevodas* and officials of the central government and deny that they had approached them with any mass discontent or a conspiracy and say that they came only in small numbers to petition them, upon such petition of the Sovereign a thorough investigation should be conducted of those city officials and, in the regiments, of the military personnel. If this investigation in cities and regiments should determine that these people really came to the *voevodas* and to the officials of the central government with genuine petitions and not for robbery purposes [as it had been reported], such people should not be sentenced to death. Those *voevodas* and officials of the central government who erroneously reported to the Tsar should be severely punished as the Tsar should determine. . . .

Chapter IV
Forgers of Documents, Signatures, and Seals

1. If someone should forge a charter of the Sovereign, or the Sovereign's signature on a charter, or if he should alter anything on an official document without the Sovereign's authorization, or the approval of either the *boyars*, or members of the *boyarskaia duma*, or of lesser officials, and forge the signature

of a clerk, or if someone should make for himself a seal similar to the Sovereign's seal, such individual, upon investigation, should be executed for such crimes.

2. If someone should steal the Sovereign's seal from the Sovereign's charters or other official documents and attach these seals to forged documents, or if he should write illegal documents and then attach such seals to them without the Sovereign's permission, such individuals should be executed and their forged documents invalidated.

3. If a person should forge some documents and then die, and after his death these documents should be discovered by members of his family or his officials, and if either members of his family or his officials should petition the Sovereign on the basis of these documents, such petitions should be investigated to determine how they obtained these documents, where they found them, and whether they were aware that these documents were forged. If, in the course of the investigation, these persons should acknowledge their complicity or knowledge that these documents were forged and that they held them for personal gains, such individuals should be sentenced to death.

4. But if the investigation should determine that they held those forged documents without being aware that they were forged, such people should not be sentenced to death; the documents must be invalidated and no one should stand trial.

Chapter V
Mint Masters Who May Counterfeit Money

1. If mint masters should make either copper, or tin, or economical money [that is, adulterated money], or if they should add copper, tin, or lead to silver and thereby cause harm to the Sovereign's treasury, such mint masters should be executed by pouring [molten matter down their throats].

2. And if gold or silver masters accept someone's gold or silver work and start adding either copper, or tin, or lead to the silver or gold, upon discovery of this [alteration] they should be knouted. And those people who were hurt by this action, that is, by [the mint master's] alteration of gold and silver through copper, tin, or lead, should be compensated for the loss suffered.

Chapter VI
Permits to Travel into Other Countries

1. And should someone wish to travel for trade purposes or other private matters from the Muscovite state into a foreign country which is on peaceful

terms with the Muscovite state, such person in Moscow must petition the Tsar, and in [other] cities [petitions are to be addressed to the local] *voevodas* for a travel permit. Without a travel permit no person should travel. *Voevodas* in cities must issue travel permits without delays.

2. If a *voevoda* should delay issuing a travel permit and thereby cause delay and a loss, and then if a petition of grievance be submitted about it [to the Tsar], and then an inquiry be held about it, those *voevodas* will incur the Tsar's great anger. And if they cause a loss they must pay it double, and this [the fine] should go to the petitioner.

3. And if someone should travel into another country without a travel permit, and having been in another state then return to the Muscovite state, and then be reported by someone that he had travelled without a travel permit for treasonous purposes or for some other foolishness, such reports about illegal travels into foreign countries without the Sovereign's permits should be thoroughly investigated. And if an investigation should establish that a person travelled into another country without a travel permit for treasonous purposes or other evil matter, such person, upon investigation, should be sentenced to death.

4. And should investigation establish that a person travelled into another country without a travel permit for trade purposes and not for treason, he should be penalized by knouting, so that others, seeing it, might learn that they should not do the same [that is, travel abroad without travel permits].

5. And in those border cities and districts where villages of the Sovereign and villages of state peasants, and hereditary and service estates join Lithuanian or German border lands, and where the Sovereign's lands thrust into the Lithuanian or German side or where Lithuanian or German lands thrust into the Sovereign's side, in such case free people and peasants living in the Sovereign's villages, or in villages of state peasants, or on hereditary and service estates, are permitted to travel through those Lithuanian or German border lands without permits from one city to another; they are also allowed to meet Lithuanian or German people; it should not be held against them that they live adjacent to those Lithuanians or Germans who live in border areas.

6. Should service or hereditary nobles of border areas hear that some of their own people or their peasants are trying to commit treason or some other foolishness, they should notify the Sovereign, and in cities they should also provide appropriate information to local *voevodas* and bring such people or peasants before them. The *voevodas* should thoroughly interrogate and investigate such suspects who had been reported upon, using all possible means, and then should report their findings to the Sovereign. Such people should be held in prison until the Sovereign decides what to do with them.

⚔ *62* ⚔

The Popular Discontent in Seventeenth Century Russia

Three features seem to dominate the history of seventeenth century Russia: 1) the steady consolidation of political power by the Romanov dynasty; 2) the rapid territorial growth of the Russian state in Asia and Europe; and 3) the violent popular discontent that for a moment threatened the very existence of the Muscovite way of life. Of the three features the most spectacular was the nationwide internal violence. Among the factors contributing to this discontent were costly foreign wars, graft and corruption of officials, oppressive taxation, the increased burden of serfdom, drought, unresponsiveness of officials to complaints, and bureaucratic high-handedness. The popular discontent assumed varied forms. In Moscow it manifested itself in a riot in 1648 and another in 1662 that cost many lives and brought considerable destruction of property. Along the Volga in the late 1660s and early 1670s the discontent assumed the form of a bloody social upheaval against the established order under the leadership of Stenka T. Riazin. Throughout Russia the popular discontent was greatly complicated by the problems created by the religious reform that split Russian society into two hostile camps: the Old Believers and the proponents of the new rituals.

The 1648 Turmoil in Moscow: A Contemporary Account

There was in the city of Moscow an eminent nobleman named Leontii Stepanovich Pleshchev, who, in his position of authority [as judge in the *Zemskii prikaz* in charge of commoners], exhibited harshness and injustice in matters that affected common people. Because of this the whole [Muscovite] society, including the commoners, frequently beseeched His Tsarist Majesty and with sincere humility begged that this Pleshchev (who, often without any actual

---

The first selection, by an anonymous Swedish observer of the Moscow riot of 1648, was taken from K. V. Bazilevich, ed. *Gorodskie vosstaniia v Moskovskom gosudarstve XVII v. Sbornik dokumentov* (Town Uprisings in the Muscovite State in the 17th Century. A Collection of Documents) (Moscow: 1936), pp. 52–59; the second from "*Akty otnosiashchiesia k istorii Solovetskoga bunta*" (Documents on the History of the Solovetskii Insurrection), *Chteniia v Obshchestve istorii i drevnostei Rossiiskikh*, (October–December, 1883), vol. 127, Part V, pp. 78–81. Translations mine. Words in brackets are mine.

cause, interrogated people and inflicted upon them—especially those he disliked—severe punishment under a pretext that they had allegedly committed
some kind of crime) be removed on account of his harshness and injustice,
and that his position be given to another individual who would be modest
and judicious. When at last, after many petitions by the common people,
His Tsarist Majesty ordered that the above-mentioned Pleshchev be imprisoned and interrogated, thanks to the efforts of Boris Ivanovich Morozov (who
as a distinguished individual, a tutor, and administrator of His Imperial
Majesty's household, was in high esteem and grace [with the Tsar] and who
earlier had been very kind toward Pleshchev, agreed secretly with him and
helped him in the matter described), the whole affair was twisted in such a
manner that Pleshchev's servants, instead of the master, were subjected to
interrogation and punishment. Pleshchev himself, thanks to Morozov's intervention as well as his own defense, which argued that he was framed on
account of hate and unjustified anger by the commoners who wanted his
destruction, was freed and the entire case was closed. But the common people
were not satisfied with such a solution and continued to petition His Tsarist
Majesty, calling to his attention all the cases of Pleshchev's harshness, and
pleading that society should not suffer on account of the actions of one individual. But this time again the people failed to get any satisfaction. Meanwhile on May 17 [1648], His Tsarist Majesty left Moscow for Troitsa, a
distance of about twelve miles, where is located a beautiful monastery named
in honor of the Holy Trinity, for the annual pilgrimage prayer, in order to
participate there in the Divine Service and to be able to return to Moscow
by June 1. As was customary, he was accompanied in both directions by the
streltsy. According to local custom, [as he was returning] the common people
[of Moscow] met him some distance from the city with bread and salt and
good wishes, asked that he accept these, and petitioned that he do something
about Pleshchev. However, not only were they not listened to, but the *streltsy*
drove them away with knouts. On orders of Morozov, who was in command
of the *streltsy*, sixteen petitioners were arrested in the Tsar's name. Then the
remaining people attempted to petition about Pleshchev to His Tsarist Majesty's wife, who followed him by half an hour, with Morozov walking behind
her. The petition was not accepted, and similarly as before the *streltsy* drove
the petitioners away. Deeply hurt by these actions, the people grabbed stones
and clubs and began to hurl them at the *streltsy*. Some of those who accompanied His Tsarist Majesty's wife, including Porsercky [Pozharskii?], were
hurt and received cuts on their faces. During this unexpected disturbance the
wife of His Tsarist Majesty asked Morozov to explain what caused this riot
and agitation, why people dared to take such a step, and what should be
done to pacify the rioters. Morozov [is reported to have] replied that on

account of this illegal act and audacity one should hang the young people
wholesale, and doubtless this would have been done immediately were it not
for the fact that the entire mob interrupted it [the executions] next day with
a new petition that gave them their freedom.

Next day, Friday, June 2, when the Russians began solemn preparations
to celebrate Ascension Day, as His Tsarist Majesty came downstairs from his
palace a mob once again tried to plead that he issue an *ukaz* on the problem
about which they had petitioned him earlier. His Tsarist Majesty asked them
why they had not presented their grievances and wishes in writing. The mob
answered that this had already been done earlier and that now they were only
asking that those who had been imprisoned [yesterday] be freed. Since His
Tsarist Majesty said that he would give them a satisfactory answer upon his
return from the church the mob was pacified. Meanwhile His Tsarist Majesty
asked Morozov with considerable indignation how he had dared to imprison
some people without his knowledge. Morozov was disturbed by this but gave
no reply. Then, when His Tsarist Majesty came out from the Kremlin he was
met by a group of rioters who once again started to talk about Pleshchev.
His Tsarist Majesty was both surprised and angered by this. He went inside
the church. After the Divine Service the petitioners followed the Tsar from
the church and when His Tsarist Majesty entered the Kremlin the entire crowd
rushed after him. Since Morozov was suspicious he ordered the *streltsy* to
close the Kremlin gates and allow no one to enter. But the *streltsy* could not
carry out this order because of the assembled multitude. Several thousand
persons had penetrated to the Kremlin square and instantly in strong language
they began to demand immediate satisfaction of their wishes and their grievances. Since His Tsarist Majesty had just sat down to the table, he sent out
to them one of his *boyars* named [M. M.] Temkin [-Rostovskii]. They detained
him under the pretext that they desired to speak with the Tsar himself. Then
another [*boyar*] went out. They tore his clothes off and gave him such strong
kicks and blows that he was forced to stay in bed for several days. Finally,
His Tsarist Majesty came out, calmed them down, and asked them about
the meaning of their persistent demand. Then the mob at first expressed a
wish that those who had been imprisoned be freed, and they were freed on
the spot. But the mob was still not satisfied with this and demanded that
Pleshchev be handed to them. To this His Tsarist Majesty replied that he
needed some time to study the whole matter, and should he find Pleshchev
guilty he promised to punish him accordingly. But the mob did not agree
with this [approach] and continued to stress that if His Tsarist Majesty did
not satisfy them [peacefully] they would gain it by force.

While this was taking place, to prevent a tragedy Morozov ordered that
all the *streltsy*, some 6000 strong, assemble [immediately] and then he directed

them to drive the riotous mob away from the Kremlin square and to put down the disturbance. The *streltsy*, however, rejected Morozov's orders and some even went to His Tsarist Majesty and declared that in accordance with their oath and their gratitude, they would willingly obey and serve His Tsarist Majesty and defend him, but that now on account of the traitor and tyrant Pleshchev they would not oppose the mob. Then they directed their talk to the mob and told them that they should fear nothing, that in this case they would not oppose them in any way; on the contrary, they would extend to them a helping hand. After that the people again began to demand that Pleshchev be turned over to them—this time with greater persistence than before. The meeting became more multitudinous as time went on. His Tsarist Majesty stepped forward again and asked the crowd not to shed blood on this day (namely Friday, which [because of the holiday] the Russians considered would be abhorrent), to calm down, and tomorrow [he said] he would turn Pleshchev over to them. This His Tsarist Majesty did only to save Pleshchev's life.

Meanwhile some of Morozov's servants, doubtless sent by their master, began to scold the guards of the *streltsy* and began to hit them for allowing the mob to enter [the Kremlin] contrary to their master's orders. In this fight one of the *streltsy* was mortally stabbed with a knife. Then the *streltsy* and the mob rushed to the palace of the Tsar, informed [him of what had happened], complained that Morozov's people were attacking them, pleaded that he protect them, and threatened that [failing to attain protection] they themselves would take revenge upon Morozov. To this His Tsarist Majesty angrily replied: "If you claim that you are strong, stronger that Morozov's servants, why didn't you protect me from them? And if Morozov's servants misbehaved themselves slightly, then you yourselves should seek revenge." After these words were spoken, the entire mob together with the *streltsy* mistakenly believing that they alone must settle with Morozov, rushed to his home and started to storm it. They were met by one of Morozov's administrators named Moisei, who wanted to calm them. But they knocked him down and killed him with blows from oak clubs. There was a rumor about this Moisei to the effect that he was a magician, and that with the aid of magic he had told Morozov a few days before this that a great danger awaited him, that two or three distinguished *boyars* would meet their death, and that he himself [Morozov] would be an object of that danger. To this Morozov allegedly responded: "Who would dare to get into his head an idea to harm us?" One can conclude from this that he [Morozov] was presumptuous and arrogant. After Morozov's steward, Moisei, was killed in such a deplorable manner, the entire people and the *streltsy* took part in pillaging and destroying Morozov's home so thoroughly that they left not a single nail in the wall. They broke coffers and chests and threw them out of the windows. They tore to pieces expensive clothes that they found, and threw money and household utensils to the street in order to demonstrate that they were motivated not by any material gain but by vengeance to the enemy. When they finished, they split into two groups. One plundered Pleshchev's house; the other the house of State Chancellor Nazarii Ivanovich Chistii. When they learned that the Chancellor had hidden in his home they angrily threatened one of his Tatar servants until finally, perhaps because he had sworn to his master not to babble, he pointed his finger to the room where the Chancellor was hiding. They dragged him from the secret hold or store room, and immediately without any pity or mercy they killed him with oak clubs. In the process they mutilated him so that it was impossible to recognize him. They then disrobed him, threw him on the manure cart in the courtyard, and left him uncovered for a day and a night. Next day his servants took his corpse into the entrance hall, put it in a wooden casket, and covered it with a mat. On the third day when the rioting subsided his servants secretly buried him. On that day they [the mob] pillaged and plundered seventy houses. Of course homes of merchants would not have been spared if the rich merchants had not asked protection from His Tsarist Majesty, who called in several thousand of the [loyal] *streltsy* who opposed the mob.

Next day, Saturday, the insane commoners appeared again before the Kremlin, this time in greater numbers than before. Since the gates of the fortress and of the city were closed, the entire mob began to demand with great shouting the delivery of Pleshchev. Then from the Kremlin someone fired several blank shots. Immediately after this all church bells rang out an alarm. In a very short time this created a great confusion as thousands of additional people gathered. Then His Tsarist Majesty, in order to divert a danger that was before his eyes, delivered Pleshchev (who was accompanied by several *streltsy*, a priest, and an executioner), yielding to the demand of the mob unwillingly and against his wishes. The mob immediately took him [Pleshchev] away from the *streltsy*, declaring that they themselves would judge him, and at once they killed him like a dog, with oak clubs in front of the Kremlin. . . .

Again the mob began to demand the delivery of Morozov as a traitor and an enemy of public welfare. His Tsarist Majesty ordered that the gates be opened and sent to the people his priest together with the Patriarch to plead mercy for Morozov. These intermediaries went thrice back and forth from the Tsar to the mob, but they gained nothing from the mob. Then at last His Tsarist Majesty went before the people with bare head and tears in his eyes, and pleaded with them for God's sake to calm down and to have mercy on Morozov, since the latter had performed great services to his father [Tsar

Michael] and had been his tutor, and was the manager of his household. However, they did not want to compromise. Finally their persistent demands led His Tsarist Majesty to propose that he would exile Morozov from Moscow, and to prove good faith His Tsarist Majesty offered the Patriarch as a hostage. The Patriarch held before himself an ikon depicting the Mother of God, which according to legend was painted by St. Luke and which enjoyed great reverence.

At this juncture Morozov's servants set the city on fire, hoping to create a division within the people. The fire caused such havoc that in the course of several hours the better half of the city inside and outside the white walls, beginning with the Neglinnaia River, burned to ashes. About 24,000 homes were consumed. Infinite treasures and wealth in commercial goods and other property burned and perished in this fire. One individual, who was a very wealthy merchant, lost some 150,000 *rubles*. Some 500,000 tons of grain worth six tons of gold also perished. More than 2,000 people lost their lives—most of them in a state of intoxication. After they had seized the loot they had begun to celebrate; then they fell asleep and were engulfed by the fire and burned. Their feast ended in tragedy. The mob paid little attention to this fire. They demanded blood, and when [the Tsar] did not deliver Morozov to satisfy them, they demanded that another well-known nobleman, Peter Tikhonovich Trakhaniotov, be given them instead. They suspected him and held him responsible for an increase in tax on salt, which had recently been introduced. At that time he was not on hand in Moscow, but was in a village several miles away. His Tsarist Majesty pleaded for a respite, agreed, and promised to call him in. And it was done so. Two days later, on June 5, he was brought to the city and they severed his head with an axe. In the home of this Tikhonovich, during a plunder, they found the seal of His Tsarist Majesty and two monetary dies. With the aid [of these instruments] he had caused a great deal of deception and cheating. As a result many Muscovites fell under suspicion of counterfeiting money, and many were imprisoned and innocently killed. There was a rumor that Morozov had worked secretly in these swindles, or perhaps directly, because by such counterfeiting he had accumulated much money and wealth and became so rich in such a short time that he had acquired a good half of the principality.

Meanwhile, Morozov, partly out of fear, partly because his conscience bothered him, wanted to save himself by a secret flight from Moscow. But he was overtaken by someone who knew him and was returned to Moscow. He would have fallen into the hands of the mob if he had not been freed by his captors, who, in return for a good amount of gold, delivered him to the Kremlin instead. Once again His Tsarist Majesty made every effort, using the Patriarch as an intermediary, to bring harmony between Morozov and the people. Nothing came out of it, however. In fact the people openly rose against the

Patriarch. They were even ready to call His Tsarist Majesty a traitor until they succeeded in gaining from him a pledge that he would exile Morozov not only from the Court but from the city as well. They agreed that if His Tsarist Majesty would not do so peacefully they would force him to it and that he must again give them a solemn pledge to exile him next day. This was done. With a strong escort of the *streltsy* Morozov was exiled to the Kirillov Monastery in Beloozero, located some 120 miles from Moscow, and in this way the demands of the people were satisfied.

The Insurrection at the Solovetskii Monastery, 1668–1676

A report from your humble servant [*kholop*], [*voevoda*] Ivashko Mereshchinov, to the Sovereign Tsar and Grand Prince Aleksei Mikhailovich, the Autocrat for All Great, Little, and White Russia.

Sovereign! On June 19, of this year, 1674, a deserter-monk named Pakhomii left the Solovetskii Monastery and I, your humble servant, interrogated this monk, Pakhomii. Since this monk told me during this interrogation that he too was your humble servant, I, your humble servant, am forwarding through Ivashko Golikov, a *streletz* from Kholmogory, this day, July 5, 1674, a [written] copy of this interrogation to Moscow to you, Great Sovereign Tsar and Grand Prince Aleksei Mikhailovich, the Autocrat of All Great, Little, and White Russia.

I, your humble servant, have left a copy of this interrogation in the Novgorod *prikaz* with the *okolnichii* Artemii Sergeevich Matveev and the *dumnyi diaks* Grigorii Bogdanov, Iakov Pozdyshev, Ivan Evstafiev, and Vasilii Bobinin. I, your humble servant, have sent monk Pakhomii to the Sumsk *ostrog* in the Solovetskii Monastery [complex] under the supervision of Ignatii, a *Sobor* monk, whom I have instructed to keep him [Pakhomii] under careful supervision in order to prevent him from leaving the Sumsk [*ostrog*] until you, the Great Sovereign, issue an appropriate *ukaz* on this matter....

During the interrogation [Pakhomii] told me that he hailed from the Pereiaslav *uezd*, Riazan [principality]; that he was a peasant from the village of Putiatin, and that he belong to a hereditary patrimony of the *okolnichii* Prince Semeon Romanovich Pozharskii. [He said that] he went to the Solovetskii Monastery about eight years ago and became a monk about three years ago. [He has informed me that] some of the greatest thieves and traitors to the Great Sovereign currently live in the Solovetskii Monastery. [These include] a deserter *sotnik* [captain], *boyar* Iashko Voronin, and another *sotnik*, Samko Vasiliev from Kem. With them are two city monks: one named Feodosii, and another called Morzh, but whose actual name he [Pakhomii] cannot recall. These thieves do not attend church, they do not pray for the

Great Sovereign, they do not listen to such prayers, they have forbidden priests and monks to say [such prayers], they do not go to confession, and generally are ignorant of the Christian faith. They do not want to surrender the city; on the contrary, they have greatly strengthened its fortifications. Priest Gerondii, who called the new books a blasphemy and who prophesied the coming of the end of the world in the year 1674, has been put in a dungeon because his prophecy has failed to materialize.

[Pakhomii has informed me that] the Monastery has enough bread supplies to last ten or more years, and fats, turnips, and minced food to last for about two years. If Klementii Ievlev had not provided these thieves and traitors with the turnips, they would not have any. . . . After Klementii Ievlev left the island, these thieves dug all the turnips, gathered mushrooms and garlic, and caught as much fish as they wanted. After Klementii Ievlev departed, one monk journeyed to the Abbot of the Solovetskii Monastery on Anzer Island, from whom he purchased 100 *puds* of turbot. A peasant named Evsiutka, who hails from the Kovda *volost*, Kola *uezd*, and who acted as an agent of Klementii Ievlev, brought 100 *puds* of turbot to these thieves in the monastery. In fact, he came twice to the monastery with the result that these thieves eat turbot to the present day.

That autumn, when Klementii left the island, this Evsiutka brought to the Monastery a conniving letter from Fadeiko Petrov, who has been confined in the Sumsk prison. In that letter Fadeiko told the thieves and traitors in the Solovetskii [Monastery] to strengthen their supplies and fortifications and not to surrender to the soldiers of the Great Sovereign. In accordance with this advice these thieves erected wooden palisades at various weak points of the town, put rock behind [these palisades] and stored enough supplies of wood to last them about ten years. They [now] call the Solovetskii Monastery their own monastery, and have appropriated for it the lands that belong to the Great Sovereign. They also have gathered great quantities of cereals and dried oat meals, which they make from barley and oats. These thieves are afraid only of 1) being burned [out] by the military, 2) of cannon balls, and 3) of the Trans-Onega soldiers. They are not afraid of the Dvina *streltsy* because they have many of their own [people] and acquaintances among them. From an imprisoned *sotnik* and a *piatidesiatnik* [sergeant] of the Dvina *streltsy* these thieves have learned that [the government's] military forces are numerically weak. As a result, some 200 people have volunteered to probe government defenses. As soon as the long and dark nights of autumn will descend these thieves plan to attack the forces of the Sovereign, especially those that are encamped in [inadequately] fortified places.

After he learned from these thieves about this sinister plot, this monk [Pakhomii] left the monastery in order to pass this information to [me] *voevoda*

Ivan Alekseevich Meshcherinov so that government military forces might be made aware of this plot. The monastery has about 300 monks and about 400 deserters. These people have locked themselves up in the monastery and are prepared to die there. They will not surrender at all. They defend thievery and priestlessness and are opposed to the new faith. Many priestless monks as well as novices came to the monastery from the towns [along the Volga], especially those thieves who have abandoned the church and the teachings of the Holy Fathers. The monastery has also attracted many deserters from among the Moscow *streltsy*, the Don Cossacks, serfs who have escaped from the *boyars*, peasants, and all kinds of foreigners, including Swedes, Poles, Turks, and Tatars. These thieves have thrown good and faithful people into dungeons and have posted guards over them. [It seems that] the root of all evil has assembled in the monastery.

The mill in the monastery has stopped working because the water level in the lake has dropped on account of the closure of the stream [that supplies it]. The people now take water for all of their needs from the holy artesian well. These [thieves] invited [me] *voevoda* Ivan Alekseevich Meshcherinov without my soldiers [to their place], in order to put me in prison, similarly as they have done to the *sotnik* and the *piatidesiatnik*. These thieves [openly] say that they want to destroy the *voevoda* as well as all other leaders. [They believe that once they have achieved this] the rest of the *streltsy* will leave the island like sheep. They have in the monastery more than sixty barrels of gunpowder, each barrel weighing about ten *puds*. The powder is buried in the Gerontiev cell. They [also] have many cannons and muskets. [It would be desirable] to set the roof of the White Tower on fire, especially since many wooden structures and wooden warehouses are located nearby. These thieves are short on clothing and shoes. They are trying to make clothes from boat sails. The latter are abundant in the monastery. When monk Pakhomii lived in the monastery he did not associate himself with these thieves and traitors. He lived in the monastery in virtual slavery because they would not let him out. When he finally escaped from the town, they fired at him with small arms. Since the monk is illiterate, he did not become involved in any questionable matters.

⚔ *63* ⚔

Provisions of Russian Protectorate over Ukraine in 1654

In 1654 the Russian Tsar Aleksei (1645–1672) and the Ukrainian Cossacks, who were the leaders of the Zaporozhie Host, signed an agreement
which temporarily formed the basis of Ukrainian-Russian relations. Because of its vagueness, the agreement of 1654 caused the development
of various conflicting views in historical literature. Some scholars have
called it a personal union, others an incorporation, and still others a
vassalage, a military alliance, and a treaty between two independent
sovereigns. Regardless of its interpretations, the 1654 agreement placed
Russia in control of a rich and strategically vital area, thereby strengthening her position *vis-á-vis* Poland and the Ottoman Empire.

A Petition of Ukrainian Cossacks to the Tsar Alexei with the Resolutions of the Tsar on Each Point, March 31, 1654

To the Great Sovereign, Tsar and Grand Duke Alexei Mikhailovich, the
Autocrat of all the Great and Little Russia, [that is, Ukraine] and the Ruler
and Possessor of many States.

His Tsarist Majesty's subjects, Bohdan Khmelnitsky, the Hetman of the
Zaporozhie Host, as well as the whole Zaporozhie Host and the whole Christian Russian world, most respectfully beg that His Tsarist Majesty grant them
what their envoys [Samiilo Zarudny and Pavlo Teteria] are to petition, and
they will serve His Tsarist Majesty, according to his orders, forever.

[Note] His Tsarist Majesty's resolutions concerning each article follow after
each one.

[The Kozaks Ask]
Article 1

That in [Ukrainian] towns the officeholders will be chosen among the natives
who are worthy of it; they shall rule the subjects of His Tsarist Majesty and
collect taxes for the Tsarist treasury honestly. [Such an arrangement is rec-

---

Reprinted by permission of the publisher from George Vernadsky, *Bohdan: Hetman of the
Ukraine* (New Haven: Yale University Press, 1941), pp. 131–140.

ommended] for the reason that in case a governor appointed by His Tsarist
Majesty should come [to a Ukrainian town] and begin to violate the natives'
rights and make new ordinances, it would be a great annoyance to them; and
if the natives themselves should be officeholders, they would rule in accordance
with their rights.

[The Tsar's Resolution]

And concerning this article His Tsarist Majesty graciously ordered that the
article stand according their petition. There shall be [elected] officeholders in
[Ukrainian] towns, *videlicet* mayors, burgomasters, counselors, assessors and
they shall collect for His Tsarist Majesty sundry taxes in money and in grain,
and shall pass them over to his sovereign treasury, [handing them] to His
Tsarist Majesty's agents; and the agents sent by His Tsarist Majesty for receiving the tax moneys shall supervise the [town] collectors, that the latter
act honestly.

Article 2

That, through the kindness of His Tsarist Majesty, the Secretary-General of
the Host will receive [yearly] appropriation of 1000 Polish *zloty* [gold coins]
for the clerks of his office; and of 300 Polish *zloty* for the secretary of the
Host; and of 100 Polish *zloty* for the secretary of the Host Court; and of fifty
zloty for the secretary of each regiment as well as for the standard bearer of
each regiment; and of thirty *zloty* for the standard bearer of each hundred;
and of fifty *zloty* for the master of Hetman's insignia.

[Resolution]

His Tsarist Majesty has graciously ordered according to their petition; and
that the money be appropriated from the local income.

Article 3

That a mill be assigned for the sustenance of each [of the following office-
holders]: the Secretary of the Host; the two Justices of the Host; the Colonels;
the Asauls of the Host and those of each regiment, because they have great
expenditure.

[Resolution]

His Tsarist Majesty has graciously ordered according to their petition.

Article 4

That concerning the artillery of the Host His Tsarist Majesty would graciously
provide for the winter quarters and food of the cannoneers and all the artillery

workers; also [to appropriate yearly] 400 gold coins to the quartermaster of the artillery, and fifty gold coins to the master of the artillery standards.

[Resolution]

His Tsarist Majesty has graciously ordered that the amount should be appropriated from local income.

Article 5

That the Hetman and the Zaporozhie Host should be free to receive envoys who since long ago have come to the Zaporozhie Host, in case they mean well; and only in case there shall be [about these embassies] something wrong with regard His Tsarist Majesty the Host should notify His Tsarist Majesty.

[Resolution]

Concerning this article His Tsarist Majesty has ordered that [the Host] shall receive and dismiss the bona fide envoys, and write truly and immediately to His Tsarist Majesty [to inform the Tsar] on what business they came and with what [instructions] they were dismissed. With regard to envoys sent by some [foreign power] on business detrimental to [the interests of] His Tsarist Majesty, these ambassadors and envoys should be detained by the Host, and [the Host] should write about them immediately to His Tsarist Majesty for his *ukase*; and they should not be dismissed without His Tsarist Majesty's *ukase*. And there should be no exchange of envoys [between the Host on the one hand and] the Turkish Sultan and the King of Poland [on the other hand], without a *ukase* of His Tsarist Majesty.

Article 6

[An abstract.] Concerning the Metropolitan of Kiev the envoys had no written instruction; and in their speeches they begged that His Tsarist Majesty graciously grant his patent conferring to the metropolitan bishop his possessions.

[Resolution]

His Tsarist Majesty graciously granted his patent confirming to the metropolitan bishop [of Kiev] and all [Ukrainian] clergy their estates they now possess.

Article 7

That His Tsarist Majesty deign to send his army to Smolensk at once without any delay in order that the enemy [that is, the Poles] should not [have time to] prepare themselves and be joined by other [reinforcements, taking into account] that now the [Polish] troops are in bad estate. [The Tsar] should not believe any Polish insinuations in case they make recourse to such.

[Resolution]

His Tsarist Majesty has already decided to set forth personally against his enemy the King of Poland and likewise to send his *boyars* and generals with ample troops as soon as the roads will be dry [after the thawing of the snow] and there will be forage for horses.

Article 8

That soldiers be hired, about 3000 or even more, at His Tsarist Majesty's will, to be stationed on the [Ukrainian-Polish] frontier to protect Ukraine [from the Poles], and that they should be stationed permanently.

[Resolution]

His Tsarist Majesty's soldiers are always available for the protection of Ukraine's frontiers and will be stationed permanently [to that purpose].

Article 9

The custom used to exist for the Zaporozhie Host to receive a salary [that is, from the King of Poland]. And now they beg His Tsarist Majesty that he should appropriate [annually] to the colonels 100 *thalers* [each]; the regimental Asauls, 200 gold coins; the Host Asauls, 400 gold coins; the centurions, 100 gold coins; the [registered] Kozaks, thirty Polish *zloty* [each].

[The Boyars' Resolution]

More than once in previous years Hetman Bohdan Khmelnitsky and all the Zaporozhie Host had sent envoys and begged that His Tsarist Majesty show them graciousness for the sake of the Orthodox Christian Faith and the holy churches of God and intervene in their favor and accept them under the [protection of his] exalted arm and should help them against their enemies. And in that time our great sovereign, His Tsarist Majesty, was not able to accept you under his protection, since there was a permanent peace between His Tsarist Majesty, and the King of Poland, and the Grand Duke of Lithuania. And whereas on the part of the King many insults and offenses were committed with regard to the father of His Tsarist Majesty, the Great Sovereign Tsar and Grand Duke Michael Fedorovich, autocrat of all Russia and ruler and possessor of many states, of blessed memory; and [with regard] to our sovereign's grandfather, the Great Sovereign and holy Patriarch of Moscow and all Russia Filaret Nikitich, of blessed memory; and [with regard] to our Great Sovereign, the Tsar and Grand Duke Alexei Mikhailovich, autocrat of all Russia, [because of all that] His Tsarist Majesty expected apologies [from the King of Poland] for all [the above-mentioned] offenses in accordance with the King's notes, and the Diet's resolutions and constitutions, and the Polish

[-Russian] treaties; and His Tsarist Majesty also desired, through his ambassadors extraordinary, to reconcile the Hetman Bohdan Khmelnitzky and all the Zaporozhie Host with the King of Poland in the following way: in case the King Jan Kazimierz should make peace with the Kozaks according to the provisions of the Zborov treaty, and would not persecute the Orthodox Christian Faith, and would remove the Uniates, in that case His Tsarist Majesty was ready to grant amnesty to those [Poles] who by insulting his sovereign honor deserved capital punishment. And with this offer [our Tsarist Majesty] sent to the King Jan Kazimierz his great and plenipotentiary state ambassadors, the *boyar* and Lord-Lieutenant of the Great Perm, Prince Boris Alexandrovich Repnin-Obolensky with associates; and those great plenipotentiary ambassadors of His Majesty spoke to the King and his Lords in Council about that peace and action offering various methods [of settlement]; and the King Jan Kazimierz and his Lords in Council did not agree with any proposal and thus brought this great thing to naught, and dismissed those great and plenipotentiary ambassadors of His Tsarist Majesty without any result. And our great sovereign, His Tsarist Majesty, in view of such numerous [cases of] incorrectness and rudeness and falsehood on the part of the King, and because of his desire to protect the Orthodox Christian Faith and all the Orthodox Christians from the Roman persecutors aiming at the destruction of God's churches and the annihilation of the Christian faith, has accepted you under [the protection of] his exalted arm. And it is for your protection that our great sovereign, His Tsarist Majesty, having raised numerous Russian and Tatar and German troops, is personally setting forth against the enemies of [Orthodox] Christianity, and is sending his *boyars* and generals with many troops as well. And for the organization of these armies, according to his sovereign *ukase*, large sums have been distributed; therefore they, the envoys [of the Kozak Host], taking into consideration such munificence of His Tsarist Majesty for the sake of their protection, should not now mention the matter of payment of the salary to the Zaporozhie Host. And when the sovereign privy *boyar* and Lord-Lieutenant of Tver, Vasili Vasilevich Buturlin did visit the Hetman, Bohdan Khmelnitsky, the latter talked with him concerning the quota of the Zaporozhie Host, and suggested that it be set at 60,000; and [the Hetman suggested] that even if there should be more Kozaks registered than this quota, it would not be detrimental to the sovereign since they would not ask for pay. And they, Samiilo [Zarudny] and Pavlo [Teteria] and other men who at that time were with the Hetman, should know about it. [Besides] His Tsarist Majesty is not aware of what the revenues are from the cities and towns of Little Russia [that is, Ukraine]; our great sovereign, His Tsarist Majesty, is sending his squires [to Ukraine] to tabulate the revenues; only after those His Majesty's squires have tabulated and computed various revenues, a *ukase* will be promulgated as considered by His Tsarist Majesty concerning the salary of the Zaporozhie Host. And [even] now His Tsarist Majesty, showing his favor to the Hetman and all the Zaporozhie Host, doth intend, according to the old customs of his ancestors, the great sovereigns, tsars, and grand dukes of Russia, to send [some] salary to the Hetman and all the Zaporozhie Host [to be paid] in gold coins.

Article 10

In case [the Tatars of] the Crimean Horde should attack, it would be necessary to oppose them, starting from the Astrakhan and Kazan; likewise the Don Kozaks should be ready [for a campaign against the Tatars]; however, the peace now with them should not yet be discontinued, and they should not be provoked.

[Resolution]

His Tsarist Majesty's *ukase* and command has already been sent to the Don Kozaks, to wit: in case the Crimean people are not stirred up, [the Kozaks] are not allowed to provoke them or attack them; in case, however, the Crimean people should be stirred up, His Tsarist Majesty would then issue orders for a campaign against them.

Article 11

Whereas the Hetman permanently keeps a [Kozak] garrison of 400 men, providing them with everything, in the fortress of Kodak, on the Crimean frontier, [the Kozaks ask] that His Tsarist Majesty would now graciously supply to the fortress food [for the men] and powder for the guns; that likewise, His Tsarist Majesty would graciously provide for those [Kozaks] who guard the Kozaks' Headquarters (*Kosh*) beyond the cataracts, since men have to be kept there.

[Resolution]

With regard to this article His Tsarist Majesty's gracious *ukase* will be issued in the future after it is established what quantities of what supplies used to be sent to these localities, and how much revenue will be collected by His Tsarist Majesty [in Ukraine].

[Concluding Remarks]

And concerning [the matter] which has been mentioned [in connection with the Article 9 of] your petition: as soon as our great sovereign, His Tsarist Majesty, will grant to the Hetman Bohdan Khmelnitsky and all the Zaporozhie Host his sovereign charter of your liberties, you must muster your men [and determine] who will be [registered] as a Kozak and who will be [counted as] a peasant. And with regard to the 60,000 quota for the Zaporozhie Host, our great Sovereign, His Tsarist Majesty has accepted and decreed it. As soon as your envoys come back to the Hetman Bohdan Khmelnitsky, you are to inform him that he is to muster the Kozaks and make the lists of their registration and send the lists certified by his signature to His Tsarist Majesty immediately.

The Charter of the Zaporozhie Host, April 6, 1654

By the grace of God We the Great Sovereign, Tsar, and Grand Duke Alexei Mikhailovich, Autocrat of all the Great and Little Russia, have granted [this Charter to] Our Majesty's subjects Bohdan Khmelnitsky, Hetman of the Zaporozhie Host, and the Secretary Ivan Vyhovsky, and the Justices of the Host, and the Colonels, and the Asauls, and the Centurions, and to all the Zaporozhie Host. In this year A.M. 7162 [=A.D. 1654], by the grace of God, he, the Hetman Bohdan Khmelnitsky and all the Zaporozhie Host have come under [the protection of] our exalted sovereign arm and have sworn an oath of everlasting allegiance to Us, the Great Sovereign, and to our sovereign children and successors. And in March [of this year] he, the Hetman Bohdan Khmelnitsky, and all the Zaporozhie Host sent their envoys, the Justice of the Host Samiilo Bohdanov [Zarudny], and the Colonel of Pereyaslav [regiment] Pavlo Teteria; and in their note to Us the Great Sovereign, to Our Tsarist Majesty, the Hetman and the envoys have most humbly begged that We the Great Sovereign grant [our favor to] him the Hetman Bohdan Khmelnitsky and to the whole Zaporozhie Host and confirm all their former rights and the liberties of the Host, which had been established from ancient times under the Grand Dukes of [Lithuania and] Russia and the Kings of Poland; also [that We the Tsar guarantee] their liberties and property rights with regard to the courts; that they be judged by their elders and that no one [from the outside] interfere with their Courts of the Host; and that [We the Tsar] not violate their former rights which had been granted to both clergy and laymen on the part of the Grand Dukes of [Lithuania and] Russia and the Kings of Poland, and [that We] grant them a charter of confirmation of [those] rights [stamped] with our sovereign seal; and that the quota of registered Kozaks be fixed at 60,000, and that it always be filled up. And that in case the Hetman by God's judgment should die, We the Great Sovereign allow the Zaporozhie Host, according to their old custom, to elect the Hetman among themselves and by themselves, and to notify Us as to who shall have been elected; and that, since the Chihirin district with all appurtenances had been assigned to the Hetman's mace, We the Great Sovereign grant it, ac-

cordingly, to be attached to the [Hetman's] mace; that [We] order that the
Kozak estates and the lands which they use for their sustenance not be taken
from them; also that the children keep the rights of their grandfathers and
fathers on the legacy left by Kozak widows. Therefore We the Great Sovereign,
Our Tsarist Majesty, have graciously commanded our subject, Bohdan Khmelnitsky, the Hetman of Zaporozhie Host, and all Our Tsarist Majesty's Zaporozhie Host, to be under [the protection] of Our Tsarist Majesty's exalted
arm, according to their former rights and privileges which have been granted
to them by the Kings of Poland and the Grand Dukes of Lithuania; and We
have ordered that these their rights and privileges be not violated by any
means, and commanded that they be tried by their elders according to their
former rights; and we have decreed that the quota of the Zaporozhie Host,
according to their own request, be fixed at 60,000 to be always filled up.
And in case, by God's judgment, the Hetman should die, We the Great
Sovereign have allowed the Zaporozhie Host to elect a [new] Hetman, according their former customs, by themselves and among themselves, and to
notify Us the Great Sovereign as to who shall have been elected Hetman;
and the newly elected Hetman shall swear his oath of loyalty and allegiance
to Us, the Great Sovereign, before [our deputy] whom We the Great Sovereign
shall appoint. And We have decreed that the district of Chihirin with all its
appurtenances which had been attached to it before be assigned to the Hetman's mace as before. We also have forbidden [anyone] to deprive the Kozaks,
their widows, and their children of their estates and their lands which they
use for their sustenance, and [have decreed] that [such estates and lands] be
[registered] with them, as before. And when ambassadors come from any of
the neighboring countries to the Zaporozhie Host, to the Hetman Bohdan
Khmelnitsky, on business concerning food, We the Great Sovereign have
allowed the Hetman to receive and to dismiss those ambassadors. And the
Hetman shall immediately notify Us the Great Sovereign from what states
and on what business those ambassadors came and with what [instructions]
they were dismissed. And in case ambassadors shall be sent [to the Zaporozhie
Host] by any [power] on some business detrimental with regard to Us the
Great Sovereign, such ambassadors must be detained in the Host, and notice
must be sent to Us the Great Sovereign at once, and without Our Tsarist
Majesty's decree [such ambassadors] should not be permitted to go back. And
[the hetman] shall not maintain relations with either the Turkish Sultan or
the King of Poland without Our Tsarist Majesty's decree.

And through Our Tsarist Majesty's graciousness let Our Tsarist Majesty's
subjects, the Hetman of the Zaporozhie Host Bohdan Khmelnitsky and Our
Tsarist Majesty's Zaporozhie Host be under [the protection of] Our Tsarist
Majesty's exalted arm, according to their former rights and privileges and all

the articles which have been written above; and let them serve Us the Great Sovereign and our son the sovereign Tsarevich Alexee Alexeivich and our successors, and be loyal [to Us] and wish everything good [to Us] and, whenever our sovereign order will be issued, to set forth against our enemies and fight them, and to be in every circumstance obedient to Our Sovereign will forever.

And concerning those other articles which the above mentioned envoys Samiilo and Pavlo in the name of Bohdan Khmelnitsky, the Hetman of the Zaporozhie Host, and of all Our Tsarist Majesty's Zaporozhie Host, presented to Us the Great Sovereign, to Our Tsarist Majesty, and the articles they submitted to the privy *boyars*, of Our Tsarist Majesty, [to wit] the *boyar* and Lord-Lieutenant of Kazan, Prince Alexei Nikitich Trubetskoy, the *boyar* and Lord-Lieutenant of Tver, Vasili Vasilievich Buturlin, and to the *okolnichii* and Lord-Lieutenant of Kashira, Peter Petrovich Golovin, and to the state-secretary of the privy council, Almaz Ivanov, We the Great Sovereign have listened to those articles with favor, and ordered to write under each of those articles what we have decreed with regard to each, and have commanded to deliver [the copy of] those articles with Our Tsarist Majesty's decree, to the same envoys Samiilo and Pavlo, and it is our desire to keep the Hetman Bohdan Khmelnitsky and all the Zaporozhie Host in Our Tsarist Majesty's gracious favor, and they shall trust in Our Sovereign favor.

This Our Tsarist Majesty's charter has been issued [and stamped] by our State Seal, in our reigning city of Moscow, in the year A.M. 7162 [=A.D. 1654], on March 27 [Julian calendar]. By the grace of God, the Great Sovereign, Tsar and Grand Duke Alexei Mikhailovich, Autocrat of all the Great and Little Russia. (Seal.).

☙ *64* ☙

Kotoshikhin's Description of the Private Lives of the Boyars and of Other Ranks of Muscovite Society

Grigorii K. Kotoshikhin (1630–1667) was a clerk in the *Posolskii prikaz* (Ambassadorial Department or Office), where he had the opportunity to encounter foreign diplomats (especially those from the Polish-Lithuanian Commonwealth, Sweden, and Denmark) and to observe the working and living habits of Muscovite aristocracy. His career was secure until it was discovered that he had divulged some state secrets to the Swedish ambassador. Kotoshikhin was removed from his post in the *Posolskii prikaz* and, as punishment, was conscripted into the army in 1664 and sent to the Polish-Russian battle front.

Kotoshikhin's army career was brief, coming to a sudden end when he refused to testify to alleged misconduct of his commanding officers. Fearing obvious repercussions, he deserted and made his way through Poland, Prussia, and Lubeck to Stockholm where, because of his past contacts with Swedish officials in Moscow, and his knowledge of Moscow's bureaucracy and of Muscovite society, he hoped for asylum and employment.

Since at that time Muscovy was the principal adversary of Sweden, the Swedish Foreign Office wanted to obtain all possible information about their secretive enemy. They encouraged Kotoshikhin to analyze for them, in writing, the working of Muscovy's institutions, its customs, and its strengths and weaknesses. He complied with their request and produced one of the most detailed, and, in many ways, the best account of seventeenth century Muscovy, its administrative structure, its economy, its society, and its officially prescribed *modus operandi*.

Presented here are Kotoshikhin's fascinating observations on private lives and wedding ceremonies of the upper classes of Muscovite society in the seventeenth century.

From Leo Wiener, ed., *Anthology of Russian Literature From the Earliest Period to the Present Time*, Part I, *From the Tenth Century to the Close of the Eighteenth Century* (New York: G. P. Putnam's Sons, 1902), pp. 139–149.

Boyárs and Near People live in their houses, both of stone and wood, that are not well arranged; their wives and children live all in separate rooms. Only a few of the greater *boyárs* have their own churches in their courts; and those of the high and middle *boyárs* who have no churches of their own, but who are permitted to have priests at their houses, have the matins and vespers and other prayers said in their own apartments, but they attend mass in any church they may choose; they never have the mass in their own houses. The *boyárs* and Near People pay their priests a yearly salary, according to agreement; if the priests are married people, they receive a monthly allowance of food and drink, but the widowed priests eat at the same table with their *boyárs*.

On church holidays, and on other celebrations, such as name days, birthdays, and christenings, they frequently celebrate together.

It is their custom to prepare simple dishes, without seasoning, without berries, or sugar, without pepper, ginger, or other spices, and they are little salted and without vinegar. They place on the table one dish at a time; the other dishes are brought from the kitchen and are held in the hands by the servants. The dishes that have little vinegar, salt, and pepper are seasoned at the table; there are in all fifty to one hundred such dishes.

The table manners are as follows: before dinner the hosts order their wives to come out and greet their guests. When the women come, they place themselves in the hall, or room, where the guests are dining, at the place of honor,[1] and the guests stand at the door; the women greet the guests with the small salute,[2] but the guests bow to the ground. Then the host makes a low obeisance to his guests and bids them kiss his wife. At the request of his guests, the host kisses his wife first; then the guests make individual bows and, stepping forward, kiss his wife and, walking back again, bow to her once more; she makes the small salute each time she kisses a guest. Then the hostess brings each guest a glass of double- or treble-spiced brandy, the size of the glass being a fourth, or a little more, of a quart. The host makes as many low obeisances as there are guests, asking each one in particular to partake of the brandy which his wife is offering them. By the request of the guests, the host bids his wife to drink first, then he drinks himself, and then the guests are served; the guests make a low obeisance before drinking, and also after they have drunk and as they return the glass. To those that do not drink brandy, a cup of Rumney or Rhine wine, or some other liquor, is offered.

After this drinking the hostess makes a bow to the guests and retires to her apartments to meet her guests, the wives of the *boyárs*. The hostess and the wives of the guests never dine with the men, except at weddings; an exception is also made when the guests are near relatives and there are no outsiders present at the dinner. During the dinner, the host and guests drink after every course a cup of brandy, or Rumney or Rhine wine, and spiced and pure beer, and various kinds of meads. When they bring the round cakes to the table, the host's daughters-in-law, or married daughters, or the wives of near relatives come into the room, and the guests rise and, leaving the table, go to the door and salute the women; then the husbands of the women salute them, and beg the guests to kiss their wives and drink the wine they offer. The guests comply with their request and return to the table, while the women go back to their apartments. After dinner the host and guests drink more freely each other's healths, and drive home again. The *boyárs'* wives dine and drink in the same manner in their own apartments, where there are no men present.

When a *boyár* or Near Man is about to marry off his son, or himself, or a brother, or nephew, or daughter, or sister, or niece, he, having found out where there is a marriageable girl, sends his friends, men or women, to the father of that girl, to say that such and such a one had sent them to inquire whether he would be willing to give his daughter or relative to him or his relative, and what the girl's dowry would be in the trousseau, money, patrimony, and serfs. If the person addressed is willing to give his daughter, or relative, he replies to the inquiry that he intends to marry off the girl, only he has to consider the matter with his wife and family, and that he will give a definite answer on a certain day; but if he does not wish to give him the girl, knowing that he is a drunkard, or fast, or has some other bad habit, he will say at once that he will not give him the girl, or he will find some excuse for refusing the request.

Having taken counsel with his wife and family, and having decided to give him the girl, he makes a detailed list of her dowry, in money, silver, and other ware, dresses, patrimony, and serfs, and sends it to the people who had come to him from the prospective bridegroom, and they, in their turn, take it to the bridegroom. Nothing is told of the matter to the prospective bride, who remains in ignorance thereof.

The dowry of the bride appearing satisfactory, the groom sends his people to the bride's parents, to ask them to present the girl. The bride's parents reply that they are willing to show their daughter, only not to the prospective groom, but to his father, mother, sister, or near female relative, in whom the groom may have special confidence. On the appointed day, the groom sends his mother or sister to inspect the bride; the bride's parents make preparations for that day, attire their daughter in a fine garment, invite their relatives to dinner, and seat their daughter at the table.

When the inspectress arrives, she is met with the honor due her, and is placed at the table near the bride. Sitting at the table, the inspectress converses with the girl on all kinds of subjects, in order to try her mind and manner of speech, and closely watches her face, eyes, and special marks, in order to bring a correct report to the bridegroom; having stayed a short time, she returns to the bridegroom. If the inspectress takes no liking to the bride, having discovered that she is silly, or homely, or has imperfect eyes, or is lame, or a poor talker, and so reports to the groom, he gives her up, and that is the last of it. But if the bride has found favor in the inspectress's eyes, and she tells the groom that the girl is good and clever, and perfect in speech and all things, the groom sends his former friends again to the girl's parents, telling them that he likes their daughter, and that he wishes to come to a parley to write the marriage contract, in order to marry her on a certain date. The bride's parents send word to the groom through his trusted people that he should come to the parley with a few of his friends in whom he has most confidence on a certain day, in the forenoon or afternoon.

On the appointed day, the groom puts on his best clothes, and drives with his father, or near relatives, or friends whom he loves best to the bride's parents. Upon arrival, the bride's parents and her near relatives meet them with due honor, after which they go into the house and seat themselves according to rank. Having sat a while, the groom's father or other relative remarks that they have come for the good work, as he has bid them; the host answers that he is glad to see them, and that he is ready to take up the matter. Then both sides begin to discuss all kinds of marriage articles and to set the day for the wedding according to how soon they can get ready for it, in a week, a month, half a year, a year, or even more. Then they enter their names and the bride's name and the names of witnesses in the marriage contract, and it is agreed that he is to take the girl on a certain date, without fail, and that the girl is to be turned over to him on that date, without fail; and it is provided in that contract that if the groom does not take the girl on the appointed day, or the father will not give him his daughter on that day, the offending party has to pay 1000, or 5000, or 10,000 *rubles*, as the agreement may be. Having stayed a while, and having eaten and drunk, they return home, without having seen the bride, and without the bride having seen the groom; but the mother, or married sister, or wife of some relative comes out to present the groom with some embroidery from the bride.

If, after that parley, the groom finds out something prejudicial to the bride, or someone interested in the groom tells him that she is deaf, or mute, or maimed, or has some other bad characteristic, and the groom does not want to take her—and the parents of the bride complain about it to the Patriarch that he has not taken the girl according to the marriage articles, and does not want to take her, and thus has dishonored her; or the bride's parents, having found out about the groom that he is a drunkard, or dice player, or maimed, or has done something bad, will not give him their daughter, and the groom complains to the Patriarch—the Patriarch institutes an inquiry, and the fine is collected from the guilty party according to the contract, and is given to the groom or bride, as the case may be; and then both may marry whom they please.

But if both parties carry out their agreement, and get ready for the wedding on the appointed day, then the groom invites to the wedding his relatives and such other people as he likes, to be his ceremonial guests, in the same manner as I described before about the Tsar's wedding[3]; on the part of the bride the guests are invited in the same way. On the day of the wedding, tables are set at the houses of the groom and bride and, the word being given the groom that it is time to fetch the bride, they all set out according to the ceremonial rank: First the bread-men carry bread on a tray, then, if it be summer, the priest with the cross rides on horseback, but in winter in a sleigh; then follow the *boyárs*, the thousand-man, and the groom.

Having reached the court of the bride's house, they enter the hall in ceremonial order, and the bride's father and his guests meet them with due honor, and the order of the wedding is the same as described in the Tsar's wedding. When the time arrives to drive to church to perform the marriage, the bridesmaids ask her parents to give the groom and bride their blessing for the marriage. They bless them with words, but before leaving bless them with a holy image, and, taking their daughter's hand, give her to the groom.

Then the ceremonial guests, the priest, and the groom with his bride, whose hand he is holding, go out of the hall, and her parents and their guests accompany them to the court; the groom places the bride in a *kolymága* or *kaptána*, mounts a horse, or seats himself in a sleigh; the ceremonial guests do likewise, and all drive to the church where they are to be married. The bride's parents and their guests return to the hall, where they eat and drink until news is brought from the groom; the bride is accompanied only by her own and the bridegroom's go-betweens. The two having been united, the whole troop drives to the groom's house, and news is sent to the bride's father that they have been propitiously married. When they arrive at the groom's court, the groom's parents and their guests meet them, and the parents, or those who are in their stead, bless them with the images, and offer them bread and salt, and then all seat themselves at the table and begin to eat, according to the ceremony; and then the bride is unveiled.

The next morning the groom drives out with the bridesmaids to call the guests, those of his and the bride's, to dinner. When he comes to the bride's parents, he thanks them for their having well brought up their daughter, and for having given her to him in perfect health; and having made the round to all the guests, he returns home. When all the guests have arrived, the bride offers gifts to all the ceremonial guests. Before dinner the groom goes with all the company to the palace to make his obeisance to the Tsar. Having arrived in the presence of the Tsar, all make a low obeisance, and the Tsar, without taking off his cap, asks the married couple's health. The groom bows to the ground, and then the Tsar congratulates those who are united in legitimate wedlock, and blesses the married pair with images, and he presents them with forty sables, and for their garments a bolt of velvet, and atlas, and gold-colored silk, and calamanco, and simple taffeta, and a silver vessel, a pound and a half to two pounds in weight, to each of them; but the bride is not present at the audience. Then the Tsar offers the thousand-man, bride-groom, and the ceremonial guests a cup of Rumney wine, and then a pitcher of cherry wine, and after they have emptied their wine the Tsar dismisses them.

After arriving home, they begin to eat and drink, and after the dinner the parents and guests bless the married couple with images and make them all kinds of presents, and after dinner the guests drive home. On the third day, the bride and groom and the guests go to dinner to the bride's parents, with all their guests, and after the dinner the bride's parents and their guests make presents to the married couple, and they drive home; and that is the end of the festivity.

During the time that the groom is in the presence of the Tsar, the bride sends in her name presents to the Tsarítsa and Tsarévnas, tidies of taffeta, worked with gold and silver and pearls; the Tsarítsa and Tsarévnas accept these gifts, and send to inquire about the bride's health.

During all the wedding festivities, no women are present, and there is no music, except blowing of horns and beating of drums.

The proceeding is the same when a widowed daughter, or sister, or niece is married off: the ceremonial and the festivity are the same.

In the beginning of the festivity, the priest who is to marry the pair receives from the Patriarch and the authorities a permit, with the seal attached to it, to marry them, having first ascertained that the bride and groom are not related by sponsorship, nor by the ties of consanguinity in the sixth and seventh generation, nor that he is the husband of a fourth wife, nor she the wife of a fourth husband; but if he discover that they are related by spon-sorship, and so forth, he is not allowed to marry them. Should the priest permit such an unlawful marriage to take place, with his knowledge or without his knowledge, he would be discharged from his priesthood and, if he was knowingly guilty, he has to pay a big fine, and the authorities lock him up for a year; but the married pair is divorced, without being fined, except the sin which they have incurred, and if they have not been previously married three times, they may marry again.

If a widower wants to marry a maiden, the ceremonial at the wedding is the same, but during the wreathing in church the wreath is placed on the groom's right shoulder, whereas the bride wears her wreath upon her head; if a widower for the third time marries a maiden, the ceremonial is the same, but the wreath is placed on the groom's left shoulder, and the bride wears hers upon her head. The same is done when a widow marries for the second or third time. But when a widower marries for the second or third time a widow, then there is no wreathing, and only a prayer is said instead of the wreathing, and the wedding ceremonial is different from the one mentioned above.

The manner of the parley, marriage, and ceremonial wedding is the same with the lower orders of the nobility as described above, and the wedding is as sumptuous as they can afford to make it, but they do not call upon the Tsar, except those of his retinue.

Among the merchants and peasants the parley and the ceremonial are exactly the same, but they differ in their acts and dresses from the nobility, each according to his means.

It sometimes happens that a father or mother has two or three daughters, where the eldest daughter is maimed, being blind, or lame, or deaf, or mute, while the other sisters are perfect in shape and beauty and speech. When a man begins to sue for their daughter, and he sends his mother, or sister, or someone else in whom he has confidence to inspect her, the parents sometimes substitute the second or third daughter for their maimed sister, giving her the name of the latter, so that the inspectress, not knowing the deceit, takes a liking to the girl and reports to the groom that she is a proper person to marry. Then the groom, depending upon her words, has a parley with the girl's parents, that he is to marry her upon an appointed day, and that the parents are to give her to him upon the appointed day, and the fine is set so high that the guilty party is not able to pay it. When the wedding takes place, the parents turn over to him the maimed daughter, whose name is given in the articles of marriage, but who is not the one the inspectresses had seen. But the groom cannot discover on the wedding day that she is blind, or disfigured, or has some other defect, or that she is deaf or mute, for at the wedding she is veiled and does not say a word, nor can he know whether she is lame, because her bridesmaids lead her under her arms.

But in that case the man who has been deceived complains to the Patriarch and authorities, and these take the articles of marriage and institute an inquiry among the neighbors and housefolk, each one individually, whether the person he had married is the one indicated by name in the marriage articles. If so, the articles are valid, and no faith is to be put in his contention, on the ground that it was his business to be sure whom he was going to marry. But if the neighbors and housefolk depose that the bride is not the same as mentioned by name in the articles, the married pair is divorced, and the parents have to pay a large fine and damages to the groom, and besides the father is beaten with the knout, or his punishment is even more severe, according to the Tsar's will.

The same punishment is meted out to the man who presents his serving maid or a widow in place of his unmarried daughter, by giving her another name and dressing her up so as to look like his daughter, or when his daughter is of short stature and they place her on a high chair in such a way that her defect is not noticeable.

When parents have maimed or old daughters, and no one wants to marry them, they are sent to a monastery to be shorn nuns.

When a man wants to inspect the bride himself, and the parents grant the request, knowing that she is fair and that they need not be ashamed of her, but the groom, having taken no liking to her, decries her with damaging and injurious words, and thus keeps other suitors away from her, and the bride's parents complain to the Patriarch or authorities: these institute an inquiry, and having found the man guilty, marry him to the girl by force; but if he has married another girl before the complaint has been entered, the girl's disgrace is taken from her by an *ukase*.

When a man marries off his daughter or sister, and gives her a large dowry in serfs and patrimony, and that daughter or sister, having borne no children, or having borne some who have all died, dies herself, the dowry is all taken from her husband and is turned over to those who had married her off. But if she leaves a son or daughter, the dowry is, for the sake of her child, not taken from her husband.

Gentle reader! Wonder not, it is nothing but the truth when I say that nowhere in the whole world is there such deception practiced with marriageable girls as in the kingdom of Muscovy; there does not exist there the custom, as in other countries, for the suitor to see and sue for the bride himself.

The *boyárs* and Near People have in their houses 100, or 200, or 300, or 500, or 1000 servants, male and female, according to their dignity and possessions. These servants receive a yearly salary, if they are married, two, three, five, or ten *rubles* according to their services, and their wearing apparel, and a monthly allowance of bread and victuals; they live in their own rooms in the court of the *boyár's* house. The best of these married servants are sent out by the *boyárs* every year, by rotation, to their estates and villages, with the order to collect from their peasants the taxes and rents. The unmarried older servants receive some small wages, but the younger ones receive nothing; all the unmarried servants get their wearing apparel, hats, shirts, and boots; the older of these servants live in the farther lower apartments, and receive their food and drink from the kitchen; on holidays they receive two cups of brandy each. The female servants who are widows remain living in the houses of their husbands, and they receive a yearly wage and a monthly allowance of food; other widows and girls stay in the rooms of the *boyárs'* wives and daughters, and they receive their wearing apparel, and their food from the *boyár's* kitchen.

When these girls are grown up, the *boyárs* marry them, and also the widows, to some of their servants to whom they have taken a liking, but sometimes by force. The wedding takes place in the *boyár's* hall, according to the rank of the marrying parties; the food and festive dresses are furnished by the *boyár*. The girls are never married to any person outside the *boyár's* court, because both male and female servants are his perpetual serfs. In the *boyár's* house there is an office for all domestic affairs, where an account is kept of income and expenses, and all the affairs of the servants and peasants are investigated and settled.

Notes

1. In the front corner, under the holy images.
2. Bending as far as the girdle.
3. "The wedding ceremony is as follows: on the Tsar's side the first order is the father and mother, or those who are in place of his parents; the second order, the *travellers*—the chief priest with the cross, the *thousand-man*, who is a great personage in that procession, and then the Tsar and eight *boyárs*. The duties of the *travellers* are as follows: they stay with the Tsar and Tsarítsa at the crowning in church, and at the table occupy higher places than the others; the *friends* (*drúzhka*), whose duty it is to call the guests to the wedding, to make speeches at the wedding in the name of the thousand-man and Tsar, and to carry presents; the *bridesmaids* (*svákha*), whose duty it is to watch the Tsarítsa, to dress her, and undress her; the *candleholder*, who holds the candle when they get the Tsarítsa ready for the crowning; the *breadholders*, who carry the bread on litters to and from church (these litters are covered with gold velvet and embroidered cloth and sable furs; the *equerry* with his suite. The third order is the *sitting boyárs*, twelve men and twelve women, who sit as guests at the tables, with the Tsar's parents, but do not go to church with the Tsar. The fourth order is *of the court*, who attend to the food and drink."

⚔ 65 ⚔

A Decree
on Runaway Peasants, 1661

Following the issuing of restrictions on free movement of the peasantry
in the middle of the fifteenth century (see Chapter 38), conditions of
Russian peasants deteriorated rapidly. By the early seventeenth century
the majority had become serfs of one kind or another, and to keep them
in that status, the nobles obtained governmental permission to search for
and reclaim those who might have escaped (see Chapter 57). By the
middle of the seventeenth century, serfdom, with its inhuman conditions,
was firmly and almost universally entrenched. Conditions were so inhuman that many serfs, indeed whole villages, fled their native places to
escape a slow death. Some of them joined various cossack bands and
others sought shelter with perhaps kinder nobles. This practice became
so common that in 1661 the government issued a new decree that prohibited the harboring of runaway peasants and specified penalties for
violators.

If alien runaway peasants are found in the possession of a lord of a manor
. . . and it is established that they have been taken in by the administrator
of the manor without the knowledge of the lord . . . this administrator should
be lashed mercilessly with the knout, so that from this time on others will
have no desire to take in alien runaway persons and peasants.

   And the fugitives should be returned to the plaintiff, along with wives and
children, their goods and their grain. And they should be sent back to their
old domiciles, to the *pomestie* estates, or to the hereditary estates of the lords
from whom they fled, in wagons belonging to those people who [illegally]
took them in. And compensation should be extracted from the people who
took the fugitives in as possessions, covering the time during which they used
the fugitives, according to a tsar's decree [of 1642].

   If, however, the owners of the hereditary or of the *pomestie* estates possess
written confirmation from Moscow that the administrator of the manor had
permission to retain runaway persons and peasants, or if it can be established

---

From *Polnoe Sobranie Zakonov Russkoi Imperii . . . 1649–1913* (Complete Collection of the
Laws of the Russian Empire . . . 1649–1913) (St. Petersburg: 1830), vol. 1, No. 307, pp.
556–558. Translation mine. Words in brackets are mine.

that the owners of the hereditary or of the *pomestie* estates themselves took in the fugitives, the administrators in these cases should not be lashed with the knout. And the great sovereign and the *boyars* have decided that from each [guilty] lord on whose *pomestie* or on whose hereditary estate a runaway peasant is found, an additional serf shall be taken, together with wife, children, goods, and grain, in addition, of course, to the compensation covering the years the runaway spent there. All these should be given to the manorial lord who formerly owned the runaway. And if more than just one runaway is found working for a lord, then one should take not only all the runaways but also one of his own peasants for each of the runaways, in order that no one else from this time on will want to harbor and use alien peasants.

⚔ 66 ⚔

Krizhanich's Observations on Russia's Potential Strengths and Weaknesses

Iurii Krizhanich (1618–1683) was a Jesuit-educated Croatian priest who took upon himself a two-fold task: the reconciliation of Eastern Orthodoxy with Roman Catholicism under papal leadership, and the concomitant unification of Slavic peoples under Moscow's hegemony. In pursuit of these goals he studied hard, travelled extensively, and in 1659 came to Moscow to begin to carry out his ambition.

Initially Moscow authorities treated him well. Soon, however, because he concealed certain details about his origin and was careless with the truth when answering questions about his background and objectives, he was arrested and banished to Siberia. During his fifteen years of Siberian exile Krizhanich wrote numerous works on history, government, politics, economics, religion, and other topics. The most important of his works in the Siberian wilderness was his *Besedy o pravleni* (Discourses on Government), which has become widely known under the pseudonym *Politika*, or more accurately *Russian Statecraft*. In this work Krizhanich provides a comprehensive analysis of Russia's potential strengths and

From John M. Letiche and Basil Dmytryshyn, *Russian Statecraft: The Politika of Iurii Krizhanich*. (Oxford–New York: Basil Blackwell, 1985), pp. 14–17, 110–111, 113–115, and 161–164. Reprinted with permission of Basil Blackwell, Inc.

weaknesses and offers valuable suggestions for transforming the country
into a major European and world power.

Although our famous [Russian] state is quite vast and immeasurable, nevertheless it is closed to trade on all sides. In the north, we are engirdled by the
Arctic Ocean and by wastelands. To the east and south, we are surrounded
by backward peoples with whom there can exist no trade. In the west—in
Lithuania and Belorussia—nothing is produced that we need, except for the
copper found among the Swedes. The Azov and Black Sea trade, which would
be very beneficial to this country, has been seized and is still held by the
Crimean Tatars. Trade in Astrakhan is hindered by the Nogai Tatars. The
Kalmucks interfere with our Bokhara trade in Siberia. As a result we have
only three safe marketplaces for overland trade: Novgorod, Pskov, and the
Archangel harbors for sea trade. But the road to the latter is incredibly distant
and difficult.

Thus it is evident, first, that this country has very few marketplaces and
that it is essential that there be more; but that without the tsar's help, no
one can organize them.

Second, that the country possesses no gold, silver, copper, tin, lead, mercury,
or good iron.

Third, that there are no precious stones, pearls, corals, and dyes at the same
time that the commonest and poorest people want them.

Fourth, that there is no sugar, saffron, pepper, cloves, nuts, ginger, myrrh,
thyme, nutmeg, or other spices and fragrances.

Fifth, that there are no olives, grapes, raisins, almonds, figs, lemons, walnuts,
chestnuts, plums, peaches, melons, or many other fruits.

Sixth, that in addition to this there are no basic and essential items, such
as cloth and other materials for wearing apparel—wool, silk, and cotton.

Seventh, that this country is devoid of stone and good lumber for construction and good clay for pottery.

Eighth, that the intellectual faculties of our people are undeveloped and
sluggish. The people are inexperienced in crafts and only slightly knowledgeable in trade, agriculture, and household management. Russians and Poles,
indeed the entire Slavic population, are totally ignorant of how to carry on
distant trade at sea as well as on land. Our merchants study neither arithmetic
nor accounting. Consequently, foreign merchants are always able to outwit
and mercilessly deceive us, all the more since they live throughout the entire
Russian land and buy up our goods at the lowest possible prices. It would
be possible to bear this if our people lived among them and could buy up
goods cheaply themselves. But our people do not live among them, and cannot
because of their natural impracticality, because of their undeveloped intellects,

and especially because of foreign envy and malice, which many of our people have experienced.

Ninth, that roads in this extensive state are long and difficult because of marshes and forests; and also that they are unsafe because of attacks by the Crimean and Nogai Tatars, and by the Kalmucks and other brigand-like peoples.

Tenth, that this country abounds only in furs, sheepskin, hemp, and most recently potash. Honey, wax, caviar, wheat, rye, flax, hides, and other goods exported from here are exported not because of their abundance, but out of necessity and because of the machinations of foreigners. As a result we are deprived of the fruits of our own land and suffer shortages in these goods.

There is only one way to help the people to meet many of their needs. Let the sovereign tsar, in name and in reality, resume control over the entire trade with other nations, as he has done in the past, and let him retain it for future times. Only in this way will it be possible to keep accounts in such a way that we neither export the many goods of which we have no surplus nor import foreign goods we do not need. In this way the sovereign tsar will be able to increase the number of marketplaces and customs officials essential to the state for conveyance of goods.

Then foreign merchants will have nothing to do here. Cloth and other foreign goods will pass through our own hands to Siberia, to the Bokharans and the Indians; to Astrakhan, to the Persians; to Azov, to the Turks; to Putivl, to the Ukrainians and the Wallachians. Conversely, goods from these nations will flow to us and through our hands to the Germans and other Western Europeans, the Poles, and the Lithuanians.

Through such activity the entire state will become wealthy, and all of its inhabitants will rejoice. The only people who will be dissatisfied will be the great merchants, whose revenues will be somewhat decreased. But one should pay no attention to their plight because this matter concerns the overall benefit of all the people. . . .

Foreigners judge us by superficial standards—they judge us only by what they can see and hear: our appearance, our language, our clothes and customs, and the way we build our houses and make our tools.

Our *appearance* is neither first nor last. Therefore, our intelligence is neither first nor last, and is adequate for the study of science if we put great effort and determination into it. It has been said that a moderate intelligence used with great effort is better than a great intelligence used carelessly.

Our *language* is very poor and inadequate. We are ignorant of our history and legends. We are incapable of sophisticated political discourse. Because of this, we lose the respect of other nations.

The *style of clothes* is a vital sign of human intelligence. Those who have devised the most appropriate style clearly surpass others in natural intelligence.

An attractive style of clothing often helps a man in achieving his life's ambitions. Conversely, a poor style of clothes does little to help anyone.

The poor style of our dress results in excessive expenditure for decoration, undermines the spirit of our soldiers, and decreases the honor of our ambassadors. In addition, long hair, beards, and shaved heads make us look ridiculous. We resemble a tribe of wooden goblins let loose among human beings.

Laws and custom determine what will be virtue and vice, justice and injustice, but we are not concerned here with these fundamental customs. We speak only of daily customs and the ruder aspects of life that manifest themselves in conversation, in types of food, in cleanliness, and similar matters.

Foreigners criticize our food as dirty, attributing it to our generally coarse and untidy way of life. This is because we put coins in our mouths, and because a commoner filling a pitcher with liquid will stick his two fingers into it before offering it to his guest. *Kvas* looks dirty when it is sold, and the dishes in which other foods are sold often are dirty.

The king of Denmark once made the following remark about our ambassadors: "If these people come often I will have to build a pig-shed for them, because any place in which they stay becomes uninhabitable for half a year, thanks to the smell they leave behind." In another country, the following was written mockingly in a popular weekly newspaper about our ambassadors: "If they go into a store to buy something, no one will enter it for a whole hour after they leave on account of the stench."

Our houses in some places are unfit for habitation. The windows are small and there is inadequate ventilation, so that people are blinded by the smoke. They nail boards under the benches, causing debris to collect indefinitely because it is impossible to sweep it out. Our carts are very poorly made, while other implements are completely worthless.

Because of all this there can be little wonder why foreigners condemn us. They also invent a great deal that does not exist. Yet the harm that stems from the inadequacy of our appearance, language, clothing, customs, and housing is still not that great. Far greater harm stems from the cause of these inadequacies, which I call *xenomania*, or craze for all things foreign. We admire every foreign item and we despise and reject our own things. We take in all foreigners, admire their beautiful appearance, resounding language, and free (but more accurately licentious) way of life, and we grant them authority over us in our own country, enabling them to devour all of our wealth and dominate us. . . .

Causes of Misfortune

The first cause of [Russia's] misfortune and poverty is *luxurious dress*. Shirts are decorated with gold and silk, boots with copper wire. Pearls are worn even by men. Nowhere in Europe do such disgraceful practices exist. Even the lowest common people wear silk clothes. Their women cannot be distinguished from the leading *boyar* ladies. Our country has no pearls—yet everyone wants to wear them. Our country has no dyes—yet everyone wants to wear colored textiles.

The second cause is the *lack of natural resources*. The country does not have any of its own precious stones, pearls, coral, or dyes; it does not have gold, silver, copper, tin, lead, mercury, or good iron. There is no silk, cotton, or wool for textiles. There is no rice and no pepper, saffron, sugar, cloves, myrrh, thyme, muscat, or other spices and aromatics. There are no fruits like grapes, olives, almonds, raisins, figs, or lemons. We lack balsam, camphor, amber, and other medicinal drugs, herbs, and roots; and we lack raw materials like limestone, clay, and good forest land.

The third cause is the *long winter*, which necessitates an enormous amount of firewood and hay and supplies for both people and livestock. The summer is short, cold, and rainy, so that abundant crops cannot be grown; and what survives is difficult to harvest because of the rains and the lack of time. As a result, it is possible to feed only a small population and to keep only a small number of livestock which, by the way, is smaller than anywhere else. Moreover, not only in Russia but among the Poles, Bulgars, Serbs, and Croats—wherever the Slavic tongue prevails—only small horses can be found. Yet everyone around us—Tatars, Turks, Hungarians, and Germans—has big, fast, powerful horses. Because our bodies are large and our horses are small, we appear clumsy on horseback. The Tatars are small, but their horses are large and strong, which is why Crimean horsemen seem to be better than our own.

The fourth cause is *evil neighbors and merchants*. The Crimean [Tatars], the Nogai [Tatars], and other barbaric peoples frequently devastate and despoil this country. At every favorable opportunity, the Swedes use deceit to take something away. The Greeks persuade us to trade much of our wealth for false gems and glass. Finally, German merchants and military officers clean out the remainder of our wealth.

The fifth cause is the *scanty population* and sparsely inhabited land. This stems from drastic and cruel laws, which will be discussed later.

Causes of Good Fortune

Whoever does not value the good things God has given him is unworthy of them. If we wish to receive new national benefits from God (such as peace, security, and prosperity), we should understand and acknowledge all the benefits that God has already bestowed upon us. (We speak here only of worldly benefits.) Just what benefits has God bestowed on this tsardom and why, as a result, should it consider itself fortunate?

The first, most important, and leading benefit is *absolute autocracy*. This is "the rod of Moses" with which the sovereign tsar can perform all necessary miracles. Under such a system of government, it is easy to correct all mistakes, shortcomings, and distortions and to introduce all kinds of beneficial laws. We will attain this if we obey the sovereign tsar, the lieutenant of God, in everything; and if the sovereign gives each layer of society appropriate privileges. In addition, we should maintain dignified relations with peaceful nations, offend no one without cause, conclude alliances with like nations, and take advantage of happy circumstances, opportunities, and divine grace.

The second cause is *safe frontiers*, because this tsardom needs fear no enemy from the Arctic Ocean. Moreover, there are no powerful kings in Siberia; only the Kalmucks and other nomadic peoples, whom we need not fear.

The third cause is the presence of *good neighbors*, such as the Persians, with whom we can trade and whom we need not fear will violate our dignity. The Poles and Lithuanians are also good neighbors. We need not fear that they will start a war provided we ourselves do not precipitate one. We can also conclude a very advantageous alliance with them. More will be said about this later.

The fourth cause is the presence of ideal *circumstances for large-scale trade*. We are capable of receiving goods from various nations and transmitting them to various other nations, as do the inhabitants of Danzig (from which practice they get rich year after year). We can carry goods from the Germans to the Turks, Persians, Cherkess, Kalmucks, Bokharans, Chinese, and Dauri, and transport the goods of these nations to Germans, Poles, and Lithuanians. We could build new marketplaces similar to Archangel, first along the Don, second in Astrakhan, and third near the Kalmucks. Lesser marketplaces could be established in Putivl, along the Lithuanian and Swedish frontiers, adjacent to the Dauri territory, and in appropriate places along the Caspian Sea. We could also dispatch our merchants to live and trade throughout the Bokharan and Persian realms, as noted earlier.

The fifth cause of good fortune consists of *favorable conditions for shipping*. We have ports on the Arctic and Caspian Seas as well as on the Black Sea. We have navigable rivers: the Northern Dvina, Don, Volga, Irtysh, Ob, and others. We possess an abundance of hemp, tar, and timber suitable for ship building, and have boats and all sorts of sailing craft; but apparently we are unfamiliar with marine transport. We should fill the Caspian with our ships.

We should devote more attention to river transport—especially in Siberia—and do everything necessary to achieve it. The value of Siberia is contingent on the use of its rivers; whoever is the master of these rivers is the master of the entire territory.

It would also be useful to discover if water routes exist from Siberia to Dauri, or China, or India; and from Magazeia and Ob to Archangel.

Clearly, we are also blessed with *domestic products*: furs, reindeer hides, colored hides, hemp, potash, caviar, fish, honey wax, grain, meat, and flax, among other things. We should conserve these divine gifts, not squander them. We certainly should sell to foreigners, but not deprive ourselves of these riches. On some goods, an annual export quota should be imposed. This can be achieved only if all foreign merchants leave the country, and if the sovereign tsar takes over the whole import and export trade. . . .

Nature has given us a prime advantage. *Our people are not ambitious.* They do not yearn for power and therefore readily submit themselves to anyone who knows their nature, who can thus easily force them to do hard work or engage in war. Most other nations are different. We are content with *simple food and drink* and do not make any special effort to prepare it. The Germans, on the other hand, never stop boasting about their gastronomic delights and their luxury. But we should neither envy them nor seek out ways to import such viands from India. *In preparing their beds*, our people do not exert any special effort either. All Germans in contrast drown themselves in feather beds.

The first major good fortune of this country is the fact that is has secure borders along the Arctic Ocean. Our second good fortune is our good neighbors: the Persians, Cherkessians, and Poles (if we could discover how to utilize them). Our third good fortune is our weak neighbors such as the Kalmucks, Samoyeds, and other Siberian natives, who pose no danger of major attacks.

A fourth good fortune lies in the resources of our land and rivers. Compared with Poland, Lithuania, Sweden, and Belorussia, Russia is well endowed and bountiful. Here grow large and delicious garden fruits, cabbages, radishes, beets, onions, turnips, and so on. In Moscow, turkeys, chickens, and eggs are larger and tastier than those available in the above-mentioned countries. The bread that commoners and rural people eat is more plentiful and delicious in Russia than in Lithuania, Poland, or Sweden. Fish, too, is available here in abundance.

A fifth good fortune of this land is the navigability of its seas and rivers, as well as the availability of various materials for shipbuilding. We, too, are capable of starting and developing an extensive overland trade system that would transport goods from nation to nation.

There are also some very good things in our *laws and national customs*. Of these the first and best is absolute autocracy. A second good custom is the closure of our borders. We deny foreigners free entry into our country and prohibit our own people from wandering outside the borders of the realm

without vital reasons. These two customs are the pillars—the heart and soul—
of this realm and should be preserved by all available means. In effect, they
should be reinforced by the expulsion of all foreigners, a matter that will be
discussed later.

Another beneficial custom is that no one is allowed to lead an idle life—
that is, no one can free himself from public and national service, be it at
court, in government offices, or in the military. In contrast, many German
nobles and burghers live in idleness and luxury, like the ancient Sardanapalu,
or like weaned-out pigs who bring no benefit to anyone.

Still another good custom is that no one is allowed to spread heresy. A
further beneficial custom and national good fortune centers in our spiritual
Palladium: we maintain sacred vigils, attend matins, participate at the Holy
Liturgy, sleep little, rise early, eat late, and restrain our bodies through a
multitude of genuflections and fastings. It seems to me that this is the most
vital factor in the preservation of our realm. This is the true and lofty fortress.
For that reason our kings and pastors should especially see to it that strict
preservation of the well-established rules of the church are in no way violated
by any modification.

A final useful custom is the method of punishment used in this tsardom—
namely the exile system, under which those who have been exiled receive
means to live, or even salaries from the ruler. In this way the tsar can punish
any guilty person without causing a popular uprising. It is bad when a well-
known and previously useful person is punished for some transgression by
being completely abandoned, as the emperor Justinian did when he blinded
Belisarius (once his military commander) and confiscated all of his property,
forcing him to live by begging.

Those who counsel that exiles should receive no sustenance, counsel poorly.
It may perhaps be that they are now useless, but providing them with food
is not useless.

Knowing our national advantages (both bestowed and acquired) we can
now compare our life with that of other nations and conclude that Russia is
richer than Lithuania, Poland, and Sweden because our people can live in
greater prosperity. Although Sweden has copper ore and Poland some silver,
these advantages cannot compare with the combined good fortunes of Russia.
However, when we compare ourselves with other, richer countries (such as
Greece, France, Italy, Spain, or England) that have vineyards, wool, silk, dyes,
and other expensive goods, and where there exists better political organization
and more developed industry, it is essential to acknowledge that the nobles
and burghers are much richer in those countries than in Russia. Even the
richest of our Russian people do not live in such luxury as do their more

common people. Any town, there, has more gold and silver—and all other goods—than all Russian towns.

It is a fact that in England, Germany, France, and other countries there are many cities which have more wealth than our entire nation—excluding the tsar's treasury. If Russia were as populous, as naturally productive, and administratively as well organized as France, it, too, would have a seat among the leading nations.

From the preceding account, the following conclusion can be drawn. We should not compete with these very affluent nations either in hospitality, dress, the splendor of our silverware, or the hiring of foreign mercenaries.

We can boast before the Poles, Lithuanians, Belorussians, Tatars, Siberians, and similar peoples about our food, drink, clothes, and silver. But if we boast about food and drink to Germans, Frenchmen, and Italians, they would simply ridicule us and consider us fools. We support this impression by getting stone drunk in front of foreigners. . . .

Finally, let us remember that although some people in these other countries live more comfortably than we do, nevertheless our peasants and poor townsmen, who make their living from handicrafts, live much better than do the peasants in those rich countries. For there, in many places, the land has been set aside for vineyards, specialized crops, cultivation of dyes, mining of ores, and similar uses, so that grain cannot be cultivated. The agriculturists and craftsmen engaged in these enterprises cannot grow grain and thus live quite poorly. Sometimes for the entire year they drink only water. All wine produced is sold. They eat bread sparingly and know nothing about *kvas*. Some eat bread made from chestnuts, sorghum, or Turkish wheat that resembles gravel more than true bread. Many regions, sometimes whole countries, consist of mountains. There grain does not grow at all, and the people must eat bread that is scant and tasteless. This is the case in Switzerland, the Tirol, and Salzburg.

Thanks to God's grace, here in Russia all people, both rich and poor, eat rye bread, fish, and meat, and they drink *kvas* if they do not have beer. As a result, peasants and poor craftsmen live far better in Russia than do their counterparts in Greece, Spain, and other countries where meat and fish are quite expensive and where firewood is sold by weight. People who live in those warm countries also suffer more during the winter from cold. They sleep there in cold rooms without ovens or fireplaces, while here we have heated rooms.

⚥ 67 ⚥

An English View of the Muscovite Tsar
and of His Society

In the seventeenth century Muscovy was inundated by west European (English, German, Swedish, French, Dutch, and other) craftsmen, merchants, and soldiers of fortune. Some came on their own initiative. Others came on the invitation of the tsar or his officials. Regardless of how these foreigners came to Moscow, or of their purpose, many Muscovites viewed them with suspicion, considered their lifestyle distasteful, and resented their behavior and contempt for everything Muscovite or Orthodox.

Most of these foreigners performed three essential services. They supplied Muscovy with the most advanced west European experience, ideas, and technology (military and industrial) that enabled the Muscovites to triumph over such of their long-standing adversaries as the Swedes, the Poles, and the Ottoman Turks. Moreover, west European ideas convinced a few influential officials in Moscow that their country trailed western Europe in science, technology, education, and other matters, and their concern laid the foundation for the great transformation of Muscovy under Peter the Great. Finally, many west European visitors left priceless impressions of Muscovy and of its people.

While their accounts of customs, habits, virtues, follies, strengths, and weaknesses must be viewed with caution, nevertheless they provide us with rare glimpses of Muscovy in the seventeenth century. The following two entries are by Samuel Collins, an English doctor who spent nine years in Moscow as Tsar Alexei's personal physician. His description of the tsar and his daily routine and his commentary on the Muscovite scene are superb and are reproduced here to clarify some misconceptions and to provide a better understanding of Muscovy.

A Contemporary English View of
Tsar Alexei and His Surroundings

His Imperial Majesty [Tsar Alexei] is a goodly person, two months older than King Charles II. He is of sanguine complexion, light brown hair, and his

---

From Samuel Collins, *The Present State of Russia...* (London: 1671), portions of Chapters 2, 4, 9, 13, 14, 15, 23, and 24. Spelling has been modernized to facilitate reading.

beard [is] uncut. He is tall and fat, of a majestical deportment, severe in his anger, bountiful, charitable, chastely uxorious, strict in his devotions, and a favorer of his religion. And had he not such a cloud of sycophants and jealous nobility about him, who blind his good intentions, he might be numbered amongst the best and wisest of princes. . . . This emperor is of a warlike spirit engaged against the Crimean [Tatars], the Poles, and the Swedes. . . . This empire has been impoverished, depopulated, and spoiled [that is, devastated by these wars] so much in ten years as it will not recover its pristine prosperity in forty. Seven years ago [in 1663] the plague carried away 700,000 or 800,000 people. And three years since, the Crimean [Tatars] carried away captive out of the borders 400,000 souls into perpetual captivity. Besides, 300,000 were consumed and killed by dint of sword in several armies. The best of the land is harassed, the rest is untilled for want of men. For in 500 *verst's* [one *versta* equals 3,500 feet or 1.06 kilometers] travel up the river [Moscow?], you may see ten women and children for one man. All things are there become scarce; everything six times the rate it was formerly, and copper money [introduced in 1662] is not valued. . . .

Return we now to our Great Emperor, who is an absolute monarch, but has a council, both general and particular, to advise with. His dominions were enlarged by his forefathers; for at first they were but dukes of Vladimir and increasing in strength possessed themselves of Moscow, or as they write, Moskva. . . . The present emperor comes of Ivan's [IV—that is, the Terrible] race by the mother's side. He had an elder brother, a hopeful prince, although he would take pigeons and pick out their eyes, saying to one: "You are a traitor!" And to another, cutting off his head: "You are Ivan, a rebellious traitor to my father and me!" But he died young. . . .

The present Emperor's name is Alexei Mikhailovich Romanov, namely, Alexei, the son of Michael Romanov. He puts many titles into his broad seal as the Spaniards do, and thus he styles himself: By the Grace of God, We Great Lord Tsar and Grand Duke Alexei Mikhailovich of all Great, Little, and White Russia; Self-upholder of Moscow, Kiev, Vladimir, and Novgorod; Tsar of Kazan, Tsar of Astrakhan, and Tsar of Siberia; Lord of Pskov and Grand Duke of Smolensk, Tver, Iurga, Perm, Viatka, and Bulgaria; Lord and Grand Duke of Nizhnii Novgorod, Chernigov, Riazan, Rostov, Iaroslav, Beloozero, Udorsk, Obdorsk, Kondinsk, and of all the northern parts Commander; Lord of the land of Iversk, Kartalin, and of the Gruzian [Georgian] Dukes; and [Lord] of many other dominions and countries, east, west, and north; Heir thereof from father and grandfather, Lord and Monarch.

The Emperor in his [coat of] arms gives the spread eagle, as descending from the Roman [Byzantine] emperors, but he carries a distinction, for he bears between the double head of the eagle a mitred crown, and in the eagle's breast St. George on horseback, which some say was added upon Queen Elizabeth's [I of England] bestowing the Order of the Garter to Ivan Vasilevich [the Terrible].

The tsarevich [that is, the tsar's eldest son and heir to the throne] is not seen by the people till he is about fifteen years old, nor by many noblemen. But then he is exposed to public view, is carried upon men's shoulders and set on high in the market place, which is to prevent impostors wherewith this land has often been deceived.

The tsar marries not out of his dominions, but takes a wife where he pleases, though seldom out of the nobility. When she dies, all the interest of her kindred and relations dies with her. Eliah [Ilia Naryshkin], the present Emperor's father-in-law, was of so mean account, that within this twenty years he drew wine to some Englishmen and his daughter [the present Tsaritsa] gathered mushrooms and sold them in the market. . . .

The Imperial Palace [that is, the Kremlin] is built of stone and brick, except some lodgings wherein His Majesty sleeps and eats all winter. For they esteem wooden rooms far wholesomer than stone. And they have some reason to think so, because their stone rooms, being arched thick, reverberate a dampness when the stove is hot. The Emperor's lodge is three stories high. His drink is brague made of oats. His bread is made of rye, which the Russians esteem a stronger nourishment than wheat. The tsar lies in no sheets, but in his shirts and drawers under a rich sable coverlid and one sheet under him. His recreations are hunting and hawking. He keeps about 300 falconers and has the best gerfalcons in the world, which are brought from Siberia. He flies at ducks or other fowl. He hunts the bear, wolf, tiger, fox, or rather baits them at his pleasure.

Whensoever he goes forth, the East Gate of the inner wall of the city [of Moscow] is shut till he returns. He seldom visits any subject, yet last year [1670?] he did, but went not in the common way, for the side of a wall was pulled down. At the birth of his children, the commoners bring him great presents, which he returns back again. But if he likes any of them, he gives the full worth. On the Saturday after Good Friday he goes into some of the prisons, examines the prisoners' crimes and delivers many of them. . . . They put very few to death here. They only whip them, which is worse than the pains of death. . . .

As the Emperor's territories are great, so is his revenue. For, *first*, he is the master in a manner of every man's estate. The son does always petition [the tsar] for his father's land. . . . He [the tsar] is heir to all who die intestate, criminally, or without heirs. *Secondly*, his customs are very considerable. *Thirdly*, the *kabacks* (or places wherein are sold *aqua vitae* and strong beer), are his royalty, some of which he farms out for 10,000 *rubles* per annum and some again for 20,000 *rubles*. *Fourthly*, his bath stoves, which are very frequent here, are a great *entrado*, for their religion obliges them to bathe freely, both men, women, and children. When they [stoves] are hissing hot, they cast cold water upon them. Some come out into the snow and tumble in it stark naked, and then go in to the stove again. *Fifthly*, he is the chief merchant in all the empire. *Sixthly*, his sable trade in Siberia yields a vast treasure brought in by the exiled slaves sent thither in disgrace. And, *seventhly*, the caviar made in Astrakhan, as also the *ithycolla* and *agaroc*, all of which he monopolizes.

All of his provisions are brought in by those who hold lands in villanage. This year a fire happened in his store house and burnt and broiled 60,000 flitches of bacon. By which you may see the Russians are no Tatars, abhorring swine's flesh. . . . When the Greek or Persian [merchants] come [to Moscow], the Emperor engrosses all their commodities at a price. To Archangel he sends great quantities of hides, wax, potash, hemp, and flax and furnishes himself with their commodities which serve him to give away amongst his subjects. For most of his graces are bestowed in silks, sables, cloth, velvet, or cloth of gold.

To his household servants he gives allowances of meal, honey, fish, nut oil, oats, beer, and mead. His Imperial Palace [that is, the Kremlin] is encompassed with a high brick wall larger by half than the circumference of the Tower [of London]. Herein are twenty-four churches and chapels. Most of them have gilded cupolas and great crosses which make a splendid show altogether. . . . Some of the chief *boyars* have palaces of stone within the walls of the Court. . . . There are also five monasteries and two or three nunneries, together with most of the *prikazes* [that is, departments of government], the court of justice, the apothecary, or the ammunition gallery.

The Tsar has officers of state as other princes have, but not of so great value. His gentlemen of the bed chamber come not into his chamber, but wait in the next room to it; and at the table also, some two or three rooms off. The Tsar is temperate in his diet. He drinks very little wine. Sometimes he drinks at meals a little cinnamon water, or oil of cinnamon in his small beer. For cinnamon here (you must know) is the *aroma imperiale*. The scent of musk and ambergris are not much esteemed, but rose water is much used at the Court and so is holy water in the church.

At the entertainment of his nobility, the Emperor sits in his chair and delivers out of his hand a *charka* [glass] of treble or quadruple spirits, which are able to take away his breath who is not accustomed to them. His Majesty is delighted to see his subjects handsomely fuddled and sometimes he will put mercury into their liquor. . . .

I shall now give you a further description of the tsar. He is a goodly person, about six feet high, well set, inclined to fat, of a clear complexion, lightish hair, somewhat a low forehead, of a stern countenance, severe in his chastisements, but very careful of his subjects' love. . . . He never appears to his people but in magnificence and on festivals with wonderful splendor of jewels and attendants. . . . His sentinels and guards placed around and about his Court stand like silent and immovable statues. No noise is heard in his palace, no more than if uninhabited. None but his domestics are suffered to approach the inward Court, except the lords who are in office. He never dines publicly but on festivals, and then his nobility dine in his presence. At Easter all the nobility and gentry and courtiers kiss the Emperor's hand and receive eggs. Every meal he sends dishes of meat to his favorites from his own table. . . .

Every year towards the latter end of May the Tsar goes three miles out of Moscow to a house of pleasure. . . . The Emperor has there most magnificent tents. His own is made of cloth of gold lined with sables; his tsaritsa's with cloth of silver lined with ermines; the princes' according to their degree. His and the tsaritsa's [tents] with those of his eleven children and five sisters stand in a circle with the church tent in the middle. There are rails and guards set musket shot [a distance] from them, beyond which no man may pass without order. For the tsar will have none of the vulgar people to be eyewitnesses of his pastimes. . . . His Majesty is jealous of gazers. . . . When the tsar goes into the country or fields to take his pleasure, he gives strict charge that none should interrupt him with petitions. . . .

In the night season the tsar will go about and visit his chancellors' desks and see what decrees are passed and what petitions are answered. He has his spies in every corner and nothing is done or said at any feast, public meeting, burial, or wedding but he knows it. He has spies also attending his armies to watch their motions and give a true account of their actions. These spies are gentlemen of small fortunes who depend on the emperor's favor and are sent into armies and along with ambassadors and are present on all public occasions. . . .

As to the tsar's religion, he is of the Greek faith and very strict in the observation thereof. He never misses divine service; if he is well, he goes to it; if [he is] sick, it comes to his chamber. On fast days he frequents midnight prayers standing four, five, or six hours together and prostrating himself to the ground sometimes a thousand times. In the great fast he eats but three meals a week, namely, on Thursday, Saturday, and Sunday. For the rest he takes a piece of brown bread, salt, a pickled mushroom, or cucumber and drinks a cup of small beer. He eats fish but twice in the Great Lent and observes it seven weeks together. . . . Out of the fast he observes Mondays, Wednesdays, and Fridays and will not then eat anything that comes of flesh. . . .

As I have nothing to say against the magnificence, splendor, clemency, and virtue of the Tsar's own person, so I have no reason to recommend the Russians' integrity, for most of them are false, truce-breakers, subtle foxes, and ravenous wolves, much altered since their traffic with the Hollanders by whom they have much improved themselves in villainy and deceit.

A Seventeenth Century English View of the Russians

The Russians are a people who differ from all other nations of the world in most of their actions. They wear shirts over their drawers, girded under the navel. None, neither male nor female, must go ungirt for fear of being unblessed. They whistle not with their lips (that they count profane) but through the teeth. . . . When they spit on anything to wipe it (as shoes for instance), they use an action not unlike sneezing. In cases of admiration or incredulity, instead of a shrug they wave their heads from one shoulder to another. Their very speech and accent also differs from other nations. It is a grand sin for them to omit *lotionem post mictum*. As we use paper in our offices to clear accounts, so Russian Ivan uses a little spade made of fir, thin shaven, like the ivory spatulas which merchants and scriveners use to fold up letters and smooth them.

In our clock dials the finger moves to the figure. In the Russian the figure moves to the pointer. . . . Because the Roman Catholics kneel at their devotion, the Russians stand, for they look upon kneeling as an ignoble and barbarous gesture. Because the Poles shave their beards, the Russians consider it sinful to cut them. Because the Tatars abhor swine flesh, the Russians eat it rather than any other flesh, although its food is the most *poganoe*, or unclean of any beast. They count it a great sin for a Russian to live with a Dutch or an English woman, but a venial *peccadillo* for a Russian woman to prostitute herself to a stranger, for they say her issue will be educated in the true ancient faith, but a Russian gets an uncircumcised child of a stranger. They prefer rye above wheat, and stinking fish above fresh. They count their miles by nineties and not by hundreds. Their New Year's day is the first of September. From the creation they reckon 7000 and odd years. To things improbable they easily give credit, but hardly believe what is rational and probable. . . .

They write upon their knees, though a table stands before them. They sew with the needle towards them and thrust it forward with the forefinger. It should seem they are bad tailors. They do not know how to eat peas and carrots boiled, but eat them shells and all, like swine. They do not pick the peas, but pull them up by the roots and carry them to the market to be sold. . . . They will sooner take the word of a man who has a beard, than the oath of one who is beardless. . . .

The beauty of women they place in their fatness [subscribing to a saying]:

"God made me fat and I will make myself beautiful." Their painting is no better than that of our chimneys in the summer, namely, red ochre and Spanish white. They paint or stain their teeth black, upon the same design that our ladies wear black patches; or, it may be their teeth being spoiled by mercurial painting, they make a virtue of necessity and cry up that for an ornament which is really a deformity. Low foreheads and long eyes are in fashion here. . . . They have a secret amongst them to stain the very balls of their eyes black. Narrow feet and slender waist are alike ugly in their sight.

A lean woman they account unwholesome. Therefore, they who are inclined to leanness, give themselves over to all manner of Epicureanism, on purpose to fatten themselves and lie in bed all day long drinking Russian brandy (which will fatten them extremely); then they sleep and afterwards drink again like swine designed to make bacon. . . .

Their greatest expression of joy upon festivals is drinking, and the greater is the day the greater are their debauches. To see men, women, and priests reeling in the streets is counted no dishonor. After a very great entertainment among the grand ladies, the lady of the feast sends her chief gentleman the next day with an "Howd'ye" to her guests to inquire of their health, or if they got well home or slept well. The lady answers: "I thank the lady for her good cheer which made me so merry and drunk that indeed I know not how I got home!". . . .

Their marriages are very solemn. A few attend the bride about 3:00 P.M. At their coming out of the church, a clerk strews hops upon the bride and wishes her children as thick as hops. Another, with a sheepskin coat turned outward, meets her and prays she may have as many children as there are hairs in his coat.

The bridegroom is led home by young fellows and the bride (being covered all over) by an old woman and the priest who marches before with his cross. They sit down a while at the table with bread and salt before them, but eat nothing. Meanwhile, a choir of boys and girls sing nuptial songs . . . bedaubed with scum of bawdy and obscenity. . . . After this they are led by the priest and the old woman to a room where she advises the bride to be debonair and buxom and exhorts the bridegroom to bestow due benevolence. Here they are shut up for two hours. In the interim the old woman attends for the token of virginity. . . . The married couples must have no earth over their heads (a ceremony strictly observed, as if mortality then ought not to be the object of their meditations), for you must know that all warm rooms are covered with earth half a yard thick to keep in the heat.

The bridegroom has a whip in one boot and a jewel or some money in the other. He bids the bride to pull them off; if she happens upon the jewel, he counts her lucky and bestows it upon her. But if she lights upon the boot with the whip in it, she is reckoned amongst the unfortunate and gets a bridelash for her pains, which is but the earnest penny of her future entertainment. The Russians discipline to their wives is very rigid and severe, more inhumane in times past than at present.

Yet, three or four years ago, a merchant beat his wife as long as he was able with a whip two inches about, and then caused her to put on a smock dipped in brandy three or four times distilled, which he set on fire and so the poor creature perished miserably in the flames. Certainly this person was a monster not a man, born of a tigress not a woman, and in no wise deserved the epithet of good, or a wife. For the heathens themselves condemn such unchristian villainy. . . .

And yet what is more strange, none prosecuted her death. For in this case they have no penal law for killing of a wife or slave if it happens upon correction. But it is a strange chastisement to kill, seeing the design hereof was never intended to end people but to mend them. Some of these barbarians will tie up their wives by the hair of the head and whip them stark naked. But this severity is not commonly used unless it be for adultery or drunkenness. . . .

Seldom a wedding passes without some witchcraft. . . . I saw a fellow coming out of a bridal chamber, tearing his hair as if he had been mad, and being asked the reason why he did so, he cried out: "I am undone! I am bewitched!" The remedy they use is to address themselves to a white witch who, for money, will unravel the charm and untie the cod-piece point, which was this young man's case. It seems some old woman had tied his cod-piece point.

The ecclesiastical law commands their abstinence from venery three days a week, namely, Monday, Wednesday, and Friday. After coition they must bathe before they enter the church. A man who marries a second wife is barred from the church but not the church porch. If [he marries] a third, [he is barred from] the communion. If a man thinks the wife is barren, he will persuade her to turn nun, that he may try another. If she refuses, he will cudgel her into a monastery. . . .

Their children are commonly strong and hardy. They give them suck not above a month or two at the most, after which they feed them with a horn or silver cup made horn-wise with dried cow-dung tied to the small end, through which they suck. At two years old they observe their fasts, which are severe. They have four [fasts] in a year, and in Lent, on Wednesdays, Fridays, and Saturdays they eat no fish, but feed on cabbage and cucumbers and coarse rye bread and drink *kvas*, which is a liquor one degree below our [English] small beer. . . .

Their penance consists of many bowings and knockings of their heads before an image and sometimes to eat nothing but bread, salt, and cucumbers and to drink water for a season. That which is *poganoe*, or unclean, may not be eaten at any time; as horse flesh, mare's milk, ass's milk, hares, squirrels, coneys, and elks. Treacle is *poganoe* because it has viper's flesh in it. Castorium, musk, and civet are not to be used internally amongst them. Sugar candy and loaf sugar are prohibited on fasting days. A knife that has cut flesh is not used for twenty-four hours. This is good policy as it happens that they are so strict else the flesh of the country would soon be destroyed. For the Russian boors, being perfect slaves, are careless of more than what serves from hand to mouth. And as for the surplus, the lord or his steward takes it away. . . .

Their burials are strange. As soon as the breath is out of the body (as we commonly express it), they carry the corpse into the church, where it abides not long before it is buried in the church yard. The wife of the deceased is obliged to howl most pitifully and hire others to do the like. Custom, not love, may possibly incite them to do it. . . . The Russians count that the greatest funeral is where there are the most women mourners. These, therefore, in a doleful tone cry out (as the wild Irish do): "Alas, my dear! Why have you left me? Was I not obedient to you in all things? Was I not careful of your house? Did I not bring you fine children? Did you not have all things in abundance?" Or, "Why would you die? Did you not have a fair wife, pretty children, much goods, good clothes, and enough brandy-wine?"

As soon as anyone is dead they open the windows and set a bowl of holy water for the soul to bathe in, and another bowl of wheat at the head of the corpse that he may eat, having a long journey to go. After this they put on his feet a pair of black shoes, and some *kopecks*, or pieces of money, in his mouth, and a certificate in his hand (from the metropolitan of the place) to St. Nicholas about his life and conversation.

If anyone dies without Confession and Extreme Unction, he is denied Christian burial. Those killed or frozen to death are brought to the *zemskii prikaz*, or office, for that and many other trials, and there are exposed to view three or four days. If any own them, they are carried away; if not, they are sent to the *bozhii dom*, or God's House, which is a great pit in the fields, arched over, wherein they put 100 or 200 [corpses] and let them rest till midsummer. Then priests go, bury them, and cover them with earth. Thirty days after burial, they read the Psalter over daily upon the grave . . . ; but what their meaning is in this I cannot understand.

In the carnival before the Lent they give themselves over to all manner of debauchery and luxury, and in the last week they drink as if they were never to drink more. Some drink *aqua vitae* four times distilled until it fires in their mouths and kindles a flame not unlike that of *Bocea di inferno* which issues out at their throat. If they have not milk given them to drink, they presently die. . . . These drinking bouts are commonly attended with quarrels, fightings, and murders. . . . Some of these going home drunk, if not attended with sober companion, fall asleep upon the snow (a sad cold bed) and there they are frozen to death. If any of their acquaintances chance to pass by, though they see them like to perish, yet they will not assist them to avoid the trouble of examination if they should die in their hands. For those of the *zemskii prikaz* will extort something out of everybody's purse who comes to their offices. It is a sad sight to see a dozen people brought upright in a sledge frozen to death. Some have their arms eaten off by dogs; others their faces; and others have nothing left but bones. Two hundred or 300 have been brought after this manner in the time of Lent. By this you may see the sad consequence of drunkenness, the epidemic distemper, not only of Russia, but of England also.

⚔ *68* ⚔

Avvakum's Account of His Sufferings

In the middle of the seventeenth century a significant religious revival, aimed at breathing new life into Russian Orthodoxy, developed in that country. Although, initially, the revival received support from the state and the Church authorities, a conflict soon developed between the proponents of the reform led by Patriarch Nikon (1606–1681) and the opponents of innovation led by Archpriest Avvakum (1620–1682). Avvakum and his followers insisted that old rituals be preserved and that lower clergy and their parishioners be given a greater voice in Church affairs. These demands were intolerable to Nikon, and Avvakum and his followers were subjected to inhuman treatment, exile, and even execution. The following are excerpts from Avvakum's own account of his sufferings between 1640 and 1667.

From *Zhitie protopopa Avvakuma im samim napisanoe i drugie ego sochineniia* (The Life of Protopop Avvakum Written by Him and Other of His Works), (Moscow: Gosizdat, 1960), pp. 59–64, 66–75, 77–78, 85–88, 92–95, 101–104. Translation mine. Words in brackets are mine.

I was born in the district of Nizhnii Novgorod, beyond the Kudma River, in the village of Grigorovo. My father, Peter, was a priest; my mother's name was Maria, or Marfa. My father liked to drink; my mother, however, was dedicated to fasting and prayer, and always instructed me in the fear of God. Once I saw a neighbor's livestock die, and that night I rose and wept for my soul before an icon, for a long time, pondering mortality and how I too must die; from that time on it became my habit to pray every night. Then my mother was widowed and I became a young orphan, and we were driven away by our relatives. My mother resolved that I should marry. I prayed to the Holy Mother of God to give me a wife who would help me to gain salvation. And in that village was a maiden, also an orphan, who constantly went to church, and whose name was Anastasia. Her father, Marko, was a blacksmith, and a well-to-do man, but when he died all of his wealth was squandered. Therefore, she lived in poverty, praying to God to make it possible for her to marry me; and by God's will this happened. Later my mother died and went to God in great glory. Because of persecution I moved to another place. At twenty I was ordained as a deacon, and two years later I became a priest; I was a priest for eight years and then was elevated to archpriest by Orthodox bishops. This happened twenty years ago; I have then been in Holy Orders thirty years.

When I was a priest I had many parishioners, perhaps five or six hundred souls. . . . Once, in those days, a young woman came to me burdened with many sins, including idolatry and other sins of the flesh; weeping, she began to acquaint me with her sins, in detail, in the church before the gospel. And I, thrice-accursed doctor, fell sick myself, burning inwardly with a feeling of guilt, and that moment was a very unpleasant one for me. I lit three candles, fixed them to the lectern, placed my right hand on the flame and held it there until my evil passion died; when I had dismissed the young woman, I laid away my vestments, prayed, and went home greatly disturbed. When I reached my house, about midnight, I wept before an icon until my eyes swelled, and prayed diligently that God remove me from my parishioners because the burden was too heavy for me. . . .

Shortly thereafter . . . an official abducted a daughter of a widow, and I pleaded with him to return the orphan to her mother; he scorned our prayer, became angry, and came to the church with his followers, who beat me unconscious. I lay there unconscious for about half an hour or more and was revived by God's sign of the hand. And he, frightened, gave up the girl for my sake. But then the devil incited him: he came to the church, beat me, and dragged me on the floor by my legs in my vestments, while I prayed all the time.

On another occasion, another official became very angry with me, came to my home, beat me, and like a dog, gnawed the finger of my hand with his teeth. And when his throat was full of blood, then he loosened his teeth from my hand, pushed me aside, and went away. Thanking God, I wrapped up my hand in a cloth and started for vespers. On the way, he jumped on me again with two small pistols, and from a close distance he fired at me; by God's will the powder exploded in the pan and the pistol did not fire. He threw it on the ground and fired from the other and it too did not fire. As befits, I prayed to God, and walking away, I blessed him [the official] and bowed before him. He, however, cursed me, but I said to him: "Ivan Ro-dionovich, let blessings proceed out of your mouth!" Later he seized my homestead, beat me, took everything away from me, and gave me no food for the road.

During that time my son Prokopei was born, who now, with his mother, is buried. I took my belongings, my wife, the unbaptized infant, and we set off on our journey, whither God would lead us, and on the way we baptized our son. . . . When I reached Moscow, I went to Archpriests Stefan and Neronov and Ivan; they informed the Tsar about me, and henceforth he knew about me. The reverend fathers gave me a charter from the Tsar and sent me back to my previous place; I dragged myself home to find the walls of my home pulled down. I again established myself, and the devil again raised a storm against me. There came to my village dancing bears with drums and lutes; I, a sinner in Christ's service, drove them away, destroyed the masks and the drums in a field outside the village, and took away two great bears. I beat one bear senseless, but he revived; I let the other free in the open field. For this Vasili Petrovich Sheremetev, who sailed on the Volga to the Kazan *voevoda*-office, took me on board, reprimanded me strongly, and ordered that I bless his son, Matvei, who had a shaven face. When I saw the image of shame, I would not bless him. As a result the *boyar* became very angry and ordered that I be thrown into the Volga, and they beat me very much. But later they were nice to me; we were reconciled in the Tsar's antechamber, and my younger brother was a confessor to *boyar* Vasili's wife. . . .

Shortly thereafter I was again driven out of that place. I went to Moscow, and the Tsar, by God's will, appointed me archpriest in Iurevets on the Volga. I stayed there only about eight weeks; the devil incited priests, peasants, and women; they came to the patriarch's office, where I attended to church affairs, and dragged me out—there were about 1500 of them—to the street and whipped me and trampled me; women beat me with hand-spikes. Because of my sins they beat me unconscious and threw me into the corner of a house. A *voevoda* came with his musketeers, took me on their horses, and rushed me to my little home; the *voevoda* stationed his men around my house. The people came to the house and raised a great storm throughout the town. The most belligerent were priests and women whom I tried to lead away from sin; they cried: "Kill the thief, the son of a bitch, and throw his body into a ditch for the dogs." On the third day, without any rest, leaving my wife and children, I left for Moscow by way of the Volga. I came to Kostroma, but there too they drove away Archpriest Daniel . . . . When I reached Moscow I reported to Stefan, the Tsar's chaplain, but he reprimanded me: "Why did you leave your church?" There was more trouble awaiting me. In the evening the Tsar came to his chaplain to receive his blessing; he saw me there and asked why I had deserted my city. And my wife, children, and household of some twenty souls, who had stayed in Iurevets, represented another concern for me, as I did not know whether they were alive or dead. . . .

While I was celebrating vespers, I was arrested by Boris Neledinskii (with his *streltsy*); they arrested about sixty people with me; they sent all the others to prison while they put me in chains in the patriarch's court. Early on Sunday morning they placed me in a cart, stretched out my arms, and drove me from the patriarch's court to the Androniev Monastery, where they chained me again, threw me into a dark dungeon dug in the ground, and where I stayed for three days without any food or drink; chained in that darkness I did not know where was East or West. No one visited me except mice and black beetles; the crickets chirped plenty and fleas were abundant. . . . In the morning [the fourth day] the archimandrite came with the brothers and led me away; they scolded me for not yielding to the patriarch, but I replied to them from the Scriptures. They took off the big chain and put on a small one. They gave me to a monk with instruction to bring me to a church. In the church they pulled my hair, poked my ribs, pulled my chains, and spat in my eyes. May God forgive them in this and the next world. . . . I remained there for four weeks.

They sent me later to Siberia with my wife and children. The journey was full of misery and only a small portion can be told here. My wife bore a child and while she was sick in a cart we drove to Tobolsk; it took us thirteen weeks to complete our journey of 3000 *versts*, half of it by cart and water, half by sled.

The archbishop gave me a church in Tobolsk. Here, in this church, great misery pursued me; in a year and one half I was accused of conspiracy against the Tsar five times. . . .

Then [in 1655] a decree came ordering that I be taken from Tobolsk to Lena because of my condemnation of Nikon and my accusation that he was a heretic. . . . So once again I got into my boat . . . and sailed toward Lena. When I reached Eniseisk, a second decree came ordering me to proceed to Dauria [past Lake Baikal] over 20,000 *versts* from Moscow. They assigned me to the regiment of Afanasii Pashkov, who had some 600 men under him;

because of my sins he was a fierce man: he constantly burned, tortured, and beat his people. Many times I tried to persuade him to stop it, and now I fell into his hands. Nikon informed him from Moscow to torture me.

Following our departure from Eniseisk on the Great Tunguska River, a storm sank my raft: the raft was in mid-stream, full of water; the sail was torn and only the deck remained above the water. My wife somehow managed to drag the children out of the water on the deck. I just looked to heaven and cried: "Lord save us! Lord help us!" By God's will we reached the shore. . . . From another raft, two men were washed away and drowned. Later we made necessary repairs on the bank of the river and sailed away.

When we reached the Shaman Rapids, some people came to meet us; two widows were with them, one age sixty, the other older; both were sailing to a nunnery. Pashkov tried to stop them as he wanted to marry them off. I told him that it was against canon law to marry off these women. Instead of listening to me and letting the widows free, he became angry and began to devise tortures for me. In another rapids, called the Long Rapids, he set out to push me out of the raft. "You don't know how to navigate the raft, you heretic! Why don't you go to the mountains! Don't come along with the Cossacks!" I was disturbed. Mountains there were high, the ravines impassable, and a stone crag stood there like a wall—you would break your neck if you tried to see its top. These mountains were full of great snakes, geese, red ducks, black crows, gray jack daws, eagles, hawks, gerfalcons, guinea fowl, pelicans, swans, and other wild birds. Many wild beasts wandered at liberty in these mountains: wild goats, deer, bison, elk, boars, wolves, and wild sheep—seen everywhere but difficult to catch. Pashkov wanted me to live in these mountains with beasts, snakes, and birds. . . . Some fifty men rushed toward me, seized my raft and pulled it to him [Pashkov], who waited about three *versts* away. . . . They tied the raft, and the executioner brought me before him. He stood with a drawn sword and in a rage. He asked me whether I was a priest or not. I replied that "I am Avvakum, the archpriest; what do you want?" He roared like a wild beast and struck me on one cheek and then on the other, and then on my head; and having knocked me off my feet, he struck me thrice with a strap on the back and gave me some seventy blows on my naked back with a knout. . . . At each stroke I said a prayer, but in the middle of this flogging I screamed: "You have beaten me enough!" He stopped. And I asked him: "Do you know why you beat me?" And he ordered them to beat me again on the ribs; and then they stopped. I was shaking all over and then fell. He ordered them to carry me to an official raft; they tied my hands and feet and threw me on the deck. It was autumn; rain fell and I lay in the rain all night. . . .

In the morning they threw me onto a small boat and took me away. Then we reached the great rapids of Padun, where the river is about one *versta* broad with three reefs stretching across. If you should miss the passage between them, you will be shattered to pieces. They brought me to the rapids. It was raining and snowing. They put a little coat on my shoulders; water flowed over my belly and spine, and I felt miserable. They took me out of the boat and, skirting the rapids, they dragged me over the stones. . . .

Then they brought me to the Bratsk fortress, where they threw me into a dungeon on the straw. I was there in the cold tower until Advent; winter reigns there during this time, but God kept me warm without clothes. I lay on the straw like a poor dog; sometimes they fed me and sometimes they did not. There were many mice and I would hit them with my cap because the fools would not give me a stick. All the time I lay on my belly because my back was sore. There were many fleas and lice. I wanted to ask forgiveness from Pashkov, but God's will ordained that I endure. Then he moved me into a warm hut where I stayed through the winter with hostages and dogs. My wife and children were exiled to a place about twenty *versts* away. Her woman servant, Xenia, tormented her the entire winter with complaints and tantrums. My son, Ivan, still a boy, visited me after Christmas, and Pashkov ordered that he be thrown in the cold dungeon with me where the dearest one almost froze to death. In the morning he ordered him back to his mother. I never saw him again. He came to his mother with frostbite on his hands and feet.

In the spring we moved forward. We had but scant provisions, as everything had been stolen; books and clothes had been taken but other items remained. I almost drowned on Lake Baikal. I was ordered to pull a towing rope on the Khilok River; it was a very difficult task and there was no time for eating or sleeping. I suffered the entire summer. People were dying from the hardship of water travel, and my feet and belly were blue. For two summers we journeyed by water, and during the winters we crossed portages. On the Khilka River I almost drowned for the third time. The current sucked me and my boat from the shore while others remained. My wife and children remained on shore; only I and the steersman were in the boat. The swirling water tossed and pitched the boat; I climbed on the boat and cried out: "Blessed Virgin help us! Our Hope, don't let us drown!" At times my feet were in the water, at times I would climb on top. The boat was carried away for about a *versta* or more and then the people overtook it. Everything was shattered to pieces. . . .

Then we reached the Lake of Irgen. There was a portage and we carried our belongings through the winter. He [Pashkov] took my workmen away and would not allow me to hire others. The children were small, there were many mouths to feed but no one to work; one archpriest built a sleigh and hauled things through the entire winter. When spring came we sailed down the Ingod River. It was my fourth summer of travel since Tobolsk. They were cutting timber there for houses and cities. Food became scarce and people began to die from hunger and continuous work in water. The river was shallow, the rafts heavy, the wardens merciless, the sticks big, the cudgels gnarled, the knouts cutting, and the suffering cruel—fire and rack; people were hungry. . . . Oh what a time! I do not know how he [Pashkov] went mad. My wife had one gown left from Moscow which had not rotted; its value was about fifteen *rubles*, but more here. He gave us four sacks of rye for it, and we managed, with it and eating grass, to live on the Nercha River for another year. He starved many people, would not allow anyone to hunt, gave them a very small space, and they were forced to wander over the steppes and fields, to cut grass and dig roots; we were with them. In the winter they would eat pine cones. Sometimes God would lead us to a mare's flesh or to bones of wild beasts which the wolves had left and which we would finish. And some would eat frozen wolves or foxes—really everything. A mare foaled, and secretly the starving people devoured the foal together with the caul. When Pashkov learned about it, he tortured them to death. And when another mare died, they all became desperate because they had pulled the foal out of her; the moment they saw the head they pulled it out, and ate the blood that came out with it. Oh, what a time! Two of my little boys died during these sufferings; with others, naked and barefoot, I roamed over the hills and sharp rocks, living on grass and roots. What did I not endure?

We suffered thusly in the Dauria land about six or seven years. Some of these were not too bad. Afanasii always slandered me and ceaselessly sought my death. . . . From the Nercha River we returned to Rus. For five weeks we travelled on ice in sleighs. He [Pashkov] gave us two small ponies for our children and belongings, so my wife and I were forced to walk, stumbling over ice. The country was barbarous and the natives were hostile. We could not afford to be separated from the horses; neither could we keep up with them because we were hungry and tired people. My poor wife trampled along and then she collapsed. Later when she fell again another tired soul fell on her; they both cried but were unable to get up. The man said: "Forgive me, lady!", and she said, "Are you trying to crush me?" Then I came and the poor soul began to complain, asking: "How long, archpriest, are these sufferings to last?" And I replied: "Markovna, till our death." And with a sigh she said: "Well, Petrovich, let us go." . . .

After we left Dauria our food became scarce; we all prayed and Christ gave us a roebuck, a huge beast which provided us with food until we reached Lake Baikal. Near the lake we came across a Russian settlement of sable hunters and fishermen. They were pleased to see us and we were glad to see them. . . . They gave us as much food as we needed; they gave us some forty fresh-water sturgeons, saying: "Here, Father, God sent them into our fishery for you. Take them all!" I thanked them, blessed the fish, and asked them to take it back with them, saying, "What would I do with it?" They entertained me there, gave me needed provisions, and after we repaired our boat we set out across the lake. . . .

I wintered in Eniseisk, and after a summer sailing I again wintered in Tobolsk. On my way to Moscow, in all cities and villages, in churches, and at fairs, I preached the word of God, taught, and exposed godless flattery. And so I arrived in Moscow after a three-year journey from Dauria; it took us five years travelling there upstream; going east we journeyed through native tribes and settlements. Much could be said about that. The natives captured me too. On the great Ob River, before my very eyes, they killed twenty Christians; they also wanted to kill me, but for some reason they let me go. Or, again on the Irtysh River, a group of natives was waiting to ambush our men from Berezov. I did not know about it and approached them at the bank, and they immediately surrounded us with their bows. I went forward and embraced them as if they were monks. . . . And they treated me kindly and they brought their wives to my wife. My wife flattered them, which they enjoyed; their women were kind. We know that if women are good then everything under Christ is well. The men hid their bows and arrows and began to bargain with me. I bought some bear meat from them and they let me free. . . .

And so I came to Moscow, where the Tsar and *boyars* received me gladly, as if I were an angel. I went to see Feodor Rtishchev; he met me, I blessed him and we spoke about many things; he would not let me go for three days and nights and later he informed the Tsar about me. The Tsar immediately ordered that I come to him and he spoke kindly to me. . . .

When they saw that I was not agreeing with them, the Tsar asked Rodion Streshnev to persuade me to hold my peace. I agreed, because the Tsar was appointed by God, at the moment he was kindly disposed toward me, and I hoped he would slowly change. They promised, on Simeon's Day, to place me at the Printing Office to correct books; I was very pleased because this sounded much better than being the Tsar's confessor. . . . After about half a year [after my return], I saw that religious matters had no success, but on the contrary rumors prevailed; and so I grumbled, wrote the Tsar pleading that he earnestly seek the old piety, defend our common mother—the Holy Church—from heresy, and place an Orthodox shepherd in the patriarchal office in place of Nikon, who was wolf, heretic, and thief. . . . From that moment on the Tsar was critical of me. He did not like [the fact] that I had started to speak again. They [bishops] would have liked to silence me, but that was impossible. And the authorities, like goats, began to leap against me, began to plot my banishment from Moscow because those Christians who understood the truth came to me and stopped coming to their service. And I received a statement from the Tsar: "Bishops complain to me against you; they say that you have emptied their churches; go again into banishment." Thus spoke *boyar* Peter Mikhailovich Saltykov. And they took me to Mezen. . . .

After half a year of suffering, they brought me back to Moscow with my two sons, Ivan and Prokopei. My wife and the others remained at Mezen. In Moscow they took us first to the Pafnutiev Monastery. Here a letter awaited us which stated as follows: "How long are you going to torture us? Join us dear Avvakum!" But since I refused as if they were devils, they flew in my face! . . .

They held me in chains in Pafnutiev for ten weeks and then they took me back to Moscow, to the room of the Cross, where the bishops argued with me. They led me to the cathedral, where they cut off my hair and that of Deacon Feodor, and then they cursed us and I cursed them.

And after they held us at the patriarchal court for a while, they transported us to Ugresha at night, to the Monastery of St. Nicholas. Here God's enemies shaved my beard. . . . They were like wolves who have no pity for the sheep; they tore my hair like dogs and left only one forelock, such as the Poles wear on their foreheads. They took me to the monastery, not via the usual road, but through marshes and mud so that people would not see me. They could see that they behaved like fools, but still they did not wish to terminate their folly. . . .

They kept me at Nicholas', in a cold room, for seventeen weeks. . . . Then they brought me again to the Pafnutiev Monastery, where they locked me up in a dark room, and, chained, kept me there for almost a year. . . . When they brought me to Moscow from the Pafnutiev Monastery they placed me in a guesthouse, and, after many trips to the Miracle Monastery, they brought me before the patriarchs of the entire Christendom [in 1667] where our [Russian] bishops sat there like foxes. I spoke a great deal with the patriarchs about the Holy Scriptures. God opened my sinful mouth and Christ put them to shame. The last word they spoke to me was this: "Why are you so stubborn? Our Palestine is everywhere—Serbs, Albanians, Wallachians, Romans, Poles—they all make the sign of the cross with three fingers; you are alone in your obstinacy and make the sign of the cross with five fingers; this is unseemly!" I replied to them the following about Christ: "Teachers of Christendom! Rome fell long ago and lies prostrate; the Poles fell with it because to the end they were enemies of Christians. Your orthodoxy is diluted because of Turkish Mohammedan oppression; you are weak. In the future you come to us to learn. By God's decree we have autocracy here. Until the time of Nikon, the apostate, under our pious princes and Tsars we had pure orthodoxy in Russia and a non-seditious church. Nikon, the wolf, decreed with the devil that men should make the sign of the cross with three fingers; but our early shepherds made the sign of the cross with five fingers, and they also blessed people with five fingers according to the tradition of our Holy Fathers, Meletina of Antioch, Theodore the Blessed, bishop of Cyrene, Peter of Damascus, and Maxim the Greek. Our own *sobor*, held during the reign of Tsar Ivan [IV], approved the usage of five fingers in the making of the sign of the cross and in blessing, as was also taught by such early fathers as Meletii and others. Likewise, at the *sobor* of the reign of Tsar Ivan, Gurii and Varsonofii, distinguished miracle makers of Kazan, and Philipp, the abbot of Solovki, were present." The patriarchs then began to think; but our [Russian] wolves began to howl and belch out words against their own fathers. They said: "Our Russian holy men were ignorant, and because they were illiterate, understood nothing. How can one believe them? They could not read!". . . I tried to defend them as much as I could, and my last words were: "I am pure and I shake the dust off my feet before you for as it is written: 'better one who would execute God's will than a multitude of godless.' " Then they cried out against me: "Take him away! Take him away! He has insulted us all." And they began to push me and to beat me; and the patriarchs themselves, about forty men, threw themselves at me. It was a great anti-Christ gathering. Ivan Uvarov seized me and dragged me. I cried aloud: "Stop! Do not beat me!" And they all sprang back. . . .

Then the Tsar sent an officer with *streltsy* and they took me to the Vorobiev hills. . . .

Then from the Vorobiev hills they transferred us to the guesthouse of the Andreevskii [Monastery] and then to the Savin *sloboda*. They treated us as criminals and military guards followed us everywhere, even when we went to relieve ourselves; it was a laughable and sorrowful spectacle. . . .

Then they brought us back to Moscow again, to the guesthouse of the Nikolskii [Monastery], where they demanded from us, anew, a statement of the true faith. . . .

Following the execution of my friends, but not me, they banished me to Pustozerie [in 1667, where Avvakum was burned at the stake in 1682].

ꙮ *69* ꙮ

A Biography of Boyarina *Morozova*

In the middle of the seventeenth century, Russian society was profoundly affected by a grave religious crisis known in history as *raskol*, or schism. Like similar religious movements in other parts of the world, *raskol* was a product of many forces and it brought many human casualties—both men and women. Among men the best known victims were: Archpriest Avvakum and Patriarch Nikon; among women, the most celebrated figures were Feodosia Morozova, widow of the *boyar* Gleb Morozov, and her sister, Princess Evdokiia Urusova.

Although the sisters were members of Muscovy's highest aristocracy, church and government authorities persecuted them brutally because they opposed the religious reforms of Patriarch Nikon. The brief biography of *Boyarina* Morozova was written by an anonymous author who apparently was quite familiar with her surroundings and sufferings and who was also sympathetic with her religious beliefs. In the nineteenth century, Russian painter V. I. Surikov depicted touchingly on canvas the *boyarina* as she was being transported to prison.

Feodosiia [Morozova], of blessed memory, was the daughter of a noble and honest father Prokopii, family name Sokovnin. He was a member of the tsar's council in the capital city of Moscow. Her mother's name was Anisiia. At the age of 17 her parents married her off to a *boyar* named Gleb Ivanovich Morozov [an influential member of the Muscovite aristocracy]. After some time she gave birth to a boy who was named Ivan. . . . Her brother-in-law, Boris Ivanovich [Morozov, 1590–1661, tutor and brother-in-law of Tsar Alexei, 1645–1676], admired Feodosiia very much. His admiration was spiritual. Whenever they talked, he always used mellifluent words advising her to be wise and religious. She had only a few years with her husband. She became a widow with a son. . . .

Sometime later, this blessed Feodosiia learned about attempts [by Patriarch Nikon] to introduce new dogmas and innovations into the Holy [Orthodox]

From N. Subbotin, ed., *Materialy dlia istorii raskola. . .* (Sources for the History of the Schism. . .). (Moscow: 1886), as reprinted in fragments in *Anthology of Old Russian Literature.* Edited by Ad. Stender-Petersen in Collaboration with Stefan Congrat-Butlar. (New York: Columbia University Press, 1954), pp. 388–402. Translation mine. Words in brackets are mine. Reprinted with permission of Columbia University Press.

Church and to modify the teachings, the hierarchal structure, and the writings of the ancient church books, its glory, songs, and prayers. As a result, the Orthodox faith found itself in a deep crisis. Many of its followers became alienated and outraged by these new innovations.

Ultimately, Feodosiia's concerns came to the attention of the tsar. On many occasions he tried to assure her that everything was fine. But she was never convinced by his arguments. Later the tsar sent to her Archimandrite Ioakim [1620–1690] of the Chudovsk Monastery and Sacristan Peter. In clear and resolute voice she rejected their arguments, accused them of promoting false-hoods, and humiliated them. Because of her accusations, on orders of the Tsar and the Patriarch, officials throughout Russia altered the appearance of the Orthodox three-bar cross. They also confiscated half of her patrimonial estates. She suffered greatly on account of her religious beliefs but resolved not to abandon them. She preferred to die for the truth.

Later, thanks to intervention in this matter by the tsar's wife, Maria [I. Miloslavskaia], Feodosiia's situation improved somewhat. Because Feodosiia led a virtuous life, the tsar's wife was very kind to her and admired her very much. Now that she had received some reprieve [from official persecution], Feodosiia organized many charities, distributed much of her own property to the needy, and [towards that end she] even purchased additional properties. She also donated some of her wealth to monasteries, gave generously to needy churches, satisfied many needs of hermits, and took care of the lepers in her home.

Then Feodosiia met the reverent nun named Melaniia [also known as Mother Alexandra, of the Zhuba Convent near Belov, in the Tula region, who was the perceived spokesperson for women of the Old Believers]. The two discussed religious matters and Feodosiia approved everything Melaniia said, and, for Christ's sake, Feodosiia adopted Melaniia as her [spiritual] mother. She submitted herself completely to Melaniia's will and, for Christ's sake, obeyed her in everything. Indeed, she surrendered her spiritual powers to Melaniia, became her obedient servant and, to her death, never disobeyed her orders. . . .

* * *

Then, discerning her virtuous mind and firm convictions concerning truth, Feodosiia's uncle, Mikhail Alexeevich Rtishchev [one of the most prominent members of the tsar's government] and his daughter Anna, who were Nikon's friends and supporters of his innovations, frequently visited the home of the blessed Feodosiia and, while there, they applauded Nikon's teachings in an apparent hope of changing Feodosiia's mind. They would, for example, say the following: "Patriarch Nikon is a very great and wise teacher; indeed, the tsar himself listens to him. The faith he has initiated is very constructive and good, and, based on new books, the church ceremony is beautiful."

After listening to his presentation, the blessed Feodosiia responded as follows: "Uncle! You are a very charming person! But, why do you praise such an enemy of God [as Patriarch Nikon], his books, and his introduction [into our Orthodoxy] of many Roman [Catholic] and other heresies? To us, Orthodox Christians, his books are repulsive and Nikon should be declared an enemy of the Church of Christ and be damned accordingly."

The gray-headed old man was compelled to say: "Oh, Feodosiia! What are you trying to do? Why have you decided to distance yourself from the rest of us? Can't you see the outcome?" And about the children who were present, he said the following: "When I look at you, you remind me of grown olive trees. We should, therefore, rejoice, celebrate, feast, drink, and be happy. But instead, there has developed a gulf between us. [Feodosiia] I beg you please abandon this discord, use three fingers in making the sign of the Cross, and so forth. Do not contradict the great sovereign and our bishops. I know that this vicious *Protopop* [Avvakum] will ruin you. You yourself know that his name is held in contempt. Do you want to die on account of his teachings? Avvakum has been damned by our bishops."

Feodosiia listened attentively to the foolish words of the old man, then she smiled and in a soft voice said: "Uncle, that is not so. Your words and your advice are incorrect! You have called the sweet thing bitter and the bitter sweet. Avvakum is a true follower of Christ. You are punishing him because he is obeying the law of his Lord. . . ."

Then Anna Mikhailovna [Rtishchev's daughter] said: "Oh, dearest sister! Nuns of [the Zhaba Convent in] Belov [the center of Old Believers] have devoured you, have poisoned your mind, and have separated you from the rest of us. You are perceiving us, your relatives, incorrectly. You have not told us anything about your only son. He is your only child. You should think about it. You should be at his bedside, sit by him, and watch him. Light a candle made of pure wax and place it in the image lamp. Then admire his face and rejoice that God has granted you such a wonderful child. Both the tsar and the tsaritsa often look at him and admire his handsome appearance. You are oblivious to this and you also disobey the great sovereign. Your stubbornness will bring the tsar's anger upon you and your household. He will order your home destroyed; you will experience great sufferings; and through your pitilessness, you will ruin your son."

[To this] Feodosiia responded as follows: "You are not telling the truth. I have not been seduced by Belov nuns as you have asserted. With the blessing of my Savior, I honor God, the Father, with all my heart. I also love Ivan, my son, constantly pray to God in his behalf, and take care of his spiritual needs." . . . Then, she crossed herself and added: "Son of God! Please save me from the unpleasant endearment! I do not want to perish by protecting my son, even though he is my only child. I love Christ more than I do my son. . . ."

Feodosiia also had a very dear sister named Evdokiia, who stemmed from the same family, was affluent and was married to Prince Peter Ivanovich Urusov [who was a member of the tsar's council]. Feodosiia often prayed to God that He grant her sister, Princess Evdokiia, the same love and affection for Christ and her own soul as she had for Christ. She heard voices telling her clearly to be loyal and assuring her to trust mother Melaniia completely. . . .

Subsequently Feodosiia started to think about additional matters and wanted very much to become a nun. She came to Mother Melaniia, kissed her hands, bowed to the ground and asked her to dress her in a nun's attire. The Mother refused to do it. She cited many reasons, including the fact that it would be improper for Feodosiia to organize a convent in her home. . . . However, seeing Feodosiia's firm resolve, faith, and determination, the Mother asked Father Dosifei, lover of Christ, to dress Feodosiia in the attire of a monk. Dosifei then tonsured her, gave her the name of Feodor, and, in accordance with the rules of the Holy Scriptures, he turned her over to Mother Melaniia. Thereafter, blessed Feodosiia, now monk Feodor, viewed herself as a member of a religious order and considered it as a great gift of God. She now committed herself to new activities, to fasting, praying, temperance, and silence. Pleading illness, she also refused to do anything around the house and delegated all important matters to her loyal servants.

Then [in 1671] came the tsar's marriage, after the death of [his first wife] Tsaritsa Mariia Miloslavskaia, to Nataliia [Naryshkina]. The blessed [Feodosiia] declined the tsar's invitation to participate, with other *boyar* wives, in the tsar's wedding. Tsar Alexei considered her refusal as a great affront, since [by virtue of her family background] she was to be in the front row and was to recite the tsar's titles. He personally requested her presence, but she declined by saying: "My feet hurt me very much. I can neither stand nor walk. . . ." Throughout the summer the tsar was very angry at Feodosiia and tried to find a way to punish her for her behavior. Early in the fall he dispatched to her home *Boyar* [Prince Boris] Troekurov with a reprimand, and a month later he sent another reprimand through Prince Peter Urusov telling her to obey [the tsar's command] and accept all of his new laws [pertaining to religion]. And should she disobey she would place herself in great peril.

She invoked God's name and responded to *boyar* emissaries as follows: "I do not know how I could have caused any harm to the tsar and am surprised by his anger at my situation. If he wishes to deprive me of my true Orthodox faith, the sovereign should not be concerned. He should know that as long as the Son of God protects me with His right hand, I have absolutely no intention of abandoning my true Orthodox faith. Also please inform the sovereign that I, poor soul, will not obey his new decrees. . . ."

After they returned, the emissaries reported her daring words to the tsar. He, in turn, was infuriated and, in order to break down her resolve, told those who were present: "It is impossible to be her friend. All of us henceforth should avoid her." The *boyars* then began to devise ways and means of accomplishing the tsar's intent. The tsar's council held many meetings trying to come up with a response to the ill-advised and rebellious behavior of a single soul. Many *boyars* and counselors, who disagreed with [the suggested harsh] measures, abstained from supporting them. But bishops and abbots, who were [Patriarch] Nikon's followers, [supported] them. . . .

Then on November 14 [1671], Feodora told her nun-superiors: "Mothers! My time has come! Each of you should go your own way and perhaps God will save you. Bless me and pray for me. In return for your prayers, God will give strength to endure the sufferings in His name." Then I kissed her and left in peace.

Then, at Shrovetide, Princess [Evdokiia] returned to her home and while enjoying dinner in a relaxed atmosphere, [her husband] Prince Urusov told her about the latest developments in the tsar's council and said: "Great trouble awaits your sister because the tsar is very angry with her. He plans to exile her from her home. . . ." Next morning, as he was leaving for the meeting of the tsar's council, his princess asked him whether he would approve her visiting her sister Feodora. He replied: "Go and bid her farewell, but do not stay there too long. I think that today she will receive the [sad] news." But when Evdokiia went, she stayed in Feodora's home till evening. . . .

[That day], accompanied by the *dumnoi diak* [high-ranking official] Ilarion Ivanov, and displaying great pompousness, Ioakim, Archimandrite of the Chudov Monastery, came [to Feodora's home]. He entered her bedroom and, seeing her in bed, informed her that he was sent by the tsar. He then asked her to get up, and, standing or sitting, to answer the tsar's questions. She refused to comply. Then the archimandrite asked her: "How do you cross yourself?" She put her fingers in accordance with the ancient tradition and said: "Lord, Jesus Christ, Son of God, have mercy on us! This is how I cross myself and this is how I pray. . . ."

[Meanwhile], *dumnoi diak* Ilarion Ivanov went into a dark storeroom where he spotted a human being reclining on a couch. "Who are you?" he asked. Princess [Evdokiia] replied: "I am the wife of Prince Peter Urusov." He was shocked as if burnt by fire and left the storeroom in haste. The archimandrite noticed his behavior and asked: "Who is there?" Ivanov replied: "Princess Evdokiia Prokofievna, wife of Prince Peter Ivanovich Urusov." The archimandrite then said: "Ask her how she crosses herself." But Ivanov declined. . . . Subsequently, he did so and reported his observations to the archimandrite, who ordered Ivanov to remain in Feodora's home, while he went to the tsar to report on his findings. When he came to the tsar, the latter was sitting among the *boyars* in the throne room of the Granovitaia Palata. The archimandrite approached the tsar and whispered in his ear: "Not only was *Boyarina* [Feodosiia] dressed in the attire of a monk, but her sister, Princess Evdokiia, was in her home, supporting her in her defiance of your decrees. . . ." The tsar then said: "If this is true then arrest Evdokiia as well." Prince Peter [Evdokiia's husband], who was there and heard the tsar's words, was shocked but could do nothing.

The archimandrite then returned to the home of the blessed [Feodosiia] to interrogate her servants. He asked them who among them followed their mistress. . . . Then he told the *boyarina*: "Because you have refused to obey the tsar and because you are very stubborn, in accordance with tsar's orders, you are to be removed from your home. . . . Get up and move!" When the blessed one failed to comply, he ordered her servants to pick her up and carry her out. Ivan Glebovich, her son, followed her to the middle of the grand staircase and bowed to her. But she did not notice him and so he returned [to his room]. They put iron shackles on the feet of the blessed Feodora and Princess Evdokiia, took them to a big wooden mansion, where they posted guards, and left.

Two days later, *dumnoi diak* Ilarion visited them. He ordered that they be unshackled and that they be freed. When Feodora refused, he instructed her servants to carry her out. They brought in a blanket, set her on a chair, and on Ilarion's orders, they carried her to the Chudov Monastery. Princess Evdokiia was also ordered to go there. When they brought them to the [Monastery's] Ecumenical Palace, there already were present Pavel, Metropolitan of Krutitsy, Ioakim, Archimandrite of the Chudov Monastery, and the *dumnoi* [*diak* Ilarion]. In a quiet voice, Metropolitan Pavel recounted Feodosiia's honors and her family background and [interrogations and arguments followed that lasted from 2:00 to 10:00 P.M.].

Then the interrogators brought in Princess Evdokiia. Like Feodora, she too answered their questions courageously. As a result, they brought them back to their former place of detention. Feodora was carried as before. They were housed on the ground floor and they were shackled. . . . Next morning high-ranking officials visited them again. They removed their old shackles from their feet and replaced them with iron chains and locks. . . . Then they put Feodora on a peasant sledge, and, to humiliate her, they took her to the Chudov Monastery through the Tsar's Gate. . . .

Princess Evdokiia was also put in iron chains and she was taken to the

Alexeev Monastery, where she was placed under strict guard. Feodora's ultimate destination was a convent house in the Pecherskii Monastery, where she was kept under strict guard consisting of two *streltsy* officers and ten guards. . . . [In her new confinement Feodora met Mariia Gerasimova Danilova, wife of a colonel, with whom she shared her fate.] Ilarion, Metropolitan of Riazan, visited Feodora frequently.

After Feodora was arrested, the tsar and his *boyars* contemplated for many days on how to punish her for her stubbornness. The tsar then ordered that her son, Ivan Glebovich, be placed under house arrest. Because of his great grief, Ivan became ill. Because of [the nature of] his illness, they were unable to cure him and he died in a few days [in 1671]. A priest, who was quite malicious, was given the task of informing Feodora of the death of her son. . . . The tsar was pleased with the news of Ivan's death because he felt that he was now free to torture his [Ivan's] mother. His anger against her expressed itself in the exile of her two brothers, Feodor and Alexei, in the destruction of her properties, and in the distribution of her estates and horses to other *boyars*. He also decreed that all of her gold, silver, pearls, and precious stones be sold. And when they destroyed her mansion, much of her gold possessions was immured. In due time the tsar mellowed somewhat and allowed two of her servants to serve her in her confinement. Princess Evdokiia was not allowed to have her servants. Fortunately, God made it also possible to assign to her a *boyar* daughter named Akulina. The previously mentioned Mariia, who was imprisoned in the Streltskii Prikaz, endured a much greater hardship than did the two sisters. Because of their ignorance, the shameless guards perpetrated against her all sorts of crimes. . . .

Then at 2:00 A.M., our three martyrs [Feodora, Evdokiia, and Mariia] were brought to [Moscow's] Post Office. Many people had gathered there. Officials put our martyrs in a very crowded room where our three saints sat in dark corners amidst a great multitude of humanity. They did not know how they would be tortured, but all were aware that, after they were interrogated, they would be sent to a prison. . . . Their official torturers were: Prince Ivan Vorotinskii [a relative of the tsar]; Prince Iakov Odoevskii [in charge of the tsar's bodyguards]; and Vasilli Volynskii [the tsar's advisor on foreign affairs].

Mariia was the first to be brought for the torture treatment. She was undressed to the waist, had her hands tied behind her back, and, after they gave her a good thrashing on the *strapado*, they threw her to the ground. Then they subjected Princess [Evdokiia] and finally Feodora for the [hot] iron treatment. . . . [Because Feodora was stubborn] authorities ordered that she hang by her sleeves, and then they whipped her, tied her hands and tortured her on the *triaska* [an instrument for torture by shaking]. She was triumphant here as well. She reprimanded her tormentors for their inhuman act. For that reason they kept her on the *triaska* for a long time. She was hanging there for about one-half hour, with the result that the rope cut to the bone. Then they had lowered her down alongside her two companions [Mariia and Evdokiia]. They also cursed them in an inhuman way, and for three hours they kept them lying in snow with hands tied behind their backs.

They also devised various schemes. For example, they placed frozen covers on their bosoms; then they brought them near a fire and burned them. Later they covered the two martyrs and put Mariia at the feet of Feodora and Evdokiia. They beat Mariia mercilessly with a whip. First they beat her back and then the front of her body. And *dumnoi diak* Ilarion told the two martyrs: "If you do not submit [to our will], you will receive the same treatment." [Our two martyrs responded to this threat as follows]: "Is it Christian to torture human beings in such a way?" Then at 9:00 P.M. they led them to their place of confinement. . . .

Later the tsar ordered that Feodora be moved from her confinement in the Pecherskie Podvorie to the Novodevichii Monastery. He also ordered that no one could bring her anything, that she be kept under strict supervision, and that she participate in the church chant. But she seldom obeyed these orders.

. . . Then the tsar decreed that she be brought to the Khamovniki [district] of Moscow. . . . Later she was sent to Borovsk [in the Kaluga region] to a horrible prison in an underground dungeon in an *ostrog* [fort]. When Feodora entered that dungeon she met there a nun named Iustina [from Vologda], who was imprisoned there because of her religious beliefs. The blessed Princess was informed that her beloved sister [Evdokiia] and their companion [Mariia] were sent far away [to different places of confinement]. For her, this separation was very painful. It resembled the separation of a child from her mother. . . . Later Tsar Alexei agreed to transfer Princess [Evdokiia to Borovsk]. . . . A short time later Mariia was also brought [to Borovsk], and they all rejoiced. They were not allowed to have any visitors in their dungeons and they suffered there very much. . . .

In the first week after Easter, *diak* Kuzmishchev was sent [to Borovsk] to investigate the problem of alleged [illegal] visits [these women had received]. Because she refused to cross herself with three fingers, he ordered that she [Iustina] be burned at the stake. He also placed the blessed Feodora and Evdokiia into a deep dungeon and put Mariia in a cell with common criminals. And what was worst of all, he ordered, under penalty of death, not to give the three any food or drink, and those who would defy his orders were to be decapitated. . . .

The blessed Evdokiia suffered in this horrible confinement for two and one-half months. She died on September 11 [1672]. Feodora tied three threads, symbol of the Holy Trinity, around her dear sister's body and informed the guards of her death. On orders of their officers, her remains were taken away. . . . After the death of the blessed martyr Evdokiia, [authorities] brought Mariia into Feodora's dungeon. . . . The blessed and great Feodora died peacefully in her deep dungeon on the night of November 1–2 [1672]. . . . At her request, she was buried alongside her sister, Princess Evdokiia. Instead of rich attire, her body was wrapped in a simple mat. Mariia died exactly one month later, on December 2 [1672].

⚶ *70* ⚶

The Story of a Rich Merchant Sutulov and His Clever Wife Tatiana

Generally speaking, until the seventeenth century, literature in Muscovy and other Rus principalities was dominated by the church, and its content was religious. This was natural since illiteracy was almost universal, with the few who knew how to read and write being ecclesiastics (priests and monks) who served, in one capacity or another, either the church or the state.

Things began to change in the seventeenth century when secular themes, including moral laxity, gradually began to appear. Most of these works were anonymous. From their content, however, it seems likely that they were composed by clerks and members of the lower-echelon classes who were familiar with corruption and other vices. Their use of the vernacular, and their local, often earthy settings, indicate that these stories were intended for the lower social strata. One of the best examples of

---

From Iu. M. Sokolov, ed., *Trudy Slavianskoi Komissii Moskovskogo Arkheologicheskogo Obshchestva* [Works of the Slavic Commission of Moscow Archeological Society]. (Moscow: 1914), vol. IV, Part 2, pp. 1–40, as reprinted in *Anthology of Old Russian Literature*. Edited by Ad. Stender-Petersen in Collaboration with Stefan Congrat-Butlar. (New York: Columbia University Press, 1954), pp. 454–460. Translation mine. Words in brackets are mine. Reprinted by permission of Columbia University Press.

the new trend is *The Story of the Merchant Karp Sutulov*. Actually, in the
best *Decameron* tradition, the story revolves around Karp's wife Tatiana,
who outwitted three would-be lovers: a merchant, a priest, and an archbishop.

Once there was a very rich and famous merchant named Karp Sutulov. He
had a very beautiful wife named Tatiana whom he loved very much. In the
town where the merchant Karp lived, his equally rich, famous, and trusted
friend named Afanasii Berdov also lived.

It happened that our merchant Karp Sutulov had an opportunity to go to
Lithuania on a business trip. So he went to his friend Afanasii Berdov and
asked a favor.

"Afanasii, my dear friend! I have an opportunity to go to Lithuania on a
business trip. I will leave my lonely wife at home. My dearest friend! Please
provide everything for my wife should she request. When I return, I will not
only thank you for it, but will fully reimburse you."

His friend Afanasii Berdov replied: "Karp, my dear friend, I would be
delighted to take care of your wife!"

Karp then went home and told his wife: "I have visited my friend Afanasii
and have asked that he take care of your financial needs [during my absence].
And he told me: 'I would be delighted to take care of your wife's needs
during your absence.'"

Then Karp instructed his wife Tatiana as follows: "Tatiana, my lady! Let
God be between us! If, during my absence, you should decide to entertain
influential women or your sisters, I am leaving you money for that purpose
so you can buy food for them. However, should you run out of money for
your needs, then go to my friend Afanasii Berdov and ask him to give you
100 *rubles* so you can buy food. I hope that this arrangement will take care
of your needs until I return. Be sure, however, to follow my advice and neither
abandon nor disgrace my bed!"

And after he finished his instructions, he left on the business trip. His wife
accompanied him for a short distance with love and joy, and then she returned
home. Then, after her husband left on the business trip, she gave many parties
for influential ladies. She enjoyed these events very much, and recalled her
husband Karp with affection.

She lived without her husband for a long time. But then she ran out of
money. And three years after her husband had left, she went to her husband's
friend Afanasii Berdov and told him: "Sir! My husband's friend! Please give
me 100 *rubles* on credit, because before my husband, Karp, left on a business
trip, he told me: 'If you should ever need money to purchase anything, then
remember, in accordance with the verbal understanding between me and my

friend Afanasii Berdov, [you are to] go to him and get 100 *rubles* for your food.' So please give me 100 *rubles* for food and charge this sum against my husband's account. When my husband returns from his business trip, he will repay you.''

But when Afanasii looked at her figure and her beautiful face, he became aroused, approached her and said: ''I will give you 100 *rubles* for food only if you will consent to spend one night with me.''

She was very embarrassed by these words and for a moment did not know what to say. But soon, she regained her composure and said: ''I cannot do such a thing without first receiving permission from my religious father. I will go and ask my priest. If he approves, then I will sleep with you.''

She then departed quickly and requested that the priest come to her home. [When he arrived] she said to him: ''My spiritual father! What advice will you give me? When my husband left on a business trip he told me: 'If you should run out of money for food and other needs, go to my friend Afanasii Berdov, who, in accordance with our mutual understanding, will give you 100 *rubles*.' Presently, I have run out of silver money for food, and, in accordance with my husband's instruction, I went to his friend Afanasii Berdov. But he told me: 'I will give you 100 *rubles* only if you will agree to spend one night with me.' I do not know what to do. I cannot do it without your—my spiritual father's—permission. What advice do you have for me?''

And her spiritual father said: ''I will give you 200 *rubles* if you agree to spend one night with me.''

When she heard these words, she became very confused. At first she did not know how to respond to her spiritual father. But then she said: ''Father! I will need one hour to give my response.''

Then, she secretly went to the home of the archbishop and said to him: ''Oh, your great Eminence! Please advise me on what I should do. When my husband, the famous merchant Karp Sutulov, went to Lithuania on a business trip, where he has been now for the past three years, he left me some money for my needs. But that money has now run out and I do not know when he will return. And before my husband left, he told me: 'If you should ever run out of money for your basic needs, then, in accordance with an agreement with my friend, Afanasii Berdov, you should go to him, and, based on my agreement with him, he will give you 100 *rubles* for your basic needs.' And so today I went to my husband's friend, Afanasii Berdov, and asked him to give me the 100 *rubles* my husband had arranged for me. But he said: 'I will give you 100 *rubles* only if you will agree to spend one night with me.' Obviously, I could not do such a thing without first receiving permission from my spiritual father. But he told me: 'If you would spend a night with me I will give you 200 *rubles*.' Of course, I could not do this [without consulting you]."

Then the archbishop said: "Leave both of them—the priest and the merchant—and spend one night with me. I will give you 300 *rubles*." But she did not know how to respond to this offer and, unwilling any longer to listen to such proposals, said: "Oh, your great Eminence! How can I escape hell?" To the question he replied: "I will pardon you for all of your sins." She then told him to come to her home at 3:00 P.M. Then she went to her priest and told him to come to her home at 6:00 P.M. And, finally, she went to her husband's friend, Afanasii Berdov, and told him: "My husband's friend! Come to my house at 10:00 p.m."

* * *

Then came the archbishop. He became very passionate with her, brought [forth] the 300 *rubles*, and gave them to her. And, of course, he wanted to go to bed with her immediately. But she said: "You must take off your old clothes. You cannot be intimate with me wearing the same clothes you wear in public and in which you praise God." And he replied: "No one has seen me in the clothes I am wearing now. And, besides, no one will see us."

But she replied: "Father! God sees all of our actions. While we may try to conceal our actions from humans, He knows everything and needs no extraordinary disclosures. God will not come with a cane to punish you or anyone for any wrongdoing. He may only send an evil person who will catch you, embarrass you, and expose you along with all other evil-minded people."

She said this to the archbishop, who responded: "But, my lady! I do not wear any attire that ordinary people wear. Can I ask you to give me some?" She then gave him her own clothes she was wearing, and when he took off the formal [clerical] attire he was wearing, she put it in a trunk and said: "I do not have any other clothes at home because I took my husband's clothes to the laundry."

Although he was willing to put on woman's clothing, the archbishop said: "Lady! I do not see any reason why I should dress in your clothes since I want to go to bed with you." But she replied: "I will help you take them off before we go to bed."

Just at that moment the priest, her spiritual father, appeared at the entry gate to her house in accordance with her previous instruction. He had with him 200 *rubles* and he proceeded to the door. She spotted him through the window and, clasping her hands, said: "God is very generous because He has now given me an enormous and great pleasure!" The archbishop responded: "Lady, why are you so happy?" And she replied: "My husband has just returned from his business trip. I had not expected him to return at this time."

The archbishop then asked: "My lady! Where should I go now to escape shame and dishonor?" To this she replied: "My Lord! I will conceal you in a chest. But be quiet there. I will let you out in due time."

And so he hid himself in a chest and she as quickly locked it. Meanwhile, the priest approached the stairs, where she met him. He gave her the 200 *rubles* and showered her with many compliments. But she replied: "My spiritual father! Why are you trying to seduce me? Are you unaware that by your spending one hour with me we will be damned for eternity?"

But the priest replied: "My spiritual child! If you sin before God without asking your spiritual father for forgiveness, how can you then please God and regain his grace?" And she replied: "Father! Are you the true judge? Do you have the power to send me to heaven or hell for eternal damnation?"

And as she uttered these words, the rich merchant, Afanasii Berdov, the dear friend of her husband, appeared at the gate of her home. He knocked on the gate. She went to the window, looked out, and, after she spotted Afanasii Berdov, the rich merchant, her husband's best friend, she clasped her hands and returned to the room [where the priest was waiting]. The priest asked her: "My child! Who is at the gate? Why are you so happy?" And she replied: "I am very pleased that you have noticed my joy. It is because my husband has just returned from his business trip and I have seen him with my own eyes."

Then the priest said: "I am in great trouble! My lady, where should I hide to escape disgrace?" And she responded: "Father, do not be afraid of death, just consider your eternal sin! You will die [sooner or later]. But, for the sin you [were about to commit] you will suffer for eternity." Then, in the room they were in, she pointed out to him another chest. He stood there in his underwear and without a belt. She told him: "Father! Please hide in that chest and, in due time, I will allow you to leave my home."

He immediately hid in the chest and she locked him in. She then went quickly to the gate to let the merchant in. The merchant came to her room and gave her 100 *rubles*. She received him with pleasure. He, in turn, admired very much her beautiful figure and her face. She noticed, and asked: "Why do you look at me this way and why do you shower me with so many compliments? Do men really praise a woman when she is very evil?" To this he responded that, in his judgment, the woman's intellect and not her beauty deserve praise. And then he added, "My lady! I will leave your home as soon as I satisfy and delight myself with your beauty."

She did not know how to divert the merchant's attention and so she ordered one of her servants to leave the room and make lots of noise. In accordance with her mistress' instructions, the servant left the room and caused a great commotion. [Tatiana] went to the window and exclaimed: "Oh, what a wonderful joy! What wonderful news! What a sight and what a wonderful joy for my soul!''

Then the merchant asked. ''My lady! Why are you happy? What have you seen at the window?'' To this she replied. ''My husband has returned from his business trip.'' When the merchant heard these words be began to run around the room and then asked her. ''My lady! Where should I hide to escape the embarrassment?'' She then pointed out a third chest and told him: ''Get in and in due time I will let you out.'' He immediately hid in the chest and she locked him in.

* * *

Next day she went to the office of the local *voevoda* and asked him to come to her house. And he thought: ''Why has this woman come here and why has she asked me to come to her home?'' To this question she responded as follows: ''Sir! I am the wife of a merchant of this city. Do you know my husband, the rich merchant Sutulov?'' To this he responded: ''Of course, I know your husband very well because he is a famous merchant.'' Then she said: ''It has been now three years since my husband left on a business trip and before he left he told me that if I should ever run out of money, I should go to his best merchant friend, Afanasii Berdov, and ask him to give me 100 *rubles*. After my husband left, I gave parties for many elite women and for women from our town and, as a result, I have run out of money. And so, I went to the home of the merchant Afanasii Berdov. Unfortunately, I did not get there the money my husband said I would. So, please, advance me 100 *rubles* and as collateral I will give you three chests filled with sacerdotal vestments and other treasures.''

The *voevoda* responded to this offer as follows: ''I see that you are the wife of a good and rich merchant. I will advance you 100 *rubles* without any collateral and when God will return your husband safely from his business trip, I know he will reimburse me.''

To this she responded: ''For God's sake, please take these sacerdotal vestments and other treasures that are in these chests so that thieves will not steal them. Then, my husband will not be able to accuse me of not having followed his instructions and to say: 'You have not trusted my good friend.' ''

After the *voevoda* heard the story, he ordered that the three chests, which apparently contained precious sacerdotal vestments, be brought in. When she left the *voevoda's* office she took with her five of his men who accompanied her to her home. She returned with them to the *voevoda's* office, bringing the three chests, and asked him to inspect the precious sacerdotal vestments. The *voevoda* ordered that the chests be opened at once. And there, in one chest he saw the merchant huddled in a night shirt; in another chest he saw the priest dressed in a shirt but without a belt; and in the third chest the archbishop dressed in a woman's clothes without a belt. When the *voevoda* saw such indecent people, dressed in shirts and huddled in chests, he laughed and asked them: "Who put you here in these clothes?"

Then he ordered them to come out from the chests. Because a clever woman had humiliated them, they resembled dead persons. They fell at the *voevoda's* feet and cried, being aware of their transgressions. The *voevoda* asked them: "Why do you cry in front of me and why do you kowtow to me? Kowtow instead to this woman, since she is the one who has exposed your weaknesses."

Then the *voevoda* turned to the woman and asked her: "Lady, please tell me how were you able to lock them in these chests?" And to this she responded that when her husband went on a business trip, he told her that [in case of need] she should ask his merchant friend to advance her 100 *rubles*. And when she went to Afanasii to get 100 *rubles*, the merchant asked her to spend one night with him. She then told the story about the priest and the archbishop and how she arranged for their timely appearances in her home, how she deceived them, and locked them in various chests.

When the *voevoda* heard the entire story, he was very impressed with her cleverness and praised her for being faithful to her husband. Then he smiled and said: "Good wife! You won the bet and the money is yours!" Then he fined the merchant 500 *rubles*, the priest 1000 *rubles* and the archbishop 1500 *rubles*. He freed all three and divided the money with the wife. He again complimented her for using her brain, for not disgracing her husband in his absence, for not allowing herself to have affairs with three men, for maintaining firm her loyalty to her husband, for bestowing great respect and honor [on her husband and on herself], and for not defiling herself.

Shortly thereafter, her husband returned home from his business trip. She told him everything that had happened while he was away. He was very pleased that his wife was so clever and that she had devised such an ingenious scheme. Her husband was indeed pleased.

Grand Prince—Tsar Ivan III, 1462–1505.

Grand Prince—Vasilii III, 1505–1533.

Tsar Ivan IV, "The Terrible," 1533–1584.

CHNES VELICH, THEODORO GIA
NOVICH, GRAN SIGNOR DI MOSCOVIA
Franco Forma.

Tsar Feodor Ivanovich, 1584–1598.

Tsar Boris Godunov, 1598–1605.

Tsar Vasilii Shuiskii, 1606–1610.

Tsar Michael F. Romanov, 1613–1645.

Tsar Alexei Mikhailovich, 1645–1676.

Tsar Feodor Alexeevich, 1676–1682.

Princess Sophia, 1682–1689.

ІОАНЪ АЛЕКСѢЕВИЧЬ ЦАРЬ И САМОДЕРЖЕЦЬ ВСЕРОССІИСКІИ

CZAAR IOANN
ALEXE WITZ
Iolius Russiae Autocrator

Tsar Ivan Alexeevich, 1682–1696.

Tsar Ivan V and Tsar Peter I, 1682–1696.

Glossary

altyn—A monetary unit in medieval Russia. One *altyn* equalled six *dengas,* or three *kopecks.*

arshin—A linear measure equal to about twenty-eight inches.

barshchina—An obligation of a serf to work on his master's estate, often with his own stock and implements.

boyar—A member of the medieval Russian aristocracy, as distinguished from the service noble (*pomeshchik*). *Boyars* received their titles from the Tsars, headed important offices, and participated in the deliberations of the *boyarskaia duma.*

boyarskaia duma—An advisory council to the Russian Grand Princes and Tsars, consisting of important *boyars,* nobles, and high church dignitaries.

chelobytnaia—Literally "beating one's forehead"; a petition.

chetvert—A fourth; a quarter; a grain measure of about eight bushels; also a land measure.

chin—Occupation or profession of a group of people.

denga (pl. *dengi*)—A medieval Russian monetary unit, borrowed from the Tatars, which ceased to circulate after the seventeenth century. One *denga* equalled one-half *kopeck.* In modern Russian *dengi* denotes "money."

deti boyarskie—Petty nobles, especially service nobles. There were different categories of *deti boyarskie* in Moscovy.

diak—A secretary; a clerk in an office of the central government in Moscow or in the provinces.

druzhina—The retinue of Kievan princes which helped them to trade, fight, and rule.

dukhovnaia gramota—A will; a testament.

dumnyi diak—Chief secretary or clerk who had the right to attend meetings of the *boyarskaia duma.*

dvorianin—A nobleman; a courtier; a member of the Russian nobility (*dvorianstvo*).

gost (pl. *gosti*)—A member of the highest ranking merchants in Moscow, appointed by the Tsar to handle his domestic and foreign trade in monopolized goods. *Gosti* could buy land and were exempt from certain taxes.

gostinnaia sotnia—A merchants' association (guild) of lower rank merchants in Moscow in the sixteenth and seventeenth centuries. The membership of the association varied from 100 to 350 members, who, though influential, did not enjoy the same rights and privileges as did the *gosti*.

gostinnyi dvor—A marketplace in Moscow where foreign or outside merchants could display their goods.

gramota—Any written document.

grivna—A monetary unit in medieval Russia consisting of ten *kopecks* or twenty *dengas,* or twenty *nogatas,* or twenty-five *kunas,* or fifty *rezanas*. Originally, *grivna* meant a circular ingot of silver.

gubernia—An administrative unit in Russia introduced by Peter I and abolished by the Soviet government in 1923.

hetman (from German *Hauptmann*)—Commander-in-chief of the army in Poland, Lithuania, and among the Zaporozhie, or Dnieper Cossacks.

igumen—An abbot; head of a monastery; Father Superior.

izgoi—A feudal serf, bound to the owner and to the soil.

kabala—A form of servitude in medieval Russia under which an individual accepted an obligation to work for a definite and agreed period of time.

kholop—A captive, a personal slave of the prince, the *boyar,* or the monastery; a dependent individual, and next to the peasant, the most numerous in Russia. There were various categories of *kholops* in medieval Russia.

kholopstvo—Captivity; slavery; a surrender of freedom because of economic necessity.

Kitai gorod—A section of Moscow on the east side of the Kremlin.

kniaz—A prince.

kormlenie—A system of local administration prevalent from the fourteenth through the sixteenth centuries in Moscow, under which local administrators, who were appointed by the Tsar, received payments in kind from the local population.

kormlenshchik—A recipient of the *kormlenie;* a local administrator and tax collector, and, as a rule, a member of the nobility.

krestianin—A peasant. In medieval Russia there were different varieties of peasants according to whom they belonged (Tsar, *boyars,* church, monasteries, and so forth).

krestnoe tselovanie—An oath affirmed by the kissing of the cross.

kuna—A marten; also a monetary unit in Kiev and Novgorod.

mestnichestvo—An elaborate code in Moscovy regulating the quantity and quality of service which the aristocracy rendered to the prince; a "trade union" founded upon genealogical principles.

namestnichestvo—A large administrative unit in medieval Russia.

namestnik—An administrator of a *namestnichestvo,* usually a high-born nobleman appointed by the Tsar.

nemets—In a broad sense any foreigner; in a narrow sense any west European (German, Englishman, Dutchman, and so forth).

nogata—A monetary unit in Novgorod and Kiev. One *nogata* equalled one-twentieth of a *grivna.*

oblast—An administrative unit in Russia; a province; a region.

obrok—Quit-rent; payment in kind or money of a serf's obligations or dues to the nobleman.

obshchina—Russian peasant village commune; also known as *mir.*

okolnichi—A courtier, and next to *boyars* the most important member of medieval Russian nobility.

okrug—An administrative unit in Russia; district; region.

oprichnik—A member of the *oprichnina.*

oprichnina—A terrorist system employed by Ivan the Terrible (1547–1584) to crush feudal aristocracy and thus to strengthen his autocratic rule.

poltina—A monetary unit in medieval Russia; one *poltina* equalled one-half *ruble,* or fifty *kopecks.*

pomeshchik—A recipient, and later an owner, of an estate; a nobleman.

pomestie—An estate granted to a nobleman by a prince in return for service, usually of a military nature.

posada—A suburb inhabited by taxpayers.

posadnik—An elected city official in Novgorod; city mayor.

prikaz—A department of Moscovy's government headed by either a *boyar* or an *okolnichi* and run by a *diak.* These departments were numerous.

prikazchik—An official of the central government in cities or provinces.

pud—A unit of weight equal to 36.113 lbs.

raba—A female slave.

rezana—A monetary unit in medieval Russia. One *rezana* equalled one-fiftieth of a *grivna.*

ruble—A monetary unit in Russia. In the fifteenth century a *ruble* was a bar of silver weighing about one-fourth pound and equal to 200 *dengas,* or 100 *kopecks.*

sazhen—A linear measure of three *arshins,* or seven feet.

sloboda—A section of town inhabited by taxpayers, or free people.

smerd—A free peasant in Kievan Rus who subsequently became obligated either to the prince or to a noble.

sobor—An assembly, usually of high church dignitaries.

starosta—A title of an elected official of a village, a *volost,* or a section of town.

stolnik—A courtier who attended the Tsar during receptions for foreign dignitaries.

strelets (pl. *streltsy*)—Musketeers in Moscow and other cities who received land and other privileges in return for military service.

sukonnaia sotnia—An association of Moscow's lower-rank textile merchants in the sixteenth and seventeenth centuries.

tiaglo—A tax or an obligation in kind or money, or both, paid by city inhabitants and peasants.

tselovalnik—A sworn man; a person who has kissed the cross; officials of local or central government in Muscovy.

tysiatsky—Commander of the city militia in Novgorod who was elected by the *veche* and who acted as commander-in-chief in the absence of the prince.

uezd—An administrative unit in Russia comprising several *volosts.*

ukaz—An edict; a statute; an administrative decree.

veche—A village or city assembly in medieval Russia which theoretically determined the domestic and foreign policy of the town, elected officials, and discharged certain judicial functions.

velikii kniaz—A Grand Prince.

versta—A linear measure; a unit of distance equal to 0.6629 miles, or about 3500 feet.

vladyka—Title of the high clergy (bishop, archbishop) of the Russian Orthodox Church.

voevoda—A military as well as administrative leader of medieval Russia, usually a high-born member of the nobility; also the Tsar's appointed official in a city or a district.

voevodstvo—An administrative unit in medieval Russia, presided over by a *voevoda.*

volost—An administrative unit in rural Russia comprising several villages.

votchina—A hereditary form of landowning in medieval Russia.

votchinnik—An owner of a *votchina.*

zakon—A legislative measure; a fundamental law.

zemskii sobor—A landed assembly in sixteenth and seventeenth century Russia, composed of free landholders having authority to deal with such major issues as war, peace, and the election of a new Tsar.

Table 1: Rus Rulers, 862–1125

Table 2: Rus Rulers, 1125–1613

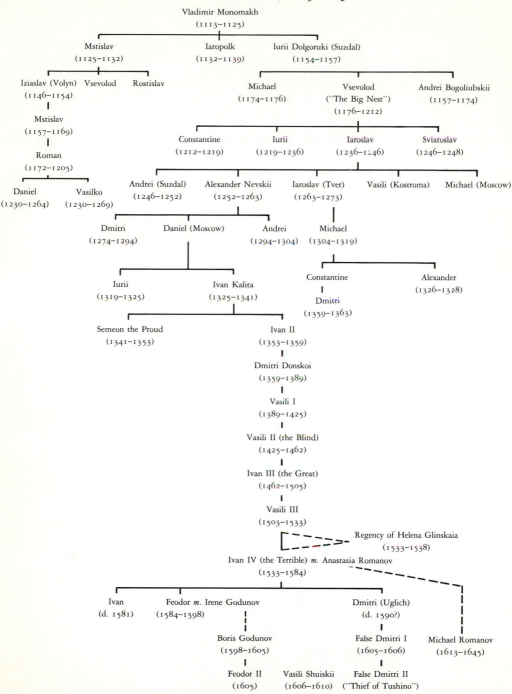

Vladimir Monomakh
(1113–1125)

Mstislav
(1125–1132)

Iaropolk
(1132–1139)

Iurii Dolgoruki (Suzdal)
(1154–1157)

Iziaslav (Volyn)
(1146–1154)

Vsevolod

Rostislav

Michael
(1174–1176)

Vsevolod
("The Big Nest")
(1176–1212)

Andrei Bogoliubskii
(1157–1174)

Mstislav
(1157–1169)

Roman
(1172–1205)

Constantine
(1212–1219)

Iurii
(1219–1236)

Iaroslav
(1236–1246)

Sviatoslav
(1246–1248)

Daniel
(1230–1264)

Vasilko
(1230–1269)

Andrei (Suzdal)
(1246–1252)

Alexander Nevskii
(1252–1263)

Iaroslav (Tver)
(1263–1273)

Vasili (Kostroma)

Michael (Moscow)

Dmitri
(1274–1294)

Daniel (Moscow)

Andrei
(1294–1304)

Michael
(1304–1319)

Iurii
(1319–1325)

Ivan Kalita
(1325–1341)

Constantine

Alexander
(1326–1328)

Dmitri
(1359–1363)

Semeon the Proud
(1341–1353)

Ivan II
(1353–1359)

Dmitri Donskoi
(1359–1389)

Vasili I
(1389–1425)

Vasili II (the Blind)
(1425–1462)

Ivan III (the Great)
(1462–1505)

Vasili III
(1503–1533)

Regency of Helena Glinskaia
(1533–1538)

Ivan IV (the Terrible) *m.* Anastasia Romanov
(1533–1584)

Ivan
(d. 1581)

Feodor *m.* Irene Godunov
(1584–1598)

Dmitri (Uglich)
(d. 1590?)

Boris Godunov
(1598–1605)

False Dmitri I
(1605–1606)

Michael Romanov
(1613–1645)

Feodor II
(1605)

Vasili Shuiskii
(1606–1610)

False Dmitri II
("Thief of Tushino")

Table 3: Russian Rulers, 1613–1917

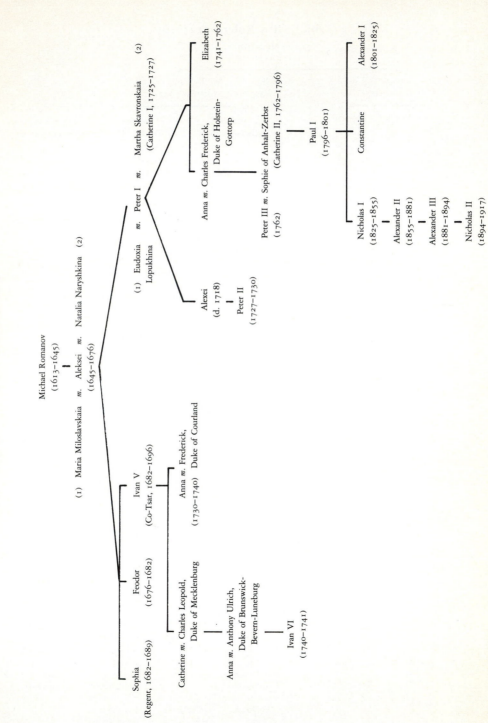

Michael Romanov
(1613–1645)

Aleksei *m.* (1645–1676)

(1) Maria Miloslavskaia

Natalia Naryshkina (2)

Peter I *m.* Martha Skavronskaia (2)
(Catherine I, 1725–1727)

(1) Eudoxia Lopukhina

Sophia
(Regent, 1682–1689)

Feodor
(1676–1682)

Ivan V
(Co-Tsar, 1682–1696)

Anna *m.* Frederick, Duke of Courland
(1730–1740)

Catherine *m.* Charles Leopold, Duke of Mecklenburg

Anna *m.* Anthony Ulrich, Duke of Brunswick-Bevern-Luneburg

Ivan VI
(1740–1741)

Alexei
(d. 1718)

Peter II
(1727–1730)

Anna *m.* Charles Frederick, Duke of Holstein-Gottorp

Elizabeth
(1741–1762)

Peter III *m.* Sophie of Anhalt-Zerbst
(1762)   (Catherine II, 1762–1796)

Paul I
(1796–1801)

Alexander I
(1801–1825)

Constantine

Nicholas I
(1825–1855)

Alexander II
(1855–1881)

Alexander III
(1881–1894)

Nicholas II
(1894–1917)

Chronological Table

860	First Varangian expedition against Constantinople.
862	Traditional date of the establishment of Riurik Dynasty in Novgorod.
882	Transfer of the capital to Kiev.
907	First agreement between Oleg and the Greeks.
911	Second agreement between Oleg and the Greeks.
941–944	Igor's expedition against Constantinople.
945	Igor's death.
945–957	Olga's rule.
964–966	Sviatoslav's defeat of the Khazars on the Volga.
967–972	Sviatoslav's expedition in the Balkans.
968	Kiev attacked by the Pechenegs.
973	Sviatoslav's death.
973–978	Iaropolk's rule.
978–1015	Vladimir's rule.
988	Traditional date of Vladimir's conversion to Christianity.
1015–1019	Struggle for power among Vladimir's sons.
1019–1054	Iaroslav's rule.
1025	Traditional date of the founding of Iaroslavl.
1034	Iaroslav's victory over the Pechenegs.
1037	St. Sophia, Kiev, begun.
1045–1052	Building of St. Sophia, Novgorod.
1054	First appearance of the Polovtsians at Kievan frontiers.
1054–1073	*Ruskaia Pravda* (Rus Justice) prepared.
1068	Invasion of the Kievan state by the Polovtsians; an uprising in Kiev against Prince Iziaslav.
1095	First election of a prince in Novgorod.

1097	Partition of Kievan Rus into patrimonial estates at Liubech Conference.
1108	Traditional date of the founding of Vladimir.
1113	Monk Nestor ends the writing of the *Primary Chronicle*.
1113–1125	The rule of Vladimir Monomakh.
1126	First election of *posadnik* (Mayor) by Novgorod *veche* (assembly).
1147	First recorded mention of Moscow.
1156	First election of a bishop in Novgorod.
1167	Destruction of Kiev by Andrei Bogoliubskii, Prince of Vladimir-Suzdal.
1169	Transfer of the capital from Kiev to Suzdal.
1185	Unfortunate expedition of Prince Igor of Novgorod-Seversk against Polovtsians.
1195	Novgorod concludes the first treaty with German cities and Gottland.
1209	First reference to Tver.
1221	Founding of Nizhnii-Novgorod (now Gorky).
1223	First invasion of Rus by the Mongols and the battle on the Kalka River.
1227	Death of Genghis Khan.
1237–1241	Invasion and conquest of Rus by Batu Khan.
1240	Alexander Nevskii's victory over the Swedes on the Neva River.
1242	Alexander Nevskii's victory over the Livonian Order at Lake Peipus.
1243	Formation of the Golden Horde.
1246	First census of the population by the Mongols in the Kiev and Chernigov territories.
1245–1247	Journey of John of Pian de Carpine to Mongolia.
1252	Emergence of Moscow as an independent hereditary principality.
1253–1255	Journey of William of Rubruck to Mongolia.
1252–1263	Rule of Alexander Nevskii.
1270	Novgorod negotiates a treaty with the Hanseatic League.
1300	Transfer of Metropolitan Office from Kiev to Vladimir.
1302	Moscow annexes Pereiaslavl, Kolomna, and Mozhaisk.
1318	Prince Iurii of Moscow acquires the Charter (*iarlyk*) of Grand Prince from the Mongols.
1322	Charter (*iarlyk*) of Grand Prince passes to Dmitri of Tver.
1325–1340	Rule of Ivan Kalita in Moscow.
1328	Ivan Kalita gets the *iarlyk* of Grand Prince.
1340	St. Sergius founds the Trinity Monastery.
1352	Black Death visits Novgorod and Moscow.

1359–1389 Rule of Dmitrii Donskoi.
1360–1362 Struggle between Moscow and Suzdal for the title of Grand Princedom.
1367–1368 First stone fortifications of the Moscow Kremlin.
1371–1375 Heresy of *Strigolniks* (Shearers) in Novgorod.
1375 Tver acknowledges Moscow as Grand Principality.
1380 Dmitrii Donskoi defeats Khan Mamai at Kulikovo.
1382 Moscow taken by Khan Tokhtamysh; first mention of firearms in Moscow; first coining of money in Moscow.
1392 Moscow absorbs Suzdal and Nizhnii-Novgorod.
1395 Defeat of the Golden Horde by Tamerlane.
1389–1425 Rule of Vasilii I in Moscow.
1425–1462 Rule of Vasilii II, the Blind.
1427 Formation of the Crimean Khanate.
1430–1466 Disintegration of the Golden Horde.
1436 Foundation of Solovetskii Monastery.
1437 Formation of the Kazan Khanate.
1439 Council of Florence attempts to reunite eastern and western Churches.
1441 Metropolitan Isidore deposed in Moscow for acceptance of Council of Florence.
1448 Church of Moscow declared autocephalous.
1453 Ottoman Turks capture Constantinople.
1458 Kievan Metropolitan assumes independence from Moscow.
1459 Formation of the Astrakhan Khanate.
1462–1505 Rule of Ivan III, the Great.
1463 Moscow annexes the principality of Iaroslavl; Moscow conquers the Mari Lands.
1463–1468 First limitations upon freedom of peasant movement.
1470 The Judaizer Heresy spreads throughout Novgorod.
1472 Moscow annexes the principality of Perm; Ivan III marries Sophia Paleologue, niece of last Byzantine Emperor.
1474 Moscow annexes Rostov.
1476 Ambrosio Contarini, the first Westerner, visits and writes about Moscow.
1478 Moscow annexes Novgorod.
1475–1479 Building of the Uspenskii Sobor (Cathedral of Assumption) in the Moscow Kremlin.
1480 Ivan III terminates the "Mongol Yoke."
1485–1516 Building of the new Kremlin in Moscow.
1489 Moscow annexes Viatka.

1497	Ivan III issues *Sudebnik* (Code of Laws).
1503	Church Council condemns the heresy of Judaizers.
1505–1533	Rule of Vasilii III.
1510	Moscow annexes Pskov.
1514	Moscow annexes territories of Smolensk.
1517, 1526	Baron Herberstein's missions to Moscow.
1525	Maxim the Greek condemned by Church Council.
1533–1584	Rule of Ivan IV, the Terrible.
1547	Ivan IV assumes the title "Tsar."
1549	First meeting of the *Zemskii Sobor* (Landed Assembly).
1550	Organization of the *streltsy; Sudebnik* of Ivan IV.
1552	Moscow captures Kazan.
1553	Opening of the northern sea route to Russia by the English (Richard Chancellor).
1555	Formation of the Muscovy Company in London and the extension of privileges to it for trade throughout the Moscow State.
1556	Conquest of Astrakhan.
1558–1583	The Livonian War of Ivan IV.
1564	First book printed in Moscow by Ivan Fedorov.
1565–1584	Ivan IV's reign of terror.
1570	Ivan IV's punishment of Novgorod.
1571–1572	Crimean Tatars raid and burn Moscow.
1577	Establishment of commercial ties with Holland.
1582	Ermak conquers the Khanate of Sibir.
1584	Founding of Archangel.
1584–1598	Rule of Tsar Feodor Ivanovich.
1587–1598	Boris Godunov acts as Regent.
1588	Giles Fletcher visits Moscow.
1589	Formation of the Office of Patriarch in Moscow.
1596	Creation of Uniat Church in Poland-Lithuania.
1597	An *ukaz* grants nobles five years to claim their fugitive peasants.
1598	End of the Riurik Dynasty.
1598–1605	Rule of Tsar Boris Godunov.
1601–1604	Years of famine.
1604–1613	Time of Troubles.
1605–1606	Rule of the First False Dmitrii.
1606–1607	Bolotnikov's revolt.
1607–1610	Second False Dmitrii.
1610–1612	Poles occupy Moscow.
1611–1612	National uprising against Poles.

1611–1617 Swedes occupy Novgorod.

1613 *Zemskii Sobor* elects Michael Romanov as Tsar.

1613–1645 Rule of Tsar Michael Romanov.

1631 Peter Mogila, Metropolitan of Kiev, founds Kiev Academy.

1634–1643 Adam Olearius makes four visits to Moscow.

1637 Don Cossacks conquer Azov; first mission from Moscow to China.

1643–1646 Poiarkov reaches the Sea of Okhotsk.

1645–1676 Rule of Tsar Aleksei.

1648 Ukrainian Cossack uprising against Poland.

1648–1649 *Zemskii Sobor* issues *Sobornoe Ulozhenie* (Code of Laws).

1649 Trading privileges of the Muscovy Company abolished.

1652 Foundation of the German settlement in Moscow; founding of Irkutsk.

1652–1666 Nikon, Patriarch of Moscow.

1653 Last full meeting of the *Zemskii Sobor*.

1654 Ukrainian Cossacks swear allegiance to the Tsar of Moscow; Church Council adopts Nikon's reforms, thereby causing a schism.

1654–1667 Russo-Polish War over the Ukraine.

1662 "Copper riots" in Moscow.

1664 Russian official, Grigorii Kotoshikhin, flees to Sweden.

1666 Establishment of postal service in Russia; Church Council deposes Patriarch Nikon.

1667 Poland cedes Kiev and Smolensk to Russia in the Peace of Andrusovo; *Novotorgovyi ustav* (New Commercial Code) promulgated; Church Council condemns Old Believers.

1667–1676 Revolt of Solovetskii Monastery against church reforms.

1670–1671 Revolt of Stenka Razin.

1672 Russians send embassies to all major European states.

1676–1682 Rule of Tsar Feodor Alekseevich.

1682 Execution of Archpriest Avvakum.

1682–1689 Regency of Sophia.

1684 Institution of formal persecution of Old Believers.

1689 Peter I deposes Sophia; Treaty of Nerchinsk with China signed.

Selected Bibliography

History of Kievan Rus, of the Mongol Yoke, and of Muscovy, which form focal points of this volume, have not received as intensive scholarly scrutiny as has the modern, that is, post-Petrine period of Russian history. This is because of the obvious language barrier and the lacunae of sources. The lack of attention applies not only to American but to Canadian, English, German, French, and Soviet scholarship as well. In spite of this, however, in recent years an impressive amount of literature has accumulated.

The items listed below are representative of many fine works that deal with the complexities of that region's past from about 850 A.D. to 1700 A.D. Because this volume is intended for readers of English, all entries are in English. They have been selected not because I necessarily agree with their interpretation, but because they might provide the reader with valuable insights for a fair, better, and more accurate understanding of perplexing issues that have been either touched on in this collection of sources or have been treated in various basic texts on Russian history.

The selected bibliography consists of two parts: Monographic Literature and Periodical Literature. Anyone interested in pursuing specific topics that have been dealt with in this collection should consult library catalogues, references cited within each item listed in this bibliography, and any other available sources.

Monographic Literature

Alef, Gustave, *Rulers and Nobles in Fifteenth-Century Muscovy*. London: Variorum Reprints, 1983.

Anderson, Matthew S., *Britain's Discovery of Russia, 1553–1815*. New York: St. Martin's Press, 1958.

Andreyev, Nikolay, *Studies in Moscovy. Western Influence and Byzantine Inheritance*. London: Variorum Reprints, 1970.

Armstrong, Terence, ed. *Yermak's Campaign in Siberia: A Selection of Documents*. Trans. by Tatiana Minorsky and David Wileman. London: Hakluyt Society, 1975.

Backus, Oswald P., *Motives of West Russian Nobles in Deserting Lithuania for Moscow, 1377–1514*. Lawrence: University of Kansas Press, 1957.

Baddeley, J. F., *Russia, Mongolia and China . . . 1602–1672*. London: Macmillan, 1919, 2 vols.

Baron, Samuel H., *Muscovite Russia: Collected Essays*. London: Variorum Reprints, 1980.

———— ed., *The Travels of Olearius in Seventeenth Century Russia*. Stanford: Stanford University Press, 1967.

Basarab, John, *Pereiaslav Treaty of 1654: A Historical Study*. Edmonton: University of Alberta Press, 1982.

Berry, Lloyd E., and Robert O. Crummey, eds., *Rude and Barbarous Kingdom: Russia in the Accounts of Sixteenth-Century English Voyagers*. Madison: University of Wisconsin Press, 1968.

Billington, James H., *The Icon and the Axe. An Interpretative History of Russian Culture*. New York: Knopf, 1965.

Birnbaum, Henryk, *Lord Novgorod the Great. Essays in the History and Culture of a Medieval City State*. Columbus: Slavica, 1981.

———— and Michael S. Flier, eds., *Medieval Russian Culture*. Berkeley: University of California Press, 1984.

Blum, Jerome, *Lord and Peasant in Russia from the Ninth to the Nineteenth Century*. Princeton: Princeton University Press, 1961.

Bobrick, Benson, *Fearful Majesty: The Life and Reign of Ivan the Terrible*. New York: G. P. Putnam's Sons, 1987.

Bushkovitch, Paul, *The Merchants of Moscow, 1580–1650*. New York: Cambridge University Press, 1980.

Buxton, David, *Russian Medieval Architecture*. Cambridge: Cambridge University Press, 1934.

Cizevskij, D., *History of Russian Literature from the Eleventh to the End of Baroque*. The Hague: Mouton, 1960.

Concevicius, Joseph B., *Russia's Attitude Toward Union with Rome (9th–16th Centuries)*. Washington: Catholic University of America, 1927.

Conybear, F. C., *Russian Dissenters*. Cambridge: Harvard University Press, 1921.

Croskey, Robert M., *Muscovite Diplomatic Practice in the Reign of Ivan III*. New York: Garland, 1987.

Cross, Samuel H., *Medieval Russian Churches*. Cambridge: Medieval Academy of America, 1949.

Crummey, Robert O., *Aristocrats and Servitors*. Princeton: Princeton University Press, 1983.

———— *The Old Believers in the World of Anti-Christ*. Madison: University of Wisconsin Press, 1970.

Dewey, Horace William, *Muscovite Judicial Texts, 1488–1556*. Ann Arbor: University of Michigan, Department of Slavic Languages and Literature, 1966.

———— and Ann M. Kleimola, eds., *Russian Private Law in the XIV-XVII c. An Anthology of Documents*. Ann Arbor: University of Michigan, Department of Slavic Languages and Literature, 1973.

Dimnik, Martin, *Mikhail, Prince of Chernigov and Grand Prince of Kiev, 1224–1246*. Toronto: Pontifical Institute of Medieval Studies, 1981.

Dmytryshyn, Basil, E. A. P. Crownhart-Vaughan and Thomas Vaughan, eds., *Russia's Conquest of Siberia: A Documentary Record, 1558–1700*. Portland: Oregon Historical Society, 1985.

Donnelly, Alton S., *The Russian Conquest of Bashkiriia, 1552–1740: A Case Study of Imperialism*. New Haven: Yale University Press, 1968.

Dukes, Paul, *The Making of Russian Absolutism, 1613–1801*. London: Longsman, 1982.

Duncan, David D., *Great Treasures of the Kremlin*. Rev. ed. New York: Abrams, 1968.

Dvornik, Francis, *The Slavs in European History and Civilization*. New Brunswick: Rutgers University Press, 1962.

Eekman, Thomas, and Ante Kadic, eds., *Juraj Križanić (1618–1683): Russophile and Ecumenic Visionary, A Symposium*. The Hague: Nijhof, 1976.

Fedotov, Georgii P., *The Russian Religious Mind*. Cambridge: Harvard University Press, 1946.

Fennell, John, *The Crisis of Medieval Russia*. London: Longman, 1983.

———— *The Emergence of Moscow, 1304–1359*. Berkeley: University of California Press, 1968.

———— *Ivan the Great of Moscow*. New York: St. Martin's Press, 1961.

Fisher, Raymond H., *The Russian Fur Trade, 1550–1700*. Berkeley: University of California Press, 1943.

———— *The Voyages of Semen Dezhnev in 1648*. London: Hakluyt Society, 1981.

Fuhrman, Joseph T., *Tsar Alexis: His Reign and His Russia*. Gulf Breeze: Academic International Press, 1981.

Gibson, James R., *Feeding the Russian Fur Trade . . . 1639–1856*. Madison: University of Wisconsin Press, 1969.

Golb, Norman, and Omelian Pritsak, *Khazarian Hebrew Documents of the Tenth Century*. Ithaca: Cornell University Press, 1982.

Graham, Hugh F. ed., *The Muscovia of Antonio Possevino, S. J.* Pittsburgh: University of Pittsburgh Press, 1977.

Grekov, Boris, *Kiev Rus*. Moscow: Foreign Language Publication House, 1959.

Grey, Ian, *Boris Godunov: The Tragic Tsar*. New York: Scribners, 1973.

———— *Ivan the Terrible*. London: Hodder & Stoughton, 1964.

Gudzy, N. K., *History of Early Russian Literature*. New York: Macmillan, 1949.

Halecki, Oskar, *From Florence to Brest (1439–1596)*. Rome: Sacrum Poloniea Millennium, 1958.

Halperin, Charles J., *Russia and the Golden Horde: The Mongol Impact on Medieval Russian History*. Bloomington: Indiana University Press, 1985.

———— *The Tatar Yoke*. Columbus: Slavica, 1986.

Hellie, Richard, *Enserfment and Military Change in Muscovy*. Chicago: University of Chicago Press, 1971.

———— *Slavery in Russia, 1450–1725*. Chicago: University of Chicago Press, 1982.

Hittle, J. Michael, *The Service City: State and Townsmen in Russia, 1600–1800*. Cambridge: Harvard University Press, 1979.

Howes, Robert C., ed., *The Testaments of the Grand Princes of Moscow*. Ithaca: Cornell University Press, 1967.

Hurwitz, Ellen S., *Prince Andrej Bogoliubskij: The Man and the Myth*. Florence: Licosa Editrica, 1980.

Kaiser, Daniel H., *The Growth of Law in Medieval Russia*. Princeton: Princeton University Press, 1980.

Keenan, Edward L., *The Kurbskii-Groznyi Apocrypha . . .* Cambridge: Harvard University Press, 1971.

Kirchner, Walther, *Commercial Relations Between Russia and Europe, 1400–1800*. Bloomington: Indiana University Press, 1966.

Kleimola, Ann M., *Justice in Medieval Russia. Muscovite Judgment Charters of the Fifteenth and Sixteenth Centuries*. Philadelphia: American Philosophical Society, 1975.

Kliuchevskii, Vasilii O., *A Course in Russian History. The Seventeenth Century*. Trans. by Natalie Duddington. Chicago: Quadrangle Books, 1968.

———— *The Rise of the Romanovs*. Trans. by Liliana Archibald. London: Macmillan, 1970.

Kollmann, Nancy S., *Kinship and Politics: The Making of the Muscovite Political System, 1345–1547*. Stanford: Stanford University Press, 1987.

Kotošixin, Grigorij, *O Rossii v carstvovanie Alekseja Mikhajloviča*. Text and Commentary by A. E. Pennington. Oxford: Clarendon Press, 1980.

Kornilovich, Kira, *Arts of Russia from the Origins to the End of the Sixteenth Century*. New York: World, 1967.

Lantzeff, George V., *Siberia in the Seventeenth Century: A Study of Colonial Administration*. Berkeley: University of California Press, 1943.

———— and Richard A. Pierce, *Eastward to Empire: Explorations and Conquest on the Russian Open Frontier to 1750*. Montreal: McGill University Press, 1973.

Letiche, John M., and Basil Dmytryshyn, *Russian Statecraft: The Politika of Iurii Krizhanich*. Oxford: Blackwell, 1985.

Longworth, Philip, Alexis, *Tsar of All the Russians*. London: Secker & Warburg, 1984.

Lupinin, Nickolas, *Religious Revolt in the XVIIth Century. The Schism of the Russian Church*. Princeton: Kingston Press, 1984.

Mancall, Mark, *Russia and China: Their Diplomatic Relations to 1728*. Cambridge: Harvard University Press, 1971.

Margeret, Jacques, *The Russian Empire and the Grand Duchy of Muscovy: A 17th Century French Account*. Trans. by S. L. Dunning. Pittsburgh: University of Pittsburgh Press, 1984.

Meyendorff, John, *The Byzantine Legacy in the Orthodox Church*. Crestwood: St. Vladimir Seminary Press, 1982.

Mongait, A. L., *Archeology in the USSR*. Baltimore: Penguin Books, 1961.

O'Brien, C. Bickford, *Muscovy and Ukraine from the Pereiaslav Agreement to the Truce of Andrusovo*. Berkeley: University of California Press, 1963.

———— *Russia Under Two Tsars, 1682–1689*. Berkeley: University of California Press, 1952.

Paszkiewicz, Henryk, *The Origins of Russia*. London: Allen & Unwin, 1954.

———— *The Rise of Moscow's Power*. Trans. by P. S. Faller. Boulder: East European Monographs, 1983.

Pelensky, Jaroslaw, *Russia and Kazan: Conquest and Imperial Ideology*. The Hague: Mouton, 1974.

Perfecky, George, ed., *The Galician-Volynian Chronicle*. Munich: Wilhelm Fink Verlag, 1973.

Platonov, S. F., *Boris Godunov. Tsar of Russia*. Trans. by L. Rex Piles. Gulf Breeze: Academic International Press, 1973.

———— *The Time of Troubles*. Trans. by J. T. Alexander. Lawrence: University of Kansas Press, 1970.

Possevino, Antonio, *Moscovia of Antonio Possevino, S. J.* Trans. by Hugh F. Graham. Pittsburgh: University of Pittsburgh Press, 1977.

Powstenko, Olexa, *The Cathedral of St. Sophia in Kiev*. New York: The Annals of the Ukrainian Academy in the USA, 1954.

Presniakov, A. E. *The Formation of the Great Russian State*. Chicago: Quadrangle Books, 1970.

———— *The Tsardom of Muscovy*. Gulf Breeze: Academic International Press, 1978.

Pritsak, Omeljan, *The Origin of Rus: Old Scandinavian Sources Other than the Sagas*. Cambridge: Harvard University Press, 1981.

Skrynnikov, Ruslan G., *Boris Godunov*. Trans. by Hugh F. Graham. Gulf Breeze: Academic International Press, 1982.

Smith, R. E. F., *The Enserfment of the Russian Peasantry*. Cambridge: Cambridge University Press, 1968.

———— *Peasant Farming in Muscovy*. Cambridge: Cambridge University Press, 1977.

Solovev, S. M., *History of Russia. The Age of Vasilii III*. Trans. by Hugh Graham. Gulf Breeze: Academic International Press, 1976.

———— *History of Russia. The Character of Old Russia*. Trans. by Alexander V. Muller. Gulf Breeze: Academic Press International, 1980.

———— *History of Russia. Rebellion and Reform, Feodor and Sophia, 1682–1689*. Trans. by Lindsey A. J. Hughes. Gulf Breeze: Academic International Press, 1989.

———— *History of Russia. The Reign of Ivan III*. Trans. by John D. Windhausen. Gulf Breeze: Academic International Press, 1978.

———— *History of Russia. The Time of Troubles*. Trans. by G. Edward Orchard. Gulf Breeze: Academic International Press, 1988.

Tikhomirov, M. N., *The Towns of Ancient Rus*. Moscow: Foreign Languages Publishing House, 1959.

Vernadsky, George, *Ancient Russia*. New Haven; Yale University Press, 1943.

———— *Bohdan: Hetman of Ukraine*. New Haven: Yale University Press, 1941.

———— *Kievan Russia*. New Haven: Yale University Press, 1948.

———— *Medieval Russian Laws*. New York: Columbia University Press, 1947.

———— *The Mongols and Russia*. New Haven: Yale University Press, 1953.

———— *The Origins of Russia*. Oxford: Clarendon Press, 1959.

———— *Russia at the Dawn of the Modern Age*. New Haven: Yale University Press, 1959.

———— *The Tsardom of Muscovy, 1547–1682*. 2 Parts. New Haven: Yale University Press, 1969.

Stavrou, Theofanis G., and Peter R. Weisensel, eds., *Russian Travellers to the Christian East from the 12th to the 20th Century*. Columbus: Slavica, 1985.

Sydorenko, Alexander, *The Kievan Academy in the Seventeenth Century*. Ottawa: University of Ottawa Press, 1977.

Szeftel, Marc, *Russian Institutions and Culture up to Peter the Great*. London: Variorum Reprints, 1975.

von Staden, Heinrich. *The Land and Government of Muscovy*. Stanford: Stanford University Press, 1967.

Voyce, A., *The Art and Architecture of Medieval Russia*. Norman: University of Oklahoma Press, 1967.

Waugh, Daniel C., ed. *Essays in Honor of A. A. Zimin*. Columbus: Slavica, 1985.

Willan, Thomas S., *Early History of the Russian Company, 1553–1603*. Manchester: Manchester University Press, 1955.

Yanov, Alexander, *The Origins of Autocracy. Ivan the Terrible in Russian History*. Trans. by Stephen Dunn. Berkeley: University of California Press, 1981.

Zenkovsky, Serge A., ed., *The Nikonian Chronicle*. Princeton: Kingston & Darwin Press, 1989, 5 vols.

Zernov, Nicolas, *Moscow: The Third Rome*. New York: Macmillan, 1937.

Periodical Literature

Allsen, Thomas, "Guard and Government in the Reign of Grand Qan Mongke," *Harvard Journal of Asiatic Studies,* vol. 46 (1986), 495–521.

———— "Mongol Census Taking in Rus, 1245–1275," *Harvard Ukrainian Studies,* vol. 5 (1981), 32–53.

———— "Prelude to Western Campaigns: Mongol Military Operations in the Volga-Ural Region," *Archivum Eurasiae Medii Aevi,* vol. 3 (1983), 5–24.

Anderson, M. S., "English Views of Russia in the 17th Century," *Slavonic and East European Review,* vol. 33, no. 80 (December, 1954), 140–161.

Andrusiak, M., "Kings of Kiev and Galicia," *Slavonic and East European Review,* vol. 33, no. 81 (June, 1955), 342–350.

Backus, Oswald P., "Was Muscovite Russia Imperialistic?" *The American Slavic and East European Review,* vol. 13, no. 4 (December, 1954), 522–534.

Blum, Jerome, "The Beginnings of Large-Scale Landownership in Russia," *Speculum,* vol. 28, no. 4 (October, 1953), 776–790.

———— "The *Smerd* in Kievan Russia," *The American Slavic and East European Review,* vol. 12, no. 1 (February, 1953), 122–130.

Bushkovitch, Paul, "Taxation, Tax Farming and Merchants in Sixteenth-Century Russia," *Slavic Review,* vol. 37, no. 3 (September, 1978), 381–398.

Cant, C. B. H., "The Archpriest Avvakum and His Scottish Contemporaries," *Slavonic and East European Review,* vol. 44, no. 103 (July, 1966), 381–403.

Cherniavsky, Michael, "Ivan the Terrible as Renaissance Prince," *Slavic Review,* vol. 27, no. 2 (June, 1968), 195–211.

———— "The Old Believers and the New Religion," *Slavic Review,* vol. 25, no. 1 (March, 1966), 1–39.

Cross, S. H., and K. J. Conant, "The Earliest Mediaeval Churches in Kiev," *Speculum,* vol. 11, no. 4 (October, 1936), 477–499.

Dewey, Horace W., "The 1550 Sudebnik as an Instrument of Reform," *Jahrbücher für Geschichte Osteuropas,* New Series, vol. 10, no. 2 (July, 1962), 161–180.

———— "Immunities in Old Russia," *Slavic Review,* vol. 23, no. 4 (December, 1964), 643–659.

———— "Political *Poruka* in Muscovite Rus," *Russian Review,* vol. 46, no. 2 (April, 1987), 117–133.

Dmytryshyn, Basil, "Iurii Krizhanich: The First Sibirologist," *Sino-Soviet Affairs,* vol. 10, no. 4 (Winter, 1986–87), 195–211.

———— "Russian Expansion to the Pacific, 1580–1700: A Historiographical Review," *Slavic Studies* (Hokkaido University), (1980), 1–25.

Esper, Thomas, "Military Self-Sufficiency and Weapons Technology in Muscovite Russia," *Slavic Review,* vol. 28, no. 2 (June, 1969), 185–208.

Evans, N. E., "The Anglo-Russian Marriage Negotiations of 1600–1603," *Slavonic and East European Review,* vol. 61, no. 3 (July, 1983), 363–387.

Fennell, J. L. I., "The Dynastic Crisis, 1497–1502," *Slavonic Review,* vol. 39, no. 92 (December, 1960), 1–23.

Fisher, Raymond H., "Dezhnev's Voyages of 1648 in the Light of Soviet Scholarship," *Terrae Incognitae,* vol. 5 (1973), 7–26.

Florovsky, Georges, "The Problem of Old Russian Culture," *Slavic Review,* vol. 21, no. 1 (March, 1962), 1–15.

Halperin, Charles J., "Soviet Historiography on Russia and the Mongols," *Russian Review,* vol. 41, no. 3 (July, 1982) 306–322.

Hellie, Richard, "Recent Soviet Historiography on Medieval and Early Modern Russian Slavery," *Russian Review,* vol. 35, no. 1, (January, 1976), 1–32.

Kerner, Robert J., "Russian Eastward Movement: Some Observations on Its Historical Significance," *Pacific Historical Review,* vol. 17, no. 5, (May, 1948), 135–148.

Keenan, Edward L., "Muscovy and Kazan: Some Introductory Remarks on the Patterns of Steppe Diplomacy," *Slavic Review,* vol. 26, no. 4 (December, 1967), 548–558.

Keep, J. L. H., "The Decline of the Zemsky Sobor," *Slavonic Review,* vol. 36, no. 86 (December, 1957), 100–122.

———— "The Regime of Filaret (1619–1633)," *Slavonic Review,* vol. 38, no. 91 (June, 1960), 334–360.

Kleimola, A. M., "Boris Godunov and the Politics of Mestnichestvo," *Slavonic and East European Review,* vol. 53, no. 132 (July, 1975), 355–369.

Kollmann, Nancy Shields, "Concensus Politics: The Dynastic Crisis of the 1490s Reconsidered," *Russian Review,* vol. 45, no. 3 (July, 1986), 235–267.

Letiche, John M., and Basil Dmytryshyn, "Iurii Krizhanich on the Wealth and Poverty of Nations," *International Social Science Review,* vol. 62, no. 3 (Summer, 1987), 99–118.

———— "Križanič's Memorandum on the Mission to Moscow," *Slavonic and East European Review,* vol. 68, no. 1 (January, 1990), 41–68.

Lind, John H., "The Russo-Byzantine Treaties and the Early Urban Structure of Rus," *Slavonic and East European Review,* vol. 62, no. 3 (July, 1984), 362–370.

Longworth, Philip, "Russian-Venetian Relations in the Reign of Tsar Aleksey Mikhailovich," *Slavonic and East European Review,* vol. 64, no. 3 (July, 1986), 380–400.

Noonan, Thomas S., "Medieval Russia, the Mongols, and the West: Novgorod's Relations with the Baltic, 1100–1350," *Medieval Studies,* 37 (1975), 316–339.

———— "The Millennium of Russia's First Perestroika: The Origins of a Kievan Glass Industry Under Prince Vladimir," *Occasional Paper, #233, Kennan Institute* (April, 1989), 1–43.

———— "The Monetary History of Kiev in the Pre-Mongol Period," *Harvard Ukrainian Studies,* 11 (1987), 384–443.

———— "Russia's Eastern Trade, 1150–1350: The Archeological Evidence," *Archivum Eurasiae Medii Aevi,* 3 (1983), 201–264.

———— "Why the Vikings First Came to Russia?", *Jahrbücher für Geschichte Osteuropas,* 34 (1986), 321–348.

Olmstead, Hugh M., "A Learned Greek in Muscovite Exile: Maksim Grek and the Old Testament Prophets," *Modern Greek Studies Yearbook,* vol. 3 (1987), 1–73.

Ostrowski, Donald, "Church Polemics and Monastic Land Acquisition in Sixteenth-Century Muscovy," *Slavonic and East European Review,* vol. 64, no. 3 (July, 1986), 355–379.

Pelenski, Jaroslaw, "Muscovite Imperial Claims to the Kazan Khanate," *Slavic Review,* vol. 26, no. 4 (December, 1967), 559–576.

Pritsak, Omeljan, "Moscow, the Golden Horde and the Kazan Khanate from a Polycultural Point of View," *Slavic Review,* vol. 26, no. 4 (December, 1967), 577–583.

Pouncy, Carolyn Johnson, "The Origins of the *Domostroi*: A Study in Manuscript History," *Russian Review,* vol. 46, no. 4 (October, 1987), 357–373.

Raba, J., "The Fate of the Novogorian Republic," *Slavonic Review,* vol. 45, no. 105 (July, 1967), 307–324.

Riasanovsky, Alexander V., "The Embassy of 838 Revisited: Some Comments in Connection with a Normanist Source on Early Russian History," *Jahrbücher für Geschichte Osteuropas,* vol. 10, no. 1 (April, 1962), 1–12.

Riasanovsky, Nicholas V., "The Norman Theory of the Origin of the Russian State," *Russian Review,* vol. 7, no. 1 (Autumn, 1947), 96–110.

Ševčenko, Ihor, "Muscovy's Conquest of Kazan: Two Views Reconciled," *Slavic Review,* vol. 26, no. 4 (December, 1967), 541–547.

Shepard, J., "Some Problems of Russo-Byzantine Relations c. 860-c. 1050," *Slavonic and East European Review,* vol. 52, no. 126 (January, 1974), 10–33.

Spinka, Matthew, "Patriarch Nikon and the Subjection of the Russian Church to the State," *Church History,* vol. 10 (December, 1941), 347–366.

Stokes, A. D., "The Status of the Russian Church, 988–1037," *Slavonic Review,* vol. 37, no. 89 (June, 1959), 430–442.

Vernadsky, George, "Feudalism in Russia," *Speculum,* vol. 14, no. 3 (July, 1939), 300–323.

———— "On Feudalism in Kievan Russia," *The American Slavic and East European Review,* vol. 7, no. 1 (February, 1948), 3–14.

Zdan, M. B., "The Dependence of Halych-Volyn Rus on the Golden Horde," *Slavonic Review,* vol. 35, no. 85 (June, 1957), 505–523.

Zenkovsky, Serge, "The Russian Church Schism: Its Background and Repercussions," *Russian Review,* vol. 16, no. 4 (October, 1957), 37–58.

Zguta, Russell, "Kievan Coinage," *Slavonic and East European Review,* vol. 53, no. 133 (October, 1975), 483–492.

———— "Witchcraft and Medicine in Pre-Petrine Russia," *Russian Review,* vol. 37, no. 4 (October, 1978), 438–448.

———— "The One-Day Votive Church: A Religious Response to the Black Death in Early Russia," *Slavic Review,* vol. 40, no. 3 (Fall, 1981), 423–432.